MW00817215

RAGGED but RIGHT

RAGGED but RIGHT

Black Traveling Shows, "COON SONGS," and the Dark Pathway to BLUES and JAZZ

LYNN ABBOTT and DOUG SEROFF

UNIVERSITY PRESS OF MISSISSIPPI / JACKSON

LIBRARY
NORTHERN VIRGINIA COMMUNITY COLLEGE

AMERICAN MADE MUSIC SERIES

Advisory Board

David Evans, General Editor
Barry Jean Ancelet
Edward A. Berlin
Joyce J. Bolden
Rob Bowman
Susan C. Cook
Curtis Ellison
William Ferris
Michael Harris
John Edward Hasse
Kip Lornell
Frank McArthur
Bill Malone
Eddie S. Meadows
Manuel H. Peña
David Sanjek
Wayne D. Shirley
Robert Walser

www.upress.state.ms.us

Designed by Todd Lape

The University Press of Mississippi is a member
of the Association of American University Presses.

Copyright © 2007 by University Press of Mississippi
All rights reserved

Manufactured in the United States of America

First edition 2007
∞

Library of Congress Cataloging-in-Publication Data
Abbott, Lynn, 1946–
Ragged but right : black traveling shows, "coon songs," and the dark pathway to blues and jazz / Lynn Abbott and Doug Seroff. — 1st ed.
p. cm. — (American made music series)
Includes bibliographical references (p.) and index.
ISBN–13: 978–1–57806-901–9 (cloth : alk. paper)
ISBN–10: 1–57806–901–7 (cloth : alk. paper) 1. African Americans—Music—History and criticism. 2. Minstrel shows—United States—History. 3. Tent shows—United States—History. 4. Sideshows—United States—History. I. Seroff, Doug. II. Title. III. Series.
ML3479.A23 2007
781.64089'96073—dc22 2006015009

British Library Cataloging-in-Publication Data available

CONTENTS

ACKNOWLEDGMENTS

When we first started pooling our research and comparing notes, about thirty years ago, we had no idea that we would be undertaking long-term writing projects together. We are grateful for having been able to hammer out a democratic working relationship capable of withstanding the years. This is our second outing with University Press of Mississippi, and we appreciate their continued interest in our work.

Thanks to David Evans and Wayne D. Shirley for their critical readings of our manuscript on behalf of the Press; and to Alex Albright, David Crosby, and Garnette Cadogan, from whom we solicited commentaries on specific portions of the manuscript.

Special thanks to Chris Ware for a perfect book jacket.

Many individuals and institutions opened their collections to us, granted research assistance, technical support, interviews, workspace, hospitality, etc. We gratefully acknowledge Linda Abbott; Alex Albright; Amistad Research Center; Eleanor J. Baker; Hayden Battle, Annie Kemp, Arely Martinez, and Patricia Windham, Interlibrary Loan Division, Howard-Tilton Memorial Library, Tulane University; Pen Bogert, Filson Historical Society, Louisville, Kentucky; Carl Brasseaux, Jennifer Cooper, and Linda Garber, Center for Louisiana Studies, University of Louisiana; Tim Brooks; Ray Buckberry; Robert Cogswell, Tennessee State Arts Commission; David and Patricia Crosby, Mississippi Cultural Crossroads, Port Gibson, Mississippi; Ken, Peggy, Julie, and Thomas David; Sue Fischer; Sarah Dave; John Daniel Draper and Erin Foley, Circus World Museum, Baraboo, Wisconsin; Emanuel Ford; Ray Funk; Byron Gill and Matthew Moss, C&A Associates; Annie and Tony Hagert, Thornton Hagert Vernacular Music Research (www.vernacularmusicresearch.com); Robert F. Houston, Philadelphia Museum of the Circus; Muriel McDowell-Jackson, Washington Memorial Library, Macon, Georgia; Bryan McDaniel, Chicago History Museum; Arthur LeBrew; Barry Martyn; Media Services, J. Edgar and Louise S. Monroe Library, Loyola University; Michael Montgomery; Bruce Nemerov and Paul Wells, Center for Popular Music, Middle Tennessee State University; Johnny Parth, Document Records; Ronnie Pugh, Nashville Room, Nashville Public Library; Bruce Boyd Raeburn and Alma Williams Freeman, Hogan Jazz Archive, Tulane University; Richard Raichelson; Erin Royal, McCain Library and Archives, The University of Southern Mississippi; David Sager; Jim Sherraden, Hatch Show Print; Jessie Carney Smith and Beth Madison Howse, John Hope and Aurelia E. Franklin Library, Fisk University; Sherry Smith; Tennessee State Museum and Archive; Rosemary Thomas, Parker High School Library, Birmingham, Alabama; Albert Vollmer; Eric Wedig, Connie Cannon, Charlotte McCrary, and Gaile Thomas,

Microforms and Newspapers Division, Howard-Tilton Memorial Library, Tulane University; Pete Whelan, *78 Quarterly*.

Finally, we acknowledge R. M. W. Dixon, John Godrich, and Howard W. Rye, compilers of *Blues and Gospel Records 1890–1943*; Guthrie T. Meade, Jr., Dick Spottswood, and Douglas S. Meade, compilers of *Country Music Sources: A Biblio-Discography of Commercially Recorded Traditional Music*: Tony Russell, compiler of *Country Music Records A Discography, 1921–1942*; and Brian Rust, who compiled *Jazz Records, 1897–1942*. We consulted these indispensable sources more often than our citations may indicate.

LYNN ABBOTT and DOUG SEROFF,

April 2006

RAGGED but RIGHT

INTRODUCTION

In 1897 an African American stage singer named Bessie Gillam, on the road with P. T. Wright's Nashville Students, drew praise from a black entertainment reporter for her "artistic rendition of coon songs." The writer took stock of Bessie Gillam's situation: "Being a young lady she has a bright future and we look forward to see her hold positions among the many bright lights now lighting the dark pathway on to the road of success for the colored race."[1]

To the modern ear, the phrase "artistic rendition of coon songs" is oxymoronic, but in context it speaks to a compelling reality of turn-of-the-century race entertainment. When ragtime made its stunning leap from African American underclass culture into mainstream fashion, it provided the first real professional opportunities for a wide range of black performers; however, every prospect was mitigated by systemic racism. The era's biggest hits weren't Scott Joplin's stately piano rags; "coon songs" were what appealed to the masses. To the popular music industry and the contemporary white audience, ragtime and coon songs were virtually synonymous.[2]

Ragtime released a pent-up reservoir of modernism in African American culture, providing the antidote to "Ethiopian minstrelsy," which had stifled the development of race entertainment for most of the nineteenth century. Just as the century drew to a close, the lid blew off, unleashing a torrent of creativity that swept thousands of black writers, performers, musicians, and entrepreneurs into the professional ranks. No individual engineered this stigmatiferous groundswell; it was shaped by popular taste, driven by the mainstream American audience.

Ragtime startled American sensibilities; and in spite of violent recoil, its formulae became the foundation of twentieth century popular music, part of a shared perception of American style and identity. In the course of this development, audiences were charmed into accepting a much broader panorama of black stage arts and music.

Aspiring black performers faced exploitative business practices and biased journalistic criticism in the northern entertainment world, and violent racial antagonism and Jim Crow prohibitions in the South. White southern audiences demanded unreconstructed minstrelsy from black entertainers, while white northern audiences resisted black musical comedy that did not prominently feature coon songs. It is surprising how much was accomplished, given the limitations. Every branch of the black stage profession included artists who saw race elevation as a part of their professional responsibility.

The word "coon" is an archaic invective that has lost currency; nevertheless, it is powerfully redolent of turn-of-the-century American racism.[3] Though meaningless and ridiculous, it remains highly offensive, and we take no pleasure in its repeated usage. However, it is impossible to investigate black popular entertainment of the ragtime era without directly confronting coon songs.

It is important to differentiate between the word as a racial epithet and the generic designation "coon shouter" or "coon song shouter," used to describe a certain kind of professional stage singer. At first, the most popular coon shouters were white women, such as May Irwin and Clarice Vance. They helped propel ragtime coon songs to prominence around the turn of the century. Ragtime rapidly paved the way for a greater authenticity in American popular entertainment, as black coon shouters, male and female, established their superiority at "portraying" themselves.

Commercially published coon songs spilled into turn-of-the-century black vernacular culture, where they seem to have served a transitional function.[4] Two-way traffic between the grass roots and the black professional stage, intensified by the popularity of ragtime coon songs, cleared the way for the "original blues."

As late as the mid-1910s, the term "up-to-date coon shouter" was routinely applied to the likes of Clara Smith, Ma Rainey, and Bessie Smith; but around 1916 they were redefined as "blues singers." This may seem an unlikely entrée for what is now called "classic female blues," but the transition reflects a dominant theme in twentieth-century African American entertainment: the triumph of the real over the false.

Our previous book, *Out of Sight*, encompasses the broadest scope of black musical activities observed during the years 1889–1895, a critical period that marked the final countdown to the commercial explosion of ragtime. In *Ragged but Right* we begin to examine the fallout from that explosion. But, we do not attempt to present an inclusive survey of black musical activity during the subsequent ragtime era. Instead, we concentrate on three attenuated avenues of professional opportunity that ragtime opened to black performers: musical comedy productions, band and minstrel companies in the circus sideshow annex, and itinerant tented minstrel shows. We have not wandered down these particular pathways at random; they stand out boldly in contemporaneous black newspaper documentation.

Our information comes primarily from the entertainment columns of the *Indianapolis Freeman*, as well as the *Chicago Defender* and other black newspapers, and from mainstream entertainment trade papers such as *Billboard* and *Variety*. The *Freeman* is a truly remarkable document of black professional stage activity, far-reaching, insightful, and uniquely representative of the thoughts and opinions of black musicians and performers. By the end of the nineteenth century, it had become a clearinghouse for black entertainment news.[5] In 1920 *Billboard* acknowledged a debt of gratitude to the *Freeman*: "The pioneer efforts of that paper to command public respect and attention for the negro performer mark the real beginning of national theatrical development for the race."[6]

Representatives of dozens of musical comedy companies, circus annex troupes, and tented minstrel shows filed reports to the *Freeman*. The most prolific among them was musical comedy star and road show manager Salem Tutt Whitney, who penned a long-running column under the apropos title, "Seen and Heard While Passing." Much of the correspondence from traveling shows is tinged with self-promotion; it seems every company had the hottest musicians, funniest comedians, largest audiences, etc. However, there are also frank accounts of racial encounters, wrecks, fires, and funerals, and hard information on rosters, repertoires, routes of travel, etc.

News from the field was augmented by commentary from staff reporters and critics. Will "Juli Jones Jr." Foster, "I. McCorker," "Tom the Tattler," R. W. Thompson, P. B. R. Hendrix, Carey B. Lewis, Billy E. Lewis, and others weighed in on every facet of the profession. The "dean of black entertainment critics," Sylvester Russell, was born circa 1870 in East Orange, New Jersey, and raised in Newark, where he attended an otherwise white parochial school. He received private tutoring in vocal culture, and served as a boy soprano with Newark's white Arcade Glee Club. As a young man, Russell became the valet of a student at Brown University in Providence, Rhode Island, where he reportedly "succeeded Flora Batson, Sissieretta Jones and Marion Adams Harris as soloist in the famous Meeting Street Church choir."[7]

Sylvester Russell, *Indianapolis Freeman*, December 27, 1902.

In 1891 Russell toured with Hicks and Sawyer's Georgia Minstrels, and then "took up concert variety and museum work" as a "double-voiced marvel, singing falsetto and baritone alternately." Around 1898 he began submitting critiques to the *Freeman*. In 1909 he settled in Chicago and became the *Freeman*'s chief dramatic critic and Chicago entertainment reporter. Russell continued to monitor black entertainment until his death in 1930, when Salem Tutt Whitney eulogized: "As a critic, Sylvester always tried to be sincere. He also tried to make his criticism constructive. He would point out the fault and then recommend the remedy. Fear of punishment, nor promise of reward never deterred Sylvester from saying what he thought about anybody. He couldn't be bluffed, bullied or bought. It meant more to him to be a critic than to eat humming bird's hearts or ride in a Rolls Royce."[8]

Russell's overriding mission was to enforce a "legitimate standard of comedy" on black performers.[9] Yet, he was not above positioning himself "in the ten cent gallery—something fierce—but I like to sit among the rowdies, I like to hear them talk—then I know what's doing."[10] Russell could also be "dicty" and spiteful; he has not been widely consulted by latter day scholars, but he is nevertheless relevant. Sylvester Russell's eyewitness accounts and insights are crucial to untangling the complexities of the ragtime era and its aftermath.

Front and center in the history of popular ragtime are the "big shows," the stunning stage successes of Bert Williams and George Walker, Robert Cole, and Ernest Hogan. During ragtime's brief reign, legitimate musical comedy was the holy grail of the black entertainment profession. Sylvester Russell supported the formal theatrical conventions of modern musical comedy as a means to escape the everlasting graveyard of minstrel farce and elevate the standards of the African American stage.

Bert Williams is the one African American performer of the ragtime era whose name is most recognized by informed observers. He is the subject of at least three books and numerous articles. So much emphasis has been placed on Williams's individual career that the larger context of black musical comedy in the ragtime era has been obscured.[11] In the salad days, Bert Williams, George Walker, Bob Cole, and Ernest Hogan were all on the same plane of popularity and accomplishment. They all shared an extraordinary moment of opportunity.

There is particular need to reassert Ernest Hogan's place in the pantheon. For many years scholars were unable to get beyond the damning title of Hogan's epoch-making hit song of 1896, "All Coons Look Alike to Me," to fairly assess his contributions to the American stage. Only in the past decade has any serious, research-driven study of Hogan's professional career been undertaken.[12]

One of Hogan's most noteworthy stage accomplishments was the Smart Set, which he originated in 1902 in collaboration with Billy McClain. Though Hogan only toured with the show for one year, his true-to-nature approach left an indelible imprint. After Hogan, Tom McIntosh, Sherman H. Dudley, and Salem Tutt Whitney each had a turn as leading man.

The Smart Set was an especially significant vehicle for constructive change on the early twentieth-century American stage. Comedian-producers of the Smart Set laid the foundation for a new era in black comedy by bringing forth recognizable characters who spoke more directly to black audiences. No other entertainment entity embodied this change so vividly.

Under Whitney's watch the Smart Set became the first big black musical comedy company to tour successfully in the South, where minstrelsy predominated. The success of Whitney's Southern Smart Set was built on more than the charisma of its star performers; the show was a haven for ragtime piano kings, among them Wilson "Peaches" Keyer, Charles "Lucky" Roberts, Eubie Blake, and Cuney Connor.

In 1914 Whitney began to complain through his *Freeman* column that another company was traveling in the South under the talismanic Smart Set name. This was Alexander Tolliver's Smart Set, aka Tolliver's Big Show, a freewheeling variety show that initiated the era of blues and jazz in tented minstrelsy. It was under Tolliver's big tent that Ma Rainey came to prominence as the "Assassinator of the Blues." Other future recording artists with Tolliver's Smart Set included Bessie Smith, Clara Smith, Trixie Smith, Leola "Coot" Grant, Butterbeans and Susie, Frankie Jaxon, and Daisy Martin. Tolliver "blended" his blues revue with a stunning array of novelty acts, including wire walkers, trapeze artists, acrobats, jugglers, and unicyclists. For the season of 1916, he attempted to fashion a blues and jazz-heavy all-black circus.

The American circus is afflicted with a pernicious history of racial discrimination. Throughout the early twentieth century, circuses exploited the popular demand for black musicians and performers while mindfully segregating and subordinating them to their sideshows. The circus sideshow band and minstrel phenomenon gained a foothold during the 1890s, and by 1910 it was becoming an institution.[13] Some of the most experienced and well-trained black musicians in the United States served as bandleaders for circus sideshow annex companies. Under their supervision, sideshow annex performers held tight to this backdoor opportunity for employment while they struggled to extricate themselves from regressive "plantation show" conventions and elevate the standards of their profession.

The repertoires of circus sideshow annex bands establish this overlooked avenue of black entertainment as central to the mainstreaming of both blues and jazz. Many future jazz recording artists spent at least a portion of their careers "jamming wind" in a sideshow tent, and many younger players were inspired by them. Black bandsmen and performers also worked in Wild West Shows, which had their own sideshow tents.

Minstrelsy has become another "forbidden" subject, lately reduced to a metaphor for historical racism in popular culture. But do not confuse the African American minstrel companies of the ragtime and blues era with their nineteenth-century white predecessors! Black minstrel companies stole the audience away from the pale imitators, thus opening a pathway of employment for hundreds of musicians, performers, and entrepreneurs. In the process, they brought elements of musical comedy, vaudeville, and circus entertainment under their all-embracing umbrella. Dispassionately appraised within its historical context, black minstrelsy requires no special exculpation.

Nineteenth-century minstrel companies gave their entertainments in theaters; but just before the turn of the century, a new form of African American minstrel show arose, "under canvas." Tented minstrelsy remained a staple of popular entertainment in the Southland for more than fifty years. African American minstrel troupes reached deep into the rural districts to provide irresistible fun, entertainment that black southerners identified with and took pride in. After all, black minstrels were professional stage performers who gathered coin and gained admiration from both blacks and whites.

Black minstrel companies made no pretense "to elevate the Negro on the stage, by laying aside the stereotype style of Negro performances."[14] Still, they managed to broadcast the latest trends in racial music, dance, and humor throughout the South. The parade bands, with their "street flash" and open-air concerts, and the canvas theaters, with their blues singers, jazz orchestras, vernacular dancers, and blackface comedians, brightened the lives of the entertainment-hungry southern masses. The fact that the minstrel heritage in the South carried into the post–World War II era reflects not only regional resistance to change but the great fun delivered by these shows.

We address the near void of substantive information on twentieth-century black tented minstrelsy with detailed histories of four of its most important exponents: Allen's New Orleans Minstrels, the Rabbit's Foot Company, the Florida Blossom Minstrels, and *Silas Green from New Orleans*. We also recover an epic tale concerning the wave of tented minstrel shows that swept over the Mississippi Delta every year at cotton-picking time.

Intrepid black tented minstrel show owner-managers such as Pat Chappelle, Eph Williams, and Charles Collier were heroes in their day; they deserve to be remembered and their legends retold. Furthermore, light must be shone on the labors and accomplishments of generations of troupers who toted the heavy baggage down rough and rocky roads. Minstrel bandsman Freddie Pratt, who trouped with the Rabbit's Foot, Florida Blossom, and Silas Green shows during the 1910s, tried to sum up the life in a poetic recitation that he called "A Showman's Dream":

> One night a showman dreamed a dream, and dreaming dreamed he died, and straightway to the pearly gates his sin stained spirit hied, and there before the saints he stood with downcast head and low. "My record's pretty rank," he said, "and I guess I'm bound below. I've smoked a lot and drank a lot—confess all, and must, and flirted, too, and then, besides, great heavens, how I've cursed." The good St. Peter looked at him with kindly, smiling eyes, but shook his head, "Don't ask," said he "a mansion in the skies." The sinner bowed, and in this strain the aged saint began: "You've gotten up at 4 a.m. and chased the train a mile, amid the train crew's gibs and jeers a-sounding all the while. And then you found, as usual, the time card's played its tricks. You've chased the wrong train once again and yours goes out at six. You've taken some gay trouper out, and spent a ten or more, and then he calmly says he has got to get up at four. You've spent your life at bad hotels, and eaten still worse meals with oleo and waiter girls, all run down at the heels. You've had your letters sent astray, your grips have wandered, too, with porters, clerks and baggagemen you're in a constant stew and once a month you see your wife, now tell me is it so?" "It is," replied the showman, as he took his hat to go. "Oh, well," said good St. Peter, as he opened the portals wide, "I'm very glad to meet you sir; just kindly step inside; we'll try to make you happy here, we'll do the best we can; you've already served your time in h— for you've been a showman."[15]

The Black Patti Troubadours, as pictured in their souvenir booklet, "Songs as Sung by the Black Patti Troubadours." This was the largest and most prestigious African American minstrel company of the ragtime era, ranked with the landmark black musical comedy companies led by Williams and Walker, Cole and Johnson, etc. The photo dates from 1897–1898, when the roster included both aging minstrel pioneer Sam Lucas, standing in the back row with top hat, and coming star Ernest Hogan, seated in the center, surrounded by the ladies of the company. (courtesy Thornton Hagert, Vernacular Music Research)

PART ONE

Coon SONGS, Big SHOWS, and Black STAGE STARS of the RAGTIME ERA

The colored man writes the "coon" song, the colored singer sings the "coon" song, the colored race is compelled to stand for the belittling and ignomy of the "coon" song, but the money from the "coon" song flows with ceaseless activity into the white man's pockets.

—**"Tom the Tattler,"** *Indianapolis Freeman, August* 24, 1901

COON SONGS AND COON SHOUTERS

In the late 1890s, ragtime sung and performed by black musicians reached the mainstream popular stage in a form ignobly dubbed the "coon song." Coon songs, with their ugly name, typically featured lyrics in Negro dialect, caricaturing African American life, set to the melodious strains of ragtime music. The designation first took hold during the 1880s, under the influence of such portentous hits as "The Alabama Coon," "I'm the Father of a Little Black Coon," and "New Coon in Town," but the real "craze" commenced in 1897 with the inception of the "ragtime coon song."

A WEALTH OF COON SONGS.

A REPRESENTATIVE list of REPRESENTATIVES in every style.

It is generally conceded that we controlled the Coon Song Successes last season. We are confident that the "PRESENT CROP," below listed, will overshadow our former triumphs in this line.

LIVELY AND BRIGHT.

★CAN'T BRING HIM BACK (Orches., with rag. chorus, ad. lib.)........ By King Kollins
★BLACK MAN FROM TROY........By John T. Kelly
HONEY, YOU'LL BE SORRY THAT YOU SHOOK ME........By Hattie Starr
★I LOVE MY LITTLE HONEY (Orches., with rag accompaniment)........By Ben R. Harney
WE ALL HAVE TROUBLES OF OUR OWN........By Loren Bragdon
BYE BYE, BELINDA........By H. Y. Leavitt
★BLACK ANNIE (with novel stop dance, and introducing the Black Annie Step)..By Hillman and Perrin
★CAPT. OF DE COONTOWN GUARDS (March Song)........By Dave Reed Jr.
RAM A JAM, OR I WANT DAT MAN........By F. J. Bryant
★AFRICA'S FOUR HUNDRED (March Song)........By Barney Fagan
BAPTIZING AT DIXON'S POOL........By Chas. Lovenberg
★NINTH BATTALION ON PARADE (March Song)........By Williams and Walker
★WHEN SARAH JACKSON'S NAME IS CHANGED TO BROWN........By Fred Statia and Paul Cohn
★THERE'S A GOOD THING GONE TO REST........By King Kollins
★COONVILLE GRAND CAKE WALK........By Dave Reed Jr.
YOU'LL NEVER FIND A COON LIKE ME........By Whitelaw and Harding

GENTEEL, YET CATCHY.

★COME BACK, MY HONEY, I'SE BEEN WAITING........By Newcomb and Statia
★HONEY YOUS'E MY LADY LOVE........ By Nat. D. Mann
★MELINDA JENKINS' WEDDING DAY........By A. Gillespie
★MY COAL BLACK LADY........By W. T. Jefferson
★DIS COON HAS GOT DE BLUES, OH! SUSIE........B J. H. Murray and F. W. Mack
★SHANGHAI LAYING FOR A COON........By Dave Reed Jr. and J. Ben Michaelis
ISE NEBER GWINE TO LUB YOU ANY MORE........By Will Waters and A. E. B. Leonard
★THAT YALLA GAL OF MINE........By Hillman and Perrin
★DAT'S ME (Male and Female version)........By Alf. Hampton and J. A. Silberger
★MY BLACK BABY MINE........By Thos. Le Mack
★LUCY LOU........By A. B. Stone
★MAMMY'S LITTLE PUMPKIN COLORED COONS........By Hillman and Perrin

In conjunction with above we can hardly refrain from mentioning our STANDING HITS:

★MY GAL IS A HIGH BORN LADY........By Barney Fagan
★MR. JOHNSON, TURN ME LOOSE........By Ben R. Harney
★ALL COONS LOOK ALIKE TO ME........ By Ernest Hogan
★I WANT DEM PRESENTS BACK........By Paul West
★HONEY, DOES YER LOVE YER MAN?........By Ford and Bratton
★RACCOON AND THE BEE........ By Ed. Abeles
★HUSH YOU BUSINESS, OH GO ON........By Sager Midgley and Maurie Levi
★YER BABY'S A COMIN' TO TOWN........By John T. Kelly

The popularity of which do not seem to wane, as they are being constantly called for, and will again be introduced by a number of companies this season.

New York Clipper, August 21, 1897. This "Wealth of Coon Songs" was part of a "Remarkable Assortment" of titles advertised by the publishing company of M. Witmark and Sons.

As ragtime reached the height of its popularity, the mainstream public was becoming somewhat obsessed with black vernacular music, dance, and poetics. This condition produced an exponential increase in professional opportunities for black entertainers and encouraged African Americans in every branch of the profession to explore their distinctive musical folklore more forthrightly. However, African Americans gained the mainstream stage only because white audiences demanded they be there. Their fortunes remained subject to the coon song–loving disposition of the dominant race and the inherited conventions of minstrelsy.

A cunning amalgam of appreciation and mockery was a cornerstone of minstrelsy and was perpetuated in ragtime coon songs. This ambiguous dynamic afforded some latitude in interpretation. Not all ragtime coon songs had the word "coon" in their title, and they were not all equally offensive in lyric content; many made use of current indigenous street slang, often reflecting a more realistic "black perspective" than earlier minstrel songs.

During the 1890s advertisements for major song publishing companies routinely included long lists of coon songs by both white and black composers. Writing in 1948, American popular music chronicler Sigmund Spaeth described ragtime piano legend Ben Harney's pioneering hit, "Mr. Johnson, Turn Me Loose," as "an early and authentic example of 'coon-shouting,' with all the abandon of the Negro style of interpretation."[1]

Disparate opinions about coon songs and the popular stage were aired in the African American press throughout the ragtime era. In December 1896, a turning point in the history of American popular music and entertainment, *Indianapolis*

Freeman theater critic R. W. Thompson expressed optimism:

The evolution of the modern stage means much to the Afro-American. The transition in popular taste—severe and pedantic critics may call it decadence—has opened an avenue fraught with vast possibilities . . .

Taste runs in cycles. Everything has its hour, and gives way to the next sensation. The Negro's chance for survival comes in his talent for versatility, to his ready adaption [*sic*] to the duty required. The legitimate outcome of this rise in the profession will be better salaries for the deserving, a higher personal esteem, and an increased dignity to the calling itself.[2]

Thompson's commentary contained an element of prophecy, but it was not long before the allied forces of race prejudice and entertainment commerce began to impinge upon his rosy scenario, forcing African American stage professionals to make uncomfortable choices. In 1901 the *New York Age* expressed the editorial opinion that matters had gotten out of control: "One of 'our companies' of the 'Coon' sort advertised recently in a Savannah (Georgia) newspaper that a certain part of the theatre would be 'reserved for coons.' The Afro-Americans of Savannah were fighting mad over it and they were right . . . The music of ragtime is tolerable, but most of the sentiment of it is false, degrading and intolerable. We want our men and women on the stage, but we want them in a decent and honorable way."[3]

As *Freeman* columnist "Tom the Tattler" pointed out, no outside force was powerful enough to suppress ragtime's raging popularity:

The American Federation of Musicians, in session at Denver last week, declared vigorously against ragtime. Ragtime has been the object of attack for the past two years by several persons of prominence. Will J. Davis, one of Chicago's leading managers, thought he had put a quietus on ragtime when he declared no performer should play his house who indulged in ragtime "coon" songs. In spite of this and several other hard raps the "coon" song, with its ragtime setting, flourishes. There are more of them on the market than ever. The Federation at Denver thought the music taste of the public had wandered so far from the ideals of Wagner, Beethoven, etc., it was cause for alarm. In unlimited numbers the people have been turning from symphonies and rhapsodies to such songs as "Ragtime Life" and "Goo-Goo Eyes." The craze has reached such proportions the prima donnas are now essaying it. Music teachers, in order to make a living, must shelve Clementi and Czerny, and teach the popular syncopation. Many a performer's sole reputation depends on his ability to dispense it.

Whether or not the Federation of Musicians can suppress ragtime remains to be seen. After all it is left to the public . . . When musicians find that nothing but empty benches will listen to a Dvorak or Brahms symphony they are likely to change their way. The public alone, I think, must do away with ragtime, and no outside pressure can affect it.[4]

In a 1904 interview, the famous black British composer Samuel Coleridge-Taylor was asked what he thought of coon songs. He dismissed them as: "The worst sort of rot . . . In the first place there is no melody and in the second place there is no real Negro character or sentiment in these 'coon' songs. However, I will not object to the term 'coon' songs. They may be that, but they are not Negro melodies." In response Sylvester Russell, the *Freeman*'s most famous African American theater critic, offered a corrective interpretation:

I deny Mr. Taylor's assertion that there is no melody in "coon" songs. They are light and airy and often full of variety, for ragtime is something that Mr. Taylor has not understood and will not understand until he visits some low Negro concert hall and sees how naturally it is executed in music, song, and dance. For, let me tell Mr. Taylor and everybody else that this low life phase of music which has electrified the world is better performed by degraded southern Negroes than by the best stage artists in existence.[5]

Russell, however, adopted a different attitude when he revisited the subject of ragtime coon songs in his *Freeman* column of June 22, 1907:

Song publishers have at last been driven to their wits' ends to fathom what kind of songs the public will stand for next. It was a gracious thing that the public got an overdose, all at once . . . [T]he change soon came when white people began to tire of wench stories and had actually become ashamed of hearing insulting darkey life insinuations set to rag-time music . . .

Some people might say: "What harm is there in a mere song?" But let me inform such people that a lot of harm has already been done. The fundamental harm dates back to what has already been rehearsed, "All Coons Look Alike to Me," "Coon, Coon, Coon," and "Nigger, Nigger, Never Die." . . .

Now, if the stubborn, ignorant class of colored actors will please cut all the self-ridicule out and if the song publishers will please kindly oblige the respectable element of the colored race by restricting race insult from comic songs, they will be doing a heap of good to a badly demoralized country.

As Russell observed, certain popular coon songs had been especially harmful in their effect, and none more so than Ernest Hogan's epoch-defining hit of 1896, "All Coons Look Alike to Me." The song's title inspired derisive humor in the white press, and incited street-level racist taunting. As late as 1928, fellow black star Sherman H. Dudley recalled that Hogan had "gained fame over night by writing, 'All Coons Look Alike To Me.' This song was a national hit. I remember when I was traveling with the 'Original Nashville Students' way back in 1899, when we were playing all one-night stands. Every time I would pass a little white child, it would start singing 'All Coons Look Alike To Me,' and those who could not sing would whistle it."[6]

Predictably, the ascendance of "All Coons Look Alike to Me" was animadverted upon by the African American press. The May 8, 1897, edition of the *Leavenworth Herald* reproduced this report from the mainstream daily *Kansas City Star* as an "Ernest Hogan Item": "A Chicago policeman shot the wrong Negro during a row in that city . . . His only excuse was: 'All niggers look alike to me.'"

Russell later contended that Hogan had written "All Coons Look Alike to Me," "not as a race insinuation, but as a popular style of literature, written for rag-time music in its earliest days."[7] The song's controversial sentiment is ascribed in the lyrics to "Lucy Jane Stubbles," the narrator's "honey gal," who has run off with "another coon barber from Virginia." In the chorus, Miss Stubbles chides, "I've got another beau, you see, he spends his money free . . . So, I don't like you no how, all coons look alike to me."

Many coon songs had more insidious lyrics, but unfortunately for Hogan, "All Coons Look Alike to Me" was adopted as the slogan of a Jim Crow society that refused to acknowledge African Americans as individuals. Many of Hogan's black contemporaries denounced the sentiment attached to "All Coons Look Alike to Me," but none held Hogan personally responsible for endemic racism. Otherwise, in fact, Hogan was widely respected as a role model in the black theatrical profession.

"All Coons Look Alike to Me" was cleverly parodied by many of Hogan's colleagues. In 1897 the *Freeman* reported on Billy McClain: "In every performance with 'Darkest America' he receives flattering remarks and encores for his rendition of 'All Coons Look Alike to Me' in German."[8] An 1898 *Freeman* review of Cole and Johnson's musical comedy *A Trip to Coontown* claimed it was "worth the price of admission merely to hear the blackest Negro in the company sing 'All Chinks Look Alike to Me.'"[9] That summer Billy Miller advised *Freeman* readers that his parody, "All Spaniards Look Alike to Me," would "be on sale soon at 25 cents per copy."[10] Later that fall, Charles H. Williams sang "All Colored Folks Look Like Little Black Gnats to Me," and Howard E. Morton came out with a contrary version, "White Folks All Coons Don't Look Alike to Me."[11]

BRAN NEW PARODIES

By JOHN RUCKER,
The Original "ALABAMA BLOSSOM"
JUST WRITTEN—"All Guns Look Alike to Me;" "She Was Bred in Old Kentucky," a sure laugh producer; A funny parody on "No Coon Can Come Too Black for Me," which is a winner; "Guess that will hold you for awhile," and "Just as the Sun Went Down" 25c Each, or the Five for $1.00. Send money order or postage stamps, and "Get in the Game."
J. HARRY JACKSON, Publisher,
318 N. Capitol Ave. Indianapolis, Ind.

Indianapolis Freeman, June 24, 1899.

The lyrics and melody of Hogan's notorious coon song have been largely forgotten, but the title still lingers.[12] At a 1927 recording session in Atlanta, Georgia, white southern banjo songster Uncle Tom Collins waxed a wide assortment of coon songs, including the epic "Tain't No Lie," which includes a joke about a blind street singer:

> *What made me laugh so much, you see,*
> *He was singing "All Coons Look Alike to Me."*[13]

When ragtime burst onto the scene during the season of 1897–1898, a new generation of white, predominantly female "negro specialists" sprang up, who became popularly known as "coon shouters." Like the earlier designations "jubilee shouter" and "camp meeting shouter," "coon shouter" described an untrained vocalist of a certain "robust degree." Famous white female coon shouters of the late nineteenth and early twentieth centuries included Elizabeth Murray, Stella Mayhew, Artie Hall, Marie Cahill, May Irwin, and Clarice Vance. These women helped popularize many songs written by black composers.

Clarice Vance was among the first to be identified as a coon shouter. A striking woman, fully six feet tall, she was born in Louisville, Kentucky, in 1871.[14] The *New York Clipper* of June 6, 1897, noted, "The coon song singer, Clarice Vance, is making a decided success with George Graham's tough negro oddity, 'I Can't Give Up My Rough and Rowdy Ways.'" When she appeared at Miner's Bowery

Theater with Scribner's Columbian Burlesquers in January 1898, the *Clipper* described her as a "coon shouter and rag time vocalist."[15]

In 1913 Vance recalled to a Terre Haute, Indiana, newspaper reporter that she had started out performing in blackface, but eventually gave it up because, "I had almost worn my face off removing burnt cork after performances."[16] A drawing of Vance in a 1906 edition of the *New York Clipper* depicts her holding a grotesque-looking blackface mask.

New York Clipper, January 20, 1906.

In 1900 Vance's repertoire included "I'm Leading a Rag Time Life," "I Don't Care If I Never Wake Up," "Don't Forget to Bring Your Money Home" and "I Hope Dese Few Lines'll Find You Well." By 1900 Vance had begun to soften her performance style, and she adopted a more genteel-sounding sobriquet: "The Southern Singer." A reviewer in the *Cincinnati Times Star* observed: "She does not make her entrance with a cake walk swagger and do a bit of buck dancing between verses. Her one object is to sing up-to-date coon songs without the aid of her feet—and she does it in a manner altogether refreshing and decidedly effective."[17] At the Alhambra Theater in 1906, Vance "came into the evening's bill in a good position, when the auditors were in a humor to appreciate the quiet delicacy of her delightful Southern songs. At Miss Vance's hands the Southern 'coon' song loses all of its roughness and becomes a sort of negro classic to rank with the old-time plantation melodies."[18]

Clarice Vance's "refined" style of coon shouting is documented on Edison cylinders from 1905 and Victor disc recordings from 1906; titles include "Save Your Money 'Cause De Winter Am Comin' On," "If Anybody Wants to Meet a Jonah, Shake Hands with Me" and "He's a Cousin of Mine."[19] To a modern listener these recordings, and the recordings of white female coon shouters in general, may evince "Negro dialect" but little else distinctive of African American musical style.

This generality, however, does not apply to May Irwin, one of the earliest and best-remembered white interpreters of ragtime coon songs. When she died in 1938, the *New York Times* recalled, "Her voice was untrained, but a beautiful natural one. Enrico Caruso once said she might go far as a real singer if she studied. Miss Irwin laughed. She said all the technique she needed was 'to take a deep breath and let her go!' To the theater-going public of her day it was enough."[20] Irwin's 1907 recording of her famous version of "The Bully" preserves her evocative, metallic timbre, but also her prodigal use of the word "nigger."[21]

On September 2, 1895, Irwin opened at the Museum Theater in Boston, in the title role of *The Widow Jones*, a "three-act farce" portraying the "embarrassments of a 'fat-fair-and-forty' widow."[22] It was through this seemingly unlikely character that Irwin introduced such songs as "I Want Yer Ma Honey" and "The New Bully" to the mainstream theatergoing public. A review of *The Widow Jones* in the *New York Times* of September 17, 1895, noted: "When she sang her new darkey songs . . . one forgot her blonde hair, her peaches-and-cream complexion, and her blue eyes; every tone of her voice, every expression of her countenance, every gesture and motion combined to create an illusion now of a lovelorn Virginia darkey, now a dangerous Tennessee 'coon.'"

When she opened at the Bijou Theater in New York at the end of 1896, in the musical comedy *Courted into Court*, the *Times* reported:

> Miss Irwin, as Dottie Dimple, a "popular actress," sings a number of new darkey songs in her inimitable way. "Crappy Dan," "Ma Lulu," and the old favorite, "Hot Time in Old Town To-Night," were . . . vociferously encored . . .
>
> The Southern negro she impersonates in "Crappy Dan" and "The New Bully" is not the old plantation darkey, happy in his bondage, primitive in his simplicity, but a product of the new civilization, the bad town darkey of the present age of transition. That he is susceptible to humorous treatment Miss Irwin proves, and the manner in which she puts him before us in all his badness and audacity, without the aid of make-up or scenic effect, is, in its small way, a triumph of art. But this same crappy Dan, with his dice loaded for "sebens" and his "'quaintance wid a gun," represents a grave social problem.

At the end of 1907, when Irwin appeared at the Orpheum Theater in what was described as her "first appearance in vaudeville in New York," a reviewer for *Variety* noted, "Time was when May Irwin was 'coon-shouter-in-chief to the American public,' but since then she has lost a good deal of her unction, and others have usurped her place. She employed but one 'coon' number, opening with 'Much Obliged.'"[23]

Perhaps the boldest white coon shouter on New York City's early vaudeville theater scene was Artie Hall. She was born in Atlanta, Georgia, around 1881, and began her stage career in her mid-teens. When she appeared at Proctor's Pleasure Palace in the summer of 1899, the *New York Clipper* reported, "Artie Hall became a favorite at once in her peculiar coon shouting and ragtime dancing." By the fall of 1899 she was trading as "The Georgia Coon Shouter:" "Her specialty consists of an artistic and true-to-nature portrayal of the idiosyncrasies of the exuberant young Negro woman of the South. Every detail, from the facial make-up to the kinky coiffure and the attempt at style in dress, is accurately reproduced . . . [S]he looks as though she might have come from 'the quarters' direct to the stage."[24]

Hall's stage repertoire for 1900 included "I'm Living a Rag-Time Life," "My Genuine Georgia Gal," and her own original composition, "I Don't Care What Happens to Me Now." A clever series of advertisements in the *New York Dramatic Mirror* was apparently intended to "authenticate" her act.

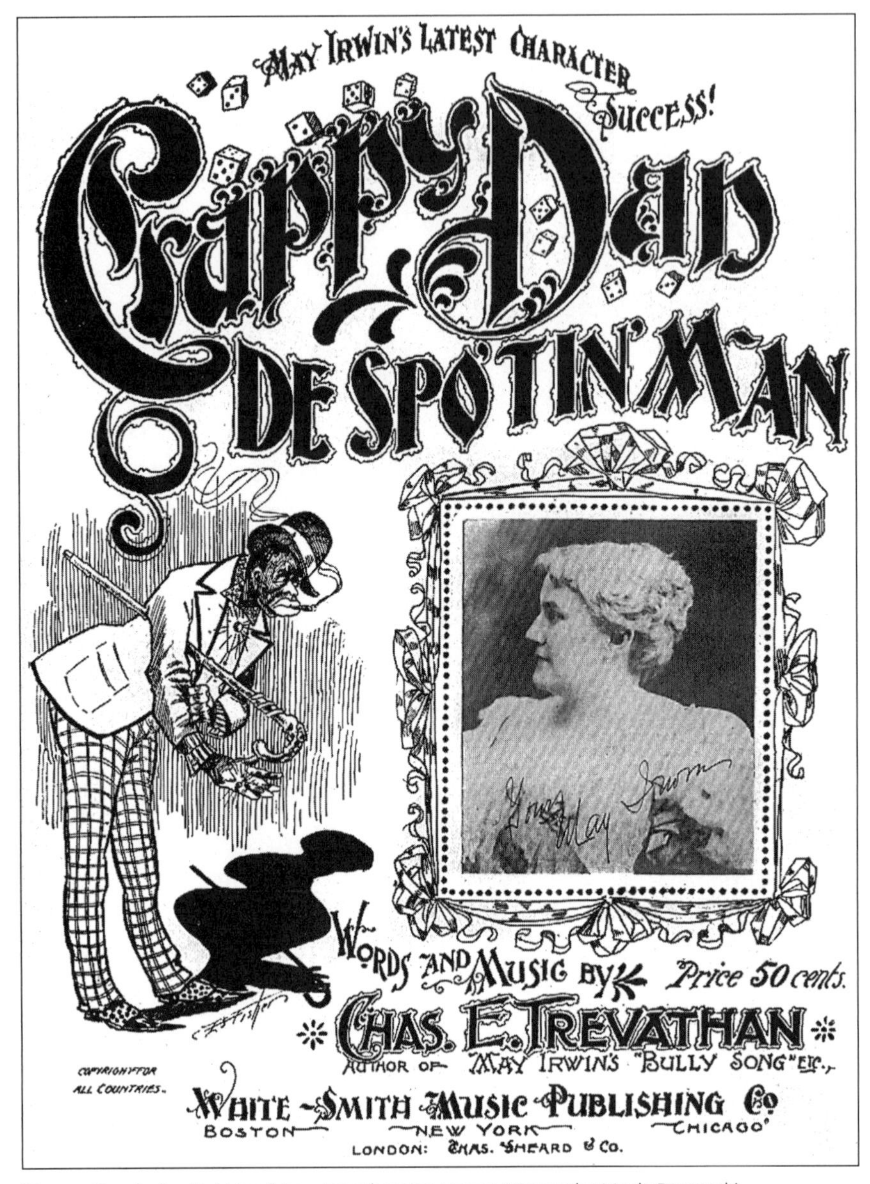

"Crappy Dan De Spo'tin' Man." (courtesy Thornton Hagert, Vernacular Music Research)

One reads: "Say, Authors! I got ma spyglass out, lookin' for a coon-song dat don't speak ob razors, gin, domestic trubbles, chickens or melons. I will gib a gold dollar for some words and an air dat don't ring in dese subjecks."[25]

In the fall of 1901 the "Georgia Coon Shouter" appeared in Boston with William A. Brady's "Uncle Tom's Cabin" Company, in the role of Topsy. Also with Brady's "UTC" was an "enormous colored aggregation," some two hundred "cake walkers

ARTIE
HALL

"Miss Artie, you is cert'n'y the onliest white woman what kin sing coon songs, and dat's de trooth."
—Ernest Hogan.

New York Dramatic Mirror, September 22, 1900.

Artie Hall in her Topsy persona. *New York Dramatic Mirror*, December 14, 1901.

and dancers," under the supervision of "solo pianist and singing comedian" Luke Pulley.[26] A photo in the *Dramatic Mirror* suggests Hall played a saucy Topsy; however, she appears to have forsaken the "modern" coon songs of her vaudeville repertoire for older race parodies like "Shoo Fly, Don't Bother Me," "Climbing Up the Golden Stairs," and "When Aunt Dinah's Pickaninnies Harmonize."[27]

Following her stint with Brady's "UTC," Hall made some appearances in vaudeville without the "smudgy aid" of burnt cork.[28] Nevertheless, her continuing success was indelibly linked to her "realistic" blackface makeup and her "'coon shouting' of extremely robust degree."[29] Hall endeavored to be virtually indistinguishable from the subject she imitated. Under Sylvester Russell's critical glare, however, certain faults were noted: "Miss Artie Hall, a Southern white coon song singer, with her natural dialect, has succeeded to qualify. Miss Hall does not seem to understand Northern culture, or she would omit songs with the word 'niggar' in them. Her greatest art is 'crying,' but she sings rag-time altogether too slow."[30]

Another of her stage peculiarities aroused adverse criticism in a 1907 edition of *Variety*: "Artie Hall . . . will persist in removing her gloves, together with wig in order to assure those assembled in front she really is a white person. If it brought applause, there might be an excuse, but the house applauds the singing, not the color." As early as 1903, Sylvester Russell had observed as much and more: "The domestic classes of white people have been cultivating a tendency of late to assert that white people can sing coon songs better than colored people. This is not true. We must not accept this 'bluff' from white people. We must disagree with them at once. The white actress who blacks her face to sing coon songs and then rolls up her sleeve to show her white arm makes no impression whatever on her audience. They applaud the song, but care nothing about her color."[31]

Some years later, on March 18, 1915, Lester A. Walton, manager of the Lafayette Theater in Harlem, related an object lesson in the *New York Age*, under the heading, "The Real and the False":

THE FAMOUS COON SHOUTER.

MRS. ROSA SCOTT,

Mrs. Rosa Scott, better known as Topsy the famous coon shouter is featuring in the A. C. Bauscher's Plantation Minstrels, singing, "I Don't Know Where I'm Going But I'm On My Way" and I'll Be Back in a Minute, But I Got to Go Now." Regards to friends.

Indianapolis Freeman, May 12, 1906.

On the bill at the Lafayette Theater Monday was a white female performer who for fifteen years has played on the big time doing a single turn. She is known in theatrical parlance as a "coon shouter." . . . Some years ago, about the time May Irwin and other white artists were in the limelight as "coon shouters," this singer in question was a big hit in vaudeville . . . She is the possessor of a good singing voice and showed such skill in making up that when, at the end of her turn, she disclosed her true racial identity, she gave her audience (that is, the white patrons) a pleasant surprise.

So after nearly sixteen years showing white people how colored people sing this variety artist was given an opportunity Monday afternoon to let the colored folk see how they chirped "coon songs" and those of the

HERE COMES the SCOTTS

ROSA SCOTT.

RICHARD SCOTT.

We are still with the Yellow Flyer of the Great PARKER SHOWS No. 1, which was wrecked on June 22, en route to Erie, Pa. Rosa Scott, the Star performer with PARKER'S GEORGIA MINSTRELS, was badly injured in the wreck, but has recovered and will be ready for work Friday night if nothing happens. Richard Scott is still in line, and is working trying to have a new act this fall. The Scotts send regards to all friends. When writing mention The Freeman.

Indianapolis Freeman, August 10, 1907.

ragtime brand. But the efforts of the lady fair under a coat of tan was not convincing, and some of the disorderly patrons in the audience showed their disapproval by hissing. It was obvious that many promptly realized in the beginning that they were not listening to the real thing . . .

When reminded that she was working before a colored audience and that she should not overdraw her character and make herself objectionable to the patrons of the house she exclaimed that she knew how colored people acted and she did not need to be given lessons in the subject.

The term "coon shouter" was also applied to African American entertainers who sang coon songs. A subtly modified designation, "up-to-date coon shouter," became signally associated with the coming generation of black female blues singers, including Gertrude Rainey and Bessie Smith. Among the forgotten legion of early-1900s African American female coon shouters were Carrie Hall, Bessie Gillam, and Rosa Scott.

The literary persona of Topsy served as an early prototype for African American blackface comediennes and coon shouters. Rosa Scott was known as "the Topsy Coon Shouter." Her photo, in costume, appeared several times in the *Freeman*. In company with her husband Richard, Rosa Scott traveled for at least three years (1906–1908) as the "leading lady" with the Great Parker Amusement Company No. 1. Her 1906 repertoire included "I Don't Know Where I'm Going But I'm on My Way," "I'll Be Back in a Minute, But I've Got to Go Now," "Preacher and the Bear," "Santa Claus," "Silver Heels," and "Loving Henry." A *Freeman* report of December 22, 1906, said, "Richard and Rosa Scott are still smiling on and are making five and six encores nightly with the Southern colored and white people . . . They always make good."

One of the first African American women to specialize in ragtime coon song singing was Bessie Gillam, a product of one of Detroit, Michigan's premier black musical families. Her father, barber-musician Charles Gillam, had been prominent in the local black string and brass band milieu until his death in 1890, while her older brother Harry appeared in local community productions like Ed Rector's Juvenile Minstrels before venturing out with some of the major black road shows of 1890–1910.[32]

MISS BESSIE L. GILLAM.

comedenne and soubrette. The above is an excellent cut of Miss Bessie. The young Miss is a native of Detroit, Mich. She was born the 3rd of May, 1880. At an early age little Bessie showed marked talent for the stage, and being of an apt and musical family, she was naturally encouraged in her natural vocation. At the age of three she participated in a concert in which she sang that ever popular song "Peek-a-boo," at that she had to be placed on a stool in order to be seen by the audience. After that from time to time she appeared in home talent concerts, until finally her marked advancement demanded recognition and in consequence of that she had the pleasure of holding the boards for eight weeks at the Wonderland Theater, (in Detroit, Mich.,) which speaks for itself. At that time she was only five years of age. At the end of this unprecedented engagement she was put in school, and at the same time she was given a musical education by her mother, (Georgie E. Gillam, a very accomplished pianist). After receiving a good school education and the art of music, she was still haunted by the desire to become an actress, to that event she was fortunate in receiving an engagement in connection with her brother, (Harry L. Gillam,) from the Georgia University graduates, under the direction of J. Edward George. They started on the road on Dec. 16th., '95, to tour the country. After a successful tour of thirty weeks, she returned home and had to remain home for a long while to patch up a sprained ankle received while in the act of preforming some grotesque work. After taking a good rest she rejoined her brother at Eureka, Kan., on Dec. 10th., 1897, to work as a team with the Nashville Students and P. T. Wright's Colored Comedy Co. She is receiving praise from press and public for her artistic rendition of coon songs and refined dancing. Being a young lady she has a bright future and we look forward to see her hold positions among the many bright lights now lighting the dark pathway on to the road of success for the colored race.

Indianapolis Freeman, April 9, 1898.

In the spring of 1896 sixteen-year-old Bessie Gillam completed a tour of the western states with the Georgia University Graduates. With P. T. Wright's Nashville Students at the beginning of 1898 she was "singing her new coon song, 'Syncopated Sandy,' also 'There's No Coon One-Half So Warm.'"[33] The *Indianapolis Freeman* of April 9, 1898, noted, "Little Bessie Gilliam [*sic*], the charming little soubrette, with Wright's Colored Comedy Co., is proving to the public that all coons don't look alike to her. She is singing 'Mammy's Little Pumpkin Colored Coon,' to perfection nightly."

At the end of 1898 Gillam was with the Georgia Up-To-Date Company, "hitting them hard nightly, singing coon songs in her artistic and catchy way." With P. G. Lowery's Vaudeville Show in the fall of 1899 she sang "All I Want Is My Black Baby Back" and "I'se a' Picking My Company Now." She entered the new century on the cutting edge of a rapidly developing black entertainment industry. On May 20, 1901, when the Rialto Theater in Memphis opened its landmark "summer season in Ragtime Opera," "Bessie Gilliam, as 'tough Lize,' was a revelation; the part was created by her and she will place it on her list as a special act."[34] Tough Lize became a stock character in black vaudeville.

One of the first black stage performers to be specifically identified as a coon shouter was Carrie Hall. She made her mark in such pioneer black vaudeville venues as the Palace Theater in Savannah, Georgia, the Domino Theater in Fernandina, Florida, and the Exchange Garden Theater in Jacksonville. On May 19, 1900, the Exchange Garden's *Freeman* correspondent called her "the Queen of coon song singers." At the Palace Theater in the fall of 1902, she was judged "second to none as a coon shouter."

Carrie Hall's early-1900s repertoire was laced with "covers" of coon song hits from the big, northern-based African American road shows, including Williams and Walker's "The Game of Goo-Goo Eyes," Ernest Hogan's "The Phrenologist Coon," and Cole and Johnson's "My Castle on the Nile." Her other offerings ranged from grassroots expressions such as "What You Going to Do When the Rent Comes Due" and "I'm Tired of Dodging Dat Installment Man," to the absurdly titled "A Pork Chop Is the Sweetest Flower That Grows."[35]

In the spring of 1903 a correspondent from the Domino Theater in Fernandina notified that, "Miss Carrie Hall, the Southern Coon Shouter, has made a big hit, rendering 'Oh, Oh, My' and 'Good Evening Mr. Johnson'" in the "musical farce of 'Miss Hannah from Savannah.'" It seems Carrie Hall was the black stage embodiment of "the exuberant young Negro woman of the South" that white coon shouters like Artie Hall were trying so hard to impersonate. In the person of Carrie Hall and African American entertainers like her, the designation "Southern Coon Shouter" indicates a pathway for the commercial ascendancy of the blues. By 1909 Hall was producing musical farces at the Royal and Pekin Theaters in Memphis, where blues was just beginning to assert its presence.

The term "coon shouter" was not applied exclusively to women. Charles Wright, better known as "C. W. Bebee," or "Bebee the coon shouter," was an African American performer who toured primarily in the South and Midwest, with minstrel companies and medicine shows and in small-time vaudeville. In the fall of 1899, at the Little Solo Theater in Houston, Texas, Bebee and his partner

Sally Cottrell sang "Baby You've Made a Hit with Me" and Ernest Hogan's "I Don't Like That Face You Wear." At the Little Solo Theater again the following spring, "Bee Bee, the 'Coon' shouter and rag time comedian," was "hitting them hard singing 'When a Coon Sits in the Presidential Chair,'" and he and Sally Cottrell performed a sketch titled "4- 11- 44."[36]

In the spring of 1901 Bebee filled an engagement at the Olympic Theater in Galveston, Texas.[37] During the summer of 1903 he appeared in Hot Springs, Arkansas, as a "lightning cake walker and dummy dancer" with King and Symmons's Southern Black Troubadours.[38]

The *Freeman* of March 26, 1904, conveyed word that "C. W. Bebee, the coon-shouter . . . is well and got out of his troubles alright and is now at liberty." In October 1904 Bebee was in Cherokee, Kansas, with the Ton-Ka-Wah Medicine Company.[39] In November he wrote the *Freeman* to say: "I am now with the Cosmopolitan Amusement Company as stage manager. We left Coffeyville, Kas., Oct. 25th for Pulaski, I. T. [Indian Territory]. We are getting ours at each performance. The week of Nov. 6 we are in Sherman, Tex."

En route to Tuscaloosa, Alabama, with Proctor's Arkansas Minstrels in the fall of 1905, Bebee was singing "'Chicken Can't Roost Too High for Me,' using live chickens and special scenery." In 1906 he was the stage manager and principal comedian with Howard McCarver's Southern Comedy Company, and he was still with them when they closed out a thirty-week season in May 1907.[40] They were preparing to reopen in July, when a *Freeman* correspondent reported: "C. W. Bebee, our stage manager and comedian, is very busy getting everything in shape."[41]

W. L McMullen (Erastus) comedian and vocalist, a well known coon song shouter, who has travelled with J. B. Morris for five years has decided to join a minstrel company this season and

would like to hear from A. G. Allen. Mr. McMullen was born in Kingston, Ont., and is 32 years old. Last winter while in Mobile Ala., he met the one is to be Mrs. McMullen this winter. Regards to all friends. Write me care of The Freeman.

Indianapolis Freeman, September 20, 1902.

W. L. McMullen was another well-regarded black male coon shouter. Brief reports in 1902–1905 editions of the *Freeman* placed McMullen in black vaudeville theaters and road shows operating in Georgia, Alabama, Tennessee, and Kentucky. McMullen notified the *Freeman* on September 6, 1902, that he was a member of "the Plantation company with J. B. Morris' Carnival Company . . . Our musical director is ably assisted by Mr. Alonzo Taylor, a clever guitarist of Augusta, Ga." The *Freeman* of December 5, 1903, relayed this message: "W. L. McMullen writes from Elberton, Ga., that Frank G. Hill and he have joined hands and that the former with his twelve-stringed instrument is making a hit."

By the dawn of the twentieth century a new style of coon song composition was coming into currency, built around the latest street slang or black colloquialism, which was almost always incorporated in the song title. Examples noted in 1898–1908 editions of the *Freeman* include "Ain't Dat a Shame," "Get Off My Money," "I Got Mine," "I'll Break Up This Jamboree," "I've Got My Habits On," "Kill It, Babe," "All In, Down and Out," "You're in the Right Church but the Wrong Pew," "I'm Going to Start Me a Graveyard of My Own," "T'ain't No Lie," etc. Many of these specific expressions reverberate in blues and "old time" country music recordings of the 1920s and 1930s. Popular songs constructed around the latest black slang or vernacular expression were commonplace in rhythm and blues of the 1940s, as well as rock and roll of the 1950s and 1960s. In fact, this characteristic method of composition, a palpable legacy of the coon song era, remains prevalent to the present day.

Coon songs and their methodology influenced indigenous African American folk music. Between 1905 and 1908, social scientist Howard W. Odum collected "negro folk songs" in Georgia and Mississippi. In 1911 he presented 110 of these songs, or fragments thereof, in an essay published in two consecutive issues of the *Journal of American Folklore*.[42] Odum's timely fieldwork indicates the extent to which ragtime coon songs mingled with African American folk music in the rural South.

In his examination of "how current negro songs arise," Odum wrote that some of the fragments and "one-verse songs" he transcribed "are representative of the negro song in the making . . . Fragments of songs are always interesting; and one wonders to which song, if to any, they originally belonged, or how they may ultimately be combined." Odum was aware that much of the material he had collected was "unfinished." He was a witness to the agglomeration of "every kind of song into one," the "mongrel productions arising from the mingling of negro song with 'coon' songs and with popular songs of the whites."

Odum claimed his survey was not concerned with songs performed on the professional stage, and that he only considered songs performed informally, within the "folk-life" of indigenous black southern communities. He described how:

> The great mass of negro songs may be divided into three general classes . . . first, the modern "coon songs" and the newest popular songs of the day; second, such songs greatly modified and adapted partially by the negroes; and, third, songs originating with the negroes or adapted so completely as to become common folk songs . . . The second class of songs easily arises from the singing of popular songs, varied through constant singing or through misunderstanding of the original versions. These songs appear to be typical of the process of song-making . . . The third class of negro songs is made up of the "folk-songs" proper.

While Odum maintained that "only those [songs] that have become completely adapted are given in this collection," a significant number of the songs he reproduced are more or less straightforward interpretations of currently popular, commercially published coon songs.

Odum transcribed a version of "Baby, Let Me Bring My Clothes Back Home," which he considered "characteristic in its adaptation of the 'coon' song into a negro song." The same could be said of other songs he collected, with titles that correspond with published coon songs, such as

"I Got Mine," copyrighted in 1901 by John Queen and Charlie Cartwell;[43] "Lookin' For That Bully of This Town;" "Dat Fortune Teller Man," which originated with Williams and Walker's 1900–1901 musical comedy *The Sons of Ham*; and "Moving Day," published in 1906, by Andrew B. Sterling and Harry Von Tilzer. It is interesting to compare Sterling and Von Tilzer's chorus with the folk "deconstruction":

It's moving day,
Pack your folding bed and get away,
If you've spent ev'ry cent,
You can live out in a tent,
It's moving day.[44]

Odum transcribed this interpretation:

It's movin' day, it's movin' day,
I'm a natchel-bohn git away,
I spin ev'y cent—go camp in a tent,
Lord it's movin' day[45]

Many songs and fragments Odum collected contain themes, phrases, couplets, and expressions also found in popular coon songs. He documented numerous improvised parodies of John Queen's "Just Because She Made Dem Goo-Goo Eyes." His transcription of "Long Tall An' Chocolate to the Bone" includes the phrase, "I'm going to start me a graveyard of my own," traceable to minstrel comedian Billy Cheatham, who performed it with Allen's New Orleans Minstrels in 1900.[46]

One of the most striking elements of Odum's transcriptions is the preponderance of phrases that became a living part of the 1920s blues recording era. Examples include, "If you don't want me, please don't dog me 'round," "I'm going where the water drinks like wine," and even, "I got the blues, but I'm too damn mean to cry." Odum was an annalist of the primordial soup of the blues, in the instant before the blues was recognized as a distinct style of song. Yet, despite what must have been extensive contact with grassroots "songsters" and "music physicianers" in rural Mississippi and Georgia, Odum does not appear to have encountered the descriptive term "blues," as he did not include it in his classifications of black folk music of the 1905–1908 period.

By the late 1890s the term "blues," which had long been used to describe a certain "low feeling," was being applied more particularly to a certain low feeling among African Americans. Coon song composers were quick to exploit this association. The *New York Clipper* of December 25, 1897, carried an ad for one of M. Witmark & Sons' latest publications, "Oh, Susie! (Dis Coon Has Got De Blues)," in which "the pleading of a melancholy 'cullud' gen'man" was said to be "vividly depicted." In 1901 black composers Chris Smith and Elmer Bowman published a "Colored Complaint" entitled "I've Got De Blues." It told of a leading member of "Darktown's elite" who was about to toast the assembled guests at a big social function, when he spied "his rival and his Lize . . . making goo goo eyes":

I'm all confused, ma gal I 'spects to lose,
I can't make no toast tonight
Because I've got de blues.[47]

Shepard N. Edmonds was a progressive black ragtime songsmith. His coon song hits were not free of race insinuation and offensive language, but there was much more to them than that. Sylvester

Russell felt that Edmonds came "very near to jubilee in his rag-time compositions."[48] Many of Edmonds's creations were subsequently absorbed into folk tradition.

Originally from Columbus, Ohio, Edmonds joined his first minstrel show in 1895.[49] He was with Isham's Octoroons in 1897 when the *Freeman* predicted: "What will undoubtedly prove the greatest hit in the line of 'coon' songs since their institution in the merry world of songs, is an exceptionally catchy melody by Shepard N. Edmonds entitled, 'Give Me Your Eye.'"[50] Edmonds's productions for 1898 included "You May Go When You Get Your Trunk Packed," "You Want to Be a Devil, But It Ain't No Use," "My Little Powder Rag," "All Dat I Had's Done Gone," and "There Are Others Who Don't Think That Way." The *Freeman* of July 16, 1898, said the latter title was "creating much comment through the East. Winn and Edmonds are featuring this one, and receiving four and five encores on it. Following is the chorus:

'Don't you think that because you're yaller,
I'm a-goin' to give you my last dollar,
Don't you think that I'm a-goin' to beg you to stay.
Don't you think that because I'm black
I'm a-goin' to coax you to come back.
For there's others who don't think that way.'"

More than forty years later, in 1942, Mississippi Delta bluesman Son House recorded these same couplets for the Library of Congress, under the title "Am I Right Or Wrong":

You may not think because I'm black,
I'm going to beg you to take me back,
Now babe, was I right or wrong.
You may not think because you're brown,
I'm going to let you dog me 'round,
No, honey, was that right or wrong.
May not think because you're yellow,
I'm going to give you my last gold dollar,
No, babe, was that right or wrong.[51]

Sylvester Russell characterized Edmonds's big hit of 1901, "I'm Goin' to Live Anyhow Until I Die" as a "genuine rag-time song perfected by class meeting music that was extracted by Edmonds for comic usage. Such is the history of rag-time, and Edmonds is one of the most perfect composers of its music."[52] On the original sheet music, Edmonds dedicated his song to "the unbleached American, Ernest Hogan," who had introduced it during a lengthy engagement at the New York Theater Roof Garden. The chorus states:

I'm goin' to live anyhow till I die,
I knows my kind of life ain't very high,
With sticks and stones you can break my bones,
You may talk all you want to 'bout me when
I'm gone,
But I'm goin' to live anyhow till I die.

Howard Odum's early field transcriptions include a garbled stanza of "I'm Going to Live Anyhow Until I Die," which he heard in the context of a work song:

I'm goin live in hell [i.e., "anyhow"] till I die,
An' I know you goin' talk about me when I'm gone,
Sticks and stones goin' break my bone.

When Alan Lomax collected a version of "I'm Going to Live Anyhow Until I Die" from a rural black Mississippi fiddle and guitar duo in 1959,

Shepard N. Edmonds, *Indianapolis Freeman*, December 25, 1897.

he classified it as "one of a family of tunes lying between black square dance music . . . and the first true instrumental blues."[53] It could be said that, in both musical style and narrative theme, Edmonds's song stands as a marker between the nineteenth and twentieth centuries in American vernacular composition. Its history on commercial recordings may have begun with a 1904 cylinder waxed in London, England, by African American entertainer Pete Hampton.[54] During the 1920s it was recorded under different titles by a variety of "hillbilly" banjoists and string bands.[55]

New York theater critic J. Harry Jackson filed this report on Edmonds in the *Freeman* of January 10, 1903:

> Shepard N. Edmonds, the well-known author "I'm Going to Live Anyhow Until I Die," "Kissing Trust," "Deed I Do," and many other popular song hits, has brought suit against J. W. Stern & Co. music publishers, to recover damages for their failure to pay royalties for several of his compositions, which he alleges they have on several occasions refused to do. Several months ago when "coon" songs were in the height of popularity, the big music publishers almost ran over themselves in an effort to secure the most successful Negro writer for their particular firm . . . Now it is alleged that the publishers are "holding back" several good songs of the Negro authors and publishing others, thereby causing complaint from the colored brother.

Sidney Perrin, another outstanding African American popular songwriter and minstrel performer of the ragtime era, complained in a 1904 newspaper interview: "If I had been paid for a number of my songs in proportion to the amount made by them I should now be retired and enjoying a fortune. I sold 'Mammy's Little Pumpkin Colored Coons,' which was one of the most popular coon songs of recent times for $5 and was tickled at the time to get the money. Another for which I received only a pittance was 'That's the Way to Spell Chicken,' which went for $15."[56]

"That's the Way to Spell Chicken" was one of the biggest coon song hits of 1902. A New York City–based *Freeman* columnist notified that it would be "sung by that clever singing comedian, Bobby Kemp" with the 1902–1903 edition of the Black Patti Troubadours. The *Freeman* of November 8, 1902, confirmed that "Bobby Kemp's Whangdoodle Comedy Four are winning laurels singing, 'That's the Way to Spell Chicken,' being the only ones to produce it South. Get it, it's a winner. It was originally written by Sydney Perrin for 'Coon's Paradise,' a coon operatic farce by J. Ed Green and Sydney Perrin."

Pioneer recordings of Perrin's irresistible "chicken song" were made by white singers Arthur

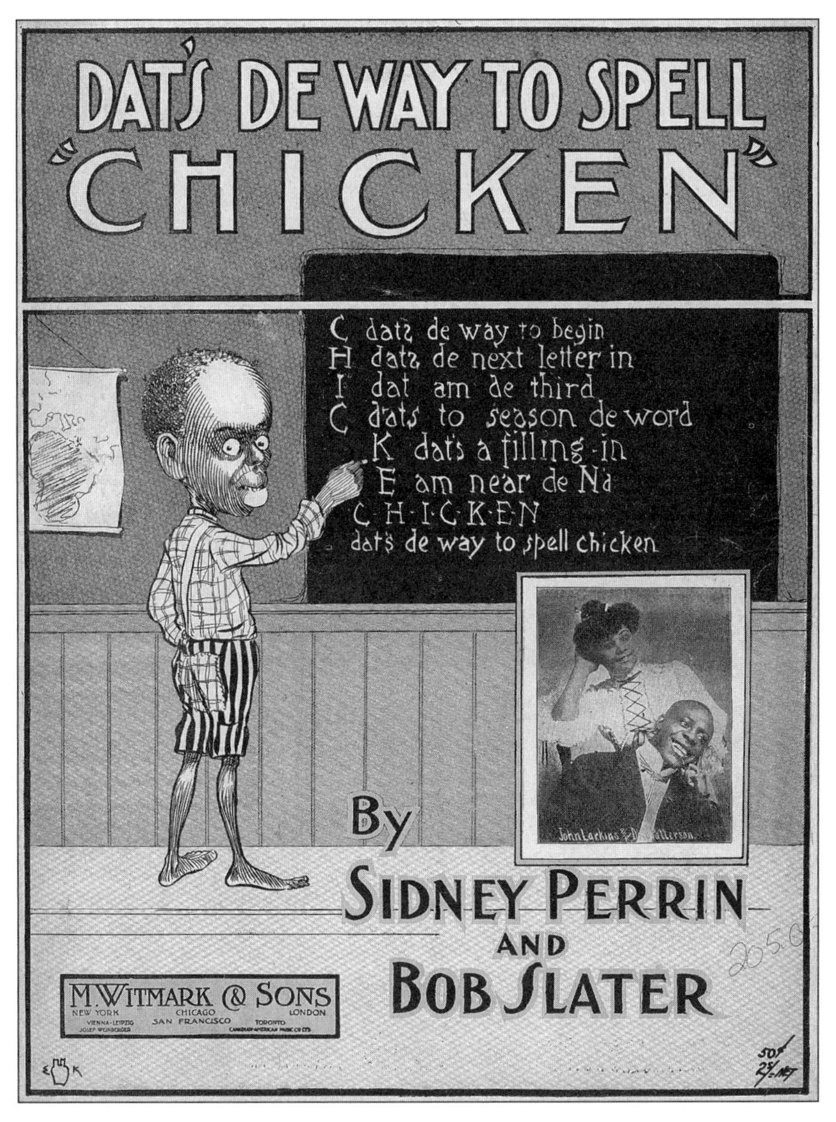

"Dat's de Way to Spell 'Chicken.'" (courtesy Hogan Jazz Archive, Tulane University)

Collins in 1902 and Len Spencer in 1903. During the first two months of 1903, the *Freeman*'s weekly "Songs and Singers" column identified at least six different white entertainers who were featuring it in their stage acts. Several "hillbilly" artists recorded it during the 1920s and 1930s,[57] and in 1967, blues legend Mississippi John Hurt incorporated its signature chorus in a medley of remembered "chicken songs":[58]

C, dat's de way to begin,
H, dat's de next letter in,
I, dat am de third,
C, dat's to season the word,

K, dat's a filling in,
E, I'm near de end,
C-H-I-C-K-E-N,
Dat's de way to spell chicken.[59]

Writing in 1904, Sylvester Russell opined: "The modern school of distinguished educated colored song writers, without complaint, have set a new example, and all the most intelligent singers in America are now singing their songs. Among these writers are Bob Cole, Rosamond Johnson, Sidney Perrin, Billy Johnson, Nathan Bivins, Al. Johns, Shepard Edmonds, Will Hamer, Will Tobias, [R. C. "Cecil Mack"] McPherson, [James "Tim"] Brymn and others."[60]

Notably absent from Russell's list is Irving Jones. Jones was one of the most successful African American composers of early ragtime coon songs. His initial professional breakthrough came with Sam T. Jack's Creole Burlesque Company, during their maiden voyage of 1890. For many years he was a headliner on mainstream vaudeville circuits, and a favorite in the theatrical centers of New York and Chicago, singing his original coon songs and performing comic monologues.

Perhaps no other coon song composer better captured the hell-bent spirit of ragtime's commercial ascendancy. At work within the iniquitous economic regime of the ragtime era, he was seemingly one of "those market informants who understand the commodity premise and [are] prepared to authenticate their cultures accordingly."[61] In any case, Jones's coon song compositions proved equally popular with singers of both races and left a lasting impression on blues recording artists of the 1920s.

Ragtime-era critics expressed mixed opinions about Jones's songs. When he signed with the Black Patti Troubadours for the touring season of 1900–1901, he was proclaimed "the very best interpreter of modern ragtime ballad and one of the most accomplished composers of songs of that class."[62] But in 1902 a different view was expressed by *Freeman* columnist "I. McCorker":

> We have it that God gives a man talent and the people afterward give him fame, but not infrequently all of us get the word "capability" confounded with "talent" and "notoriety" with "fame." After Irving Jones became notorious by having written "Get Your Money's Worth," "Let Me Bring My Clothes Back Home," etc., the people pronounced him famous, and he has gone on the loud tenor of his way ever since, grinding out coon conceits with a fecund mind which might be envied by Chas. K. Harris, who works off two or three sentimental spasms a day. And Jones is never in so felicitous a frame of mind as when he is "composing." But we have no doubt that Jones has made money from his products, and the Negro has so few avenues open to him from which to make it that we are glad the Rag-time Millionaire has bagged some of the coin of the realm.[63]

Jones's coon song hits of 1898 included "Take Your Clothes and Go" and an "answer" song, "Let Me Bring My Clothes Back Home." Both were popular on the minstrel show routes. The Quaker City Comedians reported in February 1899 that their star comedy team held forth "for 25 minutes of continuous howling from the audience, in which they introduced: 'Take Your Clothes and Go' and 'Let Me Bring My Clothes Back Home.'" "Let Me Bring My Clothes Back Home" jumped quickly and deeply into tradition. Paul Oliver has noted that Howard Odum collected it in the field

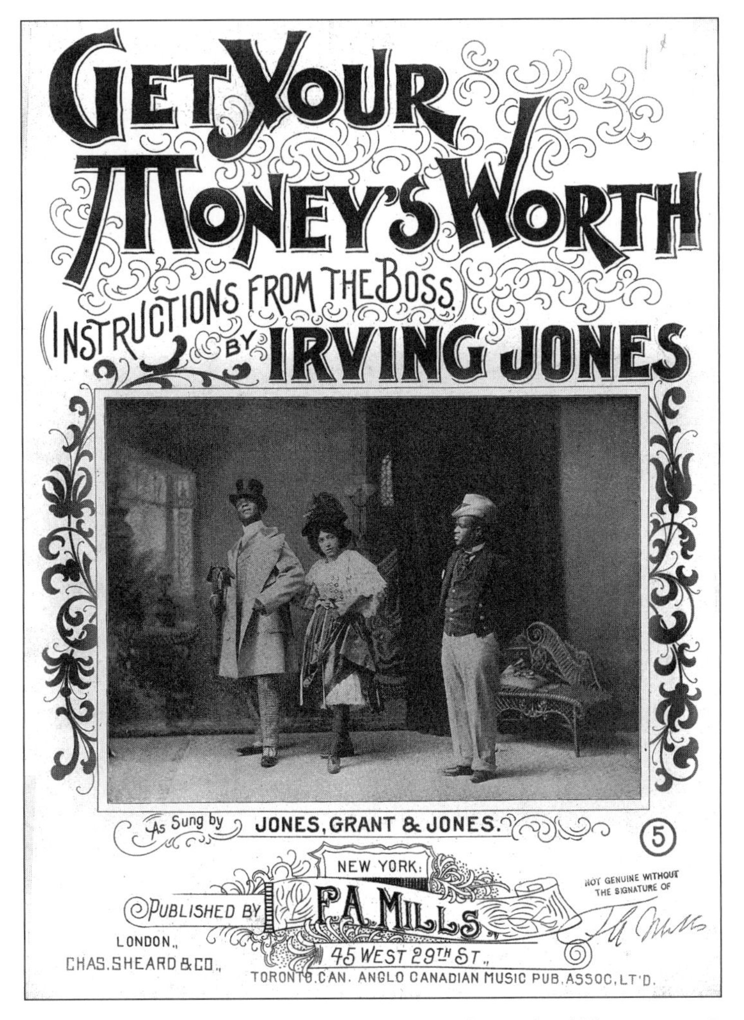

"Get Your Money's Worth." (courtesy Center for Popular Music, Middle Tennessee State University)

only a few years after it was published and that Texas guitarist-songster "Henry Thomas recorded it in a medley entitled *Arkansas* in 1927."[64]

In the spring of 1900 Jones's newest coon song composition broke out along the minstrel show routes. With Oliver Scott's Refined Negro Minstrels in Tennessee that spring, James White "added to his repertoire that funny meaning song of Irving Jones, 'My money never runs out,' and is making a wonderful hit." And with Cummings and Alexander's Uncle Tom's Cabin Company, Tom Jefferson was "hitting them hard with the song, 'My Money Never Give Out.'"

Jug band banjo legend Gus Cannon recorded "My Money Never Gives Out" twice: for Paramount in 1927, and for Victor in 1930.[65] Cannon's interpretation weds the Irving Jones song to another popular coon song of the same period, "I Don't Care If I Never Wake Up." The two songs are built on similar chord progressions, and

"I Don't Care If I Never Wake Up." (courtesy Hogan Jazz Archive, Tulane University)

Cannon stitched them together in the manner of "floating verses":

There's a certain yellow coon lives in this town,
He's as lazy as he can be,
At a Chinese laundry he hangs around,
"I likes my hop," says he.
But the other day this man got drunk,
And a pipe full of dope he bought,
He went to sleep, dreamt he was rich,
And then to himself he thought,
(chorus)
"Well! I don't care if I ever wake up . . ."[66]

I am a coon who is a financier,
I'm known as the rag-time millionaire,
I wake up with a million dollars every morn',
And I throw away ev'ry dollar that is soiled or torn,
If all of my money was stacked up high,
I know that my coin would reach the sky,

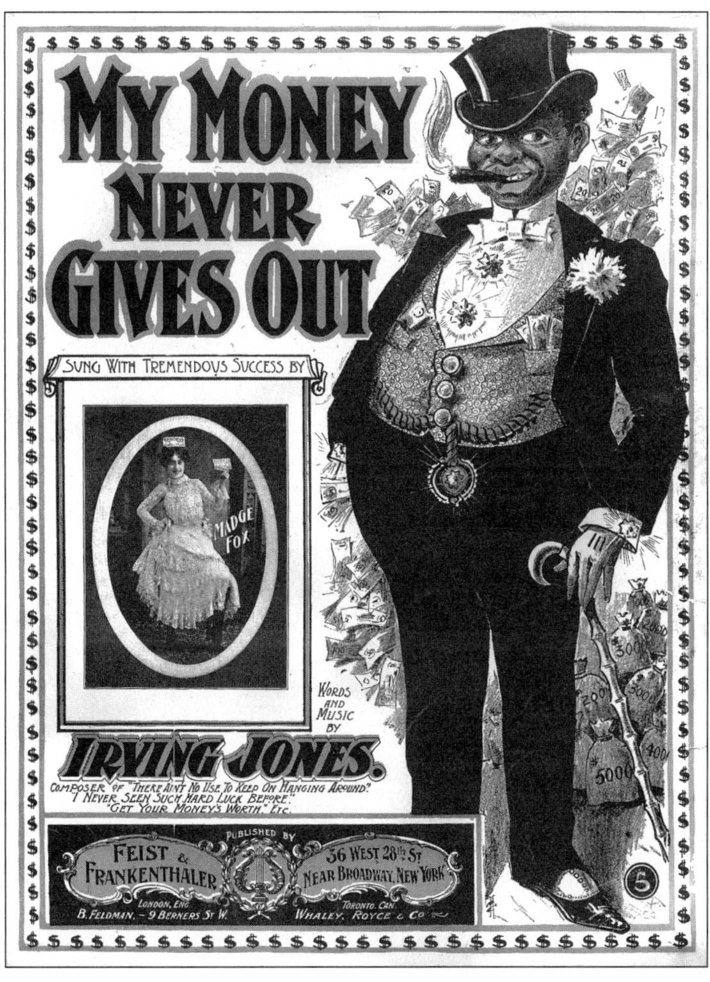

"My Money Never Gives Out." (courtesy Hogan Jazz Archive, Tulane University)

For Vanderbilt or Gould I do not care
nothing about,
I've got so much money it never gives out.
(chorus)
My money never gives out . . .[67]

Tailoring the lyrics to suit his style and taste, Cannon removed the word "coon" from both songs in his recordings of "My Money Never Gives Out."

Irving Jones followed "My Money Never Gives Out" with another "coon fantasy," "The Ragtime Millionaire," which also made a resounding hit with black performers. With Gideon's Minstrels in the spring of 1901, Bobby Kemp was "certainly a 'Ragtime Millionaire,' that being the song he features." At Ninaweb Park in Louisville, Kentucky, that summer, John Tolliver was "singing 'I am a ragtime millionaire,' and is making good." During the fall of 1902 Al Boyd reportedly sang "Ragtime Millionaire" while playing through New Mexico with the Old Plantation Minstrels. In 1928 a race recording of "The Ragtime Millionaire" was made

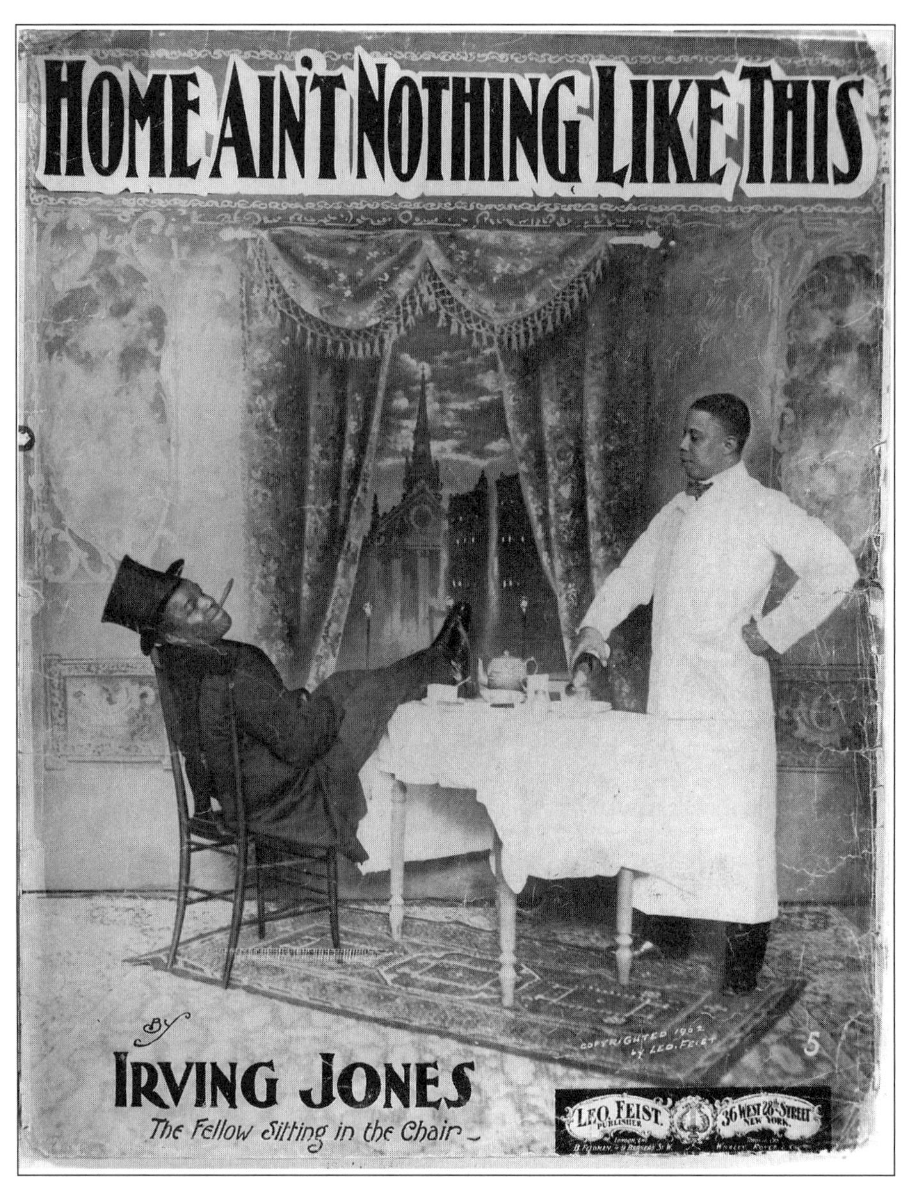

"Home Ain't Nothing Like This." (courtesy Michael Montgomery, Montgomery Archives)

by Tidewater, Virginia, barber-guitarist William Moore.[68]

An advertisement for Jones's 1902 hit "Home Ain't Nothing Like This" took a paradoxically apologetic tone: "Seems hard—but people will have coon songs—we must supply their needs and demands—Ernest Hogan at Keith's recently sang a new and humoristic darkey song, 'Home Ain't Nothing Like This' by Irving Jones, receiving no less than a dozen encores—Irving Jones sang it himself at the New York Theatre, with similar results."[69]

In 1903 critic P. B. R. Hendrix reported from Chicago that, "Irving Jones, for the past two weeks playing our leading vaudeville houses, cleaned up everything. The Bufays [i.e., white performers] hate for him to be on the bill with them for they have to work so hard to make a hit with the audience."[70] When he showed at the Pekin Theater on State Street in the fall of 1910, critic Carey B. Lewis wrote, "Irving Jones. My, who would not laugh at this human wit . . . his monologue is full of bright, characteristic philosophy, showing close study of the humorous Negro character and his delineations were as clearly defined as a well cut Cameo. He was simply immense."[71]

An item written in 1924 by *Chicago Defender* entertainment editor Tony Langston provided an update: "Irving Jones, the famous comedian and songwriter, who started in the show business when Hector was a pup . . . has been tying the show in knots at the Academy theater, Chicago . . . Irving has been on the water wagon for years . . . He has some real bookings and will be busy for a long time."[72]

In 1925 Jones went out with the Famous Georgia Minstrels, in what was said to be "his first tour with a minstrel show."[73] A report from the "Georgias" in the *Chicago Defender* of August 15, 1925, had him singing "Pawn Shop Blues." Irving Jones remained active in the profession until his death in 1932.

As the twentieth century progressed, the public's appetite for coon songs began to wane, and African American commentators became more outspoken in their condemnation. Sylvester Russell conducted an interview with stage genius Bob Cole, published in the *Freeman* of October 7, 1905, in which, to the critic's apparent surprise, Cole sounded a keynote regarding the use of the word "coon," a word that had played a prominent role in his rise to show business fame. Cole now asserted:

> The word "coon" is very insinuating and must soon be eliminated . . . I am going to crusade against the word "coon" . . . the best class of white people in America abhor the word "coon" and feel ashamed whenever they hear it used. In London [Cole] found it used as common slander. Here [Russell] asked Mr. Cole how it was he had named his comedy of several years back "A Trip to Coontown," he replied, "That day has passed with the softly flowing tide of revelations."

Cole's declaration was somewhat unprecedented and may have influenced subsequent developments. Chicago-based *Freeman* columnist "Juli Jones Jr." had this to say in a December 5, 1908, article titled, "From The Heart Of Dehomey": "The Lincoln [Theater on State Street] offers the dear Uncle Wesley Lumly in 'The Honolulu Boys,' yet the show is billed 'Honolulu Coons,' which is a bad bill for taste to present to the public. The word 'coon' has lost its usefulness years ago."

The use of the word "coon" in popular song greatly diminished after 1910.[74] The descent of coon songs was almost a foregone conclusion by January 2, 1909, when an especially bitter commentary appeared in the *Freeman* under the headline "Coon Songs Must Go":

> "Coon" songs after the great damage they have done to the American colored man, are now dying out. Although "rag" time melody may live forever, the words "coon," "nigger" and "darkey" are now being omitted by song writers. Usually some fictitious name as "Sam Johnson" and "Linda Lue" are used in the lines of poetry instead of the word "coon" which is very offensive to the colored race and makes the hair raise on their heads

when they hear it. There is a great difference in composers of 20 years ago to the later day poets. The authors who wrote "Suwanee River," "Old Black Joe" and others like those, songs that will live forever, never used bad words, slang, etc. Nowadays the composers have no respect for good people, no thought of elevating, careless of hurting good innocent people, they rush their horrible junk on the market for sale. Out for graft, they use slang, hurried-up poetry—anything that will sell quickly. The colored writers not knowing the harm they were doing, took a stick to break their own heads, by writing "coon" songs. The old authors seemed to write with a good sympathetic feeling toward the race and the more popular their songs, the more sympathy we got. If we only had such writers now!

The first "coon" song was composed by a little insignificant, sawed off and hammered down west India [*sic*] banjo player by the name of Chas. O'Brien, in San Francisco in 1892. He sang on an excursion boat and passed the hat. A white man, a music publisher heard him sing, invited him to his store where he and O'Brien rigged up a song called "Mah Angeline." It was published and played by all the bands and sung everywhere, being a new wrinkle in the way of music. Bert A. Williams was at that time singing for the price of chili and beans at a side show on Market street, San Francisco. He heard this new song, gave it the name of "Dora Dean," and claimed himself the author. O'Brien sued Williams' publisher and it went to court. The judge declared it a vulgar song because in it were [*sic*] the word "coon". But he decided that both parties would have the authority to publish and sell the song. Bert Williams sent his song east and O'Brien stood his ground and sold them like hot cakes. Soon after, Earnest Hogan got some white man to publish "All Coons Look Alike." The music was catchy, the words were amusing, and the title page disgusting in their attempt to portray a typical Southern Negro.

Two thirds of the white people today don't know that colored men write songs. It's hard to make them believe that Gussie L. Davis, one of the most popular song writers this country ever produced, was a Negro. White composers, now seeing that there were money in "coon" songs, they all commenced to write. They soon discovered that it didn't require education, talent, refinement or anything that was really good to write a "coon" song. All they had to do was to get two verses and a chorus of anything bad they could say about the Negro in a humorous way, put the words to rag time or a slow drag tune to suit the words, and in the poetry use the word "coon" as often as possible, and their fortune was made provided the song became popular. If it never was played by Sousa's band or sang on the Orpheum Circuit, the song was "shelved" or "pigeon holed." There are as many "coon" songs published today and lying on the shelf—never sung, never introduced, as there are drops of water on a rainy day. It used to cost $40.00 to publish a song, now they have dwindled down to $2.00, with a royalty of three cents per copy to the author.

Within the last five years the more trash put into a song the better it sold, even if it only lasted a month. Four years ago the air was rank with "coon" songs. Every song of Southern melody, or ragtime was titled a "coon song." Williams & Walker are a great deal to blame for being the originators and established the name "coon" upon our race. They met a white man in San Francisco by the name of McConnell who put them on the circuit. In order to achieve success or to attract the attention of the public they branded themselves as "the two real coons." Their names accompanied with "coon" songs was soon heralded North, East, South and West. As much as to say the Negro has now changed his name! He is no more human, but a "coon." His new nickname was now printed in large type without quotation marks. Williams & Walker and Ernest Hogan were not old enough then to know the harm they had brought on the whole race. They needed the money, what little they received, and the white people needed the laugh on the ignorant and the largest amount of money they made in the speculations. Colored men in general took no offense at the proceedings and laughed as heartily on hearing a "coon" song as the whites. But where the rub came is when the colored man was called a "coon" outside of the opera house. Instead of the whole race raising up in arms and protesting against such slang used in songs and such horrible caricatures on the title pages, they good naturedly joined in the chorus, "All Coons Look Alike to Me."

Within the last few years I notice the colored writers have cut out the word "coon" in their poetry. Some few white ones still use it and the latest agony is "If the Man in the Moon Were a Coon." Songs sell as well now without the word "coon" as they did when they were chuck full of "coon." Every colored man and woman of any pride, whether educated or not, becomes grossly insulted when called a "coon." Yet he can't go to a theatre nor listen to a phonograph without being told that he is a "coon." The name "coon" in a song, we understand, is only meant as an assumed name, just to amuse or cause laughter while you are hearing the song or seeing the play; but it don't stop there. A show goes to a country town—some low down, loud-mouth "coon shouter" sings "Coon, Coon, Coon," or some other song that has plenty of "coon" in it, with an emphasis on the word "coon." Then the people, especially the children, are educated that a colored man is a "coon." What was meant for a jest is taken seriously. Before the show came the people were afraid to call a black man a "coon." Or they may have wanted to show him some respect by calling him "colored." But now they think it's all right and he won't mind, because it's all in fun and it's in all the songs. In this way and many other ways too numerous to mention, "coon" songs have done more to insult the Negro and cause his white brethren, especially the young generation, to have a bad opinion of good Negroes as well as bad Negroes, than anything that has ever happened. Just imagine Booker T. Washington or some of our worthy bishops or other great men of our race walking on the street on their way to lecture on "How to Educate the Race," and they hear a lot of trashy boys singing, as soon as they see the colored man, "Coon, Coon, Coon," or "Bill Simmons," or anything that comes in their mind as a sly way of insulting the gentleman of color.

Dr. Talmadge was outspoken in denouncing nicknames in print. In fact, great men never allowed such slang as "coon" and "nigger" in print. Occasionally the word "darkey" was used. They had more respect for the race. History says that mankind is the highest of animals and that Adam named every living thing. He never intended a human being to be called a "coon." Congress called the American Negro "colored" to distinguish them from the genuine African. If Congress had given us the name "coon," the slang slinging, so-called Americans would have, no doubt, called us "colored" just to be contrary and insulting. A song writer once told me that he objected to using the word "coon" in his poetry but he had to because it rhymed with moon, loon, tune and spoon. It's only one syllable and easier to articulate than the word Negro or colored. Now, then, if the law had in the beginning made it a penalty for any compositor to set up in type the word "coon" and "nigger" in songs and plays, and had demanded or enforced respect for the race there would be less prejudice, ill feeling and trouble between the races. But the time will come when a spade will be called a spade. Certain slang and nicknames should be abolished, even if it cost bloodshed—the same as it did to abolish slavery.

The inhabitants of Butte, Mont., are most all Irish. Two years ago a burlesque show came there and posted lithographs caricaturing and ridiculing the Irish. The company was arrested, the house closed and bills torn down and the show had to leave town. Four years ago a bill was introduced in the Pennsylvania Legislature to cut out cartoons in newspapers, but it didn't pass. The voters against it were bought up by the Associated Press. Ireland might have been free today only for the songs they published against England. Do you know that a song can touch the heart? They bring laughter and tears, sympathy or ill feeling, especially when the writer gets personal or when he is writing for himself—careless of whose feelings he may hurt. Abraham Lincoln once wrote a harsh letter to a man and after considering how the man might feel over it, he threw the letter in the stove. Every composer who writes a song with the word "coon" in it should do the same.

The author of "Coon Songs Must Go" blamed Ernest Hogan, Bert Williams, and George Walker in particular for "establishing the name 'coon' upon our race." However, it was under the guidance of these same entertainment leaders that a generation of African American performers reached the popular stage and forever altered the face of American entertainment.

The Big Shows

In the late 1890s, the public's fascination with ragtime brought about a confluence of creative and commercial purposes, resulting in unique and unexpected opportunities for black entertainers. Significantly, it led to the creation of financial mechanisms for the original road productions of a handful of African American comedian-producers. Bob Cole, Bert Williams, George Walker, and Ernest Hogan directed all-black musical comedy productions, known in the profession as the "big shows." These big shows were considered the pinnacle of black accomplishment on the professional stage during the ragtime era. Heavily bankrolled by white theatrical investors, they made seasonal tours, appearing in large mainstream theaters with casts of forty to sixty people or more.

Musical comedy was the popular commercial trend, and the big shows dared to compete with white companies, even on Broadway. Their productions were as elaborately staged and costumed as any white show. Testing the boundaries of "coon comedy," they offered a new-fashioned, in-crowd slant on African American life and thought that made them unique in the entertainment universe. Even in the entrenched mainstream theatrical establishment of New York City, the big shows demonstrated that black producers and performers were capable of things white performers could not reproduce.

Also included in the select category of big shows, the Black Patti Troubadours represented another stream in the evolution of black entertainment. Like the shows led by Hogan, Cole, and Williams and Walker, this was an elaborate, oversized, reliably financed, all-black production that appeared in mainstream theaters. However, while the black stars of the other big shows exercised considerable creative control, the white proprietors of the Black Patti Troubadours, Voelckel and Nolan, retained strict authority over their productions. Moreover, while the other big shows engaged in the development of "legitimate" musical comedy, the Troubadours were an African American minstrel-variety show, albeit the biggest and the best on the road.

The Black Patti Troubadours opened their maiden season in Boston, Massachusetts, on September 7, 1896, and continued to run the roads until 1915. Their annual tours covered the length and breadth of the United States and much of Canada. From Jacksonville, Florida, to Vancouver, British Columbia, no section was overlooked or avoided. Inside the profession the Troubadours were known as a "woods outfit," because they played many one-night stands in small towns and isolated regions. However, they also filled week-long engagements in practically every major American metropolis, including New York City, Chicago, and San Francisco. At the end of their forty-five-week tour of 1899–1900, the *Freeman* summarized:

> During the season about to close these merry entertainers have travelled over 28,000 miles and given nearly 500 performances in nearly every principal city

of the United States and Canada. It is estimated that over one million theatre goers have been entertained by the Troubadours this season. From a pecuniary point of view it has been a highly profitable one for Messrs. Voelekal [*sic*] and Nolan . . . It was the first colored company to receive recognition from theatre patrons in the better class of houses. While the coon song, rag time, the buck dance, and cake walk predominate in the performance, yet there are moments when these talented singers give expression to some of the sweetest melodies selected from the standard Grand and Comic operas.[75]

Reviewers described "a stage show that is as varied as it is entertaining, and the kind that is enjoyed without the aid of a libretto or an interpreter. It is a rapid fire medley of song, story [and] dance with Negro melody, darky fun, the buck dance, the cake walk, stunning specialties and coon shouts, happily interspersed and climaxed by selections from the standard operas."[76] The Troubadours' program deliberately counterposed expressions of high and low art. As one *Freeman* columnist explained: "[The] interspersing of high and low comedy including plantation scenes were notable and in keeping with the public demand as seen from the manager's viewpoint."[77] Under Voelckel and Nolan's control, the show was designed to appeal to the masses and conform to what mainstream audiences considered acceptable from black entertainers.

Unlike the big musical comedy shows, the Black Patti Troubadours were able to tour with success in the South, where their identification with minstrelsy afforded easier entrée.[78] The racial composition of their southern audiences differed from place to place; however, segregated seating was the general rule. When they appeared in Chattanooga, Tennessee, on April 1, 1908, "The balcony was given over to colored people, and it was crowded . . . The body of the house contained only a sprinkling of white people, which, taking the real excellence of the production into consideration, was somewhat strange."[79] One week later, at the Avenue Theater in Louisville, Kentucky, they attracted "a large and appreciative audience made up mostly of white people." The Louisville engagement marked "the first time that a colored performer received a bouquet at the theatre in this city. It was given to Madam 'Patti' after singing 'My Old Kentucky Home.'"[80]

The Troubadours' main attraction was their prima donna namesake, Sissieretta Jones, the "Black Patti," universally accepted as "the greatest singer of her race." For nearly a decade, unyielding racial segregation had kept her from the mainstream opera platform.[81] Now, in a sort of compromise, she sang selections from operas within the context of a hard-traveling minstrel and variety show.

To accentuate the Black Patti's special talents, the Troubadours formulated an opulent "operatic kaleidoscope" as a signature element of the show. It featured Madame Jones with a select chorus, singing excerpts from classic and comic operas. She typically performed the "Miserere" from *Il Trovatore*. She also made cameo appearances in the olio, where she was invariably called upon to perform "Suwanee River." During the season of 1905–1906 she starred in an adaptation of *H. M. S. Pinafore* that obviously impressed Sylvester Russell:

Madam Sissieretta Jones as Josephine, surprised everybody beyond expectations . . . After she rendered her principal solo, "Sorry Her Lot, She Loved So Well," to the few who are advanced in the language of music it was easy to discern why Black Patti is still the supreme cantatrice of her race. So perfect was she in her articulation that her diphthong enunciation carried the day in vocal significance. "Farewell, My Own" was also delivered with much sympathy and pathos. Singing a role in "Pinafore," which has been heard so often by white prima donnas, shows how superior Black Patti's voice is, to those who are really capable of judging. The maturity of this voice of continual sweetness, methodically schooled, means years to its preservation.[82]

Almost every season, the proprietors of the Black Patti Troubadours hired different star comedians and producers, billing them just below Madame Jones. The top comedian of the first season's tour was Tom McIntosh, with support from Bob Cole, Billy Johnson, and Hen Wise. The great Ernest Hogan was the feature of the next two seasons, supported by Billy and Cordelia McClain, Irving and Sadie Jones, Sidney Perrin, and others. In 1907 a *Freeman* reporter observed that, "Nearly all colored performers of any repute have been members of this remarkable company, with the exception of Bert Williams and S. H. Dudley."

The Black Patti Troubadours reveled in vernacular music and dance. Ragtime and coon song singing existed alongside, and on a more or less equal footing with, opera singing. The company's most prominent female ragtime specialist was Mattie Phillips, "a dashing octoroon from North Carolina," still in her teens when she joined the show in 1897.[83] A critic immediately noticed, "she sings her 'coon' melodies in such a painstaking manner that she never fails to bring forth a hearty recall."[84] In the spring of 1898 a reporter enthused that "her fancy steps in the first act, when she sings 'Mr. Johnson, Turn Me Loose,' set the audience wild, and her idea of the poetry of motion in the cake walk is wonderful to behold."[85] Later that fall Mattie Phillips "won herself a place in the olio,

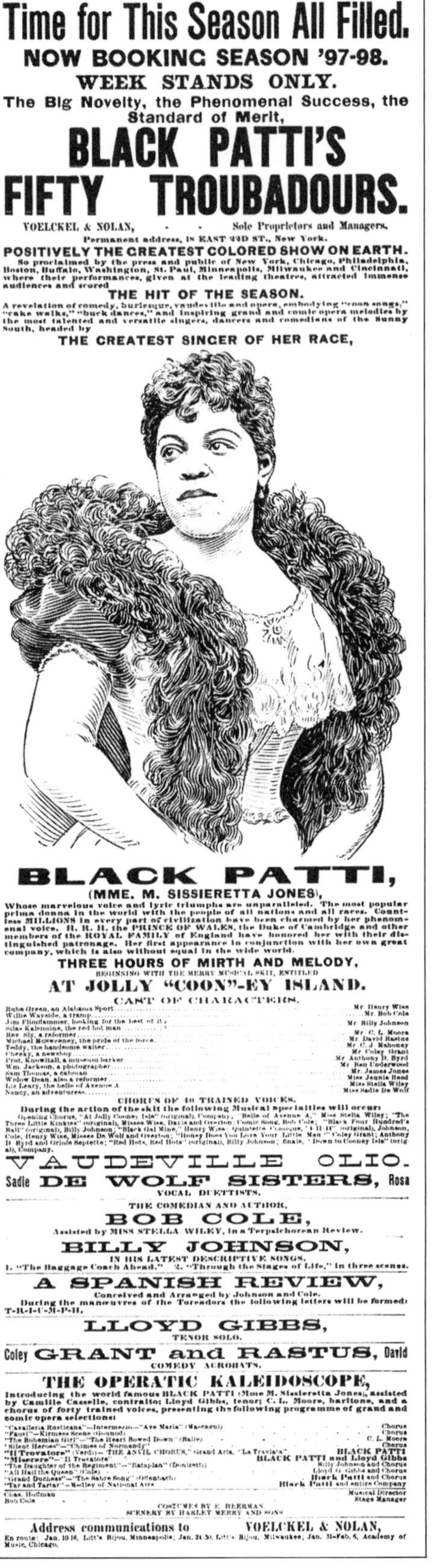

New York Clipper, January 16, 1897.

and is filling it with the ease of an old professional. She nightly brings the house down with her 'coon songs.'"

During the season of 1898–1899 Mattie Phillips's repertoire included "Give Me My Money" and "Anna Eliza, My Rag Time Gal." In the fall of 1899 a correspondent dubbed her the "Rag Time Whirlwind." In 1902 Phillips ventured into mainstream vaudeville. At the Roof Garden in Philadelphia that summer, she joined hands with John Bailey to put on "a very clever sketch in which they introduce the novelty 'rag-time' shadow dance."[86] That fall she played the Unique Theater in Brooklyn as a member of Walter Smart and George Williams's New Octoroons.

In the fall of 1903 "Miss Mattie Phillips, late of the 'Black Patti' Company," was said to be appearing in Paris, France. She was back with the Black Patti Troubadours by the fall of 1904.[87] During the season of 1905–1906 she "displayed all her old-time charm and grace of style in her grotesque dancing and singing of rag-time songs."[88]

On October 28, 1899, the Black Patti Troubadours' *Freeman* correspondent informed that, "Ida Forcen [*sic*], coon song singer and buck and wing dancer, joined us in Chicago." When they played Chicago again in the spring of 1901, "Ida Forcen, the little Chicago sunbeam, was greeted at every performance by rounds of applause. Everyone still remembers 'You're Just a Little Nigger,' it being her master rendition." In 1902 the same Ida Forsyne toured with Ernest Hogan in the original edition of the Smart Set Company. Back with the Black Patti Troubadours in 1903, she was billed as the "unbleached soubrette."[89] Ida Forsyne went on to garner international acclaim for her "Russian dancing."[90]

Another member of the Black Patti Troubadours who featured artistic interpretations of coon songs was Emma Thompson. A *Freeman* notice of April 26, 1902, explained that, "In her rendition of coon songs, Emma Thompson was compelled to respond to applause four and five times. She is an excellent coon song shouter in the same school from which we get our May Irwins and Elizabeth Murrays."

Beginning with their first tour in 1896, and continuing for more than a decade, the Black Patti Troubadours opened their show with a "musical travesty," a one-act farce comedy skit with music. It was a "free-for-all" variety production with plenty of "low" comedy, song and dance, and no pretense of a coherent story line. Though elaborately costumed and choreographed, it was not to be confused with prestigious, modern "musical comedy."

The musical travesty presented during the Troubadours' inaugural tour was Bob Cole and Billy Johnson's "At Jolly Coon-ey Island," a "laughter-provoking skit which serves as a curtain raiser and a vehicle to give free scope to the company's comedy and singing talents."[91] The title is a takeoff on "At Gay Coney Island," a successful mainstream musical comedy of the time. For the Troubadours' second season, Ernest Hogan came aboard and overhauled the skit, as described in a Chicago daily paper, quoted in the *Freeman*:

> Whoever loves "coon" comedy, "coon" songs and dances, "coon" cake walks and every form of "coon" entertainment should go to the Shiller this week, where the Black Patti Troubadours are disporting themselves. It is a great show they give, a fast and furious medley of everything laughable and melodious, and nothing but the genuine "coon" article. The performance opens with a thoroughly characteristic farce in one act, and much action, called "At Gay Coon-ey

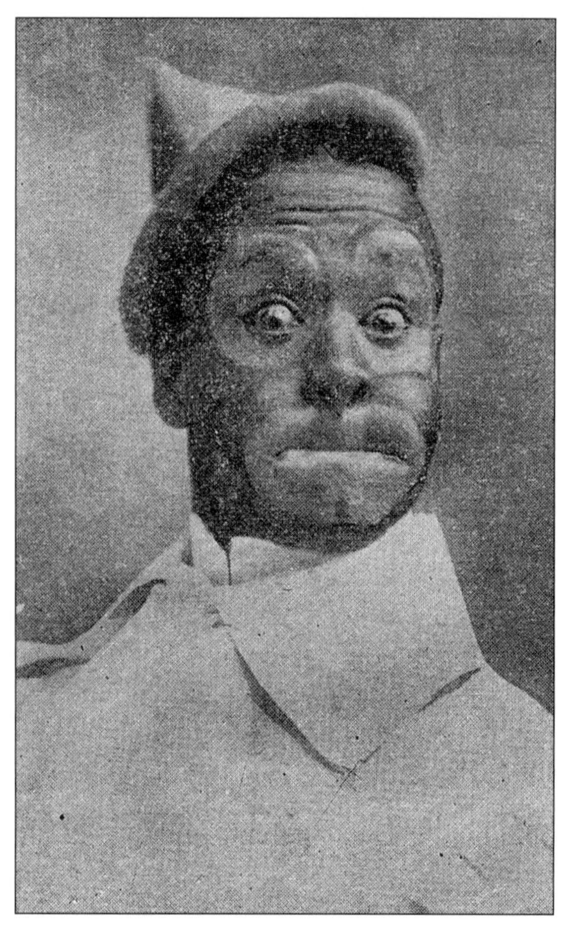

Ernest Hogan, as pictured on the sheet music cover of "My Gal's de Town Talk." (courtesy Ray Buckberry)

Island." It is the work of Ernest Hogan, who is the life and spirit of the performance, and whose rag-time songs set every foot to pattering. It is nonsense, but it is very characteristic nonsense and immensely funny.[92]

If "Coon, Coon, Coon" was the pop-music anthem of the ragtime era, the cultural history of the banal, oppressive, archaic racial epithet has remained largely hidden. The word "coon," in itself meaningless and ridiculous, is a vexing reminder of unresolved aspects of modern American history.

Ernest Hogan once told a newspaper reporter that he had "first conceived the music of . . . 'All Coons Look Alike to Me,' while walking through the park alone at night, in an Eastern city, and when his fortunes were at their lowest ebb."[93] After twenty years of hard knocks in the minstrel field, the stunning success of "All Coons Look Alike to Me" earned Hogan an unprecedented sum in royalties.[94] He was proclaimed the "King of his Race" by mainstream devotees of coon songs, ragtime and blackface comedy. Hogan was ready and able to grasp the opportunity and do something constructive with it. He played an essential, transitional role in the evolution of American comedy. At the time of Hogan's death in 1909, Sylvester Russell flatly rated him "the greatest colored comedian-actor America has ever produced." Another eulogist made a revealing comparison with the classic minstrel comedians Sam Lucas, Billy Kersands, and Tom McIntosh:

It was among these that young Hogan received his first impressions . . . He was essentially a burnt-cork man, but being young was susceptible to present-day influences . . . He presented the glimpses of the past, and presented phases of the present at their best. He was a mimic of the highest order. Not a dull moment when Hogan was on . . .

He gave glimpses of the pathetic and other qualities essential to the higher stage. Here were bits of as refined comedy and dashes of true drama as one would care to see and hear. Notwithstanding this, he seemed to take real delight in the minstrel phase of his work. His hilarity will be remembered when he sang with his company that stirring piece, "Is Everybody Happy?"[95]

Years later, in 1928, S. H. Dudley raised a brief testimonial to Hogan in an article he wrote for the *Pittsburgh Courier*, headed "Uncle Dud Writes of Old Stars": "Hogan was a great actor. I remember when he headlined in vaudeville; he sang

New York Clipper, July 3, 1897.

'Emancipation Day,' and when he finished the song instead of dancing the chorus he pantomimed it so real that you could just imagine you were looking at 'Emancipation Parade.'"

Hogan's blackface characterizations began to unveil a "black perspective" in stage humor. An April 1900 review in the *Evening Bulletin* of Honolulu, Hawaii, stressed his naturalness and "ease of manner," qualities that were new to "authentic" black minstrelsy:

> Ernest Hogan and his company of colored minstrels opened at the Orpheum Saturday night in a happily selected program . . . Ernest Hogan is undoubtedly the star. His natural flow of wit and humor at all times is almost enough to make one wish they did not know how to laugh. No one could be more natural or unaffected than Mr. Hogan. The ease of manner is refreshing and one needs something refreshing after they have enjoyed to excess as everyone seemed to have Saturday evening, his every effort . . . It was a pleasure to hear the composer's idea of his own song and woe to those who try to sing "All Coons Look Alike to Me" hereafter.[96]

Before 1897, Hogan had achieved recognition as a coon song writer, producer of *In Old Tennessee*, and leader of the Criterion Quartette. He stepped up to the big time as principal comedian with the 1897–1898 edition of the Black Patti Troubadours. Acknowledged as the "especial bright star" of the show, Hogan held the stage for twenty minutes with his blackface monologue and songs. He reportedly featured Williams and Walker's "Not a Coon Came Out the Way He Went In," along with his stump speech "What is Man?"[97] It seems he also introduced "his side splitting 'Turkey Carving' turn," which he recycled in 1902 with the original Smart Set Company.[98]

In the summer of 1898, between seasons with the Black Patti Troubadours, Hogan headed the cast of *Clorindy; or, The Origin of the Cake Walk*, a playlet with libretto and lyrics by Paul Laurence Dunbar and music by Will Marion Cook. It was included in the vaudeville entertainment staged by E. E. Rice at the Casino Roof Garden in New York City under the title, "Rice's Summer Nights." *Clorindy* was "so vividly successful it remained on the bill most of the summer," establishing a landmark in black entertainment.[99]

The *Freeman*'s annual "Christmas Number" for 1898, an elaborate pictorial celebration of the African American stage, gave over its entire front page to Ernest Hogan. It said he was currently commanding "the largest salary that any colored man has yet been given." In the spring of 1899 Hogan left the Black Patti Troubadours in mid-tour and returned to New York, where he continued to enjoy prosperity and celebrity. He submitted this ragtime credo to the *Clipper*, in the words of an Irving Jones coon song hit: "I'm living easy, eating pork chops greasy. Always got money to give my Honey, I'm always picking on the bone of a chicken, I'm living easy, I certainly am living HIGH."[100]

Contrary to this carefree pronouncement, Hogan was driven by an obsessive work ethic. On June 1, 1899, he set sail for Sydney, Australia, with the M. B. Curtis Afro-American Minstrel and Vaudeville Company, a monumental combination that included Billy McClain, N. Clark Smith's Pickaninny Band, Madah Hyers, Katie Carter, Tom Brown, Siren Navarro, Muriel Ringgold, and other great African American stage stars. Shortly after their arrival, manager Curtis left them stranded. Stepping into the breach, Hogan took charge of the company, and they successfully resumed their tour as Hogan's Minstrels.[101]

In March 1900 Hogan and most of his company left Australia for Honolulu, Hawaii, to fill an extended engagement at the Orpheum Theater. Afterward, they were unfairly denied steamship passage from Honolulu to Vancouver, British Columbia. Hogan re-engaged his company at the Orpheum and filed a civil rights suit against the Canadian-American Royal Mail Steamship Line. In June 1900 it was announced that he had won the lawsuit. He was awarded $2,250, and other members of his troupe also received cash settlements.

By August 1900 Hogan was back in New York City, "playing an indefinite engagement at the New York Roof Garden, where his coon song singing is a strong feature."[102] Following the murder of a New York City policeman by a black man that month, white mob violence was randomly directed against African Americans on the streets of Manhattan, and, according to a brief report in the *New York Dramatic Mirror* of August 25, 1900, Hogan was one of the targets: "There was a genuine 'hot time in the old town' on Wednesday evening last, when a terrible race riot occurred . . . and every black man found on the street was terribly beaten. Among the victims of the mob were Ernest Hogan, the 'unbleached American,' and George Walker of Williams and Walker, both of whom were playing in theatres in this city, and whose business compelled them to be abroad just when the riot was at its worst."

A more detailed report in the *Freeman*, quoting from what was identified as the "New York Journal," specified that, while Walker was victimized, Hogan actually managed to elude the mob:

> The wild uncontrollable passion of the mob was best shown on Broadway at 12:30 o'clock this morning, when that popular comedian and song writer, Ernest Hogan, was chased like a wild beast with a pack at his heels.
>
> The rioting was wholly unknown to Hogan, when he left the Cherry Blossom Grove, where he had been doing his turn as usual.
>
> "All Coons Look Alike to Me," Mr. Hogan's own composition, had been rendered, to the applause of a large audience. Hogan, fashionably dressed, stood on the curb, twirling his cane.
>
> A cry came from Forty-fourth street and Eighth avenue, and a mob of five hundred men, armed with clubs and stones, surged over toward Broadway. Hogan

was seen. "Get the nigger!" was the chorus. Hogan dropped his cane and started down Broadway on a run. The mob followed and for the next three minutes it had a life and death race for Hogan.

At Broadway and Thirty-seventh street Hogan was almost in the hands of his pursuers. It would have been all over with him in a minute if he had not darted in an open door of the Marlborough Hotel.

Detective Madden, who ran up from Thirty-fifth street, stood at the door and with a drawn revolver kept the crowd back while Hogan was taken through to the Thirty-sixth street entrance and sent away in a cab.[103]

In the fall of 1902 Hogan went out at the head of the famous original Smart Set Company, only to quit at the end of the season and return to vaudeville. Late in 1903 he produced and starred with his wife Mattie Wilkes in *The Missionary Man*, a "satirical exaggeration, in one act," which successfully toured a mainstream New England vaudeville circuit and received this review from a Bridgeport, Connecticut, daily:

Ernest Hogan, called the "Unbleached American," made the greatest hit on the bill. He was supposed to be an automobile chauffeur. There was an explosion and he made his entrance tattered and torn with a steering wheel in one hand and a rubber tire in the other. When he got to singing the audience repeatedly recalled him and would not allow him to stop. When he invited the audience to join in a whistling chorus the gallery nearly blew the roof off. He was assisted in the sketch by Miss Mattie Wilkes, who, as Mrs. Angelica Scattergood, added considerably to the success of the little comedy.[104]

During the summer of 1904 Hogan presented the same skit, this time paired with Henrietta Vinton Davis, a noted African American "dramatic reader" and student of the classical stage. The *Freeman* of October 22, 1904, commented:

Those who follow the movements of theatrical performers will remember the pronounced hit made this summer at Atlantic City by Ernest Hogan and Miss Henrietta Vinton Davis who appeared for two record-breaking weeks in the former's choice vaudeville skit, "The Missionary Man." It proved to be a vehicle in which both showed to such excellent advantage that they have decided to accept a number of joint engagements with vaudeville circuits like Keith's, Castle's and the Orpheum's. They opened Sunday night for a week at the Grand Opera House in New York and were received most cordially . . . Miss Davis has long desired to make an incursion into the vaudeville arena, but has lacked a suitable vehicle.

Hogan again made theatrical headlines in June 1905 when he brought his Memphis Students to Hammerstein's Victoria Roof Garden. The Students embodied Hogan's novel concept of a twenty-five-piece chorus, with many members doubling on stringed instruments, predominantly mandolins and guitars. He presented them in a half-hour specialty called "Songs of the Black Folk," featuring soprano Abbie Mitchell. A description in the daily *New York World* tempts the modern imagination:

The roof garden fairly reeked with melody. There was a fervor in the rendering of the songs that could never have been supplied by white singers. The musical oddity involved was that each player sings in a different part from that which the instrument he played called for. For instance, the manipulator of the double-bass was a tenor and the man who picked the airs on a mandolin sang in basso profundo a hundred fathoms deep. All the singers were picturesquely dressed except Hogan who displayed the African fondness for an evening suit and an opera hat.

"Ernest Hogan and his Memphis Students celebrating the Fourth of July," *New York Clipper*, July 8, 1905.

> The songs, which were written by Will Marion Cook, the colored composer, all had the plantation swing. "Barbershop" harmony and broken measures were mingled in fantastic confusion. The audience could not get enough of the specialty and it proved to be one of the best numbers that Oscar Hammerstein has ever offered.[105]

By early August 1905 Hogan's Memphis Students had completed one hundred performances at Hammerstein's Victoria Roof Garden, and Sylvester Russell testified: "Ernest Hogan and his Memphis Students . . . has been the star event of the black regime of summer."[106] The Memphis Students seem to have appealed directly to the sophisticated New Yorker's fashionable appreciation of black folk music. During the course of their Victoria Roof Garden engagement, Hogan and his Memphis Students made an impromptu appearance, by special invitation, at a convention of the National Negro Business League, where Booker T. Washington was the keynote speaker. Sylvester Russell, who was there as Hogan's personally invited guest, described how the Memphis Students had "come on and assisted Mr. Hogan in a new coon song about chicken, with mandolin and guitar accompaniment, that set the vast audience crazy."[107]

Early in September, the Memphis Students closed their run at Hammerstein's. Hogan seems to have tried to hold the group together for a future production, but some of the members had other plans. The *Freeman* of September 30, 1905, reported that Hogan had obtained an injunction in New York State restraining Abbie Mitchell from singing in any company other than Hogan's Memphis Students. Nevertheless, shortly thereafter, Mitchell and a summary aggregation of Memphis Students stole off to Europe.[108]

Meanwhile, Hogan launched his big, new musical comedy production for the season of 1905–1906. According to Sylvester Russell, rehearsals were marked by friction between the star and his adoring but hard-pressed company. Reporter Carle B. Cooke attended a "full stage rehearsal" at the Harlem Opera House, which began "at one o'clock Sunday and lasted until after four. The new management, Hurtig & Seamon, were delighted with the work, and Stage Director, J. Ed Green and Mr. Hogan granted the whole company a two days' rest which came none too soon . . . Although the company is worked down and full of cold from such long and exceptionally hard rehearsing, they have accomplished some great work."[109]

The blockbuster show took shape under the working title *The Birth of the Minstrel* but opened under the name *Rufus Rastus*, which Carle B. Cooke found unacceptable:

> It is too bad that Ernest Hogan has allowed his ungrateful managers to change the name of his new comedy company which has been largely advertised by that pretty and fitting card, "The Birth of the Minstrel." The letter heads issued for the show now read: "Rufus Rastus," "A Real Coon Show." How shocking and our dear "Uncle Rube" [Hogan] is striving to rise to a quality plane, too. It is sad that so good a drawing card as Ernest Hogan would stand for such provincial labeling of such an able aggregation as he is heading.[110]

When *Rufus Rastus* played Chicago in November 1905, *Freeman* reviewer P. B. Ross Hendrix noted:

> It is one of the best shows ever brought to Chicago . . . The costumes are costly and rich, for which the management have spent $30,000. The beauty of the future for the production is that there are so many performers who have been stars, stage managers, etc., in other companies, and their combined strength, with the excellent chorus, will keep it on the waves of success. J. Ed Green, the best stage manager in the business, barring none, deserves great credit for the rehearsing and casting of the play in such a manner, making it a scorcher wherever they appear. Mr. Hogan could not be surrounded with better support than at present . . . They turned them away in Detroit, Cleveland and here also by the hundreds . . . Mr. Hogan, with the assistance of J. Ed Green is making it hard for others to follow him, for he certainly has a show.[111]

J. Ed Green, *Indianapolis Freeman*, December 21, 1907.

J. Ed Green was among the most progressive performer-managers on the African American stage. For two years he was stage manager of the Black Patti Troubadours. In 1904, he became stage manager of the Smart Set Company. Before coming to *Rufus Rastus* he assisted Hogan in staging the Memphis Students at Hammerstein's. The following year, Green was hired to manage the stage of the newly opened Pekin Theater in Chicago.

Sylvester Russell credited Green as the "discoverer" of the *Rufus Rastus* company's brilliant

NOTED DIRECTOR AND COMPOSER.

PROF. H. LAWRENCE FREEMAN.

Prof. H. Lawrence Freeman is the successful director of music of Ernest Hogan's Rufus Rastus Company and the splendid music heard in this company is the result of his careful training. He is the composer of some of the best and catchiest musical numbers that are so popular just now. Prof. Freeman has several compositions in preparation that will be published very soon.

Indianapolis Freeman, October 6, 1906.

young musical director, H. Lawrence Freeman, an instructor at Wilberforce University who was "perhaps the most promising composer of his race." Russell's only advice to Freeman during his tenure with *Rufus Rastus* was to "bring his music down—down to the level of a weaker and wiser generation of warblers. If he will do this and also commence at once the development of rag-time music as a classical composition he will do us two lasting favors that will tend to complete his reward of greatness."[112]

The cast of *Rufus Rastus* numbered sixty-five performers, including Henry Troy, Harry Fiddler, J. Leubrie Hill, Theodore and Anna Cook Pankey, Carita Day, and Muriel Ringgold. Hogan, as usual, was the overly ambitious star. As one reporter noted, "Mr. Hogan is working as never before. After keeping his audience laughing and applauding for three hours, he is forced to take a curtain call at the end of the last act."[113] Sylvester Russell turned in a slightly backhanded assessment: "Of Ernest Hogan who now shines so bright in his artistic ascendancy that criticism can scarcely reach him, it can be said that he succeeded in holding his audience to a 'top-notch' pitch of laughter for every moment he has lingered inexcusably overtime upon the stage."[114]

Rufus Rastus made its first New York City appearance on January 29, 1906, at the American Theater, before a "congested standing room" audience. Russell reported:

> Mr. Hogan's . . . greatest achievement was the quaint song, "Oh Wouldn't It Be A Dream," responded by an invisible chorus that was most excellent. His performance in the minstrel scene including the song "Is Everybody Happy?" was something that can never be duplicated by white comedians, and this scene comes as a refreshing treat to white people in New York . . . Hogan's love scene, with Miss Carita Day was clever and far reaching. Hogan has much work to do alone, in soliloquy, in the play.[115]

The ragtime era presented a producer-performer like Ernest Hogan with new opportunities to advance the standards of the black

Indianapolis Freeman, June 1, 1907.

theatrical profession. He was mindful to incorporate "love scenes" in his all-black cast productions, which not only broke ground, but added another degree of "naturalness." The set designs for *Rufus Rastus* also brought complimentary notices; the mainstream *Brooklyn Citizen* judged: "The stage setting is very elaborate, the last scene in the first act showing a palm bower at the Ponce De Leon Hotel in Florida being especially fine. The interior of Madison Square Garden with a row of boxes along the back of the stage was also realistic. Ernest Hogan stands without peer in the class of 'funny coons,' and he was at his best last night."[116]

Through the spring of 1906 *Rufus Rastus* toured the East and Midwest, closing in New York City in June. For the second season of *Rufus Rastus*, Hogan brought Tom Logan into the cast. Logan was probably Ernest Hogan's closest confederate in the profession. Few black stage performers were more experienced at character parts than Tom Logan: "He is one of the very few Afro-American artists in the country who can appear to equally happy advantage in straight roles, grotesque character work, such as Chinese, Italian, Dutch, Jew and other impersonations, and in Negro comedy of every variety, from the minstrel end man to the Apollo of fashion."[117]

Early in 1899 the *Freeman* published a biographical sketch of Logan, noting that he "attributes his success to the painstaking training of Mr. Hogan."[118] Later that year, Logan went to Australia with Hogan, in M. B. Curtis's Minstrels. In 1901 Pat Chappelle brought Logan south to serve as stage manager for his *A Rabbit's Foot* Company.

In the fall of 1901, when Lew Hall brought his Ragtime Opera Company to Church's Auditorium in Memphis, he installed Logan as stage manager and producer: "The amusement loving public feel duly grateful to Tom Logan, who has staged some of the most generally satisfactory first parts ever seen here."[119]

At the beginning of 1902 Logan went to Tampa, Florida, where he worked at the Mascotte and Buckingham theaters. That spring he staged a skit said to be "head and shoulders above the average road attraction that visits our city. The first act depicts the 'ups and downs' of the average 'Jig-walk' [i.e., black] performer—his 'flush times' when the

Indianapolis Freeman, April 19, 1902.

'Ghost' walks, his 'medium' times between pay days, his 'tough' times when the manager has 'ducked with the coin,' and the ingenious plan they adopt to get back to 'Good Old New York Town.'"[120]

Logan had charge of the stage at Ninaweb Park in Louisville, Kentucky, each summer season from 1903 through 1905. A visitor to Louisville wrote: "Logan is stage manager at this beautiful Louisville summer resort . . . The company's program is adroitly balanced to please both those who fancy the Negro in plantation garb and those who like to see him do his 'swell' or 'straight' work. Tom Logan in the varied roles of legitimate actor, grotesque comedian, dramatist, song-writer, manager and producer is equally painstaking and loyal to the demands of art."[121]

In September 1906 Ernest Hogan and company played the Park Theater in Indianapolis, where an enthusiastic reviewer judged: "The 'Rufus Rastus' company will stand as a splendid type of the possibilities of the Negro on the stage up to date, and the performance showed what the audiences have been educated up to receive."[122]

At the end of 1906 Hogan was invited to write an article on "The Negro in Vaudeville" for the first anniversary edition of *Variety*. In it he prophesied the day when "the colored artist [would] play more serious lines than he does today." He also acknowledged that his own progress and the progress of black entertainers in general had been directly linked to coon songs: "With the advent of 'coon' songs came the colored people into variety in large numbers. To the popular demand for 'coon' songs the writer believes he owes much, for it was shortly after he wrote the first syncopated 'coon' song ever written, 'Pasmala,' followed by 'All Coons Look Alike to Me,' that he made his debut on the Eastern vaudeville stage."[123]

Hogan would certainly have been a candidate for the "more serious lines" that he saw on the horizon. By 1907, however, his health and energy were almost exhausted. *Rufus Rastus* was in Columbus, Ohio, on April 13, 1907, when he decided to call it quits. The *Freeman* of April 20 reported, "Mr. Hogan will devote his time to his air-ship, while the other members of the company will either rest or accept other engagements." A report the following week sounded incredulous: "Without any notification ceremonies the 'Rufus Rastus' company closed . . . and why they closed so suddenly no one knows . . . although everyone springs a different reason . . . Air ships and air castles for Ernest Hogan. Everything must be aloft."

Hogan's "air ship enterprise" was first mentioned in the *Freeman* of June 16, 1906. Fellow performers were initially amused by Hogan's interest in air ships and air shows, but they grew concerned when it began to divert his attention from the stage. On February 2, 1907, the *Freeman* stated, "Hogan's Air Ship Company seems to be more than a dream. Announcements are out in the leading theatrical papers promising a flight of the air ship thousands of feet in mid air, and high-class vaudeville attractions for aerodrome patrons. The machine will be in charge of the well-known navigator Ray Stevens, and 'big things' are promised this summer—in the air."

A large advertisement appeared in the *Freeman* touting the "J. P. Parks–Ernest Hogan Air-Ship Company"—"Managers of Parks, etc., write at once for open time." On August 3, 1907, *Variety* published an announcement from Olympic Park in Newark, New Jersey, that Ernest Hogan, "with his Wolverine Airship, will race with Archie Griffen in his balloon on Sundays and make flights daily." Not much more is known about Hogan's airship enterprise, but for many years thereafter the already popular phrase "taking the airship route" had a special meaning among black stage people: to lose one's head under the pressures of success.

After shutting down his *Rufus Rastus* company, Hogan returned to the vaudeville stages of New York City, appearing as a "single" through most of the summer of 1907. A racially charged incident occurred that summer, when a white florist had Hogan arrested for loitering in front of his shop on Twenty-Eighth Street near Broadway: "Hogan declares that he is interested in a music publishing firm which has offices in the same building . . . and protested in court that he had a perfect right to stand on the sidewalk."[124]

In August 1907 Hogan once again called rehearsals for a new play, *The Oyster Man*, with backing from Hurtig and Seamon. But when the company opened in Lima, Ohio, on September 26, after seven weeks of intense preparation, the *Freeman* relayed a worrisome report: "Mr. Hogan is quite ill and required the services of a physician throughout the entire performance."[125]

The Oyster Man was well received, especially such musical numbers as Carita Day's "I Can't Keep My Eyes Off of You" and Hogan's "Contribution Box." However, Hogan's health failed a few months into the season, and the play was forced to close. Lester Walton wrote in the *New York Age*: "Despite prospects for a prosperous season Hogan had to retire on account of a general breaking down. Mr. Hogan has been in ill health since his new show opened, as he attempted too much during the rehearsals of 'The Oyster Man' last summer. Besides assisting in composing the music and writing the book, 'the unbleached American' staged the show and made his speaking part entirely too much work for one man."[126]

Muriel Ringgold, Character Comedienne.

Muriel Ringgold, who was an understudy of Ernest Hogan, has turned out to be a finished performer. In looking over her work one is impressed with what might be called her entireness. Take for instance, her first number. Here she is clothed in a billowy fashion, resembling the sea as much as possible. She sings "Bobbing Up and Down," also in imitation of the sea. She becomes seasick, taking it off fine. Her next number " By Myself Alone, Nobody But Me" is a complete change. She is now decidly male, but a char-

MURIEL RINGGOLD, COMEDIENNE

acter which she does well. It is rather boobyish, calling for movements in keeping and eccentric dancing. In her final number the "Junkman's Rag" is featured. Here she shows the same careful, thoughtful performer who values her art and tries to get the most out of it. All of her work was nicely received.

Indianapolis Freeman, May 23, 1914.

It was reported in the spring of 1908 that Hogan was recuperating at a sanitarium in Rutland, Massachusetts. The profession moved on, still very much under Hogan's influence and example. He had been a generous mentor. His expertise was conveyed into the broader black stage world, particularly the ripening southern vaudeville theater world, through his most successful protégés J. Ed Green, Tom Logan, and Muriel Ringgold.

Muriel Ringgold first gained attention with the Black Patti Troubadours in 1898, when Hogan was their star comedian. She was a sensation in her dance specialty, and the Troubadours' correspondent may not have exaggerated in calling her "the best dancer of all colored or white artists in the business."[127] However, Muriel Ringgold did more than dance; she also created memorable comic characters. Black theater critic W. Milton Lewis

WATTS AND RINGGOLD.

Indianapolis Freeman, March 10, 1917.

identified her in 1906 as "a protege of Mr. Hogan's . . . It is thought she has no superior as a dancer. She hopes to become a celebrated comedienne."[128] Hogan almost certainly wrote characters into his productions with Ringgold in mind.

In 1899 Ringgold went with Hogan to Australia, where she portrayed Topsy in the M. B. Curtis Company's rendition of *Uncle Tom's Cabin.* She joined Hogan and McClain's original Smart Set in 1903, assuming a role that seems to have been written for her: the mysterious Moana, subject of the hit song, "My Sweet Moana," originally featured in the 1902 Hawaiian production *My Friend from Georgia.*

In the cast of *Rufus Rastus* Ringgold played the important part of Snowflake. Mainstream theater critic Helen Green wrote a distasteful but informative review in which Snowflake's appearance in the opening scene is briefly described: "Small, stiff braids stuck out from her head above her squatty little nose. She made faces, and was a pert and active pick, always dancing." At the close of Act One, "Snowflake, with her braids elegantly arranged, and a nice new dress, made her brown legs fly in a buck dance."[129]

Sylvester Russell was bewitched by Snowflake: "Miss Muriel Ringgold . . . was the most fascinating giddy little creature you ever saw and later in the play her dancing showed that she has few, if any equals."[130] When *Rufus Rastus* opened its second season in the fall of 1906, the *Freeman* reported that "Muriel Ringgold, 'Snowflake' is ill in New York, and has little hope of returning to the stage." Ringgold did manage to recover, and a note at the end of the year advertised that she was available for work. When she appeared in Hogan's *The Oyster Man* during its abbreviated season of 1907–1908, a reviewer assured that, "as a Topsy, she has neither peer nor equal."[131]

Muriel Ringgold's famous eccentric dance specialty and her comic Topsy caricature place her at the forefront of an important byway of black female performers. Ringgold, Kate Milton, Katie Carter, and Ida Forsyne all shared the identical specialties, and they all became internationally acclaimed entertainers. Ringgold remained on the stage for at least another quarter century, much of it in a blackface-comedy team act with Ernest Watts.

During the spring of 1909, as Hogan's condition deteriorated, the *Freeman* published several retrospectives on his career. One columnist recalled a backstage meeting with Hogan:

> I saw him smear on the black grease paint. A slight tremor came over me; but he was used to it, slapping it on as if he liked it.[132] I saw him coming off the stage with the stage laugh all over his face, bowing, rebowing, and then bowing again, and then saw the laugh go off almost terrifyingly suddenly as soon as he got out of the sight of the audience. Then I saw him wash the grime off, and "Richard was himself again" . . . the violent contrast made the heart ache. Behind was the lifeless mechanisms—grinning masques—reminder of the final day when all have gone to their destinies.[133]

Ernest Hogan died at 7:30a.m., May 20, 1909. He was forty-four years old. His death has been alternately attributed to tuberculosis and paresis. Sylvester Russell wrote:

> The shock which the theater-going public received . . . when the newspapers gave out that Ernest Hogan had died, can hardly be estimated. All the profession was cast in gloom. All the colored actors, especially in New York and Chicago, were horror stricken with grief as

"My Sweet Moana." (courtesy Ray Buckberry)

> the news was passed up and down the familiar haunts and avenues of the popular theatrical thoroughfares . . . [W]e are reluctant to part with our dear deceased friend, Mr. Hogan, who was not destined to endure to the end. If there ever was a popular actor, and one beloved by all classes of people of every race, individually and collectively, it was Ernest Hogan, and long may his name remain sacred in the ideals of his race's history.[134]

Lester Walton, "Music and Stage" editor of the *New York Age* and manager of the Lafayette Theater, was a friend and business associate of

Hogan's and was privy to many details surrounding Hogan's death:

After a lingering illness of seventeen month's duration, the well-known comedian succumbed to the disease of which he had been for some time a victim, but only after a hard fight—a fight which he so valiantly fought for nearly two years . . . Death came to the "Unbleached American," as he styled himself, on the morning of Thursday, May 20, at the family residence, 1002 Brook avenue, Bronx . . . [T]he citizens of New York City, irrespective of color, turned out in large numbers and paid their last respects . . . Men high in the theatrical profession, business men and hundreds who greatly admired Ernest Hogan during life, showed their respect at death.

Funeral services were held over the remains from the Church of St. Benedict, the Moor . . . , under the rites of the Catholic Church, Father O'Keefe officiating.[135] So crowded was the church that many were unable to obtain admission . . . The active pallbearers were composed of some of the leading colored members of the theatrical profession. They were Bert A. Williams, Bob Cole, J. Rosamond Johnson, Alex Rogers, Charlie Hart and Bob Slater . . . After funeral services at the church the body was taken to the undertaking establishment [C. Franklin Carr Burial Company, 266 West Fifty-third Street], where the public was permitted to look upon the face of the widely known comedian for the last time . . . Sunday afternoon the body was shipped to Bowling Green, Ky., the home of the deceased, and was accompanied by the mother . . . The remains were interred in the family plot Tuesday . . .

[D]eath removes from our midst a useful man, one of unspotted reputation, who has served well his people and his generation . . . That the stage loses one of its greatest colored comedians in the death of Ernest Hogan is admitted by all. But aside from the loss of one whose talents as an actor are well known, the colored members of the theatrical profession also lose one who might be termed, in many respects, a "Moses" of the colored theatrical profession . . .

It was a few years ago when the writer [Walton] was then a reporter on a St. Louis daily that he met "the Unbleached American," who was the leading comedian of the Smart Set Company. It was Ernest Hogan who finally induced the writer to come East to act as his personal representative during the second season of the Rufus Rastus Company . . . The comedian's motto at all times was: "Give all the theatrical profession an opportunity to make good; bring out of the chorus the ones who are doing their work well, and give them a part in the cast." . . .

Ambition was one of the causes of Ernest Hogan's illness and ultimate death. He was versatile, and it was a difficult matter to keep him from displaying his talents at all times. He assisted in writing his last show, besides composing many of the songs, staging all the musical numbers and playing the leading role. Coupled with his theatrical work, the interest he gave other matters made his life a strenuous one and many who saw him rehearse "The Oyster Man" Company were not surprised to learn of his illness . . .

Just how far the colored profession, in fact, the entire profession, is set back by the death of Ernest Hogan the writer will not attempt to even surmise; but it has sustained a great loss, for there is no one at this time to take his place.[136]

Hogan is buried in a family plot at Fairview Cemetery in Bowling Green, Kentucky. In the fall of 1917, while playing an engagement in Bowling Green, Billy Arnte and members of his Dixieland Troubadours Company visited the gravesite, accompanied by Hogan's mother and sister. According to the *Freeman*, "The Carnival Band played a sad dirge, while members of the company placed a number of beautiful floral tributes upon the last resting place of their fallen comrade." Arnte was quick to note "evidences of neglect of the great actor. There is no stone to mark his last resting place." He vowed to "start a fund to be used for the purpose of securing a stone to mark the spot where [Hogan] is playing his last stand."[137] As of this writing, however, only Hogan's father's grave has a marker.[138]

Bert Williams and George Walker comprised the most successful African American comedy team of the ragtime era. Billed as the Two Real Coons, they rose to fame on the strength of their original coon songs and blackface humor. George Walker offered this explanation: "We thought that as there seemed to be a great demand for black faces on the stage, we would do all we could to get what we felt belonged to us by the laws of nature. We finally decided that as white men with black faces were billing themselves 'coons,' Williams and Walker would do well to bill themselves the 'Two Real Coons,' and so we did. Our bills attracted the attention of managers, and gradually we made our way in."[139]

Like Ernest Hogan, Williams and Walker worked through conventional minstrel stereotypes to create more honest, three-dimensional characters, capable of sustaining "legitimate" musical comedy.[140] In a 1902 essay on "Minstrels, Comedians and Singers," *Freeman* commentator "I. McCorker" maintained:

> White folks have claimed all along, with some degree of truth, that they can outdo the Negro in the aping of himself, but they now admit that they have stubbed their toes on [Bert] Williams, who refuses to enter into horseplay or overdo his character for the plaudits of his patrons. He is a natural born comedian, and he was born funny. And he could find no better partner to help him out in his fun making than George Walker, than whom no man looks sleeker in evening dress.[141]

In the fall of 1896 Williams and Walker began an "unlimited engagement" in vaudeville at Koster and Bial's Theater in New York City. Their popular cake walk specialty was described in the *Freeman*:

> One pair holds the floor at a time, and the men's manner are in strong contrast. One chap is clownish, though his grotesque paces are elaborate, practiced and extremely timed, while the other is all airiness . . . Pointed shoes, tight trousers, red and white striped shirt front, and shining silk hat are not a bit out of harmony with mock diamonds that are as big as marbles . . . Away up stage he and his partner meet and curtsey, she with utmost grace, and he with exaggerated courtliness. Then down

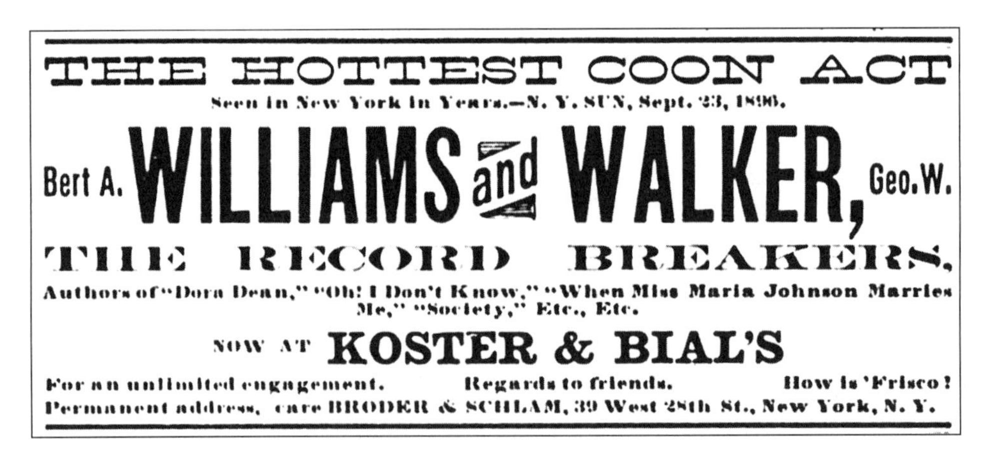

New York Clipper, November 7, 1896.

they trip, his elbows squared, his hat held upright by the brim, and with a mincing gait that would be ridiculous were it not absolutely in its harmony with the general scheme of airiness . . . The other chap's . . . joints work jerkily, but he has his own ideas in high stepping, and carries them out in a walk that . . . ends at the other side of the stage. Then the first fellow takes both women, one on each arm, and, leaving the other man grimacing vengefully, starts on a second tour of grace.[142]

In the fall of 1898 Williams and Walker went out at the head of a touring company of twenty-five people. At Koster and Bial's in November, "Williams and Walker, with their 'coontown' production, were still popular, their dances, songs and cake walks being received with marked favor."[143] The "'coontown' production" referred to was *A Lucky Coon*, the musical comedy vehicle for Williams and Walker's first "big show."

During the early months of 1899 Williams and Walker's Own Company played *A Lucky Coon* from New York to Chicago. A note in the *Freeman* of January 21, 1899, informed that, "Mr. Harry T. Burleigh, the accomplished musical director, has closed with Williams & Walker's Own Company." Burleigh was no devotee of ragtime music; years later, he publicly denounced the influence of ragtime and jazz on the spirituals. Burleigh's connection with Williams and Walker in 1899 indicates the breadth of ragtime's influence.

On June 22, 1899, George Walker married the company's rising female star, Ada Overton, a physically striking woman, as Sylvester Russell observed: "Ada Overton Walker is not only lucky in having nice hair but her color and skin are perfect. Her complexion is a light shade of brown without a blemish."[144] Ada Overton Walker was proud to be unmistakably African American, and this helped her open new stage horizons for race women, in her pioneering role as the "dark soubrette."

Over the next several seasons Williams and Walker produced a bold succession of musical comedies. Their business relationship with Hurtig and Seamon enabled them to stage their productions in an atmosphere of relative artistic freedom. As their personal manager Charles L. Moore explained, "The booking, time, scenery, etc., is attended to absolutely by Hurtig & Seamon; the booking of people, writing of plays, lyrics, staging, etc., is under direct supervision of Williams & Walker."

Williams and Walker assembled a top-flight staff of writers for their shows. Jesse A. Shipp, fresh out of Sam T. Jack's Creole Burlesque Company, was their playwright; Will Marion Cook was their chief composer, and Paul Laurence Dunbar wandered into this unfamiliar world as their lyricist. These men abandoned the ubiquitous vehicle of "plantation pastimes" in favor of contemporary themes—black college life, the back-to-Africa movement, etc. For the season of 1899–1900 they introduced *The Policy Players*, which told "the tale of the doings of a policy fiend, who has won a large sum of money on policy and wishes . . . to enter and mingle with the colored 400 and the many difficulties that he encounters in so doing."[145]

Williams and Walker's vehicle for the season of 1900–1901 was *The Sons of Ham*, an "Afro-American improbable musical comedy by Steven A. Cassin and Jesse A. Shipp," in which the two stars played college students at "Risk University," supported by a cast of fifty people. It toured as far west as Indiana and closed in New York in May 1901. That fall they put out a revised version of *The Sons of Ham*,

Indianapolis Freeman, October 1, 1904.

and the *Freeman* of October 12, 1901, reproduced a review from the mainstream *New York Telegraph*:

> Williams & Walker still exploit "The Sons of Ham," and this week they are crowding the Bijou Theatre, in the sad borough [Brooklyn] . . . It is one of the weeks when the black friend and brother is given a chance to sit even in the boxes and they crowd about the house in droves . . .
>
> Williams is really a clever chap and is possessed of more unction than some of those who strut the Broadway stages and are accounted great. Some of his lines are capital and a departure from the regulation coon comedy . . . In place of the fortune telling coon that was used in the second act he is now a head doctor and reads bumps. For this reason, he has a song, "The Phrenologist Coon" that is as good as the other, but for an encore he has "My Castle on the Nile," which is one of the best things he has ever sung . . . It has good swing and is catchy as to air.

This reviewer was especially taken by Ada Overton Walker: "A new departure is the dark soubrette. Ada Overton Walker has developed a sprightliness and comes close to being the regular farce comedy soubrette. This is something new in this class of show, and . . . marks the trend of

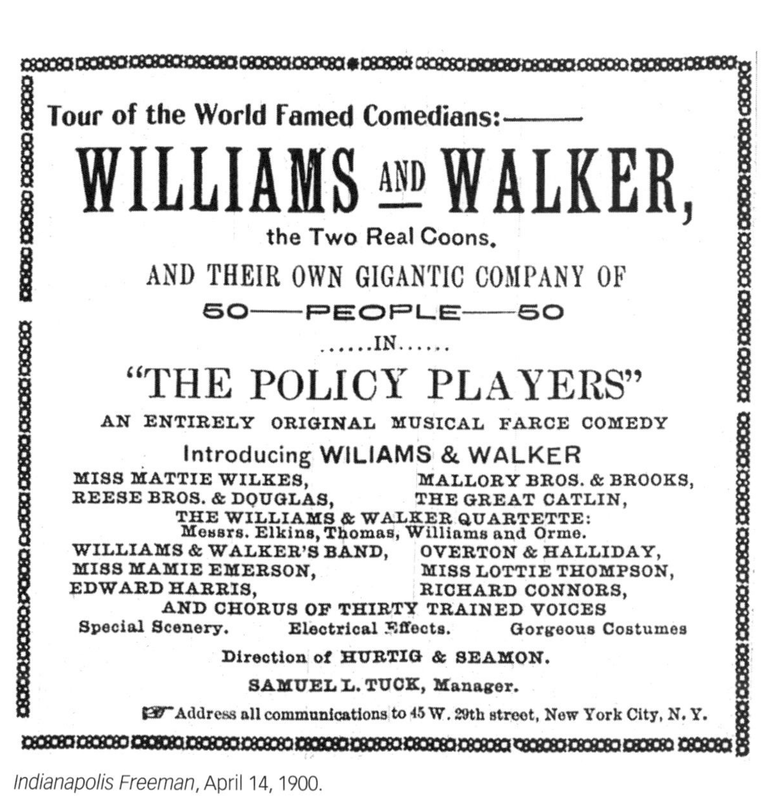
Tour of the World Famed Comedians:——

WILLIAMS AND WALKER,

the Two Real Coons.

AND THEIR OWN GIGANTIC COMPANY OF

50——PEOPLE——50

......IN......

"THE POLICY PLAYERS"

AN ENTIRELY ORIGINAL MUSICAL FARCE COMEDY

Introducing WILIAMS & WALKER

MISS MATTIE WILKES, MALLORY BROS. & BROOKS,
REESE BROS. & DOUGLAS, THE GREAT CATLIN,
THE WILLIAMS & WALKER QUARTETTE:
Messrs. Elkins, Thomas, Williams and Orme.
WILLIAMS & WALKER'S BAND, OVERTON & HALLIDAY,
MISS MAMIE EMERSON, MISS LOTTIE THOMPSON,
EDWARD HARRIS, RICHARD CONNORS,
AND CHORUS OF THIRTY TRAINED VOICES

Special Scenery. Electrical Effects. Gorgeous Costumes

Direction of HURTIG & SEAMON.

SAMUEL L. TUCK, Manager.

Address all communications to 45 W. 29th street, New York City, N. Y.

Indianapolis Freeman, April 14, 1900.

'coon' comedy. This company has already made a big advance over the old octoroon shows, and now more sweeping changes are apparently underway."

Race pride and the need for "sweeping changes" are reflected in Ada Overton Walker's published comments. As one journalist noted:

It is decidedly instructive to talk to Mrs. Walker and to discover her attitude toward the white and black actress, theater managers and toward the theater-going public, which is filled with every conceivable prejudice against a Negro . . . "You haven't the faintest conception of the difficulties which must be overcome, of the prejudices which must be left slumbering, of the things we must avoid whenever we write or sing a piece of music, put on a play or a sketch, walk out in the street or land in a new town," said Mrs. Walker.[146]

In 1907, with her star still rising, Mrs. Walker changed her first name from Ada to Aida, lending operatic proportions to her ascendancy.[147]

While presenting *The Sons of Ham* in New York during October and November 1901, Bert Williams recorded several songs for the Victor Company, including the show's biggest hits, "The Phrenologist Coon," "My Little Zulu Babe," and "In My Castle on the River Nile."[148] At Lexington, Kentucky, in December 1901 a *Freeman* correspondent assured, "Williams & Walker have given Lexingtonians a great treat . . . Chicken stealing gags and crap game songs are conspicuous by their absence." When they played Chicago at the end of the year, Sylvester Russell noted, "The Zulu Babe is a special treat and shows what unusually clever work Williams and Walker can do with new ideas."[149]

Indianapolis Freeman, March 18, 1911.

"My Castle on the River Nile," words by Robert Cole and James Weldon Johnson, music by J. Rosamond Johnson, is a first-rate example of a sophisticated turn-of-the-century ragtime coon song. While the clever lyrics are constructed around ludicrous racial allusions, they are neither crude nor unwholesome. A popular black quartet, the Deep River Boys, recorded this song in the 1940s.[150] Certain nuances and inflections suggest that the Deep River Boys may have been familiar with Bert Williams's 1901 recording; however, they sing the song in swing tempo, while Williams recorded it more slowly, wringing the full value out of the lyrics. The chorus:

In my castle on de river Nile
I am g'winter live in elegant style
Inlaid diamonds on de flo'
A baboon butler at my do'

When I wed dat princess Anna Mazoo
Den my blood will change from red to blue.
Entertaining royalty all the while
In my castle on the Nile.[151]

For the season of 1902–1903, Williams and Walker staged the latest Jessie Shipp–Will Marion Cook–Paul Laurence Dunbar collaboration *In Dahomey*, which told of two young men with "more brains than money," who "join a syndicate for the development of Dahomey (a la Bishop Turner), and finally gain control of the colony of emigrants which they have taken from the state of Georgia. Walker becomes the King and Williams his prime minister."[152] *Freeman* commentator J. D. Howard expressed favorable sentiments:

> Much credit is due Mr. [Jesse] Shipp for overcoming the many drawbacks consequent upon the putting together of a real "coon" comedy. He has succeeded in giving to the people a bunch of fun perfectly clear from all offensive innuendoes and acceptable to every class . . . So nicely is the story told that the prejudiced whites in front are beguiled into a profound interest, even though the characters appear in beautiful gowns and full dress suits.[153]

When *In Dahomey* debuted at Stamford, Connecticut, on September 8, 1902, Sylvester Russell

Williams and Walker in Zulu costumes. This photo was inset on the sheet music cover of "My Little Zulu Babe." (courtesy Thornton Hagert, Vernacular Music Research)

noted that Bert Williams's "rendition of 'Everything Going Out and Nothin Comin In' created a furore."[154] Russell reserved special praise for Ada Overton Walker, who "owns the stage for a short spasm of time, very short and all alone, but let us thirsty creatures be thankful even for that." Another auditor observed, "Her work is not only a distinct departure from any yet attempted by a colored woman, but a genuine novelty, insomuch as it is not exactly like any now being done by white women."[155]

One of the most popular songs from *In Dahomey* was "The Jonah Man," a "hard luck coon song" sung by Bert Williams, with whom it became synonymous. A front-page headline in the *Freeman* of January 31, 1903, announced, "'The Jonah Man' Will Try His Powers Of Voodooism In A Theater On Broadway In New York City."

In Dahomey opened at the New York Theater on Broadway, February 18, 1903, and according to the *Freeman* it drew a large, responsive crowd despite "the severe criticism of a local daily, from a prejudicial standpoint." A reviewer noted, "The color line has been drawn during this engagement, a certain part of the house being set apart for the colored people; nevertheless they are there at each performance, arriving in automobiles, coaches, coupes and afoot attired in evening gowns, Tuxedos and swallowtails, just the same as the 'white 400.' At the opening performance there were over one thousand colored people in the house."[156]

In Dahomey's six-week run on Broadway ended on April 5, 1903; on April 28 the company sailed for London, England. By the end of 1903 Williams and Walker's *In Dahomey* Company had given more than two hundred performances at the Shaftesbury Theater. They also gave a "command performance" for King Edward at Buckingham Palace, the occasion being the ninth birthday of Prince Eddy.[157]

Williams and Walker returned to the States in July 1904, and on August 27 began a new touring season with a revised production of *In Dahomey*. Sylvester Russell assessed:

> Bert A. Williams is today the world's greatest natural Negro delineator, his bits of race comedy opiates are all to the good and several miles in advance of . . . Lew Dockstader or any other comedians of the white race who black up their faces . . . His rendition of "I May Be Crazy, but I'm No Fool" made the house resound with screams . . .
>
> George W. Walker seems to have developed with time in his artistic element as a kid gloved comedian . . . and his song "Me and de Minstrel Band," with a minstrel parade chorus march was a very novel feature . . . The incidental Spanish dances led by Ada Overton Walker were beautiful to behold. Mrs. Walker sang "Why Adam Sinned." . . . Her most pretentious effort was a song called "A Rich Coon's Babe" . . . The seats being all sold out and without an extra word of encouragement from New York newspaper critics foretell the rate of speed at which the Negro will soon be, through foe and flame, advancing.[158]

At the end of the summer of 1905, under new management, Williams and Walker began rehearsals for *Abyssinia*, their largest, most ambitious production to date. They were still in rehearsal when Sylvester Russell informed, "Williams & Walker's plans have suddenly terminated and all the news that has been ventilated concerning their new management and production is off."[159] Russell later explained that the "Hackett-Dockstader managers could not stand for a $30,000 production and 110 people, so they flim-flammed the two famous actors and the thing fell through."[160]

On December 16, 1905, in the premiere edition of the mainstream music business journal *Variety*, a columnist who called himself "Corks Recivivus" spelled out the white racist slant on Williams and Walker's success to date:

> All the same, it must gall to see some chap who might be a waiter if it wasn't for the variety stage copping the money that ought to go to us if it wasn't for the coons and the dramatic headliners. It must kinder hurt to see the black type goin' to the black man and the white man getting the yellow or mulatto end, but they seem to hit the bank roll for about all they need for crap money, while the chap with the white skin and old act can go yell all he wants to.
>
> Williams and Walker pulled down $1,750 from Willie Hammerstein and $2,000 from Proctor. That's the answer. What's the question?

With *Abyssinia* in limbo, Williams and Walker returned to vaudeville. The *Freeman* of December 9, 1905, noted that they were headlining an all-star bill at Proctor's Fifty-eighth Street Theater, with support from several members of the *Abyssinia* company. Williams was "still handling his 'Nobody' with undiminished success. He has added seven new verses."[161] At the same time, Ada Overton Walker and "her ten 'Abyssinian Maidens'" were appearing at another local vaudeville house, and the Williams and Walker Glee Club was entertaining at Hurtig and Seamon's Theater.

George Walker had initiated the sixteen-voice Williams and Walker Glee Club during the touring season of 1904–1905, as a way to "keep the young men of the company in touch during the summer months and also furnish them employment."[162] The Glee Club's director and manager was William C. Elkins, a thoroughly schooled singer from Washington, D.C., with a long history in the entertainment business. During the World's Fair summer of 1893, Elkins was heard with Edith Pond's Midnight Stars.[163] He toured abroad with Isham's "Oriental America" before joining the Williams and Walker Company in 1899 as director and baritone voice of the Williams and Walker Quartette, which reportedly "attempted heavier stuff" than the average vaudeville quartet. Between 1923 and 1929 vocal groups under W. C. Elkins's direction recorded spirituals for several commercial recording companies.[164]

With Elkins in the original Williams and Walker Glee Club were "J. L. Hill, Memphis, Tenn.; Henry Green Tapley, Chicago, Ill.; Sterling C. Rex, Philadelphia, Pa.; Charles Henry Young, St. Louis, Mo.; Charles Henry Moore, Cincinnati, O.; Charles Lincoln, New Haven, Conn.; Theodore Lawrence Pankey, Little Rock, Ark.; James Escort Lightfoot, Hamilton, Canada; J. Mantell Thomas, Philadelphia, Pa.; Adolph Henderson, Pine Bluff, Ark.; Arthur H. Payne, Cambridge, Mass.; Lloyd G. Gibbs, Baltimore, Md.; Lewis Henry Saulisbury, Washington, D.C.; and Modeste Bel Guillaume, New York, N.Y."[165]

The roster included many famous names of early black vocal quartet and jubilee singing history. James E. Lightfoot had distinguished himself with the Canadian Jubilee Singers. Sterling Rex and James Mantell Thomas were veterans of the Dinwiddie Colored Quartet of pioneer recording fame.

The *Freeman* of August 19, 1905, noted, "A few days ago the Williams & Walker Glee Club paid a visit to Dr. and Mrs. Booker T. Washington,

W. C. ELKINS
Director of Vocal Music and Manager of the Glee Club.

Indianapolis Freeman, October 20, 1906.

THE SONG THAT HAS TIPPED THE NEW YORK SINGING PROFESSION IS
IOWEN M. LAWSON'S
HOT TAMALES
Send late programs and stamps.
We have "JULIE MY JEWEL," A pretty Song by ANDREW B. STERLING and GEO. L. SPAULDING.
And "VISIONS OF HEAVEN." A Sacred Song, sung by 1600 Professionals.
All Bands send for "HOT TAMALES." LAWSON will be pleased to hear from all friends.
ADDRESS ALL MAIL TO GEO. B. JENNINGS CO., 105-107 W. 4th St., Cincinnati, O.
BEING FEATURED AT EVERY PERFORMANCE BY THE
WILLIAMS and WALKER
GLEE CLUB,
And an Enormous Success at All New York Theatres.
Reference: LEW DOCKSTADER, ERNEST HOGAN and HARRY BROWN. Played by all Bands, DUSS, INNES, HALLOWELL and others.
A good title, good words, and you can bet all you've got on the music. It's a hot rag for piano and band, and full of tricky tricks. New York singers can get it at
THE GOTHAM ATTUCKS MUSIC CO.,
No. 42 W. 28th St., New York, N. Y.
HAVE IT PLAYED. OUR EASTERN DISTRIBUTORS.

New York Clipper, December 9, 1905.

at their summer home at South Waymouth, Mass., and was delightfully entertained by the distinguished educator and his charming wife." Later that fall the Glee Club made a "distinctive hit" at a New York meeting of the National Negro Business League, where their rendition of an "anthem by Cole & Johnson" was praised in particular.[166] When the opening of the 1905–1906 touring season was delayed by problems with management, the Williams and Walker Glee Club went into vaudeville.

Meanwhile, the *Freeman* of March 3, 1906, informed that *Abyssinia* had finally gotten on track:

> Jesse A. Shipp and Alexander Rogers, authors of the new Negro comic-opera will soon be enjoying the fruits of their three year's labor on "Abyssinia" which the white element in theatricals are only half willing to style a musical comedy. "Abyssinia" is indeed a Negro play to be proud of, and the grand and diversified score of music composed and arranged by Prof. Will Marion Cooke . . . Bert A. Williams and . . . George W. Walker, along with Jesse A. Shipp and a few other colored writers and performers are to be credited with the final accomplishment of founding and substantiating a new school of American comedy and also of music.

Shortly thereafter, *Abyssinia* opened at the Majestic Theater on Broadway under a new white backer, Melville B. Raymond. In the *Freeman* of March 17, 1906, a New York–based stage correspondent celebrated the current three-pronged invasion of New York by the big shows:

> The three greatest colored American plays in the world are now engaged in the metropolis. Rufus Rastus Extravaganza is a great hit in the West End theatre in Harlem, "The Smart Set," made famous by Mr. Hogan and later Mr. Dudley, opens at the Murry Hill theatre in 42nd street, and Shipp and Rogers' "Abyssinia," with music by Will Marion Cook, is scoring at the Majestic in Broadway and 59th street, and is indeed a worthy achievement of Negro ideals, playwrights and performers.

As soon as it opened *Abyssinia* became a special target of prejudiced New York newspaper critics and self-interested white performers. According to Sylvester Russell, "Alan Dale and other [white] critics pronounced it a failure and accused the two talented comedians of trying to be too much like white people."[167] By the end of March *Abyssinia*'s brief run on Broadway was over. Russell later noted that it had "played only to half-full houses during the last two of its three weeks' engagement. The show had then been cut down from 110 to less than 60 people."[168] In his column of May 19, 1906, Russell lodged a bitter complaint:

> When Abyssinia first saw the light of day at the Majestic Theatre in New York last February, the

A SCENE F OM "ABYSSINIA" THAT WILL A PEAR AT PARK THEAT R OCTOBER 8, 9, 10.

Indianapolis Freeman, October 6, 1906.

> critics commented on the idiosyncrasy of the play and its fitness to please or displease Americans who have white skin . . . from a point of racial humor, rather than the true merits of the playwright and the performer . . . If color is the ground upon which white critics build their nests, it is up to the black critic to throw rotten eggs . . . Let this be the last time that otherwise critics of New York will overlook art for the mere mortification of color.

When *Abyssinia* was presented at Convention Hall in Washington, D.C., in April 1906, the *Freeman* noted, "This will be Williams & Walker's only appearance in the South." Their success in the nation's capital was confirmed by a "surprisingly cordial" review in the mainstream *Washington Post*, which was known for its disdain of "what the local papers wish to term 'coon shows.'" The *Freeman* optimistically editorialized: "The triumph of the Williams and Walker engagement [at Convention Hall], literally translated, means that another year will find 100 ,000 Negroes of Washington in possession of a theater of their own, where such desirable attractions can play as often and as long as the people want them, independent of the grudging condescension of white managers or the patronizing superciliousness of white audiences."

In September 1906, the Williams and Walker Company opened a second season of *Abyssinia* at the Grand Opera House in New York. When they reached Indianapolis in October, a philosophical *Freeman* reviewer cited *Abyssinia* as "another evidence of the progress of the Negro actor. There were indications of fetters still, that hold the Negroes to certain lines . . . but there were further evidences of the greatest strides made . . . It stands to reason—art—the best, is the result of sufferings of pain and which in the nature of things are the chief assets of the race."

Abyssinia closed in Atlantic City, New Jersey, on May 11, 1907. Williams and Walker returned to vaudeville for the summer, staging their latest "concoction of music, singing and dancing," "On the Road to Bandanna Land," probably an excerpt from their new musical comedy for the coming season, *Bandanna Land*. For this production, playwright Jesse A. Shipp chose a contemporary setting in the state of Georgia. Bert Williams portrayed "one 'Skunkton Bowser,' a simple-minded Negro" who inherits a sum of money and, with encouragement from his friend Bud Jenkins, played by George Walker, entrusts his funds to a "syndicate of colored men," "formed for various purposes along the line of real estate investment."[169] At the Majestic Theater on Broadway in February 1908, a reviewer assured, "The Negroid atmosphere is there."[170]

It was reported that Dr. Booker T. Washington "slipped into the balcony" of the Majestic Theater to see *Bandanna Land*.[171] Washington was outspoken in his admiration of Bert Williams; in 1910 he told a reporter, "There are a quality and flavor about Bert Williams' humor which indicate that it is the natural expression of a thoughtful and observing mind."[172]

In the fall of 1908 Williams and Walker launched a second edition of *Bandanna Land*, which a *Freeman* reviewer said "brought out all of the old time humor and situations common to the early successes in minstrelsy":

This does not imply that the show is built along "jube" lines . . . It has often been said that the time has not yet come when the white people will listen to the sorrows of the Negro on the stage. The time may not "be here," but it is encouragingly near at hand if the

BANDANNA LAND.

"Bandanna Land" is a real artistic achievement, representing as it does a distinct advancement in negro minstrelsy. Realizing, perhaps, that the white public is chronically disinclined to accept the stage negro in any but a purely comedy vein and having at the same time a natural desire to be something better than the conventional colored clown whose class mark is a razor and an ounce or two of cut glass, Williams and Walker have approached the delicate subject from a new side. They—or some one for them, it does not matter who for purposes of argument—seem to have argued: "if they won't have us in a semi-serious vein, perhaps they will accept us as picturesque." If the purpose of "Bandanna Land" is to compromise upon "picturesque" as between grotesque and serious, it works out splendidly.

The ex-vaudeville pair maintain a good middle path. Since they must be comedians at least they can be funny in some other way than by stealing chickens, "shooting dice" and using razors, the three conventions which have somehow or other come to be the inevitable earmarks of the comic negro. That they have steered clear of these hackneyed subjects and still manage to make themselves acceptable entertainers argues a good deal at once for their business sense and professional skill.

If Williams and Walker exacted from the members of their supporting company the same admirable restraint they exercise over themselves, they would have a much more effective organization. Just now the effect of the piece is rather marred in places by the unfortunate efforts of several ambitious colored persons to be polite actors. While the two principals labor with complete singleness of purpose to be entertaining, several of their subordinates insist upon taking themselves seriously, by an attitude that is entirely confined to themselves and in no wise shared by the audience. Fortunately these few are very subordinate and their posings and mouthings were reduced to an almost harmless minimum. The desire to pose seems to work in inverse ratio—the more important the part the smaller the apparent desire to be taken seriously, until at the top Williams and Walker are to be entirely absolved from any desire to be dignified. This is not advanced as a novel discovery nor is its application to be confined to the present discussion.

"Bandanna Land" has found substantial success at the Majestic Theatre, where it is now in its fourth week with an almost unbroken record of capacity business. No small part of the credit for this result is due to Will Marion Cook, who wrote the music, and to the splendid singing organization. The score is full of surprises, crisp little phrases that stick in the mind and are distinctly whistleable, and several of the lyrics that go with them are excellently done. "Ain't Gwine to Be No Rain" is one of the best. There is an attractive quaintness about the lines that remind one rather of the inimitable "Uncle Remus" rhymes, and the plan of printing the lyrics on the program turns out to be an excellent idea in this case. Let us hope, however, that the scheme doesn't spread to Broadway. Imagine having the book and lyrics of "Funabashi," for example, handed to you in printed form!

J. A. Shipp and Alex Rogers are credited with the writing of the book and lyrics. To tell the truth there is a good deal of book. It tells a whole plot and requires much straight dialogue to make plain, but the straightaway manner they have of plunging into explanations and getting them over with recommends itself. It may be crude, but it saves time and gives that much more opportunity to Williams and Walker for their clever funmaking.

Alexander Rogers also has an important role in the piece, and is one of the few principals who consents to talk in negro dialect. Most of the other men—and pretty much all the women—employ a form of speech that is Bostonese in its purity—and then some. Henry Troy was one of the worst offenders in this respect.

Abbie Mitchell and Aida Overton Walker are principals among the women. Both have the pick of the musical numbers and with their fresh, clear voices add a good deal to the musical department. Likewise they wear much fine clothes—really fine clothes by any standard, not feverish stage raiment—but their contribution to the comedy was not considerable. Miss Walker scored a three-base hit at her first appearance with a capital song called "Kinky" and a lively incidental dance.

Bert Williams has a novelty number called "Me to Me Is Me." It went extremely well. Indeed, with that grotesque dance of his almost any sort of a song would bring applause, but "Me to Me" is not in the same class with "Nobody." The march number, and the popular hit of the whole piece goes to George Walker. It is a whoop bang piece called "Bon Bon Buddie," and rather reminds one of "H-a-r-r-i-g-a-n." It is used in the working up of the finale to the second act, and for the encore Williams and Walker do their burlesque cakewalk dance.

The humor of the piece arises from the relations of Skunkton Bowser (Williams) and Bud Jenkins (Walker). Skunkton has come into a fortune, and Bud, a companion during his travels with a minstrel troupe, and the familiar "wise coon," appoints himself Skunkton's guardian in the administration of the funds. Skunkton finds it difficult to understand the intricacies of high finance as interpreted by Bud, particularly when Bud's financing works itself out in terms of $10 suits for Skunkton and $80 raiment for Bud. Skunkton's timid and clumsy remonstrances against this system and Bud's half-angry accusations of ingratitude keep the fun bubbling without let up. The pair have never had a better line of talk or more skilfully devised situations.

The last act rounds the entertainment out nicely with what programs take delight in describing as "a riot of color and whirlwind motion." The situation, which introduces a big dancing and singing finale, is adroitly managed. A syndicate of colored men own a certain tract of land adjoining a recreation park, to the owners of which they are willing to sell out at a profit. In order to make themselves as objectionable as possible as neighbors they organize a big noisy negro jubilee, and this makes the closing scene. The feature of this was a burlesque of the "Merry Widow Waltz," which, if it is a rather overdone subject, had at least the merit of being a variation. The dance was a capital bit of "rag" and won solid applause.

Rush.

Variety, February 22, 1908.

MASONIC THEATRE, LOUISVILLE.

MATINEES, Monday, Wednesday and Saturday.

Week Starting Monday, FEB. 22d.

MR. F. RAY COMSTOCK Presents
The "Society Fad" of New York City for over Four Months

Williams and Walker

(Who Made Colored Show Folks Famous)
In Their Great Success

'Bandanna Land'

Book by Shipp & Rogers—Music by W. M. Cook.

AIDA OVERTON-WALKER'S SENSATIONAL DANCE, ***"Oh, You Devil"***

Hear the Big Song Hits

"You're in de Right Church but de Wrong Pew,"
"Tired o' Eatin' in de Restaurants,"
"Drinkin'," "Bon-Bon Buddie,"
"Any Old Place in Yankee Land is Good Enough for Me,"
"I'm Just Crazy 'Bout You,"
"Hard to Love Somebody,"
"Down Among the Sugar Cane" and
"In My Old Home."

THE ONE UNIQUE NOVELTY MUSICAL SHOW OF THE SEASON.

Indianapolis Freeman, February 20, 1909.

beautiful eulogy "to the bandana handkerchief," so pathetically rendered by George Walker . . . is to be considered as a "feeler."[173]

Fatal illness brought a sudden end to the famous team of Williams and Walker. When *Bandanna Land* reached Indianapolis in February 1909, the *Freeman* announced that, "Aida Overton Walker has given up the stage and remains at home."[174] At their next engagement, in Chicago, George Walker suffered what was at first described as a nervous breakdown, and later as a "fatal paresis." He withdrew to his New York home, and died in 1911 without ever returning to the stage.

In the fall of 1909 Bert Williams went out as the lone star of a new musical comedy, *Mr. Lode of Koal*, and in 1910 he began his landmark run as a headliner of the otherwise all-white Ziegfeld Follies, insuring his reputation as the most famous African American comedian of his generation. By the time he signed with Ziegfeld, Williams was the last comic star of the original big shows left standing.

Aida Overton Walker resumed her career in 1909 with the Bob Cole and J. Rosamond Johnson musical comedy production *The Red Moon*. Later

"Oh! You Devil Rag." (courtesy Thornton Hagert, Vernacular Music Research)

she had a successful run in mainstream vaudeville. In 1911 a black Chicago weekly paper reported that she was "keeping pace with Bert Williams, and is getting the top vaudeville figures."[175]

No one was better equipped to produce black musical comedies during the ragtime years than Bob Cole. In Sylvester Russell's opinion, Cole had "no equal as a producer, no superiors as an actor, coon song singer, coon song writer or Negro comedy writer."[176] The critic "I. McCorker" allowed that, "Bob Cole emphasizes a coon song about as well as any man on stage . . . If comedy is ever to be 'elevated' by colored men . . . from farce into the legitimate, its elevation must come through such representatives as Bob Cole."[177]

Cole began his steep rise to prominence in 1891, as a member of Sam T. Jack's Creole Burlesque Company, with whom he traveled, on and off at least, for the next several years. During the season of 1895–1896—his last with the Creoles—Cole was partnered in a popular song and dance act with his future wife, Stella Wiley.[178]

Cole's career gained momentum in the fall of 1896 when he was made stage manager for the inaugural edition of the Black Patti Troubadours. According to an early review in the *New York Clipper*, Cole was "one of the brightest bits on the bill . . . a witty young man, who handles himself and his stories in commendable fashion." He developed his famous gentleman-tramp character, "Willie Wayside," while touring with Black Patti, and also began an important partnership with Billy Johnson, who had come to the Black Patti Troubadours from Isham's Octoroons.

Cole and Johnson had first crossed paths as early as December 1894, when they were both listed, along with Stella Wiley, on the roster of Billy Jackson's Colored Minstrels in an historic engagement at Worth's Dime Museum in New York City.[179] Their first significant collaborative effort was the musical farce-comedy skit, "At Jolly Coon-ey Island," which served as the "curtain-raiser" for the Black Patti Troubadours' initial tour. Trouble arose when Cole suddenly left the Black Patti Troubadours in May 1897 and took all the music scores with him. As reported in the *Clipper*, "Bob Cole, the former stage manager of the Black Patti Company, was charged with the larceny of the orchestral music of 'At Jolly Coney Island [*sic*].' According to Manager Nolan, Cole was noticed after Sunday's performance prowling around the orchestra, and at the evening entertainment the music could not be found. At the police court Cole was bound over in $1,000 bail for trial."[180]

Cole apparently spent some time in jail before bail could be raised. Finally, on June 5, 1897, a grand jury "refused to find a bill against him."[181] The jury accepted Cole's claim of authorship and ownership of the music Voelckel and Nolan had accused him of stealing.

In the fall of 1897 Bob Cole and Billy Johnson brought forth the first full-fledged, critically acknowledged black musical comedy, *A Trip to Coontown*. It encountered immediate opposition from the white theatrical establishment, as Cole and Johnson described in a letter to the *Clipper*, published March 5, 1898: "At the beginning of the season untiring efforts were made by some traveling managers to stop the booking of this attraction." Despite resistance, *A Trip to Coontown* enjoyed a successful first season and propelled Bob Cole to the forefront of his profession.

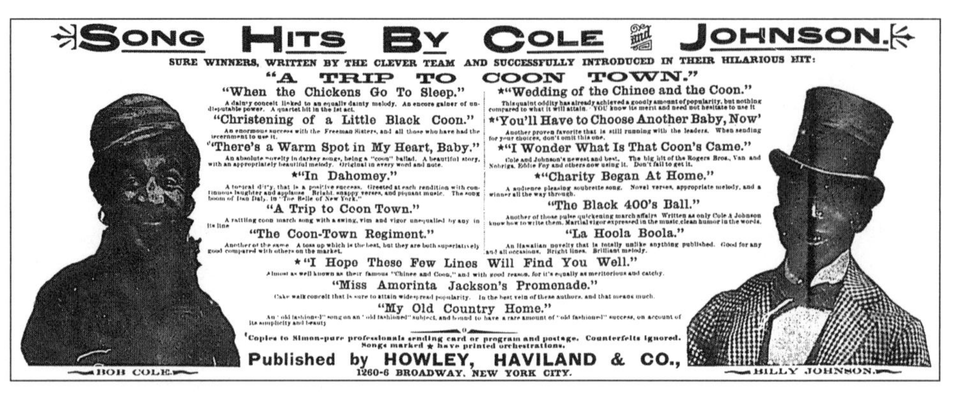

New York Clipper, September 24, 1898.

A Trip to Coontown featured fifteen original Cole and Johnson songs, including "I Wonder What Is That Coon's Game," which is echoed on a black string band recording from 1928, under the title "Mysterious Coon."[182] Outstanding members of the original cast included Tom Brown, Robert A. Kelley, Jesse Shipp, the Freeman Sisters, Hen Wise, and Lloyd Gibbs. In April 1898, when they showed at the Third Avenue Theater in New York City, the *Clipper* made a telling declaration: "The production is first class in every particular, and fully carries out the provisions of the title, 'a musical comedy.'" As late as 1902 Sylvester Russell asserted, "No Negro comedy has yet been put together to equal 'A Trip to Coontown' in plot or completion. Williams and Walker have just arrived to where Cole and Johnson left off; and all other comedy stars are three years farther behind."

Midway through the second season of *A Trip to Coontown*, Cole and Johnson relayed this note to the *Freeman*: "We opened at the Alhambra Theatre, Chicago, Feb. 26 [1899] to a packed matinee and turned many away at the evening performance. This is our fourth engagement in Chicago within three months. Mr. Billy Johnson, one of our stars, is now in the cast, after being compelled to lay off three weeks on account of having his hands frozen during our last Chicago engagement."[183]

In New York during the summer of 1899, between touring seasons, Cole and Johnson and select members of their company appeared in vaudeville at the mainstream society Casino Roof Garden, sharing the bill with white performers. That fall, when they began a third season of *A Trip to Coontown*, the *Freeman* called Cole and Johnson "a credit to the race," declaring, "It has always been the motive of Messrs. Cole and Johnson to elevate the Negro on the stage, by laying aside the stereotype style of Negro performances and opening up a new field for the more ambitious Negro on the stage."[184]

At the Park Theater in Indianapolis in the fall of 1900, the *Freeman* described:

> colored people coming out in large numbers [to see] Messrs. Bob Cole and Billy Johnson, who sing original coon oddities . . . Mr. Cole in the title role of a tramp, is a performer of rare talent, and with his famous bull dog "Bo" . . . and his singing of "I Must 'O Been

Dreaming" and "Picking on a Chicken Bone" never failed to bring down the house in a tremendous way. Mr. Johnson as Jim Flimflammer, the bunco, is also a rare professional and handles the "straight" of the play in masterly style . . . Sam Lucas, being an aged man in reality, plays the grand old man of Coontown with an air of perfect ease and reflects much credit on the show; as he is a well-to-do old man in the play a parlor in his Coontown home is staged very beautifully. Solos are rendered by Miss Edna Alexander, leading soprano, and Lloyd G. Gibbs, famous tenor, and the reception of the Prince from Dahomey, who is none less than the very comical Bob Cole. The show terminates with Cole & Johnson in their grand Oriental frolic in conjunction with the Coontown carnival.[185]

A Trip to Coontown encountered economic difficulties during its fourth season and, on April 11, 1901, Cole and Johnson filed for bankruptcy. It was reported in the *Clipper* that they had "liabilities over $3,000 and no assets." This resulted in the shelving of *A Trip to Coontown* and the dissolving of Cole and Johnson's partnership. According to Sylvester Russell, "It was quick significant history. Mr. Cole had nothing to lose in the separation except to be retarded in his progress of becoming a legitimate comedy star, while Billy Johnson is left weeping in the wilderness." As Russell predicted, Bob Cole's fame and prestige only increased, while Billy Johnson settled into a less conspicuous career in mainstream vaudeville.[186]

Cole immediately engaged himself in a successful songwriting partnership with brothers James Weldon and J. Rosamond Johnson. In an article in the March 1902 issue of the *Colored American*, Cole informed: "I was never so busy as I find myself at present, dramatizing a novel of Negro life for Mrs. Caroline H. Pemberton, writing in corroboration [*sic*] with James W. Johnson. The libretto for Will Marion Cook's opera, 'The Cannibal King,' also libretto for Willis Accooe, and preparing several big musical numbers for Klaw and Erlanger and May Irwin in collaboration with Rosamond Johnson and James W. Johnson. I have little time to idle away."

Sylvester Russell, who was anxious to see Cole return to the business of musical comedy production, expressed that, "While the new parlor song writing team is a howling success, Mr. Cole's future comedy prospects should not be overlooked." In July 1902 Cole wrote a new musical farce for Voelckel and Nolan's Black Patti Troubadours, titled *A Coontown Circus Day*. Around that same time, he chose Rosamond Johnson to be his new stage partner. Russell opined that:

In selecting a new partner by the name of "Johnson" to succeed Billy, Mr. Cole has secured the right man in Rosamond Johnson for his immediate necessity, to help him write songs . . .

[At Keith's Boston Theater] Cole and Johnson entered the stage in a parlor scene wearing evening dress suits. The lion's share of applause fell upon Mr. Cole for his very artful rendition of their own coon songs, "I Must-a-been-a-Dreamin'" and "Oh, Didn't he Ramble" were masterpieces of art.[187]

J. Rosamond Johnson was a gifted singer, pianist, and composer, but he had no prior dramatic stage experience. Consequently, for the first few years of their partnership, Cole and Rosamond Johnson confined their stage performances to vaudeville, playing mainstream theaters mostly in the northeastern states. Their act consisted almost entirely of piano and vocal selections, primarily

Indianapolis Freeman, October 20, 1900.

Indianapolis Freeman, October 20, 1900.

Indianapolis Freeman, October 20, 1900.

their own original songs. The *Freeman* reproduced this notice from the Rochester, New York, *Herald* of October 21, 1902:

Mr. Johnson played a piano solo well indeed—brilliantly in fact. It sounded like Godard's "Second Mazurka." Then he sang a German lied—"Still wie

SOMETHING NEW.

THE ORIGINAL
BOB COLE
COMEDIAN.

Authors and Composers of
"The Maiden With the Dreamy Eyes"
"The Owl and the Moon."
"Tell Me, Dusky Maiden."
"Come Out, Dinah, on the Green."
"My Castle on the Nile."
"The Old Flag Never Touched the Ground."
"Oh! Didn't He Ramble."
"My Heart's Desire"
"I Must a' Been a Dreaming."
"Mandy, Won't You Let Me Be Your Beau?"
Etc., Etc.

"The world is always ready to receive talent with open arms."—HOLMES.

THE NEW

BOB ROSAMOND

COLE and JOHNSON

"America's Greatest Colored Entertainers."—KEITH.

Presenting an Act which is unanimously conceded by both press and public to be *the best constructed,* more artistically executed, more *heartily welcomed* and vociferously applauded than any Colored Act now seen in America.

KEITH'S { PHILADELPHIA HOUSE, - June 16, "Phenomenal Hit." UNION SQUARE, N. Y. - " 23, "Veritable Triumph." BOSTON HOUSE, - - - - July 13, "Watch and See."

N. B.—In reviewing COLE and JOHNSON'S record for the past twelve months, you will notice that they have had the honor of appearing before more Distinguished Personages than any two like entertainers.

A REMARKABLE RECORD. ENGAGEMENTS EXTRAORDINARY.

U. S. Senator W. A. Clark of Montana, at his palatial residence in Washington, D. C.; U. S. Senatorial Body and Chief Executive Theodore Roosevelt; Mr. Irving and Miss Ellen Terry; Farewell Boston Dinner (per arrangement of Mr. H. B. Sire); Mrs. Stuyvesant Fish; Mr. Oelrich; Mrs. Jack Gardiner, Boston; The Vanderbilts, the Goulds, the Bacons, the Rothschilds, Mr. Chas. Schwab, Mr. Jim Brady, Mr. David Belasco, Mrs. Leslie Carter, Miss Lillian Russell, Miss Anna Held, Miss May Irwin, Mr. Chas. Hawtrey, DeWolf Hopper and a host of other notables.

SOMETHING NEW.

ROSAMOND JOHNSON

Baritone and Pianist.
Student of Boston New England Conservatory

Have written successful musical numbers for the following distinguished and well-known managers:

Klaw and Erlanger,
Messrs. Sire Bros.,
Florenz Ziegfeld, Jr.,
Geo. W. Lederer,
Primrose and Dockstader.

For private engagements address COLE & JOHNSON, care J. W. Stern & Co., 34 E. 21st St., N. Y.
For public engagements address W. S. BENTHAM, Associated Vaudeville Managers Exchange, St. James Bldg., New York, N. Y.

ONE WHOLE YEAR AT SIRE BROS.' NEW YORK THEATRE.

New York Dramatic Mirror, July 12, 1902.

Die Nacht" . . . then Mr. Cole interposed and insisted on a little ragtime. So they gave selections from a repertoire of their own songs. Mr. Cole singing them and Mr. Johnson playing the accompaniments and sometimes joining in with a vocal echo. They gave: "Mandy, Won't You Let Me Be Your Beau?" "There's No Use in Asking, Cause You Know the Reason Why," "My Castle on the Nile," "Tell Me Dusky Maiden," an irresistible travesty on the "Floradora" sextette and "Must a Been Dreaming," the last named including a clever imitation of Dan Daly by Mr. Cole. No such rag-time was ever heard in Rochester. If the coon song is to endure, let it be done by such artists as Cole and Johnson. They have reduced ragtime to an art and they are its interpreters par excellence.[188]

Cole and Rosamond Johnson played the entire month of December 1902 at Keith's vaudeville house in Boston. At the beginning of 1903, a front-page article in the *Freeman* said of Cole, "He has written more popular songs and plays than you can shake a stick at, and made a world-wide reputation as one of the greatest character actors in America by playing the part of a tramp in 'A Trip to Coontown,' a famous musical comedy of which he was co-author with Billy Johnson, his former partner."[189]

During 1904 and 1905, Cole and Rosamond Johnson wrote songs for Klaw and Erlanger's all-white musical comedy productions, including *Humpty Dumpty* and *In Newport*. It was apparently under Klaw and Erlanger's management that they went to Europe in 1905. A *Freeman* report of June 2, 1906, said they were "still scoring success in England with their refined singing act."

After more than four years in mainstream vaudeville, Cole and Johnson announced that they were going out on a "starring tour" for the 1906–1907 season, in an original musical comedy titled *The Shoo-Fly Regiment*, produced by Melville B. Raymond.[190] The show's hit songs included "The Ghost of Deacon Brown," sung by Cole and chorus, "Who Do You Love," sung by female impersonator Andrew Tribble, and "On the Gay Lunetta," sung by Theodore Pankey and chorus. The tour opened on August 27, 1906, at Cumberland, Maryland. At the Park Theater in Indianapolis in March 1907, near the end of the season, a *Freeman* reviewer was favorably impressed:

The comedy work was particularly good; it had a finish which made it very taking . . .

The plot of the "Shoo-Fly Regiment," if it may be thus designated, was more discernible than noted in other shows. The "thread" was fairly continuous and strong, holding the interest to the last as to the final outcome of the Negro regiment sent to do duty in the Philippines. Some very excellent scenes and some good acting were noted on the soldiers' arrival at their destination.

Mr. Bob Cole, who played the part of the janitor of the industrial school, and also other parts in keeping, was at once a favorite . . . He is an especially good actor; no exponent of light comedianism, and of his class, has any advantage over him. The audience could have stood more of Bob Cole.

J. Rosamond Johnson assumes a legitimate role . . . His part appeared somewhat experimental, but on the whole good. Of course the searchlight of criticism will be directed toward him owing to the advanced step taken . . . He acquitted himself well, in view of the bits of acting permitted him . . .

The play is rich in special attractions—strong people that had good telling parts and opportunity to make good . . .

The "Bode of Education" was an amusing creation. Among its members was Sam Lucas, the dean of the Negro stage . . . He yet moves very gracefully on his feet . . .

"Ophelia, the Village Pride," by Andrew Tribble, was exceedingly well done. All must give it to Tribble; he is the goods. His characterization was great. Theodore Pankey as "Lieutenant Dixon," was quite a hit. Pankey is fairly a matinee idol, when he arrives in his white suit de regiment, he is a furore. His speech to the troops when off to the war was beautiful and stirring . . .

Singing is one of the strong features of the show. Many of the songs and the music generally were prepared by J. Rosamond Johnson. Besides the notable singing of Miss Wise was that by Anna Cook, who has a beautiful voice. Mr. Johnson has an excellent baritone voice which he uses to advantage. In fact he is an all around musician, finding himself at home at the piano, where he has the rare ability of doing a "rag" or classic

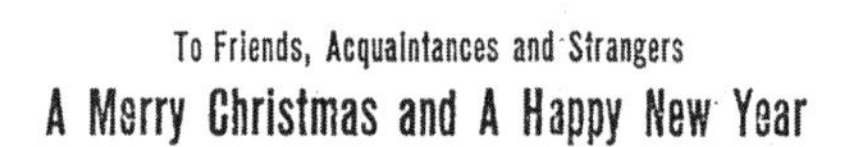

Indianapolis Freeman, December 23, 1916.

equally well. Mr. Henry Williams, musical director, is a prize. He is a man of eminent ability, having had the advantage of the best teachers at home and abroad.[191]

The Shoo-Fly Regiment spent much of its initial tour on an adventurous sweep through the South, extending as far as Galveston, Texas, in a succession of one- and two-night stands. When questioned by a newspaper reporter about *The Shoo-Fly Regiment*'s first season, Bob Cole described a series of adversities:

Yes, we had a pretty rough time of it. When our original manager, M. B. Raymond, failed, we were left in Darkest Texas, with an indebtedness of some $12,000, which included printing, railroad transportation, back salaries, etc., all of which we assumed. Among other things we carried for the greater part of the season, four sheriffs with attachments, which have since been vacated and although we made no money for ourselves, we have paid off all obligations and will start off in the fall with a clean slate. Our route has not been of the best, but we have made good wherever we went.[192]

In a sense, the southern leg of the tour was capped at Ruston, Louisiana, where the show had to be canceled "on account of prejudice . . . having received notice that Negro shows were not needed there."[193]

In the fall of 1907 Cole and Johnson took *The Shoo-Fly Regiment* out for what appears to have been an abbreviated second season. In the summer of 1908 they went into rehearsal for *The Red Moon* with a cast that included Sam Lucas, Abbie Mitchell, Theodore and Anna Cook Pankey, Fanny Wise, Andrew Tribble, and Bessie Brown. The title referred to "the old superstitions of both races that furnish the characters of the comedy. The red moon is an omen of bad luck with the old fashioned Negro, and when the moon shines red, to the Indian it is the Great Spirit's call for them to follow the warpath." The story focused on the interactions of "a Negro-Indian half-breed girl," played by Abbie Mitchell, with "a ragtime pianist and a shabby genteel coon show manager" who were "masquerading as a doctor and a lawyer," played by Johnson and Cole, respectively.[194] Andrew Tribble added his comic touch as "Lilly White, the washerwoman," singing "I Ain't Had No Lovin' in a Long Time" in his convincing "wench" costume.[195]

According to a plot outline in the *Freeman*, *The Red Moon* opens at a Government school for Indians and Negroes at "Sunshine Land." Minnehaha is the "half breed" daughter of a Negro woman connected to the school and an Indian chief who deserted her in infancy. The chief suddenly returns to reclaim his daughter and take her to the "Land of the Setting Sun." With the aid of Red Feather, "a bold, bad Indian student at the school who is in love with Minnehaha," the maiden is forcibly taken away. In Act II, the curtain goes up on an elaborate mountain setting, the "Land of the Setting Sun." After various musical and comic machinations, Minnehaha is rescued by the resourceful Negroes Plunk (Johnson) and Slim (Cole) and returned to the school, her home, and friends. In Act III, Plunk gets to marry Minnehaha, and they live happily ever after.[196]

The Red Moon proved to be an unmitigated success. From the Great Northern Theater in Chicago, in October 1908, a reviewer raved:

They have the real goods in "The Red Moon." This piece has crossed the line "no classic colored shows" that has been drawn by the managers and press. They flatly turned back "Abyssinia;" now they are face to face with another. The whole Chicago press is lauding "The Red Moon." The theatregoers are packing the house at every performance. Has sentiment changed in the last two or three years[?] . . . The music is the best that was ever offered by Negroes . . . The comedy was exceptionally light; nothing to scream at, but keep smiling . . . There never was such a collection of colored girls . . . A well laid out story, acted to the line, dressed and staged. "The Red Moon" is the hit of the season.[197]

As the tour progressed, informative reviews came from Indianapolis and Louisville. J. D. Howard wrote from Indianapolis:

The show is positively an innovation inasmuch as it is an introductory measure of absolutely new characters and impersonations to the stage so far as colored performers are concerned . . .

In [Act II] is put on one of the most pretentious and best dressed song numbers I have ever seen staged by colored performers. The song was "On the Road to Monterey," sung by Theodore Pankey, backed by a chorus of exquisite sweetness both in voice and costume . . . Mr. Cole is very funny and Mr. Johnson shows to good advantage as a finished and much improved actor over his efforts of last year.

There is a bit of evolution interwoven throughout the story that is sure to have a beneficial effect upon the American whites as regards their opinion of the Negro. They have succeeded in bringing out to a nicety the natural degenerate tendency of the Indian and show correspondingly well the ambition and progressive tendency of the Negro . . .

The best received song numbers were "On the Road to Monterey," "Big Red Shawl," "I Ain't Had No Lovin' in a Long Time," and the "Pathway of Love." The endorsements, business and "yellage" scored by the "Red Moon" were general and tremendous.[198]

At the Avenue Theater in Louisville, *Freeman* critic Carey B. Lewis exclaimed:

We doff our hats to Messrs. Cole and Johnson. They are here sweeping the town like a cyclone. They have broken the record of the venue in point of attendance and quality of the class of performance. It is conceded to be the greatest musical vehicle that has been on a local stage this season . . .

The Cole and Johnson company is without peers on the American stage today and the aggregation does more to give the white Americans an example of what the Negro can do in higher departments of musical comedy than any show we have seen. "The Red Moon" is quite a step forward from the "Shoo Fly Regiment" so far as dramatic coherency is concerned. The theme is more finely drawn and clear cut and the action is made to revolve around the grand central idea of a little love romance.

Under the personal direction of Mr. James Reese Europe, the chorus is full, strong, sweet and brilliant . . . Miss Abbie Mitchell, the prima donna is graceful, artistic and charming . . . [Andrew] Tribble as Miss Lilly White, the washer-woman, always makes good and causes the gallery gods and the whole audience to laugh a plenty.[199]

Sylvester Russell gave his approval to *The Red Moon*, but not without reservation. He specifically objected to Rosamond Johnson's "pianologue," done "in bar room style this season, with his hat on, and with a big special three legged piano which crowds the chorus from the stage."[200] A March 20, 1909, commentary in the *Freeman* expressed the opinion that the general public was still unprepared to support "Negro plays" as such: "Now it is reasonably certain that if circumstances warranted a straight play from curtain to curtain, it would be given. But we have shreds and patches, and simply because the public will only pay for what it wants

. . . The 'Red Moon,' Cole & Johnson's show, has gone further in the matter of presenting a complete play. Even that presentation is mixed—part opera, more or less serious, part comedy."

A contemporaneous report postulated that, with increasing support from black audiences, Cole and Johnson were at last making a profit from *The Red Moon*: "It is thought they are making money very fast this season. It is also said that it is only within a year or so that the combination crossed the financial deadline . . . The boys are growing popular and special with the race."[201]

The complex critical response to the play was partly explained in the *Freeman* of May 29, 1909:

> The New York correspondent of the Chicago Tribune found space to comment on Cole & Johnson's "Red Moon." He said, among other things, that the "Red Moon" was set and arranged in such a way as not to offend the white race or infringe upon white actors. This has been the cry of nine-tenths of the white writers on negro shows. It looks like trying a dumb man because he can't talk. How can the Negro imitate the white man successfully? On the other hand, the white man has stolen his minstrel, his songs and his cake walks.

By the summer of 1909 Ernest Hogan was dead, George Walker was irreversibly ill, and Bert Williams was set to join the Ziegfeld Follies. With hopes for the future of big African American musical comedy productions resting heavily on Bob Cole, the second season of *The Red Moon* was anxiously awaited. To bolster the bill, Aida Overton Walker was contracted to appear as a "special attraction." The show's white backers apparently sealed the agreement by promising to make her the star of her own big show the following season. In response to this surprise announcement, Abbie Mitchell, Minnehaha, resigned from *The Red Moon* Company in a fit of pique. Andrew Tribble, the show's celebrated Miss Lilly White, also withdrew.[202]

The second edition of *The Red Moon* opened in October 1909 to crowded houses. Sylvester Russell allowed that it was "perhaps the best musical comedy upon the American stage . . . all completely changed and originally new . . . notable improvements have been effected." He especially liked the new song, "Don't Tell Tales Out of School," sung by Cole and Johnson in a "singing and dancing quartet" with Fannie Wise and Leona Marshall.[203] Other new songs included James Reese Europe's "Pickaninny Days," the "Red Moon To-da-lo—Two Step," and J. Rosamond Johnson's "Bleeding Moon," which Russell called a "tuneful blessing." As rendered by Fannie Wise, it "fairly arose to an unexpected height of vocal sweetness and expression."

At the Park Theater in Indianapolis, *The Red Moon* drew an honest, straightforward review:

> We do not exaggerate when we place the Cole and Johnson show on an equal footing with any of the white shows of like character . . . Messrs. Cole and Johnson are studious, and are endeavoring to attain perfection in their chosen profession. This is particularly noticeable in the music department and regrettably absent in the elocutionary department. Cole himself would appear to a better advantage if he would speak louder and more distinct; lack of expression sometimes spoils the effect of his well-aimed jokes . . . In the theatrical world the "finales" of this show are being highly commented upon . . . they are excelsior.[204]

In Chicago, Sylvester Russell commended Cole and Johnson for "maintaining a standard of ability, and not one of complexion, and the dark faces of men and women in the chorus look better for a race of mixed colors rather than the impression by all yellow girls who look like white and create prejudice." Aida Overton Walker was the subject of particular attention: "[Her] appearance always calls for silence, and then applause as she enters on the stage. Whatever it is that seems to check one's breathing goodness only knows. You see her play a pickaninny child, you sigh and wait a while, then you see her dance, but after the dance is over you see her as the real soubrette that she is."[205] Another correspondent remarked, "If girls looked and acted like [Aida Overton Walker] in 'Pickaninny Days,' then why can't we have those days always? I want to go back to them."[206]

Shortly after the season closed, Bob Cole suffered a nervous breakdown that abruptly ended his brilliant theatrical career. Ten months later he was dead. As Sylvester Russell explained:

> It was on the morning of October 8, 1910 that Mr. Cole broke down while appearing at the Fifth Avenue Theatre, New York in vaudeville, with Rosamund Johnson, and on October 14 he became hopelessly insane as a result of overwork and had to be sent to Bellevue.
>
> About a month ago Mr. Cole became so rational and quiet that he was permitted to be removed to a sanitarium in Amityville, Long Island . . .
>
> [He died] August 1, 1911, when either in a fit of despondency or a sudden return of insanity he deliberately walked into the stream and was drown in Catskill creek, where in the mountains he had been taken for his health and summer vacation.

A great appreciator of Cole's art, Russell assessed:

> He was an excellent artistic dancer; his comedy was of a high order and full of natural and educational wit. His

COLE & JOHNSON

The Greatest Afro - American Actors on the American stage.

IN THEIR CELEBRATED PLAY "THE RED MOON" ARE PLAYING TO CROWDED HOUSES AT THE GLOBE THEATRE.

Slim Brown, the lawyer they don't expect .... Bob Cole
Plunk Green, the doctor they don't expect .... Rosamond Johnson
Bill Gibson, the saloonkeeper .... Henry Gant
Bill Armour, the butcher .... Wesley Jenkins
Bill Webster, the barber .... Sam Lucas
Bill Simmons, the whitewasher .... Benny Jones
John Lowdog, the old chief .... Arthur Talbot
Red Feather, an educated brave .... Frank Brown
Eagle Eye, the tribe's scout .... Harry Watson
Spread Eagle, the medicine man .... Sam Lucas
Lucretia Martin, the old chief's wife .... Elizabeth Williams
Amanda Gibson, the saloonkeeper's wife .... Mollie Dill
Minnehaha, the old chief's child .... Leona Marshall
Lilly White, the washerwoman .... Tootsie Allen
Nakomis, the tribe prophetess ....)
Truscalina White, her actress daughter ....) .... Fanny Wise
Sambco Simmons ....) (.......... Edgar Connor
Sally Simmons ....) Bill Simmons' Kids (.......... Pearl Taylor
Susan Simmons ....) (.......... Daisy Brown
Sunshine, Truscalina's sister .... Aida Overton Walker
Flaming Arow, an Indian maid .... ———

The Gibson Gals—Mayme Butler, Lulu Coleman, Blanche Deas, Ida Blueford, Bessie Simms, Pauline Haukney.

The Dancing Picks—Daisy Brown, Marion Potter, Bessie Oliver, Pearl Taylor, Lottie Gee, Millie Dean.

The Aida Girls—Marie Young, Mattie Harris, Marjorie Sipp, Rebecca Allen, Gertie Townsend, Anna Jarret.

The College Boys—Frank DeLyons, William Phelps, Lewis Mitchel, Herbert Sutton, Samuel Craig, Harry Watson.

The Policemen—Nelson, Tunsell, William Patterson, Frank Hill.

Indian braves, squaws, villagers, guests, etc.

SYNOPSIS OF SCENES.

ACT 1.—Swamptown, Virginia. Sunshine Land.
ACT 2.—The Land of the Settling Sun.
ACT 3.—Bill Gibson's Parlor. Swamptown.

Incidental to Act II, Aida Overton Walker, as Flaming Arrow, will execute an aboriginal dance entitled "Wildfire." The medicine men have lighted their medicine pots. The girl, seeking a love potion to administer to her unrequited lover, without consulting the medicine men, attempts to get possession of the same. Her every effort is met by tongues of flame.

MUSICAL NUMBERS.

Musical Director, James Reese Europe.

ACT I.

Opening Chorus .... Company
"The Same Old Moon is Shining" .... Herbert Sutton and College Boys
"Keep on Smilin'" .... The Four Bills
"Don't Tell Tales Out of School" .... Slim, Plunk, Minnehaha and Truscalina
"Pickinniny Days" .... Aida Overton Walker and Picks
"Pliney, Won't You Come Out in the Moon Light" .... Slim and Ada Girls
Finale .... Ensemble

ACT II.

Prelude .... Mayme Butler and Company
"Bleeding Moon" .... The Prophetess
"The Big Red Shawl" .... Plunk and Chorus
"On the Road to Monterey" .... Red Feather
Wildfire Dance .... Aida Overton Walker
Finale .... Company

ACT III.

"Red Moon To-da-lo"—Two Step .... Chorus
"Sambo" .... Sambo and Chorus
Pianologue .... Plunk
"Hoola Woola" .... ———
"Run, Billy Possum, Run" .... Slim
Old Songs .... ———
"Phoebe Brown" .... Aida Overton Walker and Girls
Finale .... Ensemble

Additional music by James R. Europe. Additional lyrics by Charles A. Hunter. Additional dances by Benny Jones.

FOR THE COLE & JOHNSON COMPANY.

Manager .... Edgar Healy
Advance Representative .... Sam Corker, Jr.
Musical Director .... James R. Europe
Stage Manager .... Charles A. Hunter
Assistant Stage Manager .... William E. Phelps
Drums .... Geo. Smith
Carpenter .... W. S. Saunders
Electrician .... Louis Potts
Properties .... John Schlesser
Wardrobe .... Belle Morgan

Chicago Broad Ax, November 20, 1909.

conception of art, costuming and stage paraphernalia was highly intellectual. In fact, as a playwright and stage producer he never had an equal, except in Jesse A. Shipp. In consideration of the fact that he was a legitimate comedian who played acting parts and without the aid of blacking his face, and I have seen him in everything from variety blackface plantation acts to the most qualified grade of high comedy, and this alone places him highest in rank, even if not so funny as Hogan or Williams . . . Cole was nearest of any actor of his race to genius . . . As a ragtime composer and lyric song writer he was the greatest of his day of any race or color and I defy any man who disputes it.[207]

Meanwhile, it was disclosed that Aida Overton Walker would not be getting her own show after all; the money men had withdrawn their support.[208] The golden era of the big shows, representative musical comedy companies that had toured the mainstream northern theater circuits since the late 1890s, seemingly came to a sudden and tragic conclusion. This development evoked stunned appraisals from the African American press, such as the following from the *Freeman* of August 13, 1910:

The Passing of the Big Companies . . . With the dropping off of the big ones, those aggregations of forty to sixty people that made their annual rounds, the question is being asked, What has struck stagedom anyhow? After knowing of Bert Williams' great success single-handed, much was not thought of the fact that his company would not get together for the coming season . . . The same kind of money is not in sight, not to speak of the relief from worry . . .

The colored theater patrons were prepared to lose Bert Williams, holding to the well-known conclusion that "our loss was his gain." The colored theater patrons were struck hard when the news flashed that Cole and Johnson, too, had joined that innumerable caravan of passing things. It was most amazing. Somehow the colored people had learned to look on the Cole and Johnson aggregation as the acme of theatrical endeavor . . .

But what is it all about? Who has done it? What has done it? The innocent little theater has had something to do with detracting from big liners. They have been infinite, however, in benefit; they have covered the land and in so doing they have made it possible for thousands of young Negro men and women to earn a living along lines best suited for themselves . . . thus everybody ought to be happy, in the language of the late lamented Hogan.

"Juli Jones, Jr." put a more pessimistic take on these developments when he wrote in his *Freeman* column of September 10, 1910:

The season of 1910 and 1911 curtain is raised on one of the most pitiful scenes the colored showman has presented in thirty years. From the very face of the dismal scene it shows that the colored actor . . . is hopelessly lost from the legitimate organized company concerned . . . One reason given is that vaudeville has taken the day, that the houses and the public demand quick shows, cheap prices, that is so and will continue to be so. Vaudeville is here to stay, but that excuse is not good enough to offer, as the reason that Cole and Johnson will not go out, that Miss Aida Overton Walker did not get her new show, that Bert A. Williams had to close his show two months earlier than the end of the regular season . . . As things stand today if there is not a quick change, which is not likely to happen, every colored actor will have to look to the South for his bread . . .

The only pleasant thing about this dismal affair is that the colored man in the South and many scattered throughout the North, have built small theaters without one bit of encouragement from the colored showman, yet this is his only salvation; the only encouragement the small house colored manager received was that the Pekin Theater in Chicago was a success, and that was all they knew . . . From these little houses we are compelled to get something out

> of the ordinary from the rising generation from every department. The little houses in the South need not whine about talent. There will be talent and plenty of it, in their fields before many moons—talent that will surprise every one. The change in one year's time makes it safe to predict that the South will be well filled with colored acts inside one year.

Vaudeville entertainment, by black performers and for black audiences, had been gaining momentum in the South since the turn of the century, on makeshift stages in saloons and public parks. By 1910 a mushrooming network of theaters was in place and reportedly doing good business. Several of these new southern vaudeville houses survived to become anchors of the Theater Owners' Booking Association, organized in 1921.

Even as press reports bemoaned the passing of the big shows, the Smart Set Company continued to present "legitimate" black musical comedies, which prompted the *Freeman* to console its readers: "Don't become too disconsolate. We have with us yet that king of funmakers S. H. Dudley, who will appear as usual." Dudley's successor, Salem Tutt Whitney, expanded the Smart Set's touring route into the Southland, and mingled with the rising generation of southern talent.

PART TWO

THE SPIRIT OF THE SMART SET

The comedian-producers of the big shows weaned mainstream audiences away from the crude character delineations of nineteenth-century minstrelsy and conditioned them to appreciate verisimilitude in black comedy representation. "Natural expression" in racial caricature became the cutting edge of black comedy. Still in blackface makeup, black comedians dared to bring forth modern, recognizable characters who spoke more directly to black audiences, creating a revolutionary dynamic that became a cornerstone of twentieth-century African American minstrelsy and vaudeville.

The Smart Set Company was a singular vehicle for constructive change on the American stage. The originators of the Smart Set were comedian-producers Ernest Hogan and Billy McClain, who had helped popularize up-to-date black vernacular music in conjunction with the new, "vaudevillized" minstrelsy of the 1890s. In 1899 Hogan and McClain shared an adventure, and a brief artistic collaboration, when they sailed for Australia as members of the M. B. Curtis Afro-American Minstrel and Vaudeville Company. Shortly after they arrived in Sydney, a local newspaper described Australasia's real introduction to ragtime, as Hogan and McClain "kept the house in splendid humor by their antics in the Rag Time opera."[1]

Collaborating again in Honolulu at the beginning of 1902, Hogan and McClain staged the

original musical comedy skit *My Friend from Georgia*. A review in the local *Pacific Commercial Advertiser* was reproduced in the *Freeman*:

> Hogan's capabilities are well known, but in Billy McClain, a former partner, he has support which is the best he has ever received. McClain is . . . the best Negro minstrel, speaking of that genius as created in the days of Carncross and Haverly, of Billy Rice and Billy Emerson [all white men], that has been seen here in years but in fact he has made some strides along the way and his poses, his quiet demeanor and his command of the situation show real dramatic instinct. [Henry "Hen"] Wise as a black face Hebrew, was fairly good, there being a straining at some points, but with all a careful representation of the anxious real estate man. Mrs. McClain was seen to advantage and the return of Laura Moss, the "bronze" Patti, with the quartette, gave a needed lift to the quality of the choruses. The best song of the evening was the new "My Sweet Moano [*sic*, Moana]," written by Wise and the music by Hogan, sung by Miss Mamie Harris. The most striking specialty was the burlesque hula "Tommy Tommy" in which Kitty Milton, Wise and Hogan (who wrote it) sang and danced, the first named giving a touch of the hula, which made the whole go so well that the trio ran out of verses and had to stop.[2]

Hogan and McClain planned to launch a "mammoth production" of *My Friend from Georgia* on the mainland, but instead they accepted an offer to star jointly in big-time white promoter Gus Hill's spectacular new production *Enchantment*, or *A Southern Enchantment*, which they revised to suit their own ideas. One African American journalist attributed the play's tropical setting to Hogan and McClain's recent sojourns in Hawaii: "This land of sunshine had great effect on the players—The land of brown people, people who approached them in color, manner, living a poetic existence. They

Billy McClain. *Indianapolis Freeman*, December 25, 1897.

got their heads together on the proposition to construct a play embodying the entrancing features of that flowery habitation."[3]

Hogan and McClain's new touring company became popularly known as the Smart Set. Sylvester Russell first committed the name to print on October 25, 1902, when he advised that, "'The Smart Set' in 'Enchantment' introducing Ernest Hogan as a featured star is now on the road." This relatively new expression—*smart set*—had come into popular usage during the 1890s as "a general designation for the extremely fashionable portion of society (sometimes with the implication of being a little 'fast')."[4] It was an oddly radical name to apply to an African American touring company, and it left an indelible mark on black entertainment history.

After attending one of the Smart Set Company's first performances, at the Empire Theater in Newark, New Jersey, on October 18, 1902, Sylvester Russell wrote one of the most enthusiastic reviews of his long journalistic career. One week later he warned, "Williams and Walker will have to look to their laurels and become deep thinkers in order to keep up with the tidal wave of the 'Smart Set.'"

On October 27, 1902, the Smart Set began a one-week run in Philadelphia.[5] On October 29, the company's outstanding Dinwiddie Quartette recorded a group of spirituals and subtly minstrelized jubilee songs for the Victor Company. One of the titles, "Way Down on the Old Camp Ground," was officially touted by Victor as a "coon shout." The Dinwiddie Quartette recordings survive to give a real taste of turn-of-the-century black barbershop harmony.[6]

After their reportedly lucrative Philadelphia engagement, the Smart Set opened a weeklong stand at the Star Theater in New York City, on November 8, 1902. *Freeman* critic J. Harry Jackson reported a packed house at every performance: "The show is running smoothly and Ernest Hogan, Russell Brandow, Ben Hunn, Jerry Mills and Billy McClain keep the audience in an uproar."[7] Sylvester Russell provided additional details: "Billy McClain wore a new mustache. Ernest Hogan in snowflake pants with angel wings had first mortgage on the audience, and a large one at that." Russell concluded that Williams and Walker's current production *In Dahomey*, "is a most intelligent organization . . . They are excelled only by Ernest Hogan's individual performance in making 'Enchantment' the funniest play of the two."[8]

Russell's infatuation with the Smart Set did not last long. In a lengthy review of December 6,

SMART SET IN "ENCHANTMENT."

The Smartest Colored Comedy Ever Produced In America.

BY SYLVESTER RUSSELL.

The unexpected has happened. The advent of a new darkey sensation, the like of which our eyes have never seen before, greets the world. The "Smart Set" is the smartest set of colored people ever put to gether, on one stage in America; and serves to introduce Mr. Hogan as a three quarter, full fl-dged star (the heavy type on the board fences being devoted to the 'Smart Set') in a spectacular musical comedy called "enchantment"

The book is said to be by Steven Casson, but the rub-a dubb of Hogan and fiddle de dee of Billy McClain, to-gether with anything else the management may have added, makes us doubt the ability of Casson to have written the entire work. However, we are not so much interested in who put the work to-gether as we are elated over the glorification of its success.

When the "Smart Set" opened at Newark, N. J., Monday, Oct 18th., for a week's stay at the new Empire theatre, I took a reserved seat in the balcony (I pay my own admission) and I was not sorry at what I saw—and did not expect to see—when the curtain went up Everything was new and costumes were varied in designs of oddity and effectiveness The scenes are all laid in Honolulu, a rich land of beauty and enchantment. When the curtain first rises you find yourself in Honolulu gardens. You are enchanted at once by the flower girls, led by Margaret Jordon a pleasing soprano The American sailors also arrive in quick succession headed by little Ida Forcen, who, later in the play, creates a sensation by her marvelous efficiency as a dancer. Nothing drags; everything moves with precision; every piece of stage craft is marked with perfection and every deed is a constant flow of wit and humor. Everybody is wide awake; nobody sleeps and everybody finds somebody to talk to without talking to the same party longer than a minute.

Something new takes place all the time and for the first time in the history of Negro comedy, "A Trip to Coontown" has been surpassed. Then Billy McClain enters upon the scene, followed by Ben Hunn and Jerry Mills.

M'CLAIN'S STARTLING CLOTHES.

Billy McClain takes his place at once as the best dressed colored actor on the stage but his style and personality will not claim him that distinction. He has suits of all shades and changes clothes every minute. Any other actor on the boards who aspires to be a "swell" will have to buy three new suits of clothes and have a new green English tailor made suit made to order, at once, to even approach him. He is more at ease in comedy than any other actor in the cast. "Sing a little tenor" is a clever little song which brings him many deserving encores.

MRS. HOGAN WEARS DIAMONDS.

Mattie Wilkes-Hogan, enshrouded in real genuine diamonds comes forth and does a little soubrette work. Her lower notes are thin but she depends on the beautiful upper tones of a well trained voice to carry everything before her. Then she shyly glides away driving her spick span, eight in hand, new rag-time oriental American horses. After a lively scene—a race track swindle by Billy McClain—the climate changes and Ernest Hogan in a new red automobile suit, rides in on his new wheelbarrow and is capsized in full view of the audience by his silly acrobatic servant, the silliest of his kind—Russell Brandow. Hogan finds himself confronted by Miss Stella Wiley and a dancing flirtation ensues, followed by a strong love scene between Miss Wiley, Miss Jordon and Ernest Hogan This is interrupted by Billy McClain who calls to see Hogan about getting into a secret order society.

Then Hogan takes a dive to the footlights and sings his latest success "I am the Missionary Man." He labors quite hard and that's what attracts attention.

The scene changes. The Dinwindie quartette comes in on its way to the Rooster's lodge and sings "Palms" in a manner unsurpassed S. C. R-x, the leader, has a light baritone voice of much sympathy and sweetness and J. M. Thomas, the basso is very fine; together with J. C. Meredith and H. B. Coyer, they make the most harmony and display the best artistic methods of any colored quartette now before the public. Hogan arrives to the Royal Rooster's lodge ahead of time. Something unusual is going to happen. The Royal Roosters lodge is to be in session and everything seems to be getting in readiness for that. Everybody gets in readiness for Ernest Hogan's diacritical dexterity.

HOGAN GETS INITIATED.

Here the comedy becomes spectacular and the liviiest scenes euer presented in Negro comedy takes place. Hogan gets initiated. Real full grown chickens with weary feathers flutter about until the masculine roosters begin to crow and the audience commences to know what fun it is to be enchanted. After this is all over Mr Hogan, chief bug a bee of the situation, comes forth to the footlights and takes his bow, and brings little Willie MClain with him—Willie bows also But there are other interesting things that happen: Russell Brandow and Pauline Freeman do a bit of love and acrobaticism. Brandow as a simpleton, is a fine comedy actor.

BEN HUNN A SACRIFICE

Ben Hunn, because of his lack of judgment becomes a sacrifice Mr. Hunn is not entirely at home in comedy and at times, when he should be acting his mind is absorbed in taking notice of McClain and Hogan when the three are together on the stage

When Mr. Hunn sings the song "Gabe" he does a rich piece of comedy work For an encore he returns to the footlights and addresses his audience in the same manner as he would in a variety theatre or minstrel show and lowers the performance to the grade of a cheap variety burlesque show. He don't stop at that; he has "self" in view and must resort to his old out of the way specialties to make a hit that will equal the modern McClain or Hogan. So he sings "Turkey in the Straw" and sets the gallery to whistling and Howling or else he dances George Tichner's old "Jinnie My own True Love," or the time worn parody, "No one could feel dead sore than a father on his' son, so kill the son of a gun." Of course the the common people accept of this. It makes the hit of the evening with the people in the gallery.

But this is not the question. The question is: Where are we at? Where is the comedy at? Mr. Hunn must remember that he is now in a modern production, which caters only to the requirements of a legitimate standard The lines of comedy is not across the footlights. When a man is on the stage alone he is supposed to talk to himself and not the people. The common element of white people (and about two thirds of the Empire theatre audience) care nothing about the boundary lines of coon comedy or anything else that colored actors may do so long as they get lots of fun. But we have got to establish these precedents ourselves and those in comedy, who do not, will be creatures of criticism and the best results are bound to follow. If Mr. Hunn will sing his "Gabie" and dance the cooler dance and stop at that, he will still be third star in the cast. He will not be able to get further than third star—not in this cast—anyhow.

The full chorus of banjo players was another treat but the rarest treat of all was the singing of Mme Cordelia McClain As a soloist she, is extremely entertaining. Her art has broadened. She has never before been heard to such as advantage as an artist and her essential qualities of skill make her to-day one of the unrivaled list of singers who approach the Black Patti.

The third act discloses a parlor scene where the guests have assembled to introduce Henry N Jackson, the Brooklyn baritone-tenor as a soloist. Mr. Jackson, since his return from abroad, has twisted his name around to H. Jackson Norris and with this name he renders Dunbar and Cook's "My Gypsy Maid" in a sympathetic style that appeals to the audience. Mr. Norris has a pleasing voice but of its light range there is a limit which he carefully surveys in favor of his education.

When the guests march out Hogan comes in hungry and intoxicated He meets Mrs McClain and suggests something to eat. At the tap of a bell, Jerry Mills a tramp waiter appears, Mr. Mills is a very capable actor in the part and does himself credit that will serve him good hereafter. Hogan carves the turkey; (where have I seen that same old turkey before?) but soon falls asleep at the table and on awaking finds Mrs. Hogan seated at the table in place of Mrs. McClain. This disturbs him favorably and they indulge at once in a strong love scene (for Hogan seems to know what love counts for in coon comedy) and the two artists sing Bob Cole and Rosamond Johnson's, "Tell Me Dusky Maiden"

The duel scene is the funniest thing of all. When Hogan, the coward, has a visit from the fair sex to bid him good bye, it racks his nerves and the appearance of two women dressed in black causes him to break down and exclaim "I see my funeral now." His appearance as a hunchback with a pillow slip up his back is also a piece of quaint perfection

HOGAN IS THE REAL STAR

Ernest Hogan is the real star of the entire production. The play is written up to him for a star part Everything points to him He is not a genuine natural born comedian. His art is that of a mechanical genius—so skillful is he as a delineator of that peculiar type of Negro character which he strives to imitate His acting of strong comedy scenes was wonderfully clever and at no time did he fall short of requirements or over act his scenes. Both in the initiation scene, and in the duel scene with Billy McClain he has established himself as an actor of intelligence and a student to his art He is not yet thoroughly at home in comedy and he will have to adopt himself to continuous endeavor rather than carelessness in order to maintain the best results of the new situation.

The "Smart Set" is said to be under the management of M. Gus Hill. For this show, New York has no terrors. They can open on Broadway with modesty, unheralded and run for the rest of the season. Its the real thing. Its the smartest colored comedy ever produced in America.

Indianapolis Freeman, November 1, 1902.

1902, he expressed concern that "its stars are going wrong." He complained that Cordelia McClain's solo had been omitted, and that "Mattie Wilkes and her eight rag-time horses were also cut out. These two features were prime favorites in the show, greatly admired and commented on by the people. The sketch substituted by Mr. and Mrs. McClain was old."

Russell's chief complaint was with Hogan's changed approach to the play's main character, George Washington Bullion. Noting that Hogan had traded his original costume, a "legitimate comedy suit," for "minstrel rags and variety stage garments," he cautioned: "If Ernest Hogan is wise he will give us comedy not farce, and it is time for him to realize that the rich Mr. Bullion should not be dressed up like a rag time coon from Memphis. Mr. Hogan is on the right road but has switched over on the wrong track. But Hogan learns fast . . . When he switches he can . . . return to the original Newark legitimate performance. Everybody would be enchanted."

In Chicago during the first week of February 1903, an enthusiastic reviewer rated the Smart Set the "greatest and only real up-to-date colored organization that has ever appeared before the footlights." A more concrete review was filed when they played Indianapolis in March:

> The Smart Set, the theatrical aggregation in which Ernest Hogan and Billy McClain are the ruling stars . . . left an impression for good as it concerns the colored people's capacity and aptitude for all lines of theatrical work.
>
> In many respects the show was a notable departure from the exhibitions of the past, in that it sought to put a better front to Negro life . . . Ernest Hogan . . . is evidently a student of nature; his comicalities and witticisms are the result of art so perfect, that it appears the individual. One would suspect Mr. Hogan to act on the street precisely as he does on stage, so near to nature is he. His power lies in his gestures, what he implies as much so as in what he says; he is a great comedian. He is also a philosopher as was proven by his dying request to his wife, "tell her to stay off of Indiana Avenue."
>
> Billy McClain makes good support for Mr. Hogan. He makes a clever villain and sport, the roles he assumes. Of course the audience is not enrapped [*sic*] with the character . . . He acted his part well, however, giving evidence of dramatic ability . . .
>
> The Rooster Lodge skit is about as clever as anything seen on the stage. The initiation is something fierce, the oldest lodge man has never seen anything like it; it will certainly do.
>
> The ensemble singing all along was good, much of which was operatic in effect and in the personnel the coon songs were good, but not so numerous as in similar shows of the past. The costuming was superb.
>
> Taking it all in all there was but very little chance for criticism.[9]

At the end of the Smart Set's historic inaugural tour, Hogan walked away. "Juli Jones Jr." later reflected that Hogan had carried the Smart Set to success, only to "have his heart crushed, to find that he had helped some of his people up only for them to show their ingratitude toward him. He threw up his hands and went it alone."[10] According to Sylvester Russell, it was proprietor Gus Hill's refusal to send the show to Europe that caused Hogan to quit.[11] Although he never returned to the Smart Set, Hogan set a standard for the comedians who followed, and his influence proved indelible. As *Freeman* commentator Will M. Lewis observed in 1905: "A few years ago the well-known organization set out before the public under the guiding genius of Billy McClain, the well-known player, who was fresh from his triumphs in Australia, and Ernest Hogan, the conceded premier comedian of the American stage . . . The first company was excellent, but large and somewhat unwieldy . . . There is no denying, however, but what the herculean effort put forth by the first managers created a sort of popular glamour in which the succeeding companies have lingered, making the name Smart Set somewhat synonymous with success."[12]

In September 1903 the Smart Set launched its second season in Boston, Massachusetts, with Billy McClain returning to manage the stage, and with minstrel warhorse Tom McIntosh stepping into Hogan's place as George Washington Bullion. Originally from Lexington, Kentucky, McIntosh had come up with Charles B. Hicks and Billy Kersands in 1870s and 1880s editions of the Original Georgia Minstrels, and he starred in some of the most popular and influential black minstrel-variety and burlesque troupes of the 1890s.[13]

In 1899 McIntosh headed the *A Hot Old Time in Dixie* Company, with a cast that included Gussie L. Davis and S. H. Dudley. When they showed in Columbus, Ohio, a local mainstream daily paper concluded that, "for the genuine portrayal of the colored man to day, they have no equal."[14] In 1900 McIntosh toured with Rusco and Holland's Big Minstrel Festival. His last engagement before joining the Smart Set was with the 1903 edition of Tom Brown's Troubadours.

After seeing the Smart Set in Hartford, Connecticut, on September 21, 1903, Sylvester Russell expressed disappointment with the direction he thought the show was taking, and he subjected McIntosh to some particularly harsh criticism:

> Before reviewing this production it is cordiality to the management and company to again state to the public that this show is one of the finest colored organizations on the road. My mission in criticizing the performers is strictly in keeping with my past methods of formulating the legitimate standard in Negro comedy . . . "Enchantment" is a farce-comedy-travesty . . . The dialogue is all farce comedy of the foolishest kind . . . Billy McClain, who has taken great pains to give a strictly legitimate performance this season, scored in a new travesty . . . He wore a new chocolate suit, cut to perfection and looked quite nobby.
>
> Tom McIntosh, who succeeds Ernest Hogan in the cast . . . plays Dr. Bullion in his own, broad, farcical way . . . After all that has been said of the impropriety of talking to an audience over the footlights in a so-called legitimate show, McIntosh must be termed a legitimate failure. The famous minstrel comedians of the past are not destined to shine in modern Negro comedy . . . His best dramatic scene was carving a chicken while in dialogue with Cordelia McClain. His acting in the initiation scene was not affective [*sic*], and his duel scene was the flattest thing he attempted, and left an aching void that was once filled by Hogan.[15]

After a month or so in the Northeast, the Smart Set headed below the Mason-Dixon Line—a pathbreaking venture for a "colored show" that was not traveling under the umbrella of minstrelsy. At Birmingham, Alabama, in late October or early November 1903, they received this review from a local mainstream daily:

> "Southern Enchantment" . . . was given at the Jefferson Theatre, the best playhouse in Birmingham, and while the greater portion of the theatre was filled with colored people, and among them some of the best members of the race in the city, there were quite a number of white folks present, some of whom state that the performance

as a whole, was satisfactory. The book and music of this play is by Billy McClain, a well-known Negro performer, and it does credit to a white man . . . Tom McIntosh, that well-known colored comedian . . . is easily one of the best comedians on the stage, and regular critics say that he is a regular fun-maker, in other words, does not entirely depend on "horse play," etc. He made a good impression here, and the large audience of colored people expressed pleasure with his efforts.[16]

It seems the Birmingham engagement was not concluded without a hitch. Billy McClain later cryptically remarked that he had been instrumental in "quelling a riot on stage in Birmingham, Ala."[17] Shortly after the Birmingham date, a correspondent for Richards and Pringle's Georgia Minstrels mentioned having just played a successful engagement in Mobile, "behind the Smart Set, who are also creating a furore around here."[18]

On November 15, 1903, the Smart Set opened a week's engagement at the mainstream Crescent Theater in New Orleans. Advance advertising touted "A New Era in the Annals of Comedy." The *Daily Picayune* released an upbeat preview: "The thousands of people who love the good old colored ragtime and the side-splitting comedy of such well-known artists as Tom McIntosh and Billy McClain, will welcome this organization, because they know that at every performance of 'The Smart Set' they will hear the latest and the best popular music of the day, as well as many operatic selections. Aside from the singing, 'The Smart Set' presents a company of dancers who are unrivalled and unequalled by any in the business." Special mention was made that, "During the engagement of 'The Smart Set,' the entire balcony will be reserved for colored people, and sufficient number of seats will be reserved on the lower floor for white persons who intended to occupy balcony seats."[19]

In reviewing the opening night's performance, the *Daily Picayune* cited certain "incongruities" in the production:

There is an attempt at a story, but it is of such minor consequence that no one thinks seriously about the quest of one G. Washington Bullion for a certain Lucinda . . . And it is good that the author of the extravaganza paid more attention to the music and arrangement of the dances and marches than to the book, and, therefore, "The Smart Set" is acceptable for those who are willing to waste a few hours. The negroes sing and dance well, but they make an incongruous picture when they wear rich costumes. And it does not sound right to Southern ears to have them dropping off their lips five and six syllable words. Yet for all this, "The Smart Set" does not descend into vulgarism, and the unpolished fun, the uncultivated singing and the natural dancing goes along for three acts with a swing. It is questionable, however, whether a first class theatre should darken its stage with such attractions.[20]

Halfway through the Smart Set's controversial New Orleans engagement, the Crescent Theater quietly advertised that, "The colored comedy company continues to give unoffensive performances with really commendable vocal accomplishments."[21] In the end, the Smart Set, the very *idea* of a "colored smart set," whose stage characters were breaking away from the stereotypes of conventional blackface minstrelsy, offended the sensibilities of New Orleans's white theater establishment. As a result, the city's playhouses barred their doors to African American touring companies. Only after the independent, black-owned Temple Theater opened in 1909 was a Smart Set company able to return to New Orleans. On November 20, 1909, six years after the Smart Set's initial southern incursion, New Orleans–based *Freeman* columnist

V. P. Thomas announced that "the Tutt Whitney Musical Comedy Company, composed of the members of the Smart Set No. 2 . . . will be the attraction at the Temple Theater":

> New Orleans has suffered the want of good, first-class shows for a long time. In fact, ever since the Smart Set played at the Crescent Theater years ago and won the unbounded admiration it did, and caused the envy and jealousy that have barred colored shows out of the white theaters from that time, there has been a popular demand among the colored people of New Orleans for the Smart Set, or shows of that class, to come back. But the coming back of such shows has been out of the question until Messrs. Kilduff and Cheevers opened the Temple Theater.

Returning north by way of Little Rock, Arkansas, St. Joseph, Missouri, and Louisville, Kentucky, the Smart Set opened a week's engagement in Cincinnati, Ohio, on February 21, 1904. No explanation was given when Billy and Cordelia McClain suddenly jumped ship the following week. A few days later, en route from Indianapolis, Indiana, to Columbus, Ohio, Tom McIntosh died of a stroke, "in the presence of the entire company, who were on the train at the time."[22]

Following McIntosh's death, proprietor Gus Hill apparently closed the show for the rest of the season. At this low ebb in the Smart Set's fortunes, minstrel comedian Sherman H. Dudley was selected to fill the role of George Washington Bullion for the season of 1904–1905. *Freeman* commentator R. W. Thompson later described how Dudley had garnered a reputation for "clean comedy methods and pronounced originality—drollery that amuses without offending the most delicate sensibilities—so it was not surprising that when poor Tom McIntosh . . . suddenly breathed his last . . . Dudley was picked out as the best natural comedian available to permanently fill his place and who could safely handle the exacting role created by such a resourceful actor as Ernest Hogan."[23]

According to retrospective accounts in the *Freeman*, Sherman Houston Dudley was born "of humble parentage" at Dallas, Texas, in 1872. In his youth Dudley worked as a jockey, and he eventually drew on this experience in his stage career. His earliest theatrical experience was with "a medicine show held on the street corners" of Dallas, in which "he sang a song entitled 'Dese Bones Shall Rise Again.'"[24]

Dudley apparently was running a show of his own by 1897, when the *New York Clipper* informed that, "S. H. Dudley's Georgia Minstrels will open their season . . . at the Grand Opera House, Galveston, Tex."[25] Later that year Dudley joined P. T. Wright's highly successful Nashville Students Company, in a team act with A. P. Harris. They proved to be "favorites in the South" with "their latest sketch entitled 'Well All Right,'" and Dudley won further favor "singing his old camp meeting Shout," possibly "Dese Bones Shall Rise Again."[26]

Dudley also found success as a ragtime coon song composer. During the summer of 1899 the *Freeman* announced, "S. H. Dudley, author and comedian, has written three of the hottest coon songs heard this season, entitled 'Dat Coon Done Put De Rollers Under Me,' 'Mr. Coon, You'se Too Black For Me,' and 'I'm The Real Thing, The King Of Them All.' They are published by Thos. Goggan & Bro., Galveston, Tex."[27]

In the fall of 1899 Dudley went out with Tom McIntosh's *A Hot Old Time in Dixie* Company, in a team act with Sidney Perrin, billed as "the original

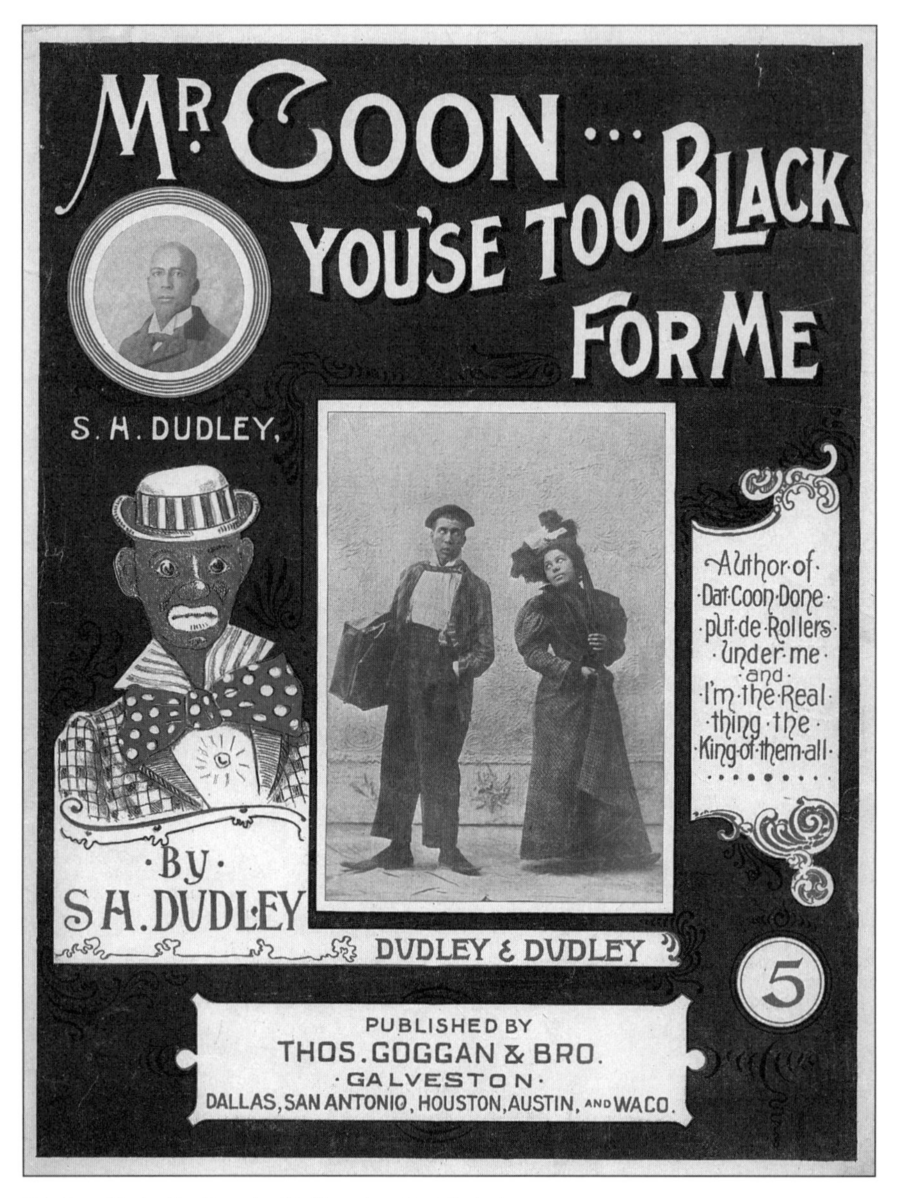

"Mr. Coon You'se Too Black for Me." (courtesy Sue Fischer)

Pumpkin Colored Coons" and making a hit with Perrin's latest composition, "Done Said All I Have to Say."[28] In the fall of 1900 he hit the road with John W. Isham's ill-fated "King Rastus" Company, which disbanded at Cincinnati in April 1901.[29] Dudley then "signed for a summer season with Tom Brown's 'Black Rat' Co.," and on June 22, 1901, the *Freeman* reported: "S. H. Dudley, the clever and versatile comedian and author, is now doing a sketch with Miss Alberta Ormes, the Octoroon singing and dancing soubrette; they are now playing parks and are a tremendous hit with Tom Brown's 'Black Rats.' Mr. Dudley is singing his latest song, 'Ma Friend.'"

Before the end of 1901 Dudley and Alberta Ormes appeared together in mainstream vaudeville as the stars of Dudley's musical farce, *A Holiday in Coonville*.[30] A few weeks later they rejoined Tom Brown to put out a show called *Coontown Golf Club*, for which Dudley and Brown wrote most of the music.[31] In New York City during the spring of 1902, Dudley "had charge of the colored people" hired to appear in a Yiddish-language production of *Uncle Tom's Cabin*.[32] He was also seen at both the Douglass Club and Ike Hines' Professional Club. At the same time, he and Tom Brown were "working like beavers putting on the finishing touches to their new farce entitled, 'Jolly Ethiopians.'"[33]

Under the banner of Tom Brown's Troubadours, *The Jolly Ethiopians* opened at Lynn, Massachusetts on Decoration Day, 1902, and toured "with success throughout the New England States." Dudley sang "I Never Sing Good Morning Carrie Now," an answer to the 1901 Chris Smith–R. C. "Cecil Mack" McPherson hit, "Good Morning Carrie," and he appeared in a team act with "lightning buck dancer" John "Dude" Kelley.[34] He and Kelley spent the season of 1902–1903 with Rusco and Holland's Big Minstrel Festival, touring the South in company with venerable African American minstrel Billy Kersands. A highlight of the season was "Dudley's laughable farce, 'The Darktown Ping Pong Club.'"[35] At Shreveport, Louisiana, in September 1902, a correspondent noted, "Although it has been four years since S. H. Dudley has made a Southern tour . . . he has lost none of his popularity and is daily meeting friends who are very glad to see him."[36] From Shreveport the company embarked on a two-month sojourn in Texas, where Dudley was billed as "The Lone Star Comedian."[37]

At the end of the 1902–1903 season, Billy Kersands severed his long-term relationship with Rusco and Holland's Big Minstrel Festival. To fill the vacuum, Rusco and Holland consolidated their minstrel enterprises under the banner of Richards and Pringle's Georgia Minstrels, and hired Dudley to be their "star and principal comedian, stage manager and amusement director" for the season of 1903–1904.[38] Rising to the occasion, Dudley introduced a new musical "afterpiece," "Jim Jackson at the Policy Shop," in which a "Negro policy game . . . speedily transformed itself into a prayer meeting when an officer was heard outside."[39] Dudley also appeared in the olio, featuring his latest coon song, "Satisfaction Babe," in a singing and dancing skit with Dude Kelley and Alberta Ormes.[40]

Dudley married Alberta Ormes in the fall of 1903.[41] They were playing through Texas with Richards and Pringle's "Georgias" in the spring of 1904 when news reached them that Tom McIntosh had died.[42] Within the next few weeks, Dudley quit the Georgia Minstrels and caught a train to Chicago, where it was announced that he "will star in the Smart Set next season."[43]

The Smart Set began its third consecutive touring season on September 10, 1904, presenting *A Southern Enchantment* in Newburgh, New York, with Dudley in the role of George Washington Bullion. Sylvester Russell was on hand to file a mixed review:

> The show is billed this season as a musical comedy but this season's production can only admit of its being

RICHARDS & PRINGLES
GEORGIA MINSTRELS

ONE S.H. DUDLEY

The above likeness is an electrotyye cut of S. H Dudley, the lone star comedian, now holding the position of stage manager and amusement director with Richards and Pringles' Famous Georgia Minstrels Co. No 1. Too much credit can not be given Mr. Dudley for the artistic manner in which he has staged this famous show. He has proven himself to be the most versatile comedian and producer the progressive managers Ruscoe & Holland have ever employed, and they frankly admit this season's show to be the best they have ever had thanks to the efforts of Mr. Dudley. With his peculiar way and original idea of delivery he can sing any song and make it go, even with the most fastidious audiences. Being possessed with the above original trait, places him in the front rank of colored comedians.

Mr. Dudley has been complimented highly by both public and press for producing and staging the most laughable afterpiece ever seen with a minstrel show "The Darktown Ping Pong Club." This act abounds with mirth and merriment from start to finish and Mr. Dudley shows to advantage in it, for he carries the comedy with a dash and vim that always elicts round after round of applause. The above act will be seen in vaudeville at the close of the season, supported by a cast of ten clever people. Wanted six bright women that can sing and dance and four men. Address all communications to 5908 Calumet Ave., after Jan. 15, 1903.

* * *

Indianapolis Freeman, October 25, 1902.

classed as a "variety stage burlesque farce" and as such the show is very good. The legitimate order of things which should have prevailed in this organization this season in particular is absent and the show suffers all the more because great comedians had formerly played the principal parts . . . After all that has been said along the lines of musical comedy in The Freeman there is no excuse for this latest edition of "Smart Set" actors who have changed the play and book from a high standard adopted by McClain and Hogan and reduced it to a variety stage attraction. But the show is a good one.

The critic was particularly hard on Dudley:

His singing of "Satisfaction Babe," assisted by Marion Smart, was highly legitimate and qualified, but he never knew it. As a recruit from the minstrel stage, he's green as grass. He knows nothing about comedy but is a very good comedian and will take rank in comedy just as soon as he learns the difference between legitimate comedy and the illegitimate variety and also how to dress for low comedy and keep it above common minstrelsy . . . There is hardly any use in trying to compare Dudley with Hogan. Hogan's conception and acting of the character of Dr. Bullion is as high as the sun over Dudley's.[44]

Russell persisted with the notion that, as a "recruit from the minstrel stage," Dudley was somehow "unworthy." In 1906 Russell unleashed his cruelest assessment of "this loathsome comedian who hails from the Lone Star State": "Dudley is simply a cold-blooded graduate of the minstrel stage. He came up to minstrelsy from hard kicks and pounds; he had hayseeded around New York long enough to become an actor on the indiscretion of discovering that his Texas dialect would serve him well brushed up with foolishness and topped off with just enough originality and brazenness to make himself a success."[45]

Russell's assaults on Dudley were finally countered in 1911, after the critic "saw fit to say something uncomplimentary" about Dudley's young son. A *Freeman* reporter editorialized that Russell had "for years had a caustic pen for Dudley and all that belonged to him. Dudley had nothing but patience, enduring whatever Russell had to give out, until Mr. Booker T. Washington came to Chicago. It was the last straw that broke the camel's back when Russell said that the kid ought to have been home in bed, rather than at the society function in honor of Mr. Washington. It was too much. Dudley met the man very soon after the event, and the world knows the rest. Russell thinks he was beat up $5,000 worth."[46] According to a report in the *Chicago Broad Ax*, Russell had Dudley arrested. Dudley was found guilty of assault, and fined $1.00 and court costs. Russell then proceeded to enter a civil suit against Dudley for five thousand dollars.[47]

Russell's reluctance to confirm Dudley's genius is not reflected in the writings of other *Freeman* commentators. In sizing up his first season with the Smart Set, Indianapolis-based columnist Will M. Lewis concluded that Dudley's portrayal of George Washington Bullion "belongs to the Hogan class; not so natively funny, but with better judgement. Dudley knows where to ring off . . . He is a finished actor, funny without apparent effort and so natural that you would not be surprised to meet the same Mr. Bullion coming down the street."[48] It was Dudley's ability to bring the street to the stage, to present more realistic, recognizable comedy characterizations, which allowed him to step into the role of George Washington Bullion, and the shoes of the immortal Hogan. Dudley revitalized the Smart Set and made it into an enduring classic of the American popular stage.

In Will Lewis's estimation the 1904–1905 edition of *A Southern Enchantment* was

no less than an index of the colored players' future, also their present status. Managers of colored companies have been often at their wits' end to know just what the public would "stand for" from colored shows. The statement will be understood by those who know the racial situation in America . . . The process of evolution is on, and by evolution I have in mind the reduction of an excessive amount of "Nigger" in the worst sense, taking on more of the Negro of "quality"—a little elimination and substitution as it were. It is taking; proving more acceptable to colored patrons, a treat to the whites who are learning to appreciate the Negro in the higher spheres—new roles. In fact, a faithful representation of colored society as it is understood is good to see—"lots" of truth mixed up with it, you know—that's where the laughs

A SCENE FROM THE "SMART SET"

Indianapolis Freeman, March 4, 1905.

come in. The colored players also prefer a little higher order of comedy or comic opera, so noted in the presentation last week, they are willing to do some coon songs, to do some buck and wing dancing, to do some low Negro stunts, but there are also artists among them that can shine and have a right through natural endowment and acquired to do so.

The change for the better is coming slowly. It does not mean that a football rush is expected for the high class, but it does mean an exit for some from the lowest variety.[49]

The Smart Set's roster for Dudley's inaugural season of 1904–1905 was stacked with supportive talent. The musical director was Leo Merriman, "under whose tutelage the entire chorus seems to be as one great organ."[50] The stage manager was J. Ed Green. The cast included John Bailey as Grafter Smooth; Lawrence Chenault as Lieutenant Mildew; Jerry Mills as Didhe Ketchum; Hattie Hopkins, Will Pierce, Julius "Jube" Johnson, and Charles "Bass" Foster; and the leading lady was irresistible "colored soubrette" Marion Smart: "She sings sentimental songs fairly well, but coon songs are her 'home.'"[51]

For at least a portion of the 1904–1905 season the Smart Set roster also included the team of

Indianapolis Freeman, March 4, 1905.

Billy and Stella Johnson. Not to be confused with Bob Cole's original stage partner, this Billy Johnson was an aspiring twenty-two-year-old southern blackface comedian. His brilliant partner, Estelle "Stella" Harris Johnson, was not long out of her native Hot Springs, Arkansas. Nevertheless, by 1904 she had already served distinguished apprenticeships with J. Ed Green at the Tivoli Music Hall in Memphis; with Will Goff Kennedy at the Buckingham Theater in Tampa; and with Tom Logan at Ninaweb Park in Louisville. Billy and Stella had also traveled together with Pat Chappelle's *A Rabbit's Foot* Company and performed briefly with the Black Patti Troubadours.

A *Freeman* report of November 12, 1904, describes Stella Harris Johnson's moment in the sun with the Smart Set, and suggests she was a magnet for the company's progressive experiments with coon shouting:

> The rendition of "The Barbecue," by Mrs. Stella Johnson, ably assisted by the chorus is a very decided feature of the show. Billy Johnson, of Memphis, Tenn., a new acquisition to the Smart Set roster, is rapidly perfecting the difficult part of Willie He He, the simpleton. The Indian song, "Birch Canoe," sung by Ed. Harris, Stella Johnson and chorus proves to be a fitting climax to the second act . . . Such a well balanced singing chorus have seldom if ever been heard, and such a bevy of pretty girls have never been brought together before. Especially attention has never been given to expression in rendering the plaintive coon melodies.

A note from Louisville, Kentucky, at the end of 1904 disclosed that Dudley's Smart Set "owned the town" while there, having sold out twelve performances at the Avenue Theater: "The wonderful popularity of colored companies in this city suggest the thought a theatre owned and conducted by reputable colored men, playing colored troupes and high grade vaudeville would pay big."[52] During the season of 1905–1906, the Smart Set evoked similar sentiments from a correspondent at the integrated, mainstream Park Theater in Indianapolis:

> All Indianapolis was there, so to speak, and as usual new sayings and songs were left in the wake. Community conditions here are such that any colored show albeit of indifferent merit will at least make

MISS MARION HENRY SMART.

One of the most pleasing actresses on the American stage is Marion Henry Smart now starring with W. H. Dudley in the Smart Set Company. Even the most severe critics have been quick to pronounce her a decided success in every particular. She is both pretty and clever and ranks with the best singers. A tremendous ovation was rendered her last season in her rendition of the song, "Teasing." Miss Smart completely captivated her audiences and was the talk of the town wherever she appeared. She has a charming personality and is a favorite off the stage as well.

Indianapolis Freeman, November 18, 1905.

good. It stands to reason that a combination like the Smart Set would be a furore. This company won a place in the affections of the people a few years ago and which it clinched as the seasons came and went, until now "Smart Set" is familiar as house words. The audiences were not made up of a particular class; thousands of whites jostled and elbowed their black neighbors in trying to see what the company had to put on this time. . .

Stage craft was manifest in the excellent settings and backgrounds, stuff made purposely for the Smart Set people. The lodge initiation scene was a thing of beauty, also the scene in the third act—a pink study.[53]

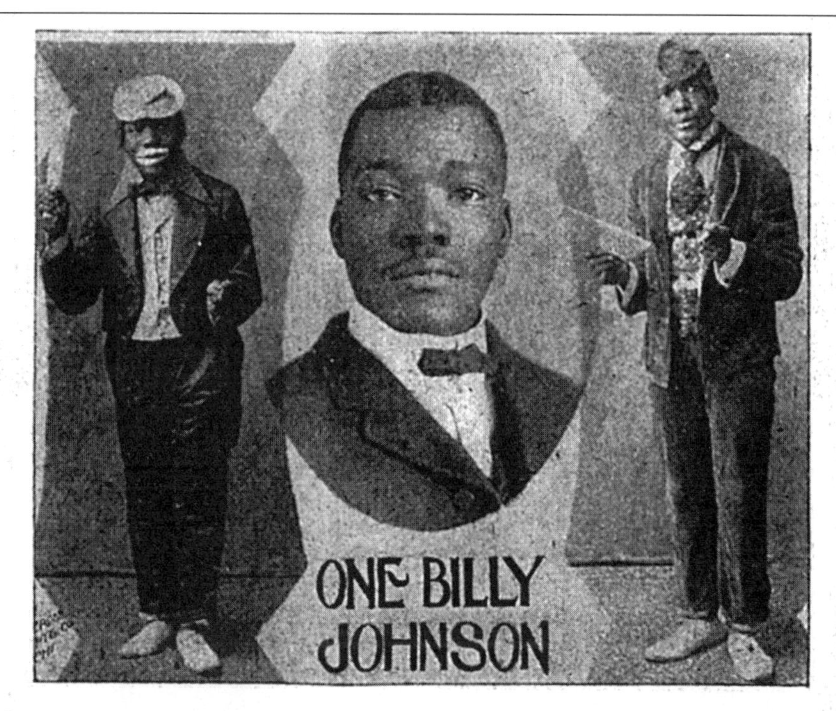

All lovers of minstrelsy will easily recognize the above picture of Billy Johnson as it is a goed one of the gentleman. Mr. Johnson was born Jan. 8, 1882, and even when a youngster was in ready demand whenever occasion called for his services for local affairs, which was quite often, for Billy could sing and dance the best of any of the boys in the neighborhood. At the age of ten we find him the leading star with the Leslie Thomas Afro-American Co. Since then he has appeared with some of the best attractions and vaudeville houses in America. The season of '96 and '97 we find him with the Primrose and West minstrels, and making good as he does everywhere. In '99 he was engaged as a special feature with Murray and Murphy, Our Irish Visitors company. He was also principal comedian two seasons with Oliver Scott's minstrels. At present, and for the past sixty weeks, he holds the honor of leading laugh maker with Mahara's operatic minstrels. Being joined recently by his talented little wife, Estelle, they now constitute the team of "The Johnsons," equal to any and surpassed by none. They will be found an agreeable and pleasant lady and gentleman in every sense of the word.

Indianapolis Freeman, October 24, 1903.

The same critic voiced a complaint about "unfrocked" girls in the show's military drill: "If anything the attire of these people grew scantier this year than ever. If the consensus of opinion had been taken, those ungowned would have been tabooed . . . On what grounds then are they exhibited?"

At the end of the season the Smart Set Company retired *A Southern Enchantment*, and in August 1906 they began rehearsals for their new vehicle, *The Black Politician*. One auditor judged: "The songs are good and the singers better. The dancers are decidedly warm and the hoe-downs put a volt or two of enthusiasm into the blood of the audience. The horse racing atmosphere shows the colored performers in their element, and everybody has both hands full of money."[54]

The plot revolved around a mayoral election campaign in the mythical all-black town of Marco, Georgia. Dudley's new character was Hezekiah Doo, "an itinerant race track tout" who becomes the campaign manager for candidate Ephriam Grindle: "Hezekiah also steps into the breach and acts as jockey for Grindle, who has a horse entered in the Great Election Day Handicap."[55]

The music for *The Black Politician* was written by James "Tim" Brymn, "who composed the entire musical score of the last two season's shows of the Smart Set."[56] Brymn was expected to tour with the show, but on November 17, 1906, less than two months into the season, a Smart Set correspondent noted, "It is with sincere and heartfelt regret that we learn we must lose our musical director Mr. Tim Broyum [*sic*] . . . It is the old tale of prejudice. Local orchestra leaders object to a colored man leading the orchestra, notwithstanding he belongs to the union and is thoroughly competent."[57]

Dudley put his early experience as a jockey to good use in *The Black Politician*. "At the close of the race scene in the second act, after . . . 'Hezekiah Doo' rides Jimmy Blackburn to victory, he brings the horse on the stage amid the glare of the footlights, the shouts of the chorus, the applause of the audience and the crash of the orchestra and band."[58]

In Cleveland, Ohio, in October 1906, a "full blooded donkey" named Shamus O'Brien was added to the cast: "It is one of the most laughable spots in a truly laughable show when Dudley brings him on the stage and upbraids him for not appreciating good treatment."[59] In Chicago a *Freeman* columnist joked that Dudley and his donkey had become "almost inseparable companions. Last Thursday Mr. Dudley and Shamus 'did' State Street, stopping in at all the principal buffets from 18th to 50th street."[60]

The most important supporting actor in *The Black Politician* was Salem Tutt Whitney, who, "besides handling the stage for Mr. Dudley and playing the part of Ephriam Grindle, is understudy for Mr. Dudley. Mr. Whitney's versatility allows him to vary from straight to comedy roles with little apparent difficulty."[61] Other members of the cast included Whitney's brother Homer Tutt as "Mayor Jackson, the one-legged relic of the civil war," and Charles Gilpin, late of Williams and Walker's Company, in the role of Remus Bareland, "a villainous type."

At Chicago in November 1906, theatergoers were "unanimous in voting the 'Black Politician' the superior of 'A Southern Enchantment,' the Smart Set's first offering."[62] Indianapolis theatergoers agreed:

> Dudley more than sustained his reputation as one of the leading comedians in the country. The play affords him excellent opportunity to show his versatility and cleverness, which is better seen in Hezekiah Doo . . . the hired booster than in George Washington Bullion, the sedate and fairly respectable old Negro, with means. . .
>
> The "Smart Set" evidently has hit on a good thing in the "Black Politician" . . . The unique features are those of the live mule and the live horse, and for which the show stands alone. Hogan had his make believe "Catastrophe," Williams "buyed" himself a make believe camel; but Dudley comes up with the "authenticated."[63]

Scene from "The Smart Set" which comes to the Park January 31, 1907, for three days.

Indianapolis Freeman, January 26, 1907.

Sylvester Russell contended that *The Black Politician* was actually an "old story, old as the hills":

In its new coat and as a new play the Dudley Politician is as good a farce comedy as one would care to enjoy . . . The essence of war and the installation of southern colored folks in politics, a little donkey, an invisible race track and a race horse, constitute the time worn relics woven together like mustard sauce to feed a hungry, ambitious three-quarter, full-fledged star, whose name is Sherman Dudley . . . This season has given us our first opportunity to see him in a part that has not been created by other actors . . . Dudley's first entrance was something uncommon for a politician. He had a razor and he carved at everything in sight like a crazy man. But let us forget it. His first song, "All In, Out and Down," hardly filled the place left vacant for a star, but he did better with "Hezekiah" . . . But it was left for Dudley's last song, "Old Black Crow," which caught on by ringing cheers from the gallery and resounding applause from all over the house.[64]

"Old Black Crow" appears to have been a minstrel-styled song with an endless supply of verses based on puns. It had a certain staying power with African American performers. Gathered together in the 1960s for a *Golden Reunion in Ragtime*, Eubie Blake, Joe Jordan, and Charles Thompson offered a version of "Old Black Crow" that included this typical verse:

I went to call on my gal named Bess,
I said, "Come down, dear,"
She said, "I'm all undressed,"
I said, "Slip on something, come down here,"
She slipped on the step and broke her ear.[65]

"All In, Down and Out," which Sylvester Russell deemed inauspicious "for a star," was a transitional song, emblematic of the process by which ragtime songs were transformed to blues. Penned by black composers Chris Smith and R. C. "Cecil Mack" McPherson, and published in 1906 by Gotham-Attucks, the first African American outpost on Tin Pan Alley, it cut close to the traditional blues idiom:

The friends you had when you bought wine
Are hard to find when you need a dime.

. . .

When I had money I was crazy to lend,
But if I ever get my hands on a dollar again,
I'm goin' to hold on to it, it's your only friend
When you're all in down and out.[66]

Bert Williams recorded Smith and McPherson's "All In, Down and Out" shortly after it was published, and a variation was recorded for Paramount in 1929 by Ben and Rufus Quillian.[67] The "down and out," or "out and down" theme has been linked to the earliest clear-cut manifestations of folk blues in the state of Texas by songster-sharecropper Mance Lipscomb, who was born in 1895 and raised in Navasota. Lipscomb claimed it was "the original blues":

First song I played that I could rememorize was, oh, about thirteen an foeteen years of age, I was bumpin on a gittah. Playin two songs: "Sugar Babe" an "Out an Down." "Out an Down" was the first blues come out in state a Texas. Represented what the blues was. Well, we playin "Out and Down," but we was playin the blues and didn't know what it was . . . We didn know nothing bout "The Blues," but we *had* the blues right *on*. Then, after while people commenced ta namin a song like that "The Blues."[68]

Lipscomb went on to recall having heard legendary street singer and popular recording artist Blind Lemon Jefferson perform "Out and Down" in Dallas:

He was doin that when I tuck the interurban up there ta Dallas, to hear him sang an play. Nineteen-seventeen: he's standin there on the ground, on the railroad tracks playin that song. He imitated the blues behind that. First man that ever knowed what "The Blues" was made outa. Well then here come "The Blues," stept in behind that song. An then they invented it from that: "The Blues" style.[69]

On the last day of 1908, Chicago-based ragtime pianist James "Slap Rags" White deposited

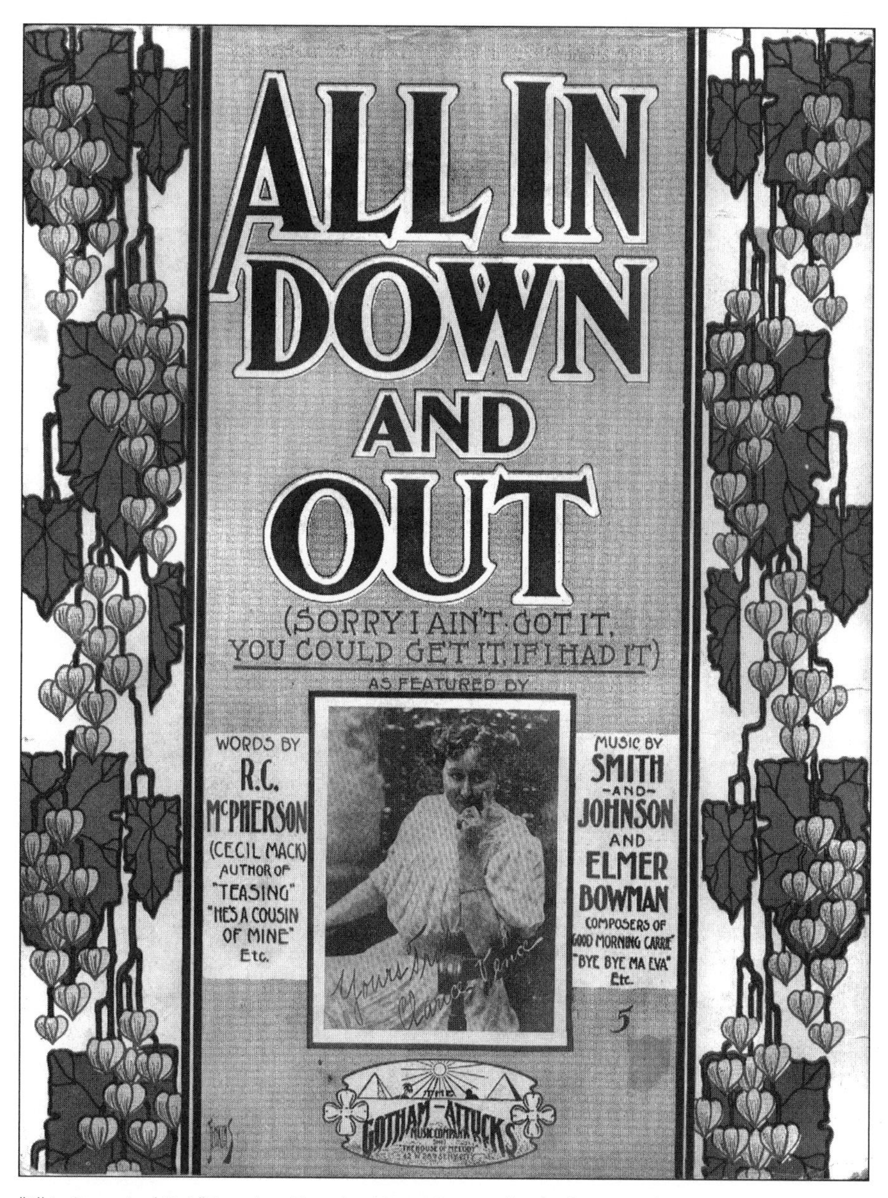

"All In Down And Out." (courtesy Thornton Hagert, Vernacular Music Research)

for copyright a variation of the "old 'Out and Down'" titled, "I Wonder If I'll Always Be Out and Down." It made an impression in black vaudeville. In January 1912 at the Crown Garden Theater in Indianapolis, "The Wilson and Davis Trio surprised the audience with a real funny travesty. Mr. Wilson's song, 'I Wonder Will I Always Be Out and Down,' scored."[70] Amos Peoples made a hit singing "I Wonder if I'll Always Be Down and Out" with the Dandy Dixie Minstrels when they appeared in Bastrop, Texas, early in 1913.[71]

In 1916 Jimmie Cox introduced his masterpiece, the ultimate commercial application of the "down and out" motif, "Nobody Knows You When You're Down and Out."[72] Textually, it relates directly back to the 1906 Gotham-Attucks publication by Chris Smith and Cecil Mack. When vaudeville blues star Mattie Dorsey took it up in 1920, she wrote the *Freeman* to "thank Jimmy Cox for his song entitled, 'When You're All In, Down and Out.' Oh boy, you should push it to the front."[73]

The Smart Set launched its second edition of *The Black Politician* at Kingston, New York, on September 14, 1907. It was said that James Reese Europe, the new musical director, and Cecil Mack "fairly outdid themselves in their contributions of new lyrics and music." Dudley was praised for retaining "that peculiar 'Dudleyism' that is so welcome, but so hard to be duplicated . . . At no time did he over act his part. Dudley . . . was the 'Black Politician' at all times—translated from the streets to the stage."[74]

The essence of Dudley's art was his true-to-life characterizations. An Indianapolis-based *Freeman* writer described Dudley's work in *The Black Politician*: "[Hezekiah Doo] is not rowdy rough, but just a common Negro, one you would meet on Indiana avenue every day . . . His replies—sorties of wit—are without effort, such as would be expected of that kind of a Negro when situations lead up to them. It is this naturalness that makes Dudley go big."[75]

The 1907–1908 season of *The Black Politician* produced the most flattering press reports Dudley had yet received. Even Sylvester Russell was moved. It seems Dudley was now giving the kind of performance that Russell had been calling for: "If the story of the politician is old, it has been made very interesting; if it needed criticism last year, it needs great praise this season, for [it] led us to witness a series of scenes that lent amazement to the best first night's performance I have ever seen . . . Mr. Dudley has given us a complete legitimate performance."[76]

Writing in 1908, *Freeman* columnist "Juli Jones Jr." reminded readers that the Smart Set had been "created by Ernest Hogan, assisted by Billy McClain, and at that time it never occurred to these gentlemen that this production, which they sent on its road to joy, would become the household word of America; neither that it would be introduced by an instrument such as is found in the personality of 'the lone star comedian,' S. H. Dudley; yet this came to pass in living history."[77]

In the spring of 1908 the Smart Set's trained donkey was killed by railroad cars at Elyria, Ohio. Dudley immediately "purchased another mule [sic], trained him, named him 'Patrick' in the incredibly short time of five hours."[78] Dudley and Patrick eventually made a famous vaudeville team. It was a sad day when Patrick was killed by a streetcar in Washington, D.C., in 1919.[79]

Dudley announced in August 1908 that the Smart Set Company would venture south during the coming season, but word came in October that they had "cancelled their southern tour, the people failing to give this excellent company of entertainers financial support."[80] Sylvester Russell editorialized: "Surely America must be very sectional when the elite of the South turns out to see Sissieretta Jones (Black Patti) and refuse to entertain Williams and Walker or the Smart Set."[81] No further explanation was provided.

At Indianapolis during the 1908 Christmas holidays, "Dudley was called back 'indefinitely' in

S. H DUDLEY ALBERTA ORMES WITH THE SMART SET

Indianapolis Freeman, October 26, 1907. Assessing "His Honor, the Barber," Indianapolis-based critic Carey B. Lewis cautioned: "Some people claim that Mr. Dudley should cease from using burnt cork. They seem to forget that it is the aim of the play to show the wit and humor of this sort of Negro, and on the stage at the same time there are forty others who are refined, cultured and dignified actors. Without this kind of wit and humor, there would be no Williams, Dudley, Cole or Steward, and colored actors could never reach the footlights."

Indianapolis Freeman, November 16, 1907.

his 'Old Black Crow.' His 'Right Church but the Wrong Pew' was great . . . Tim Brymn presided at the piano and at times wielded the baton. Brymn is efficient in either capacity . . . Everything starts off in order under Mr. Brymn and stays in order."[82] But the *Freeman* of February 27, 1909, notified that, "When the Smart Set was in Paducah, Ky., it had to get along the best way it could without an orchestra. The white orchestra drew the color line on the negro piano player."

At the end of the 1908–1909 season, the Smart Set's original proprietor Gus Hill apparently sold

Indianapolis Freeman, December 19, 1908.

out to New York City–based entertainment businessmen Barton and Wiswell. The next season witnessed the advent of *two* Smart Sets. The original company, with Dudley at the helm, was qualified as the "Northern Smart Set," while a new company, built around Dudley's former understudy Salem Tutt Whitney and Whitney's brother Homer Tutt, was initiated as the "Southern Smart Set."

Dudley's Northern Smart Set came out with a new musical comedy for 1909–1910, *His Honor, the Barber*, written by white playwright Edwin Handford. In Sylvester Russell's opinion, "Mr. Handford has given us a new story, and one which, if not built upon entirely original ideas, is at least interwoven with unexpected scenes and situations that are unusually logical and meritorious in their relation to a theme." Dudley starred in the character of Raspberry Snow, "an ambitious barber, an old-time edition, who lived in the days when the fondest dream of a colored barber's expectation was to acquire the honor of shaving the President of the United States of America."[83]

The music for *His Honor, the Barber* was "written expressly for the S. H. Dudley company by those eminent colored writers of music and lyrics, J. T. Brymn, Chris Smith and James Burris."[84] Among the titles were "No Use Working All the Time," "Corn Shucking Time," "Watermelon Time," "Big Cry Baby in the Moon," "Isle of Love," and Dudley's feature hit, "Come After Breakfast, Bring 'Long Your Lunch and Leave 'Fore Suppertime."

"His Honor, the Barber" debuted on September 11, 1909, at Plainfield, New Jersey, before a large audience, "white and black." According to Herbert Amos, a member of the cast, Dudley's portrayal of Raspberry Snow established him as "one of America's greatest black-face comedians":

In using the adjective blackface perhaps some of my readers may become imbued with the idea that

> Mr. Dudley's method of entertaining is relegated to the old style of burnt cork. This is a mistake, however, for his method of comedy does not impress you with the mere fact that he is under cork. He first impresses one as being a keen portrayer of the technical demands of stage deportment. In doing this he shows you that as a present day comedian he is as far above the old-time minstrel man as the rocks of Gibraltar are above the Mediterranean Sea.[85]

In Chicago during the 1909 Christmas holidays, *His Honor, the Barber* was reviewed by Sylvester Russell, who was now willing to concede

Indianapolis Freeman, December 25, 1909.

that there could be "no doubt that Mr. Dudley to-day, with a good play which enables him to make people scream, is the funniest comedian since the final exit of the great unbleached American [Ernest Hogan]." Russell's only quibble with *His Honor, the Barber* was that, "All the music and dancing was trotted off at such record breaking speed that time and art were beat to a frazzle . . . Prof. Brymn's music is more lively than tuneful . . . His ragtime numbers are all good, and even if 'Isle of Love' did fall short of sensuous veneration, the professor will not lose his job."[86]

The season of 1910–1911 saw Dudley's Northern Smart Set in a fantastic final production of *His Honor, the Barber*. Aida Overton Walker—now "the pet of New York's exclusive '400'"—was an exciting addition: "Her impersonations of her husband, the late George W. Walker, in her song 'That's Why They Call Me Shine,' appealed to everyone, not only from art's standpoint, but in it there lay a bit of sentiment."[87] Sylvester Russell pointed out that "her male attire and conception of the part was decidedly clever." She returned to the stage in a dazzling "Spanish costume" to sing "'Porto Rico' by Cecil Mack (McPherson), Ford T. Dabney and Jas. T. Brymn, in which Mr. Dudley added very skillful and intelligent bits of comedy pantomime to the scene, a dancing creation in which both in their different lines collectively received an ovation."[88]

Chicago Broad Ax, December 3, 1910.

On January 13, 1911, Dudley's Northern Smart Set played a one-night stand in Shelbyville, Indiana, and drew some perceptive comments in the *Freeman*:

> Tom McIntosh, Ernest Hogan, Tom Logan and the inimitable George Walker have passed into the beyond, but Sherman H. Dudley lives! . . . This year's Smart Set Company in "His Honor the Barber," cannot be outdone in costume, song, story and stage business . . . From the opening chorus, "No Use Working All the Time," on down to the grand finale, everything went like clockwork . . . What strikes you most forcibly about the acting of Dudley is his clean cut wit and the magnetism he carries with it . . . You laugh at him because he is so true to nature . . . His latest song successes are "Almighty Dollar" and "You Needn't Come at All," the latter being an answer to "Come After Breakfast, Bring 'Long Your Lunch" . . . The thing remarkable and away from most comedians, is Dudley's bright idea of making you "crack your sides" by . . . saying things worth saying—that fit the occasion—and leaving out the "rubber lip" stunt. No one of us has not seen the character that he portrays right in our midst . . . The chorus, this season, is the best traveling . . . Like one great organ they sing in tune and color that "gets the hands" from every part of the house. The present company . . . gives us high hope for the future history of colored musical comedy companies, for Mr. Dudley is keeping open the place long ago made by Hogan, Williams & Walker, Cole & Johnson and others.[89]

The arrival of Dudley's Smart Set at the Park Theater in Indianapolis on March 13, 1911, was greatly anticipated: "For days the theatrical horizon has been scanned with the hopes of discovering this bunch, one of the very last of the big aggregations that now seems of a golden age."[90] By 1911 Dudley had been in the spotlight long enough for black audiences and critics to begin to put him in historical perspective. The Lone Star Comedian had managed to add a chapter of his own to the "golden age" of black musical comedy productions.

Dudley launched a new vehicle for the season of 1911–1912, *Dr. Beans from Boston*, in which he starred as Gymnasium Butts (Dr. Beans). The book was by Dudley and Henry Troy and the music and lyrics by Henry H. Creamer and Will H. Vodery, the new musical director. When *Dr. Beans* descended on Washington, D.C., in the spring of 1912, Dudley drew praise for his "dancing specialties" with "Philadelphia girl" Daisy Martin, and for his "peculiarly original talents" in general: "By methods purely natural he keeps his audience in a constant roar of laughter, and one sees at all times the rollicking, happy-go-lucky son of Ham that he meets every day, and there is scarcely a realization that he is in the presence of a skilled actor who knows how to artistically 'hold the mirror up to nature.'"[91]

The *Freeman* of August 24, 1912, announced what turned out to be Dudley's final season with the Smart Set, in a "reconstructed and greatly improved version of 'Doctor Beans From Boston'" with additional music composed by James Reese Europe: "Mr. Dudley will only visit larger cities next season, owing to the demand for his personal attention in connection with his circuit of theaters."

Dudley's theater circuit initiative was inspired by the painfully obvious need for venues willing to host black touring companies and showcase black vaudeville artists. Dudley first articulated his vision for a national chain of independent black theaters in a 1907 *Freeman* interview. He had just finished a performance of *The Black Politician* and was "still clad in the grotesque habiliments of the wily 'Hezekiah Doo,' with his expressive eyes sparkling through the burnt-cork makeup of the part." The interviewer noted:

Mr. Dudley is an enthusiastic believer in the future of the Negro Thespian. He sees with the eye of a prophet a chain of theatres, controlled by a syndicate of Negro managers, duplicating in every city in the country where there is a considerable colored population, the triumph that is being achieved by the new Pekin at Chicago, managed by the enterprising and indefatigable Robert T. Motts. If the managers will only get together and furnish the opportunity, Mr. Dudley is confident that the professionals will be ready to supply "the goods" that draw the people and put the money in the strong box. The white people like pure Negro comedy, up-to-date Negro music and folk lore, so if the entertainment at a Negro house is of the best quality and good order is maintained, they would give a generous support, and of course the Negroes will be there early and often. Not only would such a chain of theatres prove a veritable gold mine in the South where the Negro is barred from the decent seats in the white houses, but the venture would not be less welcome nor less successful in the larger cities of the North. . .

What Mr. Dudley says is worthy of serious consideration by the moneyed men of the theatrical world. A vast Negro syndicate . . . controlling bookings of the standard companies and operating a string of desirable playhouses from the Atlantic to the Pacific, is not "an iridescent dream"—it can be worked out into a tangible, productive reality. There are millions in the comparatively undeveloped mine of black-face comedy.[92]

While primarily devoting himself to his theater circuit after 1912, Dudley never fully retired from the stage, and he was always remembered for his glory days with the Smart Set.

Back in 1905, *Freeman* reporter W. Milton Lewis had acknowledged a special dynamic in the Smart Set: "The public is studied through the presentation—the pulse of public sentiment is felt—the status of race progression somewhat analyzed and set down. In short, what the public is willing to 'stand for' from colored performers is made known by the reception accorded. The Smart Set as a type of stage accomplishment is a means of sizing up the Negro on the stage—what he is per se—a chronicling of the process of the evolution. This company has kept pace with public sentiment."[93]

Under Dudley's stewardship the Smart Set spanned the gap between the conventions of minstrel farce and the modern characteristics of black musical comedy; it also achieved a higher development of bona fide self-referential humor and vernacular music and dance on the American stage.

The last "legitimate" heir to the Smart Set Company was Salem Tutt Whitney. Whitney was not a southerner but, with the introduction of the Southern Smart Set in 1909, he became the Smart Set's official ambassador to the South and carried the Smart Set legacy into the era of blues and jazz.

Whitney was born in Logansport, Indiana, on November 15, 1876, and raised in Indianapolis.[94] He recalled having made his first professional tour with the Puggsley Brothers Tennessee Warblers in 1894.[95] An 1897 *Freeman* report identified him as the Tennessee Warblers' "vocalist and comedian," in company with William A. Baynard, "trick and descriptive pianist"; Baynard's sister, Emma A. Baynard, "prima donna soprano"; and others.[96]

From 1898 until 1904 Whitney served as stage manager, principal comedian, and "lion basso" of the Oriental Troubadours, apparently an offshoot of the Tennessee Warblers. Mainstays of the roster included William Baynard and his sister Emma, who became Whitney's first wife; "Southern tenor" C. H. Puggsley, "in his impersonation of Auntie Clo"; soprano Lillian Brown, "the Boston Nightingale"; and the Taylor Sisters, Nettie and

Jennie, who "always held the spectators by their skillful handling of the banjo, mandolin and cornets."[97] These skills had been imparted to the sisters by their father, Charles Taylor, Sr., whose Philadelphia neighborhood barbershop served as a "pleasant rendezvous for musicians from all over the city."[98] Nettie Taylor remained an important fixture of Whitney's theatrical enterprises for the next ten years.

The Oriental Troubadours operated "principally in Pennsylvania and New Jersey," showing in "the best houses" during the winter, and "under canvas" during the summer. Their winter tours ran from mid-October of one year through mid-April of the next.[99] It seems their favorite show stop was Ringing Rocks Park in Pottstown, Pennsylvania. They opened their summer season of 1901 there in May, and when they returned in October to close out the tour with a two-week engagement, a *Freeman* correspondent noted it was their "seventh date there in three seasons, for a total of nine weeks, a record that any company might envy."[100]

In November 1902 the Oriental Troubadours were "presenting 'The Ex-President of Liberia' a musical comedy with eighteen star actors headed by Salem Tutt Whitney."[101] At some point before the spring of 1904 they reorganized as Baynard and Whitney's Famous Troubadours.[102] A correspondent boasted in 1905 that they were "carrying twenty or more people, entirely owned and controlled by colored men. The company during the summer travels under canvas with a band of twelve pieces, playing week stands, changing programs nightly, making it the first colored repertoire show in the country."[103]

The roster of Baynard and Whitney's Troubadours for 1905 included Charles W. Williams, comedy juggler; Sarah Venable, coon shouter; DeRose, female impersonator; Montrose Douglass, trick bicyclist and wire walker; and Homer Tutt, who came in "as an understudy to his brother, Salem Tutt Whitney, in the leading comedy roles." It was also noted that, "The band under the direction of Nettie Taylor is the best and largest we have yet had on the street." One of the musicians was Nettie's brother, violinist Charles Taylor, Jr.[104]

In August 1905 Whitney left Baynard and Whitney's Famous Troubadours "to take charge of the stage with the Smart Set Company." Touring with S. H. Dudley's Smart Set for the next two seasons, he pulled his younger brother into the

SALEM TUTT WHITNEY.

Indianapolis Freeman, February 9, 1907.

company, and they became an inseparable team. In a 1909 statement, Whitney explained their different last names: "My real name is Salem Tutt. 'Whitney' was given or rather forced upon me by L. E. Puggsley of Puggsley Brothers Tennessee Warblers, about fourteen years ago . . . I liked my job [touring as a bass singer with the Warblers], for which I was receiving $4 almost every week, and rather than lose the job I kept the name. I like it myself now and shall be known to the theatrical world as S. Tutt Whitney. Homer Tutt is my full brother, but the team will be called Whitney & Tutt."[105]

For the season of 1907–1908 Whitney and Tutt jumped from Dudley's Smart Set to the Black Patti Troubadours. Whitney served as "Principal Comedian and Stage Manager," Tutt as "Straight Man and Character Artist." Their tenure with Black Patti appears to have marked their introduction to southern audiences, and by one account they quickly succeeded in making their songs and sayings "bywords . . . throughout Dixieland."[106] At Chattanooga in the spring of 1908, the mainstream *Daily Times* exclaimed, "Whitney is any amount funnier than [white minstrel counterparts] Dockstader or Fields. And why shouldn't he be? His black-face comedy is the genuine article . . . It was worth while being present to see the colored comedian if only to hear the uncontrolled shouts of the galleries. For with comedians of his own race upon the stage and only a few of the 'white folks' below stairs the Negro literally takes the check-rain [*sic*] off his emotions and demonstrates his approval by ecstatic roars of laughter."[107]

HOMER TUTT

Who has made a great hit this season as the wooden leg soldier in "The Black Politician" and is engaged for the summer months with S. H. Dudley's "Jolly Ethiopians"

Indianapolis Freeman, March 23, 1907.

During the summer of 1908, between seasons with the Black Patti Troubadours, Whitney and Tutt reconnected with William Baynard in Eph Williams and William Baynard's Troubadours, and Whitney developed the original conception of *Silas Green from New Orleans*, portraying the misadventures of a stranded minstrel troupe. He incorporated it in the 1908–1909 edition of the Black Patti Troubadours as "The Barnstormers," with himself in the role of Silas Green.[108]

On the night of November 13, 1908, Whitney's wife Emma "passed away at her home, 2041 Lombard street, Philadelphia . . . after an illness of over six months."[109] Whitney immediately closed with the Black Patti Troubadours and made his way home. Around this same time, brother-in-law William A. Baynard was hired to manage the Lincoln Theater, a black playhouse in Knoxville, Tennessee, and he talked Whitney and Tutt into coming down to produce a stock company. The *Freeman* of December 26, 1908, reported:

> The reopening of the Lincoln by S. Tutt Whitney and the new Lincoln Stock Company was a most auspicious occasion. The seating capacity of the house was entirely inadequate, standing room being at a premium, and fully three hundred persons were turned away from the doors. The elite of Knoxville turned out in large numbers, the best families of the city being represented. The show, a one-act musical comedy, "The Strollers," by S. Tutt Whitney, was . . . one jolly round of mirth, music and song . . . Whitney . . . appeals to the intelligence of his audience, and amuses without resorting to horseplay or vulgarity. The work of Homer Tutt is also deserving of special mention . . . In dress he is the legitimate rival of George Walker. The dancing of Sam Gardner was above the ordinary . . . Sank Simms displayed real talent . . . Mamie Gardner sang and danced . . . The song hits of the show were "It's Shouting Time," sung by John Johnson; "Oh, My, Miss Mandy," introduced by Homer Tutt; Nettie Taylor and the "Merry Widow Quartette" were encored again and again. S. Tutt Whitney sang his own composition, "I Ain't Going to Let Nobody, Nobody Make a Fool Out of Me." Prof. [Henry] Watterson and Lawrence ["Buss"] Williams furnished the music, and it was of a high order. Mr. Carl F. Johnson, proprietor and W.A. Baynard, manager, are assured of the enthusiastic support of the Knoxville theater-going public.

In March 1909 the Lincoln Stock Company presented "Mr. Whitney's latest musical comedy, 'The Tenderfoot,' with special music by Homer Tutt and Trevor L. Corwell,"[110] an Englishman and, "incidentally, the best white man with a colored show in the business." After having emigrated to the States in 1891, Corwell served a five-year stint with the Second United States Cavalry Band, then led "a varied career as bandmaster and musical director with small circuses and road shows of all kinds and conditions." Just prior to connecting with Whitney, he served four years with the Rose Melville Company, of *Sis Hopkins* fame.[111] Corwell's musical skills, business acumen, and social philosophy proved important to Whitney's success.

On April 10, 1909, the Lincoln Theater closed down for the summer, and Whitney and Tutt took their stock company on the road. That summer, while holding down the stage at the Lyric Theater in Newport News, Virginia, members of the Whitney Stock Company attended a reception for Booker T. Washington. By Whitney's own account, "Dr. Washington appeared delighted to meet the different members of the company, and said he was glad to note the progress colored performers are making in the theatrical world. He inquired very earnestly after the health of George Walker, and expressed sorrow for the death of Ernest Hogan."[112]

The *Freeman* of July 17, 1909, broke the story that "Salem Tutt Whitney will star this season in the 'Smart Set Show'—Southern—under the personal direction of John J. Nolan, of the firm of Barton, Wiswell and Nolan Co., Inc." These veteran white promoters of black shows saw Whitney as "a disciple of the old school of comic character delineators" whose recent record with the Black Patti Troubadours assured "immense success for the 'Smart Set Show' South of the Mason and Dixon Line," especially in "colored circles," where anticipation over the arrival of the Smart Set was said to be equaled only "by the universal popular interest manifested at the coming of Santa Claus."

For their inaugural tour of 1909–1910, the Southern Smart Set presented an adaptation of *A Southern Enchantment*, which they titled *George Washington Bullion*. Whitney starred in the title role. The "orchestra" comprised Lincoln Theater Stock Company veterans Henry Watterson, piano, and Lawrence "Buss" Williams, drums, augmented by violinist George Rhone. The leading lady was Daisy Martin, and the supporting cast included Homer Tutt, William A. Baynard, Nettie Taylor, Sank Simms, and Sam and Mamie Gardner.[113]

Mamie Gardner's journey with Whitney's Southern Smart Set was relatively brief, but Whitney was nevertheless proud to note years later that, "Little Mamie Gardner Smith, one of the charter members [of the Southern Smart Set], is now basking in the Spotlight as one of the greatest singers of ragtime and 'Blues' songs that has ever made a record for the edification of a Victrola loving public."[114] He was referring to Mamie Smith's 1920 recording of Perry Bradford's "Crazy Blues," the first big hit of the blues recording era.

The song hits of *George Washington Bullion* included "Strutting Sam," "Smile On, Sue," "You's My All in All," and the runaway hit of the show, "Dat's Sufficiency." The company chorus, under T. L. Corwell's direction, was labeled the "best singing and dancing chorus of its class or color"; and one of the specialty acts, "The Mississippi Maids," with Lavinia "Babe" Brown, Mabel DeHeard, Ethel Marshall, Lida Marshall, Hallie Dean, and Blanche Simms, was said to be "the dancingest lot of dancers that ever danced."[115]

S. TUTT WHITNEY AND J. HOMER TUTT.

The rise of these Hoosier comedians has been nothing short of phenomenal. Their first appearance with any of the big shows was with the Smart Set Company in 1905-06, when Mr. Whitney filled the position of stage director and understudy, while his brother, Homer, enacted the role of the "one-legged soldier." They next appeared as leading comedians with Black Patti Troubadours, capturing the entire South by their clean, intelligent comedy and high-class work. In two seasons they have made their funny sayings bywords, and their songs are being sung throughout Dixieland. The brothers, for such they are, despite the difference in names, were born in Logansport, Ind., later moving to Indianapolis, Ind., where they resided until they entered the show business. Both are graduates and are not only comedians and producers, but accomplished musicians, writing or assisting to write all the music for all the productions they are with. They will no doubt be accorded a warm welcome when they appear in the East and Middle West.

Indianapolis Freeman, August 7, 1909.

Whitney's Southern Smart Set made its debut at the White City Theater in Norfolk, Virginia, on August 9, 1909. For the next few weeks they played one-night stands in southeastern Virginia and the Carolinas, then journeyed west to Bristol, Tennessee, and plunged southward. Show stops included Chattanooga, Tennessee, September 9; Decatur, Alabama, 10; Pine Bluff, Arkansas, 13; Little Rock, 14; Hot Springs, 15; and Texarkana, 17. The Southern Smart Set bounced around Texas for the next two months. A reporter in Denison said they "set this 'burg' wild . . . Everybody is singing 'Sufficiency' and 'Smile on Sue.'"[116]

Whitney observed that, in the black communities, "The hospitality of the Texans seems unbounded. Everywhere the company has been sumptuously entertained—in Dallas by the

Calhoun and Monday Social Clubs, in Fort Worth by Jones' Social Club, in Waco by the Elite Social Club, and a royal banquet by the Clover Leaf Club of Houston."[117] Outside the black communities, however, a different reality prevailed. Correspondence from Corsicana, dated November 13, 1909, chronicles a crisis in the company's fortunes:

> The season of the "Smart Set" Southern Company closed here on the first of the month, under the management known as Barton, Wiswell and Nolan, with everyone paid to the last penny and all with money to go where they pleased. But all remained with Whitney and Tutt, who will take them from here to . . . New Orleans, La., where they will put on four or five shows from the pen of Tutt and Whitney.
>
> This company has been playing one-night stands . . . in the heart of the South . . . In some towns they were unable to obtain anything to eat or a place to lodge; then making 4 o'clock trains in the morning and these trains averaging ten miles an hour, taking all day to cover forty miles, often too late for a matinee. At one place the men had to make a guard line around the women to keep the white men from assaulting them, and they all carry .48 revolvers. T.L. Corwell, the white manager, remained with them in the "jim-crow" cars, and did all he could to cheer them. In going over this route everyone was satisfied that a blunder had been made in sending them without a private [railroad] car.
>
> John J. Nolan, who was formerly an owner of this company, has been doing some unscrupulous work with the firm of Barton & Wiswell, and warnings have been sent to every newspaper for publication advertising all theatrical folk not to trust him. Mr. Nolan was to have secured a private car, "Nellie," but it never came, and Barton & Wiswell were not aware of the fact for some time afterward.

Whitney further noted that when "the company could not get sleeping accommodations, although Mr. Corwell had free access to the hotels, he would sit up all night in stations with the company, not willing to enjoy comforts, in which his people could not share." The Southern Smart Set rededicated itself as the Whitney Musical Comedy Company, and with Corwell replacing Nolan as "pilot," made their way from Corsicana to New Orleans to open a week's engagement at the Temple Theater, playing "exclusively for colored patronage." They made "such a terrific and instantaneous hit" that the Temple held them over for three additional weeks. During their second week, they staged "The Star of Zanzibar": "The story . . . tells of one Sam Slick (Homer J. Tutt) trying to emigrate the colored folks of America to . . . Africa, and to do this he needs the help of 'Ezy' Amos (Salem Tutt Whitney) . . . [W]hen they arrive in Africa the natives mistake Amos for the king whom they had been taught would come from some foreign land . . . and thus he saves his friends from being eaten up as well as himself." One feature of the play was a "Zulu King song and drill by Whitney and chorus," which may have been the specific inspiration for New Orleans's well-known Zulu Social Aid and Pleasure Club and its outlandishly costumed Mardi Gras parade.[118]

From New Orleans, the Whitney Musical Comedy Company made its way north. At Logansport, Indiana, "Friends white and black vied with each other to make the homecoming of the Tutt Brothers a grand success."[119] After winding up the season at North Vernon, Indiana, on May 31, 1910, Whitney, Tutt, and seventeen members of the company caught a train to Newport News, Virginia, to provide summer stock for the Lyric Theater.

"Going Some"
THE
Whitney Musical Comedy Company
HEADED BY
Salem Tutt Whitney

SALEM TUTT WHITNEY

AND
Homer Tutt

HOMER TUTT

SUPPORTED BY
MISS DAISY MARTIN
And a Company of Unequalled Excellence.

LOOK AT THIS RECORD

The Whitney Musical Comedy Co. opened on November 8 at the New Temple Theatre, New Orleans, for one week, was such a terrific and instantaneous hit that the show was retained for a second and then a third week, and at the end of the third week was actually COMPELLED to cancel a week of the road tour to meet the great demand for another week. Not in the history of theatricals in the South has this record been even approached, let alone equalled. And that is

"GOING SOME"

Managers of first class colored theaters should communicate at once and secure this great show before the Northern tour, as this show plays city time after Jan. 1.

ADDRESS
T.R.Corwell
Manager.

Send Communications in regard to time to
B. H. Nye
Representative
As per Route.

Indianapolis Freeman, December 11, 1909.

Safely ensconced in Newport News's black-owned We-Us Hotel, Whitney reflected on his initial experience with the Southern Smart Set:

> The faculty to see something funny in the most sordid of subjects, the dexterity to turn a seemingly hopeless situation into a laugh, has been and will be the saving grace of the Negro race. . .
>
> [O]n November 30 at Corsicana, Texas, 2,000 miles from home, Mr. Nolan imparted the sad tidings that the Smart Set No. 2 (Southern) had expired . . .
>
> There we were, strangers in a strange land . . . Mr. Corwell said, "Whitney, what will we do?" I said, "We will hold together, stay out and fight to the finish," and it is of that fight I am now speaking . . . Under the careful (I might say parental) guidance of T. L. Corwell, the Whitney Musical Comedy Company covered 12,000 miles in a season of less than six months . . . It would take an extra edition to enumerate the experiences of those six months. We ran the entire gamut: we played one nighters, two and three days, week stands, and also stock. We rode passenger trains, freight cabooses, trolleys and wagons. We slept in bed and out of bed . . . Sometimes we made money, sometimes we didn't. Most times we didn't . . . Our only capital was an unlimited stock of nerve and perseverance . . . We were making a success out of failure . . . Now our sixth sense gets to work and we can find something funny in the whole thing. In fact, it is our best joke. We laugh and the future looks bright, brimful of happy prospects.[120]

Whitney's optimistic attitude was justified. His company had rescued the Southern Smart Set and preserved its great legacy. Barton and Wiswell contracted to finance the company for the season of 1910–1911, with T. L. Corwell continuing as "pilot." Their musical comedy offering was a revised *George Washington Bullion*, with Homer Tutt as Bullion's friend, Sam Cain; W. A. Baynard as Bullion's nemesis, Grafton Smoothe, Sam Gardner as "Major Johnson, the old man with the wooden leg"; and Sank Simms as "Sureto Ketchum, attired in a thousand rags."[121]

The play had minimal plot and plenty of action. The first scene concluded with Bullion waving his razor and singing "I'm a R-U-L-E-R," and the second scene ended in a "general slash up, when Bullion gets his razor into play again." In another scene, "Bullion misses his chicken dinner, by being detained by Smoothe and Ketchum. After a lively scrap he finally gets to the dining room in time to get the leavings." During the second act, "a war ensues. Indians, soldiers and civilians are slain," and Major Johnson, with his wooden leg, "outruns everybody." Finally, there was the classic comic duel between Bullion and Grafton Smoothe. Homer Tutt and Daisy Martin sang the old hit, "Oh, Miss Mandy" until mid-season, when they replaced it with Tutt and Watterson's "That Loving Rag Time Glide." One of the biggest hits of the season was "'Mammy's Golden Rule,' in which seven girls do a regular buck dance."[122]

During this season the Southern Smart Set managed to thread its way through Texas "without one whit of trouble, though at times trouble seemed unavoidable." A commentator half joked that, in order to maintain a low public profile during their Texas sojourn, the women of the company dressed as "ordinary cotton pickers" and "wash women," and the men, except for Tutt, who "maintained his dudish look and therefore was adjudged the boss of the gang," dressed as "jobmen" and "compress hands." The star player took a different tact: "Determined not to put on any open air dancing stunts, Mr. Whitney generally appeared as a Texas ranger of the frontier type . . . ready to round up a herd of Texas steers."[123]

One thing Whitney came to appreciate during the 1910–1911 season was the deep reservoir of "native talent" that existed in the South: "It is really harder to please a colored audience in the South than in the North," he confessed. "There are performers in the South drawing $12 per week that can dance rings around our best Northern dancers and sing a coon song incomparably."[124] He later reiterated, "Every other man or boy one meets on the street corner is a natural-born comedian, so a comedian has his work cut out for him before he faces the audience. If one is a dancer, he need not go far to find a barefoot boy who can eclipse one's best effort."[125]

An article in the *Freeman* of January 7, 1911, celebrated Whitney's "excellent work by way of composing songs and playlets. Of his many songs are the following: 'The Man that Rules the Town,' 'My Spanish Maid,' 'I Ain't Built that Way,' 'Love You Best of All,' 'Linda, Be My Lady Lou,' 'O, My Miss Mandy.'

"A few of his playlets are as follows: 'Prince Bungaboo,' 'Blackville Strollers,' 'Two Jolly Tramps,' 'The Recruit,' 'Derby Day,' 'Hodge and Hodge.'"

In addition to writing songs and playlets, Whitney was a prolific essayist, and he left a large body of work in the *Freeman*.[126] In 1911 he launched a weekly column under the heading, "Seen and Heard While Passing," which served as an outlet for his original poems, anecdotes, and philosophical ramblings, as well as a diary of the progress of his show business career. The March 4, 1911, installment of "Seen and Heard While Passing" celebrated the Southern Smart Set's return to northern pastures:

"Back to God's country." More than one of the company made use of this expression as we crossed the river into Cairo, Ill. For nearly seven months we have been travelling south of the Mason and Dixon line, where one is eternally reminded, if there be a drop of negro blood in his veins, that he or she is a Negro. Where one is continually confronted by such signs as, "For Negroes Only," "This Side for Blacks," "Niggers Not Allowed," until it becomes nauseating—where everything is "Jim Crowed" but the air you breathe.

I have been asked, "How do you stand it?" In the first place, I think colored people are naturally philosophers. Secondly, when one learns to attend strictly to one's business, with conduct becoming a lady or gentleman, one will find that he or she can get along almost anywhere. Thirdly, the colored people of the South are prodigal with their hospitality. To know them is to like them. When you give them a good show their enthusiasm is unbounded, and their praise unstinted. If there be any colored people in the North who think the Southern Negro is asleep, let them awake from their lethargy. Negroes in the South own homes that would grace Fifth Avenue, New York. In many of the smaller towns they own whole business blocks. They are engaged in nearly every line of business. Their professional men are keen, intelligent and thrifty. Farmers owning large plantations are common, and Negroes can produce competent workmen in every line of manual labor...

I believe the "Jim Crow" to be a blessing in disguise. It will establish a unity of purpose and a self-reliance as nothing else could possibly do. It is God's smelter. The Negro is being tried by fire, but in God's own time he will come from the grueling test, refined even as pure gold.

I take this opportunity to thank the colored people of the South and Southwest for their support, their many courtesies and abundant hospitality, and will look forward to my next season's tour through the South with pleasurable anticipation.

For the Southern Smart Set tour of 1911–1912, Whitney introduced *The Mayor of Newtown*, starring himself as Mayor Lem Lee; his brother Homer as Lee's rival, Sam Jackson; and Sam Gardner as "a peg-legged veteran with a doubtful war record, but the possessor of many medals." Whitney was responsible for the season's biggest song hit, "I Ain't Nuthin', Never Had Nuthin', Don't Want Nuthin' But You." Also popular was the Whitney-Watterson collaboration, "Keep a Movin' Rite Along," which admonished listeners to, "Stop yo' talking 'bout the wedder; better git yo'sef togedder."[127] In another popular feature, "Ethel Marshall, with J. Homer Tutt, added many gyrations to the 'Grizzly Bear,' the 'Turkey Trot' and the 'Bunny Hug.'"[128]

From the Howard Theater in Washington, D.C., the latest edition of the Southern Smart Set embarked on what Whitney described as their "triumphal march through Dixie, the land of sugar cane, corn and cotton, 'possum, coon and yam, where the watermelon is the national flower, the land of moccasins, rattlesnakes, centipedes, mosquitoes and corn whiskey; the land of oranges, bananas, magnolias, balmy breezes and the mockingbird; the land of pretty women and homely men; the land of hospitality, contradictions and inconsistencies."[129]

At San Antonio that fall they "filled the galleries of the Grand Opera house to overflowing with a dark-hued but joyful and cheering audience. And the white people in the pit caught the enthusiasm." In Austin they encountered an infestation of grasshoppers: "The lights from the stage attracted them in great numbers, making it almost impossible to speak or sing. They were piled several inches deep in the trough of the foot-lights." The reason the Smart Set lingered so long in Texas every fall was finally spelled out: "Everywhere is heard the songs of the cotton pickers and the whir of the gin mills. Everybody has money during the cotton-picking season, and they spend it with a happy prodigality."[130]

Whitney found cause for optimism in the fact that, during the 1911–1912 season, "our colored patrons have been able to see the Smart Set show for the first time from any part of the house in . . . Albany and Americus, Ga.; Orangeburg, S. C.; Florence, Wilmington, Raleigh, Winston-Salem and Greensboro, N. C."[131] Before the season was over, however, they endured a close encounter with a lynch mob.

During the summer of 1912 Homer Tutt married Blanche Thompson, "a Baltimore girl" who became the Southern Smart Set's new leading lady. They opened the season of 1912–1913 in Hampton, Virginia, with new musical director Wilson "Peaches" Keyer of Charleston, South Carolina, "a pianist of exceptional ability."[132] Their new play, *The Darktown Politician*, reportedly featured "twenty original musical compositions, ranging from rollicking rag time to grand opera." According to a reviewer in Lexington, Kentucky, "The jubilee scene in the second act, introducing a medley of plantation songs and dances, was a real treat. It not only pleased the Negroes in the balcony and gallery, but was exceedingly entertaining as well to the white people in the audience."[133] New to the roster were Richmond Puggsley, son of original Tennessee Warbler R. C. Puggsley, and Leigh Whipper, who

SEEN AND HEARD WHILE PASSING

A Mob at Close Range.

By S. Tutt, Whitney.

While in Cordele, Ga., I had my first undesired opportunity of seeing a real mob ready for action. Two seasons past, in Spartansburg, S. C., they attempted to lynch a Negro the day after we left the city. Again in Greenville, S. C. the stage hands very cordially extended us an invitation to remain over until the next night and see a genuine lynching bee. We arrived in Clarksville, Texas, about eight hours after they had lynched a Negro. But in Cordele, the rape was committed and the mob formed about two hours before show time.

Luckily for us, a 6 o'clock rehearsal had been called and we were at the theatre when the excitement started. As soon as the deed was discovered the mob made direct for our car. There is no telling what would have been the fate of us men had we been on the car at the time. For passion and reason are not analogous, and Judge Lynch has a way of executing his victims and trying the case afterwards.

The operahouse in Cordele is situated above the firehouse and jail. This was another fortunate circumstance for us, because our rehearsal was witnessed by several firemen and policemen, who gave willing testimony that no member of the company could have been guilty of, or accessory to, the crime.

When Mr. Corwell, our manager, learned that a rape had been committed and a Negro accused, he hurried to the operahouse and informed us of the fact. He warned us not to go in the streets and to leave the theater en masse immediately after the show. He then took every precaution to safeguard the company from molestation.

While "making up" we could look from our dressing-room window and see the mob standing on the sidewalk below. Men with faces drawn and pale from suppressed passion, whose thirst for vengeance made them ready to ignore the laws of God and man. Men, who after they had reeked their bloody revenge, were scarcely better than the hapless victim they had destroyed.

"It was an orderly mob." I read this from a newspaper account of the tragedy. Is it possible to imagine anything more incongruous than an "orderly" mob? As well speak of a "peaceable murderer." But then if one is up in mobology, it is easy to know what a Southern newspaper means by "an orderly mob." This mob did not run rampant up and down the streets, shooting or beating every unfortunate Negro that crossed its path, but was satisfied with the life of the perpetrator of the henious crime.

At show time it was pouring rain. This was also fortunate for us. Water seems to have a cooling effect upon the passions of man and brute. Most of our colored audience came to the theater in carriages. The mob lined up on either side of the entrance and, after quietly inspecting each carriage, its occupants were allowed to pass within unharmed. There was a very good crowd of colored people and a few whites. They enjoyed the show immensely and seemed entirely unconcerned about the brewing tragedy. One fireman remarked: "Some strange nigger done it; none of our home niggers would do such a thing." He was right in his surmise.

After the show we were permitted to go to the car without suffering any indignities from the mob. The only evidences of hostility were the glimpses one had of Winchesters, shotguns and revolvers, which sight chased cold chills up and down our vertebrae.

The supposed perpetrator of the crime was captured during the night and an almost undisputable chain of circumstantial evidence was established. The mob awaited only the return to consciousness of his victim before they put on the final act of the tragedy. We did not leave Cordele until noon next day. Curiosity impelled me to go up town. On every corner were crowds of grim and determined men. The most unconcerned man I saw was the chief of police. He was asked: "Do you think there will be any trouble?" "No," he slowly drawled, "I don't think so. I did not know anything about it myself until past midnight." The deed was committed about 6:30 p. m.

About an hour after we left Cordele, the girl regained her senses. The identification was completed, and in less than an hour what had been a human being, hung from a tree riddled with bullets, while four or five hundred men must answer to their God for the crime of murder.

There is nothing to be said in extenuation for the crime of rape. Although I cannot concieve of any but an insane person doing any such thing. Be the crime what it may, it does not justify lynching. Statistics do not prove that lynching diminishes crime, but it does generate a disregard of the law, which is dangerous for any commonwealth. Lynching is an incubator for murderers. Americans, by ignoring this evil, which is spreading like an insiduous disease, are sowing the wind. O, God, what will the harvest be?

Indianapolis Freeman, March 30, 1912.

replaced Sam Gardner as "Major Jinks, the one-legged war veteran."[134]

The Smart Set came to the black-owned Majestic Theater in Nashville at Christmas, 1912. The *Globe*, Nashville's local black weekly newspaper, proclaimed: "'The Smart Set' came this season with new costumes and scenery throughout, new songs and new dances and in some respects a new story . . . to say nothing of the niftiest bunch of Creole beauties ever seen on any stage. They made a special hit with the Dixieland Drill, the Ragtime Jubilee in plantation songs, and original

Indianapolis Freeman, December 28, 1912.

interpretations of the Bunny Hug, Teddy Bear, Sooie Rag and other similar compositions."[135]

After the close of the 1912–1913 season, the Southern Smart Set became the *only* Smart Set, "owned by Chas. E. Barton, managed by Trevor L. Corwell, and headed by Whitney and Tutt." For the season of 1913–1914, Salem Tutt Whitney's Smart Set launched a new vehicle, *The Wrong Mr. President*, with Charles "Lucky" Roberts, "king of all ragtime pianists," replacing "Peaches" Keyer as musical director.[136]

Indianapolis Freeman, December 20, 1913. In 1913 Wilson Keyer married singing and dancing soubrette Lottie Gee. The *Freeman* of December 30, 1916, noted that Wilson and Lottie Gee-Keyer were "jointly entertaining the large clientele of Haynes dining rooms" in New York City. In 1921, Keyer played piano on Ethel Waters's first recording session, and in 1922 he recorded with Lucille Hegamin.

On August 24, 1914, Whitney's Smart Set opened their season at S. H. Dudley's American Theater in Washington, D.C., presenting *His Excellency the President*:

> The scene is laid at "Ginger Springs," a popular health resort in Georgia, and the story deals with two lively tourists of color, who have more philosophy, humor and appetite than cash. They are gentlemen of leisure in reduced circumstances and "blow into town" just in advance of an exiled President and secretary of state of Haiti, traveling incognito while awaiting the outcome of one of the periodical revolutions in their native land. The landlord and his ambitious and fashionable young wife mistake "Bud White" and "Dan Jenkins" for them, and attribute their trampy aspect to their previously announced desire to keep their identity concealed. The soldiers of fortune . . . readily assume the role and . . . the "messes" they get into as the bogus president and secretary of the Haitian republic furnish a vehicle for fun that [Whitney and Tutt] take advantage of to the full . . . The play is on the lines of last year's . . . but stronger because of the speedier action, more closely-knit story and greater prominence of Haiti than Liberia in the spotlight of the activities today.

Replacing "Lucky" Roberts as musical director was Clarence G. Wilson, "a Washington boy" with a degree from Howard University. New song hits included "I'm Just a Pickaninny All Dressed Up" and a "square dance" song, "Ye Old Quadrille." In one special feature, Blanche Thompson and Hattie Akers, with respective partners Tutt and Whitney, demonstrated "their original dances, The Hawaiian Tango, The Salem Hesitation and Tutt's Totolo."[137] Also given as "Tutt's Todalo," the latter was adapted for use in the grand finale, "in which the entire company works in single file marching order, making several trips across the stage and through the wings."[138]

At the Temple Theater, New Orleans, in December 1914, "The Temple Orchestra, under the leadership of Armand J. Piron, contributed effectively to the success of the Smart Set show." Whitney reported, "Our engagement was not only a financial success, but it was also the social event of the season . . . A sumptuous banquet was spread for the Smart Set Company at Vic DuBois' new place, corner Gravier and Rampart streets, by the Young Men's Social Club . . . W. M. Benbow, well known in vaudeville circles, was the general manager." Also, "A. Metoyer, director of the Tuxedo

Indianapolis Freeman, December 20, 1913.

Indianapolis Freeman, January 16, 1915.

Indianapolis Freeman, January 16, 1915.

Brass Band, and wife entertained J. Homer Tutt, Blanche Thompson, Salem Tutt Whitney and Emma Jackson at a gumbo dinner."[139]

In February 1915, Whitney was proud to announce that, "'I'm Neutral,' written and composed by T. L. Corwell, J. Homer Tutt and your correspondent, is a decided hit everywhere."[140] Later that summer, Bert Williams recorded "I'm Neutral" for the Columbia Graphophone Company.

At the Lafayette Theater in Harlem, toward the end of the season, Whitney's Smart Set attracted such notables in the audience as Bert

HOMER TUTT AND BLANCHE THOMPSON,
With Smart Set Co., Lyceum Theater, Jan. 18, 19, 20.

Indianapolis Freeman, January 16, 1915.

Williams, Bill "Bojangles" Robinson, James Reese Europe, Abbie Mitchell, Chris Smith, and Dr. W. E. B. Du Bois.[141] At the Grand Theater in Chicago in December, Sylvester Russell labeled Whitney's Smart Set "the largest and best colored show on the road . . . it has a place second only to the late Cole or Hogan and Williams & Walker. Surely J. Lubrie Hill has never exceeded this production and Dudley never had one to equal it."[142]

Whitney's Smart Set had reached the top of the African American entertainment world. Back down South, upstart companies were beginning to trade on the Smart Set name. Whitney first complained about this practice at the end of 1914:

> Word reaches us that a company of colored players are touring the South and in an effort to delude the public and maintain a parasitical existence from the reputation of this company, are styling themselves as the Northern Smart Set Company, under the management of a man named Tolliver . . . [T]he purloining of our title by Mr. Tolliver gives us little concern. However, our management may ask for a reckoning. The fact that he is giving employment to some boys and girls who need it compensates somewhat for his latrociny [*sic*] and makes him welcome to this bit of advertisement.[143]

Three weeks later, Alexander Tolliver posted a response from Gadsden, Alabama:

> On seeing an article in The Freeman wherein you accused me of using the name "Smart Set" in an effort to delude the public, will state in reply that I became a member of this company last April . . . known as Chas. Collier's Smart Set, under canvas . . . I did not bring the name with me or have anything to do with organizing the show. It is their show and I presume they can call it anything they like . . . But so far as I am concerned, I have no desire whatever to use the name Smart Set. Have not and will not at any time . . . I am prepared to fight life's battles and I trust you will not mislead the public any more by using my name through the theatrical journals in such a manner.

Whitney let the matter slide until the fall of 1915, when he discovered that Tolliver's Smart Set was playing just ahead of him in North Carolina. He lashed out in his "Seen and Heard While Passing" column of November 13, 1915:

> Last season we had occasion to remonstrate with one Mr. Tolliver, who was at the time playing Atlanta, Ga., with a company of which Tolliver was the head, for the illegal use of the title, "Smart Set." His answer, denying

that he had appropriated the title, and that he did not need to resort to the theft of the title to gain popularity and money, was published in The Freeman.

Since that time I have received circulars and bills with this heading: "Coming, Tolliver's Smart Set Company, the Greatest Colored Show on Earth." Since the beginning of our Southern tour Tolliver has made it his business to play his company in towns just ahead of the real and only Smart Set. Not satisfied with filching a title and traveling on the merits of another and better company, he has circulated reports . . . that his was the No. 1 Smart Set company and that the legitimate company following was the No. 2. If this be true, Mr. Tolliver is not only a plagiarist but a perjurer, and without the honor that is sometimes accredited to thieves.

The Smart Set company is the oldest established company of colored players extant and well merits the distinction of being the greatest of all colored shows, so Mr. Tolliver's canvas aggregation of 10 and 20-cent players has done us little injury. I am personally acquainted with many of the performers employed by Mr. Tolliver and I know them to be first class in their line of work. They are in no wise responsible for Mr. Tolliver's latrociny [*sic*] and this knowledge has led me to restrain my management from legitimately persecuting their manager. At present Mr. Tolliver's company is playing "Dodge" time, dodging the real Smart Set Company and its great show, "George Washington Bullion Abroad."

Two weeks later Tolliver shot back:

Now in regards to the name Smart Set. I think the name can be used by any one that sees fit to use it. It is being used by the Smart Set Athletic Club of New York; also the Smart Set Base Ball Club of Brooklyn, N. Y. A club of young ladies of Back Bay in Boston, Mass., call themselves the Smart Set. We also have a very noted magazine called Smart Set. P. T. Barnum had a circus show, also the Ringling Bros. Mr. Whitney has a Smart Set. Why not I? . . . It's not the name that I am using that's worrying you; it's all these real performers that deliver the goods and this truly great show that is the talk of the universe. My show just suits the public in every particular. That's why I turn them away at each and every performance . . . Can you rehash George Washington Bullion and make it stand such a test?

With a simple question—"Why not I?"—Alexander Tolliver demolished the sovereignty of the title "Smart Set." To bolster his claim to it, Tolliver provided a list of his "real performers that deliver the goods":

Evelyn White, Nettie Perry, Ramsey and Brown, sister team; Clara Smith, Grant and Grant, Poteete and Hawthorne, Legge and McGinty, sister team; Frank Chapman, Rainey and Rainey, Lewis Bros, Trixie Smith, Wells and Wells, Eddie (Peg) Lightfoot, Williams and Williams, Joddy Edwards, King Williams and dogs, Walton Duo, H. H. Puggsley, Barringer and Barringer, Aaron Tolliver, (Buzzin) Wayne Burton, Frank Jackson, Ada Lockhart, Wooden and Wooden, Alexander Lovejoy, Madam Tolliver and myself and eight piece orchestra. Managers that know these people, know their ability as performers.[144]

Tolliver's troupe was an unabashedly *southern* Smart Set. Most of the performers were southerners, and they were a force to be reckoned with on the southern road show routes. From 1914 to 1917, Tolliver consistently presented blues and jazz artists of the highest caliber to huge, predominantly black audiences in most every section of the South.

Alexander Tolliver was a visionary producer and manager, but not in the spirit of musical comedy that had long been associated with the name "Smart Set." Tolliver's Smart Set was a freewheeling variety show that initiated the era of blues and jazz in tented minstrelsy. By 1914, when Tolliver's Smart Set came of age, blues was being routinely featured in black vaudeville houses. But Tolliver went one step further, to harness the commercial energies of blues and jazz in a barnstorming "blues revue." His big tent was extraordinary in many different ways, but it was perhaps most important as a platform for the wider popularization of female blues singers and "shouters" in the style later referred to as "classic blues."

After seeing Tolliver's Smart Set in Richmond, Virginia, during the summer of 1915, S. H. Dudley informed the *Freeman*:

> I had the opportunity to witness the best show under canvas I ever saw, in Toliver's [*sic*] Smart Set . . . If more of our colored shows would copy after the Toliver bunch, it would help to elevate the Negro profession. The show is the talk of Richmond and playing to capacity every night. I must give Mr. Toliver great credit from a showman's standpoint. To begin with, it is the first canvas show I ever saw without a band and parade. I myself, with all of these year's experience, would have thought it foolish to even think of such a thing; next, had he told me that I could make money by charging 10 cent admission, I would have laughed at him, but if you could only see this tent, with a seating capacity of 3,000 and can stand at least 300 more, he has about half of the seats reserved for 10 cent extra and all you can hear is 'I was down to the Smart Set last night and could not get in.' The company is now in its third week there. The reason for doing so well is that the show is well staged, the chorus work is snappy, costumes are good, the vaudeville is good also, but a little too long. The redeeming feature of the vaudeville is that it is a variety. He has three novelty acts to blend the bill. If managers of colored theatres would put on the same kind of bill, they would do well or much better. Toliver himself appears to good advantage in the show and taking things as a whole, he is responsible for the success of the company . . . I can only say that it was a great show and will continue to have success for they have what the public wants and at the right price.[145]

Dudley was quick to insert that he did not approve of Tolliver "infringing on the title 'Smart Set,' for we all know who made the name 'Smart Set' famous . . . [I]f Mr. Toliver would just change the name of his show, it would be a wise move and . . . get him just as much money, for he has got a great show."

After crossing paths with Tolliver's Smart Set during the closing weeks of 1915, even Salem Tutt Whitney had to admit that Tolliver had "a very good canvas show":

> A night's lay-off in Montgomery, Ala., gave many members of our company an opportunity to see Mr. Tolliver's show, which was closing a week's engagement in that city. All agreed that they had been enjoyably entertained. My brother, J. Homer Tutt, stated that . . . the performance was full of "pep" and "ginger" from start to finish . . .
>
> The above does not excuse Mr. Tolliver from using the Smart Set title. It took us time, labor and money to make the Smart Set title a by-word in the South. The title "Smart Set" stands for the highest achievement in the theatrical art with colored people the country over. The idea of seeing the Smart Set show for 10 and 20 cents, no doubt, contributed largely to the enormous crowds Mr. Tolliver claims attended his shows.[146]

Born in Richmond, Virginia, in 1887, Alexander Tolliver made his initial impression on the entertainment profession as a novelty artist, specializing in trick roller skating, particularly buck and wing dancing on skates.[147] He and wife Mabel were active as early as 1908, when they toured with

Downie's Uncle Tom's Cabin Company, as members of a vocal sextet.[148] Their roller skating act was first noted in the fall of 1909, when they were billed as the "Whirlwind Tollivers."[149]

Toward the end of 1910 the Tollivers were making the rounds of black Midwestern vaudeville houses, in a trio that included Alexander Tolliver's alleged brother Jesse. At the Monogram Theater in Chicago a correspondent advised, "The Tolliver Trio was a merry singing, dancing and comedy act. Al and Jessie Tolliver are two young roller skaters who dance with much agility of suppleness, and Mabel Tolliver, who is the happy possessor of a great voice like Anna Cook Pankey, won great applause, and if she were a cultivated singer she would be unrivaled."[150] In her role as a variety stage Black Patti, Mabel Tolliver became known for her interpretations of "The Holy City," "Last Night Was the End of the World," J. Rosamond Johnson's "Bleeding Moon," and other "classy" songs.

In 1911 Tolliver performed his roller skating act with the Down In Dixie Minstrels, and the following year he and Mabel traveled with J. H. Boyer's Fashion Plate Minstrels. In November 1912 they appeared at the Auditorium Theater in Philadelphia: "Tolliver, the sensational roller skater, won much admiration for the many difficult figures he cut in his act."[151] A few weeks later the Tolliver Trio made an appearance at the Crescent Theater in New York City: "Madame Tolliver is heard to good advantage in her feature number 'If All My Dreams Were Made Of Gold.'"[152]

Sylvester Russell's "Chicago Weekly Review" column of October 11, 1913, contained this garbled description: "The Tolliver Trio was among the new faces seen at the Monogram Monday night, with a crippled comedian who really danced, a prima donna who actually sang, and a roller skater who virtually danced." The following week the *Freeman* noted, "The one-legged comedian of the Tolliver Trio, who collapsed on the stage of the Monogram Theater on the last day of his engagement, is reported to have gone violently insane." This report likely refers to Eddie "Peg" Lightfoot, the one-legged dancer who became an important feature with Tolliver's Smart Set.

Toward the end of 1913, Alex and Mabel Tolliver began an abbreviated season with P. G. Lowery's Dixie Fashion Plate Minstrels.[153] In Iowa during the early weeks of 1914, "Mabelle Tolliver was seen rehearsing a new skating act."[154] Lowery's Dixie Fashion Plate Minstrels closed their season on February 1, 1914.[155] Some time between April and August 1914, Tolliver began his fateful association with C. W. Park, an ambitious white financier of African American minstrel enterprises. An advertisement appeared in the *Freeman* of July 18, 1914, seeking "first class colored performers in all lines" for C. W. Park's Musical Comedy Company of Charlotte, North Carolina. An August 22, 1914, correspondence from this company identified C. W. Park as its sole owner; Charles Collier as manager; Tolliver as stage manager; and clarinet legend William "King" Phillips as orchestra leader. One highlight of the show during this time was a "Tango Contest," in which members of the company "select their partners from the audience . . . and to music furnished by Director King Phillip's capable musicians, each couple in turn dances the latest steps. A handsome or suitable prize is awarded by the management."

During the fall of 1914, Park's Musical Comedy Company rolled through the Carolinas, performing to turn-away crowds under a tent that

MADAM TOLLIVER, PRIMA DONA Tollivers Smart Set Co.

Tollivers' Smart Set Company, that show that made such a hit upon its last appearance in this city will again raise their tents on Brook Avenue and Mitchell Streets. Little need be said of this wonderful aggregation as they are known throughout the country as the largest and best colored show on the road. Since the last appearance here a large number of new faces has been added to the already large troupe.

Director Tolliver says he now has the largest colored show that ever appeared under canvas. In addition to the new acts on the program, every face seen on their last appearance in this city will again appear behind the footlights to greet their many friends.

The price for the show is always the same, 10 cents to everyone and 10 cents extra for reserved seats. Special matinees for ladies and children Thursday and Saturday, 3:00 P. M. Matinee prices, 10 cents to everyone. No extra charges for reserved seats.

Show grounds located Brook Avenue and Mitchell Streets.

Richmond Planet, October 2, 1915.

reportedly accommodated more than twelve hundred people. The strong lineup featured Evelyn White, "America's foremost coon shouter." White apparently never made commercial sound recordings; nevertheless, she was a central figure in the popular ascent of the blues. She often teamed with Bessie Smith and other legendary blues queens in southern vaudeville houses and tent shows. White scored what was probably her greatest success during the mid-1920s, as "the famous Dixie blues singer" with the *Silas Green from New Orleans* show. Also on Tolliver's bill was the husband-and-wife team of Grant and Grant, baritone Isaiah and soubrette Leola. Later known as "Coot" Grant, Leola had been on the stage since early childhood. She recalled how, at age seven, she was drafted into a minstrel company headed by the Cheatham Brothers, and traveled to Europe with them in 1901 as a "pickaninny dancer."[156]

Park's roster grew so large during the month of October 1914 that a correspondent quipped, "If another dozen come on next week we will have to change the name of the show to 'Ben Hur.'" Newcomers included Henry and Loretta Wooden, with their novelty unicycle act; and Prof. A. A. Wright, cornetist, who had recently completed his first season as director of the sideshow annex band with Sparks Brothers' Circus.

Another addition was the "husband-and-wife" team of Jones and Jones, "exponents of genteel comedy . . . always a hit and their act is never complete without singing the 'Blues.'" The male member of this team was Happy Jones, a "clever comedian, singer and dancer." The female member was Clara Smith: "Among the members of the company she is affectionately called 'Miss Blue.'"[157] A *Freeman* ad of November 28, 1914, described her as "A Rattling Good Talker and Queen of the 'Blues.'"

An outstanding blues recording artist of the 1920s, Clara Smith had appeared on black vaudeville stages in the Carolinas and Georgia as early as 1911. Her name was associated with blues singing in black theater reports as early as 1912, when she went on the road with the Billy King Stock Company. In 1913 she toured as a single on the fledgling S. H. Dudley Theater Circuit. With Park's Musical Comedy Company in November 1914, Clara Smith was "stopping the show. She sings all kinds of 'Blues,' and it's a common occurrence for her to receive a silver shower, as the South is 'Blues' crazy."[158]

Backed by C. W. Park's "unlimited resources," Alexander Tolliver produced a show that held great power over southern audiences of both races. An update from Augusta, Georgia, appeared in the *Freeman* of November 28, 1914: "Both white and colored pay numerous visits to the big show and pronounce it the best ever. New costumes from the New York costume house arrived last week and are quite an elaborate addition to the ensemble numbers. Business is still above the average. This is our final week for the big waterproof pavilion, as we go from here to the capital city of Atlanta and play the Morton theater indefinitely."[159]

For the season of 1915, owner C. W. Park removed his name from the marquee. Notices and advertisements in the *Freeman* now referred to "Tolliver's Big Show," while handbills and ads in local black community papers en route announced the coming of "Tolliver's Smart Set."

Given free rein, Tolliver developed a unique concept in entertainment, something that was never reproduced on a comparable scale—a variety show that blended his legendary roster of blues singers and jazz musicians with the most ambitious African American "novelty" lineup that had ever been assembled. Tolliver's prototypal "blues revue" was also rife with "Acrobats, Trapeze Artists, Bicycle and Unicycle Experts, Roman Ring Wonders, Hoop Controllers and Barrel Jumpers," wonderful acts whose rightful place in the mainstream American circus was barred by impenetrable racial segregation.

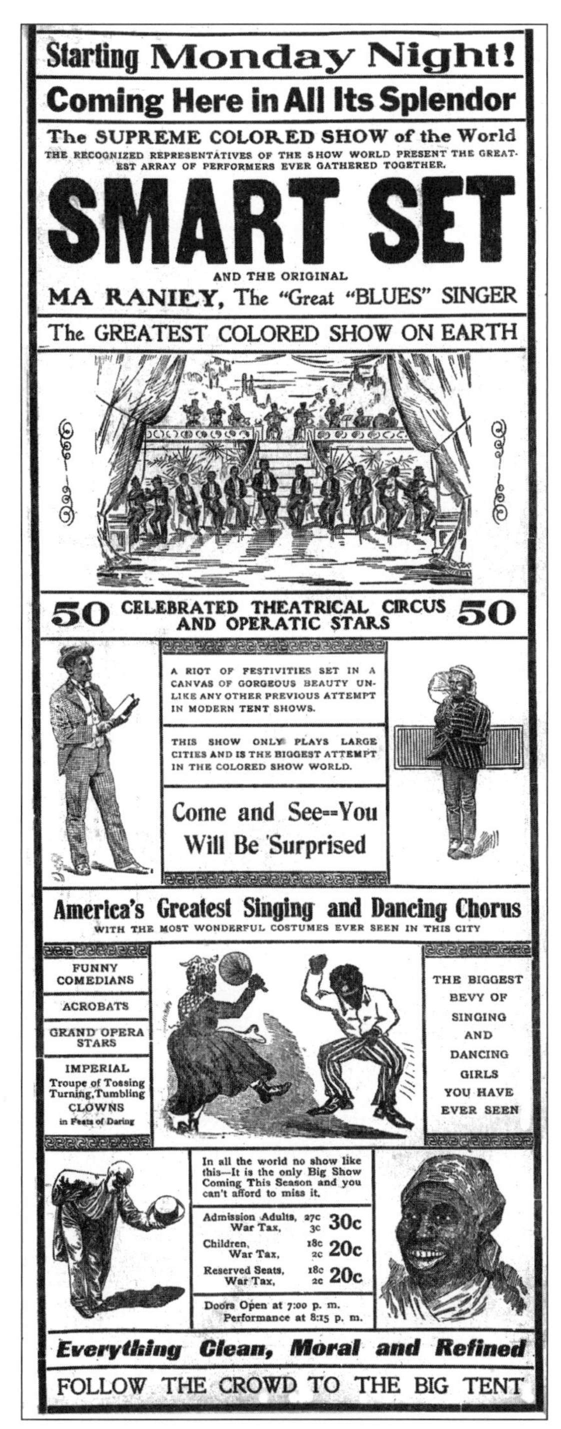

Handbill for Tolliver's Smart Set. (courtesy Chicago History Museum)

The Tolliver show opened in late March 1915, playing through the Carolinas. On May 1, 1915, the *Freeman* carried this ad:

> WANTED! For Tolliver's Big Show, The Largest and Most Complete Colored Show in Existence. Novelty Acts of every description . . . Good singers and dancers; I want singers who can really sing and dancers who can really dance. This is positively the largest colored show on the road, backed by real money and brains . . . We play week stands, one show a night, no parades . . . Address all communications to Alex. Tolliver, care Tolliver's Big Show, Charlotte, North Carolina.

The proliferation of future race recording greats on Tolliver's roster is uncanny. Clara Smith and "Coot" Grant, holdovers from the previous season, were joined in 1915 by sixteen-year-old Jodie Edwards, originally of Marietta, Georgia, and fifteen-year-old Susie Hawthorne of Pensacola, Florida. During their two years with the Tolliver show, Edwards usually sang and danced with Eddie "Peg" Lightfoot, while Hawthorne typically did her singing, dancing, and talking in a "sister team," coupled with Ma Rainey, Evelyn White, or some other Tolliver soubrette. Edwards and Hawthorne later admitted that they had "started living together as husband and wife" while traveling with Tolliver but had not yet teamed up on stage.[160] They later became famous as Butterbeans and Susie.

When William and Gertrude Rainey joined Tolliver's ranks in 1915, "Pa" Rainey was chronically ill, and he was rarely in condition to perform. On the other hand, "Ma" Rainey, who was already one of the better known "coon shouters" in the South, rose to prominence as the premier blues star of Tolliver's Smart Set, billed as "The Assassinator of the Blues."

Butterbeans and Susie. (courtesy Hogan Jazz Archive, Tulane University)

H. B. Howard, known as "Caggie" or "Keg," was Tolliver's musical director and pianist for the 1915 season. Howard had recently completed an extended tenure at Charles Bailey's Arcade Theater in Atlanta. Other members of Tolliver's band included trombone great Freddie Pratt and "sensational trap drummer" Willie "Tutan" Richardson, who assured *Freeman* readers, "I'm from Mobile, Ala., but feature the Memphis Blues."[161]

Alexander Tolliver was an avid student of choreography. Dance was a primary component of the Big Show, which featured such premier eccentric dance specialists as "national champion" one-legged dancer "Peg" Lightfoot and the revered "King Nappie" Lewis. In a latter-day conversation with Berta Wood, Leola "Coot" Grant rated King Nappie "in the genius class" of dancers. She recalled how he had patterned a dance routine "from the natural walk of Ma Rainey's husband, Pa Rainey. Coot demonstrated and it was hilariously funny . . . The head moves forward and back like a duck walking in a slow, easy . . . manner."[162]

Tolliver's dance program also included the stellar team of Wayne "Buzzin" Burton and Frank D. Jackson, who joined the show on July 5, 1915.[163] Burton was the acknowledged "King of Buzzin'," a dance step said to be the predecessor of Truckin'.[164] He and teenaged Bessie Smith had barnstormed together over black vaudeville theater routes for more than a year, beginning in the spring of 1912.[165] Burton's present partner, alternately billed as "Little" Frank Jackson and "Clever" Frank Jackson, eventually "personalized" the spelling of his last name and became known as Frankie "Half Pint" Jaxon, cabaret star and prolific race recording artist.[166]

For the season of 1915, Tolliver's Big Show performed in a 160-foot round-top tent, seating 3,000 people, with a forty-foot stage. The show's opening chorus, which included thirty-two performers, was a special focus of Tolliver's musical production talents.[167] Famous African American trapeze specialist Al Wells headed the company's impressive array of novelty artists, and he became Tolliver's right-hand man, ascending to the role of "general superintendent and master of transportation." Wells also served as the company's faithful *Freeman* correspondent, and his communications of 1915 and 1916 document Tolliver's great achievements.

Wells described Tolliver's most radical stage innovation: "One of the features of the big show is our stage in the center. When Tolliver first spoke of this last season a number of performers and managers as well, said it would never go, the public wouldn't stand for it, a stage in the center without scenery don't look the part. Well, Mr. Tolliver is making it go. It is all in knowing how. The singing and dancing chorus numbers put on by Tolliver are making a great hit, and are a big surprise to the profession. I think the stage in the center has come to stay."[168] In the early 1950s, singer and dancer Artie Bell McGinty recalled to jazz historian Charles Edward Smith that Tolliver's chorus numbers had been presented "in the round, with four groups of dancers to face the four quadrants of the audience."[169]

The show was in North Carolina in June 1915 when Wells declared, "It takes three cars to carry our outfit now, and to see the glad rags the bunch are wearing, it doesn't look as if there was a 'panic on.'" Wells went on to note, "Mr. Tolliver never fails to make the audience roar, with his jailhouse monologue."[170]

On June 28, 1915, Tolliver's Smart Set commenced the first of two brilliant weeklong summer

AL WELLS.

Al Wells, general superintendent of Alexander Tolliver's big show, the largest colored show under canvas, was made a 32nd degree Ancient and Accepted Scottish Rite Mason in Atlanta Consistory, Friday night, Nov. 17. He is also the well-known novelty artist and with the assistance of the Gaines brothers, does seven different novelty acts. They are featuring their wonderful double trapeze act which has been a sensation all season.

Indianapolis Freeman, November 25, 1916.

runs in Richmond, Virginia, Tolliver's hometown, where their audience base was expanded by a National Negro Exposition taking place at the State Fairgrounds. Tolliver pitched his tent at Thirtieth and Q Streets, and then at Mitchell Street and Brook Avenue. Both appearances were well advertised in the local black weekly *Richmond Planet*.

Through August and September the show continued its sensational run in Virginia with a series of engagements in the Tidewater region, where Rainey and Rainey were said to be "going great nightly." The Raineys were already well

"THE SMART SET" COMING

Tolliver's Smart Set Co., the largest and best colored show on the road, will arrive here tomorrow to commence a week's engagement, commencing Monday, 28. This company carries 80 colored performers, the best in the business, also a water-proof canvass seating over 5,000 people. All of the best novelty acts of the race are with this show. Wells and Wells, trapee performers, keeps the audience holding their breath, with their dare-devil feats in mid-air. The Woodens, trick bicycle riders, are the best on the road today. H. H. Pugsley, the barrel jumping acrobat, is the best of his race and keeps you laughing all the while. Alex Tolliver, the producer of the show, is of Richmond birth, and can be seen here in his fancy skating act. Mme. Tolliver, the prima dona, has a voice that is in competition with "Black Pattie." The Hamtree Chorus, containing over 80 voices, assisted by a large orchestra, makes music that one seldom has the chance to hear. The "Big Tent" will be located on 30th Street, between Q and R Streets. The admission price is 10 cents to every one and 10 cents for reserved seats. Doors open at 7 P. M. Performance starts at 8:30 prompt.

Richmond Planet, June 26, 1915.

known in these parts, having played the Lyric Theater in Newport News for nearly six months back in 1911. Al Wells reported from Newport News in August 1915:

> As usual the musical numbers are going great and Tolliver's big show is a by-word in every household and street corner . . . On Saturday night, the 14th, after our regular performance, there was a buzzin' contest held between Buzzin' Burton and a performer known as Dollar Bill. The audience was to decide who was the winner by applause and before the show we were told it was impossible for Burton to win, as Dollar Bill had his crowd and sure enough he won with his crowd. But if Dollar Bill would consent with Burton somewhere that neither one is known, Dollar Bill would run a poor second.[171]

While they were showing in Newport News, Ma Rainey, Clara Smith, and other female members of the show were initiated into the Majestic Lodge of the Court of Calanthe. In September 1915 Clara Smith and Leola Grant formed a "sister team" and left the Tolliver show to try their luck in vaudeville.[172] Buzzin' Burton also returned to vaudeville, leaving Clever Frank Jackson to form a new team with "dainty little singing and dancing soubrette" Nettie Perry, enacting "a little boy and black face wench."[173]

During a return engagement in Richmond in September 1915, Trixie Smith joined Tolliver's ranks, performing the blackface monologue and blues songs that had already made her popular in vaudeville. In October, after an extraordinary seventeen weeks' stay in Virginia, Tolliver's Big Show closed at Roanoke and headed south, ahead of the encroaching winter weather: "This show has left a warm path for other shows to follow in the state of Virginia."[174] They were dropping through the Carolinas when Al Wells first hailed, "Ma Rainey assassinates the blues."[175]

Early in November Wells wrote from South Carolina, communicating Tolliver's ambitions for the season to come: "After such a tremendous success this season with his show, Mr. Alexander Tolliver has decided to put before the public the

TOLLIVER'S SMART SET RETURNS

Tolliver's Smart Set Company, the show that made such a big hit with everybody upon its appearance under canvas in our city is here for a return engagement. This show is positively the largest Colored show in America and there is little doubt that they will enjoy a large patronage. The Management announces the addition of several new acts which make an added attraction to the theatre goers of Richmond. The large water proof tent will be located on Churchhill, corner Q. and 30 Streets.

The price of admission will remain the same 10 cents to everybody and 10 cents extra for reserved seats.

Special matinees will be given Thursday and Saturday at 3 P. M. for the ladies and children—matinee price ten cents, with no extra charge for reserved seats.

Richmond Planet, September 25, 1915. The photo captures Tolliver in formal attire and roller skates.

largest aggregation ever attended by a colored manager—a Negro circus—and he deserves great credit for undertaking such a large job. He wants to hear from all colored novelty acts suitable for a circus. Watch The Freeman for his ad."[176]

A few weeks later, the *Freeman* published a grandiloquent announcement from Tolliver himself: "I am now preparing to put before the public the largest and grandest colored show ever on earth, employing nearly two hundred colored artists, no whites . . . I am going to present for the public's approval, the first and only negro circus."[177] Tolliver made a point of employing only African American workers, even in such positions as ticket sellers, ushers, and property men, positions that most white-owned black touring companies delegated to whites.

Meanwhile, Tolliver's Big Show/Smart Set continued its southerly course. At Macon, Georgia, "singing and dancing soubrette" Susie Hawthorne was "cleaning up nightly singing 'The Memphis Blues' and 'That Animal Rag.'"[178] At Mobile, Alabama, "On Thanksgiving day after the show we were all surprised by being invited to a big turkey dinner given by the manager . . . A large table was spread on the stage, seating the entire company, canvass men and all. We were served in first class style by Ma Rainey . . . We all had a lovely time and enjoyed ourselves very much. It was in the wee small hours of the morning when we all departed for home."[179]

During the course of their Mobile engagement, "We also met the Whitney Smart Set . . . and a number of them was out to the big top to see the show on Saturday night . . . The weather was a little cool the first part of the week, but turned warm the last half. The big top was heated with eight big salamanders which made it very pleasant. Everything is still running smoothly and everyone is still holding on, as what we understand from reliable parties things are not very pleasant in vaudeville at present, and here the ghost walks every week."[180]

With the close of their touring season in sight, Al Wells reflected on the booming success of Tolliver's Big Show/Smart Set: "Any time that you give the people just what they like at a price that reaches them all, you are going to get the crowd. When you produce a show with a big opening and closing musical number, and run down a ten to twelve-act olio, change your shows each night with the admission only 10 and 20 cents you have given the public what they want."[181]

On December 6, 1915, "the Big Show invaded New Orleans, and yes, friends, it was a riot . . . On Monday night when the doors were open the crowd extended back for a whole block at 7:45 we stopped selling tickets and turned away more people than we had on the inside and when the curtain rose we received a grand ovation. The show is the talk of the city and the colored people here say it is the greatest show to ever play here, barring none."[182]

Indianapolis Freeman, December 25, 1915.

Tolliver and company established their winter headquarters in New Orleans, where they remained open to good business. The *Freeman*'s "Special Christmas Issue" for 1915 included a three-quarter page spread on Tolliver's upcoming Circus and Musical Extravaganza. Before the end of the year, the big new four-pole "white top" that would house the "Negro Circus" arrived, and there was word that three "auto trucks" had been purchased to haul the show to and from the railroad cars in which it would travel.[183]

On January 1, 1916, "After ten successful months under canvas the big show opened a two weeks' engagement in the Temple Theater . . . to the biggest crowd this theater has played to for many years."[184] Tolliver's Big Show/Smart Set was held over at the Temple Theater for three additional weeks. Halfway through the extended engagement Al Wells noted, "There are a number of performers singing the 'blues' but when Ma Rainey sings them, nuff said. She has to take three or four bows every night."[185] In addition, "A short drama by Ma Rainey, Mrs. Susie Edwards, Arthur Williams, Eddie Love and Joddie Edwards made a big hit."[186]

During the course of their winter's stay in New Orleans, members of Tolliver's company acquainted themselves with the local scene, attending dances at St. Katherine's Hall and

LUELLA WELLS.

Of the team of Wells and Wells, the first and only lady of her race to perform on high trapeze. For the past nine months they have been with Tolliver's big show, doing two acts, one on the stage under cork and the other working from the top of tent closing this act with a headspin and a forty-foot flying breakaway, which has been one of the feature acts and a sensation on the show. They are booked for Tolliver's Negro Circus, season 1916.

Indianapolis Freeman, December 25, 1915.

Magnolia Brown!

Singing and Dancing Comediene

Just clcsed a successful season with Tolliver's Big Show Will be seen on Tolliver's Circus and Musical Extravaganza Season 1916

A Merry Christmas to All Friends.

Luella Albert

Wells and Wells

Trapeze Artists

Original, Unique, Sensational; a Novelty of Comedy and Skill

A Merry Christmas to All Friends

RAINEY & RAINEY

Assassinators of the Blues. Just closing a successful seasrn with Tolliver's Big Show. Booked with Tolliver's Circus and Musical Extravaganza Season 1916. A Merry Christmas to all Friends

Indianapolis Freeman, December 25, 1915.

haunting the various cabarets and vaudeville theaters along South Rampart Street, where they reportedly encountered Virginia Liston and Hambone Jones, Lena Leggett, Little Willie Jackson, Harry Bonner, Beulah Henderson, Alma Hughes, and other memorable performers.[187]

At least one of the local cabaret performers, Lena Leggett, was recruited for Tolliver's Circus and Musical Extravaganza. Though little remembered today, Lena Leggett and her two younger sisters, Josephine and Henrietta, all became well-known soubrettes of the 1920s. Other new "finds"

Indianapolis Freeman, August 26, 1916.

included the Gaines Brothers, a New Orleans–based novelty team whose specialties included "acrobatics, wire-walking and barrel and fire escape." In combination with the Woodens and Wells and Wells, they formed an unprecedented "Afro-American acrobatic troupe."

New Orleans was a particularly advantageous place to assemble a band in 1916, and Tolliver put together a stunning collection of jazz pioneers: Fred Kewley, clarinet and leader; Willie Hightower, cornet; Alvin "Zoo" Robertson, trombone; David Jones, mellophone; H. B. "Caggie" Howard, piano; J. W. Craddock, string bass and tuba; and Eddie "Rabbit" Robinson, drums.

Fred and Elizabeth Kewley joined Tolliver's rehearsals in February 1916: "Mr. and Mrs. Fred Kewley have arrived and they take hold just like two veterans. The band and orchestra are cleaning up with all the numbers."[188] Kewley may be one of the most important forgotten figures in early jazz history. He was professionally active by 1909, when he toured with Pat Chappelle's *A Rabbit's Foot* Company. In October 1909 he joined A. G. Allen's Minstrels, and toured with them for the next two years. During that time he was featured in a popular saxophone quartet which also included William "King" Phillips. For the season of 1911–1912, Kewley served as orchestra director and clarinet soloist with Eph Williams's Big City Minstrels. He married Elizabeth, a singer from Savannah, Georgia, on November 10, 1912, and they traveled together in 1914 with the *Silas Green from New Orleans* Company, with Fred in charge of the band and orchestra. Kewley returned to A. G. Allen's Minstrels for most of 1915, then signed with Tolliver.

WILLIE HIGHTOWER

Great [illegible] Cornetist's with Alexander Tolliver's Big Show

Indianapolis Freeman, July 1, 1916.

FRED. KEWLEY

Fred Kewley, the orchastra leader of Tolliver's Smart Set Company, is undoubtedly the premier Colored clarinetist of today, in or out of the profession. He stands second to none in his line. Not only as an instrumentalist, but as a band and orchestra leader, having been brought up under the splendid leadership of three leading bandmasters from the Kneller Hall College of Music, London, England. He is a native of British Gaians, South America

Indianapolis Freeman, September 16, 1916.

Alvin "Zoo" Robertson. (courtesy Hogan Jazz Archive, Tulane University)

Eddie "Rabbit" Robinson. (courtesy Hogan Jazz Archive, Tulane University)

David Jones, *Louisiana Weekly*, April 10, 1926. (courtesy Amistad Research Center)

R. (KEGG) HOWARD,

Indianapolis Freeman, December 28, 1912.

J. W. Craddock, *Indianapolis Freeman*, December 31, 1910.

Trombonist Alvin "Zoo" Robertson was born in New Orleans in 1891. He was identified in the *Freeman* of January 30, 1915, as a member of the local community-based Young Olympia Orchestra, along with John Marrero, Simon Marrero, Jimmie Noone, Dave Depass, Joseph Saturnin, and Buddy Petit: "These boys are hot as mustard." Robertson toured with Kit Carson's Buffalo Ranch Wild West Annex Band before joining Tolliver's Big Show. He is best remembered for having recorded with Jelly Roll Morton in 1923.

Legendary mellophone player turned saxophonist David Jones was born in Lutcher, Louisiana, about forty-five miles upriver from New Orleans, around 1888.[189] Jones's year with the Tolliver show marks the visible beginnings of his illustrious professional career. Shortly after touring with Tolliver, Jones played with Fate Marable's Band on the riverboat *Capitol* before joining King Oliver's Band in Chicago in 1921. With cornetist R. Q. Dickerson, Jones headed Robinson's Syncopators, one of the most celebrated black jazz bands of the early 1920s. After touring the Pantages Theater circuit, they became the Cotton Club Orchestra in 1925, recording for Columbia under that name, with Jones on alto saxophone.[190]

Jones went on to run a popular music school in New Orleans. In 1929, while playing with Lee Collins at the Astoria Gardens on South Rampart Street, the Jones and Collins Astoria Hot Eight recorded four sides regarded as jazz classics. Lee Collins had this recollection of Jones: "Davey could teach and play any instrument . . . While I was working in the District, he would come and sit in with my band and play any instrument that he picked up. One night I talked him into bringing his mellophone with him. I never heard so much mellophone barrelhouse playing before in my life."[191]

Cornetist Willie Hightower was born in Nashville, Tennessee, in 1889, and was brought to New Orleans at the age of six. His father and mother were both musicians. His early musical influences included Freddie Keppard, King Oliver, and Arnold Metoyer. He played with Armand Piron's Band before joining the Tolliver show. As he recalled in a 1958 interview, "Somebody came into New Orleans for performers, scouting around, and they heard of me, and they wanted to hear me play. And that man was, his name was Alexander Tolliver. He was with the Smart Set; Mr. Parks [*sic*], what was Parks' name . . . C. W. Parks."[192]

Pianist H. B. "Caggie" Howard was originally from Norfolk, Virginia. He was active in southern vaudeville by 1910, when he was identified as the house pianist at the Luna Park Theater on Decatur Street in Atlanta. He went on to play at the "81" Theater on Decatur Street, preceding Eddie Heywood, Sr.

Drummer Eddie Robinson, known as "Rabbit," is believed to have been born in LaPlace, Louisiana, about twenty-five miles upriver from New Orleans, where he and trombonist Kid Ory came of age together as members of the Woodland Band, before 1910. Prior to joining Tolliver, he was playing at the Iroquois Theater on South Rampart Street. As Willie Hightower recalled in 1958, "Rabbit" Robinson was "a good one" who had studied with Walter Brundy, the highly respected drummer with John Robichaux's Orchestra.

Veteran circus annex and minstrel show bassist J. W. Craddock was summoned to Tolliver's Circus and Musical Extravaganza from Carrollton, Georgia. He started out with the show, but was replaced early in the season by New Orleanian John Porter. New Orleans cornetist Arnold Metoyer also rehearsed and even opened with the show, but withdrew shortly thereafter.

On February 15, 1916, Tolliver began rehearsals for his circus, while performers and band members continued to arrive from out of town. Among the late arrivals were Joe Jalvan and wife, the foremost African-American jugglers of the era. Jalvan had traveled through Australia and South Africa with Orpheus McAdoo before the turn of the century and had also performed in Europe. Another late addition was Daisy Martin, a former leading lady with S. H. Dudley's Smart Set and a future race recording artist.[193]

On Saturday, February 26, 1916, New Orleans witnessed the unveiling of Tolliver's Circus and Musical Extravaganza:

> [T]he doors of the big mammoth tent was thrown open to the public and the 5,000 people that passed through had the pleasure of seeing the greatest Negro show on earth, with a large stage in the center and people seated all around and with all kinds of aerial apparatus hanging at the top of the tent, with our band playing all the latest circus music, with Peg, the one legged clown, Slim Jones, our seven foot clown, assisted by seven others, and with our large chorus in elaborate costume, who are a sight to be seen. Mr. Tolliver has produced the greatest dancing chorus ever seen under canvas . . . the principle chorus workers are Misses Lena Leggett, Tressie Leggs, Artie Bell McGinty, Lizzie Kewley, Magnolia Brown, Susie Edwards, Rhoda McNeal, Gertrude Rainey, Mary Williams, Alice Gaines, and Mme. Tolliver. Arthur Williams, Jodie Edwards, two Lewis brothers, Wesley Michel, Charles H. Coffey, Eddie Love and John McNeal . . .
>
> The novelty acts are doing 14 different acts, seven acts the first half and seven the second half of the week . . .

CHARMING DAISY MARTIN
With Smart Set Company.

Richmond Planet, September 2, 1916.

> Ma Rainey, the assassinator of the blues, is still as popular as ever and was greeted with a big ovation . . .
>
> Alexander Tolliver deserves great credit for putting out such a large aggregation. It is a sensation to the colored profession. Tolliver is just a young man, 28 years of age, and only been ahead of a show as producer a few years. Yet year after year he has produced something different and all of his shows has met with great success, and with this show that he has this season he can rightly be called the Barnum of the Colored Race. The show is booked solid in the city of New Orleans for four weeks.[194]

The following week Al Wells reported:

We are on our second week in the big city and business is good. Sunday, the 5th, the new top was crowded. We are having the pleasure of seeing Madi Gras [*sic*]. Some of us have often heard of Madi Gras that is held in New Orleans each year. This year we are here to see it. The city is beautifully decorated. The streets are crowded with visitors, as thousands are coming in each day . . . There is a parade every night and day. The floats and costumes that are worn are very handsome. The king will visit the city Monday at noon. He will go to the mayor's office and get the key and Tuesday morning turn the city wide open. Pa Rainey said it is open wide enough now for him . . . Magnolia Brown is cleaning up nightly in her new act, that of impersonating Charley Chapman [*sic*]. Alex Tolliver, the animal trainer with his horse and camel is always a riot. The misfit army, Al Wells, Peg Lightfoot, Slim Jones and Joe Jalvan are a big hit and never fail to get a big laugh. The Jalvans wonder workers are in a class by themselves when it comes to juggling; they keep the audience wondering what they will do next. Madame Tolliver made a hit Sunday night singing two of the latest songs out . . . The dancing trio, the Lewis Bros. and Joddie Edwards, are cleaning up nightly; any buck dancer will certainly have to step some to beat them. Ma Rainey: Yes, she was there. Nuff said.[195]

In his next report, Wells touched on the events of Mardi Gras Day: "We won't forget it very soon, as on Monday and Tuesday, March 6 and 7, Tolliver had one of the auto trucks out with the bunch in it and we all had a fine time. Caggie Howard wanted to wear a mask, but Tolliver told him that it wasn't necessary, just look natural. Tolliver says he never realized what a band leader had to contend with until he became leader of his clown band. 'I don't know what other leaders use to lead their band with, but I use a baseball bat.'"[196]

Before leaving New Orleans, Tolliver polished his troupe to a hard shine. At every performance during their final week in New Orleans, "we had to widen the space for the white audience," which included such "prominent people as . . . G. W. Swan the circus man, and all of his performers, and they all say Tolliver has the newest novelty in show business."[197]

Tolliver's Smart Set opened in Mobile, Alabama, on March 20, 1916. A company correspondent described their reception: "The people here could hardly believe it was Tolliver's new show that had returned. The size of the tent, the new outfit and the large number of performers that he is carrying took them off their feet . . . It was reported after we left Mobile last November that Mr. Rainey and Eddie (Peg) Lightfoot had died, and when they entered the stage here they received a big ovation . . . Fred Kewley, the well-known clarinet player has his orchestra playing some very fine selections before the show each evening and has the audience calling for more."[198]

During the Mobile engagement, Ma Rainey appeared in a popular comedy act with Ed Love. While showing in Montgomery the following week, company members paid a visit to Howe's London Circus: "Ma Rainey wanted to join the elephants in their ball game, but Pa Rainey wouldn't let her."[199]

The 1916 edition of Tolliver's Smart Set was one of the most brilliant entertainments in the history of the African American stage. But, for all its grandeur and innovation, it fell short of Tolliver's advertised goal of an "all colored circus." There was no parade, no real menagerie, etc. Tolliver did not have the assistance of experienced circus veterans. Once his company left New Orleans, the word "circus" was rarely mentioned in his *Freeman* advertising and correspondence. Later in the season, Salem

Alex. Tolliver's
Big Show!
The Greatest Colored Show!
On Earth
A 4 Pole Tent
With a 40 Foot Stage in the Center
Something New and Novel
Having a Record of Showing to
36,000 People in One Week!
Featuring the Fastest
Singing & Dancing Chorus
Ever Produced
And Carry a Variety of Acts that are Above the Average

Maybelle Tolliver! Some Voice, Some Singer A BIG FEATURE On the Big Show

Eddie Peg Lightfoot The One Legged Dancing Wonder ALWAYS A RIOT

Elizabeth Kewley! Singing and Dancing Soubrette. Not the Greatest, but Holding her Own,

Lewis Bros. The Stepping Boys IN HIGH CLASS Buck and Eccentric Dancing

H. B. Howard Better Known as "Caggie" Pianist and Composer.

Prof. Fred. Kewley Clarinetist And Orchestra Leader.

Are a Few of the Acts that are Helping to Make
The Big Show Go!

Indianapolis Freeman, July 1, 1916.

Tutt Whitney offered these apt reflections: "The Tolliver aggregation contains more high-class Colored novelty acts than ever before assembled with a Colored company. However, this does not constitute Mr. Tolliver's idea of a Colored circus. The Colored circus bee is still buzzing underneath his bonnet. One of these days it will escape and the country will be electrified by the advent of a thrilling, hair-raising, nerve-shattering Colored circus."[200]

On April 3, 1916, Tolliver's Smart Set opened in Birmingham, Alabama, where Wells reported, "The city is full of performers. They were out to the big top at each rehearsal and those that were not working were out at night to see the show. Bruce & Bruce, Tommy Parker and Baby Mack, Perry and Washington, Hill Sisters and Claybourn Jones are some of the well-known performers that are here working."[201]

The following week they moved their tent to a location in West Birmingham. Wells reported extraordinarily good business:

> Monday night we turned them away and every night throughout the week the big tent was packed to the limit. 36,000 people paid admission in the six days, a record that is hard to beat. And yet Tolliver says the show is not big enough. He has purchased another [railroad] car, an 82-foot steel car. He says he don't intend to stop until he has a 10-car show . . .
>
> Each night we had 2000 or more white people, some of them the most prominent people of the city . . . There has been a great number of performers out to see the show and after they see it they shake their heads and say, "Tolliver has some show." The show is running like clock works, every act making it warm for the act following. Fred Kewley, clarionetist and orchestra leader, keeps in touch with the best musical publishing houses in this country . . . John L. Porter bass player, sends regards to Mose McQuitey. Davie Jones, melophonist, sends regards to J. H. McCammon of the Virginia Minstrels. Alvin Robinson sends regards to Robt. Stevenson and John Wilson . . . Eddie Robertson, drummer, sends regards to Armond J. Piron and Clarence Williams. Willie Hightower, cornetist, sends regards to Freddie Keppard, of the Creole Band.[202]

Shortly after this report was filed, Zoo Robertson left the show and went back to New

Orleans. That summer he signed on for a month-long tour with "a seven-piece ragtime Creole band" headed by Clarence Williams and A. J. Piron, and including Joe Oliver and Sidney Bechet.[203] Back in New Orleans that fall, he sent word that he was "now at local cabarets."[204]

During the week of April 17, 1916, Tolliver's Smart Set played in nearby Bessemer, and the week after they pitched their tent in South Birmingham, "making 4 weeks here in this city. That's going some for a big tent show that seats 5,000 people . . . such a large spread of canvass first surprises them, then when they get on the inside and see the stage in the center with seats all around it, two big grand stand [*sic*], all kinds of aerial apparatus hanging in the air and other things too numerous to mention, it gets them in that come again habit."[205] At a final location in Birmingham during the week of May 1, Al Wells noted, "Maybelle Tolliver, in classy and up-to-date songs, also Ma Rainey, singing the blues, never fail to score."[206]

On May 8, 1916, after seven weeks in Alabama, Tolliver opened in Atlanta to stiff competition: "a good show at 81 Theater, 91 Theater, feature pictures at the Auditorium and W. C. Handy's Band, the composer of the Memphis Blues, a very strong opposition. Yet we had a big, successful week." Wells made special note of "Peg Lightfoot and Edwards, a dancing team that will make them all step some. It is a three-legged dancing team that really delivers the goods." Also, "Ma Rainey still sings the blues and singing them as only Ma herself can sing them."[207]

There was a scent of trouble later that month when "Henry Wooden, the well-known bicyclist . . . closed with the big show to become manager of a big musical comedy company, not as large as the big show, but almost its equal. The name of the show will be Wooden's Bon Tons. Mr. Wooden has been successful in engaging some of the best acts in the colored profession."[208]

Henry Wooden's new enterprise was backed by "congenial and respective manager and owner" James A. Park, presumably related to Tolliver's backer, C. W. Park. The Bon Tons featured the same mix of blues singers and novelty acts that distinguished Tolliver's Smart Set. During the summer of 1916, the Bon Tons' two-piece orchestra paired pianist Lottie Frost with Tolliver's former drummer Willie "Tutan" Richardson: "They tear the house down nightly with their late orchestrations and cleans with 'The Memphis Blues.'"[209]

Henry and Loretta Wooden were not long gone from Tolliver's Big Show when Al Wells assured, "Mr. Wooden's place in the double trapeze act has been filled by Charlie Gaines and the act still continues to be a big hit." Reports from the Carolinas over the next few weeks informed that Susie Edwards and Ma Rainey had formed a team and that King Nappie Lewis and his brother were "doing a buck and eccentric dance in fine dress . . . Another feature of the show is Prof. Fred Kewley and his orchestra, as they play some heavy overtures that attract the attention of both colored and white people."[210]

From Raleigh, North Carolina, Wells reported, "The show is well-known and well liked here among both white and colored people . . . Ma Rainey is still there with the Blues. She has been appointed wardrobe mistress on the big show. The team of Lightfoot and Edwards has received some very popular songs lately. They haven't as yet decided what they will use, ragtime, or sentimental. I think Peg favors rag."[211]

On June 26, 1916, Tolliver's Big Show/Smart Set began a week's stand in Petersburg, Virginia, where, "after the opening night's show it was as Tolliver says in his monologue (Peaches to the World)."[212] From Petersburg they moved into the Tidewater area, where blues singer Clara Smith rejoined the show, less than a year after she and Leola Grant had left to work in vaudeville.[213] In the meantime, Clara Smith had reconnected with Happy Jones in a vaudeville troupe led by Buzzin' Burton, described in the *Freeman* of December 18, 1915: "Buzzin' Burton's funmakers, with Mamie Vaughn, this week at the Dixie Theater, Pacomope [*sic*, i.e., Pokomoke] City, Md. The company is Happy Jones and Clara Smith. Carrying my own pianist, Prof. Wm. Burton. Doing nicely. Regards to Frank Jackson."[214]

PEG LIGHTFOOT
Peg Leg Dancer with the Tollivers Smart Set Company.

Richmond Planet, August 5, 1916.

From Norfolk, Virginia, week of July 24, 1916, Al Wells informed: "Ma Rainey is singing several new songs and cleaning up as usual. Maybelle Tolliver is still scoring big in classic songs. Clara Smith, the well known coon shouter, is still putting them over in great shape. King Nappie Lewis, the buck dancer, is another one that is getting his (some stepper). Leggs & McGinty, sister team, never fails to do 15 minutes of laughter. Also Peg Lightfoot & Edwards, a laugh from start to finish."[215]

They played Newport News the following week: "Ma Rainey is going big as usual singing Down Home Blues. Also Daisy Martin singing, Everybody's Man Is My Man."[216] New acts on the roster included the comedy team of Johnny Hudgins and Helen Bumbray in a "Black Charlie Chaplin" skit and the Two Musical Seminoles in an "Indian act" that featured "the World's youngest left handed xylophone player."[217] Tolliver and company rounded out their 1916 summer season with a succession of heavily advertised weeklong stands in Richmond. Al Wells observed: "The people of Richmond, both white and Colored doesn't seem to get tired of this show, the way they turn out. Coming from miles around, following it from different parts of the city, and every performer gets their share of applause."[218]

Mr. Hudgins, the black Charlie Chaplin, of the team of Hudgins and Bumbray, now starring with Tolliver's Big Show.

Johnny Hudgins *Indianapolis Freeman*, August 12, 1916.

TOLLIVERS SMART SET HERE AGAIN NEXT WEEK.

Commencing Monday night, August 14, Tollivers Smart Set Company will open on Brook avenue and Mitchell Street for a week's engagement. Nothing can be said too good for this show as it is known by every man woman and child in the city of Richmond. Carrying over one hundred performers, the best in the colored race. It is considered a treat to the people of Richmond.

The mammoth canvas theatre seating over 5000 people resembles a circus and is so arranged this year that everyone can see be cool and comfortable. Many new faces are seen with the show and almost all of those popular ones of last year. Aerial act, novelty acts, singing and dancing and the Great Ham Tree Chorus go to make up over a three hour show. This is positively the largest colored show in America and was reorganized in Winter quarters in New Orleans under the personal direction of Alexander Tolliver, director and Albert Wells, general superintendent and aerial director.

Mr. Wells is a member of the act, Wells and Wells, whose picture appears in another part of this paper. Mr. Wells is considered the foremost aeriel actor of his race. Lula Wells, his wife does the famous fade-away drop from the dizzy heights of the top of the tent. This act alone is worth the price of admission.

Madam Rainey, singer of the "Blues," Daisy Martin, of Smart Set fame, the famous "Woha" Indians Musical Act, Peg Lifhtfoot, Peg Leg Dancer and others too numerous to mention will be seen on next Monday night in the wonderfully lighted tent.

This is a clean, moral and up-to-date show, you can take the children to see. Special matinees throughout the week for the special convenience of children. The price will remain the same, 10 cents to everyone and 10 cents for reserved seats. Do not forget the date and location and remember this is the Big Show you all know. Doors open 7:00 P. M., show starts 8:15. Show grounds, Brook Avenue and Mitchell Streets.

Richmond Planet, August 12, 1916.

Alexander Tolliver's marriage seems to have ended when Mabel quit the show late in the summer and returned to her family home in Scranton, Pennsylvania.[219] Al Wells gave an update on the Big Show as it appeared in September 1916:

> After a big singing and dancing opening chorus then comes the following acts: Peg Lightfoot, the one-leg dancing wonder, single, then for a change team with Joddie Edwards. Ma Rainey, Clara Smith and Evelyn White (all singles), who are assassinators of the blues and coon shouters that are hard to beat. Martin and Washington singing, dancing and talking. Tressie

Indianapolis Freeman, July 1, 1916.

Leggs, singing and dancing; Knox and Ramsey, singing, dancing and talking; Tolliver monologue and roller skate dance. Now comes a line of novelty acts that are hard to beat. Great Adams, trick bicyclist. Roxie Caldwell, the atheistic girl [*sic*], who deserves great credit. Her work consists of hoops and chairs. Charles Gaines in a novel fire escape act; Albert Gaines, wire walking; Wells and Wells, high trapeze act; Gaines Bros. acrobatic act; Wells and Gaines, ring act; Wells and Gaines Bros. in a double trapeze act; then the acrobatic troupe, five in number, goes to make up the largest and greatest Colored show in America.[220]

In Winston-Salem, North Carolina, during the week of September 24, 1916, "Ma Rainey sang 'One Beautiful Morning' and 'I'll Be Gone,' and cleaned up." Pa Rainey was "still on the sick list."[221] A report the following week notified that he had "gone home for a two or three week's visit in Columbus, Ga."[222] In Greenville, South Carolina, during the week of October 9, "Ma Rainey, when appearing on the stage, received a great ovation, she sings Lonesome Melody and Morning, Noon and Night. Everybody knows Ma Rainey and what she can do, so nuff said."[223]

"Morning, Noon and Night" was a 1916 sheet music hit from Chicago-based publisher Will Rossiter. Perhaps it was the "Ma and Pa" reference in the chorus that attracted Ma Rainey to the song:

I've got the "weary blues," and I don't know what to do,
I'm so blue,
It's all because I'm dead in love, in love with you . . .
Morning, noon and night,
I don't feel right,
My poor heart keeps on a-yearning,
Cause Ma wants her little loving Pa,
Morning, noon and night.[224]

On October 16, 1916, Tolliver's Big Show began a one-week stand in Augusta, Georgia:

Started selling tickets at 6:30; stopped selling at 7:45, turning away about 500 people, but they stood on the outside and listened to the music, for we have a fine orchestra. Fred Kewley, leader and clarinetist; H. B. Howard, piano; John [sic] Robinson, drums; John Porter, bass; David Jones, alto; Willie Hightower, cornet. We have another member to join this orchestra, Mrs. Elizabeth Kewley, wife of Fred Kewley . . . this being her first time to appear in public, as a clarinetist, she must be given great credit . . . Watch for another addition, Lena Leggett, alto, will be seen in public soon . . . We also have with us Kid Owen, the great eccentric buck dancer, and the sister team of Leola Grant and Mattie Lewis. This sister team has a very

Indianapolis Freeman, July 1, 1916.

fine act as two school girls doing a nice line of talk and dancing and singing.[225]

Al Wells related that during the week of October 28, 1916, while appearing in Charleston, South Carolina, members of the Tolliver show "were invited to the Jenkins Orphanage Home, 20 Franklin street, and I was much impressed by the great work that was being done by Dr. Jenkins."[226] One great work was the Orphan Band, which raised funds for the Home, and graduated more than a few players onto the minstrel routes and beyond.

While showing in Savannah, Georgia, on November 4, Tolliver's great horn player David Jones was married to soubrette Lena Leggett, "on the stage, before a large audience, by Rev. Singleton, pastor of the St. Phillip A.M.E. church of this city."[227] Two days later the show opened in Macon, where Susie Edwards and Evelyn White "put their work over in great style," with "Miss White singing 'If You Only Had My Disposition, You Could Love Me All the Time,' and Mrs. Edwards singing 'Everybody's Man Is My Man.'" Also, "Clara Smith (coon shouter) holds her own singing the Yellow Dog Rag and Chinese Blues."[228]

A few weeks later, Al Wells reported news of another wedding en route:

Mr. Eddie Robinson, of New Orleans, better known as "Rabbit," trap drummer of the Tolliver's Big Show, and Miss Gertrude Jackson, of Atlanta, Ga., were married Nov. 20th, 1916 . . . The company wishes them success and happiness through life.

H. B. Howard, better known as Caggie, piano player with this show says Hello, Zoo, we are now in Birmingham and had the opportunity of visiting the pig mouth and cow lip station. Hightower was there, too. I guess you know the rest piled up the cord wood. Grey hounds couldn't jump over 'em. ha, ha, ha![229]

Tolliver decided to spend the winter in Birmingham, where his white backer C. W. Park was currently based. On December 2, 1916, this ad appeared in the *Freeman*:

WANTED! Open Time in Colored Theaters for Alex. Tolliver's Big Show! The Largest Colored Show in the World—Presenting the new War Melo-Drama in two acts, by Alexander Tolliver, "The 9th and 10th Cavalry," an up-to-the-minute Dramatic production, using real horses and soldiers in uniform. A carload of special scenery and effects, including A Big Musical Comedy Ballet and Beauty Chorus Interspersed With 12 Feature Vaudeville Acts—Music by Prof. Fred. Kewley's Symphony Orchestra—Making a combination of the Most Elaborate, Stupendous and Meritorious Colored Show ever offered in America. Playing One and Three Nights and Week Stands. Managers or Theaters wanting a real Box Office Winner, wire Charles W. Park, Booking Agent, DeSota Hotel, Birmingham, Ala.

There is nothing to confirm that Tolliver's "new War Melo-Drama" ever went into production. In any case, Park and Tolliver severed their relationship that winter, following one of the most successful touring seasons in black entertainment history. After an all-too-brief winter's layover, Tolliver and company journeyed from Birmingham to Jacksonville, Florida, to kick off a new season on January 1, 1917; not under canvas, but at the local Strand Theater.[230] Back in Birmingham, C. W. Park started recruiting performers for a separate, replacement version of "Tolliver's Big Show." He spelled out his full intention in a February 1917 advert:

Wanted For The Great Tolliver Show! A Producer—Capable of putting on a singing and dancing chorus of 60 people. Require 12 to 15 minute numbers. State experience. Address mail to C.W. Park, Box 192, Birmingham, Ala.—Warning Note: Alexander Tolliver is no longer connected with this show in any manner what so ever. This is the original Tolliver Show playing only under canvas and the Management will in no way be responsible for any debts or contracts made by Alexander Tolliver's small show now playing the picture houses of Florida.[231]

Park revealed a bit of malice in the way he expunged Tolliver's name from the show. He initiated a contest in the *Freeman*, inviting readers to submit suggestions for a new name:

> The announcement by the manager of the Big Tolliver Show . . . that the show would go out bigger and greater than ever this season, but under a different name than the above title, came as a distinct surprise to the "Freeman" and the colored show world as well inasmuch as the Management offer a cash bonus of $10.00 to any colored person suggesting a proper fitting title to fit the magnitude of this show, which is the largest organization of its kind in the world . . .
>
> This Contest is open to all colored people and no suggestions by white people will be considered . . . This show embraces Musical Comedy, Novelty Acts of every description, Minstrel and Circus Acts, but carries no animals of any kind . . .
>
> The show will be under the personal direction of C. W. Park.[232]

Park informed the *Freeman* that he received 461 submissions during the first week of the contest. Subsequent "puff" articles created an air of excitement about the contest to rename "the big show, which toured the country last season known as Tolliver's Smart Set." On March 15, 1917, Park announced the winner: "The Colored Aristocrats."

The trumped-up contest and new name made desirable publicity in the pages of the *Freeman*. However, when Park's company opened its touring season eleven days later in Savannah, Georgia, a large ad in the black weekly *Savannah Tribune* proclaimed the return of the "Tolliver 'Smart Set.'" An accompanying article added: "The colored aristocrats of the big show business, the great Tolliver 'Smart Set' in the big tent at 32nd and West Broad streets will be the big event." The roster included Tolliver's estranged wife Mabel, "who was in excellent voice," plus "Sheik Hadji Tahar, with his tossing, tumbling Arabians and beautiful Egyptian girls," and Mr. Dinah Scott, "king of buzzers."[233]

Trading on the notion of continuity from Tolliver's Smart Set, Park's Colored Aristocrats developed a similar mix of blues singers and novelty acts. Black entertainment trailblazer Will Benbow was hired to manage the show, and he secured a first-rate blues queen in future Paramount recording artist Mattie Dorsey, "the girl with the loud voice and everlasting steam pipes. This lady is given the credit of being the world's greatest blues singer of her race and when she sings those blues, all you can hear them say is, 'sing 'em gal, sing 'em,' and she leaves them spellbound."[234]

Late in their 1917 touring season the Colored Aristocrats' roster was reinforced by black vaudeville's brightest blues star, Butler "String Beans" May.[235] In September, when the company came to Nashville, they were still advertising themselves as the Smart Set. The *Globe*, Nashville's culturally conservative African American weekly, assessed: "String Beans featured as the 'funniest man on earth' heads the Smart Set Co. which holds the boards on 10th Ave. near Cedar all this week. They have an aggregation of comedians, singers, dancers and musicians, all said to be talented performers of exceptional ability. They carry a bevy of girls, but the show is rotten."[236]

Whatever the reason Tolliver and Park decided to part company, there is no denying the unprecedented triumph of their previous season. From Jacksonville, Tolliver crowed: "The Tolliver show [for] the year 1916 broke all records in the colored show world . . . Did you know the Tolliver show carries more performers than any other

COMING!
ALL NEXT WEEK!
THE ORIGINAL
"SMART SET Co"
Under Water Proof Canvas
The Largest Colored Show on Earth
PRESENTING
STRING BEANS
THE FUNNIEST MAN ON EARTH
AND NEARLY
100 SINGING, DANCING, CHORUS
Admission 10 Cents to Everyone. Reserved Seats 10c Extra
SEATS FOR 5000 PEOPLE
ONE WEEK COMMENCING
Monday Night, September 10th
Doors Open 7:30. Show Starts 8:15
Show Grounds Located Cedar St. & 10th Avenue
Remember:- This is Not a Small Show but the
LARGEST COLORED SHOW ON EARTH

Nashville Globe, September 7, 1917.

colored show on earth? . . . Did you know the Tolliver show played to more people in 1916 than any other colored show on earth?"[237]

Tolliver would never reach such heights again. Once he lost his financial backer, he began to lose key members of his Big Show. Orchestra director Fred Kewley seems to have departed while the show was still in Birmingham. A *Freeman* report of January 13, 1917, placed Kewley and his wife in Memphis, rehearsing a new musical act that they planned to present in vaudeville.[238] Al Wells also decided to leave. The *Freeman* of February 10, 1917, identified Wells and his wife as newcomers with F. S. Wolcott's Rabbit Foot Company. By 1920 Wells was running a show of his own, known as Wells's Smart Set.

The loss of Al Wells brought a halt to regular correspondence from Tolliver's Big Show. Finally, on March 24, 1917, a report was submitted by Telfair Washington:

After three successful weeks in Atlanta, Ga. we opened at Macon on March 12, at the Douglass theater to capacity houses with overwhelming success. Lightfoot and Edwards present a blackface patter with material that is refreshing. Their act is replete with innovations. Both members of this team scored heavily. Hawthorne and White, those girlie girls, added wonderfully with their budget of new melody and high stepping.

Leggs and McGinty's new offering (Just Kids), singing, dancing and refined comedy, was generously applauded. Telfair Washington and Zudora Johnson offered their comedy oddity with songs and dances, which was convulsively pleasing. Gertrude (Ma) Rainey was given a tremendous ovation, which registered her a great hit. The votes for favors goes to Bessie Smith. She found it decidedly easy to corner the popular honors. Our latest addition is that one George Bell, seven foot six inches gloom dispeller. His comedy antics has never failed to put even the dullest audience into a laughing mood.

The show continues with Mr. Tolliver's farce comedy, "The Borders of Mexico," which Mr. Tolliver displays with wonderful comedy. The offering is a laughable one; unique stage settings elaborately costumed with exceedingly clever situations. Our big feature is the Johnny Boy Chorus, 12 charming damsels in male full dress attire.

Mrs. Susie Hawthorne Edwards has been some what sick and under the doctor's care for the past week. The writer wishes to mention that she is progressing favorably while papa Joddie is strutting about regarding himself as an important personage.

Our combination orchestra, under direction of Willie Hightower, with Eddie (Rabbit) Robertson at the drums, plays the show without any worry, and also renders some sweet and classy selections, overtures, rags, reveries, gallops, meditations and exit marches as well. Why, isn't that enough music?

By the spring of 1917, Tolliver had lost his wife, his financial backer, his historic lineup of novelty acts, half of his musicians, and most of his *Freeman* publicity, but he still had a great blues revue, bolstered by the addition of Bessie Smith. Unfortunately, Bessie Smith's tenure with Tolliver's Big Show passed without further commentary. By the fall of 1917, she had reportedly returned to southern vaudeville theaters.

Clara Smith left the Tolliver show and took up with Wooden's Bon Tons. A note from the Bon Tons, posted from Montgomery, Alabama, on May 18, 1917, warned: "Clara Smith, the black 'Sophia Tucker,' says be on the lookout coon shouters."[239] Three months later she was "still singing the 'Blues' as loud as ever with her big voice."[240] During the summer of 1920 Clara Smith was the "nonpariel blues singer" with Al Wells's Smart Set.[241]

Telfair Washington informed from Charleston, South Carolina, in April 1917, that:

Eddie (Peg) Lightfoot, Charleston's favorite, was generously applauded. Evelyn White and Susie Hawthorne, those two girls in songs and dance diversion, scored a deserved hit. Joddie Edwards, the eccentric buzzer, rocked the house. The Leggs-McGinty combination was irresistible, bowed off amid thunderous applause. Zudora Johnson and Telfair Washington in their odd hits of nonsensical chatter, were convincingly pleasing. Gertrude ("Ma") Rainey the popular singer of the blue note melody, carried off the big honors. Willie Hightower, Lottie Frost and Eddie (Rabbit) Robinson are our musical bugs. George Bell, the seven-foot and eleven inches joy distributor is a real feature . . . [T]he show continues with a farce comedy, 'The King of Africa,' from the pen of Mr. Alex Tolliver, with Mr. Tolliver in leading comedy role.[242]

Tolliver's jazz orchestra was reduced to three pieces, under Willie Hightower's direction. Pianist Lottie Frost joined during the Charleston engagement, replacing Caggie Howard.[243] A native of Charleston, Frost had attended the New England Conservatory of Music in Boston before taking over the piano at Charleston's Dixieland Theater in 1914. In 1916 she toured with Wooden's Bon Tons.

For nearly all of the summer of 1917, the travels of Tolliver's Smart Set were confined to a small circle of mining towns in West Virginia. At Gary, West Virginia, on July 3, 1917, Willie Hightower and Lottie Frost were married.[244] In June and July Tolliver ran want ads for musicians, novelty acts and "attractive looking girls who can really sing and dance."

When the West Virginia coal town tour ended, around September 1, 1917, Ma Rainey returned to southern vaudeville. Later that month, a *Freeman* report from the Queen Theater in Chattanooga, Tennessee, declared her "a decided hit with her blues for home sweet home."[245] Jodie and Susie Edwards also headed for the southern vaudeville houses, and an October 6, 1917, report placed them on a bill at the 81 Theater in Atlanta, in a team act with Butler "String Beans" May. It marked a turning point in their career. The following year they emerged as Butterbeans and Susie.

After finishing the summer season with Tolliver, Willie and Lottie Hightower briefly took charge of the orchestra at the Lincoln Theater in Cincinnati, Ohio.[246] In the fall of 1917 they went out with C. W. Park's Colored Aristocrats.[247] By the end of the year the Hightowers and drummer Willie Campbell were serving as the "jazz orchestra" with the Augusta Mines–Boyd Harris Show at "the New Colored Theatre" on the corner of Fifth and Mobile streets in Hattiesburg, Mississippi.[248] Willie Hightower's return to Park's Colored Aristocrats in 1918 was interrupted by a short hitch in the military at Camp Pike, Arkansas. In 1919 he reengaged with Tolliver's Smart Set, and in 1920 he and Lottie traveled with Wooden's Bon Tons. In 1921 the Hightowers settled in Chicago and immersed themselves in the musical life of the city.[249]

In September 1917 an abbreviated "Tolliver aggregation" with Peg Lightfoot and Big George Bell played theater engagements in Philadelphia and New York.[250] Lightfoot apparently departed shortly thereafter.[251] In November Tolliver's Smart Set opened at the 81 Theater in Atlanta, and a few weeks later they were noted in Jacksonville, Florida. In December a *Freeman* report revealed:

> The Tolliver Smart Set . . . is now in Charleston, S. C. meeting with great success. Mr. Tolliver has made considerable changes in his company for an extended tour of the South . . . Among the new people connected with the company are Beatrice Johnson, Nina Davis, Minstrel Morris, Margaret Dockett, Mrs. Susie Hughes, the Strayhorn Children, Prof. Attrice Hughes musical director and orchestra leader is busy getting his band together and musicians are coming every day. There will be several lady musicians connected with the band. Mrs. Alexander Tolliver is the advance agent of this truly great show, and she keeps the show well booked ahead.[252]

Reportage in the African American press indicates that during Alexander Tolliver's 1914–1917 heyday, hundreds of thousands of black southerners, and tens of thousands of whites, heard blues and jazz performed under his big tent. Although Tolliver never regained the prominence that he enjoyed during the mid-1910s, when he was dubbed

HIGHTOWER & HIGHTOWER.

Willie H. Hightower, a virtuoso leader of band, orchestra and vaudeville work, accompanied by wife, Mrs. L. Hightower, beter known to the profession as Lottie Frost, pianist. They are now featuring a few of their own original Jazz numbers, which will be published soon. Mr. Hightower is

preparing for his third season, after finishing the season with C. W. Parks's Colored Aristocrats. He is preparing to fulfill his contracts for 1918 as band and orchestra leader for the show. Would like to hear from all good musicians, as we expect to have a good band and orchestra. Address all mail to W. H. Hightower, 10½

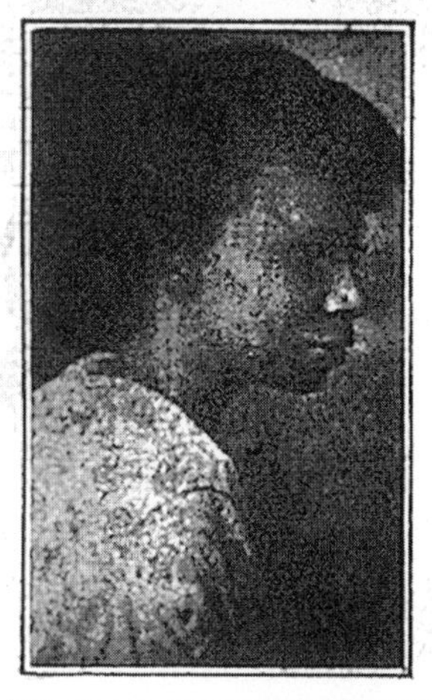

America street, Charleston, S. C. Read this and imagine how Mrs. Hightower tickles the ivories. She is a feature of her own original numbers. Both say, "Lood out, friends, we are coming through." With many good wishes, a Merry Xmas and a Happy New Year to all friends in and out of the profession. All mail can reach them at their home, 10½ America street, Charleston, S. C.

Indianapolis Freeman, December 29, 1917.

ALEXANDER TOLLIVER
THE BARNUM OF THE COLORED RACE
General Manager and Producer of the Largest and Greatest Colored Show on Earth. Something New and Novel in the Show World. The Show is Meeting with Tremendous Success. Mr. Tolliver Has Made Wonderful Progress, Being Only 28 Years of Age. The Youngest Manager in the Business, But Improvement Is His Motto.

Indianapolis Freeman, July 1, 1916.

"the Barnum of his race," he continued to direct successful road companies for at least another decade.

Salem Tutt Whitney was tied to an older musical sensibility and must have been somewhat uncomfortable with the commercial onslaught of blues and jazz characterized by the advent of Tolliver's Smart Set. In the summer of 1915, when the controversy over the Smart Set name was only beginning to heat up, Whitney wrote:

> It is truly disheartening . . . to produce something new, something classy and truly worth while, to have that act only receive a small measure of appreciation . . . What is the use of creating a sketch that makes an intelligent appeal and have it a "frost," while another actor may sing the "Blues," "Ball the Jack," tell a smutty joke or make a ridiculous reference to racial characteristics and be the hit of the bill? . . .
>
> Managers are often criticized for allowing a certain class of actors and acts to play their houses, but full houses prove that the managers are only giving the public what it desires.[253]

In the fall of 1916, when Tolliver was breaking all records with his big southern tent show, Whitney complained one more time about the lifting of the title "Smart Set":

> We certainly believe that the Tolliver aggregation possesses enough of strength and merit to draw large crowds into their capacious tent without infringing upon the rights of the Smart Set title. We had hoped that a sense of fairness and justice would have deterred those responsible for the Tolliver Shows from a continued use of the title made famous by the great comedians, Earnest Hogan, Billy McClain, Tom McIntosh and S. H. Dudley. Up-to-date we have been disappointed in our expectations.[254]

In March 1916, another pretender to the "Smart Set" title, the Georgia Smart Set, opened its inaugural season with blackface comedian Ernest Watts as stage manager and his wife Muriel Ringgold Watts as headliner. The following year, a revamped edition of the Georgia Smart Set featured future blues recording star Viola McCoy. Finally, in the spring of 1917, Salem Tutt Whitney relinquished the Smart Set title, but not without claiming the high ground, as noted in the *Freeman*:

> Mr. T. L. Corwell, for eight years manager of Whitney & Tutt's Smart Set Company, wishes to

> announce that, owing to numerous Smart Set companies that are inflicting themselves upon a patient public, that in the future this company will be known as WHITNEY & TUTT'S SMARTER SET. This title, also SMARTEST SET, IS FULLY PROTECTED BY COPYRIGHT . . . Whitney and Tutt have made the Smart Set title a byword. They are now willing to relinquish that title to the bunch of plagiarists, imitators and pirates infecting the South, and take the title of SMARTER SET, that their many friends may be able to distinguish from these others, and not be tricked or bunkoed by the petty title grabbers.[255]

By 1916, Whitney was beginning to open his musical comedies to a certain "refined element" of blues singing. His 1915–1916 edition of *George Washington Bullion* concluded with a scene that highlighted the new James Vaughn composition, "Old Kentucky Blues."

Whitney's roster for 1916–1917 included pianist Eubie Blake along with a triumvirate of female blues singers: Blanche "Billie" Young, "masculine in voice, and name only," who sang "You May Come Back Just Too Late";[256] Sweetie Matthews May, String Beans' estranged wife, who "led the chorus in 'Sweet Melodious Blues'"; and Juanita Stinette, whose version of "The Weary Blues" "passed right on to opera . . . It was the very height of blues singing."[257]

"Lucky" Roberts returned as Whitney's musical director for 1917–1918. Whitney had been boosting Roberts in his "Seen and Heard While Passing" column since their first meeting in 1913, and noted on June 24, 1916, that Roberts was "the only 'ragtime' pianist who has succeeded in making an acceptable record for the Victor machine [*sic*]."[258] While playing Little Rock, Arkansas, in the fall of 1917, Whitney's Smart Set spent an informal afternoon in company with piano legend Blind Boone, who "simply reveled in the playing of Lucky Roberts."[259]

Also returning for the 1917–1918 season was Daisy Martin, "the famous soubrette," who sang "Irresistible Blues" and "Please Don't Trifle with My Heart."[260] Whitney sang "It's Hard to Keep a Good Man Down," and Mattie Brooks displayed her skill in "racial buck and jazz . . . especially in leg movements which astounded in dexterity."[261] Whitney confessed during the summer of 1918 that, "A little bit of the 'Blues' and the 'Chimey,' JUDICIOUSLY INSERTED in acts or shows, ADD SPICE AND 'PEP' AND PROVE ENJOYABLE, but a 'BLUES' revival and a 'CHIMEY' contest IS A SUPER-ABUNDANCY."[262]

Tolliver's Smart Set could be accused of having provided a "super-abundancy" of blues. Conversely, it could be credited with having achieved the full realization of the blues on the American stage. Under Tolliver's direction the most promising southern talent, especially female blues singers, gained much wider recognition.

The military draft caught up with Alexander Tolliver in 1918. That fall, after three months' service, he received an honorable discharge and headed to Mobile, Alabama, to "get his Big Show together."[263] Tolliver kept his Smart Set on the road through the 1920s, occasionally visiting big cities on sweeping tours, but often relying on regional "tank towns" and mining camps. In the fall of 1924 he announced through *Billboard* magazine that "his show, which has toured Pennsylvania, Delaware, Maryland, West Virginia and Kentucky this summer under canvas, will be kept out all winter, playing theaters." The tour was reportedly Tolliver's "seventh consecutive trip thru Kentucky and West Virginia."[264]

WHITNEY & TUTT,
Manager and Owners.

W. R. ARNOLD,
General Advance Representative

-0-
ALL
ORIGINAL MUSIC
BY
DONALD HAYWOOD
and M. RIDLEY
BOOK AND LYRICS
BY
WHITNEY & TUTT
-0-

NAMES TO CONJURE
WITH IN THE WORLD
OF ENTERTAINMENT
16TH ANNUAL SEASON

SALEM TUTT J. HOMER
WHITNEY & TUTTS
SMARTER SET
COMPANY
BIGGEST SEASON'S SUCCESS
CLEAN WHOLESOME COMEDY

PRESENTING
A
FIRST CLASS MORAL
AND
REFINED MUSICAL
COMEDY
CONSISTING OF THE
BEST
COLORED SINGERS,
DANCERS
AND COMEDIANS

"NON-SENSE"
The Little Giant of Musical Comedies.
1Act, 3 Scenes.

All Star Cast. -----
Salem Tutt Whitney.
J. Homer Tutt
Chas. Hawkins. Char.
Claren ce Nance. Comedy.
Baynard Whitney. Tenor.
William Taylor. Dancer.

Bronze Beauty Chorus.
Miss Nona Marshall
" Bobby Lee Fredrick.
" Arlyne Brooks.
" Jewel Thomas.
" Alesia Buchanan.
" Ruby Williams.

Miss Ida Forsyne.
Worlds Greatest Russian Dancer.

The Famous Melody Maids.
Miss Mabel Ridley, Americas' Song Bird.
Miss Arlyne Brooks, Subrette.
Miss Frankie Watts. Contralto.

Mr Cuney Conner.
Mu sical Director.
****
Special Scenery & Costumes.
****

Prop List.
6 Old or new grips or suit cases.
1 Pick & shovel.
1 Fire axe.
1 Box covered, with red clothe or paper.

FIVE SHOWS
BEING PRODUCED
THIS SEASON
BY
WHITNEY & TUTT
NAMELY
"NON-SENSE"
"COME ALONG MANDY"
"UP AND DOWN"
"WHEN MALINDA SINGS"
"WHO STRUCK JOHN"

ALSO WRITERS OF
SUCH SUCCESSES AS
"OH! JOY!"
"GEO. WASHINGTON"
"BULLION"
"MY PEOPLE"
"CHILDREN OF THE SUN"
ALONG WITH
"BAMBOULA"
"NUT BROWN GAL"
"MAYOR OF NEWTOWN"
"DARKEST AMERICANS"
AND
DOZENS OF OTHER
UNANIMOUS SUCCESSES

EVERY DAY IN EVERY WAY WE ARE GETTING BETTER
AND BETTER

Smarter Set Company mailer. (courtesy Douglass Theater Collection, Middle Georgia Archives, Washington Memorial Library, Macon, Georgia)

Well-known performer Leigh Whipper took over the business management of Tolliver's company in November 1924. Whipper considered himself "'a star in the high grass' when it comes to routing and managing shows," and advised *Billboard* that Tolliver's show "would not be permitted to lose a single performance from now on."[265] They played the Palace Theater in Memphis the week of November 24; and on December 22 and 23, "Alexander Tolliver and his Smart Set minstrels," with a ten-piece band, played the Dreamland Theater in Monroe, Louisiana: "Tolliver, in his original character of 'jail-house,' was received warmly."[266]

In 1925 Tolliver's Smart Set was counted among the big attractions on the famous Theater Owners

Tolliver's Smart Set

Bigger, Better, Grander, than ever. The Show the People Know. A Merry Xmas to All.

MRS. ALEXANDER TOLLIVER

The above portrait is a likeness of Mrs. Alexander Tolliver, Secretary and Treasurer of Tolliver's Big Show, one of the few successful colored shows now traveling. This show is owned and controlled by Alexander Tolliver, who is none other than a regular showman. The company is having great success on their Southern tour, and wish everyone a Merry Xmas and a Happy New Year.

Indianapolis Freeman, December 22, 1917.

Booking Association (TOBA) black vaudeville theater circuit.[267] At the Lyric Theater in New Orleans, Tolliver took part in a special "midnight frolic for a white audience," billed as "the world's champion Negro roller skater."[268] He was cruising the southern reaches of Florida in 1926, when a note in the *Chicago Defender* informed, "The veteran Tolliver and his company of 16 people are giving Miamians one of the laugh hits of the season. Tolliver in his jailhouse attire mounted on roller skates causes the audience to nearly go into convulsions . . . The chorus is well dressed and the girls are nice looking. The show carries their own jazz band."[269]

Tolliver's second wife, Edna, was active for many years in the management of his Smart Set. Briefly reflecting on Tolliver's career in a 1928 edition of the *Defender*, columnist Coy Herndon noted: "[H]is energetic little wife did the advance work, just like any other agent, with a bundle of paper under one arm and a bucket of paste in the other. Many of the towns in the coal fields were close together, and she walked rather than wait for a train. In the course of a few years the Tollivers have climbed the ladder of success, own a block of property in an exclusive residential section of Bluefield [West Virginia], and their home is a paradise on earth."[270] They were still on the road in the summer of 1930 when the *Defender* reported, "Tolliver's Smart Set show is at Wilmington, Del., this week."[271]

The name "Smart Set" seems to have appeared spontaneously, originally attached to a company under the guidance of Ernest Hogan and Billy McClain: "The title was a happy thought, proving that sometimes there is more in a name than suspected."[272] Subsequently adopted by a succession of notable stars and companies, the genius spirit of the Smart Set Company continued to resound for generations. Modern jazz pianist Jaki Byard recalled that, as a young man, around 1948, he "went on the road with a Negro review—Larry Steele's 'Smart Set,' for which he wrote some of the music . . . and worked in the band along with Thad Jones, Gigi Gryce and Jimmy Crawford."[273]

Indianapolis Freeman, September 27, 1919.

PART THREE

BLUES for the SIDESHOW TENT

Have you noticed that nearly every circus on the road has a colored aggregation taking care of the side show? Dear colored performer, please take care of the opportunity given you and don't squabble yourself out of a job.

—"The Parrot in the Theater Loft"

Indianapolis Freeman, May 14, 1910

Only since the 1980s has there been any significant representation of African American circus performers under the big top. In his 1990 study, *The American Circus: An Illustrated History*, John Culhane reveals that in 1968, "Irvin Feld introduced to the circus a troupe of basketball-playing unicycle riders, the King Charles Troupe, and proudly billed them as 'the first all-black circus in America' . . . When he hired the King Charles Troupe, Feld told me, 'there wasn't a black person in the circus.' One of his executives . . . said, 'Kid, you're gonna have total rebellion . . .' But that closeminded executive had not noticed the times changing . . . By 1984, Ringling Bros and Barnum & Bailey Circus had black clowns, black showgirls, and since 1983 Satin, the first black aerial act."

Turn-of-the-century African American minstrel shows were havens for aerial acts, animal acts, magicians, jugglers, acrobats, wire walkers, etc. The exclusion of these acts from circus big tops was purely a result of popular race prejudice. In 1916 Al Wells, trapeze artist and general superintendent of Tolliver's Smart Set, wrote: "Colored novelty acts have never had the chance that our white brothers have had, nor do they get the salary . . . When I first went to New York City with the first Colored aerial-act to play the city, Al Wilton . . . told me he never heard of a colored trapeze act . . . but when I changed the act to a Cuban act and called it Los Cubanos, the three Garcia Bros., we then played the time, also other time that could not see a Negro trapeze act."[1]

The majority of published histories politely ignore patterns of racial discrimination that are a skeleton in the closet of the American circus. In treating the black performer as an "invisible man," much circus history has been obscured or overlooked. The pages of the *Indianapolis Freeman* unveil details of a far greater involvement of African American performers in the circus world, and in Wild West shows, than has been previously acknowledged or documented—not under the big top, but in colored companies presented to the public in the sideshow tent alongside "freaks and curiosities." This overt expression of disrespect permitted white spectators to enjoy black entertainers while maintaining "a certain ironic distance."[2]

Sideshow annex companies were divided into two departments, band and minstrel. The band took part in the daily street parade, along with the larger white circus band, the menagerie, etc., usually with its own colorful bandwagon. The white band provided music under the big top, the main circus tent. Black bands almost never played under the big top. Within the sideshow annex, the colored company presented a minstrel show, typically consisting of an old-time "first part" and an "olio," incorporating singers, dancers, comedians, and specialty acts, accompanied by a small orchestra of seldom more than ten pieces. The minstrel orchestra also provided incidental music for the rest of the sideshow attractions, and struck up overtures between the acts. Select members of the annex company might finally be summoned to the big top to participate in an "after concert," for which the audience usually paid an additional small admission fee.

The oft-used term "sideshow annex" seems to have applied equally to the separate sideshow tent, and to the colored company that performed within the tent. For decades, practically every big circus on the road had a black band and minstrel company attached to its sideshow, performing on the streets and inside the sideshow tent before people of all races, from the Atlantic to the Pacific, and from the southern reaches of Canada to the Gulf of Mexico. During the 1910s, these companies constituted a significant pathway for the dissemination of ragtime, blues, and jazz. Their success can be largely credited to an extraordinary group of African American bandmasters, Renaissance men whose musical prowess was matched by managerial skills, tough-minded perseverance, and a "ready adaptation to the duty required."[3] During the 1890s, exemplary band leaders like J. O. McNutt, James Wolfscale, and Solomon P. White helped clear the way for this avenue of professional opportunity. By the turn of the century circus sideshow annex companies were providing employment for a large and growing number of African American musicians and performers.[4]

Without question the central figure in this sphere of entertainment was Perry George Lowery, known as "P. G." Lowery was not only a great cornet player and an astute businessman; he was a legendary teacher and a model of excellence for subsequent generations of black musicians. In 1915 Salem Tutt Whitney asked, "Who does not know P. G. Lowery? Certainly not any in show business. And all who know him love him. White and colored pronounce him to be a prince of good fellows. He is recognized as one of the greatest cornetists. Framed upon the wall of his home in Columbus [Ohio] is a trophy won in a contest with twenty white musicians. Mr. Lowery is a great bandmaster, yet he is unassuming; reticent of his own accomplishments, he becomes eloquent when singing the praises of some other musician."[5]

Lowery was born in Reece, Kansas, in 1870. During the 1890s he studied at the Boston Conservatory of Music and became an able, enthusiastic instructor in the entire range of band instruments.[6] A measure of Lowery's conservative, disciplined approach is reflected in an exchange with *Freeman* critic "Tom the Tattler," who complained in his column of February 8, 1902, that colored bands tended to play too loud: "It seems as if it is a contest to see which horn can make the loudest report . . . A white man with his horn looks upon himself as part of the whole, while the colored man with his instrument . . . looks upon it as a disgrace for him not to be heard above the rest . . . Our bandmasters and musical directors should strain every effort to curb this spirit to outdo each other." Lowery responded: "Tom the Tattler—Accept my special compliments on your article in The Freeman about 'Our Colored Band.' Bandmasters, who have not had the proper training, clip that article and study it. Take heed, let it be seed sown in good ground. If we had more Band Masters with the judgement you manifest, our colored bands would play like our white ones. The noise will be turned into music. May all musical directors be benefited by your article is the best wish of—P. G. Lowery."[7]

In 1899 Lowery was engaged to head the band and minstrel company attached to the Forepaugh-Sells Brothers Circus, where he quickly ignited popular support for black entertainers in the sideshow tent. On April 23, 1900, he began a second season with Forepaugh-Sells: "One of the principal attractions of the parade was P. G. Lowery's band of 14 selected musicians, his bandwagon being the largest on parade, a brilliant blue, trimmed in gold color—his band uniformed in a dark blue new uniform trimmed with gold braid. Every department is much larger this season. Lowery opened with a band of 14, orchestra of 8, a lady quartette and Mr. William Sherrah's Quartette from Kansas City, Mo., making a company of 22 people."[8]

Popular demand for up-to-date black vernacular music opened the circus sideshow to African American performers. Although P. G. Lowery's Concert Band and Vaudeville Company was capable of rendering a repertoire of difficult classical overtures, patriotic airs, and waltzes, their main fare with the Forepaugh-Sells Circus was ragtime. Their sideshow offerings for 1900 were delineated in the *Freeman*: Mrs. Tina Gillam sang "Just Because She Made Dem Goo Goo Eyes" and "Every Race Has a Flag But the Coon;" Mrs. Nettie Lewis rendered "You Tell Me Your Dreams and I'll Tell You Mine"; "My Little Zulu Babe," "Errand Man," and "the great coon song success," "I Ain't Got No Friends or Family Now"; and Mrs. Edna Farrell contributed "Sing Me a Song of the South" and some "neatly selected coon songs" such as "The Honolulu Dance," "I Wouldn't Leave My Home If I Were You," and "My Baby Gal." Stage manager Al T. Gillam sang "Ernest Hogan's latest, 'The Congregation Will Please Keep Their Seats' and Williams & Walker's 'If You Love Your Baby Make Them Goo Goo Eyes.'" Ed Heater, "better known as 'Fish,'" sang "I Ain't Got No Time to Be Your Baby" and the Nathan Bivens composition "Warm Baby from the South." Finally, the Sherrah Quartette made "great hits with the ballad 'Sweet Norine' and all the rest of their quartette selections," including "Little Georgia Rose" and "My Lady Lu."[9]

The Sherrah Quartette consisted of manager and basso William Sherrah; first tenor William Johnson; second tenor William Spencer; and baritone F. R. "Ace" Brooks. During the season of 1900 they were one of the most popular acts in the sideshow, "singing all the latest sentimental and coon songs of the day."[10] They also appeared under the big top as a special feature of the after concert, "where they never fail to please."[11] When the 1900 circus season closed, the Sherrah Quartette continued under P. G. Lowery's management, in connection with W. I. Swain's Original Nashville Students. Brooks and Sherrah, "better known as the 'easy going' Brooks and 'White Child,'" doubled as the company's principal comedians, and Spencer served as chorister.[12]

Among the musicians who toured with Lowery in 1900 was Charles Elgar, a young Creole violinist from New Orleans. Lowery's *Freeman* correspondent called him "the French boy."[13] Elgar directed the sideshow orchestra and played second alto in the band.[14] He eventually settled in Chicago, playing his violin at local church and community musicales and in the city's increasingly potent cabaret and dance hall scene. A Chicago news column in the *Freeman* of February 9, 1918, informed that, "Charles Elgar's Creole orchestra is now engaged at a large amusement café on the northwest side"—Harmon's Dreamland Ballroom, where they held forth until the summer of 1922.[15] Elgar's Creole Orchestra is documented on commercial recordings from 1926.[16]

Other key musicians in Lowery's outstanding band of 1900 included euphonium player Mose McQuitty, tuba player William May, and drummer Skip Farrell. Farrell was one of the first to be proclaimed "king of trap drummers."[17] He and wife Edna King Farrell were present for Lowery's first two seasons with the Forepaugh-Sells Circus. Farrell threw down the gauntlet in the *Freeman* of September 15, 1900, challenging "any drummer in the world for any amount, backed by Forepaugh & Sells' Bros . . . Now, come on or get back."

Mose McQuitty had come through the band with Wright's Nashville Students, under Lowery's direction, in 1897. Reunited with Lowery for the Sells-Forepaugh Circus tours of 1899 and 1900, McQuitty was said to be "stinging 'em on his new four-valve Boston musical euphonium."[18] He continued as a featured euphonium soloist with the Nashville Students under bandmaster Harry Prampin in 1900; with the Geyer-West Minstrels under Fountain B. Wood in 1901; with Mahara's Minstrels under W. C. Handy in 1902; and with Mahara's Minstrels again in 1903, under John C. Haywood. McQuitty's outstanding show business career continued unbroken until his death in 1937.[19]

William May's life in the circus annex world defies comparison, just as his skills as a tuba player apparently defied criticism. A *Freeman* commentator summarized in 1920: "The name Wm. May is sufficient, the name stands for the best bass in the business."[20] May was especially highly regarded as a soloist: "His hard steady tone, technic, execution and phrasing has placed him as the peer of all bass soloists."[21] William May and his cornet playing brother Thomas, of Wichita, Kansas, had been playing with the Sells Bros. Circus annex band even before P. G. Lowery's arrival. As members of Solomon P. White's band, they were with the Sells sideshow at least as early as 1891.[22] Fifty-one years later, when Lowery made his final tour with the Cole Bros. Circus, his tuba player was William May.

Sideshow annex companies acquired a loyal following in black communities encountered along the circus routes; beneficial relationships were established, and musical interaction was common. En route with the Forepaugh-Sells Circus at Memphis, Tennessee, on Sunday, September 16, 1900, P. G. Lowery's band was feted by the "Young Men's band of that city. The affair was one of best ever witnessed by the four big bands of the 'big trick.' The crowd gathered at the band room on Beale street at 9 a.m., and paraded to the Jackson Mound car, headed by P. G. Lowery's Concert band, the Greenville, Miss., band and the Young Men's band of Memphis, under Prof. Love. The music furnished by the Young Men's band was a treat to the circus bands and visiting band. The white circus band met us at the gates of the park and a rousing musical time was spent by the big bands."[23]

A "golden age" of sideshow annex bands seems to have commenced in 1910. On July 9, 1910, a photograph of P. G. Lowery appeared on the front page of a special *Freeman* entertainment supplement with a caption identifying him as the originator of circus annex "Minstrel and Vaudeville—A Recent Phase of the Show Business." The accompanying text proclaimed: "Since Lowery's initiative all have fallen in line—the little ones and the big ones—until at this time no less than fourteen white tents are giving employment to big colored companies . . . The number promises to increase since the features have proven popular, hence mean money to show managers."

An essay in January of the following year elaborated:

> The present outlook is that there will be more circuses carrying colored companies this season than ever before. Most of the circuses offer engagements to both ladies and gentlemen in their band and minstrel departments. This branch of the profession was first introduced in 1899 by Prof. P. G. Lowery, with the Forepaugh-Sells circus in Madison Square Garden, New York City, with a company of twenty-three musicians and performers. He then opened an avenue that is now offering engagements to over four hundred musicians and performers. Previous to this time the circuses only carried a band of not exceeding ten pieces. At that time S. P. White was the highest promoter, being the only colored or white bandmaster carrying a circus to Australia, South America and to other foreign countries.[24] Returned from the work in 1898, taking up concert work strictly, and today he wields the baton over one of the best concert bands in the United States, the Ninth O. N. G. band [i.e., the Ohio National Guard Band of Columbus, Ohio].
>
> Since the close of the season of 1910 we find six circuses are advertising for colored band and minstrels that have never carried a colored company before . . . By the combination of the band and minstrel it gives a larger band, so much so, as to handle popular and standard overtures. We hope to see all of the bands capable of handling overtures like P. G. Lowery's and R. Roy Pope's.

Indianapolis Freeman, July 9, 1910.

> A few of the hustling managers that are busy arranging for the season of 1911 are P. G. Lowery, for the Hagenbeck-Wallace, Prof. R. Roy Pope, for the Ringling Bros.; James Wolfscale for the Forepaugh-Sells; Wm. Reid for the Floto Show; Bismark [Ferris] for the Two Bills, and H. L. Rawles for the Howe's Great London show . . . We look forward to the greatest season ever known in the history of the circus business.[25]

The circus sideshow business, an attenuated avenue of professional opportunity, held challenges, rewards, and disappointments for every African American bandleader, musician, and minstrel involved. R. Roy Pope's Annex Band traveled with the Ringling Bros. Circus for several seasons. Pope was a young cornet player from Indiana, an alumnus of the famous Original Pickaninny Band, long-standing feature of the popular mainstream play *In Old Kentucky.*[26] A *Freeman* commentary of May 14, 1910, neatly described the functions of Pope's annex band with the Ringling Bros. Show:

> Prof. Pope and his band, gaily uniformed, held a conspicuous place in the parade and rendered music that brought applause from admirers all along the line. The organization furnishes the greater part of the entertainment in the Annex. The fifteen men, with pretty dark blue, well-fitting uniforms, are correctly arranged on a raised platform, seated on red-covered chairs, with the director in the center. Selections are given at the introduction of each wonder and accompanying each feat and at intervals. The minstrel part is exceptionally good. The jokes are all new and clean. The middle is taken care of in a faultless manner by Mr. William Walker, while the comedy is splendidly given by Messrs. James Jackson, Walter Hinson and Whitney Viney. The singing is very good, showing to an

P. G. LOWERY AND COMPANY WITH WALLACE—HAGENBECK CIRCUS

Indianapolis Freeman, July 9, 1910.

> advantage the well-controlled voices of the different men. The orchestra, led by Mr. W. E. Barbour, violinist, is particularly pleasing. There is no doubt whatever as to the excellency of this organization . . . Every detail is under the personal direction of Prof. Pope.

Most annex companies carried at least a few female performers, but some carried only one, often a novelty "female interlocutor"; and some carried none at all. R. Roy Pope directed an all-male band and minstrels. Pope intended to forge bold departures with the Ringling Bros. Show, which would elevate the status of his band and relieve him of minstrel duties altogether. In January 1911 it was announced:

> The coming season, beginning in March, will bring to the profession another new idea in the musical line. Three seasons ago the Ringling Bros. circus did not carry any colored musicians, in fact no colored assistants in any line. This aggregation, known as the largest and greatest on earth, will by persistent efforts of the efficient band director and cornetist, Prof. R. Roy Pope, carry an exclusive concert band without minstrel and without women. Last season Prof. Pope was the first of band masters to discard women performers and

this season he takes the initiative in eliminating the minstrel part. The band will be composed of fifteen select musicians, who will render daily programs and afternoon concerts only.

It has been Prof. Pope's ambition and purpose to convince his employers and the public that the Negro can measure with other races in the musical profession, without the addition of the "Aunt Dinah" and "Uncle Eph" acts, and his efforts have been rewarded. It is also his desire to show that this opportunity will lead to the highest standard of musical perfection among Negro musicians.[27]

The following season, a correspondent for the Ringling Bros. Circus Annex Band boasted that, "In each and every city Prof. Pope is highly praised for having the best band of its size ever traveling with a circus—twelve men in all—both in appearance and conduct and ability. It would be very nice, indeed, if some of our other colored band leaders would drop that old 'Befo' De Wah' dope and advance as the world does; and they would find that the Ofay will appreciate it much more. If you are a performer, go into vaudeville or with an opera show. Band leaders, be band leaders, and let the producers and stage managers' business alone, and try and help the world forget forty-five years ago."[28]

There is considerable pathos in Roy Pope's heartfelt efforts to elevate standards and maintain dignity, carried out as they were within the context of a circus sideshow tent. Pope's band performed alongside "Mlle. Corretta, midget; Frank Lention, the three legged boy; Geo. Wells, the smileless man; Chas. Tripp, the armless wonder; Grace Gilbert, the girl with the auburn beard; Bombay, the royal bugler from Siam; Gondio & Apexia, the pinheads from India; Piramel & Sami, the double-bodied East Indian brother and sister; Prof. A. Roberts's

R. ROY POPE.

Indianapolis Freeman, July 17, 1909.

trained bears, monkeys, dogs and man-like apes; and Supromoni, the snake charmer."[29]

R. Roy Pope gave up his position with the Ringling Bros. Circus after the season of 1912, passing the leadership of his band to trombonist P. A. Venable. No explanation was given for his withdrawal. After a one-year hiatus, during which time he served as instructor of the Peoples's Band of Dayton, Ohio, Pope went back to Ringling Bros. for the season of 1914. When they played Indianapolis a reviewer noted, "The popular bandmaster and his musicians were seen in the parade. In the sideshow they were also making music to the delight of all. He put on some ragtime operas among his other selections and the colored element of the side show patrons showed signs of the Eagle

R. Roy Pope and his circus annex band. (courtesy Thornton Hagert, Vernacular Music Research)

Rock and other motions of similar brand. The white folks also caught the feeling and got rather wobbly. All liked it very much."[30]

On May 18, 1914, the Ringling Bros. Circus played "day and date" with the 101 Ranch Shows at Easton, Pennsylvania. A Ringling Bros. reporter noted that the 101 Ranch paraded first, and "then the big show paraded next. Both shows did a turn-away business in the afternoon while the Ringling show did capacity business in the evening also. Prof. Pope's band without minstrel proved to the public and both managements that minstrels are not needed. He gave a thirty minute concert in the afternoon playing Sells Floto Triumphal march, Remick's Hits No. 13 overture; Handy's Memphis Blues and Revelation March. This is an every-day affair and takes well."[31]

Prof. Pope and his wife, who was also a trained musician, spent the winter of 1914–1915 back in Dayton, Ohio, "teaching the Peoples' band, a union organization, and playing with the celebrated Willis-Warmack-Willis Trio." They were in Chicago for the opening of Ringling's new season in April 1915: "Mrs. Pope . . . will be with the show this season featured as the only colored lady saxophone soloist enroute with a circus."[32]

A report in September 1915 described Prof. Pope's up-to-date musical program: "Side show number one, where Pope's band is the feature, is doing a great business and the price is 25 cents. Prof. Pope is featuring 'Old Folk's Rag' and 'Down Home Rag' by Wilbur C. Sweatman; 'Memphis Blues,' by Handy; 'Salad Dressing Rag,' by Frank Terry, and 'The Florida Blues,' 'Eagle Rock Rag,' 'High Ball Rag,' the three latest numbers in ragtime, by William King Phillips. All of the above numbers are by colored writers."[33]

Obviously proud of his position and his band, Pope made it known that, "Each one of these musicians are first-class and, as has always been the rule on the Ringling show, these people are also first-class in their deportment, receiving praise everywhere for this, which only goes to show that the circus life is not as some narrow-minded people deem it, low and degrading, but strictly a business proposition of high standard and elevating to the Negro musician."[34] Nevertheless, at the end of the 1915 season Pope notified the *Freeman* that, "He has quit the circus business for good. He will locate permanently in Dayton, O[hio]. Prof. Pope will have charge of an orchestra, and will be otherwise interested in music."[35] In 1927, comedian-producer Tim Owsley confirmed: "Roy Pope, one time band leader of Mahara Minstrels, Ringling Brothers' big side show band and many other traveling organizations, is now located in Dayton with his wife and family and doing well. He is still in the music business, but has said good-by to road life."[36]

The Barnum and Bailey Circus, "The Greatest Show on Earth," opened its exhibition season each year with an extended engagement at Madison Square Garden in New York City. From 1912 through 1918 their sideshow band and minstrel company was under the direction of Prof. James Wolfscale. Born in Chillicothe, Missouri, around 1868, Wolfscale was a true pioneer of circus annex minstrelsy, "known by every man, woman and child in the business."[37] He reportedly began his circus career in 1890, after having toured for several years with minstrel organizations.[38] In 1902 the roster of Wolfscale's Plantation Minstrels, "in mighty union with Sells & Down's Circus," included Lawrence Cheatham, as well as the celebrated cornet player J. H. McCamon, who left Wolfscale mid-season to take charge of the band with Allen's New Orleans Minstrels.[39]

Wolfscale reengaged with Sells and Downs for 1903, as the J. E. Wolfscale Vaudeville Company. His roster of performers included "Misses Essie Williams and Sallie N. Lee, late of the Forepaugh & Fish Wild West show. The ladies are well pleased with the new company, as every member of the band seems to be a gentleman, and they being the only colored ladies with the company, they expect a pleasant season." Essie Williams made "a tremendous hit with 'What the Band Played.'" Sallie Lee sang "Taking a Trip Up the Hudson" and "the popular waltz song, 'Mollie Greene.'" Other featured performers included stage manager Walter Rector, singing "In Sunny Africa," "I Know Your Face But I Can't Call Your Name," and "If You Can't Be the Bell Cow, Come Fall in Behind"; Ed Williams singing "Honey Boy" and "I Got Mine"; Nat Black singing "If Time Was Money, I'd Be a Millionaire" and "When the Cold Winds Begin to Blow;" and O. D. (or Addie) Crumwell, "still telling them how to spell 'Chicken.'"[40]

1907 found Prof. Wolfscale's Concert Band and Vaudeville Show attached to the original Cole Bros. Circus. Apparently, this was the year

Wolfscale first brought his sons Roy and Troy into the band. Roy played cornet and eventually doubled as interlocutor in the minstrel show. Troy was a trap drummer who doubled on alto horn: "while quite young [they] are very accomplished musicians and give promise of a bright future in this line of work."[41] Eventually, a third son Ray also joined the band, on alto horn. Roy, Troy, and Ray Wolfscale became staples of their father's circus annex band and minstrels.

In 1911 Wolfscale's company traveled with the Forepaugh-Sells Circus. At the end of the season it was announced that Wolfscale had signed a contract with the Barnum and Bailey Circus for the following year. There was nothing ordinary about "The Greatest Show On Earth." When the new season opened in April 1912 it was reported: "One of the features in Barnum & Bailey's big spectacular production, 'Cleopatra,' is Wolfscale's Band, mounted on camels, appearing as Egyptians in Egyptian costumes. Never before has a band been seen on camels, playing. As it is very odd and very difficult, the camel band is a big hit."[42]

Wolfscale used eight people in his 1912 sideshow minstrel first part. Herman Brown and Willie Brown held down the extreme ends. Herman Brown sang "My Only Pal," "You're My Baby," "You'll Want Me Back," and the proto–blues anthem "All Night Long." Willie Brown contributed "his eccentric dancing and singing 'I've Got You, Steve' and 'I Am Going Crazy.'"[43]

In addition to Wolfscale's band and minstrels, the Barnum & Bailey sideshow harbored famous African Americans among its roster of "freaks and curiosities." One was "Zip the What Is It," described as "kind of a halfway creature. He looks as if he might be the missing link."[44] "Zip," who was originally recruited into the show by P. T. Barnum himself, was said to have celebrated his sixty-fifth birthday April 5, 1913: "He amuses the people daily, playing his violin and directing the band."[45]

Another African American "curiosity" was Princess Wee Wee, known as the "doll lady." She was an extraordinarily small, perfectly proportioned person, "pretty and cute personified."[46] At the beginning of Barnum and Bailey's 1916 season, Princess Wee Wee was declared "the hit of the Freak Department at Madison Square Garden."[47] Under the tutelage of Prof. Wolfscale and his wife, Princess Wee Wee emerged as a full-fledged song and dance artist. She joined the famous Whitman Sisters Company in 1925.[48] The following year, while playing the Howard Theater in Washington, D.C., the Whitman Sisters Company visited the White House and were presented to President Calvin Coolidge, "who expressed great pleasure in meeting the perfect little lady, Princess Wee Wee."[49]

With the Barnum and Bailey Circus in 1913, Wolfscale's fourteen musicians were purported to be "the most popular band in the parade, because they give the people what they want, besides playing heavy marches and all the popular songs and latest rags."[50] Inside the "kid top," the sideshow tent, old-time minstrel veteran J. Ed Hunn served as stage manager and took the center spot in the minstrel, singing "Take Me to That Swanee Shore," "Keep on Loving," and "Our Little War at Home, Sweet Home." Willie Brown and Earl Terry held down the two ends. Terry sang "Oh, You Georgia Rose," "You Certainly Look Good To Me," "Ragtime Melodies," and "The Undertaker Man;" while Brown featured Irving Berlin's "Snooky

Ookums," "Waiting for the Robert E. Lee," and "Fifteen Cents."[51]

Prior to the start of the 1914 season, the *Freeman* announced that Wolfscale had "received a telegram from the management of Barnum & Bailey Circus to furnish them with a band of thirty-five pieces, to be one of the features of the big new spectacle in Madison Square Garden, New York, and for the road season of thirty two weeks. It was not only a surprise to the profession, but to Mr. Wolfscale himself as well. At last we are to have a traveling colored concert band, not merely talk, but a positive fact."[52]

Wolfscale opened the 1914 season with a concert band of thirty-two pieces. It was the largest sideshow annex band on the road, the crowning achievement of Wolfscale's long career as bandmaster. Barnum and Bailey began the season as usual, with a five weeks' run at Madison Square Garden. They presented "The Wizard Prince of Arabia," a "stupendous spectacle" produced by Alf T. Ringling. Wolfscale's full band appeared as Arabian musicians "in the finale of the big ballet dance spectacle stage, and play 'The General Felix Agnus March.'"[53]

Concluding their long engagement at Madison Square Garden, Barnum and Bailey finally opened under canvas on April 20, 1914, in Brooklyn. A special feature of their street parade was the presence of two colored bands, the concert band split into two sixteen-piece units. The season reached its halfway point with Wolfscale's large band still intact:

> Prof. Wolfscale's band this season of thirty-two pieces is a credit to all colored traveling musicians inasmuch as it shows how much they are in demand . . . They are featuring the heaviest marches, latest popular music and rags . . . As a rule most side show managers just want noise from a colored band. The reason for this is because they don't have a large enough band to do anything but jam. Prof. Wolfscale has shown the management of the greatest show on earth that with a big number of colored musicians you can play concert music and other kinds and with as much expression as the big show's concert band.[54]

Wolfscale's Plantation Show for 1914 was as elaborate as his marching band. It appears to have featured an all-male cast. J. C. "Frosty" Moore served as stage manager, and Earl Terry and W. B. White were the principal comedians. White sang "Pork Chops" and a parody on "You Made Me Love You," while Terry featured "That Dogging Rag" and "I'm Crying Just For You," performed as a duet with Ben Wolfscale, presumably another relative of the director. Sonny Gray "as Rastus" sang "Down in Chattanooga," while Joseph Sudler and George Sharp, the two trombone players in Wolfscale's band, enlivened the "plant" show with "The Dynamite Rag." Sudler also "scored a decided hit as Ephraim." Other features of the show included champion eccentric dancer Taggert Hartgrave, "the boy with the insane feet"; the Comedy Quartette, Earl Johnson, Joe Sudler, M. O. Russell and Tom Grey; and Ed Hall as "the baby 'Snookums.'"[55] The following year, versatile Joe Sudler joined the Lyric Theater Orchestra of Kansas City, under the leadership of W. Benton Overstreet. Sudler went on to play cornet with Charles Elgar's famous dance band in Chicago.[56]

Barnum and Bailey reduced the size of Wolfscale's aggregation to twenty members for the season of 1915. This may have been the reason he initially threatened to cancel his engagement with

WOLFSCALE'S BAND AND VAUDEVILLE COMPANY.

Bottom row standing, left to right—Lewis Ford, Roy Wolfscale, Bebely Walker, Ernest C. Smith.
Center—J. Ed. Hunn.

Freeman representatives had the pleasure of seeing the famous Wolfscale's band and vaudeville folks last week when Barnum and Bailey were showing in Indianapolis. James Wolfscale, head of the organization, made it very pleasant for them, introducing them to his sons who are members of the band and other members of the band and vaudeville company.

They put on a show that was highly entertaining to the crowds that jammed their tent. Comedians, dancers and coon song shouters were among the attractions.

Top row standing, left to right—Earl Terry, Bennie Stratton, Jas. McDonald, Fred Garland, Troy Wolfscale, Joe E. Herriford, Ray Wolfscale, Jas. Wolfscale, Willie Brown.

Indianapolis Freeman, June 7, 1913.

the circus and "spend the summer at his home in Chicago."[57] A few weeks later he changed his mind, and when the circus opened at Madison Square Garden the *Freeman* reported: "Professor Wolfscale's band again was one of the big features of the new gigantic spectacle 'Lala Bookh' [*sic*] . . . Again this season Prof. Wolfscale will have two bands in the parade . . . The minstrel is under the stage management of Mr. Slim Mason. He is featuring 'Rufus Johnson Harmony Band,' and 'Aba Daba Honey Moon.' Mr. Leon Gray is featuring 'St. Louis Blues' and 'Du Dah Dey,' while Earl (Stoggy) Johnson as a Chinese impersonator, is featuring 'Chinese Blues' with great success."[58] A later report clarified that, "'Mio San,' the Chinese blues song by Mr. Johnson, dressed as a Chinaman, singing out in the audience, assisted by Slim Mason and Leon Gray, is the feature of the show."[59]

Stage manager Elvis "Slim" Mason was a well-respected veteran minstrel performer. As the 1915 season with Barnum and Bailey's sideshow progressed, Mason added new numbers to Wolfscale's minstrel first part: "He is using 'Moonlight on the Mississippi' for an opening chorus." Taking the stage as an end man, Mason introduced Chris Smith's new song hit, "Goofer Dust." When not otherwise occupied, Mason also beat the bass drum on parade. In turn, trombonist William Moorehead doubled as a singer in the minstrel, offering titles like "Sooner or Later," "Take Me to the Midnight Cakewalk Ball," "When It Is Circus Day in Dixie," and "My Bird of Paradise." Popular vaudeville performer Leon Gray contributed "Squeezing the Mule," "It's Too Late Now," and "Sophie Tucker's song success 'The Broadway Blues.'"[60]

Blues and emerging jazz were increasingly significant in Prof. Wolfscale's musical program during the 1915 and 1916 seasons. In the fall of 1915, when trombone player Fred "Cat" Garland declared himself the company's champion checkers player, the *Freeman* correspondent hastened to add, "But say, you ought to hear Cat play the Florida Blues."[61] The band was also playing "Jogo Blues." In 1916 Wolfscale's band rang in Jelly Roll Morton's signature "Jelly Roll Blues" and "Pace and Handy's big hit, 'The Hesitating Blues.' We have had more calls for this number than any other we play."[62]

The arrival of Wolfscale's circus annex company was cause for celebration in black communities up and down the line. Following their 1915 Indianapolis engagement, a *Freeman* reviewer noted, "The minstrel part was greatly enjoyed and especially by the colored people who make the side show a specialty. When it comes to side show proprietors the show people ought to be thankful for colored people."[63] At Dallas, Texas, on Sunday, October 8, 1916, Wolfscale's band was feted by the local Knights of Pythias Band: "The day was very much like Old Settlers' Reunion, as we met three minstrel companies there. The Georgia Smart Set were . . . at the Star Theatre . . . Members of the Virginia Minstrels and members of the New Orleans Minstrels, who were playing nearby towns, came over to spend the day. This probably was the largest number of performers and musicians that ever met in one city at the same time . . . The companies spent the evening at the colored theatres, after which the rest of the evening was spent at the Honorary Ball at the Auditorium Hall, given in honor of the B. and B. Colored band."[64]

SLIM MASON SNAPPED BY A FREEMAN PHOTOGRAPHER

During the engagement of Barnum & Bailey shows in Indianapolis recently "Slim" Mason, one of the leading funmakers with Prof. Wolfscales Company,

"SLIM" MASON.

was snapped by The Freeman photographer as he was strolling on Indiana Avenue. "Slim" is a neat dresser and a big hit with the ladies.

Indianapolis Freeman, June 26, 1915.

James Wolfscale's son Roy, the cornet player, did not troupe with his father in 1916. Instead, he joined John Wickliffe's Ginger Band of Chicago, and he was present for their historic

SLIM MASON,
That Funny Fellow, as He Appears Daily with Prof. Wolfscales' Company, with the Barnum & Bailey Shows.

Indianapolis Freeman, July 3, 1915.

1916 engagements at Schlitz Palm Garden in Milwaukee and the Gruenwald Café in Minneapolis, which introduced entertainment patrons of these two midwestern metropolises to a new style of dance music. In December 1917, a special report to the *Freeman* asserted: "J. H. Wickliffe and his famous Ginger Band will settle all questions with the Dixieland Jazz Band about who are the originators of the jazz music. At least Milwaukeans, both white and colored, have decided among themselves that there is no better bunch of real musicians for playing anything from Tannhauser to the Livery Stable Blues than Wickliffe's Ginger Orchestra."[65]

Meanwhile, at Madison Square Garden in the spring of 1916, James Wolfscale's eighteen-piece band and minstrels were featured in Barnum and Bailey's "new spectacular pageant—'Persia.'" In the sideshow Prof. Wolfscale did away with the old-time minstrel first part in exchange for a modern vaudeville show. The stage was managed by Sam Good, assisted by Slim Mason.[66] "Dance craze" songs were prominent in the repertoire. Earl Johnson contributed "Dancing the Jelly Roll."[67] Slim Mason's feature, "Walking the Dog," "using the dance movements" was "a sensational hit."[68]

Shelton Brooks's "Walking the Dog" was the biggest dance song sensation since "Ballin' the Jack." It hit the marketplace in the spring of 1916, and quickly saturated every avenue of American entertainment, on both sides of the color line. Everyone took it up, from Butler "String Beans" May to the Original Dixieland Jazz Band. Its great popularity inspired other "dance craze" hits such as Spencer Williams's "Steppin' on the Puppy's Tail" and William Benton Overstreet's "The 'Jazz' Dance," both published in 1917. These songs were the terpsichorean anthems that introduced jazz into American popular culture.

Now listen Honey 'bout a new dance craze;
Been 'riginated for about ten days,

. . . .

You were all crazy 'bout the "Bunny Hug,"
'Most everybody was a "Tango Bug,"
But now, and somehow,
The funny Dog walk is all the town talk,

JOHN H. WICKLIFFE'S GINGER ORCHESTRA,

Styled America's Greatest Jaz Combination, Now at the Regent Theater, Indianapolis.

The John H. Wickliffe's Ginger Orchestra Combination is filling a four weeks' engagement at the Regent theater, the first orchestra of Colored players that has appeared at that house. They have been a scream since the beginning of their engagement two weeks ago.

John H. Wickliffe.

Mr. Wickliffe is the founder and general manager of the organization. He is further known as the sensational drummer. In fact, he is an all-round expert in his corner—a master of the traps.

Darnell Howard.

This young man is a little wonder, a very wizard of the bow. He is born to the instrument, having all of the qualities of expression and tone of the great orchestra leaders and bandmasters. He is not more than seventeen years old. It is a positive joy to see and hear him.

Roy A. Wolfscale.

Mr. Wolfscale, cornetist, is well known in musical circles. He usually puts his time in with his father's bunch of the Ringling Bros.' Shows. His father is head of the music of the annex.

J. Ed Greene.

Mr. Greene is of splendid personality and thoroughly in love with that strangest of instruments, the trombone, that does so much execution with so little data, such little direction as to how to do it.

R. J. Scott.

Mr. Scott deals in that soft-voiced instrument, and reedy, the clarinet, which has its counterpart in love's soft impeachment—the very Pipes of Pan, "who plucked a reed by the river." He knows what to do with it.

Anthony Spaulding.

Mr. Spauling presides over the instrument that is wholly an orchestra, or a lesser part, if one so chooses. He is skilled in his playing.

Lockewood Lewis.

Mr. Lewis is the entertainer or the interlocutor.

Miss Rena James.

Miss James is well known to the profession, having appeared at the Crown Garden theater a few seasons ago. Entertainer is the part assigned her and which she is well qualified to fill.

The orchestra is the leader of dance music. Just can't keep still when the Jaz combination plays. It will appear at the Washington theater Saturday evening.

Indianapolis Freeman, October 28, 1916.

(chorus)
Get 'way back, and snap your fingers,
Get over Sally, one and all,
Grab your gal, and don't you linger,
Do that slow drag 'round the hall.
Do that step, the "Texas Tommy,"
Drop like you're sitting on a log;
Rise slow, that will show
The dance called Walkin' the Dog.[69]

At the close of the 1916 circus season, Wolfscale began a tour of vaudeville houses in an act titled

Moonlight on the Levee, with a company of sixteen people featuring Princess Wee Wee, Slim Mason, Sam Good, and Wolfscale's brass band. Music for this act was written by James "Slap Rags" White and William Benton Overstreet. When the show came to Chicago early in 1917, critic Sylvester Russell wrote: "Princess Wee Wee, the colored midget star, flooded the Grand theatre and turned people away at every performance last Monday evening in 'Moonlight on the Levee' a good levee act . . . The tiny Princess danced Walking the Dog and electrified on the finish."[70]

Moonlight on the Levee toured successfully throughout the winter, closing at the Bijou Theater in Orange, New Jersey, on March 24, 1917. The *Freeman* reported: "All members of the company open . . . March 29 with Barnum & Bailey circus at Madison Square Garden for a season of 32 weeks . . . members of the act will make up James E. Wolfscale's real circus band of 20 pieces, which will be one of the big features of the big new spectacle."[71]

Traveling with a circus could be dangerous. Each year, the *Freeman* published numerous reports of train wrecks, animal attacks, fires, and "blow downs," with the big top collapsing in heavy winds. In June 1917 a correspondent from Wolfscale's Annex Band relayed this news: "We encountered our first blow down of the season at Uniontown, Pa. when a windstorm came up, just ten minutes before the afternoon performance started. The big top was carried high in the air and came down on the heads of the spectators. Several were injured. It was impossible to give a night performance."[72]

In North Dakota later that summer, Wolfscale's sideshow orchestra was "featuring a new dance hit, 'Shake Ol' Brown' by R. P. Akard, some dance number."[73] Akard's own *Freeman* advertisement for "Shake Ol' Brown" advised, "That's just what you'll want to do when you hear this rag."

Following the 1917 circus season, Wolfscale's aggregation again appeared in vaudeville theaters with *Moonlight on the Levee*, billed as "Princess Wee Wee And Her Jass Band Company." According to the *Freeman*, the company consisted of Princess Wee Wee, Ida Forsyne, Edna Parker, Slim Mason, Tommy Woods, Jessie Schaffer, James Wolfscale, Johnny Brown, Willie Green, F. Ford Lewis, Kilmer Jackson, and Troy Wolfscale: "Little Princess Wee Wee is the big feature. Slim Mason with his comedy is always a big hit. Miss Ida Forsyne and Tommy Woods hold down the dancing part of the act and more than please at every performance. The jass band and Jessie Schaffer as Mammy also receive their share of honors."[74] When the company played Gibson's New Standard Theater in Philadelphia a correspondent informed: "They represent the crew of the 'Rosa Lee' (a Mississippi steamboat) in songs, buck and wing dancing on the levee, the Princess joining in. They also have a jazz band who demonstrate their ability in playing jazz music with the Princess as director."[75] William Benton Overstreet's "On The Rockin' Rosa Lee," one of the big song hits of the 1917 season, was almost certainly featured in this jazz band's program.

Wolfscale did not open the 1918 season with the Barnum and Bailey Circus. William H. Reid was initially bandmaster, but Wolfscale soon returned. The *Freeman* correspondent assured, "Mr. Wolfscale has the reputation of carrying one of the best colored bands traveling, despite the draft calling so many good musicians, the band is right

GIBSON'S

New Standard Theatre

SOUTH STREET AT TWELFTH

JOHN T. GIBSON, - - - - - - - Owner and Manager

WEEK BEGINNING **FEBRUARY 5**

Last Vaudeville Engagement to
Satisfy Public Demand

ENGAGEMENT OF

PRINCESS WEE WEE

AND

Jez Band Co.

Has been extended to week of Feb. 5

Jule Weaver & Co.

8 PEOPLE 8
In Burlesque, Comedy, Drama

BRADFORD & JEANETTE BURRIS COMPANY

In Sargent Ham of 15th Dist.

THE DUNHAMS

Marvelous, Sensational, Gymnast

THE SMALLEST COLORED WOMAN IN THE WORLD

7 Big Features 7

Every Friday, Amateur Contest. See them get the hook. 2 Prizes Awarded

Matinee Daily 10c. Nights, 2 Shows 10, 15, 25c. Box Seats Reserved by phone, Walnut 4631, 7755.

Philadelphia Tribune, February 3, 1917.

up to the standard. This makes the seventh season on the greatest show on earth for Wolfscale's band, which is always a big feature."[76]

The 1918 season was Wolfscale's last with the Barnum and Bailey Circus. In 1919, Barnum and Bailey combined with Ringling Brothers' Circus, and P. G. Lowery was tapped to head the sideshow band. Wolfscale began the 1919 season with the John Robinson Circus, but by August it was reported that he had returned to his home in Chicago. He apparently never toured with a circus band again. James Wolfscale died in Chicago, on October 21, 1921.[77]

Cornet player Arthur A. Wright's experience as stage manager for P. G. Lowery's Minstrels with the Hagenbeck-Wallace Circus during the season of 1913 no doubt helped prepare him to take control of the band and minstrels with the Sparks Circus the following year. The Sparks Circus opened its season at Concord, North Carolina, on April 11, 1914, and finished at Seneca, South Carolina, seven months later, having traveled a reported 12,000 miles without missing a single performance or losing a sideshow performer. They did experience a blow down during the first week of July, at Redwood Falls, Minnesota. None of the performers were hurt, but one member of the audience was injured and the company lost most of its wardrobe. A few weeks later, at Wahpeton, North Dakota, members of the company "visited the Ringland [*sic*] Bros. graveyard, where a number of the workingmen that was killed in a blow down a few years ago are buried."[78]

Wright's band enlivened the 1914 season with "some classy rags and marches." Mack Carter was stage manager for the minstrel production, which featured Miss Cleo Poteet, Dorothy Burton, Eugene Peterson, and Mr. and Mrs. Sam Kennedy. Their song repertoire included "All Aboard For Dixie," "I Wonder Where My Lovin' Man Has Gone," "My Tango Man," "Memphis Blues," "St. Louis Blues," "Floating Down the River," "The Dangerous Rag," "When The War Breaks Out in Mexico (I'm Going Back to Montreal)," "I've Got the Rumitiz," "Just for Tonight," and "Who Paid the Rent for Mrs. Rip Van Winkle."[79]

A. A. Wright took charge of the Sparks Circus sideshow annex again for 1915. Important additions to his company included Mose McQuitty, the vastly experienced euphonium and tuba player, and Rastus Airship (aka Edmond Madison), a celebrated eccentric dancer who gained entrée to the main circus tent as a feature of the after-show. Wright's band showcased William "King" Phillips's latest hits "Eagle Rock" and "High Ball Rag." A letter in the *Freeman* from trombone player Horace Harrison of the Georgia Minstrels, proclaiming his supremacy in playing Phillips's "Florida Blues," provoked a quick rejoinder from Wright's *Freeman* correspondent: "Isaiah Wilds, our trombone player, says that he noticed an article in The Freeman written by a trombone player claiming that he is killing every devil playing the trombone and featuring the 'Florida Blues.' Now, this fellow must remember that there are people playing the 'Florida Blues' and getting all there is in it, also there are trombonists that he has not met lately."[80]

Mose McQuitty wrote the *Freeman* that spring to assure that the Sparks Circus sideshow was "one of the best under canvas this season," with "Wright's minstrels opening," followed by Berta Wren, "lady bag puncher, mind reading and palmistry"; Millie Dick, "snake enchantress"; James Hartte, magician; Ray Dick, "Punch and Judy"; and Mable Buel, "trunk mystery." McQuitty counted nine pieces in the parade band, and he detailed a five-piece orchestra that suggests an emergent jazz band: "Bob Oliver, clarinet; Baisey [*sic*, Boisey] Gray, cornet; Jas. McDonald, trombone; M. McQuitty, bass; Isaiah Wilds, traps."[81]

Another report from Wright's annex band during the 1915 season preserves an example of uncommon benevolence. While the Sparks Circus was in Helena, Georgia, it was discovered that a young man by the name of Babe Steel, who had been traveling with the Nashville Amusement Company, was being held in the local jail in lieu of a small fine, "for a trivial offense, but this is Georgia, and Georgia is h--l." Arthur Wright took up a collection among the sideshow performers and quickly raised the sum necessary to free Babe Steel: "So men remember, all troopers are subject to a shake down some time, so don't turn them down."[82]

Wright remained in charge of the Sparks Circus Annex Band and Minstrels through the end of the decade.[83] Future blues recording artist Viola McCoy appeared with Wright's minstrels in 1916, singing "Scaddle De Mooch" and "Daddy," and Cleo Poteet was heard singing "Dancing the Jelly Roll" and "Aba Daba Honeymoon."[84]

Prof. Arthur Wright's band, with Al. G. Barnes' Circus.

Billboard, March 17, 1923.

Mose McQuitty, who had trouped with many companies for more than two decades, expressed his satisfaction with the sleeping accommodations provided by Sparks that year: "Mr. A. A. Wright has fine quarters for his band and show, I dare say the best of any show on the road, as Mr. Sparks fixed up the end of his last year's sleeper for the colored band and we are all proud of the same. We have six double berths and eleven people; a nice wash room and clothes closet and a vestibule and sleeper."[85]

Sleeping facilities for black circus performers could be a point of contention. For many years the Sells-Floto Circus did not carry a black band and minstrel company in connection with its sideshow. The reason was provided in a 1912 *Freeman* commentary: "The whole band quit on account of poor accommodations they received on the show."[86] *Freeman* reporter Billy Lewis visited the Sells-Floto show when it came to Indianapolis in September 1914, and he made note that there were still no colored performers in the sideshow.[87]

Apparently, Sells-Floto had reinstated a colored annex company by 1923, when well-known African American minstrel performer and *Chicago Defender* columnist Coy Herndon inspected their sleeping cars and found "musicians and performers of the Race" sleeping "three high." Herndon observed that it had been the practice "for a number of years with shows of this kind to make Colored performers sleep three high. It must be a matter of, 'Oh, well, they will stand for it,' as they certainly do not deserve it." Pointing out that "No circus side show is complete without a Negro band and a minstrel show, or some kind of entertainment from them," he asked why all the white performers got to "sleep two high, and the colored performers have to sleep three high?" Herndon finally explained, "For the benefit of those who do not know what is meant by three high, is a regulation berth on a Pullman sleeper with an extra berth put in the same space."[88]

Slide trombonist James A. Harris rode with the Gollmar Bros. Circus as its sideshow colored band director for at least six consecutive years, from 1912 through 1917.[89] The Gollmar Show was a small circus, "the greatest of all little ones, making it hot for the big ones."[90] Its annex company appears to have been all male. An informative report from the Gollmar Bros. sideshow was published in the *Freeman* of June 6, 1914:

> From Madison [South Dakota] we jumped to Bridgewater and had a real "circus day," it being 90 in the shade. The boys were extended a special invitation after the show to a dance given that night by the Ofays. They all attended and enjoyed themselves to the highest. From Bridgewater we jumped to Chamberlain, where the Indians for miles around had camped two days waiting for the circus. Next was Tyndall, where we experienced a real Kansas windy day; and, at that, the natives showed that they enjoyed the show by largely attending in the afternoon, but at night we were visited with a real storm, giving but one show. Mr. Slim Mason, our hustling stage manager, keeps the boys up on the latest popular "stuff" and song "hits." No "plantation" stuff over here. Mr. Jim Green (Capt. Jenks) is still making them laugh with his funny antics. Eugene Hopkins is only "hitting the high ones" on his cornet on parade . . . Roscoe Copeland takes plenty of hands on his song "Where the Red, Red Roses Grow," which he puts over with plenty of feeling. Frankie Robinson certainly makes them take notion singing "This Is the Life." Elmer Scott has them patting their feet when he sings "Camp Meetin' Band." James Harris is featuring a trombone solo, "My Hero," and they certainly give it to Jimmie.[91]

Harris' Band and Minstrels integrated generous portions of blues and incipient jazz into their 1915 and 1916 programs, featuring "The Florida Blues," "The Memphis Blues," "Pray for the Lights to Go Out," "Walking the Dog," and others: "Our little minstrel never fails to make good in every town on the route, and the band gets its share, playing all of Pace and Handy's music."[92]

By the middle of the decade, blues had become a special attraction that sustained the popularity of African American entertainers under the sideshow tent. Prof. John Eason's Annex Band with the Yankee Robinson Show may have been the first circus band to include a blues song in its repertoire. On November 9, 1912, it was revealed through the *Freeman* that trombonist Frank Terry "has just finished a band arrangement of Baby Seals' 'Blues,' and is making a daily hit with it." "Baby Seals Blues" was one of the first published blues songs.[93] It had been on the market only a few weeks before Eason's Band performed it for the patrons of the Yankee Robinson Circus sideshow annex.

Prof. Eason's band had an eventful 1912 season with the Yankee Robinson Circus. At Cheyenne, Wyoming, in July, "During a terrible wind and rain storm our tents were blown down and torn into ribbons, breaking poles, ropes and stakes just as if they were only toothpicks, and in the panic several people were hurt. The sideshow was the only tent that stood the terrible wind."[94] A few weeks later, a band member wryly joked, "We have a very brave bunch of boys over here. Boys that will stand in front of cannons, guns and knives, but believe me, a little gust of wind will make them haul, and they are not too proud to show the rabbit, but they are a jolly good bunch after all."[95]

Later that season, the Eason bunch ran into trouble of a different hue: "While playing Big Spring, Texas, the colored band was not allowed to make the parade and worse still had to have four deputy marshals stationed on each side of the band stage besides the stake and change wagon. Can you beat it in a free and civilized country? . . . Instead of sending missionaries to foreign countries, we need them right in the United States."[96]

In 1913, Prof. Eason headed the annex band with the Frank A. Robbins Circus. This band included Charles Creath, the popular cornet player from St. Louis who recorded in the 1920s as the leader of Creath's Jazz-O-Maniacs. Creath was with the Eason band, traveling with Yankee Robinson's Circus in 1915, along with another future recording artist, clarinetist Arnett Nelson. The show opened its season at Adel, Iowa, on April 22, 1915, with a correspondent noting: "Prof. John Eason's band and minstrels is the feature attraction of the sideshow annex. Mr. Fred Buchanon, the manager, says Mr. Eason has the best twelve people together this season he has ever had . . . Our eight-piece orchestra is something grand, the best that has ever been with any side show, so boys, you see it can't be beat."[97] A later report added,

Lizzie Miles. (courtesy Hogan Jazz Archive, Tulane University)

"Mr. Arnett Nelson is screaming with 'Down At the Barbecue.' Mr. Sam Smith is featuring 'Nighttime Down in Dixieland.' Mrs. Ozella Smith is singing 'Broadway Blues.' Mrs. Lena Hulett is singing 'Back to the Carolina You Love.'"[98]

No veteran of circus sideshow annex minstrelsy enjoyed a longer or more impressive career in popular music than Lizzie Miles. Between 1922 and 1939, this memorable New Orleans native recorded more than seventy titles, mostly blues, often accompanied by legendary jazz musicians.[99] After World War II she made a remarkable career comeback and reigned through the 1950s as the matron saint of the New Orleans "jazz revival." During the formative years of her career, 1914–1918, Lizzie Miles toured the country with her first husband, bandleader J. C. Miles, in his circus sideshow annex company.[100]

J. C. Miles was a native of Indianapolis. In April 1912 he accepted the job of assistant manager, announcer, and ticket seller for the Alabama Minstrels, a traveling show under the proprietorship of C. L. Erickson. In February 1914 Miles wrote the *Freeman* from Roanoke, Virginia, to say the show was "doing fine business throughout the Virginias, Carolinas and Tennessee. We closed our tent show season at Norfolk recently, and are now playing the finest and best theaters throughout these sections."[101]

In a 1958 appearance on the old Dave Garroway television show *Wide Wide World*, Lizzie Miles said she had started singing at a very early age at lawn parties, and then joined her first traveling show at age fifteen: "Then a man named Elmer Jones, Mr. E. H. Jones offered me a bigger salary than I was getting. Mr. Jones owned the Alabama Minstrels . . . and he and his brother—they got the Cole Bros. Circus. That was a five-car circus and I was with them."[102]

Freeman reportage reveals that on April 2, 1914, J. C. Miles concluded his engagement with the Alabama Minstrels, and he and Lizzie opened the 1914 season with Jones Bros. and Wilson's Three Ring Circus, managed by C. L. Erickson's uncles, Elmer and August Jones: "Mr. Miles has charge of the colored band and minstrels, which is the feature attraction of the side show."[103] After opening at Norfolk, Virginia, on April 7, the show dipped into North Carolina, then worked its way back up through Virginia to Maryland and Pennsylvania, where Miles reported in mid-May: "Our band and minstrels, although only eleven strong, is the feature of the Annex, featuring principally the latest rags and popular airs. And who says that the 'Blues' won't go in this section. It goes bigger here than it does in Bam [i.e., Alabama], as they follow the big band wagon in vast throngs, yelling can be constantly heard, 'Give us some more of yer Memphis Blues' . . . Mrs. J. C. Miles is the only one of her sex in the company. She sings her favorite song, 'Goodbye, My Own Dear Heart' and sells the copies like hot cakes."[104]

Correspondence in June told of "capacities, turn-aways and no rain." There was also this special request: "Mrs. Lizzie Miles would like to hear from her sister, Edna Benbow, of the team of Benbow and Landry."[105] Edna Landry Benbow, Lizzie's half-sister, was also a performer, teamed during this early period with southern vaudeville pioneer William Benbow.[106] She later recorded as Edna Hicks.

The Jones Bros. Circus season ended at Flat River, Missouri, on October 24, 1914. Two weeks later, Mr. and Mrs. Miles joined the Jones Bros. Alabama Minstrels No. 2 Company. J. C. Miles reportedly served as interlocutor and solo cornetist in a twelve-piece band led by Frank Moland. When the Alabama Minstrels No. 2 closed its season at Houston on Christmas Day, J. C. and Lizzie headed to Lizzie's hometown New Orleans for a visit with her mother and half-sister Edna, who was currently entertaining at the Poodle Dog cabaret.

J. C. and Lizzie spent the remainder of the winter with J. C.'s family in Indianapolis. They opened the 1915 season with the Jones Bros. Circus at St. Louis, Missouri, on April 14: "Our band and minstrel is again the feature attraction of the big side show annex, although each and every member of the band and minstrels with the exception of Mr. and Mrs. Miles are new to the aggregation."[107]

A report in mid-May plugged the minstrel portion of the show, noting, "Mrs. Miles sings 'Wonderful Boy,' with great success. She is also interlocutor."[108]

The Jones Bros. Circus was working its way through New Hampshire and Vermont in June 1915 when an update from Miles's band and minstrels assured: "At this writing we are all O. K. as usual. Our little band of eleven pieces is still with it, and still creating much excitement all along the line, as we have drifted almost entirely from the standard marches and have gone into the popular ragtime stuff which seems to be more desired by the public in this region. They certainly like 'He's a Devil in His Own Home Town,' and the 'Jogo Blues.' We only do one concert each afternoon. Our feature number now is Remick's hits No. 15. Must sound good, for applause is positive whenever same is rendered."[109]

In July the band and minstrels spent more than a week out on Long Island, New York. As the summer waned, they headed west, then south, and they were down in Texas by mid-October. In November, while plowing across northern Louisiana, they crossed paths with J. C. O'Brien's Famous Georgia Minstrels No. 2 in Ruston: "Here was one happy day, as it was spent on both trains, first aboard our Pullman, 'The Virginia,' and then on O'Brien's handsome 'Ruth.' And at the finish . . . everybody was feeling mighty good, I tell you, as no one seemed to talk in his same tone. Ha! Ha!"[110] The last week of the 1915 season was spent in the heart of the Mississippi Delta, playing Indianola, Greenville, Rosedale, Cleveland, Clarksdale, and Jonestown, where the circus closed on December 6.

In 1916 the Jones Bros. Circus went out under the name Cole Bros. Circus. A letter from J. C. Miles published in the *Freeman* of February 26, 1916, notified that he and Lizzie were in Arkansas, "located at Hot Springs having baths and preparing for the opening of our season with Cole Bros.' Circus which opens here March 29th":

> On our way [to Hot Springs] we stopped over at Memphis, Tenn., where we enjoyed an exceedingly nice time at the residence of my friend Mr. William (Tuba) Thomas. Here we managed to assemble a number of my professional friends. Among them were Mr. William (King) Phillips, composer and writer of the famous Florida Blues; Mr. Jasper Taylor, Mr. Walter Lee, Mr. Thomas himself and several other prominent musicians and performers were present. A proficient pianist was also on hand in the person of Mr. Buddy Gilmore, who more than entertained during our hours of pleasure. A swell luncheon was gotten out by the Madam and Mr. Thomas, which, of course, was a feature number on our bill. We also took in several shows while in the city, and must speak well for Porter and Porter, who were at the Metropolitan, as they seemed to be favorites, judging from the applause they received. Furthermore, I am a fair judge myself. I also visited the music publishing establishment of Pace & Handy. Here you will find quite a staff of musical employees, who, together with Messrs. Pace and Handy, extend a cordial welcome to all professional folk at all times. With a tremendous stock of music to select from, I succeeded in securing quite a few copies. Among them were "Joe Turner Blues," one of Mr. Handy's latest numbers. Here's another "whang" for you blue lovers [*sic*] . . . J. C. Miles, 125 Water Street, Hot Springs.

At the beginning of the 1916 season Miles reported: "Our band and minstrel show is about at its normal size, having ten people in all. But we will be somewhat larger in a few days as we expect to add three more musicians and Mrs. Miles will make the fourteenth member. Our minstrel part is all new and elaborately costumed."[111] Three weeks into the season they were "finishing Arkansas, with Oklahoma, Kansas and Missouri to follow." Haley Walker, the troupe's alto horn and violin player, reported:

> We have added one more to our band, making it ten in number, and expect to add two more soon . . . With six doubling stage and Mrs. Miles as conversationalist, completes the seven chair semi-circle supported by our elevated six-piece orchestra . . . No-Sir-Ree-Bob. Not the best band on the road. Neither do we play William Tell in rag time and Poet-and-Peasant backward, but we do play some very pleasing overtures that we consider suitable for the amount of [instruments] we have . . . Remick's hits, popular song numbers and standard marches. And the several "blues" happen to be our long suit, and as for our ability in putting over each number we attempt, ask musicians in the cities we have played or the public in general or the management. Go further than that; try and make it your business to meet us during our long season.[112]

Miles noted on May 20, 1916, that his band and minstrels were still the hit of the "Big Annex of Wonders . . . Mrs. J. C. is the conversationalist and is featuring a number of late songs, among them is the great craze 'Mother.'" In closing, Miles sent regards to trombonist Freddie Pratt, and added, "We play in and around Chicago all this week." While playing Hammond, Indiana, on May 23, J. C. and Lizzie visited the sideshow band traveling with Howe's Great London Shows, and were "nicely entertained by members of Prof. [R. N.] Jackson's Band." At Michigan City, Indiana, on May 25, the Cole Bros. Circus "gave a charitable performance within the walls of the Indiana state prison to more than 1800 prisoners. Circus acts with the horses, ponies, elephants, clowns, etc. were to be seen. The acts that went the biggest with the prisoners were the elephants dancing the 'Cooche,' the band playing the 'Blues,' and when Mrs. Miles sang the 'Hesitating Blues' the riot commenced. A happy day for the boys within."[113]

By August the company was in Colorado, "more than 7,000 feet above sea level, the temperature being fine and cool, but the atmosphere is so light that we can scarcely gather wind to blow our instruments."[114] They dipped through the southwestern states, "showing daily to thousands of soldiers and Mexicans" in the border towns of Arizona and New Mexico. After playing through Texas, they made a long jump to the West Coast, closing the 1916 season in Fullerton, California, on December 8 and setting up winter quarters at Riverside, "which is only a street car ride from Los Angeles."

The J. C. Miles Band and Minstrels opened their 1917 season with Cole Bros. Circus on March 7 with a roster of twelve. Most were veterans of the previous season. Over the next three months they played one-nighters through California, Nevada, Utah, Wyoming, Idaho, Montana, and the Dakotas. In July, while the circus was in Oregon, they were visited by one of J. C. Miles's sisters: "Yes, J. C. is one happy fellow these days. His younger sister is here on the show with him and his wife. She is paying a joyous visit, looking at the elephants, feeding the monkeys and hearing the band play . . . When we play Pendleton, Ore., the home of our visitor and J. C.'s brother, we will pull off a real one. Our entire company is rehearsing to put on an eating act that day. Some grease slinging, I'll tell you."[115] J. C.'s brother Willis had "travelled for many years with various shows" before establishing himself as "a noted race horse trainer and driver" with a comfortable home in Pendleton.[116]

From Oregon, the circus headed back east through Idaho and Utah, Colorado, and Kansas, a blur of one-night stands. In September they turned south into Arkansas and Louisiana. Correspondence of September 29 found them headed for Texas and a "long season South," with Lizzie "featuring all the latest and up-to-date songs and taking care of the semi circle as conversationalist."

An October 27, 1917, report said Miles and his bunch were "in Texas indefinitely." In mid-November they played the season's final string of dates, along the Kansas City–Southern Railroad line in southwest Louisiana: Opelousas, November 12; next day, De Quincy; then north to DeRidder, Leesville, Many, Mansfield, and Shreveport, where the Cole Bros. Circus made its winter quarters. From there, Lizzie and J. C. dropped down to New Orleans to visit family.

J. C. Miles and company attempted to tour as an independent operation for the first part of the fateful season of 1918. Their timing could not have been worse. Musicians and performers were being drafted into service in World War I, and harsh restrictions on rail transportation were brought to bear. Miles's inevitable return to the Cole Bros. Circus was announced in a letter to the *Freeman*, published July 27, 1918:

> J. C. Miles and his sixteen merrymakers mostly musicians, and all performers . . . will resume duty with the Great Cole Bros. (world-toured shows) on playing-dates at Sedalia, Mo., the middle of August. The big minstrel show that was to be launched last spring was called off on account of the great shortage of musicians which of course derived from the world's war, and the show that we now have was immediately arranged, hit the trail and proud to say has done an excellent business, playing week stands with a repertoire of six complete shows, giving an entire change of program nightly. Our band will perhaps be featured with the big circus riding the number one band wagon in parade and playing the circus program, as the white band here at present is very low in number on account of the draft. This of course would take us completely away from the side show as heretofore, would also mean a somewhat larger band for us, as we are only eleven strong at present. So you musicians watch for our ad in the old reliable Freeman, also the Billboard.

It seems Miles's band actually did get to play the number one wagon and the main circus program. In a 1958 interview, cornetist Amos White recalled having been with Miles's company when they rejoined the Cole Bros. Circus at Sedalia. The memory was hardened by the fact that he had spent a night in jail there for not being able to produce his draft card: "We were playing the big show then. They had no white band on the show."[117]

If any event of 1918 cut more deeply into the ranks of traveling shows than the draft, it was the great Spanish Influenza epidemic. By November 1918, virtually every company that wrote the *Freeman* had some sad story to tell. One famous anecdote from Lizzie Miles's comeback years concerned her own personal bout with the flu. She gave a detailed account on Dave Garroway's *Wide, Wide World* in 1958: "Well, that was back during the World War I, during the flu epidemic. It was the end of the season and we were on our way to winter headquarters at Shreveport, Louisiana. Everybody on the train nearly came down with the flu. Every little town we'd come to they'd stop and try to get a doctor or a nurse or somebody to come and take care of the sick ones. I'd been doing

J. C. MILES DEAD.

The many friends of J. C. Miles, in the profession, will be grieved to learn of his death, which occurred in Shreveport, La., October 19th, of the influenza. Mr. Miles was well known in the musical world and at the time of his death was bandmaster with the Cole Bros.' circus. The remains were buried at his home in Indianapolis, Indiana.

Indianapolis Freeman, November 16, 1918.

what I could to take care of them, and they told me I'd better be careful or I'd come down with it. Well, I did and I got so sick I went out of my head and they had to take me off the train. They put me in this little town in a sanitarium and twice there they thought I was going to die."

Tragically, J. C. Miles did die on that train to Shreveport. As reported in the *Freeman*: "Jno. C. Miles, noted bandmaster and musician, passed away October 19, 1918, while en route to Shreveport, La., Cole Bros. World toured shows winter quarters. His wife is suffering from the same complaint, which was an attack of influenza and pneumonia."[118] After recuperating at her mother's home in New Orleans, Lizzie Miles started looking for club work. Her circus annex days were over.

Black sideshow entertainment was not strictly confined to the circus. By the second decade of the twentieth century, Wild West shows had begun to diversify their customary exhibitions of cowboys and Indians. They often included a sideshow tent, where, out of sight and seemingly invisible to historians, black performers were at work. The *Freeman* published reports from black bands and minstrels in the sideshows of the original Buffalo Bill Wild West Show, Miller's 101 Ranch Shows, Kit Carson's Buffalo Ranch Show, Young Buffalo's Show, Circle D Wild West, and Old Buffalo Wild West Show, among others.

Clarinetist and bandleader Bismark Ferris was born in Texas on July 9, 1881.[119] He directed the annex band and minstrel company known as Ferris's Satisfied Musical Entertainers, which occupied the sideshow tent of the Sells-Floto Circus for the seasons of 1908 and 1909. In 1910 and 1911 Ferris's Satisfied Musical Entertainers went out in connection with the Buffalo Bill Wild West Show: "Ferris furnishes a band in the side show and a complete minstrel for the concert in large arena."[120] The star of the minstrel production was Clarence Rucker singing "Play That Barber Shop Chord." Among the other minstrel performers were Harrison Blackburn, "our famous buck and wing dancer, singing 'Phoebe Jane';" Billy Moore singing "Fussy Rag"; Mrs. Juanita Pace singing "That Teasing Rag"; and Catherine Patterson singing "Italian Rag."[121]

Between seasons, Ferris spent a few weeks at home in Waxahachie, Texas, with his wife and children.[122] He and his Satisfied Musical Entertainers returned to the Buffalo Bill Wild West Show for the season of 1911:

Professor Bismark Ferris, director of the Annex Band and Concert aggregation with the Buffalo Bill's Wild West Show, has gotten together a company of extraordinary strength and merit. Unlike any other big show carrying a colored contingency, this show presents Professor Ferris' company of singers and dancers as the sole and only offering of the concert and after-show in the big top at the conclusion of each performance . . . They give a show lasting about three-quarters of an hour . . . The first part is replete with catchy and well-rendered songs, opening with a medley chorus of popular airs, which set the people to whistling. The ends are taken care of by Messrs. Harrison Blackburn, Billy Moore and James Shaw as tambos, and Norris Grigsby, Bud Borders and Ben Borders as bones.

Harrison Blackburn was repeatedly encored with his song, "Cannibal Love," while Ben Borders was a riot, singing, "Let Other Folks' Business Alone." As a monologist, Norris Grigsby told them a few things and then some more. Mr. Ried Conner makes an ideal interlocutor and handles his work with dignity and precision. Billy Moore is a good character man, and his eccentric dancing is sure to cause him to be heard from. "Any Old Way You Cook Chicken Is Good Enough for Me," sung by Norris Grigsby, was put over in a very pleasing manner. Mr. Grigsby is a comedian of much promise. "The Honey I Love So Well," sung by . . . Oglesby's "Rambler Quartet," with Mr. Oglesby as second tenor, was heavily applauded, and they had to respond to several encores.

Mr. Bismark Ferris, the leader of the band and director of the colored contingency, is a man of wide experience in this line of the show business and has had the Buffalo Bill Annex Band and Concert Company under his direction for some time. He has been with the show several seasons.

Harrison Blackburn, known to the profession as "Baby," is a funny little fellow with a natural comicality in his work that knocks them a twister. His versatility as a performer was amply demonstrated in his impersonations of the aged darkey. At no time did he appear to exaggerate or overdraw the character . . . "Baby" is stage manager for the company.[123]

Sylvester Russell met Ferris and his Satisfied Company when the show came to Chicago: "Buffalo Bill's Wild West pitched its tents in the black belt of the South Side four days last week. It was announced as Colonel Cody's farewell trip, and drew great crowds of mixed people. The show was better than ever and filled with as much variety as a circus. I visited the show in a party consisting of Mrs. Billy Kersands, Mrs. Jessie Helsear [*sic*] and Arthur Maxwell. I was introduced to the quartette and the band, who had never seen the critic before and the meeting was happy . . . These people serve in the Buffalo Bill concert or side show and draw big crowds."[124]

By 1920, Bismark Ferris was out of the sideshow annex business; a widower with five dependent children, ages five to fourteen, he was residing in Los Angeles and directing the Ferris Family Company.[125] Ferris gave his children musical instruction, and under his direction they capitalized on the current jazz and blues fever. Ferris played saxophone and clarinet; thirteen-year-old Lucille played saxophone and clarinet; fourteen-year-old Theresa played violin and banjo; and eleven-year-old Amie was featured as a blues "chirper," trap drummer, and all-around entertainer. *Chicago Defender* columnist "Ragtime" Billy Tucker spied them in a show presented by the famous Spikes Brothers at Gaumet Auditorium in Los Angeles in 1922: "This little family is a whole show in itself, and you can see that the father, Bismarck [*sic*] Ferris, has something to be proud of . . . They play

Bismark Ferris's Satisfied Musical Entertainers. *Indianapolis Freeman,* July 29, 1911.

everything from jazz to classics and from grand opera to overtures, and brother, 'they wear them all out' . . . the Ferris Family is good enough for any of the big-time houses back East."[126]

Another exemplary Wild West show of the 1910s, not to be confused with the Buffalo Bill Show, was Young Buffalo's Wild West Show.[127] W. L. Horne's Minstrels were attached to Young Buffalo's Wild West Show for the seasons of 1911 and 1912. They were in New York State in the summer of 1911, when a *Freeman* correspondent wrote: "It is my greatest delight to go down town visiting the parade and hear the remarks about the three bands. Everyone hollers put the colored band in front. Everyone goes wild when the band plays 'That Rag,' 'Miss Trombone,' 'Carolina Rag,' and 'Aggravation Rag' . . . R. L. Davis certainly makes a hit with his Susanna Sue and his buck and wing dancing . . . Wm. Moore is . . . singing 'What Has That Man Harrigan Done?' Jasper Taylor may not please the men, but the girls go wild when he sings 'Stop, Stop, Stop.'"[128]

During the season of 1912, Jasper Taylor served as an end man in Young Buffalo's minstrel first part, singing "You'll Never Know the Fool I've Been Till I Am Gone Away."[129] Late that summer the Young Buffalo Show was "playing the lots around Chicago . . . Our minstrel show is still scoring a hit. Miss Alice Edwards, our soubrette, is meeting with great success, and always pleases the audiences when she sings 'Stop That Bear Cat Dance, Sadie,' and 'Mammy's Shufflin' Dance.' Jasper Taylor still keeps the audiences screaming with his funny sayings and always receives applause when he sings 'I Am Going to Join That Minstrel Band.'"[130]

Indianapolis Freeman, April 21, 1917.

Jasper Taylor was born in Texarkana, Texas, in 1894. In a 1959 interview, he indicated that his stints with Young Buffalo marked the beginning of his professional career: "I went out on a circus. It was a Wild West show; I call it a circus. The Young Buffalo Bill [*sic*] Wild West. I just went out for the summer months. And I would always go back home to school during the winter months. But, that's how I really got started, professionally. They had a regular brass band on a side show, and a minstrel, and the band . . . Every town we visited, the band would play on a wagon, a special wagon." He said their repertoire consisted of marches and ragtime tunes: "I don't recall any blues, just a make-up blues, some trombone player had."[131]

Rather than going home to Texarkana at the end of the 1912 season, Taylor jumped from the sideshow annex of Young Buffalo's Wild West Show to the band and orchestra of Geyer's Dandy Dixie Minstrels, where he came to the fore as a trap drummer, under the influence of orchestra leader Mahlon Wilson. Taylor spent the winter of 1913–1914 in Memphis, playing with Eckford's Orchestra at the Monarch Club and Café.[132] By the summer of 1914, he was stationed in St. Louis, Missouri, as the trap drummer with "Prof. Jimmie Harris, Jr. and his challenge orchestra of the Booker Washington Theater."[133] As a drummer and washboard player, Taylor became a bright star of the early jazz era and logged a fairly prolific recording career, both under his own name and as a sideman with such legendary bandleaders as W. C. Handy, Freddie Keppard, Jelly Roll Morton, and Jimmie O'Bryant. In 1925, when Taylor was touring mainstream theaters with the famous Joe Jordan Orchestra, *Chicago Defender* columnist

Washboard Harmony

Jasper Taylor, a member of Jimmie O'Bryant's famous original Washboard band and originator of that weird rhythm known as "washboard harmony," will soon tour the United States.

Jasper has no equal and is regarded as the greatest exponent of "washboard" artist in the world. He is now in rehearsal with O'Bryant's famous Washboard band for a national tour of the country in order that his many friends and admirers may see him in person. He has just signed a long term exclusive contract with the Paramount company, so that his many admirers will be able to get his phonograph records while he is on the circuit.

JASPER TAYLOR

Chicago Defender, August 15, 1925.

Dave Peyton called him "the world's greatest novelty drummer."[134]

The premier Wild West company of the early 1910s was the Miller Bros. 101 Ranch Shows. The proprietors were the sons of Colonel George W. Miller, founder of the enormous and prosperous 101 Ranch in Oklahoma, "a monument of the Old West" and "an empire within itself." Apart from its functions as a working ranch and farm, the 101 Ranch was a major tourist attraction where grand productions and rodeos were regularly staged, featuring the legendary African American Oklahoma cowboy Bill Pickett. After Colonel Miller's death, in the spirit of "a true glimpse of ranch life," the Miller brothers and showman Edward Arlington launched their traveling 101 Ranch Shows in 1908.[135]

Through the seasons of 1913–1916, the 101 Ranch's sideshow annex was under the direction of violinist and bandmaster L. K. Baker. Baker's annex band and minstrel company was one of the most progressive of the era. Veteran comedian Sam "Doc" Ford was the interlocutor, and a frequent correspondent to the *Freeman*. During the autumn of 1913, Ford described various incidents of the current tour:

> We are now entering into "Bam," and we may add, with fear and trembling lest at any time we make a mistake, and, oh, well . . . as the old song goes, we simply place our lives in the hands of God. We certainly . . . don't approve of that segregation that is forced upon our people by the government by the people and for the people. We had the pleasure of playing Ponca, Okla., and some of the boys took advantage of the chance offered and made a visit to the 101 Ranch and had a swell time, as the Miller brothers know how to entertain. We met the original king of the bull ring, William Pickett, who is on the ranch this season and

busy training a herd of buffaloes for the big show next season, and say, it will certainly be some act.[136]

When the 101 Ranch Shows came to Indianapolis in September 1914, *Freeman* reporter Billy Lewis recorded his impressions:

The minstrels were good and enjoyable. The great crowds of colored and white people were kept laughing all of the time . . . This fun was mostly due to Sam Ford and Wm. Nash, who were the end men. Ford told good jokes in a good style, also put over some good songs. Nash sang "Rag Time Sal," did eccentric dancing and told some very funny ones. Both are clever men . . .

Ford sang "Send Me My Overcoat." Nash sang "Way Back Home." The skit, "Throwing the Deacon Out" caught 'em just right, the white folk and the colored folk. [Charles] Brown sang "Way Down in Dixie Land."[137]

White heavyweight boxing champion Jess Willard was the 101 Ranch Shows' main attraction for the season of 1915. Willard had achieved national celebrity by capturing the title from legendary Negro champion Jack Johnson on April 5 of that year. One scholar of Wild West shows has noted that the 101 Ranch's owners "profited from the crowds that flocked to see Willard, but headlining an athlete rather than a frontier hero indicated that Wild West shows required something extraordinary to make money."[138] A member of the sideshow annex contingent allowed that Willard was "a great attraction, and . . . very sociable to all."[139] When the 101 Ranch played McAlister, Oklahoma, on October 7, 1915:

Mr. Jos. C. Miller, the lion-hearted joint owner of this aggregation, carried several features of the show to the State prison there to entertain the prisoners and each number was roundly applauded. The music was by Prof. Baker's band. Jess Willard, the big champion, was presented amid cheers. Also cowboys and cow girls came in for great applause.

Our old plantation show was well received and we are well pleased to know we were able to shed a ray of sunshine in the lives of those poor fellows. When our band struck up the "Memphis Blues" it was a riot.[140]

L. K. Baker's twelve-piece band featured "Handy's repertoire of blues, also King Phillips' sensational 'Florida Blues,' and 'Fess' Baker always wears a smile because he has surrounded himself with a band of gentlemanly musicians, clean and refined, and no booze fighters or agitators."[141] In June 1916 one of Baker's gentlemanly musicians, P. L. Jenkins, informed that, "While showing Washington, D. C. on Decoration Day, we were on parade coming up broad historical Pennsylvania avenue and when passing the Capitol building our band played W. C. Handy's great hit 'Hail to the Spirit of Freedom.' We were cheered to the echo. President Wilson, who viewed the parade from an upper balcony, was seen to bow, smile and applaud by clapping his hands. We considered this as quite a compliment to the race, Prof. Handy being one of the foremost colored writers."[142]

After the 1916 season the Miller brothers sold their interest in the 101 Ranch Shows to former partner Edward Arlington, but retained exclusive rights to the 101 Ranch name.[143] In 1917 the show toured as the Jess Willard–Buffalo Bill Show. L. K. Baker's bunch remained at the head of the sideshow annex. When the show came to Indianapolis early in September, Billy Lewis described:

The parade was a surprise because of its good quality. Thousands lined up, the small boy and girl, of course, being in the majority. And there were the elephants without which a parade is no parade to the American hope. There were other parade essentials, including Indians, cowboys and girls, the bands and the indispensable calliope—that classic tailpiece.

My business was mainly with the side show, where I met Mr. L. K. Baker, the genial bandmaster . . . Baker's men seemed to be in the best of humor. They discoursed music most sweetly. He keeps all of his old fellows, who like wine, improve with age. Will Nash is on the end in the minstrel show, and James Anderson is also an ender, while the grand ole man, Doc Ford, is in the middle and says, "Gentlemen, be seated"—as he oft has said before . . . All nationalities were there and they all managed to laugh at Nash and Anderson . . . Their leading songs are the "Dangerous Rag," and "A Long, Tall, Brown Skin Gal Will Make a Preacher Lay His Bible Down," sung respectively by Nash and Ford.[144]

Another hit for Doc Ford that season was "Dog Gone Triflin' Blues."[145]

L. K. Baker's band maintained an especially cordial relationship with the Pace and Handy Music Company. Some of the *Freeman* correspondences from Baker's company read like advertisements. In August 1917 they submitted these two items:

Prof. Baker has just received and added to his already fine repertoire Prof. Handy's latest hits, "Beale Street Blues" and "Joe Turner Blues." They both have that peculiar dreamy effect. All leaders will do well to get in touch with the Pace-Handy Music Company, as no repertoire can be complete without some of Handy's "Blues."[146]

We have just received a copy of Prof. Handy's sensational hit "Beale Street Blues." No lover of music should be without this and other numbers by Prof. Handy; each of his tunes is a careful blend of sweet dreamy harmony set by the master musician's hand. The Pace-Handy Music Company . . . is truly termed the home of the "Blues."[147]

W. C. Handy's influence on the Jess Willard–Buffalo Bill Show seems to have extended beyond the confines of the sideshow tent. A September 29, 1917, letter from Baker's bunch contained news that, "Sanders's Big Four Jazz Band of Memphis, Tenn. joined September 19 at Little Rock, Ark., to play for our Hawaiian Village on the Midway. They are making good daily, featuring W. C. Handy's great hit 'Beale Street Blues.' The roster is as follows: George Burke, violin, Commodore Sanders, banjorine, Emmett Williams, first guitar, Van Matlock, second guitar." Sanders's Big Four finished out the 1917 season, closing in Jacksonville, Florida, November 3rd. Afterward, they reportedly returned to Memphis.[148]

Comedians Doc Ford and William Nash also added to the proliferation of blues in the Jess Willard–Buffalo Bill annex. Nash was a comedian-singer and second trombonist in the band.[149] In 1915 he was said to be "daily rehearsing 'The Yellow Dog Rag,' W. C. Handy's great hit." In 1916 Nash was "scoring daily, singing the Skidmore Music Company's great hit, 'Pray for the lights to go out.'"[150] This song had been introduced in 1912 by African American vaudeville blues pioneer Butler "String Beans" May. Somehow Will E. Skidmore gained control of it, and used it to launch a very successful "Deacon Series." In 1917, Doc Ford featured another title from Skidmore's "Deacon Series," "It Takes a Long, Tall Brown Skin Gal to Make a Preacher Lay His Bible Down." These songs were eminently suitable for the Baker Company's perennial afterpiece, a comic skit titled "Aunt Hester's Party," or "Throwing the Deacon Out." As described during the 1913 season, Ernest Williams played "the Deacon" to Nash's "Aunt Hester" in the minstrel portion of the show: "Billy

Indianapolis Freeman, September 8, 1917.

Nash is still cleaning up about 'steen times every day as Aunt Hester, and little Ernest Williams is bringing up the deacon-like Si Brown, and is still doing his inimitable dance at each performance. The boys all predict that he will fall from the stage and kill himself."[151] Baker's Minstrels were still closing with "Aunt Hester's Party" when Billy Lewis reviewed the show in 1917. Lewis called it "a comic classic built for show purposes and which wears like leather."[152]

During the season of 1917, the Jess Willard–Buffalo Bill Show was visited by Prince Oskazuma, one of the most colorful figures in the field of sideshow entertainment. Born in 1865, he had been in the public eye since the early 1890s, when he toured as a lecturer on African customs, claiming to be a native of South Africa educated in Great Britain.[153] By 1894, Prince Oskazuma, "African Warrior, Lecturer, Mimic, Fire Fiend," was traveling with the Sells and Renfrow Circus. During the season of 1901 he was with the Buffalo Bill Wild West Show, and he spent many succeeding years on the road with various circuses and Wild West shows. At the time of his visit with the Jess Willard–Buffalo Bill Show, he was a member of the Superior Shows Plantation Band and Minstrels, in the annex of the Coop and Lentz Circus: "The famous black scout Prince Askajuma [*sic*] is a wonder in the side show. He holds his audience spellbound. As an announcer and ballyhoo man he can not be beat."[154]

Oskazuma developed a special relationship with the Native Americans on the Wild West Shows and, as a result, acquired the nicknames "Hawk," "Cherokee Charlie" and "Black Scout." In conjunction with his 1917 visit to the Jess Willard–Buffalo Bill Show, Oskazuma announced that he had "signed an agreement with Mr. Francis Nelson, charging Hawk [*sic*] to book and handle all Sioux Indians and make contracts for them, with medicine shows, vaudeville houses, parks, fairs, expositions, Wild West, circus and carnivals and any out and indoor engagements. Francis Nelson is Indian agent and superintendent of the Indians with the Big Jess Willard and Buffalo Bill show. Mr. Nelson is a nephew of Frank C. Goings, mayor and chief of police of Pine Ridge Agency, S. D., and the Sioux Indians are particular friends of the Black Scout and have adopted him in the tribe."[155]

Years later, in 1923, *Billboard* reported: "Prince Oskazuma, who goes out with the Dobyns Carnival this season . . . has spent the spring season in organizing the American Indian Brotherhood and in trying to create an old folks home for colored actors."[156] In Charleston, South Carolina, that fall, he was "spending his spare time boosting the interests of the Jenkins Orphanage . . . the bands of which have played in the streets of every big city in the land."[157] By the end of 1923, Oskazuma, "Renaissance man," was in Savannah, Georgia, promoting prize fights: "There's no limit to 'Osky's' ambitions."[158] Back in Charleston at the end of 1924, the Lincoln Theater engaged "Prince Oskazuma with his Indian display to stage an exhibition in the lobby. The stunt proved a good ballyhoo for the film house."[159]

Oskazuma had trouped with Young Buffalo's Wild West Show during the seasons of 1913 and 1914, when they carried "three colored races in the street parade, also the side show." Counted among these "colored races" was "Chief Panakiea, of Condo, Ceylon, who entertains the people with the custom dances," and "Chief Tevi and his troupe of ten genuine native Africans, who are quite an attraction in the street parade." William H. Reid managed Young Buffalo's nine-piece sideshow band for 1913, in combination with the Famous Tennessee Minstrels and Toad Quartet of dancers and singers. The show also carried "a Negro calliope player, 'Old Doc' being his name. He sure plays some ragtime in the street parade and the calliope never stops playing from the time the parade leaves the lot until it returns." The same report indicated that "Prince Askazuma" was "holding his own with his fire act. He is the first American Negro that has the pleasure of being general side show lecturer and announcer as well as assistant managing director of Young Buffalo's Wild West Shows."[160]

Young Buffalo's Wild West Show played Indianapolis in the summer of 1914, prompting this descriptive commentary:

> The minstrel annex and band were features at the show grounds. Here were a group of colored minstrels, players, band people, under the direction of Edward Rucker. The band was also seen in the parade. Rucker is a genial, whole-souled leader whom all of his people like. They work willingly and cheerfully, and the audience falls right in with them . . . The band plays pretty airs of all kinds, suiting the music nicely to the work in hand. When the snakes were exhibited it played a charming waltz; somehow it fitted that exhibit; others were of similar propriety . . .
>
> In the minstrel part Eddie Porter, Webster Rucker, John Briscoe and Ethel Rucker do some nice quartette work. They do a bit of real minstrel work when Miss Ethel rings out in the good old way: "Gentleman, be seated." Then the fun is on; jokes, songs and so forth. And they go big. Little Congo Cropp did a dancing turn in which he put a touch of 'balling the Jack.' And in the language of Dunbar, you should have heard those colored folks yell. Our folks were there in force. The sideshow managers have much to be thankful for, in that there are plenty of colored people in the world.
>
> Ethel Rucker does the "International Rag" and "This Is The Life" in a nice, taking style, with a good voice. Webster Rucker features "Get Out And Get Under" and "Can't Get Any From Here," and does them well. Among those seen while making the rounds was Oscar Zuma [*sic*], of whom one hears so much. He was eating fire right along . . .
>
> The show was good, all parts of it. Crowds flocked to see it, thousands of people. Some . . . expected to see elephants. But nothin' was doin' along that line. It was plenty good enough without the pachyderms."[161]

The Jess Willard–Buffalo Bill Wild West Show did not go out in 1918. Annex bandmaster L. K. Baker took over the fourteen-piece annex band with the Hagenbeck-Wallace Circus, a position that had previously been occupied by the great P. G. Lowery. On June 22, 1918, the Hagenbeck-Wallace Circus was involved in one of the worst train wrecks in circus history. More than eighty performers were killed in a rear-end collision with an empty troop train near Hammond, Indiana. Fortunately for the L. K. Baker Band, the car they were traveling in was not affected by the accident.

In October 1920, L. K. Baker's Annex Band and Minstrels were traveling with the John Robinson Circus: "As we are now in the Sunny South we are playing Blues and Rags until we can't get our folks to leave the side show."[162] For some reason the John Robinson Circus had a particularly difficult time keeping a bandleader in their sideshow annex; no less than ten different men filled the position between 1914 and 1920. The minstrel stage roster was more stable, thanks to Eugene Clark and his son Robert, who occupied the Robinson Show tent for a considerable portion of the decade. Eugene Clark and his brother Joseph Clark, Sr., were the progenitors of Louisville, Kentucky's first family of African American minstrelsy. Both had been members of Whallen and Martell's historic "South Before the War" Company during the 1890s. Eugene was born in 1857 and claimed to have been in the profession since 1879.[163]

In 1914 the John Robinson Circus sideshow minstrel featured Eugene and Joe Clark as their end men, and Annie Hicks as interlocutor: "When Eugene and Joe Clark get through the first part, you have to take your hats off to them, as you know what they can do." Annie Hicks sang and danced in the olio, accompanied by "the two little picks, Fred and Gertrude, [who] pick up enough change off the stage to keep them in clean clothes." The sideshow band was under the direction of John B. Forrester. It was said that, "out of five bands in the parade, the colored band gets the best of it, when they put on 'Memphis Blues' and 'Oh You Brown Eyed Baby Rag.'"[164]

Eugene Clark headed the Robinson minstrels again in 1915, while the band was under the direction of Jerry Martin. A detailed report from Robinson's Famous Shows informed:

> The band is putting over some of the standard pieces but not all. We have some that we feature which all on the show love, as well as the public. Some of the numbers are as follows: The Jogo Blues, The Memphis Blues, Yellow Dog Rag, and the Jungles Blues, which has made us a hit everywhere. The minstrel is getting theirs at every performance. Freddie Clark, our 12-year old buck dancer, wins the heart of both the white and colored people in his dancing act. Corina Adams has left a hill for all other girls of her age to climb when they play the towns we have played. She is using Winter Nights, and The Rag Picker. Anna Hicks, our interlocutor, is still featuring Balling the Jack, Yellow Dog Rag, and Keep It Up. There is but little to say of our end men, the Clark Brothers, as they are known by all young and old performers to be the big hit of the minstrel closing.[165]

Eugene Clark's Minstrel Company, including Joe and Freddie Clark and Annie Hicks, traveled with the La Tena's Circus for the season of 1916. That year, George L. Polk, of Smyrna, Delaware, brought his band and minstrel company into the John Robinson Circus sideshow tent: "Miss Mable Adams our dainty little sobrett [*sic*], is scoring daily, singing 'Are you from Dixie.' She knows just how to put it over . . . Last but not least Little Maggie Legare Motto is successfully singing 'Walkin' the Dog.' Believe me, little Motto knows how to walk the dog, and loading up the mandolin. Motto leaded that mandolin so heavy that the stage fell down."[166]

The Robinson Circus began their 1917 season with cornetist R. N. Jackson at the head of their sideshow band and minstrel. Jackson had spent

Eugene Clark's Band and Minstrels. *Indianapolis Freeman,* July 31, 1915.

the previous season at the head of the annex band with Howe's Great London Circus. He placed an ad in the *Freeman* of February 3, 1917, soliciting "Musicians of all kinds! Must double B. & O. and B. & S. [band and orchestra and band and stage]. This season all must play standard music. Accommodations will be the best." Jackson had an abbreviated, apparently unhappy tenure with the John Robinson sideshow. Several months into the 1917 touring season a Robinson Show correspondent described: "Our band and minstrel roster has changed somewhat since the last writing. Prof. T. Everett White has the band over here now . . . T. E. White, cornetist and leader, in fact, a very efficient one . . . seems to understand his work and people better than his predecessor, who absolutely refused to cooperate with his co-workers in a manner to gain their friendship or respect. Everything is like clockwork now—no stubbornness or overbearing 'amateurs' to try and cramp human feelings."[167]

Prof. White was enlisted into the Robinson Show from the Big Six Orchestra of Greenwood, Mississippi, one of the best-known African American community musical organizations in the South. The Big Six Orchestra played for dances and other entertainments on both sides of the color line and occasionally made tours through Mississippi. They often entertained the black minstrel companies and circus annex bands that passed through Greenwood, and occasionally provided work for professional musicians who were anxious to get off the road.[168] Conversely, members of the Big Six Orchestra were sometimes called upon to reinforce the depleted ranks of shows traveling through Mississippi.

In November 1917, at season's end, the *Freeman* published a summary report from the Robinson Circus:

> The old saying . . . "All's well that ends well," has proven very true with us, for everyone has had a very prosperous season, and now at the end each individual can show a bank roll and is prepared to meet the winter with a smile . . .
>
> The show opened April 17th at Macon, Ga., and closes Monday, Nov. 12th, at Brownsville, Tenn., in the meantime we have traveled 11,518 miles, traveled 17 states, lost only four days, four half days and missed 17 parades, some record, isn't it? . . .
>
> While playing Baton Rouge, La., Yazoo, Miss., Clarksdale, Miss. and Greenwood, Miss. in the last two weeks, each of the local orchestras gave special dances for Prof. White's band and minstrels . . . you may know we enjoyed ourselves, and will not forget the events soon . . .
>
> Prof. White goes back to the Greenwood's Big Six orchestra.[169]

The following year Robert Clark, of Louisville's famous Clark family, took charge of the Robinson minstrels, and W. S. Jenkins directed the sideshow band. However, without explanation, they were both soon replaced by a band and minstrel company under the leadership of Marcus Veal Chaney. Chaney, who was also known simply as Marcus Veal, had served as bandmaster with the Rabbit's Foot Minstrels in 1917. Correspondence from the Robinson Circus in the *Freeman* of June 1, 1918, told of "Marcus Veal's Band and Company": "Without saying too much, this is one of the best eleven piece bands on the road bar none." The chief comedians were Frank Tousell and Archie "One Nighter" Blue: "One Nighter Blue is singing with great success one of his own compositions, 'You Can't Ball the Jack.' Frank Tousell is knocking them with his new song 'What a Time I'd Have If I Had Everything My Way.' [G. E.] Glasco is singing America's greatest patriotic ballad, 'Don't Bite the Hand That is Feeding You.' The public takes it."[170]

In 1919, Eugene Clark's Black Devil Minstrels were back on the road with the John Robinson Circus: "Eugene Clark is still doing his same old tambourine playing and it is a knockout."[171] Veteran bandleader James Wolfscale, recently deposed from his longtime position with the Barnum and Bailey Circus, headed the John Robinson annex band for several months, but an August report said that he had returned to his home in Chicago and the band was now under the leadership of Bernie Buckhana.

Eugene Clark was in the sideshow of the Walter L. Main Circus for the season of 1920. A company report said, "Eugene Clark is still the favorite in all towns with his tambourine solo and the manager of the Walter L. Main Show is so well pleased with him that he is going to put him out with his winter minstrels." However, the following week Clark was involved in an accident, "breaking one rib and fracturing another, also dislocating his shoulder falling from his car. He will be laid up for a few days."[172]

The instability that characterized John Robinson's sideshow annex band was not the norm. In general, steady employment and a reliable paycheck were the most attractive aspects of circus sideshow work. As one circus correspondent remarked, "Some think that these ships are rough riding, but they never sink."[173] Letters from Howe's Great London Circus sideshow annex in 1914 contain some interesting commentary regarding upper and middle level management, among other matters:

> W. H. McFarland, who is manager of the side show, is a friend to the colored boys in every particular, and has the proud distinction of being the first man to put a colored minstrel with a side show and has employed some of the leading colored performers in the business today, and [has] fruitfully assisted in cutting out the segregation idea . . .
>
> Sanford Gordon, known as "Beans," is the big noise in the show, and Bessie J. Ward scores daily in her song, "Who Will Be With You When I'm Far Away." Tommy Jones gives a few lessons in buck dancing much to the edification of the side show patronage . . .
>
> Jerry Mugiran [*sic*], the affable proprietor, is all smiles these days and always has a good word for the boys, though some have abused their privileges with the show. After he reprimanded them with a fine they got back in their original places again.[174] Mr. Fred Asal, better known as Milwaukee Whitie, the astute manager of Howe's Great London Shows, is a gentleman high in the esteem of all connected with this circus, and has proved himself quite a diplomat on several occasions . . .
>
> Gordon the comedian, still racks the nerves of the side show patrons with his songs "The Blues," and "Beans," his trademark. He has just purchased a new red comedy suit from Al Derby, the bag puncher, and an opera hat from one of the performers from the big top . . .
>
> A few of the performers follow their profession in leisure hours. Willie Grantlin, the violin and alto player, runs a hand laundry. Theo Thomas, the cornetist, runs a cleaning and pressing club. Lewis Gilbert, the band master, runs a casino tournament every afternoon. The Darktown barbershop is operated by Richard Matthews.[175]

R. N. Jackson, cornetist and bandleader from Nashville, Tennessee, who suffered a disastrous season with Robinson's annex in 1917, had spent 1916 as head of the sideshow band and minstrels with Howe's Great London Circus: "Our band does not handle 'William Tell,' 'Morning, Noon and Night' or any of the large overtures. Just simply marches, gallops and Blues."[176] That summer they claimed to be "the only circus band featuring or playing the 'Schill Blues.'"[177] "Memphis Blues," "Alabama Jubilee," "Walking the Dog," and "Lucky Boy" were also performed in the sideshow annex of Howe's Great London Circus during 1916.[178]

Their 1916 tour began in Montgomery, Alabama, on April 4, progressing through the states of Alabama, Tennessee, Maryland, Virginia, and Ohio. By June Jackson's Annex Band and Minstrels were reportedly sojourning westward, and having a rather unpleasant time of it: "Some towns in the northwestern states a colored man is a peculiar curiosity to the residents. Some of them will use that vulgar name, nigger, which is very overbearing to hear coming from the lips of intelligent white people."[179] "It seems as if we have a jinx this season. From Sunday, June 24 until July 1 we have encountered nothing but rain . . . At Park Falls, Wis., [a] delay was caused by the breaking down of the pole wagon, and this caused us to be late again in our parade. If the jinx is in the side show band and we can find him out, right there he is fired without any two weeks' notice. The writer is not superstitious, but still has that funny feeling toward a jinx."[180]

R. N. Jackson was still in the circus annex business in 1925, serving as sideshow bandleader for the Hagenbeck-Wallace Circus. For a part of that season, legendary vaudevillian Wayne "Buzzin'" Burton managed the sideshow minstrel stage.[181]

P. G. Lowery's band was the nobility of circus sideshow annex entertainers, and wherever they traveled dances, dinners, and parties were given in their honor. Traveling with Lowery in the annex of the Hagenbeck-Wallace Circus in 1913, one performer confirmed: "Five receptions were tendered P. G. Lowery and company the past week. Who wouldn't want to be with the best colored company under canvas?"[182] Professional association with P. G. Lowery conferred real status and tangible benefits. Pride of association is reflected in this Lowery Company *Freeman* report of June 14, 1913: "The band is making rapid progress. Each member is striving hard to be able to add credit to the world-wide reputation of Mr. Lowery as a bandmaster, and to be able to play with credit in any band in the United States."

When the Hagenbeck-Wallace Circus came to Harrisburg, Pennsylvania, in 1913, a local correspondent observed, "The Barnum & Bailey show, also the 101 Ranch were in our city with colored companies [attached] . . . but as soon as Lowery's band played their first number one could see a vast difference in Lowery's band and the bands with the other companies . . . When hearing Lowery's band, one can easily tell they are from the Lowery school."[183] The perception of Lowery's organization as a rolling conservatory was reinforced in subsequent *Freeman* correspondences: "P. G. always freely shares his schooling, which he paid very dearly for in Boston."[184] "P. G. Lowery's band is known as the 'School of Music.' The best musicians in the profession are from the Lowery School."[185]

Promising young musicians were naturally attracted by the prospect of touring under such a leader. Horace Eubanks figured prominently among the prodigies in Lowery's annex band for 1913. A note from Lowery's Band and Minstrels that summer informed that the "rising young clarinetist" had already been "the recipient of many complimentary remarks as the result of the superb tone he has accomplished since being in Mr. Lowery's employ. His clarinet is prominent in forte as well as piano passages and in the near future he will be classed as one of the best in the colored profession."[186] Horace Eubanks's clarinet can be heard on several 1920s jazz recordings, notably a 1923 coupling with Jelly Roll Morton's Jazz Band that also includes trombonist Alvin "Zoo" Robertson, who trouped with Lowery in 1920.[187]

Lowery's minstrels with Hagenbeck-Wallace attracted almost as much praise and attention as his band. A. A. Wright served as stage manager for the 1913 edition of the sideshow minstrel, in addition to playing cornet in the band. A June 28, 1913, *Freeman* report provides details:

> The members of the minstrel first part all strive hard to give the public the latest and most popular songs published, hence their rank as the best minstrel show under canvas. Stage Manager A. A. Wright calls rehearsal promptly every Monday morning and nearly all turn on a new song every week.
>
> The daily program is divided into three different shows. The first show opens with J. L. Edwards singing "Floating Down The River," followed by Miss Callie Vassar, our versatile interlocutor, singing "My Man" to a finish. "Slow Kid" (U. S.) Thompson closes with his characteristic song, "Fifteen Cents."

> On No. 2 show, Carrie Gilbert scores heavily singing "I Want My Man." Miss Gilbert has fast come to the front as a soubrette of the classy kind. J. Bryant, our baritone, renders "Dinah Lee" effectively, then comes Earl Grandstaff that Memphis boy, singing "That Dangerous Rag" and "Sooey Dance" in a way that is bound to go over.
>
> The third show completes the song repertoire with Mrs. J. L. Edwards, prima donna, who handles that beautiful ballad, "When I Lost You," with all the taste and finish that characterizes our best sopranos. Tony Barefield, basso profundo of known fame, sings "Out Where the Breakers Roar" in his own pleasing manner and always wins the favor of the most fastidious.

U. S. THOMPSON (SLOW KID).

With the Hagenbeck-Wallace Shows.

U. S. Thompson (Slow Kid).

U. S. Thompson (Slow Kid) is one of the chief funmakers with the Haggenbeck and Wallace circus, and has been for a number of seasons. He is singing one of the latest songs, published by the Buckeye Publishing Company, "I've Got the Rumatiz." He also sings, "It Was Me." They both are

easy winners. He is seeking to find out why Mr. Sam Walker is using the added name of Slow Kid. He is advised to make a clear distinction between the two Thompsons. He intends to work with his wife this coming season in vaudeville. The two are bound to make good, as they are of the same type. Letepha, his wife, will be remembered for her clever Spanish dance which she did with a burning lamp on her head.

Indianapolis Freeman, September 5, 1914.

Freeman reporter Billy Lewis judged Callie Vassar to be "a splendid interlocutor. Her voice rings out clear and distinct. She takes charge after the opening chorus. Her singing numbers are 'In My Harem' and 'My Man.' She is a winner and a favorite of the crowds."[188] Vassar, a St. Louis native, apparently joined Lowery's company in 1908, and she remained for many seasons. Among the songs she sang in 1912 was "Mammy's Shuffling Dance."[189]

For the 1914 season J. L. "Junk" Edwards, a well-known vaudeville comedian, replaced A. A. Wright as stage manager for Lowery's minstrels. Anatole Victor led the orchestra; Callie Vassar was interlocutor; and "with Junk Edwards and Slow Kid Thompson on the extreme ends you can rest assured that the comedy is always kept at a high pitch. In fact, all the performers work to and accomplish the same end, please the public and the management."[190] Ulysses S. "Slow Kid" Thompson sang "It Was Me, Kid" and "While Dancing Around"; Junk Edwards sang "Down in Chattanooga," "Smother Me with Kisses," "O That Band," "The Good Ship Mary Ann," and "That Colored Regimental Band"; Amos Peoples gave "Let Bygones Be Bygones" and "Keep Out of My Dreams"; Carrie Gilbert sang "Just for To-night" and "You Won My Heart"; Earl Granstaff gave "Ballin' the Jack" and "I Love the Ladies"; Leslie Davis sang "Twentieth Century Rag" and "Reuben Tango's Huskin' Bee"; Hattie Edwards performed "Don't Blame It All on Broadway" and "You and the Moon"; and James Jackson sang "Ragtime Dream" and "Camp Meeting Band."[191]

Callie Vassar's 1914 song repertoire included "Get Out and Get Under" and "On the Way to Mandalay."[192] When she gave out with "The Memphis Blues" that fall, the company reporter called her "our own Sophia Tucker."[193] Following the 1914 season Callie Vassar formed a "sister team" with her daughter, Sophia Vassar, to play in vaudeville. She traveled with Morgan's Mighty Minstrels in 1915, while Lowery was heading the band with Richards and Pringle's Georgia Minstrels. A December 18, 1915, report said, "Callie is a coon shouter from her heart and will be seen in vaudeville after the closing of the season, with her daughter, 'Sofa' [*sic*]. The team will be known as the 'Two Coon Shouting Fools.'" In May 1923, Callie Vassar recorded four titles for the Gennett Record Company, accompanied by jazz legend Richard M. Jones.[194]

Trombonist, minstrel performer, and assistant stage manager Earl Granstaff was with Lowery's Company in 1913 and 1914. During the 1914 season Granstaff and Lester Davis worked up a musical novelty act for vaudeville, "rendering the classics and some real hot rags."[195] At the 81 Theater in Atlanta in 1915, "They caught the audience from the start. Granstaff kicked them with his dancing and comedy playing of the trombone at the same time. Too much credit can not be given Davis for mastering a seemingly impossibility, playing the Rosary on two cornets at once . . . Their regular closing, a medley, called for an encore which they answered with the blues."[196] Granstaff went on to play trombone with Will Vodery's 807th Infantry Regiment Band in France during World War I.[197] In the early 1920s, he participated in recording sessions with Johnny Dunn's Original Jazz Hounds and Mary Stafford's Jazz Band.

The Hagenbeck-Wallace Circus played P. G. Lowery's home town of Eureka, Kansas, on October 16, 1914, but according to a *Freeman* letter from Granstaff, a dangerous mishap spoiled the occasion: "The parade had just left the lot, and for some reason or other, it stopped, leaving the back wheels of our band wagon on a short bridge. The bridge gave way so quick that it threw P. G. who was sitting right on that part, out over the side of the wagon and down into the creek; a distance of 20 feet, on his head and shoulders. We picked him up almost unconscious and he was hurried to the nearest doctor in an automobile. It was a very sad accident, and it happened when his mother and other relatives and friends were visiting him. He's improving rapidly, as he was in good health at the time. We were all shaken up pretty badly, hands, legs and arms skinned, and horns bent. But we are very thankful because it could have been worse."[198]

This report prompted a similar story from a member of the 101 Ranch Shows' annex: "In reading of our distinguished friend, P. G. Lowery's mishap in falling off the band [wagon] brought to my mind of the incident of our bass drummer's aerial act which he performed when we were returning on parade in Lynchburg, Va. We had almost reached the lot when one of the low wires caught him under the chin and lifted him and the bass drum clear out of the seat and with the bass drum still between his legs he hung suspended in the air until after it had stretched until his feet were within a foot from the ground when it broke. Lucky boy Pole, but he is careful not to repeat the act, while if he would put it before the public it would be a scream."[199]

P. G. Lowery's Band and Minstrels did not travel with the Hagenbeck-Wallace Circus in 1915. Instead, Lowery served as bandmaster for Richards and Pringle's Georgia Minstrels. The *Freeman*

P. G. Lowery and Band aboard their Hagenbeck-Wallace Circus bandwagon. (courtesy Circus World Museum, Baraboo, Wisconsin)

explained why: "He refused the engagement because the manager requested his men to double canvas. P. G. informed the manager he would leave . . . and at once notified his band of his firm stand and the same was heartily endorsed by his band and every band director in the circus business—such as Mr. Wolfscale, Roy Pope, James Harris and others."[200] "Doubling canvas" meant that, in addition to their regular duties in the sideshow tent and on parade, Lowery's men would have doubled as "roustabouts," driving and pulling stakes, getting the white tops up and in order. No wonder other sideshow band directors supported Lowery's firm stand. If Hagenbeck-Wallace had convinced Lowery's prestigious organization to double canvas, many other circuses surely would have followed suit.

Hagenbeck-Wallace was made to suffer for its mistake. Lowery and his company were greatly missed from the sideshow. As the 1915 season closed, R. Roy Pope was able to tell the *Freeman*: "I am proud to know that the Hagenbeck-Wallace management are forced to seek Prof. P. G. Lowery's services to regain the patronage of old that they have failed to get this season without him and his classy company of musicians and singers."[201]

By the time Lowery's Band and Minstrels returned to the Hagenbeck-Wallace Circus, P. G. had married the company's soubrette Carrie Gilbert. During that 1916 season she was said to be "holding her audience spell bound" with songs like "Close to My Heart" and "Morning, Noon and Night."[202] At the same time, Miss Essie Williams was "setting the audience wild in singing 'Walking the Dog.'"[203] Lowery's Minstrels also featured a male vocal quartet consisting of Irvin Richardson, Maylon Hall, Jakie Smith, and Tony Barefield. All four members of the quartet doubled in the band. The band was featuring Handy's "St. Louis Blues," and was said to be "the best formation of any band on the road—two clarinets, three cornets, two altos, two trombones, one baritone, two basses, monster E and double B, bass drum and snare drum and bells."[204] Jakie Smith appears to have been especially versatile. A note that fall said he was "featuring 'Pray for the Light to Go Out,' and with his theatrical knowledge and stage salutation he entirely stops our show with the many encores."[205]

A Lowery company report told of some hard traveling in Kansas: "September 24 we rode all day from Hiawatha, Kan. to Ft. Scott, Kan. On arriving we had one team of horses killed by the M. K. & T. railroad, and a driver severely injured. It was dusk and neither party could see on account of a sharp curve." On the bright side of the Fort Scott engagement, "We had the father of all musicians in our parade . . . in person of Mr. Levi Payne. He has one son in the band, Mr. Elmer Payne, our solo clarinetist."[206]

Between the 1916 and 1917 circus seasons Lowery placed a want ad in the *Freeman*, seeking "good comedians with good voices, who can make good balahooing. Preference given those who play banjo or guitar."[207] An effective ballyhoo was necessary to insure good attendance in any sideshow. Through this ad, Lowery was attempting to replace Prince Mungo, "the greatest single ballahoo man in the business,"[208] who had enticed patrons into the Hagenbeck-Wallace sideshow tent during the 1916 season. Prince Mungo was purported to

PRINCE MUNGO, DESCENDENT OF THE BHOGIRATTES.

One of the ethnological features of the Sells-Floto Annex and curio department is the exhibition of Prince Mungo, a direct descendant of a tribe of Bhogirattes. Prince Mungo is known by the managers of side shows and museums all over the country as a distinct box office attraction. His weird native songs and dances are both amusing and instruc-

tive, and he is capable of giving ten minutes of strange and fascinating amusement. Prince Mungo has traveled with all of the large circuses and is considered one of the best attractions ever imported from the Philippine Islands. As a bally-hoo proposition he stands without a peer, as this is one of his strongest assets, both in front of a kid show top or in the lobby of any theater. Prince Mungo will be at liberty after October 15, and invites correspondence from all reliable managers. Address as per route of Sells-Floto Circus in The Freeman.

Indianapolis Freeman, September 16, 1911.

be a native of the Philippines: "His weird native songs and dances are both amusing and instructive . . . As a bally-hoo proposition he stands without a peer, as this is one of his strongest assets, both in front of a kid show top [i.e., a sideshow tent] or in the lobby of any theater."[209] In 1916, while seated on the sideshow bandwagon on parade with Hagenbeck-Wallace in Oklahoma, "Prince Mungo had a narrow escape by a low wire catching his chair, which is high upon the wagon, and nearly threw him to the ground. He is the feature of the side show in this section of the country."[210]

1917 was a busy year for sideshow band and minstrel companies in general. Frequent updates were published in the *Freeman* from Wolfscale's Band with Barnum and Bailey; J. C. Miles's Annex Band with the Cole Bros. Circus; Arthur A. Wright's Band with the John W. Sparks Show; Eugene Clark's Band with La Tena's Circus; P. A. Venable's Band with Ringling Bros.; Bismark Ferris's Band with A. G. Barnes Circus; T. E. White's Band with John Robinson's Circus; R. H. Loveless's Band with J. H. Eschman Circus; Edward Rucker's Band with the Yankee Robinson Circus; L. K. Baker's Band with the Jess Willard–Buffalo Bill Wild West Show; and J. S. Riggers's Band with Coop and Lentz Three Ring Circus. Elmer H. Payne's Band with the Honest Bill Shows was said to be the only colored band featured under the big top during that season.[211]

The Hagenbeck-Wallace Circus opened their 1917 season in Indianapolis. The *Freeman* said it was

> A great day for a circus, last Wednesday, the finest of the year . . . The parade moved along in its erstwhile majesty, more resplendent than what we usually get to see because of the newness and freshness of everything. Indianapolis was the first stand . . .
>
> The side show has its own peculiar worth, besides the curiosities there was P. G. Lowery and his band of colored players and his minstrels—worth the price of admission—fifteen cents, please, everything gone up.
>
> The band in some respects is new but it blazed away in the old form and made them like it. The colored people for whom the side show management should be thankful were at their posts as usual, seeing and being seen.
>
> The minstrels made a hit with all the white people, many of whom were not [illegible word] Negro minstrelsy, but they liked it just the same. A good fetching show that got the applause.[212]

Lowery's Minstrels for 1917 featured Charles Beechum, Jakie Smith, Mack Carter, and Charles Creath, end men; Callie Vassar Hill singing "Hide Away Down in Iowa," Olga Beechum singing "What Do You Want to Make Those Eyes at Me For," Carrie Gilbert Lowery singing "Paradise Blues," Charles Beechum singing "Pray for the Lights to Go Out," and Jakie Smith singing "It Takes a Long Tall Brown Skin Gal to Make a Preacher Lay His Bible Down."

In 1915, following a stint in the annex of the Yankee Robinson Circus, cornetist Charles Creath joined Drake and Walker's Bombay Girls, a "stock" company touring black vaudeville theaters. Salem Tutt Whitney later recalled that the Drake and Walker Company "was about the first Colored organization to carry its own jazz band."[213] Creath remained with Drake and Walker until April 1917, when he jumped to P. G. Lowery's band and minstrels.[214] However, he reportedly suffered an attack of rheumatism and was forced to leave the show mid-tour, returning to his home at 1200 Kansas Avenue in East St. Louis, Illinois, for a rest.[215]

En route in May, Lowery had a reunion with King Phillips and W. C. Handy in Cincinnati, and a visit with Mr. and Mrs. R. Roy Pope in Dayton, Ohio. When the circus reached St. Louis, locals were obviously eager to honor their native daughter Callie Vassar, "the peer of all female interlocutors," with parties and receptions: "Miss Vassar, who appeared in the city during the week of June 11th, with the Hagenbeck & Wallace circus, and P. G. Lowery's entire company was feasted and entertained beyond the margin of pains and expense."[216] Clarinetist D. W. Batsell said he had a good time: "O you sherry and champagne. Those week stands are certainly enjoyable."[217]

From Florence, Alabama, by way of Sherman, Texas, D. W. Batsell exemplified the dynamic relationship between minstrel bandsmen and music education in black communities.[218] During the winter of 1910–1911 he fronted Batsell's Orchestra, "one of the best colored orchestras in the South. They are now touring the southern states."[219] In March 1911 Batsell signed with the Sunny Dixie Minstrels: "He will remain with the company until May, when he will go to Nashville to join Prof. C. M. Davis, Concert Band, touring with Mazeppa, the educated horse."[220] By August Batsell was "playing with Prof. W. C. Handy's orchestra at Memphis, Tenn., and teaching a band at Ellendale, Tenn."[221]

Closing with W. C. Handy before the end of 1911, Batsell went home to Florence and revived his independent orchestra: "We are playing all classes of music and are featuring all the late music produced by our composers. Just received a copy of Wilbur C. Sweatman's rag, 'Down Home,' which is just what I want for an encore."[222] By mid-May 1912 he was back "en route with the Professor C. M. Davis musical enterprise of the Mazeppa Shows."[223] Three months later he was "resting up and teaching the 'Lebanon Union Band,' at Lebanon, Tenn."[224] The *Freeman* described the band's "great success . . . using all music arranged and written by Mr. Batsell. It's 'The Blues' that captures the laurels."[225]

Batsell joined forces with trombonist B. H. Martin, a fellow Mazeppa Show alumnus, and on April 19, 1913, "Batsell and Martin's band, orchestra and minstrels opened . . . at Oxford, Pa., with Downie and Wheeler's combined circus for eight months and carrying eighteen people." Batsell and Martin were re-engaged with the Wheeler Brothers' annex for the season of 1914.[226]

Batsell also started marketing sheet music from his home in Florence. The *Freeman* of February 7, 1914, carried an ad for his "latest rag-time number for piano solo," "Sweety Won't You Be Kind to Me:" "Send 15c in stamps and receive a copy and be convinced that it is the greatest rag since my 'Alabama Blues.'"[227] Batsell stayed with Lowery through the summer of 1917, and he returned for the season of 1919.

1918 was a catastrophic year for the nation, and the sideshow annex bands suffered right along. The increased war effort put a strain on the railways, which were mobilized to transport large numbers of troops and military supplies. A "war tax" was placed on nonessential rail travel and the state of Florida put a temporary embargo on all road shows using private railroad cars. By autumn 1918 annex bands were having a difficult time maintaining adequate manpower, as the draft took a heavy toll of musicians and minstrels. Nearly every sideshow company was advertising in the *Freeman* for replacement musicians. Then, in October, the Spanish influenza began its rampage. Major American cities were quarantined; no movement in or out was permitted. Many performers contracted the flu, and many shows suffered great financial losses or were forced to shut down for the season. Lowery did no circus work in 1918, a seemingly calculated decision that removed him from the difficult circumstances which traveling musicians contended with that year. Lowery spent 1918 directing an African American community band at a munitions plant in Nitro, West Virginia.[228]

Outdoor show business began to recover in 1919. One auspicious event of that season was the appointment of Lowery's Band and Minstrels to occupy the sideshow tent of Ringling Brothers and Barnum and Bailey's newly combined mammoth circus. Chicago columnist Sylvester Russell observed: "When the Ringling Bros. and Barnum & Bailey Combined Circus came to the city, I took a run down to Grant Park to call on P. G. Lowery the band master. I saw little Princess Wee Wee in the menagerie and shook her hand. The difference between an African and an ape was seen in a side show cage. Aside from that, everything was lovely and the goose hung high."[229]

By this time the United States had experienced a generous exposure to jazz and blues in the somewhat indecorous context of the sideshow annex. A July 12, 1919, letter from Prof. Irvin Brown's band and minstrels, traveling in Tennessee with the Gentry Bros. Circus, described their program, in which three blues singers participated: Fisher Handy singing "Alcoholic Blues"; Effie Moore Brady, "Kansas City Blues"; and Pearl Alford, "Tishomingo Blues."

In the spring of 1920 correspondence from F. Bennett Hargrave's Band and Minstrels traveling in Mississippi with the combined forces of the Rhoda Royal Circus and Old Buffalo Wild West Show proclaimed: "Our Jazz Band, under the leadership of Mr. Hargraves packs the side show at every performance." The band consisted of Hargrave on mellophone, with two cornets, a trombone, a baritone horn, trap drums, and bass drum.[230] Cornet player Bert DeLeo joined Hargrave's band later that spring, and by June he had taken Hargrave's place as manager.[231] DeLeo was in the sideshow annex business as early as 1911, when he toured with Prof. Grant Cooper's Band and Minstrels, in connection with Kit Carson's Buffalo Ranch Wild West Shows.[232] While heading the annex with the Rhoda Royal Circus he made a special point of featuring blues and jazz hits of the day. In July 1920 he noted, "The band is in good trim using all the latest Jazz and blues, just what the public looks for when they see a colored band. This little twelve piece band is said to be the life of the parade."[233] Later that fall, he wrote:

> I have added some new clever people to the band and stage. Have Fred Jenkins and wife, and Kilmer Jackson and wife. The girls are what I call real poney girls [*sic*] with Mr. Jenkins, Leroy Wilson, James King and Kid Wallace on end which makes a very lively first part, using all the latest songs. A great many are published by Pace & Handy. Fred Jenkins sings with great success, "You Can't Keep a Good Man Down." Leroy Wilson, "Blind Man Blues," which always pleases the public. Mrs. Louise Jackson "Sphinx" and "You Can Have It, I Don't Want It." Mrs. Lillian Jenkins "Saxaphone Blues" and "Jelly Roll." Our idea is to try and keep up with the times and to travel over the territory. We like to give our patrons a little surprise . . . using the real up-to-the-minute songs.[234]

In 1920 "jazz band" became the operative term on the circus routes. Judging by *Freeman* reports from various sideshow annex companies that year, both the public and the performers had "gone jazz crazy":

Al G. Barnes' Greatest Wild Animal Circus: "The kid show [sideshow] is simply a dream, headed by . . . Jap Lovelace's red hot jazz band, who sets 'em wild daily. Boys, this is some show this season."[235]

Walter L. Main's Shows: "Our band, with Louis Gilbert as leader is now up to the standard of any jazz band on the road. Miss Viola Guest . . . is doing fine and making a big hit singing the 'Jazz Band.'"[236]

"Circus Friends Meet—The Wallace-Hagenbeck Circus and the Howe's Great London Circus passed each other . . . at Oxford, Nova Scotia, Canada . . . Jazz bands playing, beer and wine flowing like water. When two colored jazz bands meet, well, it's some jazz."[237]

P. G. Lowery may have had the hottest jazz band on the road in 1920, showcasing new compositions by African American composers including the dedicatory "P. G. Blues" by H. Qualli Clark and "Trombonology" by N. C. Davis of Nashville.[238] A note that spring informed that, "P. G. Lowery, the greatest colored bandmaster of the greatest jazz band in the world," was also "featuring two Skidmore song hits for the season. Carrie Lowery is singing them to the patrons of the world's biggest circus—Ringling Brothers-Barnum Bailey. Carrie sings both to a fare thee well . . . 'I'm Gonna Jazz My Way Right Through Paradise,' and 'Never Let No One Man Worry Your Mind.'"[239] Lowery's sideshow orchestra, under saxophonist Walter Coleman, was similarly written up: "Coleman's Jazz Orchestra, with Ringling Circus, is claimed to be one of the best on the road this season. He has promised to make everyone feel like dancing when they begin to play. Mrs. Carrie Lowery is featuring all the latest songs, accompanied by Coleman's Jazzers."[240]

Recapping the events of the 1920 season, a correspondent reported:

October 27 marked the closing date of the most successful season experienced by P. G. Lowery and his band. The entire season was one ideal trip, opening in New York City, March 25, traveling through thirty states. P. G. Lowery's band did great credit to themselves, also their director in the six weeks engagement in the Madison Square Garden, New York City. The engagement consisted of the grand entry and playing a feature act in the big show performance, including full salary and expenses . . . The formation of the band was very good and the parts were artistically handled by each member. William Blue, the clarinetist from St. Louis, proved himself a feature in the band. Next comes the cornet section, consisting of Thomas May, the old reliable circus performer, who has held the solo seat for years, assisted by R. Q. Dickerson, one of St. Louis' best cornetists, ably assisted by Richard Jasper of Huntington, W. Va. The alto section was 1st class. This rank was filled by Ed Tolliver, of Washington, D. C., and C. W. Evans of Louisville. Both of these were well up in the circus business. Next to mention was the trombones. This end was handled by R. H. Horton, of Chicago, H. Lankford, of St. Louis, and A. H. Bass, of St. Louis. Too much can not be said of the three men. Winston Walker of St. Louis and A. Zoo Robinson [*sic*] of New Orleans, were the two baritones of merit. Mr. Walker bids fair to be the greatest baritone of his race, while Mr. Robinson not only is an artist on baritone but a 1st class trombonist. Walter Coleman, the saxophonist from Columbus, O., led the orchestra and doubled in band. The name Wm. May is sufficient, the name stands for the best bass in the business . . . Last but not least, is the drum section. This part was manipulated by Jas. Holmes, of Melford, Del. and Victor Miller, of Chicago, Ill. Mr. Lowery wishes to thank each and every one for their conduct and courteous work in making the Lowery band a pattern for all bands.[241]

Jazz legend Alvin "Zoo" Robertson had been a member of Homer Butler's Annex Band and Minstrels, traveling with the Walter L. Main Circus for the first several months of the 1919 season, but he joined Lowery's band mid-tour, replacing a trombonist who had left to take up other work.[242] Robertson spent the winter with John Robichaux's Orchestra at the Lyric Theater in his hometown New Orleans, and then rejoined Lowery for the start of the 1920 circus season. He played trombone with Lowery's band in 1919 and switched to baritone the following year. On August 30, 1920, the multitalented Robertson "laid aside his euphonium and closed his circus engagement . . . Will now be seen and heard at the piano in J. W. Walker's Syncopated Dance Orchestra."[243]

R. H. Horton of Chicago was one of three trombonists with Lowery's 1920 band. He is very likely the Robert Horton who recorded with Johnny Dunn's Original Jazz Hounds in February 1922. Interestingly, Robert Horton was replaced on Dunn's next recording session by Earl Granstaff, another graduate of "the Lowery school."

St. Louis's thriving black music community had for years been a source of talent for Lowery's Band and Minstrels.[244] Lowery's 1920 band featured a remarkable array of St. Louis jazz musicians who ultimately contributed to an impressive legacy of jazz recordings. Harvey Lankford is heard on 1924 recordings by Fate Marable's Society Syncopators and a St. Louis session recorded for Okeh Records in 1925 by Benny Washington's Six Aces. R. Q. Dickerson and William Blue are both present on the classic jazz recordings of the Cotton Club Orchestra (1925 and 1927) and Cab Calloway's earliest sessions (1930–1931), as well as the Missourians' recordings (1929–1930). Blue appeared on sessions with Louis Armstrong and the Henry Allen Orchestra, and is also heard on recordings made in St. Louis during the mid-1920s by Dewey Jackson's Peacock Orchestra and Charles Creath's Jazz-O-Maniacs. Creath's recording sessions feature a third "Loweryite," Horace Eubanks on clarinet. The *Chicago Defender* of August 7, 1926, reported that Creath's orchestra was, "at the present time . . . working on the steamship St. Paul, one of the largest pleasure boats plying the Mississippi. They are rated as the best orchestra in St. Louis. Mr. Creath has been under the weather for five weeks . . . Horace Eubanks, our old Chicago boy, has taken up leader's duties."

In 1922, R. Q. Dickerson and New Orleans saxophonist David Jones organized Robinson's Syncopators, a noteworthy jazz band which spent much of 1923 and 1924 on a triumphant tour of mainstream theaters. *Chicago Defender* critic Tony Langston reviewed their act at the Grand Theater on State Street: "'Robinson's Ten Syncopators' headed by R. Q. Dickerson, the famous 'preachin' and prayin' cornetist,' is the headlined attraction here this week. The big act is just off a more than successful trip over the Pantages circuit and they are showing plainly just why they have been accorded the honor of being the best act of the sort . . . They give a musical program which varies from a bunch of harmony which is almost sanctimonious to a wild scramble of blues and jazz which has the folks out front by the ears."[245] In 1925 Robinson's Syncopators settled in at the Cotton Club in New York City and became known as the Cotton Club Orchestra.

Lowery's roster never again featured so many illustrious jazz musicians as it did in 1920, and after the season ended his band was no longer referred to as a "jazz band." A brief review of Lowery's Ringling Bros. and Barnum and Bailey Circus Annex Band for 1921 described it as "a body of picked musicians . . . The band gives an hour's concert every day, consisting of standard overtures. Lee Graham, the general manager, especially praised the band on the rendition of 'Morning, Noon and Night,' 'Maritana' and 'Il Trovatore.'"[246]

At this juncture P. G. began to focus more of his attention on training bands in Cleveland, Ohio, where he made his home. His work with the Silver Seal Ladies' Band in 1922 drew special notice: "This band is without a doubt the best ladies' band of color in this country. Their advance has been wonderful under the teaching of P. G. Lowery. One can easily detect the technique taught by Mr. Lowery in their rendition of serenades and tone poems."[247]

Two members of Lowery's band, Calvin Ivory and H. L. Arrington, were alumni of Birmingham, Alabama's first black high school, and its increasingly famous Industrial High School Band, under the direction of John T. "Fess" Whatley. When the circus came to Birmingham in October, the current Industrial High School Band turned out in a body, and Lowery reportedly "made a short visit to the Elks Rest to hear the I. H. S. Orchestra play for the Annual Soiree of the Iroquois Club." Lowery presented the high school bandsmen with an orchestration of "Shrine of Liberty," which the Industrial High School Band performed in their first concert of the 1923 season.[248]

In 1923 Lowery left his post with the Ringling Bros. and Barnum and Bailey Circus. He spent the next three years in Cleveland, teaching music and training local bands. Lowery's departure "left an awful gap to fill . . . but Thomas May, his standby for years, has stepped in his leader's shoes with a wonderful band and exercises business qualities as did P. G."[249] Performer and *Chicago Defender* columnist "Ragtime" Billy Tucker saw the Ringling sideshow band when the circus came to California in 1923 and wrote: "They create as much excitement as three or four ordinary bands, but the presence of P. G. Lowery was in need and easily noticed. I'm like Sonny Clay: 'It ain't but the one and that's P. G.'"[250]

Lowery returned to the Ringling Bros. and Barnum and Bailey Circus annex in 1926. He still had "a crack band," which played "all of the standard overtures along with the scintillating popular music,"[251] but the band was no longer in the thick of the latest commercial trends, as it had been a decade earlier. By 1926 blues and jazz were no longer novelties; they had permeated the commercial mainstream, and this may have influenced the repertoire of sideshow bands in favor of standard overtures.

Lowery's engagement with Ringling Bros. ended in 1931, but his career in the sideshow continued for eleven more years, with the Robbins Bros. Circus, the Downie Bros. Circus, and the Cole Bros. Circus.[252] Lowery died in Cleveland, Ohio, on December 15, 1942, but not before he completed the 1942 circus season at the head of the Cole Bros. sideshow band and minstrels.

William May, master of the bass horn, remained with Lowery's band to the very end. He and his brother Thomas had united with P. G. in the Forepaugh-Sells annex in 1899. Thomas May left the "Lowery bunch" in or around 1930. Other old-timers who trouped with P. G. on his final tour of 1942 included trombonist Harvey Lankford, a veteran of Lowery's famous 1920 jazz band; minstrel Noah Robinson, who had performed with John Eason's Band and Minstrels in the Yankee Robinson Circus in 1915 and traveled with Lowery as early as 1927; and multi-instrumentalist Ben Goodall, who traveled with James Wolfscale's Band in the Forepaugh-Sells annex in 1911 and was on Lowery's band roster by 1929.

According to circus historian Robert F. Houston, 1948 was the final year the Ringling Bros. and Barnum and Bailey Circus carried a traditional black sideshow band and minstrel. The annex bandmaster for that landmark season was Arthur A. Wright, who had played solo cornet and managed the stage for P. G. Lowery way back in 1912 and 1913. Wright had directed the annex band of "The Greatest Show on Earth" since the 1930s.[253]

P. G. Lowery was idolized by his contemporary musicians, and there is ample evidence that the "Lowery school" was a primary factor in the development of modern African American popular music and jazz. In the book *Oh, Didn't He Ramble: The Life Story of Lee Collins, As Told to Mary Collins*, the great New Orleans jazz cornetist testified:

> One thrill I remember was the night that P. G. Lowery came to the Astoria [i.e., New Orleans's Astoria Gardens]. Lowery, who was from Cleveland, Ohio, was with the Barnum and Bailey Shows and was known as the greatest cornet soloist. He could make C over high C like it was nothing at all; he was the greatest of all time. The way he blew made goose pimples come over me; I had never heard a cornet player like him in my life before . . . Bunk Johnson told me once that he worked under P. G. Lowery and that he went with the circus on a tour of Europe. I don't know if that was true or not, as Bunk did a little stretching of the truth from time to time, but I do know that it was a great thing for all the musicians to listen to Lowery when he came to New Orleans with the circus.[254]

Phonograph records have long been the major jumping-off point for blues and jazz scholarship. The fact that Lowery and his band made no recordings has had a profound effect on the place he has been accorded in American music history. Old recordings are relatively easy to access, certainly a more convenient and enjoyable reference tool than old newspaper accounts or oral histories, and more familiar to the general public. However, far too much focus on the commercial recording industry has distorted the prevailing concept of the history of American popular music. It seems to be accepted as a matter of faith that mainstream America was first introduced to blues through the medium of phonograph records. But long before blues records became available, the compositions of W. C. Handy and other blues writers were repeatedly performed in street parades and on circus lots in countless locations throughout every inhabited part of the United States and much of Canada. Generally speaking, white America was introduced to the blues by sideshow annex bands of the World War I decade.

PART FOUR

“UNDER CANVAS”: African American TENTED MINSTRELSY and the Untold Story of Allen’s New Orleans Minstrels, the RABBIT’S FOOT Company, the FLORIDA BLOSSOMS, and *SILAS GREEN* from New Orleans

The great African American minstrel companies of the 1890s—Mahara’s Minstrels, Isham’s Octoroons, the Black Patti Troubadours, Richards and Pringle’s Georgia Minstrels, etc.—all held forth in mainstream theaters. The onset of ragtime made possible the full realization of “genuine” African American minstrelsy; by the turn of the century, black minstrel performers had seriously undermined their white counterparts, especially in the South. In response, the powers that be attempted

to choke off access to mainstream theaters in the southern states. Richards and Pringle's Georgia Minstrels were traveling in Alabama in 1903 when their *Freeman* correspondent reported: "I hear of late that it is going the rounds of the public in general that as far as [white theater magnates] Klaw & Erlinger are concerned there will be no more colored shows booked in the South over their circuit, as they seem to think the colored shows are taking the bread out of the white companies' mouths."[1] That same year a *Freeman* editorial referred to "organizations touring the Southland under canvas, whose aggregation of talent evokes encomiums from Negro-hating journals, yet denied admittance to perform in a regular theater controlled by white men."[2]

Just before the turn of the century a new breed of African American minstrel show rose up in the South, "under canvas." The southern tented minstrel show came into its own around 1900, reached its artistic peak in the years before World War I, prospered through the 1920s, survived the Depression years, and struggled into the late 1950s before giving up the ghost. Living out of Pullman railroad cars and blanketing the Southland with "canvas theaters," shows like Allen's New Orleans Minstrels, the Rabbit's Foot Company, the Florida Blossom Minstrels, and *Silas Green from New Orleans* staked out a new frontier of African American entertainment.

Landing in a new town almost every day, they announced their arrival with a street parade featuring a smartly uniformed marching brass band. The parade generally culminated at the center of town, with the band "circling up" for an impromptu concert. In the afternoon there might be a challenge baseball game, with a minstrel team squaring off against the locals. In the evening there was an open-air concert and ballyhoo in front of the tent, followed by the actual show.

The show usually opened with a tambo-and-bones-styled minstrel act, followed by the olio, and concluding with a musical farce-comedy production, or afterpiece. A stage orchestra accompanied all three parts. The primary singers of ragtime, and eventually blues and jazz, were the blackface comedians and coon shouters. Vocal quartets, as native to minstrelsy as the banjo, also made a specialty of singing the latest ragtime songs, while the minstrel bands and orchestras gave their own vivid forecast of popular directions in race music.

Like their theater-based antecedents, these new black tented minstrel shows captivated many white southerners, and they established a special rapport with black southerners. Their portable tent theaters afforded greater access to back-country towns, and allowed a bit of leeway in negotiating Jim Crow laws and customs. There were southern towns that blacks were forbidden to enter; yet black tented minstrels were often permitted to perform in such places.

At most southern show stops, whites and blacks enjoyed tented minstrel shows, but always with segregated seating arrangements. The complexion of the audience varied according to locale. Most stops brought out a predominantly black crowd, but usually with a fair representation of whites. At Clinton, North Carolina, in 1908 the *Freeman* correspondent for A. G. Allen's Minstrels noted, "This was the first colored show to visit Clinton since its formation, and the tent was crowded with both races at each performance."[3]

Excursions into the western states were altogether different. When Allen's Minstrels dropped into Texas from Oklahoma in the fall of 1901, "It had been three weeks since we had seen a colored person and you know how glad the boys were to get to Ft. Worth . . . Well we have been in anti Negro towns for about three weeks. Some of them where colored people have not been seen for seventeen years."[4] A 1913 report from Anadarko, Oklahoma, informed that Allen's Minstrels were "among the Choctaw and Apache Indian tribes, and ugh, ugh, heap big show, heap good music, heap good, heap good, is the daily comment of these proud but fast disappearing red men."[5]

Show stops in "all-colored towns" provided rare opportunities to play for exclusively black audiences. At Boley, Oklahoma, on August 9, 1909, members of Allen's Minstrels "were handsomely entertained by the citizens. This is a pure colored town and offers many inducements to colored settlers. After the show the orchestra played at the palatial residence of C. W. Perry for an hour, after which the Misses Perry entertained with vocal and instrumental selections and solos, the entertainment lasting into the wee sma' hours of the morning. This town is the king of its kind and the citizens, from the mayor down deserve much credit."[6] In the fall of 1913 Allen's Minstrels played Mound Bayou, Mississippi, another "strictly colored town. The people are very progressive and the town is a credit to the race. We showed to a very handsome and intelligent audience."[7]

There are reports of blues singing in southern vaudeville theaters as early as 1910, but documentation of blues singing under the minstrel show tents did not creep into the *Freeman* until 1914. In Oklahoma with the Sunny Dixie Minstrels that spring, end man Wee Willie Nelson was "sure some class when he sings the 'Memphis Blues.'" That fall the star comedian with Huntington's Mighty Minstrels, Jolly E. Davis, was "bringing the house down with 'his original blues.' He sings them like no one else can." A report from Barfield's Georgia Minstrels in the spring of 1915 described Lucille McGinty, "leaving them spellbound with the 'Low Down Blues.'" A few months later, the Comedy Quartette with J. C. O'Brien's Georgia Minstrels made a hit singing "It's a Long Way to Tipperary" and "The Blues."[8]

By mid-decade blues singing had begun to make a permanent home in tented minstrelsy. W. C. Handy's early blues compositions, particularly "St. Louis Blues," "Hesitation Blues," and the vocal version of "The Memphis Blues," initiated the trend. Allen's New Orleans Minstrels, the Rabbit's Foot Company, and *Silas Green from New Orleans* all carried blues singing specialists in 1915. In 1916 the blues specialist with the Florida Blossom Minstrels was Bessie Smith. By the end of the decade all African American minstrel companies were expected to carry at least one "real blues singer"; from the 1920s onward, minstrel shows were a primary platform for "classic" female blues singers.

African American minstrel performers of the early twentieth century, often working in blackface, became successful purveyors of authentic, up-to-date black vernacular music and dance. They gradually transformed the ancient stereotypes of "Ethiopian minstrelsy" into vehicles for the development of racially self-referential humor and the advancement of modern African American popular music. Nevertheless, tented minstrel shows do not appear to have pioneered in the commercial ascendancy of vocal blues.

Instrumental blues was a somewhat different matter. References to minstrel show bands and orchestras playing blues tunes infiltrated the *Freeman* almost immediately after the first significant wave of blues compositions hit the marketplace. Minstrel bandleaders generally employed the latest blues sheet music productions by black composers but did not reach into the "raw" folk music per se. The minstrel bands were comprised, for the most part, of well-rounded players who took pride in discoursing "high class" selections. While they made the most of "Memphis Blues," "Dallas Blues," "Jogo Blues," and "Florida Blues," they may have preferred to demonstrate their mastery of the conventional band repertoire.

The Georgia Smart Set Minstrels expressed in 1917 that their fifteen- to eighteen-piece band used blues as a form of "seasoning": "The band renders standard marches, selections, popular airs, [and] rags, trimmed and seasoned with a few Blues."[9] Similarly, Mahoney's Mobile Minstrels advised that their "real hot" eleven-piece band under the direction of Yazoo City, Mississippi, resident R. J. "Dickie" Anderson did "not feature the Blues. Classics and popular music is the forte, and a very few Blues to taper off things."[10]

Some of the earliest *Freeman* references to blues being played by minstrel musicians came from J. C. O'Brien's Famous Georgia Minstrels. This troupe claimed to have been on the road since 1889.[11] In 1910, when they started filing reports to the *Freeman*, they were playing winter dates in theaters and summers under canvas, with show stops extending from Mississippi to Minnesota.[12] In 1911 they started showing exclusively under canvas, and narrowed their travels to Arkansas, Missouri, Kansas, Nebraska, Oklahoma, and Texas.[13] In 1912 they moved their winter quarters from Houston, Texas, to Brunswick, Georgia, and adopted a solidly southern route. In Virginia that summer their fifteen-piece band was playing "Down Home Rag" in the evening concert, and their "famous Texas clarinetist" G. W. Warford was "cleaning up in the last act, playing 'The Blues and the Dream [*sic*].'"[14] Still with O'Brien in 1915, Warford was reportedly "making good with his 'Texas Blues.'"[15]

In Virginia during the summer of 1914, O'Brien's minstrel band featured "Baby Seals Blues" in its evening concert.[16] That fall the company correspondent wrote from North Carolina:

> Now here comes the Georgia Minstrel band, headed by Prof. G. W. Ayers, and assisted by seventeen solo musicians, featuring all the latest rags and popular overtures. We have some blues; we have "The Memphis Blues," "The Jo-Go Blues," also the "Baby Seals Blues," and we give the gigs [*sic*, i.e., African Americans] all the blues they want and you can just see them walking dogie [*sic*] when our band is playing. O, my, how Mr. [Horace] Harrison can play that slippery horn when they play the "Baby Seals Blues." Our band is also handling "Poet and Peasant," "Flowers of Italy" and the overture "William Tell," and win the hearts of all music loving people.[17]

"Walking dogie" appears to have been a grassroots African American dance step specifically identified with emerging blues and jazz. O'Brien's *Freeman* correspondent observed people "walking dogie" on the parade routes at least twice during their 1914 sojourn in Georgia and the Carolinas. This was two years prior to the publication of Shelton Brooks's monumental "dance craze" hit, "Walking the Dog."

In 1915 Prof. Ayers and his band were "still the center of attraction" with O'Brien's Georgia

Minstrels, "playing standard and medley selections, rags and blues."[18] By this time O'Brien was also running a "No. 2" company that included a fourteen-piece band under Prof. C. A. Holloway, playing "everything in music from 'The Florida Blues' to 'Poet and Peasant.'"[19] In Texas that fall the "No. 2" band made "the hit of the season. Believe me, Prof. Holloway knows just what to give the gigs. He is featuring the Florida Blues, Memphis Blues, also the Jo Go Blues and you can just see them rocking in their seats."[20]

In 1916, Prof. Ayers's fifteen-piece band dominated the "No. 1" company's street parade, "marching in their long red English walking coats and high red beavers, filling the streets with some very classic marches and a Bunch of blues of all kinds, which is everybody's favorite and seems to please all that see and hear them. And when Prof. G. W. Ayers circles his band up on the square at night for concert—Peaches."[21]

In Virginia that summer they presented their evening concert "as follows: 'Poet and Peasant,' 'Operatic Ray [*sic*],' 'Bunch of Blues,' 'Remick Hits No. 15,' 'Light Cavalry,' and closing the concert with the big favorite, 'The Weary Blues.'"[22] That fall they incorporated some recent publications from Clarence Williams and A. J. Piron—"Prof. G. W. Ayers' band is still pleasing the people with his latest rag time music, such as 'Brown Skin,' 'I Can Beat You Doing What You Doing Me'"—and they also played "Walking the Dog."[23]

Before the end of 1916, the band with O'Brien's "No. 2" company came under the direction of Prof. Charles H. Booker, of Greenville, Mississippi. Prof. Booker was an exemplary tent show bandleader with a keen ear for the blues and its commercial potential. He had most recently served with Robinson's Old Kentucky Minstrels, who had advised in the *Freeman* of February 26, 1916: "Professional musicians, watch for the latest in Blues. Within the next few days Prof. Booker will put before the public his own composition, 'The Mississippi Blues.'" Two weeks later there came an update: "Professor Booker put on his Mississippi Blues for the first time and wants it understood by all in the profession that he predicts it to cap the climax of Blues."

On April 7, 1917, O'Brien's "No. 2" company filed this report:

> While we have had great competition in the way of shows, like "The Rabbit Foot," "Silas Green," "Florida Blossoms," "The Kentucky Minstrels," "Huntington Minstrels" and "The Great Johnny J. Jones Great Shows" . . . the show-going folks say that the Georgia is the best . . . Prof. C. H. Booker, Jr.'s big concert band is going big nightly and has a nice program. Poet and Peasant, Vampire, Bohemian Girl . . . and Little Jim Powell is just bending the clarinet when the band plays the West Texas Blues.

"West Texas Blues" was Prof. Booker's latest composition. O'Brien's "No. 1" company band also put it to use: "This band is playing all standing [*sic*] overtures, such as 'Poet and Peasant,' 'Light Cavalry,' 'Flowers of Italy' and featuring the West Texas Blues, which is quite a hit."[24]

Prof. Booker eventually settled in Memphis, where he and Howard Yancy formed the Yancy and Booker Music Publishing Company, with a Beale Street address. Their first publication, in 1919, was "West Texas Blues."[25] "West Texas Blues" was recorded in 1921 by Edith Wilson, in 1922 by the Tampa Blue Jazz Band, and in 1924 by the composer's own Jazz Band.[26]

The 1915 edition of O'Brien's "No. 1" company included a "rube" band in its parade: "First in line is our fife and drum corps; second, Jim Green and his rube band, of eight pieces; third, our strutters, better known as the red coat boys; fourth, Prof. A. G. Ayers and his band of sixteen pieces; fifth, the joy wagon, with the funny boys; sixth . . . our calliope."[27]

A "rube band" was a small, comically conceptualized and costumed "country" brass band. The repertoire of the rube band with O'Brien's Minstrels was particularly focused: "Jim Green's Rube Band discourses the various blues."[28] According to O'Brien's *Freeman* correspondent, Jim Green's Rube Band was actually "too good to be called a Rube band. The Blues and rags they play makes 'em clamor for more. It is composed of the following: W. E. Mason and Eddie Alford, cornets; James Green and Leroy Drayton, trombone; Ed Knightingale and Willie Speaker, tuba and baritone; Johnnie Harris and Wm. Jones, snare and base drummers."[29]

Not every tented minstrel show had a calliope; those that did made it an additional outlet for instrumental blues on the parade routes. In Georgia with O'Brien's Georgia Minstrels during the spring of 1914, "Mr. Mancy Williams keeps them walking dogie when he plays the Blues on the steam calliope."[30] In 1916 the calliope player with Mahoney's Mobile Minstrels, Fred Sedberry, was "there with the goods and he plays a bunch of late music, 'Morning, Noon and Night,' 'Little House on the Hill,' 'The St. Louis Blues,' 'Walking the Dog' and others."[31]

One of the most striking phenomena in the history of African American minstrelsy is the flood of tent shows that spilled into the Mississippi Delta every year at harvest time. The effect, if any, on the impending tide of "country blues" can only be suggested, not investigated, here. Tent shows customarily followed the harvests and other signs of seasonal prosperity in regional laboring communities. The best time of all for tent shows was cotton picking time in the Mississippi Delta.

During the fall of 1915 tent shows were stacked on top of each other in the Delta. Robinson's Old Kentucky Minstrels reported from the crossroads town of Bobo late that year: "We have been only a few days behind Prof. Eph Williams, Big Silas Green Co. and also the Rabbit Foot Co. . . . A show in town every day in the week and all do a big business . . . Rosedale, Miss., and Greenville, Miss., were banner houses for the season."[32] At Rosedale, members of the Old Kentucky Minstrels "had the pleasure of shaking hands with J. C. Miles and his happy bunch from the Jones Circus."[33]

In September of the following year the Silas Green Company reported:

> Well, we are still in Mississippi, playing to large crowds, and the way people turned out, why, it seemed as if we were the first show to enter town, but we were not, for there are several others, such as the Kentucky Minstrels, J. C. O'Brien, the World's Follies and the Wooden's Bon Tons, and in spite of all we are turning them away nightly . . . The Bon Tons showed Jackson, Miss., one week, as they stated . . . and they were the talk of the town all Sunday and Monday, but when Prof. Eph [Williams'] Silas Green Co. opened their doors Monday night, and taking 800 people, paid admissions, and about 75 comps, why it didn't seem as though the Bon Tons had ever been there.[34]

Later that fall Silas Green's *Freeman* correspondent told how Silas Green and Mahoney's

Mobile Minstrels "Met For A Battle At Greenville, Miss." The battle was enacted through "A Bucking Parade and Concert":

Well, it seemed as though both shows were waiting for one to break the ice on the streets, though each show was at a different depot, and it was unhandy to see which one would leave their car first, but again it appeared that both shows must have left at the same time, only Silas Green had picked their concert spot and was playing when Mahoney's Mobile parade was sighted coming nearer and nearer, until they reached where Silas Green was. And, believe me, those darkeys were looking some hot and playing some music. Silas Green Band left the circle first, after receiving many hands from both white and Colored.

The reporter assured that "Silas Green carried the crowd" that night:

At 6:45 p.m. the ticket box was surrounded with crowds of people and the crowd kept on coming, and at 8:00 p.m. there were fully 800 people, and at 8:15 the ticket box was closed, having sold tickets amounting to 1,448 paid admissions, not including the many people who gave up their fares at the side entrance to Prof. Eph Williams, and the turnaways looked to be 200 or 300 persons, and some of them were the life savers for the Mahoney Minstrels. In all my traveling with tent shows last night was the first time to see men hanging to the centerpoles to see a show . . . It appeared as if the whole show were a riot . . . Prof. A. D. King's twelve-piece band . . . took the crowd like Grant did Richmond, only they left Prof. Anderson's band to take what ground they could. So, A. D. King's band took 1,448 citizens of Greenville and Prof. Anderson's band took the remainder, which was something like two hundred, although music is music.[35]

A Silas Green representative telegraphed news of another "battle" that fall: "The Sun Bros. and Silas Green clashed at Hollandale, Miss., Oct. 25. Results, S. R. O. for Silas Green. At 8 o'clock that night less than fifty paid admissions were under the Sun Bros.' big top tent."[36]

During the harvest season of 1917 the influx of tent shows to the Mississippi Delta reached the saturation point. Silas Green was among the first to arrive:

Prof. Eph Williams Famous Silas Green From New Orleans Show Co. made its appearance in the Miss. Delta on Wednesday, September 26, to a packed house at Grenada. In fact we filled it to the overflow. The big crowd was loud in praise of the biggest colored show en route, and said the performance was the best ever given in the city of Grenada. On September 27 the show makes Greenwood, Miss., where it is assured of big success.

Sun Bros. Circus is billed at Grenada for October 8; Wallace Circus is billed at Durant on October 4; Barnum Circus is at Greenwood, Miss., on the 11th. There are at this writing 31 shows in the Miss. Delta. The reason of this is cotton is selling at 30 cents a pound. Money is plentiful and shows are coming fast and furious.[37]

Max C. Elliott, a "famous wildcat agent" who handled advance publicity for various shows, filed this report in the *Freeman* of October 27, 1917:

I will now give you an idea of what shows are now in the Cotton State of Mississippi.

In the first place, the State is overrun with one and two-car shows, theatrical companies and carnivals are a thing of the past when it comes to the good old State of Mississippi. Carnivals are barred out of the biggest lot of the towns, while theatrical companies have to make big jumps in order to find houses to play in.

Nearly all the circuses have made the state and have cleaned up. The Barnum and Bailey circus came first followed by the Wallace Circus, Sun Bros, John Robinson, Sells-Floto and the Hagg [*sic*] circus. Now comes the rumor of the Ringling show and the Cole Bros. In the minstrel game first to come was the Mobile Minstrels, followed by the Rabbit's Foot, A. G. Lions [*sic*, Allen's] Minstrels, Prof. Eph Williams, Silas Green shows, Hunt's Old Kentucky Minstrels, Brown and Bowers White Minstrels Under Canvas, Jones Bros. Georgia Smart Set Minstrels, Worden's Alabama Minstrels, Campbell Bros.' New Orleans Minstrels, Joe Herbert's Greater Minstrels, Pete Worthley Florida Blossoms, and G. A. Corbin Minstrels, Price and Bornell's Minstrels. And they are doing a big business, in fact, reaping a harvest from the American Cotton Picker, as the colored people and white people of Mississippi like plenty of minstrel companies. Of the minstrel companies under canvas will say I have seen but two and they were Robert Russell Company under canvas and the Eph. Swain Company. The Swain Company is run by Mrs. Swain, as W. I. Swain is in the army. I met one musical show under canvas, white, Johnny Calvin Company. He packed them in at Greenville the night I saw the show.

On Thursday, October 11, 1917, four major tent shows converged on the little town of Greenwood. The *Freeman* published a New Orleans–based newspaperman's eyewitness account:

October 11, at Greenwood, furnished enough shows for Greenwood, Mississippi and vicinity to last them the next ten years. With the greatest show on earth, Barnum & Bailey, and their gorgeous parade, viewed by thousands along the line of march, was closely followed by the Georgia Smart Set Minstrels, then A. G. Allen's Minstrels, at four-thirty came Old Kentucky Minstrels, from what I understand from various agents of the above latter shows, it was planned to "buck" the Georgia Smart Set Show, as it was their first visit in that State.

I took time and visited both the other shows to see if it was really their intentions and soon found out that they had decided to do so but upon going to the tent of the Smart Set soon found that they were packed in like sardines and paid little or no attention to their two competitors.

Their band and parade far exceeded their opposition and really I was surprised to see such a congress of performers after having been bored by so many of these "plantation shows" which recently have styled themselves minstrels . . .

I am now on my way to New Orleans, where I shall again take up my duties with the Picayune Times and through my many moments of repose in the future, I shall always think of Greenwood, Miss. and the surplus shows that I witnessed.[38]

A correspondent for the Georgia Smart Set Minstrels told it this way: "Mississippi is some minstrel show state. At Greenwood, Miss., we had the pleasure of shaking hands with Prof. Wolfscale, of the Barnum shows, also the A. G. Allen's Minstrels and the Kentucky Minstrels; can anyone imagine the old time feeling when three minstrel shows and a circus the size of the Barnum circus strikes a town the size of Greenwood, Miss. Everyone seemed to be satisfied with the business and, not boasting, but the Smart Set management is more than pleased with our night's receipts."[39]

The bass soloist with A. G. Allen's Minstrels, George E. Glasco, was inspired to poetry:

Strange things happen in this world
We all know every day,
But what I tell you of seldom happens in this way.
Just picture four of our greatest shows
In one little town one day
All fighting for the good old coin,
In that good old show folk way.
First came the Barnum & Bailey shows

In all their glory arrayed,
The Old Kentucky Minstrels, Georgia Smart Set
Bunch were there and was some more street parade,
Then came that mighty minstrel show
That's cleaning up everywhere
And really not a bragging, boy, I tell you she's a bear
And when the curtain rose upon a sight that's really rare
One had to look real closely to find a vacant chair.
Mr. Quine was smiling for we'd more than got our share
A. G. Allen's New Orleans Minstrels
Is the last I've mentioned here.[40]

In the immediate wake of the great 1917 Greenwood, Mississippi, tent show convergence, Max C. Elliott reported that "a number of towns are closed. The past week the writer was in Ruleville, Lulu [*sic*], Belzoni, [and] Moorehead [*sic*] and found them all closed to shows of all kinds . . . It is a safe bet Greenwood will be closed and the show people themselves are to blame. Eighteen shows have made Clarksdale in the past month. And still they come to Mississippi."[41]

The Florida Blossom Minstrels noted in the fall of 1920 that they were headed for the "cotton fields of Mississippi, where we expect to meet all the shows." But A. G. Allen's Minstrels lingered in Louisiana, where they claimed to be doing "the same good business as usual, being the only minstrel show under canvas in this part of the South, as all the rest 'got the gold fever, so to speak,' and rushed to Mississippi, bad as the days of 49, twas a shame that the wonderful Delta turned out like the fable of the 'Fox and the grapes,' so sour."[42] The heyday of prosperity may have started to wane by 1920; nevertheless, minstrel show traffic remained heavy in the Mississippi Delta for decades to come.

To an appreciable extent, the annual flood of tent shows reflected the loyalty of the region's minstrel show–loving African American population. During the fall of 1925 a correspondent for the Silas Green Company told the *Chicago Defender*:

> I imagine that if one wants real show news the present situation in Mississippi should not be overlooked. It isn't such a large state, but it's one of your greatest cotton states and has a great Race population of real show-going people. At one time this season there were many shows in the state at the same time, all sparring for an advantageous position and to stay in the money spots. There are Walcott's Rabbit's Foot company, Holtkamp's Georgia Smart Set, Roger's Florida Blossoms, Huntington's Mighty Minstrels, Hunt's Sugar Foot Green from New Orleans, Erickson and Darbin's Virginia Minstrels, and Collier's Original Silas Green from New Orleans. Not one of these shows carries less than 30 performers and some 50 or more . . . I forgot in naming the shows playing the state to mention, besides the minstrel shows, Lasses White Minstrels (white), Ringling Bros. Barnum and Bailey circus and the Sparks circus. As fast as one agent posts a bill telling of the coming of his show, another agent covers it, telling about his show—some battle.[43]

Allen's New Orleans Minstrels

Very little has been written about Allen's New Orleans Minstrels. At the peak of black minstrelsy's popularity, Allen's Minstrels were the peer of any tented minstrel show on the road, including the Rabbit's Foot and Silas Green. For decades they carried a more than impressive roster of black musicians and stage performers.

Originators of Tented Minstrelsy

A. G. ALLEN'S NEW ORLEANS MINSTRELS

THE WORLD'S LARGEST MINSTREL SHOW.
TWO BIG BANDS. A TRAIN OF CARS.
ONE HUNDRED PEOPLE.
TRAVELS THE YEAR ROUND.

A. G. ALLEN, General Director. GEO. W. QUINE, General Manager. JOHN H. OAKS Treasurer.

WANTED—Good Musicians and Performers that double. Also good Novelty acts. We use Colored talent exclusively. Address: GEO. W. QUINE, Manager, care The Free man, Indianapolis, Ind., or National Printing Co., Chicago.

Indianapolis Freeman, June 16, 1900.

Allen's New Orleans Minstrels originated in Chicago, Illinois, in 1899, under the proprietorship of three northern white men: A. G. Allen, president and advance agent; George W. Quine, on-site manager; and John H. Oakes, assistant manager and treasurer. Oakes bowed out early, but Allen and Quine continued in earnest. Billed as the "Originators of Tented Minstrelsy," they helped set the course for African American minstrel companies in the South, traveling by rail and showing under canvas.

After debuting in Chicago on May 15, 1899, Allen's New Orleans Minstrels crisscrossed Illinois for about three months and then plunged southward. A note in September said they were "still en route South and gathering in all the money . . . The ghost still walks every Monday after dinner." In a grueling succession of one-night stands, they proceeded to cover the southern states and stretch out into "Indian Territory." At the beginning of 1900 they were in Louisiana, headed east. They showed in New Orleans, then played across the Mississippi-Alabama Gulf Coast to the Florida panhandle. By March they were up in Georgia. Rambling through the Mississippi Delta in April, they reported, "Everything is lovely and the goose is hanging high." At Greenville they were tendered a "grand reception" by local residents: "Champagne by the case was opened; a table spread . . . and we were royally entertained until half past four next morning. At five o'clock we left for Wyona [*sic*], drawn by special engine."

On April 26, 1900, they opened a weeklong stand at Nashville, Tennessee, and fetched this telling review from a local mainstream daily:

> Allen's New Orleans troupe of colored minstrels gave a performance last night in a tent at the corner of Spruce and Madison streets. The tent was crowded and several hundred were refused admission. The performance as a whole was creditable, while some of the features were especially good. The dancing was above ordinary and the singing excellent. Some of the jokes were a trifle antique, but the majority were original. The end men were as pleasing in their entertainment as the most critical could wish. The aggregation will give four more

performances in the city. To-night they will show at the corner of Wharf Avenue and Green street. While the show is given in a tent the performance differs in no other way from that of other minstrel troupes. The introduction in which all the members occupied the platform and took part in the fun making was perhaps the best part of the entertainment. The specialties in the second half, however, pleased the crowd, and especially the colored portion. That part of the audience predominated and was liberal in applause and laughter.[44]

On the night of their first anniversary, May 15, 1900, Allen's Minstrels were in Charlotte, North Carolina. To commemorate the occasion, the proprietors "gave the members of the company a grand banquet after the show . . . It lasted until three oclock in the morning."[45] By the end of July they had played through Virginia, West Virginia, Ohio, Tennessee and Arkansas. A note in August informed that, "For the past week we have played six towns from three to eight miles apart . . . While in Joplin, Mo., we met Messrs. T. Williams, A. Fuller and C. Williams, proprietors and managers of a swell colored saloon. They gave us a good time for the better part of a week, as from each town we played, electric cars ran to Joplin." Two weeks later they were "in Indian Territory, doing a nice business." At Kingman, Kansas, they were "entertained by Mr. Tuck Turner, the wealthiest colored man there."

In late September 1900, Allen's New Orleans Minstrels descended into Texas. They were slated to play Shreveport, Louisiana, on October 24 and 25, but:

after reaching the town the morning of the 24 just as the parade was about to start three officers walked up and said it cost us $150 to parade and $50 to show that night, so Manager Quine called the parade off. The streets were crowded with people waiting for the parade. We didn't show but left there that night for Atlanta [i.e., Atlanta, Texas, just across the Louisiana-Texas state line], where we played the following night to good business; a number of people came six or seven miles, saying they heard the two bands that distance. Our proprietors have entered suit against Shreveport.[46]

On Christmas Eve they showed at Ballinger, Texas, and on Christmas Day they played San Angelo:

At the last named place the people were prepared for us. The parade left the cars 11:45 and when we reached the square the porches were crowded with men and boys, who had bundles of fire crackers, and as the parade passed, fire crackers fell in showers, but the boys gave them no attention and marched ahead. The intention was to break up the parade, but they were unsuccessful. Mr. Viccas, one of the oldest, quietest and best liked members of this company, had his left eye injured by the bursting of a cannon cracker. That night we showed at the opera house to a packed business.[47]

One week later the *Freeman* correspondent notified: "The boys are wearing smiles on their faces because they heard that 10 more days puts us out of Texas. It is true that we broke the record for business in Texas this season, but we want some other country for awhile."

No significant break in their touring schedule was reported until the end of 1905, when the *Freeman* correspondent informed, "We have only a few more stands, and will reach Jacksonville, Fla., about December 25, for a three weeks rest, after which a new production will be presented." Subsequently, it became customary to take time off in Florida at Christmas.

WANTED QUICK

NEW ORLEANS MINSTRELS

Twenty Musicians, Two Strong Teams (Men)
One Sketch Team, Six End Men.
Name lowest salary. Tickets advanced to responsible parties to any part of the United States. GEO. W. QUINE, Manager.

——ROUTE——

Camden, Ark., August 3d.	Sherman, Texas, August 10th.
Stamps, Ark., August 4th.	White Wright, Texas, August 11th.
Texarkana, Ark., August 5th.	Wolf City, Texas, August 12th.
Mt Pleasant, Texas, August 6th.	Commera, Texas, August 13th.
Mt. Vernon, Texas August 7th.	Granville, Texas, August 14th.
Sulphur Springs, Texas, August 8th.	Plano, Texas, August 15th.

Indianapolis Freeman, August 1, 1903.

Florida was the preferred winter destination for tent shows. At Pensacola in February 1902, Allen's Minstrels pitched their tent on the corner of Chase and Baylor streets and drew a crowd in spite of unseasonably cold weather. Their *Freeman* correspondent noted:

> They are flooded with small shows in Florida, but nearly all have no merit or no show to amount to much to offer to the public. Therefore they can't expect anything else but poor business. There are several street fairs and all kinds of fakes and robbers but the people are pretty well on to that class of people, and the sooner they are, the better for legitimate shows. Our show is doing the same old banner business in all of the old territory we have ever visited and have come in contact with these street fares [*sic*] yet we have the first street fair to meet that we did not close when we played in the same town on the same date, and I think we have met them all. Florida will support a good colored show when you have anything to offer them.[48]

Cruising the Florida panhandle at the beginning of 1903, Allen's Minstrels reached Apalachicola on January 12. To get there they had boarded a ferry for "a 32½ mile trip across the arm of the Gulf of Mexico, which was enjoyed by all, as we had a bright, sunny day. The boys and girls sat upon deck singing 'In the Good Old Summer Time.'"[49] By the end of February they had made their way to the southernmost reaches of the state: "We arrived in Key West at 6 p. m., which was too late to pitch our big canvas. We played in the opera house, with no parade. The house was sold out at five minutes to seven . . . turning away about 400 people. Well, to make it short, we played to five packed houses and not withstanding we sailed from Key West at 10:30 p. m., which was thirty minutes after our last show, we had a good sized audience to have a handshake and get a farewell glance at us."[50]

In February 1912 Allen's Minstrels became the first show "to cross Flagler's new oversea road from Miami to Key West down through the Everglades, and over a part of the mighty Atlantic."[51] In the fall of 1913 they jumped directly into Florida from the Mississippi Delta and played Pensacola on

Thanksgiving Day, to "turn away business." A few weeks later, however, the *Freeman* correspondent complained that, "Since that stand business has only been fair, as this is mostly turpentine country and turpentine is being made at a loss to the operators, therefore money is very scarce with the people." Manager Quine further complained that licensing fees in Florida had been "raised so high that it is almost impossible to break even. For instance, take the city of Tampa, the city license is $100 and the state and county is $112.75, making it $212.75 to play Tampa one night." They resolved to "play what towns we make in the State mostly in opera houses and get out of Florida as soon as the weather permits."[52]

Allen's Minstrels rode the rails in a modicum of style, a "three-car show" carrying upwards of eighty people, including canvasmen, roustabouts, and a company cook. In the spring of 1900 they acquired a new "Wagner sleeping coach which . . . will accommodate fifty-eight people. We believe it to be the finest car in the minstrel business." Members of the company held a decorating party in the spring of 1901: "Now to pass through this car one would imagine they were passing through the streets of Cairo or on the midway of a street fair."[53] By 1909 their sleeping coach had acquired a name: "Ida May." At Waco, Texas, in 1911, they upgraded from Ida May to a new eighty-five foot palace car: "By direction of the management it has been named '999.' It is one of the swellest pieces of rolling stock today traveling on American soil."[54]

Their tent was billed as a "spacious, automatically heated canvas theater," illuminated by kerosene-powered chandeliers. Canvas and kerosene were a volatile combination. At Weldon, North Carolina, in 1901, Allen's Minstrels "had the misfortune of having our tent burned to the ground through the carelessness of our chandelier man, who got his hair and clothing scorched, but fortunately no one was hurt. The accident happened just before the evening show. That night and the two succeeding evenings we showed in opera houses to packed houses, and lost only three days to the fire. Our new tent is much larger than the old one."[55]

The bandsmen with Allen's Minstrels got new uniforms and street clothes almost every year. The street parade was the first point of contact between the show and its potential customer base. It was up to the band to provide a brilliant and lasting impression. Not only did they have to sound good; they had to look good, both on and off the parade routes. At Ft. Worth, Texas, in the fall of 1901, "The boys received their raglans . . . from Chicago and after the parade put them on and went out. They were the talk of the town." In 1910 a note informed that, "Geo. W. Quine, our affable and genial manager, has just received and supplied our band and walking gents with long coats and opera hats at an expenditure of $412. The boys certainly look swell in their new toggery."[56]

The parade band was topped off by an acrobatic "rube bandmaster." A note in the summer of 1900 informed that, "Billy Deyart, our rube, holds the crowd in the street." According to a 1905 correspondence, "The band and Perry Black as 'Rube' leaves them yelling." During the summer of 1915, "Jermon White, as the rube band master," was "doing double twisters in the noonday parade."[57]

The original leader of Allen's minstrel band and orchestra was Prof. James S. Lacy, but his stay was brief. In the fall of 1899 the position fell to Prof. J. H. McCamon, who remained in charge for the next fifteen years. Every year when the company played Paris, Texas, Prof. McCamon's home town, he and his wife hosted a reception at their 714 South Twenty-Third Street residence, following the noonday parade. The company's *Freeman* correspondents often sang McCamon's praises. A note in 1902 said, "All bands following him had better 'come clean' as we are something tight." A 1904 report informed, "Prof. McCamon's big concert band is too warm to be fooled with, as they handle nothing but heavy overtures and selections." In 1909 a correspondent acknowledged Prof. McCamon's "perfect directing and the band's sweet music, from classical to ragtime."[58]

During their earliest years of operation Allen's Minstrels fielded two full bands in their noonday parade, which then combined forces for the evening concert. Players came and went at a dizzying pace, jockeying from one show to another. In November 1899 Prof. McCamon had "his big band of thirty people in good trim, and the two bands on street parade, continually playing, cause quite an excitement in every town." In 1904 *Freeman* readers were advised, "Prof. McCamon continues to add musicians to his big concert band. He has now twenty all sight readers." A note in 1905 assured, "Our band of fourteen pieces . . . is the talk of the streets."

In addition to noonday parades and evening concerts, the band played for various special occasions. At Tuskegee, Alabama, in the spring of 1901, "the boys paraded out to the Booker T. Washington School grounds and the band rendered several selections, which the college boys and girls went wild over."[59] At South Boston, Virginia, later that summer, "Prof. McCamon's big concert band was asked by the mayor to play a few of their choice selections for the benefit of the laying of a corner stone for the Masonic Temple; they did so and returned to the cars with bundles of bouquets."[60]

Sometimes the band was obliged to play for funerals. The worst tragedy in the history of Allen's Minstrels occurred at Dunnellon, Florida, on February 5, 1906, when tuba player Joe Ravise, of Pine Bluff, Arkansas, was shot and killed by the town's white sheriff, for no apparent reason. Ravise's remains were "taken in charge by the K. of P., and buried with fraternal ceremonies. The band under the direction of Prof. J. H. McCamon, played a funeral dirge."[61]

Although Allen's Minstrels consistently employed top-notch musicians, most of them, like the intrepid Prof. McCamon, have fallen away from the public record. A select survey of some of the bandsmen who traveled with Allen's Minstrels is in order.

At New Orleans in January 1900, Prof. McCamon engaged tuba soloist Frank Castry, who was capable of "cracking window panes with his $125 tuba." Castry left Allen's Minstrels before the spring of 1903. In 1905 he was leading a Knights of Pythias Brass Band in Biloxi, Mississippi, and by 1908 he was touring with the Sells-Floto Circus.

Another notable tuba player with Allen's Minstrels was William "Tuba" Thomas, who served from 1909 to 1912. On July 8, 1912, Thomas closed with the show and went home to Memphis: "Address 317 Beale avenue." The following day, at Dyer, Tennessee, he was replaced by Mose McQuitty. Two months later, McQuitty "received a new $160 monster E flat bass, direct from the factory of York and Sons. It certainly is a beauty and Mr. McQuitty proceeds to jar the ground and windows."

Among the trombone players who passed through the ranks of Allen's Minstrels, female soloist Nettie Goff was a charter member of the company, before jumping to Mahara's Minstrels, to play under W. C. Handy. In Cuba with Handy in February 1900, she was "causing the people to stand in open-mouth wonder at her brilliancy."[62] Back with Allen's Minstrels in the summer of 1903, "Miss Nettie Goff, with her trombone solos, leaves them screaming nightly."

Trombonist Harry Massengale joined in the spring of 1900. Massengale was originally from Cincinnati, Ohio. His stay with Allen's Minstrels was brief, but his career proved long and eventful. In the spring of 1916, when jazz first came up for recognition in Chicago, Massengale was strategically located at Teenan Jones's Elite Cafe on State Street, playing in a four-piece orchestra headed by Tony Jackson.[63]

In 1902 Prof. McCamon recruited fifteen-year-old "Master Henry McDade, the coming young slide trombonist" from Knoxville, Tennessee. According to the *Freeman*, McDade's whole family was musical. His twelve-year-old brother George was said to be "a wonder, playing a B♭ cornet and lead violin."[64] When Allen's Minstrels showed at Knoxville that spring, George McDade also joined. That summer, George left to become a member of P. G. Lowery's Musical Enterprise, but Henry remained with Allen's Minstrels.

En route during the fall of 1903, Henry McDade devoted his free time to the Nonesuch Club, a pleasure club organized among members of the company. At Shawnee, Oklahoma, the Nonesuch Club sponsored a banquet, with music furnished by "Prof. Henry McDade's famous orchestra." One week later, at Fort Smith, Arkansas, "The N. S. C. gave its second banquet . . . Song, mirth and music were the crowning features . . .

Master George McDade age 13, the youngest orchestra leader and cornet soloist the world has ever known.

MASTER GEORGE MCDADE

The above cut is a perfect likeness of Master Geo. McDade the boy wonder. Little George was born in Knoxville, Tenn., Jan. 23, 1890. He commenced the study of music at the age of ten—the cornet was the first instrument—his advancement was so rapid he then took up the the study of the violin and today he stands among the best leaders in the business regardless of his age. Beside his wonderful accomplishment on the two instruments, he possesses the most remarkable ear so accurate and true he can at anytime tell the exact tone made on any instrument. He is justly honored the wonder of the 19th century.

The following is from the pen of P. G. Lowery: "I consider Master Geo. McDade a cornetist of rare ability, a boy of wonderful good ideas, on both violin and cornet. With good teaching Little George will out rival any cornetist of his race before he leaves the ranks of boyhood. Keep your eye on the new star from Knoxville. May he ever progress is the wishes of his admirer.

—P. G. LOWERY."

Indianapolis Freeman, October 10, 1903.

Prof. H. S. McDade's orchestra opened with Scott Joplin's master piece, 'The Entertainer,' and closed with 'Maple Leaf.'"[65]

In the spring of 1904, Henry McDade joined his brother George in P. G. Lowery's sideshow band with the Forepaugh and Sells Circus. Back with Allen's Minstrels in 1906, he met a grisly fate:

> Henry McDade, principal trombonist . . . en route with A. G. Allen's Minstrels, while in Wickliffe, Ky., received a message that his father was ill at Knoxville. He purchased a ticket for Cairo, expecting a reply from home, the depot agent instructed him to catch the caboose of a fast freight. In the daring adventure he was pulled under the moving train and both legs severed from his body. He was promptly cared for by members of the company and sent directly to the hospital at Cairo, Ill., accompanied by his companion and brother, Band Master McCameron [*sic*]. He died at 10 p.m., May 29. His remains were prepared for shipment to his home in Knoxville. The father, mother and relatives have the sympathy of the entire company.[66]

In 1908 Allen's Minstrels engaged Kansas City–based trombonist and "hoop roller" Pearl Moppin. By 1908, Moppin had served with almost every other southern tent show on the road, including Silas Green, the Florida Blossoms, and the Rabbit's Foot Company. He stayed with Allen's Minstrels for at least two years; and he played from show to show until 1924, when he finally gave up "the professional hardships for the services of train porter on the Missouri Pacific railroad."[67]

In Louisiana at the end of 1912, Allen's Minstrels picked up "one of the very best trombonists before the public," Amos Gilliard. Gilliard had come through the Jenkins Orphanage Band of Charleston, South Carolina, during the early

Indianapolis Freeman, February 7, 1914.

1890s,[68] and had been jumping from show to show for at least ten years before landing with Allen's Minstrels. Within a month of joining Allen's Minstrels, he was "winning applause daily, rendering Pryor's great hit, 'The Patriot,' as a trombone solo."[69]

One mark of status among black minstrel show bands was to become a "gold band," sporting all gold instruments. The 1909, tenth-anniversary edition of the band with Allen's Minstrels appears to have been one of the first to attain this goal. In

February 1909, G. B. Brooks, "the battle-scarred veteran of E flat cornet fame," was "holding his own with his new C. G. Conn solid gold instrument." Two months later, Pearl Moppin received a gold Holton trombone, and Ellwood Johnson received his "gold trumpet-model cornet, also Holton make, thus making our whole cornet section all gold. With the advent of these two instruments our band has a complete set of the very finest instruments of any traveling band, barring none, the full set costing a slight margin over $1,300."[70] Later that summer, Prof. McCamon "received a new gold trumpet model cornet . . . We will soon be supplied with all gold instruments from the cornets to the bass, this creating a new era for colored bands."[71]

In Oklahoma during the summer of 1909, Pearl Moppin was "rendering 'Tuberose Polka' at high noon daily," while Ellwood Johnson was "rendering 'Patriot' polka cornet solo, thus completing a quartette of soloists actively engaged in solo work in our band."[72] Johnson also showed talent as a composer. In the spring of 1910 he completed a march entitled "The Battle of Fuqua," which he dedicated to the company's female impersonator, C. Adam Larose.[73]

The aspiring "gold band" included a formidable reed section. William Phillips joined at Daytona, Florida, in February 1909: "with him our band will number fourteen experienced musicians, all good, no blanks."[74] In Oklahoma that summer, they added J. C. Singleton. Fred Kewley, who went on to lead the historic 1916 edition of the band with Tolliver's Smart Set, came aboard at New Bern, North Carolina, that fall.

At this point, Prof. McCamon placed an order for "a quartette of Boehm system saxophones of Carl Fischer. On their arrival he will immediately put on a saxophone quartette: Fred Kewley, soprano; Robert H. Gant, alto; William Phillips, tenor; J. C. Singleton, baritone."[75] Shortly thereafter, the *Freeman* correspondent confirmed, "Prof. McCammon's saxophone quartet is appearing nightly," playing "everything from classical to ragtime." J. C. Singleton drew special notice for "playing 'Asleep in the Deep' as a saxophone solo." In the fall of 1910, Singleton was replaced by Robert Miller, who was soon "receiving much praise from the public and press, for playing 'Roll On, Thou Dark and Deep Blue Ocean,' as a bass saxophone solo, with the assistance of the quartette."[76]

During the spring of 1911, saxophone quartet veterans Kewley, Gant, and Miller "joined hands in a new musical act, Mr. Kewley posing as the professor, Mr. Gant as a musician looking for work and Mr. Miller doing comedy." During the summer of 1912, "Robert Miller as Sippi and P. L. Jenkins as Uncle Hickory, two tramp musicians," put on a ten-minute act titled "Serenading Under Difficulties."[77] The following year, Clifford Brooks played straight to Miller and Jenkins's two tramp musicians in "Nancy Brown's Serenade," featuring "Silver Threads Among the Gold," "Waiting for the Robert E. Lee," and Shelton Brooks's "All Night Long."[78] During the summer of 1914, Robert "Sippi" Miller and William "Vipty" Fisher were "still going strong with their musical act."[79]

The stage orchestra with Allen's Minstrels comprised from six to twelve pieces. A roster of the 1899 edition of the stage orchestra listed Paul L. Cross, first violin; Joe Jourdon, second violin; Henry Lane, clarinet; Alfonso Guiguesse, cello; Tom Tolliver, cornet; Milton Vassar, cornet; Will Saunders, trombone; James Randolph, double bass; and J. T. Cox, trap drums."[80]

Cornetist and violinist Milton B. Vassar and his cornet-playing brother William C. Vassar were first mentioned in the *Freeman* in September 1898, as members of the band with Melroy's Real Colored Minstrels. The Vassar brothers hailed from St. Louis, Missouri, where they were associated with Cooperidge's Famous World's Fair Band and Orchestra. A St. Louis reporter proclaimed: "As a colored local organization I am perfectly safe in stating they are in a class by themselves."[81]

Milton B. Vassar was traveling with Allen's Minstrels as early as August 1899. According to report, he closed with the show in September 1900; and by November 1901 he was bandleader for the *A Holiday in Coontown* Company. By 1916 Vassar was working in Chicago. That spring, Sylvester Russell listed him among the members of Dave Peyton's Grand Theater Orchestra on State Street. Later that summer, he was identified as violinist and leader of the Phoenix Theater's four-piece orchestra.[82]

Trap drummer J. T. "Polly" Cox was the father of Little Jimmie Cox, the future composer of "I'm on My Last Go Round," "Nobody Knows You When You're Down and Out," etc. During the summer of 1901 Allen's Minstrels played a three-night stand in Richmond, Virginia, "the home of our trap drummer, J. T. Cox," and Cox's hometown cronies showed the band members "such a time that they 'don't care if they never wake up.'"[83]

In the summer of 1903, Cox "had to close in Atlanta for treatment." He laid out all winter at Portsmouth, Virginia, and when he returned in 1904, he was "handling the traps as good as ever." Cox finally left Allen's Minstrels for good in the fall of 1908, to try his hand at managing a southern vaudeville theater stock company.

Members of the stage orchestra with Allen's Minstrels experimented with a variety of stringed instruments. In the fall of 1900 cellist Alfonso Guiguesse "received a Washburn guitar" and J. H. McCamon "bought a mandolin; their orchestra will consist of seven pieces: two mandolins, three guitars, one bassoon and one violincello."[84] In the summer of 1902 clarinetist-violinist F. F. Viccas was "getting along nicely on his German Zither."[85]

In the fall of 1912, Allen's Minstrels acquired clarinet and violin player Marcus Veal Chaney, who quickly ascended to the position of orchestra leader. In 1914 Chaney "was made the proud possessor of a fine violin from his father, Wm. T. Chaney. His father traces the violin back as far as 1723. Among those who have performed upon it is the famous 'Ole Bull,' whose name is written on the inside."[86]

The orchestra played for all three parts of the stage show. A description of the show was supplied in 1904:

Our first part opens with a medley of songs after which Perry Black sings "Malinda's rag time ball,' Napoleon Black sings 'In the valley of Kentucky," H. S. Smith sings "I got a feeling for you" and "Chicken," then E. J. Looney sings, "When the blue skies turn to gold," then our interlocutor Mr. Charles Rue excuses Mr. Black and Smith and introduces J. Wise and Chas. H. Williams. Mr. Wise sings, "Good bye Eliza Jane," then comes Augustus Stevens, female impersonator, skirt and serpentine dancer one of the best, then Chas. H. Williams sings, "I'm thinking of you babe all the while" and "Sunny Africa." The Acme Quartet then closes the first part. Our olio is very strong opening with J. Wise, then the Wottses [*sic*] in their singing and talking act which is good, then Clemo Harris that boneless man, then Williams and Stevens in their novelty act a very laughable plot from start to finish entitled "A Partner Wanted" which pleases all classes; then Perry Black in buck-dancing to the sextette of ladies and gentlemen singing "Dusky maiden." The show closes with "Bad Mike from the territory," by H. S. Smith assisted by company.[87]

Tented minstrelsy's chief dispensers of up-to-date ragtime songs were its male blackface comedians and female coon shouters. Allen's Minstrels maintained a stable of six or more blackface comedians. One of the first was Philip Owens, from Paducah, Kentucky. In the summer of 1899 Owens made "a big hit on the end singing his new song 'Take Your Time Black Man.'" At the end of the year he introduced "Who dat sayed chicken in this crowd." In 1900 he added at least two more chicken songs to his repertoire, "I've Got Chicken on the Brain" and "The Congregation Will Please Keep Their Seats, Kase This Bird Am Mine," and he also found favor with the Tin Pan Alley atrocity "Every Race Has a Flag But the Coon." On April 10, 1901, after a brief illness, Philip Owens died on the road at Johnston, South Carolina, at the age of twenty-six.[88]

A comedian known as "Black Diamond" was listed in the fall of 1899, but by the spring of 1900 he had left the show and was "giving open air exhibitions to the public at Houston, Tex. One of his tricks is the placing of four billiard balls in his mouth."[89] Also listed that fall was Charles H. Williams, of Kansas City. During the summer of 1900 Williams was said to be "hitting 'em hard singing, 'My Hannah Lady, Whose Black Baby Are You.'" In Texas at the end of the year, he sang "I Don't Like No Rough Head Gal." His repertoire of 1901–1903 included "I Don't Care If I Never Wake Up," "Mr. Johnson, Shut Dat Door," "Things Ain't the Same, Babe," and "I Am Coming Home." In 1902 Williams teamed with the company's premier female impersonator, Augustus Stevens.

In 1900 Allen's Minstrels brought in William "Billy" Cheatham, who claimed to have been "Borned in old Kentucky, where the 'Rock and Rye' is pure."[90] Cheatham had already charted an adventurous career. At St. Louis, Missouri, in 1898 he and his brother Lawrence had assembled a traveling minstrel show that included ragtime pianist Tom Turpin and his protégé Louis Chauvin.[91] Correspondence from Allen's Minstrels in the fall of 1900 informed that Cheatham was making good singing "I'm Going to Start a Little Graveyard of My Own," with Pearl Wyatte chiming in on the chorus from the audience.[92]

Cheatham was still singing "I'm Going to Start Me a Graveyard" when he closed out at Bessemer, Alabama, in 1901. His song resonated long after his departure. When character comedian Norris Grigsby joined Allen's Minstrels in 1909, he was imitating a hunchback, singing "Lovin' Time"; by 1910 he was "posing as Bad Bill Dugan, the man with a private graveyard."[93] Country recording artist Gid Tanner included a verse of "I'm Going to Start Me a Graveyard of My Own" in a 1925 medley titled "Old Time Tunes"; blues singer-guitarists Jim Jackson and Furry Lewis both recorded versions of it in 1928.[94]

In the fall of 1901 Allen's Minstrels picked up a coon song singer from Columbus, Georgia, known as "Hot" Jimmie Wise. Wise came in singing "I Can Stand Your Color But Your Hair Won't Do," which had been introduced by Sam Lucas in 1898 in *A Trip to Coontown*. When Lucas sang it in Memphis at the beginning of 1901, it seemed "to catch, as this city is full of heads that have felt the pulling of hot iron, and the sticking of hair straightening glue. Say boys, it won't be long before some bald headed girls will be seen, caused by the using of those preparations."[95]

Jimmie Wise stayed with Allen's Minstrels for the better part of a decade. At the end of 1902 he and Hattie Beecham were "praying for Bill Bailey to come home." In the summer of 1903 Wise was "spelling chicken," a reference to Sidney Perrin's "Dat's de Way to Spell Chicken." Wise's hits of 1905 included "Things Ain't the Same, Babe" and "I Certainly Am Feeling Bad." In February 1909, after an indefinite absence, Wise rejoined Allen's Minstrels at Tampa, Florida: "Home again, Jim." A few weeks later he staged a skit entitled "The Recruiting Officer and the Coon." His song hits of 1909 included "Back to Kentucky, Where I Was Born," "Gee, Ain't I Glad I Am Single," and "That's a Plenty."

In the spring of 1910 Jimmie Wise applied his "unique drollery" to a topical number, "Oh You Jeffries, Oh You Jim." Later that summer he staged a new first part, "laid in Zululand, introducing Messrs. Worlds Davis, German White, Anthony Rucks, Norris Grigsby, Leroy White and J. J. Perry as the six educated Zulus."[96] At San Augustine, Texas, in the early weeks of 1911, Wise sang "the southerners choice of all songs, 'Casey Jones.'" His other hits of 1911 included "Oh What Would I Do for a Girl Like You" and "Lord Have Mercy on a Married Man."

In 1912 Wise came out "garbed as Deacon Brown, from Georgia . . . singing 'You Can Lead a Mule.'"[97] He also made a hit with the Irving Berlin composition "Ragtime Violin." A note on June 22, 1912, informed that Wise was finally closing out with Allen's Minstrels and going home to Columbus, Georgia. Ill health was cited. When the company played Mobile, Alabama, at the end of 1913, "Jimmy Wise, our ex-stage manager and comedian, now stage manager and producer at the Pike theater at Mobile, gave in honor of the Allen's Minstrels one of the swellest and grandest affairs of the season."[98]

Black entertainment trailblazer Will Benbow joined Allen's Minstrels at Birmingham, Alabama, in the spring of 1902, and he and fellow newcomer Sank Simms teamed up to sing "Zulu Babe." A note in July informed that, in addition to his stage work, "Ben Bow has the waiter and porter job and is proving a good fellow in that line." In October Benbow took the stage as a "silver tongued tenor," singing "I Want a Photograph of You." A letter in November said he had almost completed his new song, "Everybody is Looking for the Installment Man."

Benbow left Allen's Minstrels in 1903. In Atlanta that summer Sank Simms also left, and Perry Bradford took his place. Bradford's stay was brief. In October, the Midway Vaudeville and Plantation Show sent news from Birmingham, Alabama: "Perry Bradford, of the New Orleans show, is with us. Bradford and Sims have joined hands once more . . . and are setting the Midway wild singing 'Show the White of Your Eyes.'"[99]

With Allen's Minstrels at the beginning of 1903, John H. Williams, of Memphis, Tennessee, who became known during the 1910s as "Blue Steel," was "leaving them screaming" with "If Dem Chickens Don't Roost Too High." He stayed with the show nearly six years. In 1906 he hit with "If My Baby Could See Me Now" and "Song of the Ragtime Boy." In 1907 he introduced "Home, Sweet Home Sounds Good to Me." In the summer of

1908, "The one J. H. Williams, assisted by the quartet," sang "What a Time." Another hit for him that summer was "Lemon Coon."

Singing comedian, old man impersonator, and slide trombone player H. S. Smith opened with Allen's Minstrels at Pine Bluff, Arkansas, in the fall of 1902. A 1903 roster listed him simply as "old man and slide." That spring Smith was said to be "doing better work on his trombone since he has been cooking his own food, as he is doing the cooking on the car." One of his song hits of 1903 was "Ain't dat an Awful Feeling." In the spring of 1904 he was singing "I Have Got a Feeling for You" and "Chicken Can't Roost Too High for Me." His repertoire of 1905–1909 included "Chicken King," "Shame on You," "Back, Back, Back to Baltimore," "I Don't Know Where I'm Going But I'm On My Way," "Get Some Exercise," "Ephriam Johnson Don't Live Here No More," "All I Get Here Is Much Obliged," "Pay More Attention to Me," and "Oh, You Loving Gal." Correspondence in the fall of 1909 said Smith "gets his nightly with his peculiar antics, singing 'When You Got No Other Place to Go, Then Home, Sweet Home.'"

Shortly before Christmas 1909, the company was involved in a train wreck, and their palace car "Ida May" was "ruthlessly smashed in two, causing serious injury to several members of our company. H. S. Smith is suffering from a fractured skull." Smith appears to have survived the accident, but on March 26, 1910, he closed out and retired to Natchez, Mississippi.[100]

Comedian-producer Sol Tibbs joined Allen's Minstrels in Texas in the summer of 1903, and by the end of 1904 he was serving as stage manager. In 1905 Tibbs made a hit singing "I Was There, But I Had No Business to Be There." That summer he was "arranging a new electrical first part, entitled 'Luna Park.'" A note on October 7, 1905, said Tibbs was preparing another new act, "The Dark Town Possum Club." Five weeks later, however, he was forced to retire from the show on account of illness, and he died shortly thereafter.[101] Tibbs's legacy included at least one published song, a "rag-medley" titled "Mama, Mama Make Cinda 'Haive Herself," which fell into tradition and reverberated for decades.[102] Fisk University educator and folklorist John Work III collected a variation of Tibbs's "Cindy" on a field trip to Coahoma County, Mississippi, in the early 1940s:

Mama, mama make Cindy behave herself!
Mama, mama make Cindy behave herself!
She keep on foolin' roun',
I'll take a stick an' knock her down,
Well, Mama, mama make Cindy behave herself.[103]

Blackface comedians with Allen's Minstrels in 1905 included Happy John Goodloe and Hi Jerry Barnes. Goodloe made good through the summer and fall, singing "On the Rock Pile" and "Sally Ann." Barnes joined at Drake Branch, Virginia, in August, and he also stayed through the fall, "cleaning up nightly" with "The Humming Coon," "Mandy, You and Me," "Nobody" and "Wonder What's the Matter with the Mail."[104]

Also new to the show in 1905 was comedian J. B. Norton, who quickly worked his way up to the position of stage manager and stayed for more than a decade. In the fall of 1905 Norton lent his voice to the show's vocal quartet: "Tom Down, Joe Norton, Charlie Rue and Alexander Dodson, the Harmonizing Four, are singing to peals of applause." At the beginning of 1906 he was singing "Farewell, That Means Good-Bye" and the Ernest Hogan classic "Is Everybody Happy." That summer Norton and John W. Dennis introduced a skit called "I Am Just from the Jungles."

In 1909 Norton made a hit with "I'm Going to Do What I Please." At the end of the year he staged a one-act farce for the after-show, featuring "J. J. Perry, the great comedian, and W. A. Dixon as Charlie One Lung Kee, the Chinese laundryman." At the beginning of 1910 he introduced "You Ain't Talking to Me." That summer, when he was forced to close "on account of continued ill health," Norton was described as "our old reliable stage manager for seven consecutive seasons . . . He goes to Beaumont, Texas, to recuperate. Address 167 Jackson ave." Rejoining in November, Norton made an immediate hit singing "I Apologize." At the beginning of 1913 he staged a ten-minute skit titled "My Friend," with William Worlds Davis as a henpecked husband; William Eldridge as the wife; and German White as "Clarence," a "dapper dude." Later that spring Norton gave out with "Play That Barber Shop Chord."

John Dennis, one of Norton's early collaborators, became another longtime member of Allen's Minstrels. A note in 1909 informed that, "John W. Dennis, the funny old man, is sending the audience into paroxysm of laughter nightly spelling 'M-u-l-e.' He will soon retire from the stage. He has purchased a cozy house in Hazen, Ark., and will locate there with Mrs. Dennis, better known to the profession as Stella Jones."[105] Dennis was still with the show in 1915.

In the spring of 1906, Dennis H. Mitchell joined Allen's Minstrels, and his rendition of Cole and Johnson's "Give Me the Leavings" was pronounced "a sure winner." That summer he scored with "Let He Who Is Without Sin Cast the First Stone." On July 6, 1907, the *Freeman* reported: "Dennis Mitchell, a popular comedian, was taken ill on the stage, while at work at the Exchange [i.e., the Exchange Garden Theater], Jacksonville, Fla., Friday night of last week, and died Saturday. Mr. Mitchell had just closed his engagement with A. G. Allen's Minstrels." In 1904 and 1905, before coming to Allen's Minstrels, Mitchell had found success on early black vaudeville platforms in Florida and Georgia, "cleaning up with one of Bob Russell's latest songs, 'Ragged, but Right.'"[106]

Future vaudeville star Paul Carter showed with Allen's Minstrels from the fall of 1908 through the spring of 1909. A note on February 20, 1909, described him as a "singing and talking monologue comedian, the man with the pants of many colors." A few weeks later the *Freeman* correspondent announced, "Paul Carter, the popular extreme end man, has composed and is singing . . . a new song entitled 'H-O-M-E' (spells home). He was recently made an Elk."

On May 10, 1909, Billy Richardson, late of the Florida Blossom Minstrels, joined at Heber, Arkansas: "He starts the house roaring nightly, doing a swell monologue and singing 'Did He Run?' and 'L-o-v-e Spells Trouble to Me.'" Another 1909 newcomer, "droll comedian" Garfield McGhee made a hit that fall singing "You Ain't Talking to Me." On March 4, 1910, "grotesque singing and dancing comedian" Ed F. Peat joined at Pensacola, Florida, offering "Come After Breakfast, Bring Along Your Lunch and Leave Before Supper Time." In Oklahoma that summer, Pensacola, Florida, native J. J. Perry came up for recognition: "He is scoring singing 'Come Right In Sit Right Down and Make Yourself at Home,' and also in the role of the fly cop."[107]

Other 1910 recruits included John Baptiste Verdun and Archie Jones, New Orleans–based "character comedians" who specialized in Hebrew impersonations. Jones closed out in the summer of 1911, but Verdun stayed on to develop their old routine into a dramatic afterpiece with himself in the role of B. Grabenheimer, "the Jewish immigration agent." *Freeman* correspondence of March 2, 1912, noted, "John Verdun as B. Grabbenheimer; Boyd Harris as 'Eph' Spuds; Worlds Davis, as 'Sally' White; German White, as Toody Roosevelt, Sally's Baby boy, and Chas. Rue, as Doctor Kill M. Quick, serve to send the audience into paroxysms of laughter nightly in the last act, entitled 'B. Grabbenheimer's African Colony,' assisted by the company." When last mentioned with Allen's Minstrels in 1914, Verdun was enacting "The Jew and the Coon," with J. B. Norton in the role of the coon.

On June 23, 1910, "high class entertainer and comedian" William Worlds Davis joined the show at Muskogee, Oklahoma, where he had reportedly been playing in a string band. Davis quickly distinguished himself as an original singer and songwriter. In August he introduced "I Don't Care," which he reportedly wrote in collaboration with William "King" Phillips. At the end of the year he brought out another original composition, "Uh, Uh, Bear, Put That Gun Down." In March 1911 Davis introduced "his latest success entitled, 'Them Big Hats and Hobble Skirts,' music by Ellwood Johnson." Later that summer the *Freeman* correspondent reported: "Wm. Worlds Davis, posing as Sallie White, the washerwoman, and Albert (Kid) Smith, as Sallie's baby boy, serve to bring the audience to their feet in applause nightly, singing 'I Don't Care,' one of Mr. Davis' own compositions."[108]

Correspondence on November 18, 1911, said Davis was "now featuring his latest song hit, 'I Heard a Pork Chop Say, Come Unto Me and Rest,' which is a decided hit." Davis's irreverent parody of a venerable Protestant hymn took wings along the minstrel show routes. With the Cracker Jack Comedy Company in 1914, "Mr. Rastus King opens the minstrel first part with his favorite song, 'I Thought I Heard the Voice of a Pork Chop Say Come unto Me and Rest,' and when he gets through, 'Peaches.'" With Marshall's Mammoth Minstrels in 1915, Billy Arnte "caused the audience to choke with laughter singing 'I Heard the Voice of a Pork Chop, Come Unto Me and Rest.'" In 1928 "I Heard the Voice of a Pork Chop" cropped up on race recordings by Jim Jackson and Bogus Ben Covington.[109]

William Worlds Davis continued to work in minstrelsy and vaudeville until his death in Chicago on August 31, 1917. According to an obituary in the *Freeman*, his body was shipped to Greenville, Mississippi, for burial. The *Freeman* summarized that, with "his little banjo, little hat and long coat and saxophone solos," Davis had been a "clever black face comedian."[110]

In addition to singing comedians and coon shouters, Allen's Minstrels employed a host of "legitimate" singers. James Hollis was commended in the summer of 1899 for his rendition of "I'd Like to Hear That Song Again." When he died of pneumonia on the road at Columbus, Georgia, on March 5, 1900, the *Freeman* correspondent eulogized him as a "phenomenal double voiced vocal—high tenor, male soprano and falsetto singer. His home was at Shreveport, La." Hollis was buried where he fell, and when Allen's Minstrels played Columbus again in the spring of 1902, "Mr. Geo. W. Quine with company turned out to visit his grave. It was a scene that will long be remembered by us. Our band played three pieces, one of them being 'Old Kentucky Home.' Mr. Hollis . . . was 28 years old . . . Mrs. Andrews, the lady who took care of Mr. Hollis, said that up until his death he sang, 'My Old Kentucky Home.'"[111]

With Allen's Minstrels in 1903, "silver voiced tenor" Fred Garland sang "Just a Chain of Daisies." In 1909, Will A. Dixon, late of the Buffalo Bill Wild West Show, joined at Norfolk, Virginia, singing "A Picture of Bygone Days." Back in Norfolk in 1911, tenor singers George Day and James Lathan both joined the show. Day featured "Silver Threads Among the Gold," and Lathan sang "You're the Ideal of My Dreams."

The original female members of Allen's Minstrels included coon shouters Pauline Cottrell and Ruby Palmer. In the summer of 1899, Pauline Cottrell made a hit singing "Certainly Was Good to Me" and "Rosa Come with Me," while Ruby Palmer scored with "I Want to Play Ball With You Papa" and "You're Alright But You Don't Get In." In addition to her solo singing, Ruby Palmer sang duets with her husband Dan Palmer, the company's first stage manager. In the fall of 1899, they added Dan Palmer's original number, "Black Eighth Regiment" to their "already hot act."[112]

At the end of 1899, Pernecia Williams, wife of comedian Charles H. Williams, was singing "Let me Bring My Clothes Back Home." In the fall of 1900, newcomer Pearl Wyatte helped Billy Cheatham bring his "Graveyard of My Own" song to the fore. She left Allen's Minstrels before the spring of 1901, when the *Freeman* correspondent noted, "One of our old members, Miss Pearl Wyatte, was glad to see us at her home, Mobile."

A report in January 1903 mentioned "Miss Hattie Beecham, our little soubrette who sets the pace singing 'Eva.'" Shortly thereafter, it seems, Hattie Beecham became Mrs. Fred Garland. Hattie Garland was touted for her "fully developed and well cultured voice." Her biggest hit of 1903 was "The Banquet in Misery Hall." She went on to record for Gennett and Black Patti in the late 1920s.[113]

Before the end of 1906 Allen's Minstrels reverted to an all-male roster; they did not reopen their stage to women until their fall 1914 tour of the Mississippi Delta. Female impersonators were a characteristic component of early African American minstrelsy and were especially important to an all-male show. The announcement in January 1907 that female impersonator C. A. Larose was Allen's Minstrels' "leading lady" simply stated a matter of fact.

One of the first female impersonators to tour with Allen's Minstrels was Augustus Stevens, who hailed from Memphis by way of Dyersburg, Tennessee, where he was born in 1882.[114] With Allen's Minstrels in 1900, Stevens made a hit singing "My Genuine African Blonde." That fall he introduced his new song, "Hot Combination," assisted by "five of our ladies, who he has been training for some time."

During the summer of 1902 Stevens appeared as "Queen Isabella," "making the hit of his life singing 'I Must Have Been Dreaming.'" His other hits of 1902 included "Gabriella Brown" and his own composition, "I'm a Winner." By the fall of 1902, Stevens and coon song specialist Charles H.

The subject of this sketch was born in Dyersburg, Tenn., January 4, 1882 His parents died a few months later, but fortunately his grandmother and aunt took him to raise. In 1885 they moved to Memphis, Tenn., and three years later he was placed in school where he stayed but two terms, for, unfortunately, his aunt died and he son and Main streets, in front of C. L Byrd's jewelry store, which supported them both for three years. In 1894 he lost his grandmother, and having saved quite a sum of money, he decided to quit the boot-black business and he then went to work at the Grand Opera House, and while there he learned considerable about the stage. His first pany disbanded and he went back to Chicago. He then joined a doctor's show where he stayed quite a while and established the reputation as one of the best female impersonators in the country. He next joined A G Allen's New Orleans Minstrels in 1899 and has been a favorite until the present, and is making nightly hits in his single turn. He

AUGUSTUS STEVENS, FEMALE IMPERSONATOR.

was compelled to abandon school and start to labor to support his grandmother. He first found a position in a clothing store, where he worked quite a while. From there he next found a place in a factory where he stayed for an indefinite period. Becoming tired of manual labor, he decided to open a boot-black stand at the corner of Madi- appearance before the public was with a home talent company, and with daily practice he was soon fit for the public eye. In 1897 he decided to see some of the world and left for Chicago, where he soon joined a company known as Bell's Novelty company, being the only colored person with the organization. But after being out two weeks the com will soon stage one of Papinta's famous serpentine dances, and next season he will be known as the Male Papinta After having been the favorite with A G. Allen's Minstrels for two years, the managers have gotten out a special paper for him which is very showy. Regards to all friends.

Indianapolis Freeman, December 28, 1901.

Williams had formed a team. In July 1903, they closed with the New Orleans Minstrels and left for Chicago to join the *Hottest Coon in Dixie* Company. When *Hottest Coon in Dixie* closed in January 1904, Williams and Stevens returned to Allen's Minstrels for the balance of the season.

Female impersonator C. Adam Larose joined Allen's Minstrels at Hartford, Arkansas, in the summer of 1906. An accomplished trombone player, Larose earned a reputation as "the only colored female impersonator doubling band in America."[115] His song hit of 1906 was "Longing for

AT LIBERTY.

C. Adam La Rose, America's only fe-fame impersonator, playing melophone in band, also presenting 10 to 12 minutes singing specialties. For the past five years with the A. G. Allen's Big Minstrels. Open for engagement after December 20, 1911. Reliable managers address C. Adam La Rose, 533 E. Solomon street, Griffin, Ga.

C. Adam La Rose in his female impersonation. *Indianapolis Freeman*, October 21, 1911.

You." The best female impersonators were able to deceive their audiences with completely believable female character portrayals, and in 1908 Larose was "still puzzling the public," singing "Won't You Be My Honey."

In the spring of 1909 Larose was "rehearsing the great Salome dance." His 1909 song repertoire included "The Old Time Rag," "I'd Rather Float through a Dreamy Old Waltz with You" and "Shine on Harvest Moon," assisted by "our famous Dixie quartette." He was also posing as "Kitty the maid" in a skit called "His Honor the Bellboy." In 1911 Larose sang Irving Berlin's "Sweet Italian Love" in dialect and costume, and sang "Shaky Eyes" in the character of "Peggy from Paris." A note in 1912 assured that, "C. A. Larose . . . still scores singing 'Play That Loving Slide Trombone.'"

In addition to "classic" female impersonators like Augustus Stevens and C. Adam Larose, there were blackface "wench" impersonators like Philip Williams, who appeared with Allen's Minstrels in 1909, "doing nicely characterizing as 'Black Sal from Dark Alley.'"[116] In 1910, comedian and dancer William Kimbrough assumed the role of "Black Sal from Dark Alley."

Among the vocal quartets who toured with Allen's Minstrels, the Little Link Quartette signed on at Austin, Texas, in November 1899 and stayed for about a year. They were joined by the Queen City Quartette in Atlanta in March 1900; one month later, at Clarksville, Tennessee, "the two quartettes were very good, being dead up to the times."[117] The baritone singer with the Queen City Quartette, James Thomas Fernando, was also an elocutionist. At the end of 1900 the Queen City Quartette broke in a new bass singer, J. H. Bailey, who was soon receiving "encores nightly singing 'Down in the deep let me sleep when I die;' he sends best wishes to West End quintette of Savannah, Ga."[118]

In the spring of 1901, the Queen City Quartette closed at Montgomery, Alabama, "and the Acme quartette taken their place," with J. T. Fernando crossing over: "The Acme quartette are all musicians as well as singers, they are, C. Burton, B. Webster, J. Fernando and C. Rue."[119] At the end of 1901 the Acme Quartette was singing "Go Way

Back and Sit Down" and "Don't Butt In." In 1902 they added "Hello Central Give Me Heaven," "Fire's Out," "In the Good Old Summer Time" and Paul Dresser's "Curse of the Dreamer."

In Oklahoma during the fall of 1903, the Acme Quartette was "nightly forced to sing again 'Hiawatha.'" It seems the band was besieged with similar demands. In Texas, Allen's *Freeman* correspondent reported, "The Ofays are very quiet; not a shot has been fired, and it seems they have forgotten their favorite word, 'nigger.' The boys are of the opinion 'Hiawatha' has taken the place of 'Dixie;' as it is, 'Boys, won't ye give me 'Hiawathey.'"[120]

The Acme Quartette's bass singer, Charles E. Rue, was identified as "a scholar of Tuskegee college" and "a very smart man." In addition to singing quartet, he played bass drum on parade and served as a "conversationalist" in the minstrel first part, attired in "a very beautiful and costly costume . . . made of silk and satin, with wig, stockings, shoes and gloves to match."[121] The Acme Quartette faded from view at the end of 1903, but Rue remained with Allen's Minstrels for more than a decade. He kept a hand in quartet singing over the years, and in 1911 he formed a group with George Day, James Lathan, and William Worlds Davis, singing "everything from classical to ragtime." When Rue finally closed with Allen's Minstrels in 1915, it was to join the Rabbit's Foot Company.

Dance was an essential element of minstrelsy. Cake walks crossed the century mark with Allen's Minstrels. An 1899 report said their audiences were "kept in an uproar from the time the curtain goes up until it drops on the last act, our cake walk of seven ladies and gentlemen." Details were provided at the end of 1900: "Johnny Lost introduces the cake walk by first doing a drum major turn, then the couples appear, handsomely dressed. A misunderstanding arises between P. Ownes [*sic*], C. H. Williams, Miss P. Spivey and W. Cheatham which closes with a shooting scrape; the curtain drops upon the scene. The audience goes out laughing and screaming."[122] Cake walks were last mentioned in *Freeman* correspondence from Allen's Minstrels in the summer of 1902.

One of the earliest vernacular dancers with Allen's Minstrels was Kid Arnte. While showing at Alvarado, Texas, in December 1900, Arnte was accidentally shot by bandsman Frank Castry: "No arrests were made as it was purely accidental and the contracting parties are strong friends."[123] A note on January 19, 1901, informed that, "Kid Arant [*sic*] is again with us, and the way he dances, one would never think he had been shot in the leg." Shortly thereafter, Arnte appeared with Billy Cheatham in a "buck and wench [*sic*] song and dance." At Kosciusko, Mississippi, later that spring, "Kid Arant, being in company with a leading young lady there, was rocked by a couple of white men; when some of us saw what was going on we drew revolvers in defense of Kid and the whites took to their heels. We are 'passing up' all the ladies now."[124]

At the end of 1901, Arnte was performing a song-and-dance with Augustus Stevens and Pattie Roberson; and he and Roberson were doubling as drum majors on parade. A report in the fall of 1902 informed that, "Kid Arnte and Patti Robinson [*sic*] are still cleaning up in their rag time contest." At the end of the year Arnte was singing the latest Irving Jones song, "Home Ain't Nothing Like This." It seems Kid Arnte was the same "Diamond Tooth" Billy Arnte who was producing minstrel shows for touring carnival companies and medicine shows as late as 1942.[125]

Among the dance specialists with Allen's Minstrels in 1904, all-around comedian Perry Black appeared in the olio, "buck-dancing to the sextette of ladies and gentlemen singing 'Dusky Maiden.'" His other song-and-dance successes included "Malinda's Rag Time Ball" and "Scissors to Grind." In 1905 Black was the "rube bandmaster" in Allen's street parade, and he appeared in the afterpiece as "Primus from 'Bam.'"

In the spring of 1909 Frank King, "the man with the educated feet," drew praise for singing "You're in the Right Church but the Wrong Pew" in conjunction with his dancing turn. That fall, King and Rastus Jones took the stage as "knockabout comedians, doing a song and dance specialty."

On July 31, 1910, Walter Neely joined the show, billed as a "solo buck dancer." Neely had previously worked with ventriloquist Johnny Woods. New dancers in 1911 included Albert "Kid" Smith, "holding his own with his nip-ups and comedy dancing;" and Body Harris, who did his "grotesque dancing" to the tune of "If He Comes In I Am Going Out."[126]

At the Gayety.

Arthur Maxwell,
Comedy Cyclist,
15 Mins. "full stage."

For the third straight week at the Gayety Theater, a "Sun Time" house, a colored act has been represented on the bill. This week Arthur Maxwell, the well-known comedy cyclist, is getting his share of the applause at this theater with his antics as a "chink" buffoon. His funny falls and fantastic mannerisms kept them screaming throughout and he made it rather hard for the team which followed him. Mr. Maxwell was one of the first colored men to adopt this method of entertainment on the stage as a profession, although several have since taken up this line of work as performers. Maxwell is an old timer, having been identified with the stage for the past sixteen years. He has traveled with all of the large colored aggregations, among them being the Octoroons, Black Patti, Oriental Americans, Rosco & Holland's Minstrels, Billy Kersand's Minstrels, Oliver Scott's Minstrels and Mahara Brothers' Minstrels. The act is booked over the Western Vaudeville circuit, but by special arrangement he will appear at the Crown Garden Theater week of the 16th.

Indianapolis Freeman, October 14, 1911.

Singing and dancing comedian J. Page Tillman joined Allen's Minstrels in 1912, singing "Jungle Band." At the beginning of 1913, Tillman and M. H. White, as "Slick and Slick," held the audience "spell-bound" with "their ten-minute dancing turn, doing twenty-four clean-cut steps."[127]

Allen's Minstrels featured an array of specialty acts. Their original "trick cyclist" was Arthur Maxwell. Maxwell was succeeded by J. Lester McDaniels, who joined during the summer of 1900. McDaniels performed in the olio and on parade. A note in the summer of 1904 declared, "L. McDanuel [*sic*], trick bicycle rider with daring feats in tramp makeup on parade causes the people to follow in droves." On the night of August 3, 1908, a different mood prevailed: "Johnny Jones, baritone player of Allen's Minstrels, was shot . . . by J. Lester McDaniels, trick cyclist, and died at 11 Tuesday morning, August 4. McDaniels was shot three times by an unknown party, but is not seriously wounded, and is now in prison at Abington, Va."[128]

One of the first contortionists to tour with Allen's Minstrels was Hi Henry Hunt, the "Alabama Wizard," who joined at Greenville, North Carolina, in the spring of 1901. Hunt doubled as a fire eater. During the early months of 1902, he performed a double contortion act with "Tutts, the little boneless wonder." When last mentioned with Allen's Minstrels in the spring of 1903, Hunt was "still eating fire and puzzling the audience."

Another "boneless wonder," Clemo Harris, toured with Allen's Minstrels through most of 1904, in a team act with Alice (or Aline) Cassell. Billed as Clemo and Cassell, they had already established themselves in mainstream vaudeville as "The Contortionistic Alligator and Prima Donna."[129] A *Freeman* report of March 26, 1904, told how:

> Clemo Harris, contortionist, while playing Shreveport, La., was standing by the bridge that crosses Red River and got in an argument about doing dangerous feats. One of the boys bet him $50.00 that he couldn't cross the top of the bridge on his hands . . . and return without resting, then do a back somersault off the bridge to the water . . . So Mr. Harris took him up and made the walk alright, but being so exhausted, when he did the somersault, after striking the water he struck a rock and injured his arm very badly. We fished him out and put him under the care of a doctor for a day or so. He is with us again and doing his act and giving the loser the laugh.

Later that summer, Allen's Minstrels played a two-night stand at Memphis, "the home of Miss Aline Cassels." Shortly after the Memphis engagement, Clemo and Cassell returned to vaudeville, and by the end of the year they were performing at a theater in Havana, Cuba.[130]

In 1908 Allen's Minstrels introduced a new fourteen-year-old contortionist: "Little Clifton Boyd is the youngest and best of his age of the race." Boyd thrilled audiences "by kissing his elbow."

On March 4, 1910, acrobats Joe and Lew Watts joined Allen's Minstrels at Pensacola, Florida. A note that summer told how "Joseph S. Watts, the peerless slack wire artist, opens our concert nightly, doing the most difficult stunts ever seen on the American stage . . . He is assisted by his acrobatic brother, L. V. Watts." For the next two years they dominated the olio with their "many funny falls" and "death-defying stunts." On August 17, 1912, the Watts Brothers closed with Allen's Minstrels and went home to 1835 Palmyra Street, New Orleans. Shortly thereafter, they began a run in vaudeville.

John Pamplin, "the Demon from the Tropics," juggler and rifle manipulator, joined Allen's Minstrels in 1912. Pamplin had been active since the early 1890s. At the turn of the century he performed his rifle manipulations in Australia and New Zealand with Orpheus McAdoo's Georgia Minstrels and Alabama Cakewalkers. During his brief stay with Allen's Minstrels, Pamplin assumed the guise of "his sulphuric majesty, the devil." An August 10, 1912, report informed that Pamplin had closed at Cape Girardeau, Missouri, and that Robert "Hot Air" Williams, "comedian and fire eater," had taken his place.

There was a challenge baseball team with Allen's Minstrels as early as 1904. They rated themselves "one of the best base ball teams traveling." In 1913 they garnered quite a bit of press in the *Freeman*. A report from Oklahoma that summer boasted, "Our ball team is still winning, sweeping everything before them like chaff before the wind, although meeting one team after another of whites . . . At Clinton, Okla., our team met the local Three-B team. This team consisted of an Indian outfield, colored pitcher and catcher, white first, second and third baseman and a Mexican for shortstop and one for centerfield—some mixture. Our team, undaunted, proceeded to take their measure, 22 to 8."[131]

Well Look Who's Here

The Boys with the Many Funny Falls

WATTS BROTHERS, Comedy Acrobats

TWO REAL BROS

JOS. S.

LEW V.

In a grotesque combination of twist and falls. Our original act,

"The Tramp and the School Boy."

Enroute care Allen's Minstrels

Will soon return to vaudeville.

Indianapolis Freeman, June 22, 1912.

The first public notice of blues being played by the band with Allen's Minstrels came in April 1914, when the *Freeman* correspondent wrote from Cuthbert, Georgia: "The people down here are wild about the 'Memphis Blues' rendered by the band on the streets and by Miller and Fisher in their musical act."[132] An update from North Carolina in May said, "The band is a scream. Daily featuring the Florida Blues, written by William King Phillips, who is the author of a number of good marches and rags." At the end of August, when Allen's Minstrels began their annual assault on the Mississippi Delta, the band was "in line and still featuring the Memphis Blues." In Arkansas at the end of the year, they played "another one of William (King) Philip's compositions known as 'The Highball Rag.' The band more than 'hits' on it."[133]

The presence of William "King" Phillips provided a personal incentive to incorporate blues in the band repertoire. As a rising blues composer, Phillips ranked with W. C. Handy, in whose band he eventually played. However, Phillips had spent much of the past two years on the sick list. A report in the summer of 1912 said he had been in Savannah, Georgia, all season, "slowly recovering from a severe illness." Phillips finally rejoined in December, only to close again three months later, "on account of serious illness . . . He goes direct to Newburn, N.C., to rest and try to regain his health."[134]

The first member of Allen's Minstrels to be identified with blues singing was blackface character comedian Emmett Berger, who was commended in a May 9, 1914, report for "screaming them nightly with the real blues." When Berger first joined the show at Jackson, Mississippi, in the final weeks of 1913, he was "singing with much success 'You Made Me Love You' and 'Snooky-Ookums.'" The only subsequent mention of Berger was a disturbing note in the *Freeman* of June 6, 1914: "The Ku Klux have punished Emmett Berger about seven times for butting heads."

Allen's Minstrels reported good business throughout their fall 1914 tour of the Mississippi Delta:

> We played one day ahead of Sunny Dixie in Yazoo City, Miss., and one day behind them in Jackson, Miss., and turned them away both nights . . . We have the strongest show on the road as a minstrel show, tent or house show. Our first part is a dream. Opening with forty people on the stage. The finale of the first part is the Battle of Mexico and America . . . written and staged by J. B. Norton. The olio is opened by Happy Howe, going back to Alabama. Then comes Norton & Verdan [*sic*], the Jew and the Coon, and they are followed by Willie Davis, the bending wonder, the boy that has no bones. Then comes Clark & Clark (Harry and Tillie) the sketch artists, which are pleasing. Their talk is good. Harry Clark makes a hit singing 'The Green Grass is All Around and Round,' and they leave the house in an uproar. Their closing 'You Keep Me Worried All the Time.' The last but not least, is P. D. Herman Yerger and wife in their house of mystery. They appear as the world's greatest magicians, making things disappear and reappear. Then comes our big last act, presenting J. B. Norton and Happy Howe as Dallas Bill and Ready Money.[135]

The big last act was titled *Two Rich Coons from Dallas*.

Arthur "Happy" Howe had joined the show earlier in the spring, bringing with him a fifteen-year history of success as a blackface comedian, most of it spent with the Rabbit's Foot Company. A note from Allen's Minstrels on June 6, 1914, informed, "Our grand old man Happy Howe, is doing well . . . with his 'Honey, Oh.'"

At Greenville, Mississippi, on October 19, 1914, Allen's Minstrels "packed them to the doors, and just think of it, it was a return date, too. We had played there not more than thirty days ago." They were still in Mississippi in late November, "playing nothing but return dates." A new addition to the roster was Hezekiah Jenkins, of the team of Overton and Jenkins, enacting "The Jew and Coon."[136]

It was during their fall 1914 tour of the Mississippi Delta that Allen's Minstrels finally reinstated their "female contingent." Among the first arrivals, Beulah Curtis was noticed in September, singing "I Am Crying Just for You." Within the next few weeks, Lillie Clark was singing "International Rag"; Bonnie Bell Drew was singing "Chesapeake Bay" and "Annaliza's Wedding Day"; and Josie Veal was singing "I Want to Be Somebody's Baby Girl."[137] At Carlton, Mississippi, shortly thereafter, clarinetist Fred Kewley rejoined with his wife, Elizabeth, who came in singing "What It Takes to Make Me Love You, You Have Got It."[138]

At the end of 1914 there was a disruption in the seemingly smooth operation of Allen's Minstrels, attributable to the malfeasance of A. G. Allen himself. Co-owner George W. Quine suddenly abandoned his longtime post, and A. G. Allen decided to take Quine's place as on-site manager. Under Allen's brand of hands-on management, morale quickly deteriorated. Things finally exploded in the spring of 1915, when bandmaster McCamon and thirteen others walked off the job. The *Freeman* of April 10, 1915, offered two different slants on what had taken place, one from bandsman Mose McQuitty, and the other from A. G. Allen. McQuitty's version was headlined, "Why Allen's Minstrels Closed":

> Mose McQuitty writes to let the readers of the Freeman know that Allen's Minstrels did not close on account of bad business as the show was making money, but Allen and wife would not let any of the money loose so the boys packed up and left. So everyone take warning as long as A. G. Allen runs the show, stay away from them.
>
> By M. McQuitty, a man who don't believe in knocks—just a warning to my friends.

Allen's side of the story was captioned, "Truth About A. G. Allen's Show:"

> Shreveport, La., March 25—I wish to state to the members of the colored profession through your columns the fact in regard to disagreement between myself and the former members of my company, fourteen of whom got off the car without a moment's notice and, of course, as they gave me no notice they violated the contract they were working under and I refused to pay them any of their hold back salary. On December 7th, owing to the financial condition of the country and the general depression in all lines of business, and as this was a tent show working out of season, I gave the members of the company their choice of closing the show or taking their chances of working for their board and promised them one-half salary if business conditions would justify it, but assured them all that I would not take any chances on losing money trying to run a tent show in the winter time under such unfavorable conditions. Since that time and up until the first of March the show did not play to expenses and I put $1,200 into the show to keep it running. After giving these people employment and feeding them all winter as soon as spring opened up and other shows began to start out they commenced jumping to other shows without giving me a moment's notice. Those that gave me the usual two weeks' notice I paid in full. The others I refused to pay any back salary which they forfeited according to contract. Respectfully yours, A. G. Allen.

A few weeks later, Prof. McCamon submitted his take: "On December 9th, Mr. Quine left the show and Mr. Allen took the show in charge on half salary, which we never received. He went broke the second week, and I allowed him to borrow money on my diamonds, which he did, and one of them is in soak as yet. When the show began to make money his so-called wife refused to let him pay off anyone and tried to force us to work. I left and thirteen others followed."[139]

Chas. E. Rue added his point of view: "I . . . wish to state that being a member of this company for fourteen years this company never had contracts, but pays salaries every Sunday. George W. Quine, being manager until December last, has retired, and A. G. Allen has taken the show and at times during this past winter while in Texas, H. McCammon, band master, pawned his diamonds to carry the show . . . When the show began making money [Allen] never appreciated the former favors. He forgot friends. People began leaving. A. G. Allen is a number one advance man, but no manager, so musicians and performers look out."[140]

Most of those who quit were immediately picked up by other shows. McCamon went to the Virginia Minstrels. McQuitty joined the Sparks Circus Annex Band: "After 14 years out of the circus business, this season, 1915, finds me back under the white tops, riding one of the wagons in parade."[141] P. L. Jenkins joined the "Handy and Eckford bands at his home town in Memphis, Tenn., where they sing, talk and play those 'Memphis Blues'";[142] and Marcus Veal Chaney took up with the Rabbit's

Foot Company. John W. Dennis wrote to say, "I am now in De Ridder, La. I have a little business pressing clothes. A barber shop also. Agent for two or three Eastern firms, and may get by. Will be north in the future."[143]

Rumors that the mutiny had forced A. G. Allen to close the show were countered by a pithy dispatch from Trinity, Texas: "The show is now run by the manager and stage manager, not the band . . . Our stage manager, Mr. Norton . . . would like for the people to know that this show is not closed and is not going to close. The ghost walks every Tuesday."[144]

Prof. McCamon shot back at the crack about the show having been run by the band:

> Now in regards to the item in last issue of The Freeman, written by the would-be stage manager, Mr. Joe Norton. If the show was ever run by the bandmaster it was run with talent and brain, not as it is now by a bunch of so-called performers and musicians out of the alleys and dives from the larger cities of Texas, and [with] due respects to the married couples on the private car. The would be married couples would be kept in their place. They were not huddled together in the same car and sections with married couples, as they are now. Some class to the Allen show now I don't think. Yours truly, J. H. McCamon. [145]

The company's new solo cornetist, J. Elmer Moore, responded to McCamon:

> In a recent write-up a gentleman made mention of the fact that Mr. A. G. Allen's band was composed of a lot of ham fat musicians and tawa bums. I wish to state that this is a very broad assertion and I take great pleasure in replying to the profession and stating that I am around here and I am not considered by the music world a ham fat. I have been connected with two of the best negro bands in America and my record is there. Write the War Department, Washington, D. C. . . . I am around here as a business musician. Let us be careful in the future and not inflict any injury upon our brother musicians . . . Remember, if that hammer strikes something solid there is a recoil."[146]

Shortly thereafter, J. Elmer Moore was appointed bandmaster, and Allen's *Freeman* correspondent warned: "Some of these people had better look out who are throwing hot shots this way because we are liable to play day and date some day, and then we will see who has the best show and band. Our band is now under the leadership of Mr. J. E. Moore . . . and when he gets through with The Old Kentucky Home it is peaches to the world."[147]

Meanwhile, Allen's Minstrels replenished their roster. On April 17, 1915, one week after the mass defection, "The only and original Happy Howe (Arthur Howe), Charlie Hervey, Arthur Cox and wife, [and] Chas. Laurendine all joined us in Lufkin, Tex." Shortly thereafter, Hezekiah Jenkins returned with new partner Clifford Brooks, featuring "Jenkinson [*sic*, i.e., Jenkins's Own] Rag."[148] A report in July said Jenkins was "screaming the house nightly with his own songs, 'Poor Me,' 'Change,' 'You're Mine,' [and] 'My Own Rag.'"[149]

One notable newcomer was Rhea Wilson, the first female blues singer to appear with Allen's Minstrels. A report from Trinity, Texas, in the *Freeman* of April 24, 1915, proclaimed, "Mrs. Rhea Wilson certainly sings the 'St. Louis Blues.'" In Louisiana a few weeks later, she sang "I Wonder Where My Lovin' Man Is Gone."

At Jena, Louisiana, on May 27, 1915, Rhea Wilson and Beulah Curtis were injured during a severe storm: "The stage blew down and both were caught in the wreckage." By June the show was in

Oklahoma, where a detailed report was filed from the town of Bokhoma:

> Our first part line-up is a scream. Jerman White opens the show with a big noise, singing his own song, 'Get Your Money's Worth.' . . . [T]hen comes Miss Rheo Wilson with "I Wonder Where My Loving Man Is Gone." Clifford Brooks don't fail to get a shower of applause nightly, singing "When the Twilight Comes to Kiss the Rose Good Night." Miss Beulah Curtis never fails to get them with "Some Boy" and "Tiptop Tipperary Mary." The one and only Arthur (Happy) Howe is still knocking them out of their seats with "I am on My Way to New Orleans." But don't forget our excellent comedian Hezerkiah Jenkins, singing his own composition, I have made it through January and February, now I am marching right on through and my own rag [*sic*]. The next is the man that never fails, W. R. Earl singing "The Cows May Come and the Cows May Go, but the Bull Goes On Forever." Then the first part is closed by J. B. Norton singing a jubilee song, assisted by the entire company. Then comes our olio, opened by Happy Howe . . . Then comes the laughable afterpiece, "Silver King and Dollar Bill." Happy Howe and J. B. Norton as Silver King and Dollar Bill . . . Many pretty songs are sung by different members of the company, such as "Some Baby Knows" by Beulah Curtis; "The Little House Up on the Hill" by Mrs. Lillie Clark; "Virginia Love" by Mrs. Hattie Cox. "The St. Louis Blues," composed by Mr. W. C. Handy of Memphis, Tenn., is put over by Miss Rheo Wilson. The show is left in an uproar when W. R. Earl as Mrs. Dollar Bill, comes from the front door, down to the stage and gets her loving husband and carries him away. The band is rehearsing William Tell for their night concert as they play one of Rhemics [*sic*, Remick's] 1915 hits on each noonday parade, and Mr. [J. E.] Moore is still playing one of his red-hot solos. Go on Moore, you are the best that has ever been heard.[150]

In July the *Freeman* correspondent noted, "Our orchestra leader, Mr. Alonzo Wilson, is featuring 'The Yellow Dog' rag, composed by W. C. Handy . . . The whole house rocks with the music while Mr. Wilson's big ten piece orchestra plays the 'Yellow Dog Rag.'"[151]

HEZEKIAH JENKINS.

Indianapolis Freeman, September 8, 1917.

Shortly thereafter, correspondence from Allen's Minstrels dried up, and the members appear to have dispersed. A note on February 5, 1916, informed that J. B. Norton, "who spent sixteen years with the A. G. Allen's Minstrels, is still at 2365 Lawrence street, Dallas, Texas. Will be glad to hear from all friends." When Hezekiah Jenkins and Clifford Brooks were heard from again, they were in Louisiana with Robinson's Old Kentucky Minstrels, "causing laughing riots nightly" with

Letterhead stationery for A. G. Allen's Big Minstrel Show. (courtesy Circus, Minstrel and Traveling Show Collection, McCain Library and Archives, The University of Southern Mississippi)

their comedy sketch, "Two Coons and a Razor."[152] Hezekiah Jenkins went on to make race recordings as a blues singer-guitarist.[153]

There was no further news from Allen's Minstrels until October 1917, when word came that George W. Quine had returned to manage the day-to-day affairs: "We have at last hit the trail. The show opened at Friar's Point, Miss., in all its glory and as good things aren't easily forgotten, neither was the reputable name of A. G. Allen . . . Our eighteen piece band, under the able leadership of Ed Farrar, will soon come into its own as the daddy of them all." The stage show featured:

> Mr. Al Boyd, interlocutor; ends, Kid Clark singing "I Can beat You Doing Me;" Frank Powell singing "Pork Chop Pollas [*sic*, Poultice] Three Times a Day;" Sam Kennedy singing "Pray for the Lights to Go Out;" Nelson Green singing "Honkey Tonkey Twins." Circle, George E. Glasco, bass solo, "On the Billowy Sea;" Mrs. Myrtle Wells, solo, "How's Everything in Dixie;" Mrs. Marie Anderson, solo, "Mammy's Coal Black Rose;" Terrance Thomas, "Hawaiian Butter Fly." . . . Grand Finale, "Walking the Dog," introducing the one and only William R. Earl, in his side splitting burlesque, "Walking the Dog as Winch [*sic*]."[154]

By the end of 1917 Allen's Minstrels were feeling the effects of World War I: "The time has come when real shows are the only ones that can stick. War tax and higher cost of living call for higher class shows that leave no chance for the public to regret paying higher prices for admission."[155] A January 1918 railroad embargo forced the show to shut down for ten days:

> On account of the serious condition of railroads not being able to transport government supplies and materials as rapidly as was necessary, the embargo was placed on all shows using private cars and classed as non-essentials. All amusements of this class were forced to close for the present, if not temporarily until the war has been brought to an end. The A. G. Allen Minstrels and Rabbit Foot Co. being the oldest two companies of the kind in the United States,

naturally in keeping with the wide reputation of both companies, both F. S. Walcott [of the Rabbit's Foot Company] and George W. Quine strained every nerve to solve every conceivable problem in order to keep these two companies out longer than any other, which they did, and Mr. Wolcott had often said that he would stay out as long, if not longer, than any company of the kind under any conditions whatever, save being closed by the laws of the United States.

Both companies closed in good order, everybody paid in full and allowed the privilege of remaining on the car, sleeping and eating a few days longer if they so desired. Those who had failed to lay aside a few pennies for such a needy time were also given a few dollars each . . . The closing of all this class of amusements left many, if not a score or more, in a very serious condition financially, but will only serve as an everlasting lesson to those who care. As a rule about 90 per cent of the people in the profession never prepare to have anything but a good time, so we should all take heed to this broad lesson and try not to let our feathers be so easily and quickly plucked out hereafter.[156]

When the embargo was lifted, Allen's Minstrels were under new management. It seems there had been some sort of coup. On February 23, 1918, the *Freeman* posted this "Special Notice to the Profession":

J. W. Brownlee, manager of Washburn's Fashion Plate Minstrels, has purchased the title, car and entire paraphernalia of the A. G. Allen's Minstrels, and will go out under this title and exclusive management March 1.

This is one of the oldest titles on the road and we will endeavor to make it the biggest and best . . .

The management never closed the show one day during the railroad difficulties, and the boys sure appreciate it . . .

Don't forget the title A. G. Allen's Minstrels, owned and controlled by J. W. Brownlee of the Washburn Minstrels.

Reports from Mississippi in the summer of 1919 appeared under the heading of "Brownlee and Allen's Minstrels": "No doubt this must seem a strange name to many professionals, but it is a standard minstrel organization traveling through the state of Mississippi in their own Pullman stateroom car. Our band and orchestra is up to the standard. Our manager Mr. Brownlee is well satisfied with the bunch he has."[157] The "bunch" included veteran singing comedian Jim Wise, bass drummer and singing comedian Archie Blue, male blues singer Lowdown Johnson, one-string fiddler James Steward, and the acrobatic Watts Brothers: "We close with an uproaring rip comedy [*sic*], 'The Pullman Porter's Return.'"[158]

On August 25, 1919, Brownlee and Allen's Minstrels played Jackson, Mississippi. A report on September 6 assured that they were still "Captivating Large Audiences Through Mississippi":

Yerger the magician holds the audiences spellbound at the mysteries performed in modern magic . . . Lowdown Johnson, king of all blues singers, is still taking up collection nightly . . . Mrs. Lizzie Crosby is having great success singing "Tishomingo Blues." We also have a rare treat in our midst in the person of Mrs. Alice St. Matthews, a female cornetist and a thorough musician of fine taste for musical art . . . Mr. George St. Michaels, our band and orchestra leader, is an artist himself . . . Little Jimmy Steward, the one string wizard, never fails to bring down the house.

A few months later, a company correspondent went on about Little Jimmy Steward, "a marvel in his line . . . his execution upon the one-string violin being performed with such ease and grace that it seems to touch every soul and compels his admirers to render attentive ear to each and every selection

The One and Only

Jim Green

Stage manager and principal comedian with A. G. Allen's New Orlean's Minstrels and originator of the Human Top, would like to hear from good people in all lines. Any of my old people or others that want to travel with a real show that never closes and the ghost with better health than an alligator, write or wire

JIM GREEN,

The Human Top, care A. G. Allen's Original New Orleans Minstrels, per address,

200 Keene St., Spartansburg, S. C.

Indianapolis Freeman, November 22, 1919.

rendered. Jimmy is what we may term out of the ordinary, and the peer of all one-string artists."[159]

Meanwhile, A. G. Allen announced that he was back on the road with his own version of Allen's Minstrels, "under the heading of Mr. A. G. Allen (himself), ably assisted by the most competent and congenial showman, Mr. Harry Hunt":

> This show is produced by the peer of Colored minstrel producers . . . the one and only Jim Green, widely known as "Shoot 'Em Up Jim, Dean of Minstrelsy." The new addition of this great outfit are Eddie (Peg) Lightfoot, the world's premier one-legged dancer, and Leon (Sonny) Gray, formerly stage manager of Tolliver's Smart Set Minstrels; also Rawlinson & Rawlinson (Odell & Creola) . . . We have a wonderful jazz band, under the leadership of Prof. John Erwin, our most worthy bandmaster. All popular selections are being rendered daily. Our motto: "Mirth, Melange and Music." . . . We have seven of the dazzling jazzing and dancing beauties of the present age, presenting all the late song numbers of the day.[160]

Three weeks after A. G. Allen reasserted himself, Brownlee and Allen's Minstrels announced that they would "be known hereafter as the Leon W. Washburn's Minstrel. Will travel through the north and west, playing in the large opera houses . . . We are having great success at present through Mississippi." Back in control of his own identity, A. G. Allen proceeded to field a strong show. An ad in the fall of 1919 promised, among other things, a "Dazzling, Jazzing, Amazing, Fast, Furious Chorus."

Among the featured performers with Allen's Minstrels in 1919–1920 were Eddie "Peg" Lightfoot, the one-legged dancer, and Leon "Sonny" Gray, the singing and talking comedian, both late of Tolliver's Smart Set. Also prominent on the roster, as straight man and "Official Announcer," was Lew Kenner, a bona fide "Grand Old Man" of the profession. Kenner was originally from New

SEASON
1920
ORGANIZED
MAY 15, 1899.

A. G. ALLEN'S
—BIG—
MINSTREL SHOW

SEASON
1920
ORGANIZED
MAY 15, 1899.

EXECUTIVE STAFF
A. G. ALLEN Manager (In Person).
CHAS. G. FRYE, Assistant Manager.
H. D. CARNEY, General Agent.
EDWARD BOYCE, Press Agent.

BERT NEALE, Tickets.
RUBE WILLIAMS, Supt. of Canvas.
J B. FURMAN, Front Door and Privileges Putting it Over With Creole Sweets.

Leon (Sonny) Gray
Singing, Talking Comedian
Greetings to All
2nd Season

John Porter
Tuba Soloist
and
Characters
2nd Season

Artee Horton
Melephone
2nd Season

Claude Curry
"Jazz"
Barytone Solist
2nd Season

R. M. Ingram
Cornetist
2nd Season

Sol Speights
Tenor and Characters
Seasons Greetings
4th Season

Clifton C. Boyd
Contortion
and
Melephone
13th Season

Warner Ford
Trombone
Greetings to All
6th Season

Duke Davis
Singing, Dancing
Comedian
Not Funny, But Good
2nd Season

Walter Motley
Singing, Dancing
Comedian
"With It and For It"
7th Season

Charles Floyd
Ballads and
Characters
2nd Season

Mrs. Artee Horton
Soprano
and
Juvenile Leads
2nd Season

JIM GREENE
Stage Manager
Producer of
The Show That's Different

Ask Those That Have Seen
"Nuff Sed"
Seasons Greetings
2nd Season

John Irwin
Band and Orchestra Leader
6th Season

Regards to All
In and Out
R. J. Simmons, Write

Eddie "Peg" Lightfoot Hoofer
Greetings to All
2nd Season

Lew Kenner
Straight Characters
Official Announcer
Greetings to All
2nd Season

Tedd The POPES May
Electric Wire Walking, Trapeze, Magic
and Characters
1st Season

Mrs. R. Greene
Soprano
and
Leads
2nd Season

Mrs. Lizzie Irwin
Alto Singer
and Bits
2nd Season

Mrs. Lucy Motley
Female Baritone
3rd Season

Mary Clark
Contralto
and Bits
1st Season

Rastus JENKINS and JINKINS Fanny
Singing, Dancing and Comedy
Seasons Greetings
1st Season

Warren Irving
Original Funny-face
and
Jazz Trap Drummer
1st Season

M. A. George
Highest Salaried
Propecinal Cook
With Any Tented
Exhibition

MUSICIANS WRITE
JOHN IRWIN

ALWAYS OPENING FOR GOOD PEOPLE
A. G. ALLEN,
Hazen, Arkansas.

PERFORMERS WRITE
4 JIM GREENE

Indianapolis Freeman, April 10, 1920.

Orleans. His momentous career began at the turn of the century and had taken him out on the leading edge of southern vaudeville.

While playing through the Carolinas in the fall of 1920, A. G. Allen placed a want ad for a "Base drummer that can double stage; Performers and sketch teams that can sing and dance, read lines and work acts; Ballad singers and quartet, also one or two good novelty acts." He warned "Honky Tonk loafers and slap stick comedians" to "save your stamps. None but those capable of working to refined lady audience tolerated on this show."[161] The show was described in the November 20, 1920, edition of the *Freeman*:

> Mr. Allen, this year, has one of the best and I dare say the largest tent minstrel show on the road today. Carrying 60 people, one private sleeper and four one-ton trucks. With a new khaki top, 70 feet round with three 30-ft. middles, built by the Goss Tent Co., of Detroit, Mich. Company wardrobes and uniforms

new and the men in blue and gold coats and caps with leather leggins and the ladies in blue and gold opera coats with parasols to match and with the Allen famous 18 piece band under the able leadership of John Erwin sure brings the folks out in any kind of weather.

The performance is under the directorship of that Jolly, jovial comedian, Jimmie Greene (Shoot em up Jim) who also is producer of the elaborate first part by the entire company entitled, "In Old Kentucky" and the rip roaring sketch, "A Raid on the Moonshiners," which has proven such a big hit that Mr. Allen has gotten out special paper for same and had it copyrighted. The personnel of the company practically remains the same except with the addition of new people in enlarging the company and a Creole beauty chorus of ten ladies. Most of the band and principal comedians have been with the A. G. Allen show for years.

Since January 1st, at Titusville, Fla., the show has played all the principal cities and few towns in Florida, Georgia, Mississippi, Louisiana, Texas, Oklahoma, Arkansas, Tennessee, Alabama, South Carolina, Virginia and North Carolina, and has traveled to date 15,696 miles and the four trucks have come overland carrying the tent. We have lost but six nights this season, and those on account of rain. We are now headed just one jump ahead of the weather for Texas and south-west for the winter.

Following a report in 1922 that Allen's Minstrels had closed, there appears to have been a revival of the name in combination with the Old Kentucky Minstrels. An April 1923 correspondence informed that:

A. G. Allen's minstrels are now in the state of West Virginia . . . Jim Green and Rastus Jinkins are holding down the extreme ends, with J. A. B. Taylor (Lasses Candy) in the interlocutor's chair . . . Enoch Baker and Rock Markham are a dancing team that meets with the satisfaction and demands of the lovers of sensational buck and wing dancing . . . Jack Taylor, the contortionist is still with the show . . . Then there is our old favorite, W. O. Franklin and his trained canines . . . The afterpiece is entitled 'All About Juanita,' written and staged by Jim Green. The story has to do with the love of two men for one little senorita . . . Walter Motley and Lucy Motley stand out as Black Snake and Alice. Rastus Jinkins and Hattie Young make good Indians. Mary Young is an adorable Juanita. Jim Green and J. A. B. Taylor are living the parts of Tony and Pedro. The duel fought by these two at the finale of the show is done with much reality . . . On the whole, the entire show is pleasing at every stand and an ofay paper in Carolina said that the staging of the show was so far from the average minstrels that if the band had not played the Irresistible Blues they would not have known it was a minstrel show.[162]

Blackface comedian Dewey Markham later shed his childhood nickname, "Rock," and came to celebrity as "Pigmeat." Still in West Virginia that summer, "The A. G. Allen's and Old Kentucky Minstrels Combined" reported "all well and happy . . . Prof. C. A. Forby, the bandmaster, is strengthening the band . . . Joe Kemp still pleases well with that enviable voice, singing 'Call Me Back, Pal of Mine.' Walter Motley frequently responds to encores with his 'Monday Morning Blueish Blues.'"[163]

When A. G. Allen died on December 27, 1926, the *Chicago Defender* reported:

The daddy of all traveling minstrel shows is dead. He died at Fayette [*sic*], N.C. . . . at the age of 62. Heart trouble was the cause. A. G. Allen was the first man to exhibit a minstrel show under a tent; that was in 1899 in Chicago, showing there for a solid year on various city lots. At the time of his death he was president of the Bill Posters union and had saved some money, he was considered a good showman but a poor manager of finance, and seldom getting a break. The artists in general feel sorry for his death and the credit he deserves for paving the way that he has kept thousands of artists may never be given him as he deserves.[164]

A company trading as A. G. Allen's Minstrels remained in circulation through the late 1920s, at least. In 1928 and 1929 the on-site manager was E. S. Winstead, who gained a reputation during the Depression era as proprietor of Winstead's Mighty Minstrels.[165]

The Rabbit's Foot Company

The *A Rabbit's Foot* Comedy Company was founded in 1900 and was still on the road in the late 1950s. Better remembered as the Rabbit Foot Minstrels, this legendary company was familiar to insiders simply as "the Foots."

According to a 1905 *Freeman* report, the founder of the Rabbit's Foot Company, Patrick Henry "Pat" Chappelle, was born in Jacksonville, Florida, on January 7, 1869. His father, Lewis Chappelle, Sr., was one of the oldest settlers of Jacksonville's historic La Villa community, having arrived in the area around 1859, as one of "a large number of ex-slaves fresh from the plantations of South Carolina . . . By trade he was a carpenter and built many houses in the city of Jacksonville."[166]

Pat Chappelle reportedly quit school after the fourth grade and became an itinerant string band guitarist. Returning to Jacksonville after "years of travel," he organized his first road show, the Imperial Colored Minstrels, in November 1898, and for the next several months they "played through the Southland with great success."

Ragtime piano king Prof. Fred Sulis was the pianist for the Imperial Colored Minstrels, which

PAT H. CHAPPELL

The above is an excellent likeness of Mr. Pat Chappell, the subject of this sketch. He was born in the City of Jacksonville, Fla., the 7th day of January 1869. where he attended the public school until he reached the fourth grade when he left the school to become a fruit vender. It was while thus employed his father bought him a guitar and by much practice and more patience he soon became very proficient. Joining hands with two other boys, he started out on a tour of the State playing in many of the leading hotels, afterwhich they went to Boston where they furnished the music on the steamboats between Nantastic Beach and Boston. While there they were highly recommended to the inaugurator of continuous vaudeville, Mr. Keith where they played a weeks engagement, making a big hit; from there they appeared at the World's Museum in Boston and were booked as follows: Doris' Museum, Eighth Ave., N. Y. City; Doris' Harlem Museum; Grand Street Museum and Mammoth Pavillion, New York City returning to Jacksonville. Mr. Chappell was engaged by a colored man Chas Woodard, at Sanford, Fla. to furnish the music in his place of business in that city remaining with Mr. Woodard two years. From there he was engaged as musician in the saloon of Messrs Walker and Hamilton in Tampa, Fla., also worked for Mr. J. H. Mays, at Tampa City; afterwhich he returned to Jacksonville and opened a pool and billiard parlor on Bay street. He leased the Bowden Block on Bridge street, for a period of five years. He repaired the building, put in a tile floor and fitted up a concert hall at a cost of $1,600. He has also purchased a fine Orchestrion for $950. Mr. Chappell has built two fine dwelling houses—one with twelve rooms the other with seven. In the management of the concert hall Mr. Chappell has been more than successful. He employs nothing but professional people and they must be up to date and writes that he has open engagements. at all times for professional people. He also gives employment to fifteen people at his place of business. On November 28, '98. Mr. Chappell organized the Imperial Colored Minstrels which played through the Southland with great success. Mr. Chappell is in business within six squares of the place he was born. His mother, father, two sisters and two brothers are at present living with him.

• • •

Indianapolis Freeman, April 29, 1899.

included twenty-six performers. In January 1899 they received a ringing endorsement from a non-professional observer in Mayfield, Kentucky:

[T]he show is strictly first class and their performance was great and the band is up-to-date. The blind cornet soloist is one of the greatest attractions of the show, also G. H. Price, the baritone singer, and F. D. Sulis, the pianist attract much attention. Prof. Sulis and Prof. Price had a special invitation from John W. Landrum, white, to go to W. L. McGhee's Café, where the elite of the city was waiting with the assistance of Blind Joe Mungrum [*sic*] the violinist white, and Prof. Sulis, and Price, they were enthralled until the wee small hours of the morning, after which a luncheon was spread and all partook of oysters, fruit, ice cream and cake regardless of color. And what makes the show great it is owned and managed by P. H. Chappell [*sic*] colored, and while in our city they made many friends among both colored and white, we hope they will come again next season. The following is the staff: P. H. Chappell, proprietor, business manager and treasurer; C. A. Jones, leader of the band and orchestra; T. H. Price, stage manager; Sam Cohen, master of transportation; Mac Perkins, assistant stage manager and property man; F. D. Sulis, secretary and pianist, and Chas. Roltare, advance agent.[167]

Blind Joe Mangrum was a white country fiddler from Paducah, Kentucky, who appeared regularly on early broadcasts of the Grand Ole Opry, and who recorded for Victor in 1928, almost thirty years after his jam session with Fred Sulis and G. H. Price.[168]

Chappelle also opened the Excelsior Concert Hall, a saloon-theater, in the La Villa community.[169] He leased a building at 125–127 Bridge Street, put in a new tile floor, and was open for business no later than March 1899. His concert hall reportedly seated five hundred people, featured "only professional talent," and "enjoyed a liberal patronage from both races."[170]

Suddenly, amidst an escalating dispute with his white landlord, J. E. T. Bowden, who also happened to be the mayor of Jacksonville, Chappelle scuttled the Excelsior Concert Hall and moved to Tampa. His arrival was trumpeted in the *Tampa Morning Tribune* of September 28, 1899:

Pat Chappell [*sic*], colored, moved from Jacksonville to this city last Sunday, and opened up a new vaudeville show-house in Fort Brooke. The first performance was given on Monday night. Chappell calls it "The Buckingham," and has flooded the city with circulars . . .

The [Jacksonville] Times-Union and Citizen of yesterday, tells an interesting and also an amusing story about the proprietor of "The Buckingham." It seems that Chappell has been conducting a similar business at Jacksonville, occupying a building owned by Mayor J. E. T. Bowden, of that city.

The Times-Union and Citizen states that it appears, when Chappell moved out of the mayor's building, he took the tiled floor and all the fixtures with him, and supposes that the property was brought to Tampa. The paper adds that he left the walls and roof.

The mayor of Jacksonville is therefore after Chappell, and there may develop an interesting local end to the story.

Chappelle countered that the tiles rightfully belonged to him, and he produced a receipt to back his claim: "Chappell [*sic*] further states that instead of the Mayor being after him, he is after the Mayor, and that he promises to bring a suit for $10,000 damages against Bowden. Chappelle claims that Bowden has persecuted him, both with his power as landlord and his power as Mayor." The *Jacksonville Times-Union and Citizen* editorialized that Chappelle was trying to capitalize on the dispute as a means of "making his presence known in Tampa, and securing a lot of free advertising in the papers of that city."[171] Eventually, it seems, the charges against Chappelle were dropped after his lawyer promised to have the contested tile flooring returned to Bowden's building.

On September 24, 1899, Chappelle and R. S. Donaldson, "one of Florida's most progressive Afro-American capitalists," opened the Buckingham Theater Saloon on the corner of Fourteenth Street and Fifth Avenue in Tampa's old Fort Brooke community.[172] Chappelle was the establishment's hands-on business manager. The original roster of performers included Billy Cheatham and Arthur "Happy" Howe, "the people's favorite." The Buckingham stood "wide open" to Tampa's ethnically diverse citizenry. As the *Freeman* of March 24, 1900, observed, "The house is crowded to the doors every night with Cubans, Spaniards, Negroes and white people." An ad in the *Tampa Morning Tribune* qualified that, "Special attention will be shown to white visitors."[173]

On December 5, 1899, Chappelle and Donaldson announced the "Grand Opening" of a second vaudeville platform, the Mascotte Theater Saloon, at the corner of Polk and Pierce streets, in Tampa "proper." From March through July 1900, reports from both the Buckingham and Mascotte appeared regularly in the *Freeman*. A commentary of June 30 assured, "These theatres have proven themselves to be miniature gold mines."

In the spring of 1900, with vaudeville flourishing at both of their theater locations, Chappelle and Donaldson made public their plans to "bring out one of, if not the greatest aggregation of Negro talent ever on the road, the coming season. They have engaged the services of the well-known writer of burlesque, Mr. Frank Dumont, of Dumont's Minstrels" to come up with a musical comedy to highlight their new venture.[174]

Dumont came up with *A Rabbit's Foot*. Opinions varied as to whether or not it actually had a plot: "'Tis said that 'A Rabbit's Foot' is an excellent vehicle for the presentation of an abundant amount of rag-time, sweet Southern melodies, witty dialogue, buck dancing, cake walks and numerous novelties."[175]

On May 19, 1900, Chappelle and Donaldson ran a want ad in the *Freeman* for "60 Colored Performers . . . Only those with reputation, male, female and juvenile of every description, Novelty Acts, Headliners, etc., for our new play, 'A Rabbit's Foot' . . . We will travel in our own train of hotel cars, and will exhibit under canvas . . . Musicians that double write quick. Can use a good Pickaninny Band. All the members of this show must be good dressers on and off the stage, and must be ladies and gentlemen."

Chappelle held high expectations for *A Rabbit's Foot.* Intending to compete head-on with the big-time northern road shows of Williams and Walker, Cole and Johnson, etc., he engaged the prestigious Hurtig and Seamon Agency of New York to book him, and hired Nick Roberts, "late of Tony Pastor's Theatre," to serve as manager. The *Freeman* of June 23, 1900, informed that, "Owing to the many flattering offers from leading theatrical managers throughout the United States . . . Mr. Chappelle has decided to play nothing but first-class theatres, instead of under canvas, as first announced . . . Prof. Frank Clermont will have charge of the three brass bands with the show, and he has secured some of the ablest musicians of today for his concert band."

NOTICE! EVERYBODY BOOKED

—FOR—

A RABBIT'S FOOT COMEDY CO.,

REPORT FOR REHEARSAL AT LAKEVIEW, N. J., AUGUST 1, 1900. SHOW OPENS AUGUST 15.

☞Can use a few more good performers—both male and female; those doubling brass given preference. REMEMBER THAT I FURNISH NO TICKETS.

PLEASE ACKNOWLEDGE THIS CALL BY POSTAL. Any one desiring to join this high class Negro show should write PAT CHAPPELLE, Tampa, Fla., at once, stating full particulars and lowest salary. Managers wanting this big attraction address our booking agents: Hurtig & Seamon, New York City.

This show will play Opera Houses from August 15, 1900 to April 15, 1901, and balance of summer under canvas. All parties holding contracts please send in the duplicates at once to Pat Chappelle, Tampa, Florida.

TO WHOM IT MAY CONCERN—This certifies that Chappello & Donaldson, proprietors of vaudeville theatres here, are well known to me, and that they are considered to be honest, honorable men and reliable for their contracts. Respectfully,

J. B. ANDERSON, Cashier Exchange National Bank, Tampa, Fla.

Indianapolis Freeman, June 16, 1900.

Over the next few weeks Chappelle announced a spectacular roster of performers. Rehearsals commenced on schedule at Lakeview, New Jersey, August 1, 1900, with the opening performance set for August 20 at the Bijou Theater in nearby Paterson. Meanwhile, Chappelle got bogged down in a contract dispute with some of his star performers. Subsequently, bandmaster Frank Clermont defected to Rusco and Holland's Nashville Students, and Chappelle's partnership with R. S. Donaldson evaporated.

In the face of adversity, Chappelle managed to open on schedule. But, for all the pretension to musical comedy, *A Rabbit's Foot* came forth in the unmistakable form of a minstrel show. The *Freeman*'s review of the debut performance did not even mention the namesake production. It did note, however, that the "Phillipino minstrel first part" was "something grand and unique"; and the olio, with Ben Hunn, Florence Hines, the Paynes, Brandon and Arlington, Bailey and Fletcher, the Betters, the Perrins and the great Gowongo, was "the strongest colored olio before the public today."[176]

On September 15, 1900, four weeks after it opened, the premier edition of *A Rabbit's Foot* was forced to close in Brooklyn, New York, "on account of poor business." It was an inauspicious beginning for one of the most enduring tented minstrel shows on record. Sylvester Russell, who had seen *A Rabbit's Foot* in rehearsal, later opined that Chappelle had come up "green from the South" and "did not possess the qualities that would meet the requirements of a better element of performers than he had been used to dealing with at his resort in Florida."[177] In response, Chappelle labeled

Russell a "trashy fool" with "an insane idea that . . . the people of the South have no sense."[178]

Chappelle returned to the Buckingham Theater in Tampa and regrouped. On July 6, 1901, he advertised that he was preparing *A Rabbit's Foot* for another tour, and on July 13 he notified that, "With the exception of a few performers and musicians the show is almost booked. Uniforms for the band have been ordered and they are bright red with black braid, and are loud enough to talk." The *Freeman* of September 14 supplied an update: "People are getting in every day for the rehearsals of this great coon comedy . . . Mr. Chappelle has engaged Col. Chas. A. Duprez as manager and J. V. McShea as advance, with two assistants. John Gaddis, the noted scenic artist of New York, has put the finishing touches to the scenery and says that it is his masterpiece. The Eaves Costume Co. of New York has finished the costumes and they are magnificent."

On October 7, 1901, Chappelle launched the *A Rabbit's Foot* Company's second season, with a roster headed by comedians Arthur "Happy" Howe, Will Goff Kennedy, D. Ireland Thomas, and Tom Logan. Their route was an unpretentious, southern route. "In Eufaula, Ala., we played against Gentry's Dog and Pony Show and turned people away. We did not think we would do it but we did."[179] At Meridian, Mississippi, "business was so dull" that they jumped to Cordele, Georgia, "to get into a territory where there is life among the people as well as money." On the way, they "visited Booker T. Washington's school at Tuskegee, Ala., and gave them a nice serenade."[180] Chappelle had advertised that he was booked up for nearly a year, but after twelve trying weeks he retreated to Tampa for an "indefinite run" at the Buckingham.

On July 14, 1902, the third edition of *A Rabbit's Foot* debuted at Plant City, Florida, "with a brand new canvass theatre, uniforms and everything new and bright as a dollar." By the end of the month they had made their way into the heart of Georgia. In mid-August they moved into Alabama and headed for Birmingham, with show stops at Ozark, Troy, Eufaula, Union Springs, Phenix City, Opelika, Talladega, and Anniston:

> The weather is very hot, but it does not affect our attendance in the least. Our show is strong, with Happy Howe and D. Ireland Thomas in the leading parts. Will Goff Kennedy is characterizing "Old Dusenberry," singing "Phrenologist Coon" and "I Got the Blues" to big success. The Johnsons, Billy and Estelle, are cleaning up with their sketch. Mrs. Johnson is singing "Hannah from Savannah" and is singing it. Billy Johnson sets them screaming with "Castle on the Nile" And "I Got Mine." Geo. Daniels is getting his with "Cindy My Black Belle, Do." Andy Williams, the famous frog man, is puzzling thousands. R. L. Gilchrist, the funny little fellow, is singing "The Leader of the Ball" and "Please Go Way and Let Me Sleep." With all the knocks this show is at last a success. It has met every pay day and all the people are satisfied. Prof. S. E. Dodd is mystifying people everywhere with his five C's on the E∞ cornet . . . Will Means is making all the slide trombone players know that he is in the business.[181]

Character actor and baritone singer Will Goff Kennedy was born in Nashville, Tennessee, in 1879, and reportedly entered the minstrel profession at the age of sixteen. His 1902 tour with *A Rabbit's Foot* marked the onset of a long career under canvas, where he eventually blossomed as a "promoter and producer of plays and sketch comedy." In the end, it was said that Kennedy "knew his business, he knew how to manage men without the whip or lash."[182]

The new bandmaster, Prof. S. E. Dodd, stayed through the 1902 season. Among the bandsmen, Will Means and William "Tuba" Thomas were both from Memphis. When Thomas closed out in the summer of 1903, he let it be known that he could be "found any time at 121 Beale street." Star comedian Happy Howe was "funnier than ever" in the elusive drama of *A Rabbit's Foot*, playing "the fake prince and princess" to D. Ireland Thomas's conception of "the fake nephew." Other features included the Buckingham Quartette and a big cake walk.

By the fall of 1902 Pat Chappelle was ready to declare unqualified success: "When we consider that all other tent shows are playing to 25 and 15c and we are charging 35c and filling the tent, why the 'A Rabbit's Foot' must be a lucky charm . . . We are getting money and forgive all the hard knockers for now they see they cannot keep a good man down."[183] Chappelle's optimism persisted even in the face of adversity: "Although we were burn out [*sic*] at West Point, Ga., on Sept. 9, losing nearly our entire outfit our managers have refurnished everything and we are now on the road again playing our usual big business . . . and all who saw the performance [at Greenville, South Carolina] dubbed it too good for a tent."[184]

"Too good for a tent" became something of a motto for the Rabbit's Foot Company. At a few of their larger show stops, including Atlanta and Memphis, they actually did play in theaters; nevertheless, they remained a tent show.

On November 9, 1902, *A Rabbit's Foot* landed at the Buckingham Theater and gave their final performance of the season. In recognition of his change of fortune, Chappelle took out a large advertisement in the "Christmas Edition" of the *Freeman*, noting in particular that he had "accomplished what no other Negro has done—he has successfully run a Negro show without the help of a single white man." This was no mean feat, and Chappelle continued to note it: "From the razorbacks up to the manager each and every member is colored."[185] "Our success is nothing short of phenomenal, especially when you consider that we are all Negroes and are here in the heart of the South. Not one pale face among us—even our advance agents are colored."[186]

The Rabbit's Foot Company opened its 1903 season at Bradenton, Florida, on April 1, carrying thirty-six performers and musicians and ten canvas men. Chappelle made a special trip to Sedalia, Missouri, that summer to purchase "the best hotel car on wheels that is used by a theatrical company. This car accommodates 40 people. It is a six wheel truck Pullman, and it has a piano on it."[187] Chappelle was proud of his company and what it represented. At mid-season he told the *Freeman*:

> The receipts of "A Rabbit's Foot" Company average more than a thousand dollars weekly, while expenses run from five to seven hundred dollars . . . Now, if one or more of our best talent used their business ideas and put out some colored shows there would not be much room left for the white man, and he or her would be considered a manager who would be doing something for his race by the white people instead of being looked upon as an ordinary servant like our noted performers are to-day . . . While this show plays under canvas it should not be looked upon as a cheap show. It should be looked upon as an independent Negro show.[188]

Chappelle liked to point out that his show was "well patronized by the best of white and colored ladies and gentlemen." However, when *A Rabbit's Foot* played Bishop Turner's Tabernacle in

A Rabbit's Foot Comedy Company......

The only real successful show traveling that is owned and managed by Negroes, has Negro Advance Agents; has Negro Ticket Sellers; all press work and rail-road contracts done by Negro management. In fact Pat Chappelle has accomplished what no other Negro has done—he has successfully run a Negro show without the aid of a single white man. Below is a likeness of himself an his celebrated all Negro organization.

The above groupe is the manager and members of the "A Rabbit's Foot Comedy," which played a successful season last summer under canvas through the states of Florida, Georgia, Alabama and South Carolina. This show is owned, managed and controlled exclusively by colored people, which is the only show to day that has no white person connected at all. This company carries a brass band and orchestra, and travels in their own private car; also carries a 60 foot baggage car, and everywhere they appeared last summer, according to the local papers, they gave perfect satisfaction in every respect We will now call your attention to each member as follows:

1. Pat Chappelle, owner and manager, who is the originator and founder of the famous coming Negro companies traveling in Ame ica He is also general manager of the Buckingham Theater, at Tampa, Fla. This popular place of amusement is owned by Chappelle Bros At this house they employ from twenty and thirty colored performers every season.

2. Lewis Chappelle, a younger brother of Pat Chappelle. He is the junior partner of Chappelle Bros. Lewis Chappelle manages the Buckingham Theater saloon while Pat Chappelle is on the road with his company.

3. D. Ireland Thomas, private secretary and stage manager. He has been in the employment of this firm more than three years and deserves much credit

4. John Hamilton, the advance agent. This young man did the advance work for the show very creditably, he being the only colored advance agent that has piloted a colored show to success. He will have an assistant next season.

5. Happy Arthur Howe, the leading comedian, who made a big hit for himself and the show. He to day is just as good a comedian as we have on the American stage, and if he sticks to Mr. Chappelle and the "Rabbit Foot," he will become very popular.

6 S E Dodd, who is the leader of the band and orchestra. We need not say much of Mr. Dodd as he is well known throughout the country as an able man in the profession.

7. Will Goff Kennedy, is a native of Nashville, Tenn.; born July 20, 1877. He has been connected with several of the leading colored shows and concert companies of this country. He possesses a good voice and a pleasing stage appearance. During the past season he was one of the principals with Pat Chappelle's "Rabbit Foot Comedy company," and wherever that company appeared he has left a most favorable impression as a refined, up-to-date minstrel and character artist. His affable ways and gentlemanly deportment makes him a favorite with his associates. He essayed the role of Uncle and premier end man. He is now with the Buckingham Theater Stock company doing first rate.

8. William Thompson, tuba player in the band and orchestra, also stage carpenter No. 1, who plays his parts with much credit.

9. Son Payne, comedian, who made a big hit for himself last season. If he continues to improve as he has for the past two years he will make a good man.

10. Lewis Williams, clarionet player in band and orchestra, who did good work as a musician.

11. Clifford D. Brooks, comedian and bass drummer, who also did good work. Mr. Brooks is also a first class quartette man.

12. William Hampton, cornet in band and orchestra and steward. He also deserves credit.

13. J. M. Gales, baritone and stage carpenter No 2, who did good work.

14. Young Roges, who performs nicely with his trained dog.

15 Miss Lizzie Roberts, a pleasing soubrett

16. Miss Iva Harris, who plays the leading lady's part nicely.

17. Miss Laura Logan, soubrett with a high soprano voice.

18. Miss Edith Thomas, a cracker jack little singer and dancer.

19. Miss Marie Law, a pleasing little soubrett.

20. Miss Pearl Wyatt, another first class singer and dancer.

21. Remus, the trained mascot, who does a number of wonderful tricks.

As a whole the company is first class and is a credit to the colored race. This company will open its season in April and close in November, 1903, using nothing but special people.

Indianapolis Freeman, December 27, 1902.

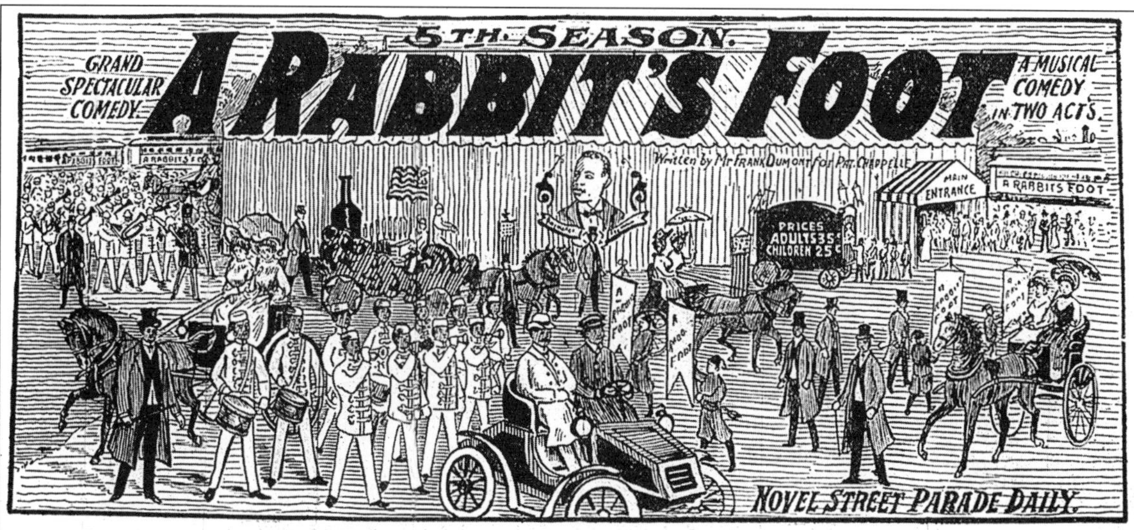

Indianapolis Freeman, January 28, 1905.

Atlanta during the summer of 1903, the mainstream daily *Atlanta Constitution* noted only black patrons, and said there "Came Near Being a Riot":

> Three or four thousand Negroes crowded around the door's of Bishop Turner's Tabernacle on Younge near Decatur street, last night about 7:30 o'clock to see a minstrel show. There was some delay about opening the doors and the crowd became impatient. When calls for the doors to open failed a lot of men and boys began to throw rocks. It looked as if a riot was pending and the police were called for . . . A wagon load of officers, all armed, hurried to the scene. The presence of the blue coats calmed the storm and the incipient riot was quelled. When the doors were finally opened the four thousand Negroes swarmed into the tabernacle like a human avalanche.[189]

The most bragged-about feature of the 1903 edition of the Rabbit's Foot Company was its street parade, "the talk of every city where we have appeared. The walking gents wear long silk alpaca haymarkets, white vests and straw beavers. The band is in regulation uniform, while the drum corps is in zouave uniforms. Our drum major is attired in red satin, and our banners are yellow and black satin."[190] Chappelle's "rubber-tire parade buggy" was also a highlight: "It is an original design and helps wonderfully to make the parade novel and up to date."

Freeman commentary in the spring of 1904 proclaimed the Rabbit's Foot's street parade "one of the finest street parades in the country for minstrels," and said it was "getting the glad hands of white and colored." A drum and bugle corps headed the parade, and "then comes Mr. Chappelle in his $2,000 automobile, manned by Hense Branson, the champion colored chauffeur of America, next comes 'Happy' Howe and D. Ireland Thomas in their Madison Square rubber tire tandem team, followed by five more teams containing two ladies each. We have ten walking gents attired in red raglans and silk hats and ten banner boys. Last but not least, the Rabbit Foot Brass Band of twenty pieces, making a parade of four squares."[191]

Prof. A. G. Jones, the new bandmaster for the season of 1903–1904, had ties to the Independent Brass Band of Natchez, Mississippi.[192] During the summer of 1903 Jones made "a big hit with his cornet solos . . . taking encores nightly, both on parade and in tent." Under his baton, the band played "Whitney Warner's latest publications, 'Lazarre Waltzes,' and also Fred Stone's latest ragtime success, 'Sue.'"[193] While showing at Bishop Turner's Tabernacle in Atlanta in the summer of 1904, Jones and leading lady Ivy A. Harris were married on the stage.

The orchestra leader for the season of 1903–1904 was Prof. E. B. Dudley. Other new names on the roster included Clifford Brooks "holding extreme end and getting his nightly singing 'Then I'd Be Satisfied,'" and the New Orleans–based team of Fred Bonnecaze and Joe Locust singing "Look into Your Baby's Eyes and Say Goo Goo."

Female performers included Pauline Crampton singing "Society"; Grace Jackson singing "Tantalizing Eyes"; "charming soubrette" Lizzie Roberts singing "Ding a Ling Ding" and "In the Good Old Summer Time"; Mrs. Grace Hoyt singing "The Jungle Queen"; and Pearl Wyatt singing "her favorite song, 'Lee a Nora Lee,'" and making "a big hit with her buck dancing." Laura Logan, late of Stowe's Log Cabin Company, joined in the summer of 1903. During the summer of 1904 she reportedly took encores singing "Since She Won That Thirty Thousand Prize," while Gertrude Brown, "the second Black Patti," late of P. G. Lowery's company, sang "Bobolink."[194]

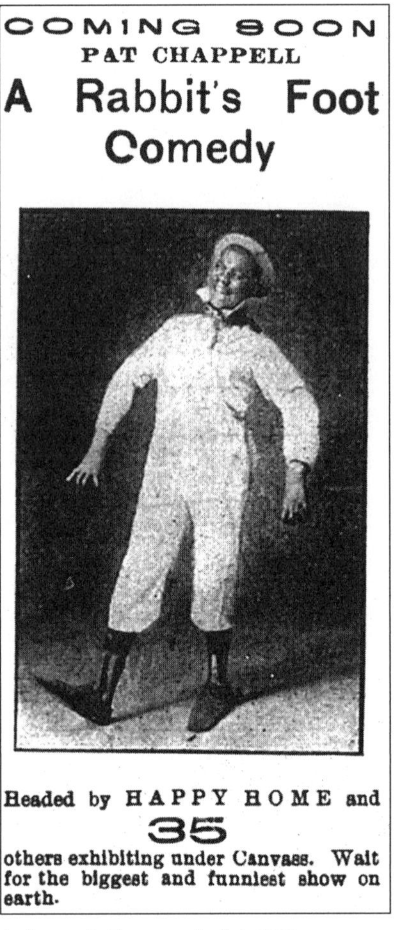

Indianapolis Freeman, April 4, 1903.

The most talked-about specialty act of the 1903–1904 season was "barrel contortionist" Charles H. Williams, who had "the people guessing how he goes in the barrel, makes a change in fire and comes out, and his chain work is wonderful."[195] Also coming in for recognition was Sam Cohen, "the greatest of all colored spielers."[196] In the fall of 1905 Cohen stepped into the role of "the fake Ebenezer" in the show's signature musical comedy production.

Star comedian Arthur "Happy" Howe was fast becoming a Rabbit's Foot institution. On return dates through Tennessee in the fall of 1903 he made a hit in his "original specialty, 'I'm Going Back to Alabama.'" His hit of 1904 was "My Queen from Zula Land." Except for a brief leave of absence in 1909, Happy Howe topped the Rabbit's Foot Company's roster of blackface comedians until 1914, when he jumped to Allen's Minstrels.

At Memphis in the fall of 1903, the Rabbit's Foot Company forsook its tent for Church's Auditorium on Beale Street, where they played three performances "to big business." At Columbus, Mississippi, on November 18, they "had the pleasure of meeting the Black Patti Troubadours." On November 25, after a two-night stand at Helena, Arkansas, they doubled back into Mississippi and played one-night stands at Clarksdale, Greenville, and Grenada. After veering over to Jackson and vicinity for a week or so, they returned to the Delta and played Natchez, Port Gibson, and Vicksburg. On January 21, 1904, they concluded their season at Green Cave, Florida, and went into their new winter headquarters at 1054 Church Street in Jacksonville.

For the season of 1904–1905, Chappelle expanded his East Coast bookings to include week-long stands at theaters in Washington, D.C., and Baltimore, Maryland. He claimed to have done nothing at all to solicit these dates; rather, "the popularity of the only Negro show with a plot caused the managers of the above named houses to offer us the dates." Seemingly on the defensive, Chappelle insisted *A Rabbit's Foot* was "not a plotless ramble, made up of threadbare jokes, songs and imperfect imitations of what has been aired to dryness by some other company. Spiced with catchy specialties, backed up by a band of eighteen pieces and an orchestra of intelligent musicians, the central idea of the play, as named in the title, is kept wholesomely in view throughout the three hours of entertainment."[197] In D.C. the show was said to have "held the town at a wonder the entire week."

Among the performers of 1904–1905 were Davis and Inman. Davis sang "Good Bye Eliza Jane," while Inman sang "Bedelia" and did some eccentric dancing. Also noted were D. Ireland Thomas and Joseph A. McMurray "in their musical act"; and the Prices, "hitting them hard in their new act, 'Carolina Volunteers.'" One of the season's most promising recruits was Charles "Cuba" Santana, a singing comedian who also played bass drum in the band. During his near three-year hitch with the Rabbit's Foot Company, Santana sang such popular fare as "On Your Way" and "Dis Ain't De Kind a Grub I Been Gittin' Down Home." At the end of the season of 1906–1907, it was reported that Santana left the Rabbit's Foot Company for the Florida Blossom Minstrels.

During the spring of 1904 Amos Gilliard, "the people's favorite trombone soloist," made a "tremendous hit daily playing the famous solo 'Eiffel Tower.'"[198] Later that fall Gilliard jumped to Rusco and Holland's Georgia Minstrels and was replaced by Pearl Moppin. In the wake of Gilliard's departure, the *Freeman* published the contents of a provocative letter that Rabbit's Foot clarinetist Lewis Williams had posted to Rusco and Holland's bandmaster in response to a recent job offer:

> Prof. Wm. Blue—Dear Sir: I . . . appreciate your valuable offer, but at present I must decline as I am under contract with Mr. Pat Chappelle, and I have no desire to give up my job for several reasons.

> First, I am a black man, and I am interested in anything a black man has, and will do all in my power to make it a success.
>
> Second, I have been with Mr. Chappelle over four years, and have always found him to be a perfect gentleman; he is always ready to help his people in any way . . .
>
> My third reason is that I was learned with this show . . . and I know that Messrs. Rusco and Holland would have never picked me up as Mr. Chappelle did and learn me, so I will frankly say that, if you were to offer me $20 per week, I would consider it an insult . . . I would never persuade a member of a colored man's show to join a show run by a white man, as you know the white man bought and sold our fore-parents, and I thank the Lord to-day that there are some young Negroes in the world they cannot buy. I am one of them that Messrs. Rusco and Holland can not buy.

The letter went on to attack Amos Gilliard, charging that he had not left the Rabbit's Foot Company of his own volition but had "acted bad until Mr. Chappelle was forced to put him off the train between stations." In closing, the letter stated:

> I trust, in the future, you will try to get other people from other places for your white bosses instead of trying to break up a colored show.
>
> We have quite a large show here—three cars, over sixty people, four horses, four rubber-tired buggies, automobile, two wagons, band of eighteen pieces, drum and bugle corps of six pieces, and we get the money for the colored people do not have to go up the side fire-escape or in back door and set in the gallery to see the show. They set where they pay for. [Signed] Lewis Williams, clarionet player.[199]

The *Freeman* of December 24, 1904, carried responses from both Amos Gilliard and Prof. Blue, implying that the letter had actually been ghostwritten by Pat Chappelle. Gilliard's remarks were pointed:

> While in Jacksonville, Fla., after leaving Chappelle's company, I received a letter signed in his own handwriting, stating that they are going to play New Orleans, and if I would join them again he would send ticket and give me back my horn he stole from me.
>
> I am now in the employment of Messrs. Rusco & Holland, who I have worked for before . . . The truth of the thing is I am in the profession as a business proposition, and not friendship altogether, and when I think I can better myself I work to that end. As I have been with both companies I preferred Rusco & Holland as the best, so I notified Mr. Chappelle weeks and weeks before hand. So, when he saw he could not keep me no longer, one night, while the train was on a run, he had his tool, San Tanna, the porter [i.e., performer Charles "Cuba" Santana], to call me about 2 o'clock in the morning, while everyone else was asleep, to have me come to his state room, and, not thinking, I went with only my trousers on, and while there Mr. Chappelle and his two brothers drew guns on me and said they were tired of my fooling, and I had to get off the train. I pleaded to them to let me go get my belongings and wait until I got to the next station but it was in vain, so I had to get off at the watering station. A brother stood on each end of the car with a gun, and as the train pulled out they threw my things, all except my horn, out the window to me . . . [Signed] Amos Gillard [*sic*], Trombonist Georgia Minstrel.

Meanwhile, the *Freeman* of December 3, 1904, informed that Gilliard's replacement with the Rabbit's Foot Company, Pearl Moppin, had been "attacked by crackers at Marion Ala.," but was "getting along nicely and will be able to work within a few days." One week later, at Warrenton, Georgia, the Rabbit's Foot Company's baggage car, "containing tents, seats, lights, etc.," was entirely consumed by fire. No injuries were reported, and the company was able to resume work after less than a week: "This is the quickest recovery on record, considering that the new tent had to come from Cincinnati, uniforms from Philadelphia and lights from New York . . . The railroad company made satisfactory settlement. We are now on route only a few days behind our original route."[200]

On January 30, 1905, the Rabbit's Foot Company slipped into winter quarters in Jacksonville. When they commenced touring again two months later, the band and orchestra were under Prof. J. C. Turner. Before the end of the season, the position fell to cornetist R. J. "Dickie" Anderson, "the boy from Yazoo, Miss."[201] The company's newest male comedian, Thomas Briggs, was also from Yazoo City. Briggs made "a big hit singing 'I've Seen Everybody But the President' one of his own compositions, set to music by our cornet player, John Anderson."[202] After the season of 1905–1906 Briggs may have decided to settle in Memphis, where he eventually became stage manager of the Royal Theater.[203] Meanwhile, his 1905 song hit was taken up by other members of the Rabbit's Foot Company. A note at the beginning of 1906 said, "Paul Carter, the bright star, singing and dancing comedian, joined us recently at Hot Springs, Ark . . . He is taking three to four encores nightly with his song, 'I've Seen Everybody but the President.'"[204] Later that summer Cuba Santana was commended for his version of the song.

New female performers for 1905–1906 included coon shouter Susie Beavers and Mrs. Lillian Rice, who was identified at first as a "charming soubrette," and later as "the prima donna, New York and southern favorite."[205] Also mentioned were John Rice, "boss canvasman," and Little Vida Rice, "an attraction in the parade."

As early as 1901, Pat Chappelle had posted an ad in the *Freeman* recruiting players for a challenge baseball team to tour the South in company with a brass band. During the season of 1905–1906, he mounted a team with the Rabbit's Foot Company. The starting lineup was almost entirely comprised of "ringers." Correspondence that fall declared, "Our baseball team has made one of the greatest records of any colored team on a diamond this season, playing 60 games and winning 53 up to September 25. They have played in ten states and claim the championship of the South and Southwest." There was a baseball team in connection with the Rabbit's Foot Company for at least the next fifteen years.

In the spring of 1906, Chappelle launched a second tented minstrel show, the Funny Folks Comedy Company, under the management of his brother, Mitchell Chappelle. To insure its success he alternated some of the biggest names on the Rabbit's Foot roster, including Happy Howe, Cuba Santana, and several of his best bandsmen. In the spring of 1907 Pat Chappelle advertised that he had "made over $50,000 in five years."[206] At the beginning of 1908, with both the Rabbit's Foot and Funny Folks companies prospering, a *Freeman* correspondent declared: "Mr. Chappelle has no equal when it comes to managing these kind of shows . . . he has proven to be the black P. T. Barnum, when it comes to the success of a Negro show."[207]

Chappelle considered himself a man of "commercial characteristics," as opposed to "the kind that debauches his life and expends his earnings on bohemian fads and fancies." He put his money into real estate, and it was noted in the fall of 1909 that, "His twenty-five modern structures in the various sections, both business and residential,

The Champion Base Ball Team of The Rabbit-Foot Company.

The above cut represents the Champion Base Ball team of the Rabbit-Foot Company, now touring the country under the management of Mr. Pat Chappelle. The team is playing ball and meeting all comers. The following is the roster: G. W. Rouland, Athens, Ga., George Washington, Goldsboro, N. C., Robert Prince, Bennettsville, S. C., pitchers and right field; James Jones, Goldsboro, N. C., L. Adams, Columbia, S. C., catchers; James Newton, Pittsburg, Pa., 1st base; Wood Adams, Goldsboro, N. C., 2nd base; Harry Martin, Pittsburg, Pa., 3rd base; Robert Gilkerson, Pittsburg, Pa., short-stop; Logan Littlejohn, Spartanburg, S. C., left field: Harry Leslie, Ashville, N. C., center field. The team has played thirty-two games and won twenty-eight, shutting out Hampton, Va., Sumter, S. C., and Chester, S. C. They desire games with all local clubs in every city in which the company appears. The comedy company, is as usual, a big succes. The company sends regards to professional friends.

Indianapolis Freeman, July 15, 1905.

of the city of Jacksonville, and the $7,000 apartment building now in course of erection, as well as a large volume of business through the Afro-American bank of his native city, are encouraging signs of race progress."[208]

When the Rabbit's Foot Company's season of 1906–1907 commenced, the band was "small" but "doing fine playing a star piece called 'Poor Jim.'" Clarinetist William Phillips came aboard in June 1906, marking his earliest known appearance in a minstrel band. He had not yet acquired the nickname "King."

The female contingent included leading lady Lulu Martin singing "Get a Man of Your Own,"

PAT CHAPPELLE, THE FAMOUS SHOWMAN.

The above is a correct likeness of Mr. Pat Chappelle, the famous showman, who is the originator, owner and manager of the "Rabbit's Foot" Company, which is now touring the country. This company carries over forty people, traveling in their own two private cars. It also carries its own teams and buggies for street parade and to move their tent and fixtures to and from the cars and the show lot. The show is now a success daily. Mr. Pat Chappelle has proven himself to be the P. T. Barnum showman of the Negro race. This season Mr. Chappelle has added a new feature to his company in the style of a professional base ball team, which plays the local club of any city that the company appears in, and during the ball game, in the day time, the 'Rabbit's Foot" great concert band gives a regular classical concert which makes the ball game a feature in every respect. The two clubs parade every day with the company, and, as a whole, Mr. Chappelle's business is a grand success everywhere it appears. As the show and ball team are both up-to date in every respect both are worthy of the great patronage that they receive. Be on a watchout for "Rabbit's Foot" as its five advance representatives will reach your city soon with William Moseley of Atlanta, Ga., as chief.

Indianapolis Freeman April 29, 1905.

"I'm Just Crazy about Him," and "Let Me See You Smile"; soubrette Gertrude Newman singing "Money Was Made for Coons to Spend"; and Susie Hendrix singing "My Hindoo Man." Lulu Martin was replaced that summer by Ida Gardner, "the Georgia nightingale," singing "Just a Little Bit of Your Love and Money" and "Making Eyes at My Man."

Joseph M. Means joined in the fall of 1906, singing "Hot Tamales" and presenting "his educated goat which does seventeen tricks." In addition to working the stage, Means and his goat were featured in the street parade. Another fall 1906 recruit, Prof. J. H. Campbell, magician, was said to leave the audience wondering when he "turns wine to water." Other performers of the season included Gracie Arnte and George McDaniels, aka "Son Payne."

Toward the end of 1906, Will and Gertrude Rainey joined the Rabbit's Foot Company, where they remained through the season of 1907–1908. Just prior to joining the Foots, they had been touring at the head of their own Alabama Fun Makers Company: "Mr. Rainey is making a hit with his 'old man' turn and 'Let Him Without Sin, Cast the First Stone,' while Mrs. Rainey is giving, 'I'll Be Back in a Minute, and I'll Do the Same for You.'"[209]

The Raineys had yet to adopt the stage names "Pa" and "Ma," and the related notion of Ma Rainey as "Mother of the Blues" was many years away. During their stint with the Rabbit's Foot Company, they were billed as "Black Face Song and Dance Comedians, Jubilee Singers [and] Cake Walkers." In spite of Ma Rainey's often cited late-1930s interview with John Work III, in which she recalled an influential 1902 encounter with what she came to realize was "blues" singing,[210] there is nothing in the existing documentation to suggest that she brought anything unique or prophetic to the Rabbit's Foot stage in 1906. In 1909 a correspondent from the Star Theater in Montgomery, Alabama, proclaimed, "Gertrude Rainey always brings down the house when she renders a late and up-to-date coon song."[211] A 1910 report from the Belmont Street Theater in Pensacola, Florida, referred to "Mrs. Gertrude Rainey, our coon shouter." Rabbit's Foot corre-

THE FREEMAN GALLERY

PAT CHAPPELLE.

Sole Owner of "A Rabbit's Foot" and "Funny Folks Comedy" Companies.

Who'd be afraid of the "kunjer" man,
I'd laugh right in his face,
And make him so all-fired mad,
He would lose his saintly grace:
If I just had a rabbit's foot,
Just like the one you've got,
I'd let him know he's not so warm
There are others just as hot.

—Garfield T. Haywood.

Indianapolis Freeman, August 11, 1906.

spondence of June 1, 1907, placed the Rainey team in context with "Arthur Happy Howe, that $5,000 comedian—the southern favorite; then comes Allen Moore, the human bed-bug. We also have with us this season the Raineys, the monologue and sketch artists. Then comes the Philadelphia nightingale, Miss Emma Goldie . . . [followed by] Miss Mary Mosly, the Floradora's teaser; then comes Joseph M. Means, better known as 'Rube, the Singing Comedian' [and] Florence Ivory, another one of our singing ladies."

A June 15, 1907, report chronicled the repertoire:

> Allen Moore, the human "Bed Bug," is singing "Mister Greenback," "All In Down and Out," and is making good. Gertrude Rainey is making a hit singing, "The Man in the Moon" and "Miss Jane." The team [Rainey and Rainey] is singing "I've Said My Last Farewell." Joseph Means, better known as "Rube" is singing one of his latest hits, entitled, "Fever's On." Miss Emma Goldie sings, "Why Can't a Girl Be a Soldier Man?" Miss Beatrice Lowe is singing, "Abraham Washington Jefferson Lee." Miss Mary Adams, "What You Going To Do When Your Clothes Wear Out."

A note in the summer of 1908 mentioned "Prof. Dick Anderson's famous concert band of twenty pieces, playing all of the highest grades of marches and overtures."[212] At Waycross, Georgia, on July 8, 1908, "the show was a big hit from start to finish":

> Happy Howe is funnier than ever in his two-act musical comedy . . . Tim Moore, who plays second edition opposite Happy Howe, is a screaming hit singing "These Dogs of Mine."
>
> Master Richard Edwards, the juvenile comedian, proved to the audience that he was the real thing.
>
> W. C. Steward took the house by storm, singing, "Who? Me? I Am Not the Man."
>
> I. A. Grant, baritone singer, is taking them to four encores nightly, singing "The Fairest Flower of All."
>
> Mrs. Beatrice Howe is singing . . . "The Meanest Man in Town."
>
> German White, our acrobatic comedian, is cleaning up singing "Miss Georgia."
>
> Daisy Williams singing "Just Help Yourself," pleases the audience.

ALABAMA JUBILEE SINGERS
BILLY RAINEY & GERTRUDE RAINEY
SKETCH ARTISTS.
Black Face, Song and Dance Comedians,
Jubilee Singers and Artists,
Cake Walkers.
Old Man's Specialty.
Enroute With A Rabbit's Foot Company.

Indianapolis Freeman, December 15, 1906.

May Adams, singing "San Antonio" with a heavy chorus, receives heavy applause.

Many other songs sung in the first act proved successful. The great Campello opened the olio with his magic act . . . The singing and dancing act entitled "Give Me Back My Eleven Dollars" was a scream. Smith and Stewart, singing and talking comedians, just mopped, opening their act in a peculiar way, not a word being said until Stewart, the comedian, wants to borrow two dollars, then fun and laughter begin. Smith feeds them with plenty of clever straight work.[213]

On August 13, 1908, the Rabbit's Foot Company played Shelby, North Carolina. After the show, "They stabled their horses and packed their tents and furnishings" and "then went to sleep in their special car":

About 8 o'clock, while all were still asleep, one of the horses kicked over a tank of gasoline, which ran down the car and into the cooking department, where it came into contact with a hot stove and exploded. The cook and six other laborers, who were sleeping in this department, were horribly burned, three of them possibly fatally. Two of the horses were burned to death, while another was taken from the car in a horrible condition. The car, which was recently built at a cost of about $10,000, and all the show furnishings were completely destroyed. The fire was so sudden that nothing could be saved.

The greater part of the members of the minstrel was sleeping in the front of the car and escaped without much difficulty, but many of them did not have time to get their clothes. The people of Shelby gave them such aid as they needed and Shelby physicians dressed those who were severely burned, some seven or eight in number, and they were sent to the Good Samaritan Hospital at Charlotte . . .

Isaiah Grant, a ballad singer from South Carolina, suffered severe burns on the face. His hands were also burned, as well as the upper portion of the body . . .

The car and some of its contents could have been saved if there had been a fire department company or even if they could have gotten water, as they had formed a very good bucket brigade, but could not get sufficient water to check the fire. The manager and owner, Mr. Pat Chappelle, did not get discouraged, but set to work writing telegrams, and in less than two hours he had an 80-foot round top on the way, which has already arrived, and called in the advance agents and started them to redating the paper, which will cause the show only to lose one week. Mr. Chappelle has four other cars and has ordered one of his new cars, which is now on the way to the show. While the loss will exceed $10,000, it will not stop "A Rabbit's Foot" Company . . . The car had $1,500 insurance on it.[214]

The show closed for the season on February 19, 1909, and laid over in Jacksonville for the next two months. Chappelle spent some of the interim time in Wilmington, Delaware, "personally looking after their palace car which is being built by the Pullman Company in Wilmington, as a Rabbit's Foot Company will carry two cars this season, and will have the finest sleeping car that will be used by any show company."[215]

On March 27, 1909, Chappelle published an open letter "of interest to managers":

> I suppose all managers of one and two-car shows know that the L. & N. Railroad will not move a small show in passenger service that carries tent and other fixtures, etc., and your car, and the I. C. Railroad compels you to pay a very high freight rate on tent, etc., and the Central Railroad of Georgia will not give you the regular two-cent rates, but compels you to pay the regular full rates, and will not move you on their local freight trains, which makes it impossible to arrive at your play dates in the daytime. All the railroads in the Southeastern Association will charge you a minimum of $25 for the movement of one car and $35 minimum when they move two cars for a company. I have investigated the whole affair, and by assistance of all other one and two-car shows I think we would be able to have the same reduced to a more reasonable rate, also have the L. & N. Railroad and the I. C. Railroad to haul a one and two-car show as they have been doing heretofore.
>
> Now, I have taken the matter up, and am in position . . . to have a few changes made . . . If this is of interest to you, write me at once and I will give you full particulars.
>
> Pat Chappelle, Mgr. and Owner, "A Rabbit's Foot" Comedy Co., Box 702, Jacksonville, Fla.

When the 1909 season commenced at Waycross, Georgia, the Rabbit's Foot Company's perennial star comedian was noticeably absent: "Happy A. Howe, the Southern favorite . . . has joined hands with Butler ["String Beans"] May, the teaser, at Montgomery, Ala., and will present a vaudeville act."[216] Willie Glenn took over the principal comedy role; John Henry Thomas assumed the role of "Parson Chickenweed."

At Talladega, Alabama, in June, Will Goff Kennedy, "one of the old original members," rejoined as stage manager. An uncharacteristic "special to the *Freeman*" later that summer stipulated that the Rabbit's Foot Company had given a "bad show" at Columbia, South Carolina, and that Chappelle was running in debt.[217] But three weeks later, "Business has at last struck the ascendancy and our show is much better and stronger in every respect than ever before. There have been several changes in personnel of company, also the show has been changed from start to finish. James Crosby, the elongated comedian, is one of the latest additions. Everybody knows 'Jim.' As a singing, talking and dancing comedian he stands pre-eminent."[218]

Happy Howe returned to the fold before the end of the year, when the *Freeman* correspondent noted: "Our trio of comedians, James Crosby, 'The Tall Talker'; 'Happy Arthur Howe,' the old-time darkey, and Will Goff Kennedy, the well-known up-to-the-minute entertainer, never fails to please . . . Bertha Thomas, Emma Goldie, Julia Jones and Mattie Parker are our soubrets. Our band, under the leadership of R. J. Anderson . . . wakes them up every day at noon . . . [Will] Goff Kennedy is successfully singing 'Come After Breakfast,' 'Transmag,' and 'The Christening.'"[219]

JAMES CROSBY

The Tall Talker and Light House of the Sea of Fun. Has made good for 30 years and never sang the Blues. He is a Comedian of merit who has sustained a well earned reputation. Now Principal Comedian and Stage Manager with the Greatest of all tented Minstrels. The owners of the company, J. C. O'Brien and Lew Arrinson, are figuring on holding him.

Indianapolis Freeman, April 28, 1917.

The season ended at Jacksonville on March 2, 1910. In June it was noted that Chappelle had been "somewhat indisposed" for the past several months, and had been "advised by his doctors to take a good long rest, of which he is now doing." He was still sick in August, when he assured that the new season's show was coming together "like clockwork." Chappelle went on to predict that "there will be a general show fight between the Negro shows this year, as all of them will have to come in the South to get any money." He complained that northern-based shows were getting preferential treatment in the theatrical papers, "But we are glad of one thing: that we Southern shows know how to put up a real fight, and are financially able to do so, regardless of the boost that is given the Northern shows."[220]

The new season finally got under way on September 12, 1910, at Valdosta, Georgia:

> Curtain rose at 8:30 on eighteen performers, and the costumes they wore were something gorgeous. They sang a medley of choruses until they were seated by the interlocutor, Mr. Joseph Means. The first song was by Mr. Edward Neeley, entitled, "I Didn't Ask, He Didn't Say—So I Don't Know." . . . The second song . . . was by Miss Julia Baynham, "Alexander." . . . The next song was by Mr. Zollie Ford, "Do Your Duty, Doctor." . . . "Cannibal Love" was the hit of our first part, sung by Mrs. Emma Skinner, our charming soubrette. Mr. Skinner sang "I Wish I Was In Heaven, Sitting Down." . . . Then came Mr. Hi Jerry Barnes, our leading comedian, singing "I Am That Hen Roost Inspector." . . . The curtain went down on the whole chorus of the first part singing "Good Luck, Mary." . . . Then came the olio . . . opened by Ford and Baynham with a clever singing, dancing and talking act . . . Then came the sensational novelty, the great Mack Allen, America's famous tight and slack wire artist . . . Then came the Woods Sister team—Isabelle Woods and Mamie Miller—in a clean little up-to-date sketch, entitled, "A Trip to Klondyke." . . . High Jerry Barnes came next in a stiff monologue, and cracked some very good jokes, which led him into his song, "Tennessee" . . . The Skinners, Emma and Verne, closed the olio, in a clever singing and talking sketch . . . Then came the last act, the "Hoodoo Man" . . . Prof. Irving Brown, orchestra leader, violinist and trombone soloist, sent the audience of fifteen hundred home well pleased with that famous march, "The Motor King."[221]

The 1908 pseudo-spiritual coon song publication, "I Wish I Was in Heaven, Sitting Down" was also performed by Leroy Knox with the Florida

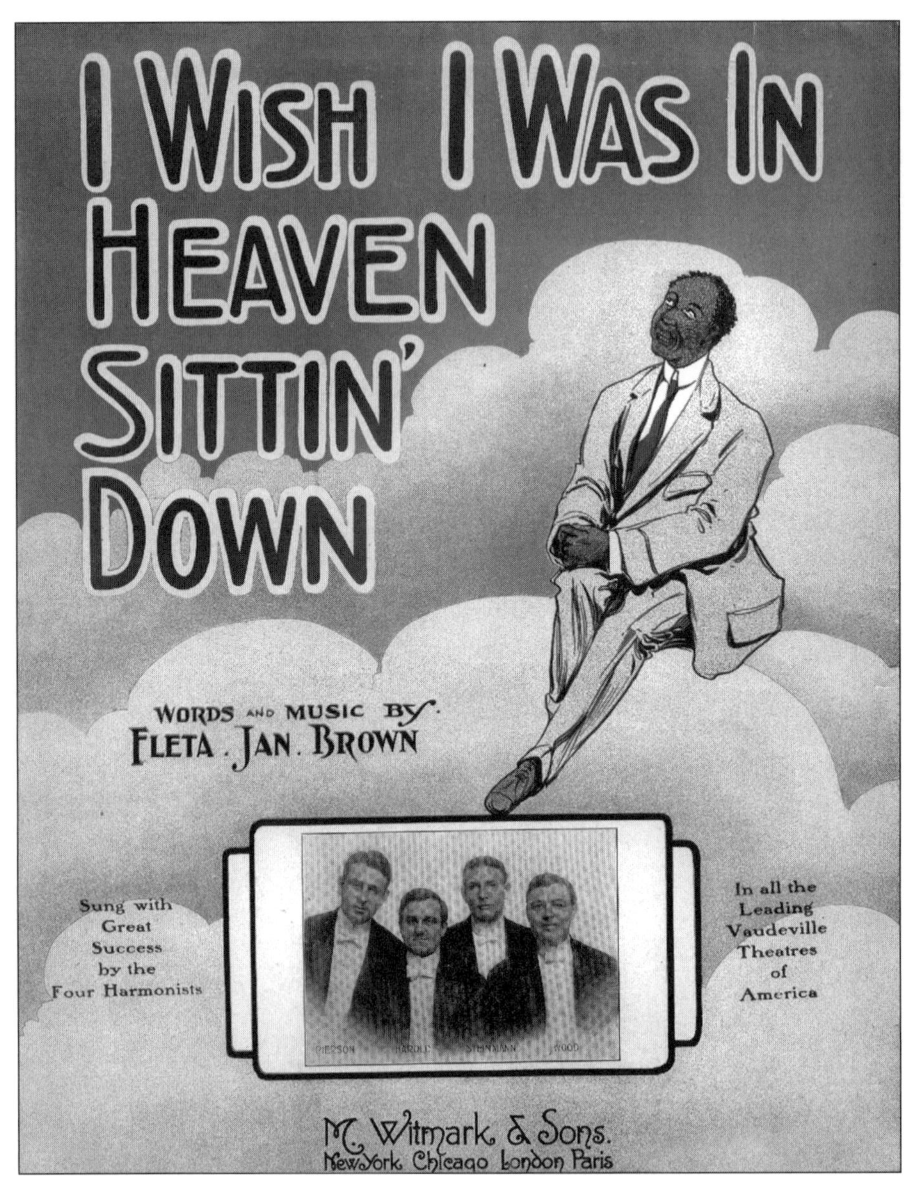

"I Wish I Was in Heaven Sittin' Down." (courtesy Thornton Hagert, Vernacular Music Research)

Blossom Minstrels in 1909, and by Richard Brown with Harrison Brothers' Minstrels in 1910. A song with the same title was recorded almost half a century later, in 1953, by the Sunset Travelers, a black gospel quartet of Memphis, Tennessee; also in 1953, another black gospel quartet, the Southern Stars of Richmond, Virginia, recorded "Tired of the Devil," which contains the phrase, "When I get to heaven, I'm gonna choose my seat and sit down." Perhaps a later generation of performers confused "I Wish I Was in Heaven Sitting Down" with a phrase from black folk tradition—"When I get to heaven, I'm gonna take my seat and sit down" (or "choose my seat and sit down"). Similarly, it is possible the composer of "I Wish I Was in Heaven Sitting Down" based its title on that same pre-existing expression.

"I Wish I Was in Heaven Sitting Down" seems to have gained special currency in Mississippi and Memphis. During the 1960s songs with that title were recorded by Mississippi Fred McDowell and by Memphis native Rev. Robert Wilkins.[222] All three late recorded versions have an amorphous, "made-up" quality, melodically related to the religious folk song "Nobody's Fault but Mine," and incorporating random verses from several well-known gospel songs and spirituals. The three recordings share no verses in common; however, the chorus is identical in all:

I wish I was in heaven sitting down,
I wish I was in heaven sitting down.
Oh angels, Lord, Lord, Lord,
I wish I was in heaven sitting down.

These late recordings retain nothing other than the title from the 1908 sheet music production, the chorus of which is:

I wish I was in Heav'n sittin' down,
With Old Saint Peter handin' me a crown;
I'd just do nothin' for eternity.
That's the place that listens good to me,
I wish I was in Heav'n sittin' down.[223]

The history of this song adduces the grab bag of floating phrases and couplets that Howard Odum registered in his research much earlier in the century. It may also reflect the influence of ragtime coon songs in tented minstrelsy on vernacular culture, especially in Memphis and Mississippi.[224]

Before the end of the season, the Rabbit's Foot band and orchestra came under the direction of Bose Gosey: "We call him the second Arthur Pryor." At Columbus, Georgia, in mid-September, Edward Neely and Beatrice Mitchell made a hit with their "'suicide' song." At Yazoo City, Mississippi, in October, under a new $800 tent, in front of 1,700 people, Ed Neely sang "the coon song entitled 'Ada, My Sweet Potatoe,'" and Beatrice Mitchell sang "That Mendelssohn Tune."[225]

At Meridian, Mississippi, Hi Jerry Barnes gave his "Hen Roost Inspector Man," and Zollie Ford sang "All Out and Down." At Bainbridge, Georgia, newcomer James London performed "his hoola boola dance." At Wigham, Georgia, "We had the misfortune to lose our beautiful $5,000 sleeping car, Chatawa, which was consumed by fire . . . The loss is felt deeply, not only by our manager, Mr. Chappelle, but by all the performers also, as a few lost everything they possessed."[226] This marked the fourth time since 1902 that a Rabbit's Foot Company car had been destroyed by fire. Three unexplained fires in the state of Georgia raise the specter of arson.

The Rabbit's Foot Show was still tucked in winter quarters on May 31, 1911, when Pat Chappelle and his wife set sail from New York City to London, ostensibly to witness the coronation jubilee and make a tour of the continent. In London Chappelle ran into Billy McClain, and admonished him to abandon his expatriate sojourn and return to the States to help direct the growing black southern theatrical movement: "if you will put your pride aside and go South where the talent is, I will guarantee that you will make more in twelve months than you will in six years where you are." However, as southern performer H. Franklin "Baby" Seals later inquired of McClain, in a letter posted from Birmingham, Alabama: "did Mr. Chappelle . . . tell you frankly and truly what you've got to go through to get this money?"[227]

Chappelle went on to claim, "I cleared twelve thousand dollars this past season, and only worked six months . . . I have an income that will keep me comfortably the balance of my days."[228] But Chappelle's balance of days was short. He and his wife returned to the States in July, and in August he aired this announcement: "A Rabbit's Foot Company will not go on the road this season, as formerly advertised, on account of my continued illness. My physician advised me that the strain would be too much for me; so all parties holding contracts will kindly consider them cancelled . . . And if life lasts and my health improves, I will be pleased to book all parties for my company for the season of 1912."[229] Chappelle retreated to the family home on the corner of Union and Johnson Streets in Tampa, where he died on October 21, 1911. His funeral cortege, headed by the Welcome Cornet Band, was said to have been viewed by thousands.

In the wake of Pat Chappelle's death, the Rabbit's Foot Company came into the possession of Fred Swift Wolcott, a white veteran manager of black minstrel shows. Wolcott was born in Onondaga, Michigan, on May 2, 1882.[230] In the spring of 1910, Wolcott's Fun Factory was playing weeklong stands in the Carolinas with twelve stage performers, a four-piece orchestra and "the most convenient canvas theater in existence, seating 500 people, equally divided for the white and colored population." The stage manager and orchestra director was Charlie Burems. The performers included Miss Willar King singing "My Little Jungle Babe"; Harry and Louise Gadston "with their acrobatic and contortion melee"; Gussie Drew, "the big-headed boy from that doggone town," singing "You'll Be Sorry Just Too Late"; and Dan Reeves "making good in his rough and tumble song and dance entitled 'I'm Glad I'm Free.'"[231]

In the fall of 1912 Wolcott notified that "The Rabbits Foot Musical Comedy Company" was "back on wheels again":

> The show numbers forty-five persons, including ten canvasmen. On the stage are twenty-nine persons, all star performers. The band consists of sixteen good musicians. Here is the personnel: F. S. Walcott, owner and manager; Ed (Dad) Howard, stage manager; George [A.] Williams, band leader; Joseph M. Means, steward. On the stage: John Means, T. H. Dumars, Joe Doukes, Billy Freeman, Carter Lockheart, Mose Watkins. Extremes, Frank Tansel and Original Happy Howe. Semi Circle, Ed (Dad) Howard, Interlocutor; Frank Dukes, Lillian Lockheart, Joseph M. Means, Lillian Dukes, Robert Reeves, Frank Means, Frank Reed, Carrie Collum, Nettie Howard. Olio, Billy Freeman, Mack Allen, Dokes and Dokes, Means, Tansel and Collum. The last act is entitled 'A Judge for a Day.'"[232]

On October 24, 1912, F. S. Wolcott's Rabbit Foot Comedy Company opened at Columbia, South Carolina:

> Billy Freeman, a clever comedian, is opening the show, singing "Another Rag." Miss Lillian Dokes is singing "Georgia Rose." Mr. John Means, comedian, is singing "Buckwheat Cakes." Mr. Jap Reed is featuring "Way Down South." . . . Mrs. Lillian Lockhart is singing "Oh, Mr. Dream Man." Mr. Joe Dokes, comedian, is singing "Just For You, Babe." Dad Howard, our stage manager and interlocutor, is featuring "Carry Mary Harry." Mr. Mose B. Watkins, comedian, is singing "Beautiful Doll, Goodbye." . . . Mr. Frank Tansel is getting his nightly, singing "When I Woke Up This Morning, She Was Gone." Mr. Happy Howe is closing

PAT CHAPPELLE DEAD.

Well-Known Theatrical Manager and Proprietor Loved by All Who Knew Him—Embraced the Hope—Touching Services at Funeral.

TAMPA, Fla.—All that is mortal of Patrick Henry Chappelle, who died at his home, on the corner of Union and Johnson streets, on October 21, 1911, was borne by loving hands to Memorial cemetery Sunday, October 29, and laid to final rest by the side of his mother, who preceded hi mto the grave just a few years ago.

The funeral services were held in the Bethel Baptist church, and were attended by a concourse of people that literally filled all space in the aisles and every approach of that spacious auditorium. The funeral party, composed largely of members and friends of the family, and escorted by about five hundred Free Masons, was headed by the Welcome Cornet band. Many carriages in which were seated the family and friends, ministers and the honorary and acting pallbearers, and others, made up this procession as it moved through the streets viewed by thousands of people.

This was not the funeral of a stranger nor was it the funeral of one who was little known. In city and state and all over the South, the name of Pat. Chappelle was familiar.

The services at the church were imposing and altogether impressive. The Rev. J. E. Ford, D. D., pastor of Bethel, was assisted in the services by Revs. James Johnson, William Nobles, Grand Master J. H. Dickerson, D. M. Baxter, D. D., and J. M. Deas. The choir rendered a service that was a distinctive feature of the occasion.

The story of this life and labors of this young man, who had just reached his forties, was fittingly told by Dr. Ford, who afterwards delivered a discourse that was peculiarly touching. His experiences at the bedside of the deceased, whose spiritual adviser he was formed a marked section in this discourse, ending in the christian's climax, the confession of Mr. Chappelle. Nor did Dr. Ford fail to admonish all in the big audience to beware of delay in the preparation for death.

Equally interesting and impressive were te words of Rev. James Johnson, who had in his life married and buried more than half of the Chappelles, including the father and mother. His long standing and intimate acquaintance with the family fortified him with facts and incidents that rendered his discourse necessarily interesting. As was true of the first speaker, so did the Rev. Mr. Johnson speak with galling frankness. He to had been the spiritual adviser of the deceased.

The great effort he found necessary to have Mr. Chappelle think seriously on matters religious gave a thrill to all who listened. But out of this hopelessness came the declaration of the fact that in his case again was the efficacy of the power to save any and all was made. Mr .Chappelle embraced his Saviour and died in a living faith.

The Rev. Dr. Baxter spoke briefly along the lines of those who preceded him, and Grand Master Dickerson made remarks emphasizing the fact that life is uncertain and short.

Many passed by and took their last look at the face of him whom they knew so well. The solemn burial service by the Masons was led by E. H. Williams, a Mason of high degree, assisted by Mr. Sherman Earle and W. A. Moore.

The long procession to the cemetery was begun, and all went well, reaching there after dark. The burial service by the Masons was there finished and the body interred. The handsome casket was of royal purple plush. The grave was vaulted and made secure by a massive stone slab.

Prof. E. W. Jackson, the photographer, made a picture of the cortege as it left the residence and as it entered and came from the church, and also made a picture of the casket in the house.

Tus as passed one of Jacksonville's young men who had won fame in his line of business, and had amassed a fortune of which any man would be proud.

In the discourses of the ministers the marked devotion of the faithful wife and the devotion of that mother who showed her love only as a mother can, were spoken of with all praise.. Mr. Chappelle's illness became apparent about one year before his death. What he did to reclaim his health, his friends know. The sorrowing wife, brothers and sisters all have the deepest sympathies of friends from all sides.

The interrment was by Geter and Baker, who rendered excellent and ample service.

Indianapolis Freeman, November 25, 1911.

Wolcott's Fun Factory, under the generic banner of "Old Plantation" minstrelsy. Fred Wolcott is positioned next to the "box office," hand on hip. His wife Catheryn Hoisel Wolcott is standing behind the box office. (courtesy Hilda Wolcott Hutchings. Thanks to Mississippi Cultural Crossroads)

the first part, singing "I Like Music With My Meals." The curtain drops with the entire company singing "In The Good Old U.S.A." The olio opens with Billy Freeman, a clever monologuist; then comes the team of Lockhart and Lockhart, Carter and Lillian, and they are a scream. Mr. Joe Means follows with a chair balancing act . . . Then comes the team of Tansel and Collins, high class singers and dancers . . . Mack Allen, America's foremost slack wire artist [is] performing all new and death defying feats. Dokes and Dokes close the olio with a singing and talking act . . . The show closes with a big act, entitled "The Coon Town High Flyers," a big musical comedy, by the entire company.[233]

In Florida a few weeks later, Estelle Williams was "making good with her wooden shoe dance"; and Carter and Lillian Lockhart were "screaming them with their line of talk and their closing song, 'Going Around the Mountain.'" Over the next several years, Lillian Lockhart proved to be an astute follower of late-breaking trends in black popular music. During the summer of 1914 she made a hit with "Floating Down the Chesapeake Bay." In the Mississippi Delta during the fall of 1915, she sang "The Hesitation Blues."

SIXTY
Performers and Musicians
WANTED
For the Original
Pat Chappelle Rabbit Foot Co.
Now Owned and Managed by
F. S. WOLCOTT
This Company will Open for Rehearsal at
Columbia, S. C., Oct. 15.
WANT

A No. 1 Band Leader, who can furnish at least a sixteen or twenty piece band; I have the Uniforms. Want Stage Manager and Producer. Want eight good looking Chorus Girls and one Lady Bugler. Want to hear from all kinds of Novelty Acts; nothing too good for this company. Will assure you of good treatment and your money every week. Will travel in two of our own private Pullman cars, making one night stands, with the best framed outfit on the road.

I Furnish All Costumes and Uniforms!

free of charge, and pay all after joining. State all in first letter, and salary. Address all mail to

F. S. WOLCOTT
Rabbit Foot Company
Columbia, S. C. P. O. Box 132

Indianapolis Freeman, October 5, 1912.

Wolcott announced at the end of 1912 that he was taking his mail at Palatka, Florida. He began to advertise the Rabbit's Foot Company in terms that Pat Chappelle seems to have consciously avoided: as a "minstrel show."

When Wolcott's Rabbit's Foot Minstrels played Orlando, Florida, on December 23, 1912, newcomer T. H. Dumas opened the show singing "I Am Satisfied." Joseph M. Means, "the man with the iron jaws," handled "five chairs with his teeth as easily as most people could with their hands." The show closed with "'Lizie Jane Spillman's Wedding,' an act that brings back memories of the old time weddings."[234]

In the spring of 1913, T. H. Dumas was still singing "Satisfied"; Happy Howe, "the star comedian with everlasting fame," was "screaming them with his song, 'In de Morning'"; and Charles "Mush Mouth" Miller was singing "Soft Black."[235] Later that summer Carter Lockhart came out with "his own song, 'Soft Black'"; and when Archie Blue started singing "Soft Black" in the spring of 1914, he identified it as *his* own song. Others on the 1913 roster included "Marvelous LaVola," the slack wire king, and Walter Lee, "better known as 'Sanks,' the old man with the doctor case in his hand . . . dishing out some medicine for the boys. Go on Mr. Lee."[236]

At the beginning of 1913, the band was augmented by Ralph Redmond, trombone; Frank Hopkins, alto; Attler Cox, cornet, and Joe White, the sensational snare drummer. "We also had two performers to join. They are Ida Cox, wife of Estler [*sic*] Cox, and Leroy White, who is well known in the business."[237] Future blues recording star Ida Cox was not mentioned again in correspondence from the Foots. In the fall of 1914 she was playing through Georgia with the Cracker Jack Comedy Company.[238]

The first person to serve as bandmaster during the Wolcott era was Prof. George A. Williams, a Detroit musician who conducted such "heavy numbers" as "Il Trovatore" and "Bohemian Girl." He also staged the minstrel first part, "In Dear Old Dixieland." Under Prof. Williams' watch, the company was lauded as a "school for musicians."[239] Williams was also a composer. A note in the summer of 1913 mentioned his "late composition in the form of a rag, which was named by Mr. Redmond as the 'Trombone Puzzle.'"[240]

Trombonist Ralph Redmond was the band's "coming Sampson." In February 1913, shortly after he joined, the *Freeman* correspondent noted, "The band is the big attraction, rendering 'Il Travatore' [*sic*] and other selections, featuring Mr. Ralph Redmond's 150 feet from the band accompaniment, with his artistic grace style tone and embellishment."[241] Redmond also played "Eiffel Tower" in the olio. Prof. Williams predicted that "with his qualified artistic ability, in daily combat with professional encounter," Redmond was "pushing all trombonists out of the ring and will soon be far in the lead as a soloist and business musician, and his own ideas on technic are wonderfully pleasing."[242]

Rounding out the trombone section were Billy Moore and Freddie Pratt. This triple-threat trombone section was also a threat on the baseball field. When the company emerged from the coalfields of West Virginia at the end of August 1913, the *Freeman* correspondent noted, "Our baseball team is playing nice ball, having lost one game and won seven. The Williamson Red Stockings won from us by a score of 7 to 5. The features of the game were the pitching of Redmond and the batting of Moore and Pratt."

Fellow bandsman Lonnie Townsend, "a cornet player of exceptional ability," died on the road that season:

> His home was at Orangeburg, S. C., where he has a host of relatives and friends. He became ill with typhoid fever on May 30, 1913, and was sent to the hospital at Charlestown, W. Va., by the members of the company on June 4th. His people located him but his condition would not allow him to be taken home. He was taken care of financially by members of the company. The benefits given for him amounted to about $350 during his illness . . . He was only on the road a few years. Ralph Redmond would like to hear from his people at once.[243]

The Foots' new snare drummer, Joe White, was born in Vicksburg, Mississippi, in 1880, and made his home in Jackson.[244] He had been traveling the minstrel show routes at least since 1909. Correspondence in the spring of 1913 referred to him as "the renowned trap drummer and sensational whirlwind eccentric street hammer head rimer [*sic*]," and disclosed that he was "using a lovely looking silver duplex drum, costing $75. Joe is featuring 'Oh, You Drummer,' which casts great reflections on Manzie Campbell."[245]

Manzie Campbell had been the drummers' drummer of African American minstrelsy for more than a decade. With Rusco and Holland's Minstrels in 1903, he drew this endorsement: "In street parades, when Manzie Campbell . . . starts one of those long rolls on the snare drum and ends in rag-time to start a march, he never fails to have a crowd around him."[246] Before the end of 1913, Joe White was pronounced "the king of the Southland, since Manzie Campbell has stayed in Chicago so long." Alliterating over his "masterly manipulations," one *Freeman* correspondent dubbed White "the Mississippi fiend."[247] White's reputation only grew over what became an incredibly long tenure with the Foots.

At Fitzgerald, Georgia, in November 1913, Wolcott's Rabbit's Foot Minstrels played day and date with the Kit Carson Wild West Show and did turn-away business. The band, under the direction of Capt. R. J. "Dickie" Anderson, was "still rendering such selections as 'Sky Pilot,' 'Bohemian Girl' and 'Il Trovatore.'"[248] At Thomasville, Georgia, in February 1914, they "packed the house, notwithstanding that the 'Silas Green Co.' showed there two days ahead of us."

Additions to the roster of singers in 1914 included balladeer and interlocutor Frank "Jap" Reed; baritone soloist Jack Thompson, singing "Till the Sands of the Desert Grow Cold"; and Mamie Johnson, singing "On the Trail of the Lonesome Pine" and "Curse of an Aching Heart."[249] A note that fall advised: "Miss Carrie White is singing 'Get Out and Get Under,' and she never fails to get hers, while Miss Brown is scoring nightly with 'All Aboard for Dixie.' Then comes our leading lady, Miss Lillian Elridge [*sic*], singing Handy's latest epoch, 'The St. Louis Blues,' which sets 'em wild."[250]

After one full year under Wolcott, star comedian Happy Howe jumped to A. G. Allen's Minstrels. Rising up to take Howe's place, T. H. Dumas "brought the bacon home when he sang 'I'm Satisfied.'"[251] Other leading comedians of 1914 included Archie Blue, Rich Brown, Bennie Sparrow, Stump Nichols, and Thirston Briggs. The *Freeman* correspondent listed them under the ancient rubric, "monarchs of burnt cork." A note that summer advised: "Thirston Briggs is some dancer and Bennie Sparrow don't fail to get his when he sings, 'I Love Her, Oh, Oh, Oh.'"[252]

Another noteworthy performer of 1914 was Robert Everleigh, the "Jelly Roll Kid." Correspondence from Kentucky early that summer informed that he was "singing 'Ich Gebibble' and is a real coonologist."[253] That fall he appeared in the olio as a "challenge buck and wing dancer in eight minutes of footology." He eventually turned up on the band roster as a clarinetist, and by 1917, "Master Robert Everleigh, formerly the Rabbit Foot Mascot," was "playing clarinet very creditably in Prof. Veal's famous band."[254]

In West Virginia during the summer of 1914, comedian and female impersonator Leroy Knox jumped to the Foots from the Silas Green Company, and took "two and three encores nightly singing 'Balling the Jack.'"[255] In Mississippi that fall, the show did "big business" at Jackson, Meridian, Clarksdale, and Greenwood. At Meridian, "the home of Miss Mary Lee Brown, our clever soubrette, we were royally entertained after the show" at a "tango ball, given in our honor, where the hesitation, one-step and tango was featured."[256]

Specialty acts of 1914 included the acrobatic Watts Brothers, Joe and Lew, and DeWayman Niles, "the human corkscrew," who "never fails to scream the audience, especially when he makes that Japanese twist. His ballad [*sic*] dance is a correct imitation of 'Pavlova,' the great Russian toe dancer."[257] At Greenville, Mississippi, that fall, Niles went through a series of contortions in "an orange-colored suit of tights, adorned with iridescent spangles and fiery brilliant rhinestones," and then returned to execute "a classy ballet dance . . . made up as a female."[258]

The big news of 1914 was that the Rabbit Foot band had become a "gold band." A note in the fall of 1913 had assured that, "The boys' gold instruments are coming in fast. Walter Lee received his gold Besson cornet last week . . . Joe White, our snare drummer received his Gold drum and sends regards to all the drummers." In January 1914 manager Wolcott wired the *Freeman*: "We have received our last two gold instruments, a double B B bass [*sic*] for Mr. Wm. Tuba Thomas and baritone for Wm. Green, which completes our gold band of fifteen pieces."

Contortionist DeWayman Niles. *Indianapolis Freeman*, January 6, 1917.

At Fort Pierce, Florida, on a Sunday morning in February 1914, the Foots crossed paths with the Florida Blossom Minstrels, "and oh, my, such a time, shaking hands and 'chewing the rag.' The citizens of Ft. Pierce had the pleasure of hearing some real music in the afternoon when both bands gave an open air concert . . . and oh, such a glittering of silver and gold."[259]

Trombonist Freddie Pratt became the show's official *Freeman* correspondent. In March 1914 he posted this notice: "Our 'Gold Band' never fails to get theirs, and is the feature of our noonday parade. When it comes to real music, we can well boast that we don't have to play the so-called 'Blues' as we are far above that standard of music."[260]

In addition to playing in the band and handling the *Freeman* correspondence, Pratt worked the stage as a "silver tongued tenor," discoursing such popular titles as "It's a Long Way to Tipperary," "Last Night Was the End of the World" and "River Shannon." He wrote from Greenwood, Mississippi, in the spring of 1914 to assure that, "The 'Gold Band' continues to feature 'William Tell,' 'Poet and Peasant,' 'Hunter and Hermit,' 'Irish,' 'Il Trovatore' and several others and the boys under Professor Anderson are rehearsing daily." After the show the band was entertained by Greenwood's Big Six Orchestra, and when the Foots hit Greenwood again that fall the Big Six entertained them again.

Shortly after their first Greenwood engagement, the Rabbit Foot Minstrels "Sundayed at Memphis," and "enjoyed a rare treat in the afternoon, when we all assembled down on the levee to witness an open air concert by the Handey & Bynum Orchestra." Their next show stop was just across the Mississippi River at Newport, Arkansas. Coburn's Greater Minstrels were also booked in Newport that night, but "after the 'Gold Band' had rendered the concert selections, and closing with Beale Ave's opera, 'Jogo Blues,' it was a settled fact that the tent would be packed."[261]

At show stops in Helena, Pine Bluff, Little Rock, and Hot Springs during the last week of April 1914, the Rabbit Foot orchestra made a hit with Handy's "Jogo Blues," while the Gold Band rendered "Poet and Peasant" and "William Tell." In Texas shortly thereafter, leadership of the Gold Band passed from Dickie Anderson to Ralph S. Redmond, with Joe White "still busting drum

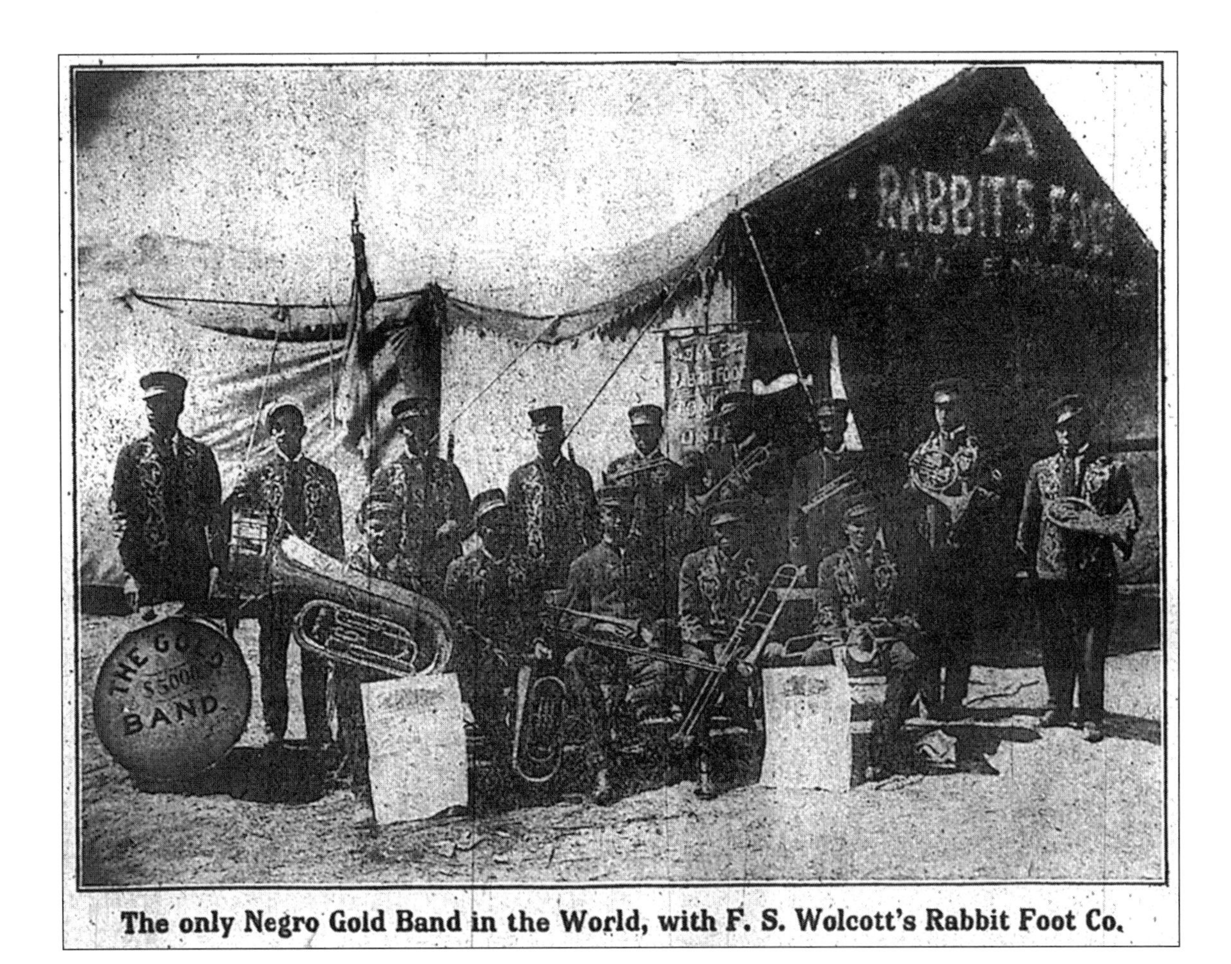

The only Negro Gold Band in the World, with F. S. Wolcott's Rabbit Foot Co.

Indianapolis Freeman, April 11, 1914.

heads." At Dallas, they "showed to a large crowd, and 'Dem Jogo Blues' set them wild."[262]

Moving into Oklahoma for the first time since the founding of the company, the Foots were forced to cancel a scheduled stop at Muskogee due to heavy rains, but they "did good business" in Tulsa the following night: "Our Gold Band was the feature of the parade, rendering such selections as 'Napoleon's Last Charge,' 'Iris,' 'William Tell' and closing with 'Memphis Blues.'"[263] When they launched their street parade at Springfield, Missouri, on a Monday afternoon in May 1914, all "the banks closed to listen to the different Andantes and Allegrettas and other movements of that beautiful selection, 'Poet and Peasant,' peeling forth from the different gold instruments of our $5,000 band, and by special request we played the 'Dallas Blues' which set 'em wild. A bystander remarked 'Dey sho do punish dem blues.'"[264]

At Bluefield, West Virginia, in July, one of the bandsmen quipped that the band was handling "an extensive rep. of opera music, also mixing in the popular stuff in such a way as to make the public like it. We can also throw away these

JOE WHITE

as he appears daily, featuring "Oh, You Drummer," on his Duplex Gold Drum, with Wolcott's Rabbit Foot Gold Band. Joe has been with this show nearly two years, and was one of the first to start the Gold Band. Regards to all friends.

Indianapolis Freeman, June 6, 1914.

gold instruments and make good with brass ones." Later that summer Ralph S. Redmond took sick, and Enoch W. Blake moved to the head of the Gold Band. From Helena, Arkansas, in November, Freddie Pratt reported, "Our superb Gold Band and Orchestra under Prof. E. B. Blake is still featuring the latest publications . . . Norman Mason, our brilliant cornet player is still featuring the high ones . . . Billy Moore, trombone player, late of the Florida Blossoms, is again with us . . . Joe White sends regards to all friends and says 'He still keeps the stick in the air.'"[265]

In a 1960 interview, Norman Mason stated that he was born in 1895 at Nassau, the Bahamas, and had started playing trumpet by age ten. In 1913 he left Nassau for Miami, Florida, and, "While I was in Miami, a fellow on a show, the Rabbit's Foot Show, heard me play trumpet, and liked the way I played so well, that he asked me to go out with the band. I traveled on the show . . . for about four years, playing first trumpet, the first couple years, and about the third or fourth year, I took the band over. And, after the War started, I got tired of traveling, and I moved to Jackson, Mississippi."[266] Gravitating from trumpet to saxophone, Mason recorded in 1924 as a member of Fate Marable's Society Syncopators.

Cornetist George Mitchell, born in Louisville, Kentucky, in 1899, recalled having gone out with the Rabbit Foot Minstrels at age seventeen, and he remembered Norman Mason as a "very good" player. Mitchell stayed on with the Foots for a year or so before returning to Louisville.[267] In 1920 he moved to Chicago, and he went on to record prolifically, including sessions with Jelly Roll Morton's Red Hot Peppers and Johnny Dodds's Black Bottom Stompers.[268]

In the spring of 1915 the position of bandmaster fell to clarinetist Marcus Veal Chaney, who had just severed his relationship with A. G. Allen's Minstrels. Shortly after Chaney came in, Freddie Pratt left for a "short vacation and much needed rest at his home, 411 Fayetteville street, Denham [*sic*, Durham], N. C." Pratt did not return. The new *Freeman* correspondent, Joe Watts, assured, "Our band still under the leadership of Marcus Veal Chaney, is giving the music loving public a treat by rendering a program from classics to rags."[269]

At Morehead City, North Carolina, on May 28, 1915, "members of the company had the honor and the pleasure of making the maiden trip on that beautiful 'Yacht Hazel.' Our parade went aboard and enjoyed a pleasant ride over to Beaufort, and after serenading the nobility of that beautiful resort, with an excellent musical program, then returning to our car, only to find the fact that Mr. and Mrs. Wolcott had planned for a fishing trip, and lots of the members went along with them."[270]

During the summer of 1915, Mrs. T. H. Dumas came out "singing those 'St. Louis Blues,'" and was pronounced "some shouter."[271] Archie Blue and Frank "Jap" Reed both closed with the Foots that summer, and Charles Rue came over from Allen's Minstrels to replace Reed as interlocutor: "Mr. LaRue [*sic*] will also take up where Archie Blue left off on the bass drum. Now Joe White is with the one he first started with, and say, but that drum section is something awful."[272]

The show's continued success was underscored in a note from ventriloquist Verner Massey: "Once you unite with the Rabbit Foot you get that gold fever . . . Those that haven't got the gold hanging around them in coins or jewels have their skin belt filled with greenbacks."[273] At Greenwood, Mississippi, that fall, they drew an uncharacteristically critical review from a local reporter: "The female section of the company is weak. It would be better if they had more women."[274]

At Christmas time the Foots took a three-week vacation in Jackson, Mississippi. Rather than dropping into Florida for the rest of the winter, they headed "far down among the Louisiana sugar cane fields" and blazed a trail westward into Texas. At Galveston on March 6, 1916, they "ran into the old reliable Richards and Pringle's Georgia Minstrels . . . We attended their show in a body . . . and on their departure from the city the whole Rabbit Foot Company bid them God speed." In the wake of that happy meeting, Richards and Pringle's trombone and violin player Albert Fredrick came over to the Foots, "thus strengthening our band and augmenting the number to thirteen members." Five weeks later, however, Frederick closed at Jacksonville, Texas, and went to work at the Park Theater in Dallas.

One notable acquisition of 1916 was on-site manager George W. Quine, who had been associated with A. G. Allen's Minstrels since their inception in 1899.[275] The season's minstrel first part featured six end men—T. H. Dumas, Robert Everleigh, and Park Wade, bones; and Richard Brown, Otto Bradley and J. T. Hicks, tambos—and two women, Lillian Lockhart and Mary Lee Brown, "our favorite soubrette." Mary Lee Brown sang "All Aboard for Dixie," while Lillian Lockhart performed an "original act" with T. H. Dumas titled "Sing Me the Blues, or I Will Leave." "Miss Lockhart is exceptionally clever in this line. She is featuring W. C. Handy's 'St. Louis Blues,' and it is a scream."[276] In the afterpiece, Dumas was "the talk of the day in his grotesque make-up as sweet papa 'skeeter' bad man, the rejected suitor of Eliza Jane Splivens"; while newcomer Park "Butts" Wade "caused no end of merriment . . . as 'Dusenberry' the nervous policeman."[277]

Multi-instrumentalist Frank Perryman joined on February 15, 1916, at Brookland, Texas. A report in April said he was "using five different instruments, playing all the way from classics down to the blues." Back in Texas at the end of the year, Perryman reportedly went big in his home town of Beaumont, "receiving much credit with his musical act and when he closes his act with his own original blues on the trombone, it's peaches."[278]

Lyric tenor Isaac Williams appeared with the Foots that spring, singing "You Are the Dawn of a Perfect Day" and dancing in a team act with Robert Everleigh.[279] Cornetist George Jefferson also scored as a vocalist, singing "Let Byegones Be Byegones" as a solo and "When I Leave the World Behind" with assistance from Mary Lee Brown and Lillian Lockhart.[280] In Arkansas and Mississippi that fall, Mary Lee Brown sang "Don't Leave Me Daddy;" Archie Blue returned to sing "Pray for the Lights to Go Out;" and T. H. Dumas sang "I Ain't Got Nobody." Jim Wise came out of retirement to front the concert band as its featured vocalist, and to produce a musical farce-comedy titled "The Pullman Porters."[281]

Back in Florida the Foots greeted the New Year in Orlando. At Deland, members of the company were treated to an "old fashioned midnight supper." While dropping through the southern reaches of the state in January 1917, Jim Wise organized a fishing club, and W. H. White "formed a domino club, consisting of eight members, which will play a series of 200 games, and the four losers are to buy the four winners a pair of Edwin Clapp shoes each."[282]

In February they reached Key West, where they were joined by Al and Luella Wells, the well-known trapeze artists, late of Tolliver's Smart Set. Al Wells immediately took over as manager of the Rabbit Foot Baseball Club and fielded a "cracker-jack" team, made up entirely of performers and musicians. He also took over the company's *Freeman* correspondence, and for the next four months he primarily talked sports: "The Rabbit Foot baseball club challenge all comers in semi-pro ball." "We certainly would like to play day and date with some of these shows that think they have a ball team." While playing in the coal mining belt around Birmingham, Alabama, that summer, Wells advertised: "We have room for a few more ball players who can double band and stage."

Correspondence from North Carolina in the spring of 1917 informed that:

> Our stage manager, George Ross, is on the job and everything is running smoothly.
>
> Our fun producers, who are assisted by an A-1 interlocutor, Al Boyd, always clean up, and why not? Such end men as Wm. Earle, T. H. Dumas, Archie C. Blue, Richard Brown, Otto Bradley and John Nick [sic] can always produce the goods.
>
> The team of Dumas and Dumas never fail to make a hit, as they put their songs and jokes over in red hot style.
>
> Miss Mamie Johnson, who has a very sweet soprano voice, is making a hit singing "You Never Can Tell." Then comes the musical wizzard [*sic*], Frank Perryman, the man who plays many instruments.
>
> The comedy acrobatic act, consisting of Luella Wells, Wm. Earl, Evans Fuller and Al Wells always get theirs.
>
> Al Boyd, in a drunken monologue, always pleases. Mr. Boyd is very good at this, as practice makes perfect.[283]

While playing through the Blue Ridge Mountains of Virginia, acrobat William Earl got to visit his hometown of Lynchburg, and Park Wade got to spend "a very pleasant Sunday and Monday, April 16 and 17, at his home in Roanoke." Crossing into West Virginia, the company found plenty of work, with "all the coal mines running full force,

Three Star Players of the Rabbit Foot Show Base Ball Team

Al. Wells, 2d baseman; Archie C. Blue, 1st baseman, and Arthur Gibbs, pitcher, with Al Boyd, catcher; Wm Earl at short stop, and Otto Bradley at 3d base, makes up the stone wall infield

Indianapolis Freeman, June 16, 1917.

and can't get laboring men enough." Amidst flush times it was noted that, "All the Rabbits are coming out for the summer with new suits of clothes and diamonds."

A May 19, 1917, report noted, "Wolcott's Rabbit Foot Got 'Em Hoo Doo'd in Kentucky . . . They just can't help going out to the show more than once down there." A headline in June proclaimed, "Wolcott's Rabbit Foot Conjures North Carolina, And Old Br'er Rabbit's Hind Leg Is Always Lucky." The correspondent went on to note: "Joe White, the sensational trap drummer,

Rabbit's Foot Company admission ticket (courtesy Emma Crisler, *Port Gibson Revielle*. Thanks to Mississippi Cultural Crossroads.)

has bought a pair of shoes that he calls buzzing shoes. He is learning to buzz now."[284] At Clinton, North Carolina, that summer, Archie Blue married Miss Mary E. Caldwell, of Durham, aboard the show's private Pullman car, "Pocahontas."

When the Foots pulled into Bessemer, Alabama, at the end of July 1917, cornetist David Phoenix of Oberlin, Ohio, received his draft notice: "Several other members of the company are looking eagerly for their names to be called next. All those within the draft limit are ready, and only await the call to arms. We hope no blood will have to be shed, but if it must be shed, let it be shed freely."[285] A few weeks later the *Freeman* correspondent posted this note: "Prof. Veal's famous Mississippi Band, for several seasons enroute with the Rabbit Foot Company, has room for several good musicians."

George W. Quine left the show that fall and returned to Allen's Minstrels. On October 24, 1917, the Foots marked their fifth anniversary under F. S. Wolcott. Wolcott had promised at the outset that anyone who stayed on with him for five consecutive seasons would receive a $50 cash bonus, and T. H. Dumas and Lillian Eldridge became the first recipients.

When the Government-imposed railroad embargo brought the show to a halt in January 1918, several members of the band regrouped at "Rabbit Foot headquarters" in St. Augustine, Florida, and hired out as the Imperial Jazz Orchestra: "Dennis West, manager, Joe White, drums; G. W. Mitchell, cornet; Norman Mason, cornet; A. C. Gibbs, trombone; J. W. McKinney, bass; B. James, violin; David James, mellophone."[286] Archie Blue went to Daytona to join a theater stock company. Marcus Veal Chaney left for Jacksonville; by June he was touring at the head of the sideshow annex band with the John Robinson Circus.

During the spring of 1918, Wolcott relocated Rabbit Foot headquarters to Port Gibson, Mississippi, about halfway between Natchez and Vicksburg on the Mississippi River. According to a local Chamber of Commerce brochure, Port Gibson was "a major slave-holding community before the Civil War and the seat of commerce for a wide area along the Mississippi River." When Union General Ulysses S. Grant reached Port Gibson during his 1863 campaign to capture Vicksburg, he reportedly declared it "Too beautiful to burn." Grant's judgment still appears on a sign as one enters the town. Though it has long been a predominantly black town, Old South customs still prevail in Port Gibson.[287]

Archie Blue, en route with Washburn's Minstrels, who is considered one of our leading bass drummers and a comedian of no mean ability, will soon be heard from as a cornet player. He sends regards to all friends in and out of the profession, especially those of A. F. and A. M. and F. C. B.

Indianapolis Freeman, October 18, 1919.

Wolcott made a splash when he brought his wife and mother to live in this scenic Mississippi town in 1918. The *Port Gibson Reveille* announced their arrival in a feature article titled "Glen Sade Place Sold":

> Glen Sade Plantation, nearly two miles north of Port Gibson, has been sold by its almost life-long owner, Mrs. J. L. Butler to Fred S. Walcott [*sic*] of Jackson, Mich., for almost $27,000. Mr. Walcott also paid C. A. Elliott, the lessee of the property $12,000 for his unexpired lease, growing crop, stock and some timber concessions, and Mr. Elliott is to manage the property for the present year.
>
> Glen Sade embraces nearly a thousand acres, and the site on the ante-bellum home is one of the prettiest in the state. For a hundred years, it has been in the Humphries family, Mrs. Butler being an Humphries.
>
> Mr. Walcott has traveled all over the country and fancied this property more than any other he has seen. He expects to spend $5000 in repairs this summer. He and his wife are now here, and his mother, Mrs. G. I. [*sic*, Carrie G.] Walcott, will soon arrive from Michigan and make her home with them.
>
> Mr. Walcott will retain the name Glen Sade, and says the place will be known as the home of the famous Rabbit Foot Minstrels, of which he has been owner for several years.[288]

When Wolcott registered with the military in September 1918, he gave his new Port Gibson address and listed his present occupation as "farmer."[289] Wolcott was an enterprising businessman, and Glen Sade was no doubt a productive working plantation, which he managed along with his minstrel company and other business interests.[290] When he first acquired the Rabbit's Foot, Wolcott served as owner-manager, and he may have continued in both capacities until 1916, when George W. Quine first came over from A. G. Allen's Minstrels and took over the responsibilities of on-site manager. Both Mr. and Mrs. Wolcott traveled with the Foots on occasion. A report in the *Reveille* of August 28, 1919, reveals: "Mr. F. S. Wolcott has joined his Rabbit Foot Minstrels. During his absence, Mr. Charles Coulter is managing his plantation."

Wolcott's Port Gibson plantation stands tall in the folklore of African American minstrelsy. Leon "Pee Wee" Whittaker, a trombonist who started running with minstrel shows during the early 1930s, recalled:

> Mr. Wolcott over there in Port Gibson—in the wintertime, when it got bad, we go out on his plantation. He had a big farm out there, you know, a big house out there for performers. If they didn't have nowhere

to go or nowhere to eat or sleep, or if you just come through there and you were a performer or a musician, you could go into that big place they had built. You could get three meals a day and three [*sic*, free?] tickets to the picture show and sleep there all winter . . . Mr. Wolcott, he was a good man. He had to be a good man to have the leading minstrel show in this country.[291]

There is not much corroborating evidence of a "big house out there for performers";[292] and nothing to indicate any egalitarianism on the part of Wolcott, who owned a black minstrel troupe but otherwise associated with Port Gibson's privileged white aristocracy. David Evans, who conducted the interview with Pee Wee Whittaker, has aptly noted that Wolcott's "whole organization seems to have been structured somewhat along the lines of a paternalistic southern plantation."[293] Patrick Henry Chappelle might have wondered just what he had wrought.

Wolcott established the Rabbit's Foot business office at the corner of Market and Carroll streets, just a couple blocks south of Port Gibson's business center. Offices were on the second floor of an odd, two-story wood frame structure; on the ground floor was a gas station that was also owned by Wolcott. The building, known as the headquarters of the Rabbit Foot Minstrels from 1918 until 1950, still stands.[294] It must have been a handsome office in its day, but it has fallen into an advanced state of dilapidation. Hardly any of the furnishings survive. One remarkable remnant is a large red leather Pullman seat, no doubt taken from one of Wolcott's private railroad cars. It is fitted into the wall of what may have been an office waiting room.

In his day, Wolcott also occupied a field just across the intersection from his headquarters, which served as winter storage space for the Rabbit's Foot Company tent, mechanical properties, etc. When they performed in Port Gibson, the Foots often set up their tent in this same field—later the site of a Jitney Jungle store.[295]

During the summer of 1919 the Rabbit Foot Minstrels reportedly played to capacity crowds in Mississippi and Louisiana: "Prof. Lewis' concert makes the public square at 12 o'clock regular, while Adams the Great is causing a stampede in trick and fancy riding . . . The stage is under the cheerful management of William R. Earl, honorably assisted by Casey [*sic*] Blue and Buckwheat Stringer." New additions included Crosby and Crosby, with "Mrs. Crosby featuring all the latest Blues."[296] The Crosbys stayed through the summer of 1920, with James Crosby serving as stage manager.

A report from North Carolina in the spring of 1920 declared:

Our first part is a grand affair and looks the picture of back in the days of old . . . T. H. Dumas opening with "Alcoholic Blues" and "I Never Miss Them," followed by Mrs. Anderson with "Mammy of Mine," some worker; Pork Chops in "They Go Wild Over Me" . . . then Mrs. Rawlinson singing "I ain't gonna give nobody none of this jelly roll.' Odell Rawlinson is next singing, "Dixie One More" [i.e., "Dixie Is Dixie Once More"], which leaves the house in an uproar. Mrs. Johnson is at her best singing "Yuma, Yuma Blues" and never misses getting her change nightly. Last but not least we have James Crosby closing the bill with that song that makes many a poor heart sad, "Let other folks business alone." Then comes our olio, with Pork Chops, Rawlinson & Rawlinson [Odell and Creola], Arthur Prince, Taylor & Taylor, T. H. Dumas and [slack wire walker] Joe Taylor . . . We are closing the show this year with the flying service on the border of Mexico.[297]

The old Rabbit's Foot headquarters building in Port Gibson, 2005. (photo by David Crosby)

By the summer of 1920 George W. Quine had returned to manage the Foots. Creola Rawlinson was singing "Never Let No One Man Worry Your Mind," and Odell Rawlinson was singing "Save a Little Change for Me." Leading the twelve-piece parade band was Arthur L. Prince, who also appeared in the olio as a juggler and hoop roller. The *Freeman* correspondent drew attention to the overall cleanliness and biracial appeal of the show: "Now we don't claim to have the biggest and best show on the road, but we do claim to have the cleanest show of this kind traveling under canvas and it takes to both white and colored." "We have a show that is clean from start to finish . . . Every joke, act, man and woman is clean and the car is kept clean." "Mr. G. W. Quine, our manager, is still smiling and proud of his company. Why? Because we have a show that pleases both white and colored."[298]

At Sylacauga, Alabama, that summer the Foots had "one of the biggest times of the season. When we arrived there, we found the Red Sox baseball team, ready to play the Rabbit Foot Giants, and I must say we had some time. At four o'clock the ground was packed. We had no park, but both white and colored turned out to see us . . . Now I want to say to all minstrels who play the city of Sylacauga, the people are fine and will give you a nice time. We had a big party that night and everybody had a fine time."[299]

Wolcott's Rabbit Foot Minstrels plowed into the 1920s without any major changes of habit. A remarkable portrait of the 1922 edition of the company comes from a published memoir of Milton D. Quigless.[300] In 1922, Quigless was an eighteen-year-old student at Alcorn A&M College, playing first trombone in the college band. That summer, he joined the Rabbit Foot Minstrel band on the road at Greensboro, North Carolina, and spent two unforgettable weeks under the baton of Marcus Veal Chaney. Quigless's pay was $15 per week. He was proud of his new band uniform, "a nice costume, light sky blue and modeled after a French army uniform, complete with a silk hat decorated with a gold-colored braid," but he was shocked to learn that the band never practiced, and that he was expected to catch new tunes "on the fly." "I was at home when we played such pieces as 'Stars and Stripes Forever.' However, when we played more popular tunes with a march rhythm I had a little more trouble."

Quigless had another shock when he entered the living quarters: "The railroad car that we were traveling in was half Pullman and half baggage car. The tent and all of the paraphernalia was stored in the baggage compartment and there were eight upper berths and eight lower berths in the other half of the car. That was all the space provided for 36 members of the minstrel troupe. The troupe slept two to a berth, which left four of us who had no berths on the car."

As for the band's nightly concerts in front of the tent:

> We played popular songs then, but everything was so fast. We'd play about four or five songs and then the audience would be invited to go into the tent to see the show.
>
> The show cost about 75 cents to get in, and you could get a reserved seat for a quarter more. For the opening act of the show, we played what would be called an overture, consisting of a medley of few popular pieces arranged by Mark Veal, who acted as orchestra director during the show . . . All during the show, the orchestra would play the songs that were sung by the performers, and the ones the dancers danced to, and during the other acts. The band would have music going the whole time, and the show would last $1\frac{1}{2}$–2 hours.

Quigless also reflected on the mechanics of Jim Crow seating: "Some white people came to the shows. Usually about one-third of the audience was white—segregated, of course. Whites were always on the right side. We used to say 'goats to the left, and the sheep over there.'"

The Foots launched their season of 1924 at Port Gibson on March 15, after having assembled at Birmingham, Alabama.[301] A note in *Billboard* that fall informed: "The Rabbit's Foot Minstrels and the Huntington Minstrels will be stored for the winter at Port Gibson, Miss. Mr. Wolcott, owner of the Rabbit's Foot show, has a beautiful home in that city and also owns the Rabbit's Foot Hotel there."[302]

Veteran performer Wayne "Buzzin'" Burton was hanging out in Monroe, Louisiana, during the early weeks of 1925, when he dispatched this news to the *Chicago Defender*:

> The "Foots" this season positively will be the best tent organization on the road. Everything new from front to back. Mr. Wolcott went to a great expense having the car overhauled, repaired and decorated and ordered all brand new scenery, wardrobe and a portable stage. Bill Campbell, the man in charge, says he has something new to offer the natives this season . . . The good car will carry an improved shower bath, designed by Mrs. Wolcott; the tank holding 300 gallons of water

> . . . Practically all the old people will return, as the postoffice box is packed each day. The opening date will be here [in Monroe] . . . Sport Akin and wife Bertha, will be among the new people for the Wolcott and Quine interests this season. Nifty pair.[303]

On-site manager George W. Quine may have left the Foots around this time. When he died at Caruthersville, Missouri, on November 1, 1929, Quine was identified in a *Chicago Defender* obituary as the manager of Huntington's Minstrels.

While touring with the rival Silas Green Show in the spring of 1925, veteran hoop roller Coy Herndon visited the Foots at Monroe, North Carolina, and critiqued their performance:

> Mr. Walcott, the owner, and Mr. Campbell, his manager, made me welcome. Rich Brown, former member of the Silas Green show, staged the show. The singing, especially the ballad singers are the outstanding features. J. A. McDonald, an ex–Georgia Minstrel, is in the line-up. Frank Smedley, the basso, formerly a member of "Chocolate Town," and John Churchill, the record singer, proved themselves favorites. The first part is beautifully dressed, but short on comedy. Rich Brown and Charles Raue [*sic*] do their team with their dummy mule, going over for a solid hit . . . A very bad mistake is made when three singles, all of which sing blues, follow each other. Five girls do "Hula Lu," similar to the Hula number Silas Green is using. The quartet is composed of marvelous voices, but being a comedy quartet, the comedy is too weak to put it over. A jazz band number followed. The last act, in which Rich Brown does the comedy and McFarland the straight, pulled many laughs.[304]

John Churchill, "the record singer," had cut two sides for Paramount in 1923.[305] Prior to joining the Foots, he had been working in black vaudeville. At the Joyland Theater in Eldorado, Arkansas, in

The "dummy mule" skit. (courtesy Edna Hackworth. Thanks to Mississippi Cultural Crossroads.)

1924, his offerings ranged from "yodeling ballads to 'Barrelhouse Blues.'"[306]

The *Defender* of April 27, 1929, announced the beginning of a new season:

> The Original Rabbit Foot company, for the past 15 years known as F. S. Wolcott's Rabbit Foot Minstrels, and recognized as Dixie's favorite show . . . will present a high-class musical comedy and will carry 50 people, including E. W. Brown's 20-piece concert band and premier orchestra. A beauty chorus of 20 high-brown beauties, carefully selected. The show will carry its own electric plant. The big tent theater will be electric

lighted, with dressing rooms on stage, one dozen large electric fans in tent. The company will be transported on the two Al G. Fields railroad cars, Dan Emmett, a solid sleeper, and Southland, a diner and baggage. Both cars are fully equipped with steam heat, electric lights and fans, offering the very best accommodations obtainable. Five hundred cushioned, easy-sitting folding chairs all numbered for coupon tickets, will be carried for reserves. Mr. Wolcott is sparing neither pains nor money to make this the outstanding one-night stand tented attraction of all America."

The Depression may have driven the Rabbit Foot Minstrels off the road for a time. After 1930, *Chicago Defender* reports from the Foots disappeared. Consequently, there is very little information about who was traveling with the show during the 1930s and 1940s. Legendry abounds, but hard documentation is sparse.[307]

New Orleans banjo player "Creole" George Guesnon recalled having joined the Rabbit Foot Minstrels in 1936. He played banjo in the orchestra, and trumpet in the band. He said the band discoursed "Liza Trombone" and "Oh, You Drummer" on parade, while the stage orchestra backed singers of popular melodies like "Blue Skies" and "Moonglow." And then "some guy would be doing something funny on the stage, so we'd play 'Turkey in the Straw' or one of those kind of things. It all depends on what act was going on . . . We had a blues singer, Big Mary . . . Mary Smith, yeah. Well, she'd come out there and sing the blues. Well, we'd play the blues for her."[308]

The *Defender* of October 16, 1937, notified that: "Delbert Payne, trombone soloist is now appearing with Sergeant King and his fourteen piece swing band playing for the 'Rabbit Foot Minstrels,' on tour throughout the Southern states. At present, the aggregation, which includes such stars as Dusty Frank Tanzel, Booty Jim, Jack Slats and a chorus of beautiful sunkissed cuties, is playing the state of Arkansas."

George Guesnon. (courtesy Barry Martyn Collection)

In the fall of 1938 *Defender* columnist Bob Hayes noted: "Roy Bowling and his sixteen piece orchestra are the big features with Wolcott's Rabbit Foot Minstrels. Joe White is still the big shot with Gold Drums as he mystifies the natives. Port Gibson, Miss. is the headquarters."[309]

News in the summer of 1939 mentioned Roy Bowling and his Royal Swingsters, plus "such outstanding artists as Hosea Sapp, Haywood Walker and Willis Harvey." Reedman Jessie Charles, who was born in 1900 in Raceland, Louisiana, recalled having joined the Foots that summer in Monroe, Louisiana. He described a fourteen- to

The Rabbit's Foot tent and fleet of buses. (courtesy Edna Hackworth. Thanks to Jerry Bangham)

seventeen-piece band, along with "about ten girls and three or four comedians" and a tent that held more than 2,000 people.

According to Charles, the Foots played small towns during the week and big towns on the weekend. They traveled in a big bus, stayed in people's houses when there was no hotel, and got paid every night after the show. The band was still parading to the center of town every day at noon, and Charles finally quit because the parade uniforms were too hot. He said that shortly after he left, the parades were discontinued.[310]

Still with the Foots in the summer of 1942, Roy Bowling and his Royal Swingsters were "dubbed the Southern Heat Wave."[311] In the fall of 1943 the *Chicago Defender* received a letter from male blackface comedian Sweetie Brown, "now heading the Rabbit Foot Shows playing through Arkansas." Brown testified that, "Hitler is a sissy compared to some of the population he has played to. Leon 'Lassus' Brown, comic; Jessie Mae Sheppard, vocalist, and Fat Heard, a 300 pound dancer, are featured."[312]

In the early 1940s, Wolcott's Rabbit Foot Minstrels typically began and/or ended their touring season with a performance in Port Gibson.[313] Locals, both black and white, attended the show. Interviewed by David Crosby in 2001–2002 for the Claiborne County Oral History Project, older African American residents Annie Wade, Harry Parker, and Nathan Jones conveyed fond recollections of the minstrel show. Annie Wade, born in 1915, assayed: "Rabbit Foot was the best time in the world." Harry Parker was also a big fan: "Went to see it every time it come in here. I was working, you know. I wouldn't miss it . . . I loved to be there. Played blues, oh, man. They played the blues . . . It was fun. I liked to go to Rabbit Foot." Nathan Jones expressed similar sentiments:

> [Wolcott] had a wonderful show. I enjoyed it. It last about two hours . . . Sometimes I liked it so well I would go back a second time to see it. It didn't come regular now. Maybe once a year. And sometimes he would skip a year. But any time he would come there, I would go to that show. I enjoyed it as much as I did the big circus show. Or even more, because I [never] been to anything like that. All the performers were black . . .
>
> You look on TV now, you don't see anything any better. Blacks and whites patronized. We didn't sit together now. White had a side and we had a side . . . Lot of whites went to that show when they came to town.[314]

Libby Hollingsworth, a member of the white Port Gibson establishment, born 1933, testified that she started going to Rabbit's Foot shows while in grammar school: "I went a lot of years in the late 30s and early 40s." She said that she would sit where she could see Joe White play the drums.[315]

The Port Gibson era in Rabbit Foot minstrelsy ended in 1950, when F. S. Wolcott sold the show to Earl Hendren of Erwin, Tennessee. Wolcott lived until July 27, 1967. He is buried in a family plot in all-white Wintergreen Cemetery in Port Gibson.

A mainstream syndicated newspaper columnist filed this story in the summer of 1954:

> The "Rabbit's Foot Minstrels" may not be the greatest show on earth, but it's about the only one of its kind you'll find these days in Dixie.
>
> The Rabbit's Foot troupe, including a peg-legged dancer, a 268½-pound blues singer with diamonds in her teeth, and a fire eater, is following the crops up and down the Southland in the all-but vanished minstrel tradition.
>
> For the cast it's a life of one-night stands, baths out of buckets and payday every day.
>
> The latter is an innovation of the company's owner-manager, Earle Hendren, of Erwin, Tenn.
>
> "If we paid off once a week some of them would be broke a day or two later," he said. "This way we avoid quarrels over loans and advances. Everybody starts the day with money." . . .
>
> The Rabbit's Foot troupe just left Memphis on its annual tour. It likes to hit town just after the big money crop is in. Folks have got more time, and cash, to spend on entertainment.
>
> In the minstrel tent they can see such performers as Peg Leg Lightfoot, who dances on one good leg and one artificial one, a fire eater, a contortionist, a man with an "iron jaw," and Mary Smith, the hefty blues singer whose smile flashes with a small fortune.
>
> "I invest my money in my teeth. I have eight inlays now," says Mary.
>
> Though the Rabbit's Foot Minstrels are as familiar as corn pones and blackeyed peas in some Southern towns, it is a new venture for Hendren, who bought the show only four years ago.[316]

"Peg" Lightfoot is the same one-legged dancer who, according to a *Freeman* report of 1913, had "gone violently insane" after collapsing on the stage of the Monogram Theater, and who, according to the *Chicago Defender* of July 21, 1923, "was beaten nearly to death by a mob of whites at Erlanger, Ky." Who could have predicted that Lightfoot would survive more than forty years in the minstrel profession?

Mary Smith, the hefty blues singer with eight inlays, was "rediscovered" in the late 1970s, and went on to garner acclaim on the international folk and blues festival circuits as "Diamond Teeth Mary." Subsequent recordings include a 1993 album on the Big Boss label. At the time of her death in 2000, Diamond Teeth Mary was said to be ninety-seven years old.[317]

Entries in the ledger books of Hatch Show Print, a Nashville, Tennessee–based print shop specializing in posters for traveling shows, indicate that Earle Hendren sold his interest in the Foots to Eddie Moran, of Monroe, Louisiana, in 1955. In 1956 an Associated Negro Press reporter informed:

> Down in the heart, and throughout the body of Dixie, there is an old 'Rabbit Foot' that's been hopping around for about 44 years and is still growing strong.[318]

What's more, there are no apparent indications that it will stop hopping when the rest of us are gone.

The full yarn about this "Rabbit Foot" is more familiar to people from Alabama to Arkansas than anyone else because as a minstrel show, "Rabbit Foot" has entertained thousands of people throughout Negro communities in the South . . . every summer that the nation sees.

Known as "F. S. Wolcott's Original Rabbit-Foot Minstrel Show", it features live entertainment of a style that most people think has long past passed, and its only rival is a similar show called "Silas Green from New Orleans."

Playing under canvas and making mostly one day stands, the cast of Rabbit Foot is all Negro with Memphis Lewis as the featured comedian and Mary Jones [*sic*] as the star blues singer.

"Foot" is backed by the band leadership of Hosea Sapp, who in his own right is a well-known performer with the outfit.

The show is made up of a chorus line of 10 luscious lovelies and has a total cast of 28. Don't forget to add the 10-piece band roughing the paid performers out to about 50 people.

Much of the familiar minstrel day jargon is still in the dialogue of the show, especially the song-and-dance routines, but the 90-minute show is climaxed with a jungle scene.

With a seating capacity of about 2,500 the stage is at one end of the big top, an 80 by 110-foot affair.

With billboards, posters and signs advertising the approach, the show comes pouring in from town to town jumping to the tunes of rock and roll songs.

The signs read "The Greatest Colored Show on Earth."

Once getting under way, the main show is followed by a 45 minute concert in which seven more acts are featured, and candy, concessions and costume jewelry is sold. Then out wiggles an exotic shake dancer and a blues singer.

Pedro Lane closes the show, but not without a little sales promotion for the next time around.

For the first thirty-eight years, Rabbit Foot was under the management of its founder, F. S. Wolcott, but since his retirement five years ago Earl Hendrin has handled the chores. This year, however, Eddie Moran will take the spotlight.

Staffed by whites as well as colored personnel, standard territory for Rabbit Foot are places like Greenwood, Vicksburg, Jackson, Miss., and Tuscaloosa or Florence, Ala.

Operating virtually on the same scale as a circus, the show hauls its equipment around in 12 big trucks.

So, if you happen to be down in the heart of Dixieland this summer, just stop and ask someone about the Rabbit Foot. They could tell you just as much about it as they could tell about themselves.

Rabbit Foot is as well known there as the weather.[319]

Drummer and trombone player Worthia "Showboy" Thomas, who was born in Napoleonville, Louisiana, in 1907, claimed to have toured off and on with the Rabbit Foot Minstrels from the 1920s to the 1950s. In 1961, Thomas showed an interviewer some special orchestrations that he had gotten from the show's last known bandmaster, Hosea Sapp. Thomas said the last time he had gone out with the Foots, around 1956, the band was down to nine pieces, "and they had cut out the parading."[320]

While no corroboration is present, it seems likely that the Foots' bandleader was the same

Hosea Sapp who played trumpet with the seminal West Coast rhythm and blues combo, Roy Milton's Solid Senders, and recorded with that band from 1945 to 1949.[321]

In a 1960 interview, Foots alumnus "Creole" George Guesnon spoke frankly about the show's late decline: "about two years ago a guy told me, said, 'We want you to come out on the Rabbit Foot.' I said, 'You must be losing your mind!' I said, 'They ain't no more Rabbit Foot out there man!' I said, 'That's a hard luck thing you got out there.' I said, 'In 1936, 1937, when I was on that show, they had a private Pullman . . . But now they travel in them old beat-up trucks, and they got to fix tires and all that stuff. It's a hardship out there now."[322]

The account books at Hatch Show Print indicate that orders for Rabbit Foot Minstrels advertising posters, etc., came to a halt in November 1957. Apparently, Hatch stopped shipping paper due to outstanding debts. A handwritten note in the ledger suggests the unpaid amount was "Charged off to bad debts April 15, 1959."[323] Some further orders were noted in December 1959, when the show was booked for a series of engagements in halls. These were the last orders noted.

The Florida Blossoms

The Florida Blossoms Company was founded at Tampa, Florida, by local race businessman R. S. Donaldson, Pat Chappelle's original partner in the *A Rabbit's Foot* Company. In the spring of 1906, three years after Chappelle abandoned the Buckingham Theater in Tampa, Donaldson reopened it under a new name, the Budweiser. Following Chappelle's example with the Rabbit's Foot Company, he used the theater as a launching pad for his Florida Blossom Minstrels.

When the Florida Blossoms made their debut on December 15, 1906, the musical director was Prof. William H. Dorsey; Will Goff Kennedy was the stage manager, and the principal blackface comedians were Billy Reeves and Billy Glenn. "Pearl Moppin, hoop controller, and Dan Randalls, wire walker, are the novelty acts. The female performers are headed by Carrie Hall, queen of coon song singers . . . The band and orchestra are, without an exception, the best on the road. The trombone section, Amos Gilliard, Pearl Moppin and George Rhone, make the natives stand up and shout. Piccolo Jones, our flute and piccolo player, is in a class to himself."[324]

Also with the Florida Blossoms during their inaugural season were the husband-and-wife comedy teams of William and Beulah Henderson and Fred Bonny and Pinkie Wallace, "the colored Dicty Doos." Another charter member was Sam Cohen, the spieler: "Sam Cohen, called the 'Jew Baby,' has made a very good reputation as an announcer, and the people never fail to come in when he is on the door." He "changes the minds of many who had no intention of going to the show."

When heard from on March 2, 1907, the Florida Blossoms were in "dear old Georgia." They were still on the road in July. That fall, R. S. Donaldson sold the Florida Blossoms to fellow African American businessmen Charles H. Douglass and Peter Worthy of Macon, Georgia, where Worthy had been operating a saloon in the 600 block of Fourth Street and Douglass had been supervising vaudeville productions at Ocmulgee Park.[325] Douglass also owned a saloon and hotel

DONALDSON'S "FLORIDA BLOSSOMS" Musical, Comedy and Minstrel Extravaganza Company,
America's Leading Colored Theatrical Organization Under Canvas,
now successfully touring the South, wants a first-class
CORNET PLAYER also GOOD DRUMMER,
MUST DOUBLE.
Performers and Musicians wanted at all times. Wanted at once first-class
BALL PLAYERS.
Jim Leslie, Bob Gilkerson, George Washington, Wood Adams, write.
PEARL MOPPIN, Captiain.
Four Good Looking Ladies Who Can Sing Wanted.
Write or wire as per route
R. S. DONALDSON, Proprietor.
WM. H. DORSEY, Musical Director. W. G. KENNEDY, Press Agent.

Indianapolis Freeman, April 27, 1907.

at 361 Broadway; his business holdings in Macon were eventually crowned by the Douglass Theater, a beacon of TOBA-era vaudeville.[326]

Setting up the Florida Blossoms' winter quarters at Ocmulgee Park, Douglass and Worthy proceeded to assemble a "big Negro minstrel, musical comedy and vaudeville organization" of thirty-six people, including a fourteen-piece band and the "largest lady chorus of any tented show extant." On March 30, 1908, they opened with a three-night stand at the park. Making an immediate impression were buck and wing dancers Lonnie and Cora Fisher; Paul Carter in "eccentric dancing and clean comedy"; contortionist Charles McKenzie; Maud and Hi Jerry Barnes in an original "bear act"; and Susie Beavers and Chink Floyd, soubrette and comedian.

Lonnie and Cora Fisher stayed on for the next two seasons. Correspondence of June 5, 1909, noted, "The Fishers, Cora and Larney [*sic*], are surprising the country with their new act entitled 'Music, Mirth and Melody.' Mrs. Fisher is sure a wonder with her feet. Larney Fisher makes the house scream with his late prescription for side pleurisy." Later that fall Lonnie was "knocking the turkey" with his rendition of "You Ain't Talking to Me." Cora appears to have fallen away from the Florida Blossoms before the end of 1909, but Lonnie remained to become amusement director, and he was still on the roster in 1916.

Paul Carter was the show's principal blackface comedy star. Coming to the Florida Blossoms from Richards and Pringle's Georgia Minstrels, he assumed the role of "Jim Jackson from Jacksonville," singing "'I Just Can't Stand Prosperity,' and also one of his own compositions, 'You Don't Look Half as Good to Me as My Straight-haired Yellow Man.'"[327] After just five or six months with the Florida Blossoms, Carter jumped to Allen's New Orleans Minstrels.

Contortionist Charles McKenzie, known as "Flying McKenzie," was famous for his "ladder drop of 25 feet." Featured in the olio for the better part of two seasons, McKenzie also got to demonstrate his versatility as a producer in a one-act skit titled "A Coon Ragtime Ball."[328]

During the first several weeks of the 1908 season the Florida Blossoms band was under the temporary direction of John W. Anderson. On May 20, 1908, designated bandmaster N. E. Perkins caught up with the show at Cordele, Georgia, along with tuba player Joe Miller, clarinetist William Phillips, singing comedian Jim Wise, and "Jacksonville soubrette" Effie Means. Under Prof. Perkins's baton, the Florida Blossoms Band of twelve to fifteen pieces played "all the latest rags and solos." The roster included cornetist Walter H. Childs, of Macon.

In Virginia during the summer of 1908, the Florida Blossoms claimed to be "setting the pace for all tented organizations with their forty-two people and two private cars." Susie Beavers was singing "Every Day She Wants Something Else"; Edith Bank was "doing nicely in her dancing and singing 'Honey Love'"; and Effie Means was "pulling down the house singing 'Down in Jungle Town.'"

In August the Blossoms returned to Macon for a month's reprieve: "Their cars are being repaired and painted and they have ordered new costumes, etc., and will look spic and span when they appear in their fall attire." On September 28, 1908, they reopened with a two-night stand in Macon. The fall edition of the band was strengthened by the addition of Otto Hurdle (or Hudle), E. N. Collins, L. W. Clark, and Howard Almond of the Barnum and Bailey Show—"Some Band."[329] At the end of the year, these four bandsmen returned to Barnum and Bailey.

The new blackface comedy star was Billie Richardson, "a scream every night as 'Kid Jones, the Gambling King from Baltimore.'"[330] Also making his first appearance with the Blossoms was John H. Williams, late of A. G. Allen's Minstrels. Williams helped fill out the olio as a monologist. Before the summer of 1909, he moved on to tour with the Whitman Sisters, who recognized him as a "coming star."

The olio opened with the Joyner Brothers, eccentric dancers, followed by Billie Richardson "with the slow drag"; Wise and Kimbrough in "The Officer and the Coon"; Charles H. McKenzie, "society gymnast"; and Garfield Smith, "tramp juggler."[331] Garfield Smith appeared elsewhere in the show as a "Southern tenor," singing "When the Sheep Are in the Fold, Jennie Dear." Another tramp juggler, Charles "Peewee" Williams, came aboard at the end of the year, along with his wife, who appeared in the afterpiece as "The Belle of the Ball."

The Blossoms spent much of the autumn of 1908 in the Mississippi Delta, "playing to capacity business." At Clarksdale in early November, they "crossed A. G. Allen's Minstrels . . . and chanced a few." They had planned to be "in the Lone Star State for Christmas," but instead they turned east, crossed Alabama, and dropped through Georgia to Florida. A page from a ledger book of "Receipts and Expenses of Florida Blossom Show" for December 7–19, 1908, notes their show stops:

Date:	Location:	Receipts:	Expenses:
December	7: Thomasville, Georgia	177.15	149.62
	8: Cairo	120.90	125.19
	9: Bainbridge	162.25	89.20
	10: Quincy, Florida	164.55	95.95
	10: Tallahassee	83.25	105.05
	12: Monticello	192.20	56.05
	13: [Sunday]		
	14: Madison	201.05	166.43
	15: Live Oak	125.00	127.55
	16: High Springs	118.15	51.89
	17: Dunnellon	213.55	117.10
	18: Ocala	158.85	164.85
	19: Plant City	183.55	61.20[332]

At year's end, the Blossoms' *Freeman* correspondent described a steady-rolling enterprise with a practical notion of their place in the entertainment universe: "[W]e get the money and don't have any lint and holly weeks. Every week is a week made. So this Southland is good enough for us."[333] They closed out their season with a two-night stand at Jacksonville, January 25 and 26, 1909. On March 29, they launched a new season at Hawkinsville, Georgia, "packing their big tent back to the door." They had forty people in tow, "featuring minstrelsy, musical comedy and high class vaudeville."[334]

The Blossoms took on a widely expanded route of travel for the season of 1909. In May they left Georgia for the Carolinas. In July they made their way through Tennessee, Alabama, Mississippi, and then back into Tennessee. In August, after three successful weeks in Arkansas, they pushed into Oklahoma, "which seems to be the colored man's land of promise ... We spent two very pleasant days in Muskogee, which is alive with colored business houses, and we were royally entertained by some of the leading young men of the town."[335] A November 20 report claimed, "The Florida Blossoms Company has been doing a banner business in the state of Texas for the last two months." By early December they were back in Mississippi, "playing S. R. O."

The bandmaster was Prof. E. B. Dudley. Among the bandsmen, John Tobias, "the boy that knows how to handle the slippery horn ... composed a rag for the band that is a cleaner. The title: 'The Blooming Blossom.'"[336] Another popular feature of the band was its dueling snare drums: "Joe White and Lonnie Fisher, the sensational snare drummers, are doing a drum duet and it's a scream."[337] This may have been Joe White's initiation to the minstrel show routes. While he trouped with the Florida Blossoms on occasion over the years, White's long-term home was with the Rabbit's Foot Company.

Star comedian Billie Richardson returned for one last season with the Blossoms. Other comedy stars of 1909 included Clarence Steward, Leroy Knox, Chink Floyd, James Jones, and Eddie Miller. Billed as "the North Carolina Favorite," Leroy Knox made a hit with "that storming song, 'I Wish I Was in Heaven Sitting Down.'"[338] He also sang "Good Evening Miss Caroline," and he scored with his female impersonation of "Mandy" in the afterpiece. Clarence Steward made a hit singing "I Didn't Ask, He Didn't Say, So I Don't Know." He also introduced "one of his own songs, 'It Ain't But One Thing Makes a Noise Like Money to Me,'" and he followed up with "There Is Only One Thing That Troubles Me and That's My Appetite." Chink Floyd sang "Fare Thee Well," James Johnson sang "Trans-mag-ni-fi-can-bam-dam-u-ality," and Eddie Miller, "our rising comedian," sang the ancient end song, "Old Black Crow."

During the summer of 1909 the Blossoms got a boost from Kid and Gussie Love. Kid was reportedly "hitting them hard with 'I Am Going to Exit,'" while Gussie was "taking two and three encores with that pleasing song, 'I'm Glad I Am Brown Skinned.'"[339] Though their stay with the Blossoms was brief, the Loves appear to have left an imprint; in the wake of their departure, coon shouter Hester Wallace was "cleaning with 'I'm So Glad I'm Brown Skin Chocolate to the Bone.'"[340]

The new specialty artist for 1909 was hoop roller Coy Herndon. Born in Palatka, Florida, in

Coy Herndon, "The Boy who put the 'oo's' in Hoops," *Indianapolis Freeman*, December 25, 1915.

The master hoop roller with his hoops. *Billboard*, Mary 19, 1921.

1892, Herndon was just starting out on what proved to be a long and successful career under canvas.[341] By way of explaining his act, the *Freeman* correspondent noted, "Master Coyden Herndon, the youngest hoop roller on the stage today, is keeping his audience spell-bound with his ghost-walking hoops. Master Herndon is keeping five hoops on his body at once, all in motion, and is making one hoop walk five strings."[342] Herndon performed his hoop rolling stunts "in Chinese costume."

Will Goff Kennedy, a veteran of the Florida Blossoms' inaugural season, returned to manage the stage, and his wife Gussie took over the role of the "Belle of the Ball" in the afterpiece. When they jumped to the Rabbit's Foot Company just a few months into the season, the role fell to soubrette Stella Smith, who made "a very pleasing Belle of the Ball singing 'Harvest Moon' assisted by a well-drilled chorus of pretty soubrettes." Before the end of the year the "Belle of the Ball" character was inherited by Katie Price, the Blossoms' latest "soubrette, coon shouter and buck dancer," known as "the Georgia Sunbeam." Price's 1909 song repertoire included "That Loving Rag," "Play that Rag," and "I Love My Husband, But, Oh, You Henry."

Correspondence of November 20, 1909, gives a sense of the afterpiece:

> Then comes the last act, "Kid Jones, the Gambling King from Baltimore," where L. L. Fisher shines as head waiter and Ed Miller as the first waiter. Geo. Crump as real "Kid Jones" can find no equal in the use of his tongue. Leroy Knox as "Mandy" makes them fall out of their seats with laughter. Nelson Green as Will Blue, Mandy's supposed beau, is out there, too. Coyden Herndon, the villain, pleases the public. J. Johnson as Slim Jim, the feather police, leaves them shouting when he enters. Mrs. Kate Price the bell of the ball is doing it with much success. Then comes Clarence Steward, the boy full of fun and laughter, as the bogus Kid Jones, and turns the house over from start to finish. Following that comes the Florida Blossom Concert Band . . . playing all the standard overtures.

At Quitman, Georgia, in January 1910, just before the end of the season, Lonnie Fisher and James E. "Happy Go Lucky" Simpson, "the Little Fellow with the Big Feet," closed with the Blossoms to take a turn at the Airdome Theater in Jacksonville, Florida. Fisher typically worked in vaudeville between tenting seasons, and recruited young talent to bring back to the show. Correspondence from the Blossoms on June 4, 1910, informed: "Mr. Fisher has two girls in the show that are cleaners with their feet. They are the Williams Sisters (Sarah and Rebecca). After the season closes they will be seen in vaudeville as the Two Popcorn Girls, under Mr. Fisher's direction." A note in July said:

> Miss Kate Price is still holding the hot corn girls down. Walter L. Long is doing a very clever monologue. Eddie E. Daye, the human corkscrew, is bending in every direction. Leroy Knox is cleaning as Miss Mandy. As a wench Leroy is a bird. George Crump, our straight man, has no equal in his line of work. Lawrence L. Fisher, doing Kid Jones, the gambling king from Baltimore . . . doesn't fail to deliver the goods. Miss Estelle Smith doing the belle of the rag-time ball and cleaning with "Boo Loo Eyes." James Johnson don't fail to hit the turkey in the streets every day at our noonday parade. Jas. E. Simpson, the little fellow with the big feet, still going with "Come Out the Kitchen, Liza" . . .
>
> Doshie Styles is doing nicely as a singing soubrette.
>
> The Williams Sisters, champion buck and wing dancers, are scoring some runs with their feet.
>
> We have a very strong band over here of 12 pieces who are wind jammers, and we have some battery section, too. They are Knox and Fisher.[343]

At this juncture, the job of band and orchestra director fell to cornetist Walter H. Childs, "a young man in age and experience, but it is plain to see that he is a real leader." Except for a brief sojourn with the Silas Green Company in 1912, Childs appears to have led the Florida Blossoms Band for the next seven years.

In Florida during the early weeks of 1911, the Blossoms found business "so encouraging that the management decided not to close, as has been usual each season . . . They are now entering into their fifth successful season, carrying two cars and forty people, and a fifteen piece Challenge Brass Band, which is the talk of each city they appear in. This show is owned and managed entirely by Negroes, carrying a daily expense of $150."[344] By October they were "in Mississippi again, playing to standing room only. This is no joke. Just out of Texas, Arkansas, Kansas and Missouri, where we

Lonnie Fisher and Rebecca Simmons, *Indianapolis Freeman*, November 2, 1912.

played 12 weeks to fine business." They were back in Florida for Christmas.

Highlights of the 1911 season included Katie Price singing "That Honkey Tonk Rag"; Mamie Johnson, "our dainty soubrette," singing "Lovie Joe"; and Hester Wallace singing "Stop, Stop, Stop" and "Come Over and Love Me Some More." Lonnie Fisher and Charlie Miller closed the first part singing "I'm Going to Florida." Fisher also appeared with a "little girl named Rebecca Simmons, and she's some team partner, believe me."[345]

Returning to the roster in 1911 was "human corkscrew" Eddie E. Daye: "He is a boneless wonder . . . doing his frog imitations." Newcomers included Ernest and Daisy Calloway, who joined at the end of the year: "Ernest is working in band and orchestra, while Mrs. Calloway sings 'That Minor Strain.'"[346]

Correspondence of August 3, 1912, placed the Blossoms in their adopted home State of Georgia. The band was under the temporary direction of Ralph Redmond, and the temporary stage manager was Leroy Knox:

> Our first part opens with a rollicking medley of popular songs by the entire company, after which Mr. Leroy White starts the flow of laughter with that real comic song, "Buckwheat Cakes." This is followed by Miss Redmond singing "That Red Rose Rag" which she is making a complete success with this season.
>
> "Plant a Watermelon on My Grave" is handed out by Mr. Leroy Knox in an interesting manner.
>
> Mr. George Ross sets everyone wondering with his song and dance, "By the Glitter of the Moon."
>
> Miss Mamie Johnson is receiving three and four encores nightly singing "Twilight."
>
> Mr. Charles Miller closes the first part with "I Thought I Heard a Pork Chop Say," which is a scream.

At Pelham, Georgia, on Friday, November 29, 1912, the Blossoms crossed paths with the Golden Leaf Stock Company and, "After both shows were over, Mr. Billy Young, better known as 'Blue,' and Jas. C. Lewis, known as 'Shorty, the Drummer,' gave a grand ball at the Elks' hall in honor of the Florida Blossoms."[347] They closed the season at Valdosta, Georgia, on December 23, and went into winter quarters at 619 Fourth Street, Macon.

Around this time C. H. Douglass sold his interest in the Blossoms, making Pete Worthy the sole owner. On June 2, 1913, Worthy's Florida Blossom Minstrels rolled out of Macon with fifty people, a new tent and "a No. 1 brass band." An early report from the road noted:

> The show has done away with the minstrel first part and is putting on a musical comedy, entitled 'Jenkins and Swipes Off to War'... The act is staged and managed by Mr. Lonnie Fisher, who is ably assisted by Mr. Charlie Miller... The parts of Captain Jolly by Tom Lockhart, and Sergeant Hart by Mr. George Crump, are very cleverly done... Special mention should be made of Mrs. Ada Lockhart, as Zenora, the Mexican maid... also Miss Rebecca Simmons and her dancing girls.
>
> The soldier quartette is also a scream. The band under Walter Childs, is one of the best on the road, and is playing the latest in classic and rag time.[348]

New to the roster, Tom and Ada Lockhart graced the olio with a "first-class dramatic act." They were no longer with the show by January 1914, when news came that Tom Lockhart had been found dead in Atlanta, Georgia.[349] In 1915 Ada Lockhart joined the rival Silas Green Company, and went on to achieve recognition as a blues singing "female baritone."

The Blossoms' most highly advertised specialty act of 1913 was the trick cyclist known as Great Adams, "holding the vast crowds spellbound, both on the street at the noon parade and on the stage at night." Another hit of the street parade was James Johnson, "knocking them in every town as rube." The star of the olio was Little Nellie Matthews, "the human frog, the undisputed queen of girl acrobats and contortionists." Little Nellie had just turned "sweet sixteen." Still touring with the Blossoms in 1918, she was qualified as "the only Colored lady contortionist, and a worthy daughter of her father, Boneless Willie, who was once the only rival of the great Marsh Craig."[350]

Stage singers of 1913 included Miss Annie Holmes singing "Down South" and leading lady Ethel Reid Cox singing "When Uncle Joe Plays a Rag on His Old Banjo."[351] This title was recorded in 1936, complete with a characteristic introductory dialogue, by the Hall Negro Quartet:

> "Hello there, Uncle Joe, how you feeling?"
>
> "Oh, good evening boys, how y'all?"
>
> "We're fine, fine. Now, Uncle Joe, what is your back doing bent over so much?"
>
> "I been working too hard here lately, son, that's what's the matter with me."
>
> "You sure you ain't been truckin' too much?"
>
> "No, I ain't been truckin', son, just working too hard."
>
> "Say, Uncle Joe, we want you to sing a song for us, you know, that you used to sing in the field down there in Chittlin' Switch."
>
> "Oh, son, I ain't sung those songs in years," I can't just go and sing it now."
>
> "Oh, can't you? Well, we had a song here we thought we'd let you harmonize with us. Can't you put a little bass in there?"
>
> "Well, I'll try to."[352]

In Florida at the beginning of 1914, the Blossoms announced that, rather than taking a winter break, they would continue open-ended. In the spring of 1915 bandmaster Walter Childs took an apparent leave of absence, to take charge of the orchestra at the Douglass Theater in Macon: "He is not using his cornet, playing violin, while Mr. Attler Cox is playing cornet."[353] The Blossoms filed few reports to the *Freeman* until the summer of 1915, when they pitched their tent in Savannah, Georgia, for an unusually long engagement of five or six weeks: "Our curtain rises on a spectacular musical comedy of twenty-four people, and elevated from the stage to the top of the canvas."[354]

Among the female singers featured during the Savannah engagement, "principal soubrette" Maggie Graham sang "Loving Sam" and "I Wonder If Anybody in Town Loves Me"; Mrs. Ethel Reid Cox sang "At the Ball, That's All" and "Down in Chattanooga"; and Katie Price sang "I Wonder Where My Easy Rider's Gone." Among the male comedians, Rastus Williams sang "Everybody Rag With Me," and John H. Williams, now known as "Blue Steel," sang "his own original composition, the 'Blue Steel Blues.'"[355] Since his last stint with the Blossoms, Williams had become a blues specialist. At the end of 1915 he introduced another original blues composition, "The Sanctified Blues."[356] In the fall of 1917 "the original blue steel monologist" appeared on the Blossoms' roster for the last time.

Others who figured in the 1915 Savannah engagement included Dave and Bertha Schaffer singing "When It's Night Time Down in Dixieland" and John and Princella Berringer singing "That Ain't No Job for Me," "I Wish I Had Some Loving Baby to Take My Troubles To," and "other latest songs." There was also a male vocal quartet, the Original Happy Four; and a black Charlie Chaplin, Clint Taylor, "featuring Charlie Chaplin walk." Specialty acts included King Williams and his company of ten trained dogs, starring "Eveline, the world's champion tango dancing dog with human brains."[357]

Another act that found favor in Savannah was a pared-down orchestra of five pieces, in effect a proto–jazz band, "rendering the latest selections." In July it comprised Attler Cox, cornet; Great Rock, violin; Julia Knox, piano; J. L. Williams, trombone; and Clifford Peeler, trap drummer.[358] A revised lineup and choice details of the repertoire were given in August: "The band of five pieces is the feature in their evening concerts, under the direction of Attler Cox, sensational cornetist, rendering the latest selections, rags and featuring 'Memphis Blues,' 'High Yellow Blues,' 'Florida Blues' and the 'Jogo Blues.' Roster of band: Prof. Attler Cox, cornet; Frank Robinson, alto; J. L. Williams, trombone; L. L. Fisher, bass drum and Clifford Peeler, our sensational trap and snare drummer."[359]

At the conclusion of their lengthy stay in Savannah, the Florida Blossom Minstrels moved inland. At Milledgeville, Georgia, late that summer, newcomers John and Bertha Idaho gave out with "Jelly Roll" and "Brother Low Down."[360] Then came the team of Clint Taylor and Rastus Williams, singing "Everybody Rag with Me." A note at the end of the year said, "The show opens with a very pleasing musical comedy, featuring Mrs. Ethel Cox, singing 'Down in Tennessee,' assisted by the following soubrettes: Misses Princella Berrenger, Bertha Shaffer, Katie Price, Bessie Smith, followed by King Williams and his dogs . . . The show closing with a very laughable after-piece, 'Milady's [i.e., Malindy's] Wedding Day.'"[361]

Prominent among the soubrettes who assisted Ethel Cox, Bessie Smith had been traveling the southern vaudeville theater routes since 1909. By 1915, when she joined the Florida Blossoms, she was at the front rank of coon shouters becoming blues singers.[362] A note from the Blossoms on January 1, 1916, assured, "Miss Bessie Smith is a riot singing the 'Hesitation,' 'St. Louis' and 'Yellow Dog Blues.'"

Bessie Smith appears to have returned to southern vaudeville in early February 1916, during a fifteen-day layover in Fort Lauderdale, only to reconnect with the Blossoms later that summer. In North Carolina in mid-July, she was said to be "singing the Hesitation Blues and St. Louis Blues to three and four encores every night."[363] She also returned to her chorus work: "This show is interspersed with a number of musical numbers by a well drilled chorus, composed of the following ladies and gentlemen: Mrs. Ethel Cox, Annie May Child, Kate Price, Bessie Smith, Quaker Jordan, Princella Berrenger, Mr. L. L. Fisher, Dave Sheffer, Ed. Whitehurst, Walter Smith, Bill Jones, Geo. Ross, Warren Thorne." Later that fall, the *Freeman* correspondent wrote from Alabama: "All of the singing and dancing numbers are well taken care of by such soubrettes as Mrs. Princella Berringer, Mrs. Ethel Cox, Mrs. Kate Price, Mrs. Annie May Childs, Miss Quaker Jordan and Miss Bessie Smith . . . Miss Bessie Smith is still singing the Blues as no one else can."[364]

While Bessie Smith was gaining stature as a blues singer, John and Princella Berringer proved to be "the acme of tongo [*sic*] dancers." Their act also featured a clarinet solo by Mrs. Berringer. Princess Regusters, "the 310 pound coon shouter" who joined the Blossoms at Daytona, Florida, early that spring, enriched the olio with her "coon shouting and dancing." The Original Happy Four Quartet remained a feature of the olio, "in rag and classic selections."

The afterpiece, *Malindy's Wedding Day*, was replaced in the spring of 1916 by *A Big Time in the Rich Folks' House*, featuring Katie Price and Mrs. Annie May Childs in blackface.[365] In Alabama that summer, Lonnie Fisher and Charlie "Mushmouth" Miller restaged their 1913 afterpiece, *Jenkins and Swipes Preparing for War*, which the *Freeman* correspondent said was "based on the war in Mexico."[366]

The 1916 edition of the band, still under the direction of Walter H. Childs, was "playing all the standard overtures, 'Morning, Noon and Night,' 'Bohemian Girl,' 'Golden Nuggets,' 'Champion' and the latest medleys. Also Prof. Handy's 'Hail to the Spirit of Liberty,' which is a credit to the writer and shows that he can put out a standard march as well as the Blues."[367] In new parade uniforms—"red Prince Albert coats, white trousers and white silk beavers"—they were said to be "Some class and a real flash." Down to twelve members that summer, the band was playing "not all of the standards, but some rags and some selections."[368]

At the head of the street parade was "Little Billy Bishop, the midget . . . a favorite everywhere." Another feature of the parade was an "electric unaphone," which substituted for a calliope: "John Berringer and his electric unophone never fail to please the crowds, as he has added all the Blues to his repertoire."[369]

The *Freeman* correspondent reported good business through North Carolina during the early fall of 1916: "Tobacco and cotton are bringing good prices and everybody has money, and is having a good time." By November the Blossoms were in the Mississippi Delta, "doing first-class business, but we had an awful sad accident befall us Saturday, November 18. A. G. Terrell, chandelier man, was instantly killed by the explosion of one of the carbide lamps . . . His remains were embalmed and sent to his home, Macon, Ga. . . . Every one else is enjoying all the blessings of life." Immediately thereafter, Pete Worthy "installed a Delco portable electric light plant, which will be quite a novelty, as this will be the first show of its kind to have its own electric light plant."[370]

At Waycross, Georgia, in the spring of 1917, the Blossoms "found the New Orleans Minstrels in opposition, and the town bedecked with flags for the arrival of several companies of United States soldiers, who are to encamp here." The war years saw many performers siphoned off by the draft; at the same time, military encampments afforded some measure of remuneration. When the Blossoms played Augusta, Georgia, in the fall of 1918, the *Freeman* correspondent noted: "There are 11,000 colored soldiers in camp here now . . . so come on all showmen and get the coin while it is here."[371]

Correspondence of April 28, 1917, identified three popular features of the Blossoms' current street parade: Slim Austin's "trombone dancing stunt"; King Williams's educated dogs; and Johnny Berringer's "electric euriphone piano." A later note qualified that, "Slim Jim Austin, the trombone dancing wonder, is featuring his stunt on the street with his new King trombone."[372] William H. "Slim Jim" Austin had developed his famous trombone dancing stunt while touring with Silas Green. His stay with the Blossoms was brief.

En route with the Blossoms on June 3, 1917, Pete Worthy received a telegram calling him to the bedside of his wife, who died that same night. The show continued without losing a day. At Covington, Tennessee, a few weeks later, "a terrible wind and rain came up and blew down our tent. Luckily none of the audience was hurt. Every one got out safely. In the excitement and shock our bandmaster, Walter H. Childs, had a hemorrhage and died in a few minutes. It was a terrible shock and loss to the company . . . The body was prepared for shipment to Macon, Ga., his home, by his widow, Mrs. Annie Childs."[373]

Shortly after her husband's death, Annie Childs returned to the minstrel routes. In the summer of 1920 she was spotted in Pennsylvania with Smith's Old Kentucky Minstrels: "Miss Anna May Childs, our dainty little soubrette is screaming them nightly, singing the 'Hooking Cow Blues' and other Jazz numbers."[374] Meanwhile, the position of bandmaster with the Blossoms fell to Attler Cox and then to Enoch Blake, who joined on April 11, 1918, after Cox received "his call to run the Huns."[375]

The *Freeman* of September 22, 1917, notified that the Blossoms had just completed a successful run through Texas: "The show now blazes forth in all new details. The new parade paraphernalia arrived last week, which is a creation by itself. The coats are of robin egg blue, trimmed in gold, with a long military cut, with trousers and hats to match." In addition, Pete Worthy "annexed six head of evenly matched Shetland ponies, with gorgeous trappings, and a new Drayon unaphone for the parade, which now gives the Florida Blossoms one of the best street flashes carried by any Colored minstrel organization."

Lonnie Fisher apparently made 1917 his last season with the Blossoms. Gravitating to vaudeville, he became a star performer and manager of the TOBA era. When the 1918 season got under way, "Gloomy" Gus Smith was in charge of the stage. Joe White came in for the season, "still making the natives gather around the small drum." The specialty acts included contortionist Nellie

Lonnie Fisher's Ten Dixie Jazz Hounds. (courtesy Douglass Theater Collection, Middle Georgia Archives, Washington Memorial Library, Macon, Georgia)

Matthews; Thomas and Thomas, "drill delineators of darkey didoes"; and Gray and Gray, "doing two distinct novelty acts: first Mrs. Gray, who is without a doubt the champion lady chair balancer and iron jaw act, and Walter Gray in his great slack wire act."

Katie Price was no longer on the roster by 1918, but Bessie Nelson, "the sedate singing soubrette," was "there with the goods and makes the natives like her." Another member of the 1918 female contingent, Grace King, received news en route that her mother had died in Kansas City, and she had to close with the show to go bury her. The *Freeman* correspondent philosophized: "Death is a debt we all have to pay and it behooves us to so shape our lives that we will be prepared to meet the grim reaper when he calls."[376]

On November 15, 1918, without warning, Pete Worthy met the grim reaper at his home in Macon, at the age of forty-nine.[377] Shortly thereafter, the Florida Blossoms came under the ownership of Oscar E. Rogers.[378] They were touring in their home state of Georgia in July 1919, when they got word that Will Rainey had died: "We extend our heartfelt sympathy to Ma Rainey." On stage with the Blossoms that summer, Zora Gibbs sang "Jassing the Blues Away" and "The Beale Street Blues." Also aboard were Leola B. Grant, who would appear on 1920s race recordings as "Coot" Grant; "eccentric monologist" Walter "Kid Sap" Miller; and "the demon of jugglery," John Pamplin. The band was under J. H. McCamon, of Allen's Minstrels fame, and the stage manager was Arthur Williams.[379]

On March 6, 1920, after two months and three days in winter quarters, the Florida Blossoms began what was billed as their sixteenth annual tour, at Fort Valley, Georgia. In August they entered their twenty-third week of the season "with only one day lost, which is exceptional with a tent show of this kind which shows that it is handled with brains and experience."[380]

During the course of the season, the legendary King Nappie Lewis performed "a dancing act not seen on every stage, including buck and wing, soft shoe and Russian dancer"; Kid Sap Miller sang "I'm Going Back to My Use to Be"; Kid Thomas sang a parody on "Somebody Done Me Wrong," and his wife Pinkie sang "Ice and Snow"; Hattie Aiken sang "I Know What It Means To Be Lonesome"; and Arthur and Mary Williams sang "Stamping the Blues Away" and "A Woman Gets Tired of One Man All the Time."[381] Finally, there was John Pamplin, the old "demon of the tropics, whose gun juggling on the streets during our noon-day parade is a sensational feature."[382]

The 1920 edition of the Florida Blossom band played "everything possible." A note in August informed that Prof. McCamon had "let the boys loose and the two jazz babies, Gus Aikens and Jimmy McLearey, cornet screamers, and Gene Aiken, the eccentric laughing trombonist, are Jazzing their way into the hearts of the people. The band is not a sensation, but they please the public in their noonday and evening concerts playing Jazz, popular and standard airs."[383] "Cornet screamer" Jimmy McLeary can be heard on 1929 and 1935 recordings with Richard M. Jones and His Jazz Wizards. Gus and Eugene "Bud" Aiken, whose legacy extended from the Jenkins Orphanage Band,[384] can be heard on a host of early race recordings.

Recollections of the Florida Blossom Minstrels are preserved in the memoirs of Dewey "Pigmeat" Markham, one of the last of the great African American blackface comedians. Markham recalled in his 1969 autobiography, *Here Come the Judge!*, that he and his wife Cecelia had joined the Blossoms at Greenville, South Carolina, in 1923:

> The show tent . . . sat about 1,500 people . . . my salary was $12.50 and Cecelia's was $10.00 a week. What with extra cash on payday, and livin' on the car all the time and gettin' two meals a day free, we was savin' money at last . . . Soon as I joined the Florida Blossoms, they gimme a big bass drum and showed me how to beat it, and I became the bass-drum player in the band.
>
> You see, after each night's performance, they'd strike the tent and load it on the car . . . a minstrel troupe could fit into one big private rail car—and we'd climb aboard and go to sleep at maybe 2 or 3 in the morning. A train would come along and we'd be hitched onto the back, and when we woke up, we'd be in a new town.
>
> Every day at 12 o'clock sharp, while the men was settin' up the tent, we'd hold a parade through town . . . We'd hire some local kid . . . to lead the way carrying the American flag, and then would come the "walkin' gents"—two or three acts from the show—and a couple big banners that read FLORIDA BLOSSOMS TONIGHT!, and finally a 12-piece band. We (the band) played all kinds of lively tunes—like "Trombone Smith" and "Shoutin' Life"—and you can bet that town knew *we* was there!
>
> By the time we marched back to the tent, it'd be all set up, and we'd spend the next couple of hours, till supper at 5 o'clock or so, band rehearsin'. The band was important to a minstrel show. In addition to the noon parade, we'd walk a mile and a half into town again in the evening, straight to the center of town, where we'd make up a little semi-circle and start playin' jazzy tunes. It was like the old ballyhoos we used to do in the gilly carnivals, and it served the same purpose. To attract a crowd. But in the minstrels we didn't call it a ballyhoo. We called it a "concert."
>
> After the show, we had to do another "concert." This one wasn't just a few numbers by the band. We threw in a couple of skits by the comics, and maybe

an act or two, and made it a real little show. It cost 25 cents extra to hang around and see this after-show concert, and while it was goin' on, the men would be dismantling the tent and cartin' away the benches.

Markham further recalled that, by the time he joined the Blossoms, the traditional "opening section, with the 'end men' and Mr. Interlocutor and the tambourines and banjos—the part most people think was a minstrel show—was gone . . . the Olio gradually took over the whole minstrel show. In fact, by the time I came along even the Olio was beginning to break up into bits and pieces—producers and writers, traveling from show to show, were introducing story lines and big dancing numbers with pretty costumes scattered between the Olio acts, and every number in the show had to fit the plot."

Finally, Markham remembered:

One of the producers who showed up to do our shows—about a year after I joined the Blossoms—was none other than Bob Russell . . . He must have been 70 or more by the time we met—he'd been a big star in theaters as well as a writer and producer—and he was a *genius*.

Mr. Russell and I became fast friends . . . Now I was bunkin' back up in the upper berth with the single fellows—my bunkmate was the drummer in the show, a little fellow named Jock. And Bob Russell had the lower berth, all to himself, under us . . . He used to coach me in all the tricks he'd learned—and he'd been in the business since the Civil War, so he'd learned them all . . . But . . . he was an old sick man by then.

In most respects Markham's recollections check out fairly well against contemporaneous reports in the *Chicago Defender*. Correspondence of September 27, 1924, placed him with the Blossoms: "Enoch A. Baker and Rock Markham, the Midnight Man, are going over the top nightly . . . Little Jock the drummer has broke all records among sensational drummers." At Winter Haven, Florida, several weeks later, Baker and Markham were still "going over the top." A report from North Carolina in the spring of 1925 informed that Enoch Baker had become stage manager, while "Rock" Markham and "Kid Sap" Miller had teamed up and were "tearing the house down."[385]

Bob Russell, the ailing genius producer recalled by Markham, was active as early as 1894, when he reportedly assisted Billy McClain in recruiting and rehearsing performers for the legendary outdoor extravaganza, *Black America*.[386] In the March 26, 1921, edition of *Billboard*, columnist J. A. Jackson called Bob Russell "the premier producer on the colored theatrical time." *Defender* correspondences indicate that, from 1922 to 1924, Russell was associated, not with the Florida Blossoms, but with the rival Silas Green Company. A September 8, 1923, report from Silas Green included this warning:

We played Huntsville, Ala., to a large and appreciative audience, and a number of reliable citizens informed Mr. Collier [the current proprietor of the Silas Green Company] that the Florida Blossoms played there a few nights previous, and made a miserable attempt to produce a part of our program.

I wish to warn the management of the Florida Blossoms Co. that the program of the Silas Green show is fully protected by copyright and any further infringement will bring about prosecution.

Bob Russell was engaged at large salary to produce the new Silas Green show, with all rights of same, and anyone doing any part of 'Oh You, Mr. Rareback,' is laying himself liable, so beware.

A report in *Billboard*, January 19, 1924, indicates that Russell was "confined with illness at the Central Hotel in Tampa, Fla. He has concluded his work with the 'Silas Green' Show, and his producing talent should promptly be grabbed by some of the many managers whose shows need such handiwork as his." Russell appears to have signed on with the Blossoms in the fall of 1924. Before the end of the year, however, he left to manage an "All-Star" revue, featuring such outstanding performers as Sam Robinson, Baby Mack, and Petrona Lazzo, on the TOBA circuit.

With the Blossoms in the fall of 1924, soubrette Elsie Gillen was "stopping the show singing 'Kansas City Man.'" The show's ten-piece band was under the direction of Prof. J. H. Witherspoon. Toward the end of the year, illness forced Prof. Witherspoon to retire to his home in Charlotte, North Carolina, and the baton fell to Prof. Elijah Nelson, formerly "cornetist and musical director of Meridian and Laurel, Miss. Band."[387] At season's end word came that, "The Florida Blossoms Show band and orchestra bunch is wintering in Macon, Ga., where they are 'gigging' until the show reopens in the spring."[388]

On March 5, 1925, the Blossoms opened a new season at Milledgeville, Georgia, with "Prof. Nelson's twelve-piece band and seven-piece orchestra." The band roster included Nelson's brother Lamar "Buck" Nelson on tuba; and John L. Porter, a veteran of the New Orleans community brass band milieu and the 1916 edition of the band with Tolliver's Smart Set, on baritone horn. Porter also played saxophone in the Blossoms' "sax quartet," along with Elmer Wheeler, Gregg A. Williams and James Buckingham.[389]

On the Mississippi Gulf Coast during the summer of 1925 the band featured trombonist Devore "Trombone Red" Graden playing "the 'Nelson Brothers' Triple Tongue Blues,' one of Prof. Nelson's own arrangements."[390] When Prof. J. H. Witherspoon returned to his post late that summer, he found "12 real jazzers" in the band. The stage show included "real blues singer" Florence Neal.

At Drew, Mississippi, in September, Rastus Smith found favor with "his song and dance, 'He's in the Jailhouse Now.'"[391] One month later the Blossoms closed their season at Lakeland, Florida, and returned to winter quarters in Macon. Members of the company went their separate ways. Prof. Witherspoon noted that he could be reached "care 81 theater, Atlanta, Ga." John L. Porter went home to New Orleans. "Rock" Markham and "Jock" Thompson signed on for a stint at the Douglass Theater in Macon.[392]

When the show reconvened at Milledgeville on February 19, 1926, Markham was back on the roster, but he left within the next few weeks. In the spring of 1927, he was "taking his with Gonzell White's company."[393] A report in the spring of 1929 advertised his new stage name: "Pigmeat Markham is doing stock at the Standard Theater, Philadelphia."[394] Meanwhile, the *Defender* of May 1, 1926, informed that the Blossoms were in Georgia, "playing to fair business": "Elonzo Williams and his 12-piece band are a big feature with the show."

In August 1927 the Blossoms played through South Carolina: "The tobacco season has opened in the state and business has picked up considerably, but the city and state taxes are extra high and 10 per cent of the gross receipts go for taxes." The roster included "Mary Johnson, our robust blues singer." At Mullins, South Carolina, they "played to a full house for the big show and also the [after show] concert, this being an opposition date to the Maxey Medicine show, which was located on the lot next to us. The medicine show being free had no effect on the Blossoms. The vaudeville and musical program of the medicine show was very good, featuring 'Fat' Hayden, the man with the owl eyes, and Bennie Sparrow and Kid Alcohol."[395]

In September they reached Mississippi, "where the show business has taken a slump, but so far the Blossoms have played to good business except Bay St. Louis. The following towns were good: Pascagoula, Biloxi, Pass Christian, Gulfport and Lumberton. At Pascagoula storms of people turned out, this being the home of 'Buck' Nelson, our tuba player."[396] Meanwhile, blues singer Mary Johnson, "who has been sick for some time, was forced to close and enter the Charity hospital, ward 28, New Orleans, La."

In 1928 the show came under a new owner, Mr. Sparks, who appears to have been the proprietor of Sparks Motor Company, a truck manufacturing firm in Macon.[397] It seems Sparks was able to link his two enterprises: "The Florida Blossoms have motorized the minstrels, discarded their Pullman car, purchased nine new special trucks, and will tour the country via gas." J. C. O'Brien's Famous Georgia Minstrels had already "tried the motor proposition" without success, but there were at least "a few circuses at present traveling through the country on trucks, seemingly with little trouble," and the Blossoms vowed to leave "no stone unturned to make the present venture a success."[398]

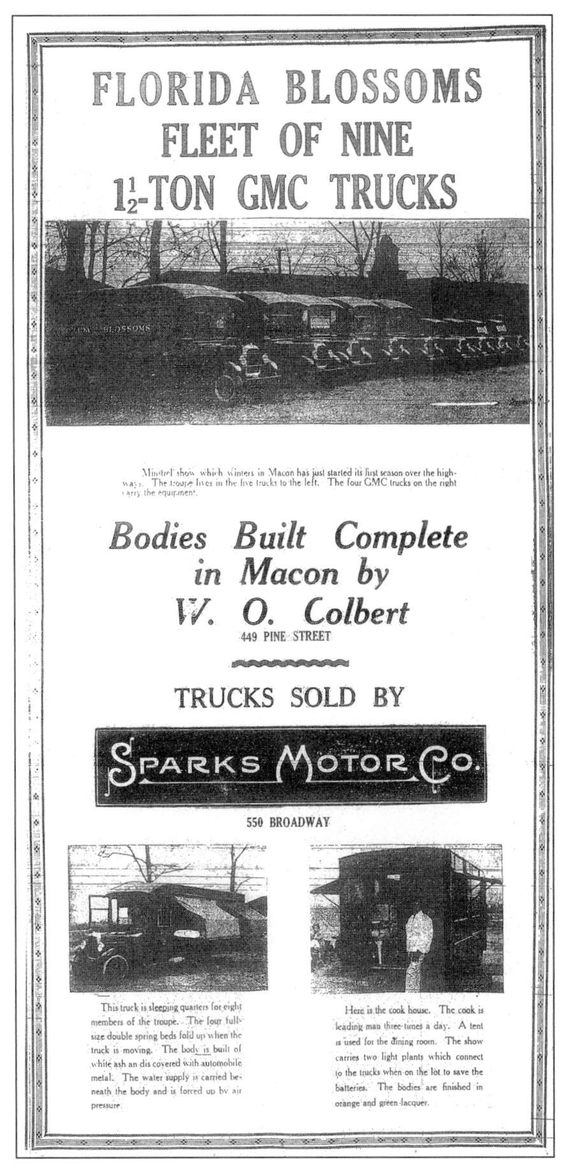

FLORIDA BLOSSOMS
FLEET OF NINE
1½-TON GMC TRUCKS

Minstrel show which winters in Macon has just started its first season over the highways. The troupe lives in the five trucks to the left. The four GMC trucks on the right carry the equipment.

Bodies Built Complete in Macon by W. O. Colbert
449 PINE STREET

TRUCKS SOLD BY

SPARKS MOTOR CO.
550 BROADWAY

This truck is sleeping quarters for eight members of the troupe. The four full-size double spring beds fold up when the truck is moving. The body is built of white ash an dis covered with automobile metal. The water supply is carried beneath the body and is forced up by air pressure.

Here is the cook house. The cook is leading man three times a day. A tent is used for the dining room. The show carries two light plants which connect to the trucks when on the lot to save the batteries. The bodies are finished in orange and green lacquer.

Macon Telegraph, March 26, 1928. (courtesy Middle Georgia Archives, Washington Memorial Library, Macon, Georgia)

A letter posted from Lexington, Virginia, in June 1928 by the show's star comedian Osby Mitchell made note of soubrette Mattie "Sweet" Spencer; prima donna Orleania Mitchell; Clifford

Pettiford, "the mystery man of India"; and Jessie Burney, singer of "blues, blues, blues."[399]

The Blossoms' season of 1931 was the last one documented in the *Defender*. The bandleader that year was Charles Love, and the star comedians were Walter "Sap" Miller and Billy Mitchell. Others on the roster included Foots Robinson, a dancer, and J. C. Davis, "the singing banjoist." Davis supplied the "low-down" on his fellow performers: "Walter Sap Miller . . . was born in La Grange, Georgia, 36 years ago and entered the show business in 1919. Billy Mitchell . . . was born at Atlanta. Foots Robinson plays the first minstrel part and is a wooden shoe artist. Foots is 39 and thumps the bass drum on parade."[400]

According to a final *Defender* report, published July 25, 1931:

> The Florida Blossoms, traveling in twelve specially built trucks, are doing good business through North Carolina.
>
> J. C. Davis is producer and has one of the fastest shows ever on the road. It opens with a minstrel first part with thirty-one people, also a twelve-piece orchestra, featuring Walter ("Sap") Miller, Happy ("Foots") Robinson, Mitchell and Mitchell, Corrine Mitchell, the south's premier blues singer, and the world's most eccentric dancer, Topsy ("Snake Hips") Hart.
>
> The afterpiece is one of continual laughter, featuring Sapp Miller and Willie Mitchell.
>
> Comedians sitting in the circle: Pierce Hart ("Snake Hips"), Billy ("Single") Terry, James Wright, Leroy Skaggs and Leroy Phillips.
>
> Ladies on the ensemble: Mrs. Vennie Davis, Mrs. Corrine Mitchell Phillips, Mrs. Lillie Mae Mitchell, Misses Rosie Tucker, Henrietta Leggett, Odessa Love, Marie Cavanaugh, Cynthia Love and Roberta Manjou.
>
> In the band, under the direction of Charles Love, are: Reeds—Elmer Wheller [*sic*] and Joe Washington. Brass—Charles Love, Amos Strickland, Audro Hooks, Earl Humphrie [*sic*]; J. C. Davis and Buck Nelson. Drums—Foots Robinson and Jock Thompson.

Among the bandsmen, trombonist Earl Humphrey was a progeny of the famous Humphrey family of New Orleans musicians. A self-proclaimed "traveling man" since the World War I years, Humphrey recorded in 1927 with Louis Dumaine's Jazzola Eight. He said the Depression flushed him out of New Orleans in 1931 and led him to Macon, Georgia, where he joined the Blossoms: "I stayed with them three years, the Florida Blossom Minstrel Show . . . We had about a twelve-piece band, brass band . . . The show consisted of about thirty-five to forty people altogether, men, women, chorus girls . . . Spread a big tent every day . . . We had sleeping vans right on the same lot where the tent would be."[401] Humphrey's testimony is the last word to date on the Florida Blossom Minstrels.

Silas Green from New Orleans

A stage character named "Silas Green" appeared as early as 1898, in Bob Cole and Billy Johnson's first big show, *A Trip to Coontown*. In the 1899 edition of *A Trip to Coontown*, old-school minstrel star Sam Lucas "scored the hit of his life as 'Silas Greene.'"[402] The particular origin of *Silas Green from New Orleans* can be traced to the summer of 1907, when veteran troupers Eph Williams, Salem Tutt Whitney, and William A. Baynard came together in a tent show headed by Sherman H. Dudley.[403]

Ephraim "Eph" Williams was born in Nashville, Tennessee, on July 19, 1860.[404] He appears to have come of age in Wisconsin, where retrospective accounts suggest he "got his early start in the saloon business" and "took up horse and pony training as a hobby."[405] Gravitating to circus work, he became "the only Negro in the world that ever owned a circus . . . He and his family were the only Colored faces seen with the show."[406]

In the spring of 1888 Ferguson and Williams's Double United Monster Shows and Trained Animal Exposition started out from Appleton, Wisconsin. That summer they stranded in Dubuque, Iowa, leaving Prof. Williams and the Bohemian Skerbeck Family of acrobats, sword swallowers, contortionists, etc., to play small towns "with the dressing room canvas."[407] Williams next launched Prof. Williams and Co.'s Circus, with the versatile Skerbeck Family. In 1891 he was said to be carrying fifty horses and 150 people.[408] From his new winter headquarters in Medford, Wisconsin, he went out every season until 1893.[409] The local Medford paper reflected on his career to date: "More than a dozen times he has been on the brink of disaster, but was saved by his indomitable pluck . . . His skin is dark, but he will come out on top yet, or know the reason why."[410]

In 1896, after a "long absence," Prof. Williams returned to Medford to take charge of the bar at the Hotel Winchester, "the bon ton resort of the county."[411] In the spring of 1897 he placed an ad in the local paper, recruiting talent for a new circus.[412] A note in the *Freeman* that summer advised: "Prof. E. Williams, of Medford, Wis., is the only Negro circus owner in America. He employs seventy-five men and owns two hundred head of Arabian ponies and horses."[413]

Prof. Williams relocated to Milwaukee before the spring of 1901, when he opened what may have been his final circus venture, Williams's Great Northern Shows.[414] Meanwhile, in 1897, Salem Tutt Whitney and William A. Baynard were touring with one of the more popular African American concert companies of the time, the Puggsley Brothers' Tennessee Warblers. Whitney was the principal vocalist and comedian, Baynard the medal-winning "trick and descriptive pianist." The Tennessee Warblers' prima donna soprano was Baynard's sister Emma, who became Salem Tutt Whitney's wife.

By 1904 the brothers-in-law were piloting a respectable little tent show of their own, Baynard and Whitney's Troubadours. In 1906 they joined forces with the Smart Set Company under Sherman H. Dudley and, when Prof. Eph Williams and his "four equine beauties" also joined the Smart Set that fall in Milwaukee, the stage was set for the rise of *Silas Green from New Orleans*.

Every summer beginning in 1903 or 1904, between the Smart Set's regular touring seasons, S. H. Dudley fielded a tent show under the title of his 1902 farce comedy, *The Jolly Ethiopians*. The 1907 edition of Dudley's Jolly Ethiopians was a notable departure in African American entertainment:

> Mr. Dudley has engaged forty colored performers for the coming season, which makes it one of the largest and strongest summer shows under canvas . . . [Dudley] has secured the services of Salem Tutt Whitney, the Hoosier comedian, to head this splendid aggregation of talent. Their mammoth waterproof opera tent has an adequate and comfortable seating capacity of 2,500 persons . . . An extra feature of the many added this season . . . will be Prof. E. Williams' dog and pony circus . . . Prof. Williams has the only rope walking pony in the world.[415]

Other features included Salem Tutt Whitney's comedian brother Homer Tutt; "lady cornet soloist" Nettie Taylor; and William Baynard's orchestra of seven pieces. The Jolly Ethiopians opened at Chester, Pennsylvania, on Decoration Day, May 30, 1907. Nine weeks later Dudley left the show to pick up again with the Smart Set. Salem Tutt Whitney and Homer Tutt also left, to assume starring roles with the Black Patti Troubadours. As Eph Williams later recalled, he and William Baynard found themselves in Phoebus, Virginia, with the remnants of Dudley's Jolly Ethiopians, and vowed to keep the show afloat as Williams and Baynard's Famous Troubadours: "Baynard agreed to go South with me if I would take the show there. I immediately furnished the capital, got out the billing matter and started on a tour across the Mason and Dixon line for the first time in my life."[416]

At Norfolk, Virginia, Williams and Baynard's Famous Troubadours picked up R. C. Puggsley, one of the namesake brothers of Puggsley's Tennessee Warblers. R. C. had served as the Warblers' star tragedian and "lion basso," business manager and advance agent. As the Famous Troubadours' advance agent, he became an increasingly important asset. In 1925, a *Chicago Defender* correspondent dubbed him "the national trade mark of the Silas Green Show."[417]

On September 7, 1907, Williams and Baynard's Troubadours reported:

> We have now been open three weeks and are glad to say that S.R.O. has been on the front ever since. The company has made good everywhere, and is acknowledged to be the finest company on the road under canvas. This is the original Jolly Ethiopians under the experienced eye of that irresistible S. H. Dudley, but the work and management was too much for him and would render him useless for the great winter season. Among the artists we are headed by Mr. Eddie Stafford, the midget comedian, who replaces the popular favorite comedian Salem Tutt Whitney. Stafford has filled the bill to the letter and is fast coming to the front. He is known as Little Silas.

By year's end Williams and Baynard's Troubadours had ventured as far south as Montgomery, Alabama, where Prof. Williams recalled having met the pastor of First Baptist Church and "arranged for a concert, which was indeed a novel and unique one, to take place at his church":

> We introduced our performing ponies on a platform built over the pool around the rostrum of the church, and this created considerable discussion among the members, some saying that Rev. Andrew Jackson Stokes was going to turn the church into a horse stable . . . That necessitated the calling of a special meeting of the members of the church by the Rev. Stokes, and in that meeting he succeeded in convincing the excited and unprogressive members of the congregation that it was purely an education exhibition and that Prof. Williams would prove that his little equine beauties could multiply and subtract mathematically, tell the time of day by the watch, write on a typewriter and demonstrate human intelligence superior to the fault finder.[418]

In May 1908, at the end of their season with the Black Patti Troubadours, Salem Tutt Whitney and J. Homer Tutt rejoined Williams and Baynard's Famous Troubadours and "stayed all summer, helping to arrange the shows." In August they made their way back to New Jersey to open the 1908–1909 season with the Black Patti Troubadours: "Salem Tutt Whitney (Happy Silas), the Hoosier comedian, will again be seen at the head of the mirth provokers . . . [He] has written what promises to be one of the best one act musical comedies ever produced by the Troubadours, entitled 'The Barnstormers.' He will enact the comedy role of Silas Green, while Homer Tutt will be seen as Suretu Walkback . . . Wm. A. Cooke . . . will assist Mr. Whitney in staging the new show, also enacting the difficult comedy role of Count-de-no-Count, a dusty knight of the road."[419]

Whitney's 1908 tour with the Black Patti Troubadours was tragically interrupted when his wife Emma died in Philadelphia. A few weeks later it was announced that Tim Owsley, "recently a big feature of the Pekin Theater, Chicago, has been engaged to replace Salem Tutt Whitney, leading comedian of the Black Patti Troubadours, at Dallas Tex., December 7." When they presented *The Barnstormers* at Bisbee, Arizona, in the spring of 1909, a reviewer for the local daily paper judged, "It would be improper to designate it as a play, although a thin spread of plot binds together the various specialty turns. In parts it is as good as anything ever seen here. This is especially true of Tim Owsley in the role of Silas Green, the rustic angel for a stranded opera troupe."[420]

After 1909, there were no further references to Silas Green in correspondence from the Black Patti Troubadours. Meanwhile, the *Freeman* of May 23, 1908, informed:

> Williams and Baynard's Famous Troubadours are making new history in the colored theatrical world, having toured the entire South under entire colored management playing to capacity and S. R. O. business producing musical comedies, with high-class vaudeville. It is the only colored repertoire company traveling that plays two and three nights and week stands with entire change of program nightly.
>
> Prof. Eph Williams and his trained ponies are making them scream with delight everywhere. W. M. Baynard, the piano specialist carries his own instrument and makes them wonder what is it? when he does his act. The company travels in its own private car, and R. C. Puggsley, the able advance representative and contractor, is handling the front in an able manner, bringing good results. Richard Stewart, the midget comedian, is certainly the coming Negro delineator. Miss Nettie Taylor, the leading lady and instrumentalist, has developed into an actress of rare ability. Mr. and Mrs. Floyd joined at Norfolk. John Johnson, leader of the band, has brought it up to a high degree. His special free concerts each evening makes them secure tickets and go inside. John Warren is playing straight and leads, and is giving a good account of himself with the tuba in the band. This company is playing return dates in all the large Southern cities to S.R.O. business. It has been out all winter and summer, and never closes. There are twenty-five people, six ponies, six dogs, band and orchestra. Williams and Baynard are proprietors. Prof. Eph Williams, manager; W. M. Baynard, director; Richard Stewart, stage manager; John Johnson, leader of band.

Williams and Baynard's Famous Troubadours had completed their summer swing through West Virginia and were headed south in the fall of 1908, when their *Freeman* correspondent noted, "Richard Stewart, the comedian, has had quite a success in his character of 'Silas Green from New Orleans.'"[421]

In 1909 Prof. Eph Williams became the show's sole owner. That spring, after a long winter season in Florida, his Famous Troubadours headed into "the Cracker State," with a two-night stand in Atlanta: "Prof. Dick Collins is in charge of the band . . . Clarence P. Jones is musical director for the show and has a fine orchestra under his baton. Ulysses Simmons, our straight man, and Harry Brown, our aged darky delineator, are two men in the right place, while Rachel Jones has created a new 'Dinah' in our plantation scene, and is mopping up in her dance specialty."[422]

By 1910 the Troubadours were traveling in two cars, a Pullman sleeper and a combination dining and baggage car. At the beginning of the year they were presenting the "genuine Negro comedy 'The Funny Side of Life.'" In April the *Freeman* correspondent wrote from Virginia to inform that, "The musical comedy, 'Silas Green from New Orleans,' which has made this company famous, is being brightened and polished up."[423] As summer came on, they moved into the coal fields of West Virginia, where they looked forward to "a glorious Fourth [of July] in their canvas theater listening to the returns of the Johnson-Jeffries fight." According to the *Freeman* correspondent, "The name 'Silas Green from New Orleans' is a byword in this section of the country, and the consensus of opinion is that our show is the best ever." In the cast that summer were William H. Mayfield as Silas Green; Thomas Price as "Bill Jones of Chicago"; Will Goff Kennedy as Uncle Ben Green; Thomas Baxter as Mr. Run-Em-In; Jennie Hale as Miss Mary Smith; and Pearl Moon as Linda Jane Green.[424]

Will Goff Kennedy had joined the show at Macon, Georgia, earlier that spring. Jennie Hale, the current leading lady, held that post through 1912, singing such titles as "Pickaninny Band" and "I'll Change the Thorns to Roses" and enlivening the evening concerts with her baton juggling. "Also, her serpentine and fire dance is the talk of the country."[425]

New to the female contingent in 1910 was Susie Cooksey, "the Indianapolis Song Bird," earlier known as "Susie Polk the Goo Goo Singing Bird."[426] At the end of the year Cooksey was singing "that great song hit of the season, 'That Barbershop Chord.'" In the spring of 1911 she was "singing 'Hide From the Light of the Moon' with much success." A note in 1912 informed, "Miss Susie Cooksey, nee Price, is making the hit of her stage career singing 'That Harmony' and that beautiful ballad, 'Way Down upon the Suwannee River.'"

Flo Russell. *Indianapolis Freeman*, December 31, 1910.

Susie Cooksey. *Indianapolis Freeman*, December 31, 1910.

MISS PEARL MOON.

The above is a photo of Miss Pearl Moon, the Virginia Dare, as Sue Johnson in a skit of that name. She is with Eph. Williams's Famous Troubadours and is greeted with great applause at every performance. This young miss is bright and witty. Her address is Box 35, Pulaski, Va. She sends her regards to the profession and wishes all a mery Christmas and a happy New Year.

Pearl Moon. *Indianapolis Freeman*, December 31, 1910.

Another important addition to the roster in 1910 was "coon song shouter" and "dainty soubrette" Flo Russell. Initially identified as "Miss Zelia B. Russell, a hot one from Pennsylvania,"[427] she was popularly characterized as "Little Flo, the ginger gal, oh, you Flo." She took the stage in "cowgirl attire," singing "that great western hit, 'My Bronco Sal.'"[428] Flo Russell remained a bright face on the roster for the rest of the decade. In 1911 she came "to the front by leaps and bounds" singing "Beautiful Rag" and "Stop! Stop! Stop!" In the spring of 1912 her rendition of "Railroad Rag" was "setting the pace for other soubrettes in her class to follow." Her hits of 1913 included "On the Trail of the Lonesome Pine" and "Rattlesnake Rag."

Before the end of 1910, the role of Silas Green fell to Thomas Price, "the Kentucky whirlwind," who also played snare drum in the parade band. During his two years as the star comedian, Price played an infinitely more grotesque Silas Green than the affable-looking character Salem Tutt Whitney had introduced with the Black Patti Troubadours. Price appears to have retired by early

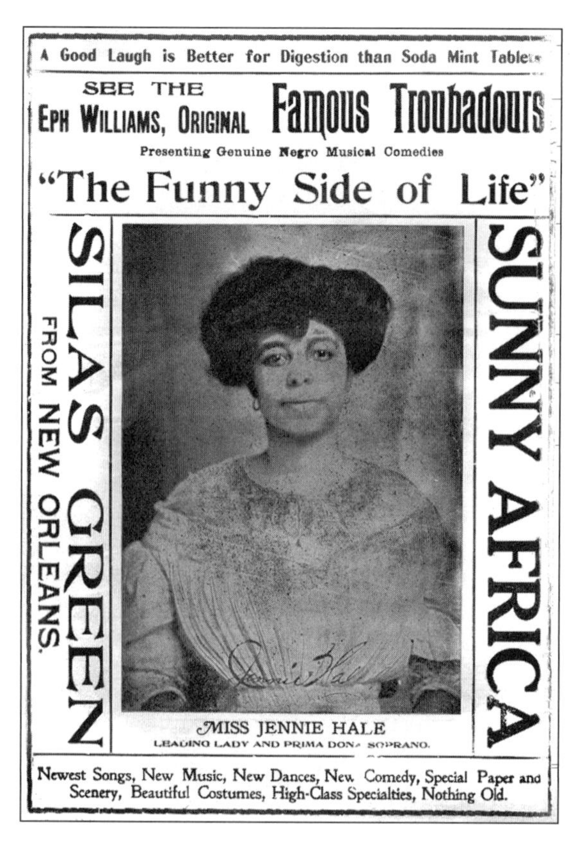

Page from promotional brochure for Eph Williams's Troubadours. (courtesy Circus World Museum, Baraboo, Wisconsin)

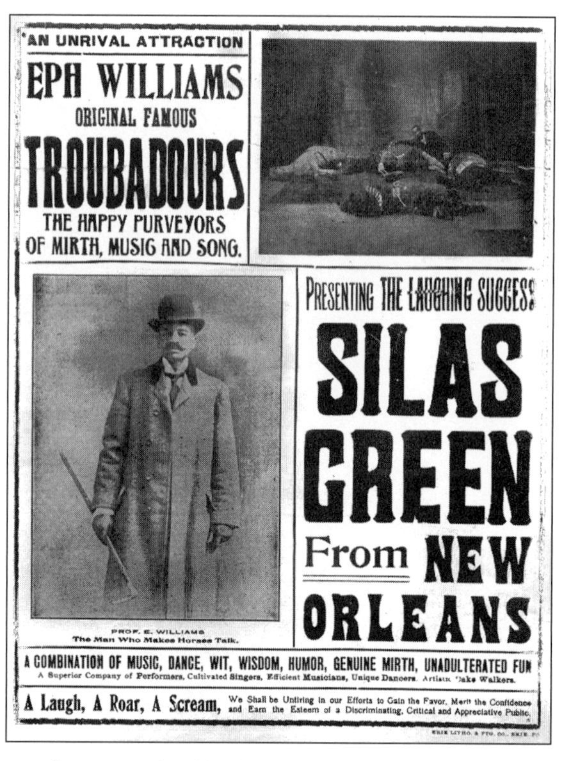

Page from promotional brochure for Eph Williams's Troubadours. (courtesy Circus World Museum, Baraboo, Wisconsin)

1913. At Charleston, West Virginia, that summer, members of the Silas Green Company were "highly entertained by Mr. and Mrs. Thomas Price [who] have a nice hotel at 510 Court street, which is open to all professionals."[429]

In the spring of 1911 the band of "twelve very well posted musicians" came under the direction of cornetist R. J. "Dickie" Anderson:

> He is a Texan and a real snappy musician and handles his band in a noble manner, playing some of the very latest selections, and the way he has his band to form their daily parade circle sets the people wild on the street. The program of his daily concert is "Diplomat March," by Sousa; "Bits of Remick's Hits, No. 7," "Medley Overture," where a quintet of ladies sing two different choruses with megaphones, and Mr. Goff Kennedy, who has a rich baritone voice, sings in the same overture, and Mr. George Israel renders "Crystal Beach," a trombone solo, with much credit. Also Maori A. Samon dances and ends with "Slipping Hank's Rag."[430]

Over the next three months the band swelled to sixteen pieces, and the *Freeman* correspondent boasted that they "never kick at any call for music . . . Thos. Price and Jake Elliott, our battery, are sending their thunder sounds and rolls, all over every place when in town . . . Jess Reeves, our principal trombonist, has his share of people around him as you know trombone players draw."[431]

LATEST PHOTO OF MRS. RHODA A. WILLIAMS.

The subject of the above cut is the bright and steady business wife of Prof. Eph. Williams, sole owner of the Famous Troubadours Comedy Company, now touring the Southern states to "S. R. O." houses nightly. Mrs. Williams is so well known that she needs no introduction to the show world. She wishes every member of the profession a merry Christmas and a happy New Year. Her address is 68 Tenth street, Milwaukee, Wis.

Rhoda Williams. *Indianapolis Freeman*, December 31, 1910.

WILL GOFF KENNEDY

Comedian, old man character impersonator, singer and Shakespearian delineator.

Nashville Globe, March 15, 1918.

L. Don Bradford and wife joined in the spring of 1911, with Bradford slipping into the role of "Mr. Jones, private secretary of Silas Green." The versatile Bradford had spent the winter of 1910–1911 painting scenery for various theaters in Miami, Florida. Prof. Williams had announced plans that winter to "float a No. 2 company," to be known as the Big City Minstrels, and he set Bradford to work painting scenery for his new show.

The advent of the Big City Minstrels was delayed by a gruesome tragedy. At Hartsville, South Carolina, in the early hours of April 8, 1911, while the Famous Troubadours were "laying on the side track," they were awakened by a cry of "fire":

All rushed pell mell out of the car . . . When on the outside they found it was not the sleeping car but the baggage car that was in flames. It was tightly closed, as there had been a thunder storm during the night. All the working crew and live stock were in the car, and everybody strained every effort to save the lives of the unfortunates . . . but not before several lives had paid the forfeit, and many seriously wounded. All the dead and wounded were canvasmen. Prof. Eph Williams rendered every assistance possible to the dead and wounded that could be had. Medical attention was procured and he then chartered a special train to take the wounded to the nearest hospital at Sumter, S. C., in company with a corps of physicians and W. H. Baynard. All is gloom around the show in consequence. Notwithstanding this terrible blow the

Troubadours opened their doors Monday April 10th at Florence, S. C., with the loss of only one day . . . The origin of the fire has never been discovered.[432]

On June 10, 1911, Prof. Williams's "No. 2" Company opened in Durham, North Carolina: "Everything new. Tents made to order by J. C. Goss, of Detroit. Lights by the Bolte-Weyer Company, of Chicago. Scenery painted by L. D. Bradford. Costumes from Great Western Uniform Company, of Chicago." To insure a measure of stability, Prof. Williams put R. C. Puggsley in charge of the Big City Minstrels, and he padded the roster with several of Silas Green's best performers, plus bandmaster R. J. "Dickie" Anderson and most of his bandsmen. Prof. R. H. Collins took charge of the "No. 1" band, which also comprised "a whopping good bunch of boys."

At Birmingham, Alabama, in November 1911, Prof. Williams "consolidated his Big City Minstrels with his Famous Troubadours," under the official banner of *Silas Green from New Orleans*.[433] Proceeding directly to the Gulf Coast, the *Silas Green from New Orleans* Company launched their winter tour of Florida "bigger, better, larger than ever":

TUTT WHITNEY AS SILAS GREEN.

Indianapolis Freeman, August 22, 1908.

Monday, December 18, we opened at Plant City, Fla., and the natives both white and colored greeted us with turn away business. Tuesday we moved into Bradenton, Fla., a beautiful town on Manitee bay. It was our first appearance there, but after our grand parade with a select concert by Prof. Collins' Cornet Band and a convincing announcement by our business manager, Mr. R. C. Puggsley, the town turned out and filled our canvas theater to its utmost capacity.

Wednesday found us in Sarasota, Fla., one of the most popular winter resorts in Florida . . . There are quite a few of our people here, all doing well, and have lovely homes.

On Thursday our next stand was Palmetto City and it gave us big business. There are only a few of our people there, but the white ladies and gentlemen came out in large numbers . . .

Friday we played a return date at Plant City . . . Saturday, December 23, we played Winter Haven . . . We spent Sunday, December 24 at Orlando, Fla., with a happy thought of what was in store for us the following day (Christmas), as we had noticed our genial manager, Prof. Eph Williams, and wife for the past ten days purchasing large numbers of bundles . . . Orlando

THOMAS PRICE, THE KENTUCKY WHIRLWIND.

The above is a reproduciton from a recent photo of Thomas Price, the Kentucky Whirlwind, as Silas Green from New Orleans, who is with the Eph. Williams Famous Troubadours. He is playing the comedy role with great success and is the coming spot

of wit and humor before the footlights. Regards to S. Tutt Whitney, Henry Waterson and Miss Tenna Weatherby. A merry Christmas and a happy New Year to all. His home address is 519 Snyder Place, N. E., Lexington, Ky.; business address, The Freeman, Indianapolis, Ind.

Indianapolis Freeman, December 31, 1910.

is a fine little city, with paved streets. There are hundreds of our people there in all avenues of business . . .

Our noonday parade here was one of Eph Williams' best efforts. The band appeared in new uniforms. Baby Josephine Williams was mounted on her newly purchased Shetland pony. Twelve walking gents, dressed in the height of fashion, eight uniformed banner boys, carrying gold and silver motto banners; six ladies, handsomely gowned, drawn in three up to date traps; Silas Green, dressed for the occasion, astride our Mexican burro Maud, who could hardly move for the kids. R. C. Puggsley, mounted on Prof. E. Williams' fiery steed acting as marshall of the day, and Prof. and Mrs. Williams leading the entire parade in their swell tandem team. The result of this parade was very much in evidence, at the box office. Our 80-foot top, with two 40-foot middle pieces, could not hold the crowd that applied for admission.

The new version of "Silas Green," as arranged by Mr. W. Goff Kennedy, our stage manager, gave the best of satisfaction . . . and the fine acting of Mr. W. H. Mayfield portraying the character of Silas Green, sent the vast audience to wonderland . . .

After the show the entire company consisting of 41 people was invited to remain by Prof. Williams and while all were waiting and wondering what was going to happen, up went the curtain, and there stood a beautiful Xmas tree loaded with handsome and costly presents and surrounded with lots of good things to eat and drink.[434]

Over the next several years Prof. Williams occasionally posted recruitment ads in the *Freeman* for his "No. 2 company," but only the Silas Green Company sent news reports. In the spring of 1912 there was this boast: "'Silas Green,' our principal comedy, bids fair to rival Uncle Tom's Cabin in popularity." One standout of 1912 was singer and "wooden shoe buck dancer" Bessie Edgington, "the little girl with the educated feet": "Her big

Indianapolis Freeman, December 20, 1913. The stylized, not necessarily personal inscription reads "Edington," but the caption below reads "Edgington." The latter spelling is used repeatedly by *Freeman* correspondents of 1912–1917.

song hits are 'When I Woke Up This Morning, He Was Gone,' 'If Some One Only Cared for Me,' and she closes with a buck dance and waltz clog."[435] In 1913 Sidney Perrin leased Bessie Edgington the rights to two of his latest songs, "Mexican Queen" and "Chop Suey Sue."[436]

Contortionist Clifton Boyd joined Silas Green in the spring of 1912: "His bending enables him to be called the boneless wonder of the 20th century." Also joining that spring was William H. Austin, identified as a "promising youngster." A note at the beginning of 1913 said Austin was "better known as Slim Jim from Savannah." Austin made news that year when he "adopted a new dance, 'The Chicken Reel.'"[437] By 1915 Slim Jim Austin was doubling on trombone, and he worked up a characteristic "dancing trombone stunt" to feature in the street parade.

The 1912 parade band, still under R. H. Collins, numbered eighteen pieces with three featured soloists: Fred Kewley, clarinet; Jesse Reeves, trombone, and R. J. Mitchell, cornet. "Jesse Reeves, Charley (Happy) Lewis and Jerry Martin, our slip horn players, never fail to raise a furore in our noonday parades. Lawrence Booker and Goff Kennedy, baritones are our harmony kids. Wm. Fisher and John Ivey, tuba and baritone, of Petersburg, Va., work together. Manzie Williams and Babe Steele are the battery."[438]

William Baynard became the company's unofficial chaplain: "In order that we may live more home-like on our private car and because we have to travel on Sundays and not get in town early enough for services of the Lord, Prof. Williams has inaugurated a special service on board the 'Rhoda,' every Sunday between the hours of 2 and 3 p.m. Mr. William Baynard, our leading straight man, has charge of these services."[439] "Mr. Baynard lectures to the members of the company every Sunday on the leading topics of the day. A lecture on the life and work of the eminent S. Coleridge Taylor was beautifully painted Sunday on board the private car Rhoda at West Palm Beach."[440]

On March 31, 1912, Silas Green's arrival at Aiken, South Carolina, was delayed by a train wreck down the line, and they had to postpone their show until 10 o'clock that night. Nevertheless, "Fully 800 people crowded the door crying for admission. White as well as colored sat on the curb stones and watched the boys erect the large and spacious canvas, eager and determined to see that great cast of performers, that has made this company the household word of everyone throughout the South, render the new and original production, 'Silas Green from New Orleans.'"[441] At Wilmington, North Carolina, they were "greeted by an audience of over eleven hundred people, notwithstanding there are six colored vaudeville houses there . . . and on Tuesday night after our show, the entire company was tendered an oyster roast, given by those prince of good fellows, Leigh Whipper, Hambone Jones and Frank Tansil, who are at the Princess Theater."[442]

In the fall of 1912 Silas Green ventured, for the first time, into Mississippi and Louisiana. On November 9, they reported:

> Our first visit to the Cotton and Sugar Cane states has been fruitful . . . The demand for return dates was so great that we played a good many and our canvass theater was not large enough to accommodate the immense crowds, especially at Jackson, Clarksdale, Greenville, Vicksburg, Baton Rouge, Greenwood and many others. Greek met Greek when we played Mound Bayou, the greatest town in the world, we think. A thrifty colored town, composed entirely of Negroes, and the best community of colored people, living like a big family. "Silas Green," the Troubadour trademark is thoroughly instilled in the minds of Mississippians and Louisianians. Our band, under the leadership of Walter H. Childs, is a feature at noonday parades, featuring Jesse Reeves, trombonist and Fred Kewley, clarinet. The company came near succumbing to the Delta malaria fever, but nearly all have recovered.

Prof. Williams's success began to manifest itself in the form of real estate. By the end of 1915 his holdings included a home in Winter Park, Florida, surrounded by "twenty acres of orange and grapefruit," a "park for Colored people at Huntington, W. Va., stores and flat buildings in Charleston, W. Va., a homestead near Blackstone, Va., a four-story flat in Chicago and lots of property in his home state, Wisconsin."[443] Members of the company also started investing in real estate. A note in 1913 informed that trombonist Jessie Reeves and singing soubrettes Susie Cooksey and Flo Russell had all purchased lots in Sanford, Florida.

In the spring of 1913, Silas Green was carrying fifty-two people and ten head of stock in two seventy-foot railroad cars.[444] Prof. Williams boasted, "They may all say what they please, but the Silas Green Company is one of the greatest organizations of its kind in existence. We spread more canvas than any other colored show of the kind on the road. We seat 1,500 people, and this show has the expense of $150 daily and has not closed in seven years. Last but not least, it has not missed a payday."[445]

They played through the Carolinas that spring: "At New Berne, Plymouth, Hertford, Elizabeth City, Washington and Kinston, N. C., our business was phenomenal," with blacks and whites attending in "almost equal" numbers.[446] Reports were much the same when they returned to North Carolina that fall. At Rocky Mount the tent was "almost entirely filled with our white patrons and as our colored friends came late in large numbers we could only give them what was remaining." At Winston-Salem, "White and colored voted us best ever."[447]

At Waycross, Georgia, Silas Green played day-and-date with the Barnum and Bailey Circus: "We were placed directly in front of our opposition, not fifty feet from the main entrance of the circus, but when our band began to play the faithful began to fall in line, and in less than half an hour the tent was filled to capacity and we had to turn them away."[448] In the wake of the Waycross engagement, the band took on a new player: "Mr. Stratton, sousaphonist of Barnum & Bailey show."

Also new to the band that fall was "sensational trap drummer" Walter H. "Dukey" Hoyt, of Hartford, Connecticut. Hoyt spent the rest of his days in Silas Green's employ, handling the snare drum on parade, and traps on stage. Other newcomers of 1913 included J. C. Pridgeon, "the one-string wonder, trick violinist and banjo player"; and Frank Smedley, the "little basso profundo." Pridgeon did not last the season but Smedley stayed on for the next five years, rendering the popular run of bass solos, including "Any Old Port in a Storm," "Asleep in the Deep," "Davey Jones's Locker," and "When the Bells in the Light House Ring Ding Dong."

Specialty artist George Baker, who had traveled with the show as early as 1910, returned in 1913 as "Marvelous La Vola, world's greatest slack wire walker." He opened with a new stunt, "turning a complete somersault in midair from the wire and returning to the wire with as much ease as if strolling in the park . . . He works sixteen feet high in midair, doing stunts that no other dare attempt." Other specialty acts of 1913 included Charles Williams, "the man who burns himself up into a new generation before the audience in an ordinary flour barrel," and Dora English, known as Queen Dora, "pleasing our audiences nightly with her serpentine fire dance and poses plastique."[449]

The 1913 season was capped by a "new version of the two-act musical comedy of 'Silas Green from New Orleans,' with new and up to date vaudeville." Leroy Knox was recruited from

QUEEN DORA,

Who Does the Serpentine Fire Dance.

The above cut is a direct profile of Queen Dora, known the world over as the only lady of color doing the beautiful electrical spectacular production, known

as the serpentine fire dance and French plastique poses. Queen Dora, it goes without saying, is an expert in her own original act and packs the houses wherever she appears. As years roll on she works with more ease and becomes more charming and beautiful . She was a riot on the American Booking Agency's time and all agents are ever ready to book the act if she but had some open time. Her wardrobe is par-excellent, she having just received some beautiful Parisian gowns for her new act, which she is now rehearsing and has an order in for her spécial scenery, which consists of three drops and one large Chinese dragon head. Critics claim that this will be the greatest attempt ever made in this special line of work. Queen Dora also carries four spot lights and lamps, everything complete. It will also necessitate the employment of two electricians. Queen Dora is prepossessing and is always abreast of the times. Regards to all in the profession. Electricians, write, care of The Freeman.

Indianapolis Freeman, November 22, 1913.

BABY JOSEPHINE WILLIAMS, ALIAS "BABY JOE," THE CHILD WONDER.

This little child takes an active part in this production. She is 7 years of age, has a wonderful voice, is a neat dancer and promises to become a star.

She wishes all a merry Christmas and a happy New Year. "Baby Joe's" address is 68 Tenth street, Milwaukee, Wis.

Indianapolis Freeman, December 31, 1910.

the Florida Blossoms to assume the character of Silas Green: "Mr. Knox bids fair to make one of the best 'Silases' we have ever had." Others in the cast included L. Don Bradford, whose portrayal of handsome, well-dressed "Bill Jones of Chicago" was said to be remindful of George Walker; Will Goff Kennedy as Uncle Ben; Flo Russell, leading lady; and Susie Cooksey as Miss Pollie. Also making an appearance was Eph and Rhoda Williams's daughter, "Little Baby Josephine . . . styled as the child wonder . . . She supports the leading lady, mingles with the chorus girls, and is seen to good advantage in the last act, in the reception given to Silas Green."[450]

Leroy Knox also performed his popular "Mandy" impersonation in a blackface team act with Slim Jim Austin: "Mandy and Slim Jim . . . stop the show." Perhaps the most important new performer of 1913 was Ford Wiggins, of New Bern, North Carolina, who initially came aboard as a "challenge buck and wing dancer." In 1916 Wiggins took over the character of Silas Green and, except for a few minor breaks in continuity, stuck with it for more than twenty-five years.

Silas Green played Christmas Day 1913 at Hattiesburg, Mississippi: "After the parade the private car Rhoda was elaborately decorated with Christmas greens, and the entire company assembled to listen to a few timely remarks relative to the occasion by W. A. Baynard, after which our genial stage manager, Will Goff Kennedy, passed out the many gifts." The *Freeman* correspondent reflected: "It is really an enigma when you stop and think that the Silas Green Show, although never closing its doors for seven years, still everywhere people are wild to see it over and over again."[451] "It seems the public never tires of the antics of Silas Green and his cohorts."[452]

On January 18, 1914, the *Silas Green from New Orleans* Company played for the first time in New Orleans. They appeared, not under canvas, but in the black-owned Pythian Temple Theater on Rampart Street. The *Freeman* correspondent noted that the locals "had read so much of the show and the scene being laid in New Orleans naturally everyone was eager to see what we could do":

> The company consisted of fifty-one people, the largest company ever playing in New Orleans . . . Mr. Leroy

Knox, the old North State comedian, assumed the role of Silas Green and he made the hit of his life . . . It goes without saying that W. A. Baynard fully sustained his reputation as an actor, and his clever work as a straight man and his many costly and beautiful costumes was a revelation. Miss Susie Cooksie, our leading lady, and Miss Millie Bradford were at their best and their new Parisian costumes were considered the finest . . . The olio consisted of Baby Josephine, the Little Dancing Wonder, who was a prime favorite; the Famous Acrobatic Artists, the Gaines Brothers; Willie Austin, The Original Slim Jim Doing the Chick[en] Reel; Prof. Chas. Williams in his master Barrel Act; Ford Wiggins, the Prince of Buck and Wing Dancers, and last, but not least, the Mighty Marvelous La Vola, who held them spellbound by his marvelous feats on the wire . . . The parade was made in automobiles and reached three blocks.[453]

In connection with their New Orleans debut, Silas Green's band and orchestra under the direction of Fred Kewley were "conceded by all who hear their music to be the best for the same instrumentation and size playing popular and standard music, featuring 'Pique Dame,' 'Morning Noon and Night,' 'Bohemian Girl,' and the colored people's national air, 'The Blues.'"[454] En route a few weeks later, the *Freeman* correspondent noted, "The band, although not a gold band, is the feature of the street demonstrations, and long and lasting is the applause when they are through peeling forth the silvery strains of the 'Memphis Blues.' A bystander remarked: 'Dey plays dem "Blues," dat's all.'"[455]

On March 9, 1914, Silas Green played for an elite gathering at the opera house in Aiken, South Carolina:

This being one of the wealthiest winter resorts in America, naturally there are gathered together the largest number of millionaires in any one place. In the audience were the Vanderbilts, Goulds, Morgans, Wilcox's and many others. But they enjoyed the show just as well as if on Broadway, N. Y., for the company was at its best knowing full well the reputation it must sustain as the greatest negro show of its kind before the American public. The costumes of the show were highly commented upon on all sides, especially the very latest costumes of Miss Susie Cooksie, who said things, sang and acted like a real actress and her one hundred and fifty dollar Japanese gown of black satin, worked with solid gold of dragons and Japanese characters was the talk of the evening . . . Mrs. Lizzie Kewley scored a hit dressed as a lady rough rider, when she sang her song "Nappie Lee." . . . The orchestra and band, under the direction of Prof. Fred Kewley, played quite a number of classical selections. Last but not least was the work of the two stars, LeRoy Knox and W. A. Baynard . . . Both Mr. Baynard and Knox make a big hit in their act, for while [Baynard] plays from the old masters, Mr. Knox does the rag time.[456]

In July they did their usual turn-away business in West Virginia:

We have a fifteen piece band that is setting the coal fields wild, featuring the famous "Florida Blues," by Wm. (King) Phillips, that well known clarinet player . . . Fred Kewley still has the band and orchestra . . . We are playing a few two night stands, playing "Silas Green from New Orleans" the first night and "The Funny Side of Life" the second. Mr. Chas. (Happy) Lewis is doing the comedy of Silas Green and Jim Jackson in "The Funny Side of Life" . . . Mrs. Rebecca Redmond is sure making a hit singing "He Had to Get Out and Get Under" and "Somebody is Coming to My House." . . . Mrs. Lizzie Kewley is still holding her own singing "At That Booly Wooly Wild West Show." Mr. Frank Smedley, the little man with the big voice, is singing "Any Old Port in a Storm," making them sit and wonder how he sings so low. Next comes Mr. Ford Wiggins . . . doing a six to eight minute dancing act that is out there. The "Great Adams" is setting them wild with his bicycle and unicycle riding . . . Last but not least come the famous Gaines Bros., Charles and Albert, comedy acrobats . . . Miss Flo Russell is knocking them [out] singing "International Rag," also Mrs. Mittie Lewis is putting over "Take Me to That Tango Tea" . . . Miss Susie Cooksey is singing "Curse of an Aching Heart."[457]

Silas Green's annual invasion of West Virginia was starting to take on the air of a homecoming festival, especially in Huntington, where Prof. Williams had bought property. On July 6 and 7, 1914, they played a two-night stand there: "Seems like every colored person in Huntington tried to come out to see 'Silas Green From New Orleans.'" On July 8 they held a "grand picnic and outing at Bellvue Park, of which Prof. Eph Williams is owner. The biggest and most eventful celebration in the history of the colored people of Huntington was held there. Mayor Floyd S. Chapman and several well known colored men made addresses."

A new addition to the company that summer was comedian S. L. Jenkins, better known as "Daddy." Originally from New Orleans, Jenkins was professionally active as early as 1910, when he appeared as a female impersonator at the Dreamland Theater in Houma, Louisiana, singing, "All I Want Is My Lovin' Louise." At the beginning of 1913, "Daddy Jenkins and Little Creole Pet" were playing through southern Alabama, with Jelly Roll Morton as their accompanist. At the Empire Theater in Dothan, "Jelly Rool [*sic*]" was "there on the piano like a ship at sea. He don't bar no rag time piano player, and when he plays the rag they call the New York Rool, he makes the audience stand up and take notice, believe me, pa."[458] Jenkins and Morton parted ways before summer's end. When Jenkins surfaced in the *Freeman* again that fall, he was "in trouble, having shot a performer. He is now in jail at Charleston, W. Va." It was in Charleston that Silas Green picked him up in July 1914. Correspondence in August said Jenkins was "featuring the Baby Seals Blues. He is forced to receive two and three encores nightly."[459]

The coalfield districts of West Virginia remained Silas Green's preferred summer destination throughout the life of the show. Mining and its attendant industries—railroading, etc.—presented a measure of opportunity for hard laboring African Americans. As one local writer observed, "This is the great coal fields of West Virginia, better known as the Black Belt of West Virginia, as the blacks greatly outnumber the whites here. The Negro is not a mere ghost in the house of Democracy."[460] A report in August 1916 assured that Silas Green "continues to get the coin in West Virginia, where everyone has money and the mines are working full blast." No local mining community was too small to exploit. After showing to "turn-away business" at Logan, West Virginia, in 1917, it was announced that, "The show will play two weeks up the Logan Hollow."

The 1915 edition of Silas Green was "illuminated by the latest and up-to-date lighting system for a show under canvas. Elegant scenic effects, gorgeous wardrobe, and the Professor is featuring the greatest colored Brass Concert Band on the road . . . It is not a minstrel or a plantation show but a three-act musical comedy, lasting two hours and forty-five minutes."[461] In spite of this disclaimer, the old minstrel format was still in evidence: "The olio opens with Ella Smith in popular songs. Then comes Willie Austin, better known as 'Slim Jim' from Savannah, Ga., cleaning them up . . . Miss Ella Simmons opens with 'At the Million Dollar Tango Ball.' Then comes back with some buck . . . Then comes Ford Wiggins, who cleans up singing and dancing. The Great Adams, Comedy Trick Cyclist, who closes the olio, is great."[462]

Correspondence from West Virginia that summer informed that:

> E. W. Blake, of Jacksonville, Fla., has joined and taken charge of the band. C. H. Coffey, the 'Topic Talker' and producer of 'Soft Black' fame, is more than making good. Edna Carter, soubrette and tango dancer, is quite an acquisition. Our Challenge Dancers, Ella Simmons, Ford Wiggins and Slim Jim Austin, never fail to meet the approval of all . . . Leroy Knox, in the title role of 'Silas Green,' is as popular as the president. He is ably assisted by W. A. Baynard, who is sure some fashion plate. He makes eight changes during the show. Miss Alice Russell, our leading lady, is some pumpkins. Albert Gaines, wire artist, acrobat and barrel mystifyer, and Elizabeth Van Clay, contortionist, are our novelty acts. Miss Ella, in the role of Lindy Jane, is pleasing. Ada Lockhart, female baritone, in descriptive songs, brings tears to the eyes of her listeners. Our Female Quartet, Misses Carter, Russell, Simmons and Lockhart, is one big hit with the show.[463]

Leroy Knox appears to have retired in 1915. Like Thomas Price before him, he went into the hotel business. A note in the spring of 1917 informed: "Leroy Knox, originally Silas Green and former partner of Miss Alice Ramsey, is now running a hotel at 507 Water street, Pittsburgh, Pa."

The new bandmaster, cornetist E. W. Blake, had been a member of the Rabbit's Foot Company band since 1908. Blake stayed with Silas Green for just over a year. His band of fourteen to sixteen pieces played "nothing but new and high class music." Among the players who joined during Blake's tenure was A. D. King, "a cornet devil" who "really makes those high registers. He is heard from the circle to the car."[464] Like Blake, King was a graduate of the 1914 edition of the Rabbit's Foot gold band. He eventually succeeded Blake as Silas Green's bandmaster.

Also new to the show in 1915, producer and blackface comedian Charles H. Coffey had cut his teeth in southern vaudeville, as a "versatile black face single." In the spring of 1916 Coffey left Silas Green for Tolliver's Smart Set but returned again in the fall, bringing with him the latest blues hit by Butler "String Beans" May, "I Love My Gal Better Than I Do Myself."[465] In the mold of String Beans, Coffey proved to be "a riot with his monologue and 'Blues.'"[466]

As producer, Coffey rewrote the signature comedy to accommodate a "dressed up" Silas Green character and some "new society dances."[467] Early in 1917 Coffey left Silas Green for the last time, to tour with the Great Pizaro Medicine Company. Shortly thereafter, he was diagnosed with a brain tumor and died on the operating table at St. Vincent de Paul Hospital in Norfolk, Virginia, on May 4, 1917, at the age of thirty-four.[468]

"Female baritone" Ada Lockhart was another 1915 Silas Green recruit. In Mississippi that fall, she was "a scream nightly singing 'St. Louis Blues.'" While her repertoire ran the gamut of popular styles, she became Silas Green's first female blues specialist. In 1916 her blues repertoire included "Hesitation Blues," J. Paul Wyer's "The Long Lost Blues," "Prof. Handy's latest blues, 'The Paradise Blues' and also Jenkins and Son's 'Kansas City Blues,' which music is making Young America whistle them in every town along the route."[469] She also plugged Pace and Handy's "Lonesome Sal."[470] In 1917 she introduced "her own quaint song, 'Neutral Blues.'"[471]

In addition to her blues singing, Ada Lockhart assumed the role of leading lady in the character of Samantha Dusenberry. During the summer of 1916 she "added to her repertoire an impersonation of

Ada Lockhart Booker and Lawrence Booker in a playful pose. (photo by Katie Bryant Abraham, courtesy Alex Albright).

'a dacint Irish lady,' sending her son to Mexico, featuring 'Barney from Kilarney' and 'Be They Friend or Foe, They're Brothers When They're Dreaming of Home, Sweet Home.'" In 1917, with trombonist Jessie Reeves as her arranger, she made a hit singing "See Dixie First," "Any Little Girl Can Make a Bad Man Good and a Good Man Bad They Say," and "When It's Cherry Time in Tokio." That fall she introduced her "two latest hits, 'My Old Rose,' a sentimental ballad, and 'Livery Stable Blues,' which she puts over in a manner to please her many audiences."[472]

On July 29, 1916, Ada Lockhart married bandsman Lawrence Booker, who had been touring with Silas Green since 1912. Booker originally came in as a baritone player but gravitated to cornet. In 1913 he became the band's assistant leader, and eventually took the reins altogether. Lawrence and Ada Lockhart Booker remained loyal members of the Silas Green Company for the rest of their long professional careers. As Ada observed in 1917, "Not quite all performers leave the tent shows and enter vaudeville, for I know of some who know when to let well enough alone and stay where they can accumulate. Everybody knows that a rolling stone gathers no moss, and as I have been in vaudeville and also opera house shows, and am now with a tent show, I wouldn't change places either winter or summer, and in the end, you will find the fellow that sticks to the bridge that carries him safely over is the fellow who comes out the best winner and ahead."[473]

During the fall of 1915 Silas Green spent eight weeks in Mississippi. On the morning of November 16, 1915, Prof. Williams left the show at Meridian and journeyed to Tuskegee, Alabama, to attend the funeral of departed race hero Dr. Booker T. Washington. Back on the show, Rhoda Williams "assembled the entire company of fifty people aboard her cars in a memorial meeting . . . The lady members of our company; Misses Alice Ramsey, Ada Lockhart, Willmet Freeman,

Prof. Eph Williams, *Indianapolis Freeman*, December 25, 1915.

Alice Gaines and Mildred Pellebon, assisted by the company, closed the meeting by singing several selections, among them, 'Shall We Meet Beyond the River.'"[474]

Toward the end of the year Silas Green reportedly booked a few indoor dates, including a three-night return engagement at the Temple Theater in New Orleans and a one-night stand at the Pike Theater in Mobile. In Florida during the early weeks of 1916, they encountered heavy competition: "At Cocoa the Coburn Minstrels played there January 25; Florida Blossoms, January 26; Silas Green, January 27, to turn away business . . . At West Palm Beach we had the Florida Blossoms on one side and Silas Green on the other side. The Silas Green show packed a four-pole tent, and at 7:30 there was not even standing room to be had." They also packed their tent in the central Florida town of Eustis, where "the audience consisted of five hundred white people and near six hundred colored."[475]

Silas Green's street parade remained a particular bragging point:

> The old reliable Silas Green company has certainly got some street parade. Headed by Prof. Eph Williams . . . After the professor has been welcomed by all the spectators on every corner, then comes the flag boy carrying a beautiful silk American flag, then the six walking gents who really look like real actors. Next comes Prof. E. W. Blake's 14 piece band which sweetens the ear of every music lover . . . And when they break loose on "Lucie de Lamanermoor" and "A Bull in a China Shop," then it is peaches and listen, when those autos roll up with as swell a bunch of beautiful and sparkling girls as can be found nowhere north or south, then it is peaches and cream. Next comes the little ponies, all Shetlands; then comes a man leading those two Great Danes, who are sometimes called lions.[476]

Slim Jim Austin's dancing slide trombone stunts were an increasingly popular feature of the street parade. A note at the end of 1916 assured, "Trombone Slim Jim Austin is daily getting his with his street dance, accompanying himself on the trombone." Austin jumped to the Florida Blossoms in the spring of 1917, and he moved on that fall to Campbell's New Orleans Minstrels. He was in Oregon with Harvey's Greater Minstrels in the fall of 1919 when he told the *Freeman*: "Our jazz dance orchestra is jazzing the ofays as usual."[477]

Silas Green's popular new stage acts of 1916 included John and Rhoda McNeil, "with their singing, dancing and talking act," and Anna Coles Morris, "our prima donna," singing "In the Garden of My Heart" and "My Mother's Rosary." The roster of specialty acts was enhanced when "Means and Means (Joe and Sally) joined us at Palm Beach with their chair balancing act and their all but talking dog 'Buster.'" By summer there were four big novelty acts: George Baker, the wire walker, "known in theatrical circles as 'Marvelous La Vola'"; Iris Boyd, "the greatest female contortionist of her race . . . Mrs. Boyd is also taking saxophone lessons under the instructions of our cornetist, A. D. King, and is progressing nicely. Keep it up, 'Mutt'"; Means and Means, "chair balancers"; and the Watts Brothers, "comedy acrobats and tumbling jesters."[478]

At Henderson, North Carolina, on May 12, 1916, Prof. Williams's brother John A. Williams suddenly dropped dead of a heart attack:

> He had just come in from off parade and was in the act of putting away the parade paraphernalia when the attack came . . . The remains were interred in Blacknal's cemetery, followed by Prof. E. W. Blake's Band, playing sweet, sad sacred music on foot, as the cortege slowly wended its way toward the burying ground. It is recorded that it was the saddest funeral that ever passed through the streets of Henderson . . . Mr. John A. Williams was a native of Murphysboro [*sic*], Tenn., and was 53 years of age.[479]

At a Mississippi show stop in the fall of 1916, after the show was over and most members of the company had gone to bed, "they were awakened about 1:30 a.m. by three serenaders outside on a nearby platform, and they rendered some very pretty music, and all the very latest songs. After several pieces were played Prof. Williams got up and went out and suited the gentlemen's taste very

SLIM JIM AUSTIN AND HIS TROMBONE—A SPPECIAL FEATURE WITH HARVEY'S GREATER MINSTRELS

Indianapolis Freeman, September 20, 1919.

much by passing around the bottle, a box of cigars and some change. They closed their serenading with our latest hit, 'Walking the Dog,' and walked away, bidding Prof. Eph Williams and the bunch a great success on their journey."[480]

During the summer of 1917 the band wavered between nine and eleven pieces, under the direction of cornetist Jeff Smith. Clarinetist Bob Everleigh joined that summer from the Rabbit's Foot

Company. Doubling stage, Everleigh offered a blackface monologue, some eccentric dancing, and the popular "preacher song," "It Takes a Long, Tall Brownskin Gal to Make a Preacher Lay His Bible Down."[481]

Gallie DeGaston graced the 1917 edition of the olio "with his screamingly funny makeup and monologue, closing with 'Any Old Tune at All.'" He also sang "If I Forget" and performed a "school kid turn" that was said to be "great, full of laughs." DeGaston got drafted before the end of the year, but a note in February 1918 said he was "expected back after having obtained his discharge . . . at Camp Dodge, Iowa."[482]

James Mack, known as "Bud," and his wife Maida joined at Roanoke, Virginia, early in the summer of 1917, and stayed through the end of the year. Their special feature was a "Hawaiian tango and whirlwind dance." Maida Mack also scored singing "Beale Street Blues" and "The Hesitation Blues."[483]

The show suffered a blow in West Virginia that summer when "Little Marytown, one of Professor Eph Williams' smallest and smartest performing ponies, died . . . from injuries received by a tree being blown down on her during a severe cyclone that raged in this section . . . Little Marytown was only two feet tall."[484]

Silas Green became increasingly dependent on its female contingent to make it through the war years. Correspondence of June 9, 1917, introduced a "bevy of new chorus beauties," including Sarita Sams, Ketturah Pettiford, Bessie Edgington, and Maida Mack. Later that summer the women took the stage in a patriotic "Drill for Uncle Sam and Our Country" and a musical comedy skit titled "Dance of Nations," featuring Ketturah Pettiford as "Zenora, Mexican Senorita"; Ada Lockhart Booker as "Ho San, Japanese Geisha Girl"; Sarita Sams as "Laughing Water, Indian squaw"; and Bessie Edgington as "Miss Liberty, the American Girl."[485] Edgington also stood out "in cornet solos and buck and wing dancing," while Ketturah Pettiford took the spotlight in a "tango dance with Silas Green," and Sarita Sams sang "The Camel Walk," "Chinese Blues," and "Honolulu, We've Got to Hand It to You."

The women of Silas Green organized a knitting and embroidery club and showed their patriotism during the fall of 1917 "by knitting for the boys who are on the firing line." Soubrette Alma Saulsby joined the show that fall, and proved to be a "dainty little worker." Her song hits of 1917–1918 included "Three Wonderful Letters from Home" and "What Do You Want to Make Those Eyes at Me for When They Don't Mean What They Say."

In 1918 Prof. Williams added another soubrette, "Miss Martha Jones, who really features the 'Tishimingo Blues.'"[486] Ada Lockhart Booker made a hit that year singing "All Bound Round with the Mason-Dixon Line" and the topical number "Just Like Washington Crossed the Delaware, So Will Pershing Cross the Rhine." She also produced a "fine patriotic drill that is a decided hit. It is composed of eight young ladies and is known as the 'Ada Lockhart Red Cross Nurse Drill.'" Veteran specialty artist John Pamplin was also with the show in 1918. Pamplin's gun drill, which he had been performing since before the turn of the century, found new relevance in the current wartime edition of Silas Green:

> The natives seemed to think that Prof. Eph Williams had brought the conqueror of the Kaiser to town and

> they came to the show like a house afire white and colored, and we certainly gave them a run for their money . . . Pamplin demonstrating the mode of manly art with his gun in the trenches in a deadly hand to hand combat and the mighty charge of the company with song as Gatling guns and Miss Ada Lockhart Booker at the head of a brigade of Red Cross nurses administering to the wounded, Silas returns with the American flag and the entire company with the audience accompanied by our orchestra singing the "Star Spangled Banner" just before the final drop of the curtain.[487]

Silas Green ventured into the season of 1918 as "the largest and best of the one-night stands." It proved to be an especially grueling season. January brought the war-related railroad embargo, which caused a "ten-day tieup" in Florida. During the previous summer, ill health had forced company favorite Will Goff Kennedy to retire to his home in Nashville, and in March news came that he had died.

Later that spring the show "met with quite a serious accident" at Franklin, Virginia:

> As we were being switched about the yard by a marble headed brakeman, he let the car get away from him and crashed into the passenger train at the station, resulting in the injury of several members of the company as well as some of the passengers on the train.
>
> Prof. Eph Williams did a heroic stunt in his pajamas in rushing out to the platform and tearing the brake lever away from the brakeman, succeeding in checking the speed of the car to the extent of saving what would have resulted in a much more serious accident than did happen.[488]

On June 12, 1918, on the road at Greensboro, North Carolina, Prof. Williams's beloved wife Rhoda died of a sudden attack of apoplexy. She was 54. Her funeral was held in Chicago, where mourners gathered at the Vernon Avenue home of family friend Oscar DePriest. "Final sacred rites of 'The Daughters of the Eastern Star' were performed by the order . . . 'Savior, More Than Life to Me,' 'I Would Not Live Always' and 'Shall We Gather at the River' were sung by the lady members."[489] Interment was at Oshkosh, Wisconsin, the city of her birth.

Eph and Rhoda Amelia Williams had been married since 1892. Rhoda had been as deeply committed to Silas Green as anyone. She traveled with the show and often had been called upon to run it in her husband's absence. Two years before she died, the show's *Freeman* correspondent acknowledged her as "one of the ablest business women of her race, and she understands the biz from A to Z."[490] Enterprising and hard working, Eph and Rhoda Williams had made a hands-on family business of Silas Green and, in spite of their nearly ceaseless itinerancy, had managed to raise four children to be "worthy examples of rising Afro-America."

The military draft loomed heavily over the 1918 edition of the show. In West Virginia that summer, Ford Wiggins—Silas Green himself—was drafted. Coy Herndon, the hoop roller, was next to go. Then, Ada Lockhart Booker's only son Earl Morgan "was called to the colors while visiting his mother." That fall the company advertised: "We can use a few more musicians at any time (out of draft age, of course)." Ada Lockhart Booker expressed measured optimism: "It is remarkable to see how Prof. Eph Williams is withstanding the many blows being struck at the theatrical business now-a-days. We have been lucky to be just leaving a town as it is being quarantined with the cost of $54 a day for the moving, extra war tax and giving soldiers to Uncle Sam, the lads being drafted on the show left and right."[491]

Prof. Williams publicly vowed that he would stay out for the winter in spite of the draft.[492] But at Rocky Mount, North Carolina, that fall he encountered an insurmountable problem: the flu. "Prof. Eph Williams closed the 'Silas Green from New Orleans' company here suddenly on October 5, owing to the Spanish Influenza epidemic. This will mark the first time in fourteen years that the 'Silas Green' Company has had to close down."[493] As the company dispersed, it was noted that bandsmen "Jessie Reeves, Norman Mason, Frank Smedley and Walter Hoyt will rest at Rocky Mt., N. C., having formed an orchestra with Wm. A. Baynard, who is located there with the A. L. C. Railroad Co."[494]

The show was back on the road by April 1919, with Ford Wiggins returning to the role of Silas Green and coon shouter Flo Russell, "one of the staunchest members of the Silas Green Co.," returning to sing "How You Goin' to Keep 'Em Down on the Farm" and "You Can Have It—I Don't Want It." R. C. Puggsley remained in charge of the advance work, and Coy Herndon was also on the roster, "still getting his mighty with those terrible hoops."[495]

"You Can Have It (I Don't Want It)" was recorded in 1924 by Virginia Liston and Sam Gray, with piano accompaniment by Clarence Williams. The lyrics are rich in double-entendre:

Gray: He can have it, I don't want it.
Liston: You mean my love and my sympathy?
Gray: Yes indeed. I mean every bit of that, what you gave to me.
Liston: Go on, don't you hang around me, daddy beat it please.
Gray: He can have it, I don't want it.
Liston: That's what you say.
Gray: I've got another sweetie now, the kind that's right.
Liston: I'm positively through with you.
Gray: Well, goodbye.
Liston: Goodnight.
Gray: He can have it.
Liston: And you don't want it?
Gray: No mama. Honey, take it away.
Liston: I'll give it to my other papa.
Gray: Honey, take it away.[496]

"Crying comedian" Turk Christian and his wife Floury were among the most recent additions. The *Freeman* correspondent made note of their act: "There is no mistaking the truth was told when a man remarked the other day, 'That thar feller would make a mule laugh,' and believe me, when he gets through crying he has his audience in tears, but they are tears of laughter. They close their act with that catchy song, 'Frenchy Coo.'" Also new to the roster were specialty artists Ted and Mary Pope: "these people rank in the first class when it comes to disrobing and robing while walking a tight wire many feet from terra firma."[497]

In keeping with the trend of wartime themes, the show's resilient musical farce comedy production was given yet another new twist "from the pen of America's greatest colored hoop roller, Coy Herndon." Titled *Silas Green and Bill Jones—Just Returned from France*, it featured L. Don Bradford in the role of "Bill Jones, a grafter," and Richard

WANTED

At Once!

For Prof. Eph Williams' Original Silas Green Show

Musicians in all lines, chorus girls, real "Blues" singer, two novelty acts; address all mail **Coy Herndon,** 1804 Myrtle Ave., Jacksonville, Fla.

Indianapolis Freeman, November 22, 1919.

Brown in a "really laughable and life-like" portrayal of "Officer Billum."[498]

As soon as he got out of the army, trombonist Freddie Pratt was placed in charge of the 1919 edition of the band. There were only nine pieces in the band, but "they certainly make some sweet music, not counting the blues they play on street parade each day." At the end of the year, Ada Lockhart Booker was "positively featuring Freddie Pratt's Overseas Blues and catching the silver as it rains each night."[499]

On Christmas Day 1919 members of the Silas Green Company assembled at Prof. Eph Williams's Winter Park, Florida, home for a "barbecued Christmas dinner under the pines." They were back on the road in February 1920 when the *Freeman* reported: "Freddie Pratt, the brilliant trombone player, so-called 'Mr. Jazz Daddy,' just closed a successful season with Eph Williams' Silas Green Co.... Mail will reach him addressed Lafayette Theater, Winston-Salem, N.C." Pratt settled in Winston-Salem, where by 1925 he and fellow Silas Green veteran Flo Russell were entrenched in the local hotel business.[500]

In the wake of Pratt's departure, Lawrence Booker took charge of the band. Among the bandsmen was soubrette Ketturah Pettiford's brother Leon "Buddie" Pettiford, "a clarinetist of class." A new bandmaster was announced that fall: "Our band, small but highly uniformed, led by Mr. James Hudson, will make you believe there are twenty-four strong if you don't count them."[501] There were actually just eleven pieces.

In a May 1, 1920, correspondence, Ada Lockhart Booker described the current stage show:

Well, here we are again, folks, back in old South Carolina for a short spell, and then on to the coal fields of West Virginia . . . The roster of our show is a good line-up as follows:

Mr. E. A. Drew, our juggling and slack wire walker, gets his nightly . . .

> Mrs. Hattie M. Gregory Lankford certainly makes them sit up and take notice when she makes those wooden shoes talk . . .
>
> Then comes that laughable team of Ingram & Ingram—Flossie and Lula—in their funny skit of talking and singing . . .
>
> Then come little Mrs. Elsie Williams Smith, in her dainty dancing and singing act . . .
>
> Mr. Rich Brown is still creating much laughter each night in his role of Officer Billum.
>
> Ford Wiggins is always a scream as Silas Green and he is also singing "Oh Death, Where Is Thy Sting" with marked success each night.
>
> We have some new faces on the show with us in the persons of Timothy Trolley, William Coleman and Luther DeGaffney, known as the Kentucky Trio.[502]

Other highlights of 1920 included Sorbert (*sic*) Ferry singing "Slow and Easy" in a "double dancing and singing turn" with eccentric comedian Isaac Martin. Also, "Our beauty chorus, led by Mrs. Elsie Smith, takes the show by storm . . . Their make up, costumes and graceful steps with harmonious singing is a perfect revelation." Finally, contortionist Clifton Boyd made a brief run with Silas Green that year. During his performance at Vicksburg, Mississippi, "Several physicians came on stage at . . . Boyd's request and examined his several contortion acts and pronounced them the marvel of the age."

That summer Ada Lockhart Booker paused to reflect: "Nine years ago there were three shows out on the road owned and controlled entirely by colored men; namely Pat Chappelle, Pete Worthy and Prof. Eph Williams. Today we have only one, that of Prof. Eph Williams' Silas Green Co., who stands alone in the field."[503] In recent years, Prof. Williams's health had been failing, and he had been forced to leave the road on more than one occasion. On December 13, 1921, he died at his home in Winter Park, Florida. Family friend Mary McLeod Bethune came over from Daytona to take charge of the funeral arrangements:

> The funeral occurred at 11:00 a. m. from the residence, which was beautifully decorated. Friends of the professor came from far and near. The service [included] a tenor solo entitled "My Home Is in Heaven," rendered by Prof. C. W. Mabury of the Hungerford school in a sweet-toned voice that made us all feel like living better lives. The funeral proceeded to the depot, whence the remains were shipped to Oshkosh, Wis., where they will be laid beside the professor's dear wife and son . . . The Silas Green show will go right along, opening in February, with Charley Collier half owner and manager.[504]

Coy Herndon noted in a eulogy that Prof. Williams had "said a thousand times, 'No white man will ever get the title of Silas Green from New Orleans.'"[505] Charles Collier was a successful race businessman of Macon, Georgia. From 1908 through 1911, he had managed the vaudeville stage at Macon's Ocmulgee Park. In the fall of 1910 he assembled Collier's Amusement Factory for a ten-day run at the Colored State Fair in Macon, under canvas.[506] In 1914 he managed C. W. Park's Musical Comedy Company, and in 1915 he broke off to head a company of his own, Collier's Smart Set. He started traveling with Silas Green as early as 1919. Said to be living out his "childhood desire to be a showman," Collier piloted Silas Green until his death in 1942.

A report from Huntington, West Virginia, in the summer of 1922 assured that, under the new regime, Silas Green was basically unchanged:

Indianapolis Freeman, November 12, 1910.

"We have a nice band and orchestra under the leadership of Prof. Lawrence Booker . . . with Bob Russell, stage manager . . . Ford Wiggins as Silas Green; Ada L. Booker, leading lady; Slim Jim Austin as Uncle Ben Green." This may have been Slim Jim Austin's last season with Silas Green.

Featured acts of 1923 included "Little Miss Bobbie Sullivan and her beauty chorus" in a rendition of the Charles H. Booker composition, "Cootie Crawl"; Johnny Coswell and Slim Golman "in their funny skit, 'The Street Sweepers'"; and soubrette Evelyn White, "treating her audiences to some of the latest 1923 numbers that have been written expressly for her use."[507]

Evelyn White quickly established herself as Silas Green's premier "Dixie blues singer" and "queen of the blues." No newcomer to the professional stage, she had cut her teeth in southern vaudeville, appearing at the Arcade Theater in Atlanta as early as 1909, on a bill with Bessie Smith.[508] In 1915 she toured with Tolliver's Smart Set, holding her own among such formidable contemporaries as Ma Rainey, Clara Smith, and Trixie Smith. Evelyn White was one of the most important female blues singers of her time but has been largely forgotten because she left no commercial recordings.

In the fall of 1923 Silas Green reported from Alabama: "Our band and walking gents, superbly costumed, accompanied by a bevy of handsomely gowned girls in decorated automobiles, parading down the main streets, never fail to attract the crowd to the circularing corner [*sic*], where Prof. Lawrence Booker's 14-piece band jazzes them up to grand selections, and when Sam Cohen, our popular announcer, announces a guaranteed attraction, the crowd shouts for joy, and jams the box office nightly."[509] Business was also good in Florida that winter because, "There was a record breaking crowd of tourists who spent the winter in Florida and hundreds of our group were there in all the cities and towns getting top prices for service."[510]

Early in 1924, soubrette Mildred Scott and bandsman Eddie Billups jumped from Silas Green to the Brown and Dyer Carnival. They were quickly replaced by Cecelia "Littlebits" Coleman and Bob Young: "Littlebits is, without a doubt, one of the fastest working chorus girls we have in the profession, and Bob is an old-timer on the clarionet." Eddie Billups rejoined the show in July, playing cornet in the band and occasionally doubling as a singer in the male quartet. At the time of his death in 1936, Billups was touring with Winstead's Minstrels. He was buried en route at Mountain Home, Tennessee.[511]

The 1924 edition of Silas Green's male quartet comprised J. C. Davis, soprano (*sic*); Mose Penny, tenor; Willie Seymour, baritone; and Johnnie "Stack O' Dollars" Coswell, bass. Ada Lockhart Booker noted, "There is great rivalry between our female and male quartets of which the Silas Green show boasts. Members of the female quartet are as follows: Alberta Fleming, Evelyn White, Helen Bombraye [*sic*] and Ada Lockhart Booker." Female quartet member Helen Bumbray, "late of the Monte Carlo Girls in burlesque . . . showed just how popular she was when she played her home town, South Boston, Va."[512] At the end of the year the *Defender* correspondent gave an update on the male quartet: "On comes the Wreckers quartet, Ed Billups, William Penny, J. C. Davis and Johnnie Coswell. Now, take it from me, they live jam up to their name, 'Wreckers.'"

In the summer of 1924, Coy Herndon returned to Silas Green, after an absence of four years. He had been living in Indianapolis, reportedly taking courses at the United States College of Chiropractic, and keeping a hand in the local theater scene. Before venturing into minstrel show life, Herndon had studied at Claflin University. Ada Lockhart Booker noted that, under his influence, "we are getting to be real high brows . . . We have readings in psychology, held by Mr. Herndon, and we find much interest therein."

Herndon continued to perform as a hoop roller, but his primary function at this point was to succeed Bob Russell as producer. For the past year Herndon had been penning a regular column for the *Chicago Defender* under the headline "Coy Cogitates," and now began to focus his cogitations on Silas Green, which he dubbed the "Little 'Barnum and Bailey' of Colored shows." In July he noted "smooth sailing" through the coalfield towns of West Virginia: "At Princeton, W. Va., four poles were put up and then we turned them away at a dollar top. At Pax, W. Va., a very small town, two poles were taxed to capacity."[513] The tent was also full at Charleston: "The Charleston people always have considered the Silas Green show a home-coming event, as the late Eph Williams invested in real estate quite heavily and at present it is controlled by Anderson Brown, one of the wealthiest and most influential Negroes in West Virginia."[514]

During their Pax, West Virginia, engagement, drummer Walter "Dukey" Hoyt fell ill and was sent ahead to Mountain State Hospital in Charleston for treatment of edema. When the show reached Charleston, the entire company went out to the hospital to pay him a visit. Three weeks later Hoyt was dead: "His grave will be visited by the company and a few minutes will be taken from our noon day concert time. His drum, which he so often beat on the streets of Charleston, will be placed in the center of the parade circle."[515]

When they played Alexandria, Virginia, in August, several notable performers dropped down from Washington, D.C., to see the show, including Lonnie Fisher, Bonnie Bell Drew, Sweetie May, and Laura Smith. Upon their return to Alexandria the following season, "the great record star" Sara Martin was there to witness the show.[516]

At Jackson, Tennessee, in September Coy Herndon observed, "The lot used by all Colored shows in Jackson is a beautiful lot in the center of the Colored park owned by the K. of P. lodge. Although the lot seems high in price, the rent goes to the lodge and the city does not charge any license for shows playing on the lot in the park. The rent for this lot is $75 a day, but where you turn them away with a seating capacity as large as the Silas Green show, it is worth it."[517]

Herndon felt the 1924 edition of Silas Green was the "best wardrobed show south of the Dixie line." In his opinion, "any parade that happens to meet Charles Collier's 'Silas Green from New Orleans' company, 40 strong, with John Ivy and his 15-piece band, all dressed in green trimmed in gold, will certainly look for a back street or an exit in the nearest alley. Thrown in for good measure to make the colors blend there are 12 high yellows and seal skin browns."[518] That fall Herndon boasted:

> It is not the policy of the Charles Collier's Silas Green show to day and date any show, but while jumping out of Mississippi . . . our advance found the Old Kentucky Minstrels billed, presenting "Shuffling Sam from Alabam," so at Hattiesburg the two shows met . . . Silas Green paraded at 12 o'clock, Shuffling Sam at 3. Everything went on peacefully, both shows putting up all their canvass. The Shuffling Sam had the up-town location, while to get to the Silas Green show you would have to pass their tent. The Silas Green band concerted a block above the other show, while they played their concert in front of their tent. In a few minutes the space between the two bands turned to a battlefield, with trombones sliding, cornets jazzing and the mighty roars of the bass horns . . . Silas Green showed to capacity.[519]

Silas Green from New Orleans had become such a venerated name throughout the South that in 1925 a rival show was launched under the copycat title, *Sugarfoot Green from New Orleans*. Silas Green charged that Sugarfoot Green was banking on the "illiteracy of the natives" to siphon off the older show's faithful following.[520] Nevertheless, Sugarfoot Green became a formidable competitor in the world of tented minstrelsy.

Writing from Mississippi in the fall of 1928, Coy Herndon informed that, "Natchez is a real Silas Green town. A few years ago we shut the Rabbit Foot company out there when the two shows met day and date." Herndon identified Hattiesburg as "another 100 per cent Silas town . . . Three years ago we closed the Sugar Foot minstrels up with a day and date performance." The boast drew a cynical response from Sugar Foot Green Company manager Harry Hunt, who asserted that, while Herndon "raves about day and dating my show three years ago at Hattiesburg . . . I had as many and possibly more in my attendance than they did . . . Then he tells of closing Mr. Walcott's Rabbit Foot show up in Natchez . . . The Silas Green show employs the same performers and the same musicians as I or Mr. Walcott. This year they work for me, and next year they are over there, and vice versa, so how can they be any better?"[521]

Ford Wiggins's long-standing position as star comedian was jeopardized in the fall 1924, when he reportedly shot and killed fellow performer Henry "Slim" Golman in the heat of a card game. According to Herndon, "Moonshine played an important part in the argument over five cents. During the argument Gollman struck Wiggins. They clinched and a shot was fired . . . Wiggins was arrested and charged with murder."[522] Within a year's time, however, Wiggins was back with the show.

When Silas Green played Fort Pierce, Florida, early in 1925, veteran minstrel bandsman Amos Gilliard, "one of the greatest trombone players of his time, and who has joined the Silas Green show 16 times in eight years," drove over for a visit from Lake Okeechobee, "where he has a small jazz band playing at a resort."[523] About a month later, Herndon reported that Gilliard had gone on a drinking spree and gotten his eye "punched out with an ice pick in the hands of a woman."[524] Herndon initially stated that Gilliard had been blinded, but later recanted this detail.

Performers on Silas Green's 1925 roster included Rich and Ketturah Pettiford Brown, "late of the Rabbit Foot minstrels"; Pearl Graham, "formerly with the Mamie Smith Review"; and "Dixie Kidd and his partner, 'Dearie,' with their educated dogs." Newcomers that summer included Leroy "Kike" Gresham and his wife Marion, in a "rube act" that was said to "tie up the show nightly, while in the cabaret scene Kite [*sic*] does his 'Winch' impersonation, for which he has no peer."[525] Also mentioned were dancing soubrettes Ebbie Burton and Elnorah Moore and a "radio style" combination known as the Deacon Four: "James Hudson, J. R. Jackson, Arthur Chick Garnett and Buddie Pettiford comprise the quartet. They all play saxophones, which range from soprano to bass, and when they broadcast 'Yearning,' 'Papa Dee Da Da,' 'Ga. Brown' and 'Bugle Blues' it's too bad Jim."[526]

At Durham, North Carolina, on June 13, 1925, "Bill Jones, age 40, born in Philadelphia, the husband of Coots Grant and a member of the Charles Collier–Silas Green company for the past three years, departed this life ... after a brief illness." His death was attributed to "leakage of the heart, enlarged liver and typhoid fever." It seems Jones had "gambled with the cards he loved so dearly up to his last moments, his last words being, 'Have you got the king and queen.'"[527]

Coy Herndon maintained a running account of the conditions encountered along Silas Green's 1925 route of travel. In the spring he complained: "Conditions in South Carolina have been anything but good for the past four or five years. In the past week a special tax has been placed on candy; a 15-cent package of cigarettes costs 17 cents; soda water costs 6 cents, and the state collects ten percent of all the gross. All shows wish for airplanes while crossing the state."[528] In North Carolina a couple weeks later, he reported:

> If you will look at the different routes carefully you will notice that every once in a while they are close to each other. It's because a careful study had been made of the country, especially its resources. For instance, Mississippi is no good until the fall of the year when cotton is marketed. Florida for its oranges and green food in winter when she has no competition to speak of, while in North Carolina, one of the greatest states in the union, has a peanut section, one cotton, then a potato section, later on the tobacco crops, but first it is the strawberry crops ... This territory has about 15 towns that can afford a show. Hundreds of laborers are migrated to this territory for the berry season which only lasts about three or four weeks. Any one of these towns will give you a capacity business ... These laborers are paid two cents a quart. Some can pick three and four hundred daily.[529]

In August Silas Green negotiated what Herndon called the "death trail" through Virginia and Tennessee: "That name could apply to any route you play through these two states. However, business gave us an even break, as farms are burned up, little or no corn for lack of rain, but the Silas

Green show has drawn rain each day until the doors open. The farmers are so elated over the rain they decide to separate themselves from a few nickels." In contrast, "reports on conditions in the Delta of Mississippi are wonderful. Cotton is the best they have had in years. Several shows are already in the Delta and a week from now will find the Little Barnum down there with one of the greatest shows they have ever seen."[530]

As they crossed the Tennessee-Mississippi state line, Herndon rejoiced: "As far as I can see, there is nothing but money in Mississippi. The streets are blocked this early with cotton . . . Several shows are down here, seemingly all of them . . . Well . . . let 'em hop on 'Little Barnum' and watch 'em hop right off, because we got 'em 52 strong, 16-piece band, 15 girls, two novelty acts . . . and a reputation that will stand the acid test, so let 'em buck cowboys, a little excitement with a couple of brass bands in a little town ain't so bad."[531]

The winter route through Florida continued to be prosperous. At Tallahassee, "The best white blood forgot their color and rubbed elbows with bootblacks to get a ticket."[532] At Tampa, "Silas Green spread its mammoth tent at Fifth and Maryland, under the auspices of a Race institution and played to 1,400 paid admissions." Locoochee, a small town "supported mostly by a large sawmill which employs many Race people, gave the show a three-pole business, the white attendants taking two-thirds of the big tent."[533]

Herndon also kept readers apprised of his stage productions. In the fall of 1924 he introduced *Silas Green the Bootlegger*: "New scenery, especially designed costumes and some unusual property effects that required Coy Herndon to visit New Orleans to have them made are all features. A rain effect, accomplished with the use of electric batteries where local connections are not available, is one unusual novelty for a tented attraction."[534]

Featured acts included the Silas Green Vamps, staged "on the order of a style show, and with seven vamps dressed in $1,800 worth of capes and gowns, causes the white folks especially to stand in their seats as Mrs. Wiggins does the part of the maid, relieves the vamps of their wraps, and they go into a unique little dance and Ford Wiggins as Silas Green does some fast strutting, finally placing them in a very pretty formation, with beautifully colored ribbons streaming from their low-neck dresses, and the vamps strut off to the time of the music."[535] Other highlights of *Silas Green the Bootlegger* included Evelyn White and her "Savannah Sand Sifters"; Romy Nelson in a wench impersonation; and Johnnie Coswell with his ten "7–11 girls," in a pantomime dice game.

At Nashville, Tennessee, on the night of August 27, 1925, Silas Green spread its tent on the corner of Thirteenth and Cedar Streets. The show commenced with a chorus of ten "Hawaiian girls"

SILAS GREEN SHOW

WANTS A No. 1 Novelty Act, Chorus Girls and Musicians. You must be "it" on and off as this is no place for boozers. Year 'round work and salaries sure. Preference given those doubling. Wire

CHAS. COLLIER

Pulaski, Va., Aug. 13; Wytheville, Va., Aug. 14; Marion, Va., Aug. 15; Bristol, Tenn., Aug. 17; Johnson City, Tenn., Aug. 18; Greenville, Tenn., Aug. 19; Knoxville, Tenn., Aug. 20.

Chicago Defender, August 15, 1925.

playing ukuleles, followed by the popular "vampire number." "Another attractive scene was the rain scene, in which real water was used. The crowd had ample chance to feast their eyes on a bunch of shapely bathing girls, who seemed to enjoy the chance of having showers of real water cast upon them."[536]

Meanwhile, the *Defender* trumpeted Herndon's upcoming production *Silas Green in a Trip around the World*, a two-act musical comedy featuring music from Clarence Williams, Maceo Pinkard, and Evon Robinson: "Evelyn White, Dixie's favorite blues singer, will lead three of the numbers, of which there are sixteen listed for the first act. Miss White will feature 'Cake Walking Babies from Home,' one of Clarence Williams' numbers, and his latest number, 'Fly Around,' bids fair to be a knockout with an old fashioned quadrille behind it."[537]

In November 1925, *Silas Green's Trip Around the World* made its debut at Ozark, Arkansas, and Herndon filed this review:

> The curtain arose on a dark house to the strains of a special arrangement of "Kentucky Home," and later three huge swings were brought into play while Miss Wiggins, Effie Smith Nelson and Alma Saulsby swung high over the heads of the audience, throwing flowers, while J. C. Davis, the silver-toned tenor, mounted on a pedestal in the audience, and a bevy of pretty girls on the stage, surrounded the leading lady.
>
> Mrs. Booker sang "Cast Away." This bit of business brought heavy applause. During the opening chorus the girls were dressed in blue satin with hats to match. Three minutes of fast dancing finished the opening.
>
> Marion Greshem, after a few minutes of unraveling the plot with "Dean Benjamin" John Wilson, sang "Sweet Georgia Brown." John Wilson as the Dean, after a little talk with newspaper reporters, sang "Fly Around, Young Ladies," a new Clarence Williams song, which went over for one of the big hits of the show . . .
>
> Ford Wiggins as Silas and Kike Greshem as Ashes screamed them on their introduction . . .
>
> Elnora Moore sang "Alabama Bound" and with her high jumps into splits was a decided hit. The girls were dressed in white Skinner satin, long coats, pleated skirts and high silk hats. Ebbie Burton gained the admiration of the audience when she sang "Everybody Loves My Baby." She and the entire chorus were dressed in beautiful feathered dresses, with the body part covered with iridescent cloth and they are still loving everybody's baby wherever Silas plays.
>
> Evelyn White sang "Cake Walking Babies," with six girls dressed in purple and lavender satin knee-length dresses, large picture hats with black plumes. They did a "strut" piece of business and wound up with a modern cake walk. Each couple gained hearty applause, while Evelyn White in her "Blues Specialty," stopped the show.
>
> The Spanish setting was beautiful, while the costumes were made of crepe de chine in flowery colors. Wiggins and Kike were extremely funny in their interrogating. The Spanish girls and their "Bird of Paradise" bit with real birds. A race-horse scene in England, with all the girls dressed as jockies, opened several situations for comedy, which the two comedians didn't overlook.
>
> No doubt the big comedy hit of the show for laughter was a telephone exchange in Alaska, with Mrs. Booker as the operator, Mildred Scott in booth 1, Ebbie Burton in booth 2, J. C. Davis doing a "Nance" character in No. 3, Kike Greshem doing his favorite "winch" character in 4, and Effie Nelson in 5. It was difficulty that the lines could be heard because the big tent fairly shook with laughter.
>
> The most beautiful "vamp" number Dixie ever saw closed the first act, with several girls dressed in

butterfly dresses and forming a living fountain with real water flowing. With the scene laid in Florida, the vamps, Effie Nelson as Persia, Mildred Scott as Japan, Alma Saulsby as Hawaii, Ebbie Burton as Cuba, Elnora Moore as France, Marion Greshem as Spain, Lillian Edwards as Canada, and Mamie Wiggins as the U. S. A., and myself, adorned in the old evening suit and silk hat, helped sell the finale.

Willie Edwards and daughter who recently joined the show, went over for a solid hit with their wire contortionist act. The last act, a penitentiary scene, with the girls doing a drill in stripes, later in pick and shovels, then suddenly turning it into a jazz drill, with Wiggins and Greshem in a cell, while the prisoners are at work and play, offer plenty opportunities for comedy, while Johnnie Coswell (Stack o' Dollars) created a sensation in the evolution trial.[538]

One week later Herndon reiterated: "It is a pleasure for me to tell the world when they ask concerning the beautiful music we are using that one of America's greatest composers wrote it—Clarence Williams." He also announced, "Silas Green will take up his trip around the world under a freshly stretched tent. It's a full 70, with a 40 and a 20, made by the Norfolk Tent and Awning company of Norfolk. It's a brown khaki, trimmed in red . . . The marquee has a double entrance, with two ticket sellers mounted on their new ticket boxes or stands, while in the background can be seen plainly the name of the owner, Charles Collier."

Herndon heaped praise on the 1925 edition of the band: "Any lover of music can get 50 cents' worth by visiting one of Prof. John Ivy's noonday concerts. By constant rehearsals and an untiring spirit and with musicians devoted to their leader he has accomplished the seemingly impossible with a minstrel band during this day and time. They are crazy over jazz and Prof. Ivy gives it to them, but when Bob Young, with his marvelous execution on the clarinet, plays 'Morning, Noon and Night' everyone says, 'It's a band.'" Other titles on the band's list of overtures included "Raymond," "Bohemian Girl," and "Opera Mirror."[539] In Herndon's opinion, Prof. Ivy deserved "the greatest credit in giving the public music worth hearing, adding just enough of the other kind to satisfy 'shimmy shakers.'"[540]

In the fall of 1925 the *Defender* published a letter from Prof. James H. Wilson, of Normal, Alabama, endorsing Silas Green's recent performance at nearby Huntsville. A veteran minstrel bandsman of the first order, Prof. Wilson had succeeded W. C. Handy as head of the music department at the Normal, Alabama, Agricultural and Mechanical Institute. He wrote: "We have coming to Huntsville each year tent shows with bands that are merely noise makers and jazz killers . . . but the band with the Silas Green company reminds me of the days when Colored troupes would have nothing but good bands. I was reminded of the days of Prampin, Lowery, Lacey, Bryant and a host of other good bandmasters."[541]

Prof. Ivy's tenure as bandmaster ended on May 17, 1926, when he died on the road at Goldsboro, North Carolina, of acute indigestion. Herndon eulogized:

A life full of adventure, full of love for his work and untiring effort to educate the younger musicians ended when John Ivy departed this life . . . The band circled in front of the undertaking parlor and played a concert in honor of their leader, "Rest in the Arms of Jesus," "Lead, Kindly Light," and "Nearer My God to Thee." So impressive was the concert the musicians came near breaking down . . . I trust the route he has taken will lead back to the God who gave him. May the next tent that houses him be the everlasting home prepared by our Jehova.[542]

Clarinetist Bob Young took over the band, and in February 1927 he counted "16 capable musicians, four clarinets, four cornets, one saxophone, two tubas, two trombones, one alto, one baritone, dressed in short orange colored uniforms, made in the 'coat sack' style, with soft fedora hats."[543] Herndon said they were "unlike most bands you see with traveling shows, who mostly specialize in noise and whose masterpiece is freak sounds in the form of moaning blues":

> There was a time when one would tell you that a band could not command and hold the attention of listeners in the South unless you gave them plenty of blues and jazz, but when you listen to the noonday concert of the Silas Green band you will agree with me that the statement is all "wet." The noonday concert program is made up of standard marches, overtures and popular melodies . . . I heard a lady at one of the concerts the other day say to another, "Gee, I wish they would play some jazz and blues, I've been standing here for twenty minutes and I ain't heard no blues yet." The other lady said, "Child, is that what you are waiting on, don't you know this is Silas Green and they don't play no blues, but when they leave here and go down to the sawmill to play, then you'll hear some blues."[544]

Coy Herndon took leave of Silas Green for the better part of 1926 to "hang out his shingle" in Miami, Florida, and test his chiropractic skills. Several new performers joined that spring, including Sam H. Gray, Joe Watts of the Watts Brothers, and legendary drummer Manzie Campbell, who now seemed to be attracting more attention as a comedian; "a polished comedian of the old school" who "gives food for thought, in as much as there is so much difference between the comedians of this day and days gone by."[545]

The most significant newcomer, Sam H. Gray, was a well-traveled and well-known bass singer, comedian, producer, and songwriter. He had recently concluded a prosperous stage relationship with Virginia Liston, with whom he had recorded for Okeh in 1924. During the mid-1910s, before he and Liston got together, Gray was teamed with Ora Dunlop, running the black vaudeville theater routes.

Gray produced Silas Green's musical comedy vehicle for 1927, *Mixed Twins*. According to the *Defender* correspondent, "Ford Wiggins and Manzie Campbell inject more comedy into 'Mixed Twins' than any other two 'runts' in the show business." Another star of the cast, wench impersonator Kike Gresham, was "the funniest female that ever put on a mother hubbard." Also coming in for praise were:

> Marion Gresham, as fast as any soubrette if properly placed; Ada Lockhart Booker, none greater as a character artist; Walter Robinson, character artist of the Lafayette Players fame of New York; Kittie Bryant [*sic*], the little dancer who is good for sore eyes to look upon; Evelyn White, Dixie's own favorite blues singer; Alonzo Moore, the greatest Race magician in the world; Hugh Turner, with a novelty that's different, playing jazz and opera upon an ordinary wood saw; [and] Elanora Grimes, known for her high kicks and splits, done in rapid fire.[546]

Sam Gray infused *Mixed Twins* with his original blues compositions, including "Shifting Gear Blues" and "Silas Green Blues."[547] One of the most successful stage acts of the season was a trio comprising "J. C. Davis, the tenor singing banjoist; Evelyn White, 'Dixie's favorite blues singer,' and

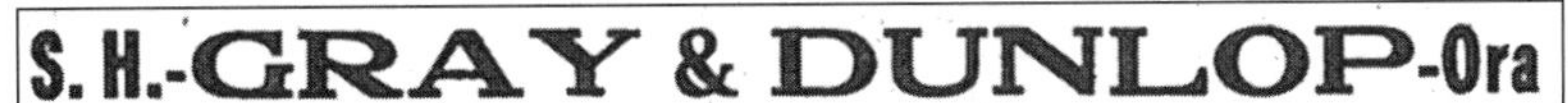

BASSO PROFUNDO CHARACTER WOMAN

Character Comedian and Soubrette Dansause

A Merry Xmas and Happy New Year

To All, In and Out of the Profession.

Indianapolis Freeman, December 26, 1914.

Eddie Billups with his talking cornet."[548] Singing banjoist J. C. Davis left before the end of the season. He was with Winstead's Mighty Minstrels in the summer of 1934, when he wrote from Bristol, Virginia, to say he had "had a peep at King Oliver's outfit, and, boy, is they ready! The king has accepted one of my numbers, 'Did You Ever Have the Blues.'"[549]

In April 1927 Bob Young was injured in an automobile accident—"deep cut in the forehead

Members of the Silas Green Company posing in front of their Pullman car. Sam H. Gray is standing third from right. Dicie Pettiford is on his left (from the collection of Dicie Pettiford, courtesy Alex Albright)

and face and sprained leg."[550] Shortly thereafter, he closed out. When the show played Rosedale, Mississippi, in the fall of 1928, "Charles Collier took several members of the company over to Clarksdale "to witness the performance of the Sparks circus . . . In the side show we met many old friends," including Bob Young, "a former band leader of the Silas Green show."[551]

In May 1927 Collier summoned veteran bandmaster Fountain B. Wood, "one of the greatest trombone soloists of our Race," from Los Angeles to take charge of the band. Wood's "first task was to get some heavy marches for the parade. His next was to eliminate the overture we were playing at the noonday concerts, 'Bridal Rose.' He said that almost every college and home-town band plays it. So instead, after he discovered he had the instrumentation and men who were capable, he chose for a selection 'Il Travatore' and as an overture 'Il Guarany.'"[552]

At Rocky Mount, North Carolina, in June, Silas Green played day and date with Bessie Smith and her "Harlem Follies": "Silas Green started its show at 8:30 p. m. on the minute to a good business, considering the time of year. 'Harlem Follies' started at 9 to a very fair business, when Bessie Smith should have turned them away."[553] They also did good business at Winston-Salem: "Winston-Salem, N. C. has a population of about 52,000 with two-thirds members of our Race. Thousands of our girls are employed in the various tobacco factories, this being the greatest tobacco manufacturing city in the world. At 12 o'clock, their lunch hour, one would imagine he was in the heart of Liberia and just at that time Silas Green with Fount Woods and his 16-piece challenge band marched up the street. So great was the crowd that was anxious to hear the band concert that special police had to be called in to keep the traffic open."[554]

Herndon made some general comments about the crowds who flocked to their noonday concerts: "The white people stand back quite a little distance, where they can hear the strains of music written by great composers and played by talented musicians. From the very beginning you can see hundreds of our people advance one foot at a time until about two feet away from the musicians, and the minute the band goes in the 'Alley,' nearly everyone is so close you can hardly see one of the musicians from any angle. They pat their feet and shake everything shakable about their bodies until the band finishes."[555]

When Silas Green played Huntsville, Alabama, in the fall of 1927, Prof. James H. Wilson came over from Normal College to inspect the band again, and he posted another letter of endorsement: "The band under the direction of Fountain B. Woods, is the best and largest that has visited us so far. Aside from playing a few jazz pieces the band attempted several standard marches and overtures. Much credit is due Mr. Woods for giving the public what they need and not so much what they want."[556] Wilson and Wood had toured together in 1902 as members of the band with Mahara's Minstrels, under W. C. Handy. Wood still had charge of the band in 1929 when Wilson reportedly sent him an original composition titled "Silas Green March."[557]

Charles Collier purchased a new Pullman coach in 1927, said to be "the last word in car construction. The car is 85 feet long, solid steel, has its own automatic electric lighting plant and ice plant . . . Henrietta is the name of the car, named after Mr. Collier's daughter." He also bought a self-contained electric lighting plant to illuminate his tent: "It's a 'Cola' electric plant, capable of giving 2,000 wattage to the tent proper. It was installed at the factory in Richmond, Va., and mounted on a Chevrolet that travels through the country."[558]

Following Silas Green's fall 1927 tour of the Delta, Coy Herndon confessed that Mississippi "has always been a life saver for 75 per cent of tented shows, just as West Virginia was for the late Eph Williams and the Silas Green show in its shuffling, I mean struggling, days."[559] Sam Gray's *Mixed Twins* ended its run that fall, when Lonnie Fisher came in to stage his latest production, *Hits and Bits. Hits and Bits* was reviewed in the October 29, 1927, edition of the *Defender*:

> Lonnie Fisher, one of the funniest comedians who ever smeared on burnt cork and a man with a New York reputation, is in charge of this season's production, "Hits and Bits of 1927," the most original show that Dixie has seen in many a day . . . The show opens with 16 girls, beautifully dressed, who go through their routine in perfect harmony. This is followed by a hold-up bit, with Ford Wiggins as Silas Green, while Freddie Durrer [*sic*] does the straight.
>
> This brings on Maxine Lopez, the dainty little contortionist. Jewell Cox, tall and symmetrical, sings "Oh Boy, What a Girl!" with a prettily dressed chorus. The quartet, with Sam Gray, Lonnie Fisher, Moses Pennie and Eddie Billups, goes over for a hit. Mamie Wiggins and Ada Booker sing a duet while six couples, dressed in Martha Washington costumes, execute steps to meet the occasion. Manzie Campbell, in the comedy role; Sam Gray, doing straight, and Henry Wooden,

Letterhead stationery for *Silas Green from New Orleans*, featuring a cameo portrait of Collier and three different views of their Pullman car, Henrietta.

the policeman, do a "hot dog" bit. The hot dog seller finally turns out to be a bootlegger and the customer a detective. Coy Herndon, billed as "America's greatest hoop roller," follows. Fred Durrer and girls sing and dance "Ain't She Sweet?" Lonnie Fisher and Kike Greshem in the comedy role, Jewell Cox and Moses Penny doing straight, do a "card bit," wherein the comedians are seemingly swindled out of their money until one of them produce five aces and plenty of ammunition to protect his spoils. "Birth of the Blues" is sung by Sam Gray and girls, who do a slow moving picture Charleston.

Princess White sings "Sitting on Top of the World," which closes the first act. After the opening chorus there is a hotel bit with a strain of comedy, in which one of the hotel maids falls in love with Silas, who is ignorant of the fact that she is a cripple. Evelyn White, Dixie's favorite blues singer, does her stuff. Marion Greshem and girls sing "You Made Me Happy." A "poison bit," with Ada Booker playing the wife, Sam Gray the husband and Manzie Campbell in the comedy part, a butler, follows. A drill, with the girls dressed as bellhops, then takes the stage; Ford Wiggins, as Silas, and Manzie Campbell follow with a comedy conversation, song and dance. The three songbirds—Josie Austin, Marion Greshem and Evelyn White—in a harmony number, hold the boards. The Woodens, world's greatest bicycling act, in eight minutes of riding anything with wheels, comes next. Nettie Coleman follows, singing "A Crazy Tune," assisted by the chorus. Lonnie Fisher, in his misfit Prince Albert suit and with a walking cane that looks as it were cut from the beanstalk that Jack climbed, does eight minutes of talk, and his parody on "Black Patti" stops the show. Princess White, in male attire, and Jewell Cox sing "Honey Bunch," assisted by the chorus, with Lonnie Fisher and Kike Greshem. The latter, dressed as a wench, does a burlesque while the number segues into the grand finale.

One of the most arresting features of *Hits and Bits* was its chorus line, comprising sixteen women "of the chocolate color variety and all of them a

The ladies of Silas Green in an informal pose. Princess White is standing farthest back, on the left. Evelyn White is standing farthest back, on the right. (photo by Katie Bryant Abraham, courtesy Alex Albright)

perfect '36.'"[560] Another highlight was Princess White's rendition of the 1925 Tin Pan Alley hit, "I'm Sitting on Top of the World."[561] At the beginning of 1928 audiences were still clamoring for her to "'sit on top of the world' just a little longer."[562]

Princess White married fellow Silas Green performer Fred Durrah and stayed with the show for the next ten or twelve seasons. Born in Philadelphia in 1881, she reportedly started touring at the age of five.[563] Trombonist Clyde Bernhardt recalled having seen her in vaudeville during the late 1910s: "a good-looking woman, medium slim, streamlined, light brown . . . with a rich, heavy voice . . . When she would start singing the blues, she would get the people under her fingers, and the men and women would be throwing money onto the stage. Then she would pull her fine dress up to her knees and show her pretty legs, and the people would go crazy. I have never seen Bessie Smith, Ma Rainey, Ida Cox, Clara Smith, Sara Martin or any of the other great blues singers, upset a theatre like Princess White."[564]

Sam Gray continued to supply original blues and jazz compositions for Silas Green's musical comedy productions. A note in the spring of 1928 informed that, "The well known S. H. Gray, who wrote 'Mixed Twins,' the show that put Silas Green over two years ago . . . has just finished three hot song numbers that will be used in the show. They are 'The Silas Green Stomp,' 'Cross-Word Puzzle' and 'Silas Green Started Jazz.'"[565] A few weeks later Gray advised that he had finished another song, "Good Gal Blues," and was writing a new song, "Mamie Has Quit Me," and a new musical comedy skit, *From Opera to Blues*.

Two other performers contributed original compositions to the 1928 edition of Silas Green: "Bettie Martin, the little Wilberforce girl, tried her hand at composing, and her first song, 'Crazy Daisies' is sure a hit. Prof. Fountain Woods will soon feature it with the band"; and cornetist Will Brown "completed a special blues number for the band. Sounds good."[566]

At Winston-Salem, North Carolina, early in the summer of 1928, Silas Green's band "gave an hour concert in front of the Lincoln Theater to a crowd that called for an extra traffic policeman. Many musicians made a special effort to hear the concert. Besides standard marches and a couple of popular numbers the band played the overture 'Oberon,' by Weber, and two selections, 'Mlle. Modiste,' by Herbert, and 'Ernani' by Verdi." Among those spotted in the crowd was former Silas Green bandmaster Freddie Pratt.[567] Several weeks later Coy Herndon wrote: "This season we are carrying the greatest concert band the South has seen in many moons, and it seems a little inhuman to me on these hot days to have a daily rehearsal, but Woods says that unless they are 'keyed up' quite often, one may hear a little jazz injected into one of his selections or overtures."[568]

In addition to their regular chores, the concert band booked after-show dances in the local communities en route. At West Palm Beach, Florida, in the early weeks of 1928, "The Silas Green orchestra played for a dance after the show and it was packed. Broadway Jones and Eubie Blake, the latter of 'Shuffle Along' fame, had just arrived in the city, and maybe we didn't have some fun!"[569] At Goldsboro, North Carolina, in the spring, "The Everett brothers . . . gave a dance at their auditorium which drew a capacity house. Music was furnished by the Silas Green orchestra. The Everett brothers gave their orchestra of eight pieces a vacation for the night." Later that fall, at Port Gibson, Mississippi, "the home of the Rabbit Foot minstrels," Silas Green did "a very nice business . . . The boys played a dance after the show and many friends motored from the delta country to attend." At Silas Green's annual Christmas party in 1929, "the orchestra boys, 12 in number, received a bonus for their dance playing—something like $150 per capita."[570]

New to the roster in 1928 was knockabout dancer Jim Green, the "human top." Green was said to have been connected, at one time or another, "with about every show of reputation that toured the South." Also making a brief appearance that year was Henrietta Leggett, of the famous Leggett Sisters from New Orleans. Leggett joined at Infield, North Carolina, "direct from Havana, Cuba," where she had been touring with Will Benbow's company. When she closed at Bristol, Virginia, four months later, the *Defender* correspondent ventured that she would "soon be seen with a Broadway production."

In April 1928 Silas Green entered North Carolina's strawberry district, a "narrow stretch of land that lies between Wilmington and Goldsboro, N. C. Many Race shows play this territory for this short but paying season."[571] In Alabama at the end of May the *Defender* correspondent complained that state and county taxes were "so high that tent shows can't exist. The lowest state tax is $250 and upwards, according to the seating capacity of the tent . . . The deplorable law enforced upon the tented shows playing in Alabama we think is due to selfish moving picture houses."[572] At Nashville, Tennessee, that fall they gave two performances in one night, "the first show, starting at 8:15, being for Race people, and a turn-away business was recorded. The midnight show for the whites was near capacity."[573]

Coy Herndon said goodbye to Silas Green for the last time that fall and did not return to the profession. By the spring of 1930, he was reestablished in chiropractics at Miami, Florida, "having been so far the only Race chiropractor to pass the state board of examiners in the state of Florida." Before the end of 1935, Herndon was admitted to the Veterans' Hospital at Tuskegee, Alabama, with what turned out to be a chronically debilitating illness. By the fall of 1937 the onetime "king of hoop manipulators" was listed in critical condition: "Special care is being given the grand old veteran as the doctors inject life giving fluid in his spine."[574] He died on March 19, 1938, and was laid to rest at the National Cemetery in Mobile, Alabama.[575]

In the fall of 1928 Lonnie Fisher called rehearsals for the latest Silas Green production, *Upside Down*. Popular features of *Upside Down* included Kike and Marion Gresham "with their rube impersonations"; Evelyn White singing the blues; and Princess White Durrah singing "That's My Handy Man."[576] Another feature was "the jazz playing of the one-armed cornet player, Carpenter."[577]

On March 15, 1929, Silas Green's band and male quartet, the New Orleans Four, were invited to broadcast over station WAOQ in Eastman, Georgia: "The band broadcast 12 noon and received so many calls that they were asked to repeat 4 o'clock that evening. Then after the show that night the quartet . . . closed the bill. Lonnie L. Fisher, second tenor; William M. Penny, first tenor; Frank Smedley, baritone, and S. H. Gray, bass."[578] When Silas Green played Eastman again in the fall of 1930, the quartet under Lonnie Fisher and the band under Fountain Wood were again heard on the radio, broadcasting "live" from the Lee Land (*sic*) Hotel.

Sam Gray left Silas Green in the fall of 1929. By this time, Charles Collier had managed to attract Tim Owsley, who had enacted Silas Green with the Black Patti Troubadours twenty years earlier. Owsley confessed that, while he had "often heard and read about the tented show entertainment," he hadn't taken it seriously "until Mr.

TIM E. OWSLEY.

Indianapolis Freeman, July 14, 1917.

Collier decided in his grand scheme of progressive show business to blend together as many different types of artists as he deemed necessary in making the tented theater equal and surpass its sister entertainment."[579] In West Virginia that summer Owsley debuted *Lucky Days*, a mélange of drama, burlesque, and vaudeville featuring music by himself and Johnny Spikes, with arrangements by Fountain B. Wood.

Silas Green played show stops in Florida from mid-December 1929 until late February 1930. Moving into Georgia, they played one-night stands at Valdosta and Waycross and then jumped to Brunswick, "where the production will rest up and do some needed repairs."[580] At this juncture, Brunswick, Georgia, became Silas Green's new winter headquarters.

From all indications, Silas Green was well equipped for the season of 1930: "Besides an all steel railroad passenger car for traveling, the rolling stock of the show has been increased to four two-ton trucks, a special built light plant truck, bill posting truck and a 1930 seven-passenger Buick for Mr. Collier's private use and he also lets the girls use it to motor about each town on sightseeing trips as we only do one show a day and no Sunday performances at all. This show always produces a new show every year."[581]

At Keystone, West Virginia, that summer, Tim Owsley unleashed his newest musical comedy, *Funny Money*, with music by Fountain B. Wood. Princess White Durrah sang "Blue" and Evelyn White sang "Can't Help It." Other production numbers included "The Same Old Silas," "All the Time in Dixie," "A Little Kiss," "Whoopee," "Dance of the Ghost," and "It's All Over Now."

During the summer of 1930, Silas Green lost two of its most celebrated female performers, leading lady Ada Lockhart Booker and blues queen Evelyn White. The *Defender* of August 9, 1930, notified that Ada Lockhart Booker was living in retirement at Daytona Beach, Florida: "She has joined the new Mt. Zion Baptist church and is choir leader." In the spring of 1932 she was commended for her part in a series of presentations at Daytona area schools: "Last week the star was featured in 'Bandana o' Yore,' an operetta of dialect songs, given at Bethune Cookman college." By the end of 1939, Ada and Lawrence Booker were

WANTED AT ONCE

FOR

Silas Green Show

Chorus girls who can sing and dance, versatile leading lady, musicians who double, novelty acts, specialties, quartet singers and cooks. Girls must send photos, also state color, height and weight. Everyone must specify ability in first letter. Tickets will be placed anywhere. Rehearsals begin March 5th. Wire or write Charles Collier, care Silas Green Show, Brunswick, Ga.

Chicago Defender, February 28, 1931.

ensconced in a "four room bungalow, smothered with roses, fruit trees, chickens and everything that makes life worthwhile."[582] Evelyn White's retirement may not have been so idyllic. The *Defender* of August 30, 1930, noted, "Evelyn White, blues singer for the past eight years with the Silas Green show, was forced by illness to retire from the show. She is at her home, 710 University St., Chattanooga."

Silas Green appears to have weathered the Great Depression better than most shows traveling under canvas. A note at the end of 1930 assured that they were still working "year round despite conditions which have forced many other travelling units off the road."[583] After a two-month layover in Brunswick, Silas Green launched its 1931 season in March, offering *Silas Green down among the Sugar Cane*, written and staged by Billiken Grimes, a refugee from the current vicissitudes of black vaudeville. Still in Georgia at the end of April, the "Barnum of little shows" claimed "great success through this section despite hard times . . . The Georgia Elks convention which sponsored the show at Savannah had them standing outside the City auditorium, which seats 3,500." The *Defender* listed some of the "things that make Silas Green's new show attractive: A peppy chorus of 18 high school graduates; Wiggin's and Manzie's peculiar experiences with voodooism; Ethel Ridley's electrifying personality; Rastus and Snow's mean way of tapping; Parthenia's colossal grin; Fisher's mastery of officiating at a wedding . . . Frank Keith's impersonations of Sophronia Windowbottom; Cornell's southern drawl; Smedley, Keith, Penny and Fisher, Medley Four; Kike's euphonious and humorous announcements."[584]

In West Virginia that summer, Billiken Grimes "issued a cast call for his new production, 'Silas Green in Africa.'"[585] When they pulled into their Brunswick, Georgia, headquarters in February 1932, the *Defender* correspondent noted: "In view of the fact that this season of depression and hardship has been unfavorable for tented aggregations this show has stood out prominently alone in braving the storm of doubt and discouragement. However, the flag is still up, and failure is a word unknown."[586]

While laying over in Brunswick, the Silas Green orchestra took up at the local County Casino Dance Hall, with "Eddie Billups, O. W. Mason, Wm. Harris, trumpets; J. C. Hudson, Oscar Lowe, saxophones; Lawrence Booker, banjo; Wm. Bryant, trombone; Billiken Grimes, piano; Mose McQuitty, sousaphone; Ford Wiggins, traps, and Donald Van Epps, master of ceremonies."[587] The *Defender* correspondent promised that the street parade for the season of 1932 would be "quite unique, featuring a beautifully gowned girl, mounted on a high stepping steed, with other novelties and a 25 piece band playing jazz and standard numbers." With the show set to open on April 4, it was disclosed that, in spite of the "tough sailing of last year," Collier was "planning to go out this season in a big way. The overflooded labor market has placed some of the topnotch performers in the reach of his purse and he is taking advantage by augmenting."[588]

Sam H. Gray returned after a three-year absence to produce the 1932 edition of the show. Like Lonnie Fisher before him, Gray came in with a "New York reputation." *Defender* reportage shows that in the fall of 1929, he had appeared at the Cosmopolitan Theater in New York City, in the cast of the *Great Day* Company. In December of that year, the former members of the Great Day Four quartet recorded four superb sides for Victor as the "Virginia Four." Gray was the bass singer, with tenors Frank Jackson and Ray Miles, and baritone Edward Ray.[589]

Sam Gray's new production for 1932 was called *Money Loafing*. In the wake of the phenomenal New York success of *Green Pastures, Money Loafing* was set to feature "a choir in spirituals and folklore songs."[590] But in June 1932, just two months into the season, Sam Gray died on the road, another hapless victim of acute indigestion.[591] A note in August advised that S. H. Dudley Jr. had been brought in to take Gray's place. Dudley was the twenty-eight-year-old son of black entertainment giant S. H. Dudley Sr., who had figured in the origins of *Silas Green from New Orleans*.[592]

SAM H. GRAY

WANT—WANT—WANT

SINGERS, CHORUS GIRLS, DANCERS, NOVELTY ACTS

Enlarge Chas. Collier's Silas Green From New Orleans company. Will place tickets from anywhere, but no advance. Wire or write Rocky Mount, N. C., June 5 and 6; Tarboro, N. C., June 7; Wilson, N. C., June 8; Dunn, N. C., June 9; Fayettsville, N. C., June 10; Smithfield, N. C., June 11; Raleigh, N. C., June 12 and 13.

Chicago Defender, June 4, 1932.

When Silas Green emerged from winter quarters on May 12, 1933, both S. H. Dudley Jr. and his famous father were listed on the roster. Dudley Jr. was listed as producer and Dudley Sr. as manager. Dudley Sr.'s presence may reflect the creeping demise of the TOBA circuit, which had consumed his creative energies throughout the 1920s.

Dudley Jr.'s production for 1933, *Keep Digging*, was characterized as an "intensely humorous and modern musical comedy with a pleasing romance that gives Silas and Lilas a role excelling in wit, humor and ludicrous situations."[593] Leading lady Cleo Mitchell starred as Magnolia, with other parts going to Joe Sheftell, Charles E. Rue, Ford Wiggins, Frank Keith and Nathan "Mess Around" Suggs. Suggs took the role of Lilas Bean, a recently developed Silas Green sidekick who would be seen in most every subsequent production.

S. H. Dudley Jr. left Silas Green before the end of the summer and was replaced by Tim Owsley. Owsley was quick to praise the show's current female blues singer: "It is a pleasure to hear Christine Barnett sing the blues. While blue singing is on the wane, this young lady has an art of putting it over."[594] At Nashville, Tennessee, that fall, Silas Green held forth in the Ryman Auditorium.[595]

The musical comedy for 1934 was *A World of Fun*, written and staged by Owsley, with music by bandmaster A. D. King. S. H. Dudley Sr. was listed as assistant business manager. Among the season's new recruits were singer and violinist Edward Harris and Kid Lips Hackett, "a sensation both on stage and in the orchestra pit. He plays 'traps' and dances." That fall the show was booked into state fairs in Arkansas and Louisiana.

The 1935 season opened April 8 at the City Auditorium in Savannah, Georgia, featuring Tim Owsley's latest musical comedy, *Share the Wealth*, a "depression pipe dream a la Kingfish."[596] "Good dance numbers, peppy girls and a hot jazz band are features."[597] After whipping the production into shape, Owsley went home to Indianapolis and left the stage to S. H. Dudley Jr. In addition to reclaiming the producer's reins, Dudley Jr. appeared in a dance routine with Velma Anderson. In the Mississippi Delta that fall, they "went over big with the Continental."[598]

During the season of 1935 Princess White Durrah attempted to modify her image. As the *Defender* correspondent explained, "Princess White has departed from blues singing, and from the continued rounds of applause received nightly in her rendition of 'Lovely to Look At' and 'You're a Heavenly Thing,' feels that blues have gone forever, and is gratified over her departure."[599] A few weeks later, however, the same correspondent noted, "Jimmy, Buster and Frankie, the dancing act, stopped the show, as did the blues singer, Princess White."

Billed as the "queen of personality," Princess White stayed at least through the season of 1938.

With Irvin C. Miller's Brownskin Models in 1943, she was "especially 'groovy' when she puts over some new Parodies in 'St. Louis Blues.'"[600] Princess White finally quit the road around 1948 to run a nightclub in Norfolk, Virginia. She eventually migrated to Newark, New Jersey, where, in 1974, Clyde Bernhardt rediscovered her at the New Eden Baptist Church, and coaxed her out of retirement to tour and record with his Harlem Blues and Jazz Band. At the age of ninety-four, she sang the title song of their 1975 album, *Sittin' on Top of the World*.[601] Princess White died in the wings of the Emelin Theater of the Performing Arts in Mamaroneck, New York, in 1976.[602]

Ford Wiggins abandoned Silas Green in 1935 to try his luck with Winstead's Mighty Minstrels.[603] He returned the following season. With S. H. Dudley Jr. as producer, the musical comedy for 1936 was *King Sambo*, starring Wiggins, with Billy Mills, Jazzlips Richardson, and others. Mills also sang in the show's male quartet. Along with the chorus line of "20 sun-kissed beauties," Silas Green's *Defender* correspondent rated the "Dummy Dance" and "Old Man Strut" by Shorty Harris and Buster Wheeler as the top numbers on the bill.[604]

In 1937 Silas Green declared itself the "oldest and largest colored aggregation traveling," and "the only one of its kind to bridge the depression."[605] At the outset of the season, there were sixty people in tow. The Pullman car was augmented by a fleet of "five Chevrolet trucks, a bus and two Buick sedans to transfer people and paraphernalia from the car to show lots."

A *Defender* report of May 29, 1937, mentioned the show's "red hot swing band," headed by "ace trumpeter" Eddie Washington. A note in October informed that, "Roy Bowling, 'hot lipped' trumpet soloist," had been added to the band.[606] Within the next few weeks, however, Bowling left to take over the band with the Rabbit Foot Minstrels.

Silas Green's 1937 musical comedy success, *I'se 'A Coming Carlusia*, was staged by "modernistic producer" Boisey De Legge, who had made his reputation during the TOBA era of African American vaudeville. It was well received in Greenville, Mississippi, that fall: "Charles Collier brought New York's Cotton club to the Mississippi delta . . . when his Silas Green company presented to a packed Greenville audience the greatest show ever seen here . . . Built around the musical comedy, 'I'se A Coming Carlusia,' the presentation is a fast, rip-roaring 'sender' from start to finish."[607]

In addition to staging the show, DeLegge performed on his musical "Bottle-A-Phone." Other acts of 1937 included Allie "Cat on a Wire" Johnson: "Walking the wire, removal of a number of garments, getting in and out of hoops and garbed as an ape, are some of the things done by Allie Johnson, to bring his act up to the standard."[608] Another standout was Harry Fiddler, "the man of a hundred faces." Active since the early 1890s, Fiddler was considered to be a "perfect Chinese impersonator."[609] With Silas Green in the summer of 1938, he and fellow old-timer Billy Mills revived an ancient skit titled "Five Minutes in a Chinese Laundry": "During the argument in the laundry, Charles Rue steps in as a peacemaker." Fiddler left Silas Green that fall to take up at the Swingland Café in Omaha, Nebraska, where "his remarkable facial changes alone" were "sufficient to transform him from a Chinaman, Japanese emigrant, woman or chimpanzee to an elegant man about town."[610]

Longtime Silas Green business manager Johnson Rooks retired in the fall of 1937 to open a

Down In Dixie

HARRY FIDDLER

Well known comedian now being featured with Charles Collier's Silas Green show. Fiddler is shown here dressed in his Chinese costume. The show is now in the Southland.

Chicago Defender, June 25, 1938.

cafeteria and beer garden in downtown Savannah.[611] He appears to have been replaced by Charles Morton of Athens, Georgia.[612] Morton was married to Charles Collier's wife's sister and was no stranger to the entertainment business; in 1910 his father founded the Morton Theater, Athens's premier African American vaudeville showcase.[613]

Silas Green's musical comedy production for 1938, *Silas and Lilas at the World's Fair*, was written and produced by Albert Gaines, of the acrobatic Gaines Brothers.[614] It featured twelve "tall, tan and terrific chorus girls."[615] S. H. Dudley Jr., who had been producing shows at the Little Harlem Café in Buffalo, New York, returned that summer to take over as stage manager.[616] In advance of their engagement at Greenville, Mississippi, that fall, the Silas Green Orchestra contracted to play for an after-show dance at Greenville's "Grand Terrace nightery."[617]

The 1939 edition of Silas Green pulled out of winter headquarters in April and followed the well-beaten path through Georgia to the Carolinas, Virginia, West Virginia, Illinois, Kentucky, Tennessee, Mississippi, Louisiana, Arkansas, Alabama, and Florida, where they closed at Fernandina in February 1940, having logged "a 10-month tour and no nights lost." A summary account of the tour noted "three deaths on the show this season: Frank Gaines, truck driver; Floyd Johnson, electrician and Oscar Lowe, clarinetist. One marriage was performed in West Palm Beach: Roy Bowling, trumpeter and Pauline Griffin, chorus girl."[618]

The season of 1940 saw Tim Owsley return to the role of producer: "A spacious bus, four cars and a fleet of six trucks are now required to carry the people when playing stands off the railroad." The *Macon Evening News* of April 17, 1940, announced an upcoming date in Charles Collier's Macon, Georgia, hometown:

> A chorus of 25 singers and dancers, a host of comedians, headed by Ford Wiggins and Billy Mills, the original Silas and Lilas, and Eddie Washington's famous Silas Green 20-piece band and orchestra all

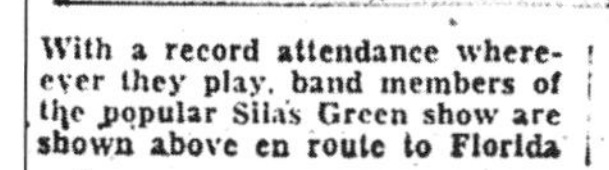

SILAS GREEN SHOW TOURS DIXIELAND TOWNS

With a record attendance wherever they play, band members of the popular Silas Green show are shown above en route to Florida where they will fill several engagements. Charles Collier, owner of the unit, says that 1937 has been a banner year for the show, despite the depression "pains" that many such groups are said to be suffering. The troupe carries many big name performers and a fine set of well-trained, beautiful chorines. Harry Fiddler is one of the show's big features, and is hitting. . . .

Chicago Defender, January 1, 1938.

combine to make the 1940 new and enlarged edition of Silas Green from New Orleans the greatest ever in the 51 years [*sic*] of this famous old epic of the true South. It will play here Friday in city auditorium.

In addition manager Charles Collier has engaged a large contingent of vaudevillians new to the field of Southern musicals. Among these are Johnny Hudgins, mimic, from Apollo theater, New York; Kid Lips Hackette, king of clown drummers direct from the Orient; Danny and Edith, rope dancers from the Follies Beregeres, Paris, France; Pedro and Delores, adiago dancers from the Cotton club; Al Gaines Brothers, acrobatic troupe from the Apollo theatre, New York; Spencer and Sparky, former tap dancing feature of Butterbeans and Susie Revue; Cherry Griffin, infamous radio star and recording fame; Cookie Howard and her three little fishes, contortion number; and Lasses Brown, minstrel star.

Admission of 55 cents will include the dance to be held after the performance. Music will be furnished by Eddie Washington's Silas Green Swing and Jive band of 20 musicians. Doors open at 7 p. m., and the performances start at 8:15 p. m. A special section of seats will be reserved for white patrons.

Two weeks later the show was written up in *Time*:

In Georgia this month an all-Negro troupe pitched its tent for a ten-month road tour. As familiar throughout the South as a statue of Robert E. Lee, *Silas Green from New Orleans* claims that this is its 51st year on the road; oldtimers can remember it for at least 38. Part revue, part musicomedy, part minstrel show, it tells, season after season, of the adventures of two Negroes, short, coal black Silas Green and tall, tannish Lilas Bean. For years the show never bothered to change its plot.

In Buffalo

SHERMAN H. DUDLEY JR.
After successfully producing shows at Club Plantation and Golden Lily in St. Louis. Dudly shuffled off to Buffalo where he has met with big success as Little Harlem's impresario.

Chicago Defender, October 23, 1937.

When the public finally started to yawn, Silas and Lilas found they had better vary their mishaps each season.

This year their troubles start when they go to a hospital with suitcases labeled M. D. (Mule Drivers), are mistaken for two medicos, end in jail. The show is garnished with such slapstick as putting a patient to sleep by letting him smell an old shoe, such gags as "Your head sets on one end of your spine and you set on the other." *Silas* gets broad at times, but never really dirty. What keeps it moving are its dances and specialty acts, its gold toothed but good-looking chorus.

Only white man in the company of 76 is the press agent. Soft-spoken, sharp-eyed owner Charles Collier has bossed the show for 18 years, recently refused to sell it for $20,000. Collier moves his troupers from town to town in a private car named after his mother, feeds their bellies, watches their morals.

After marching through Georgia, *Silas Green* will circle the South, winding up in Florida next February. His big tent, holding 1,400 people, is usually filled at prices up to a dollar. Negroes in the audience outnumber whites about three to one. If the show has any trouble with whites, it never plays that town again.[619]

Later that fall the show's "musicomedy" was restaged by S. H. Dudley Jr., under the title *Dr. Beans From New Orleans*. The title is redolent of Dudley's father's musical comedy hit of 1911–1912, *Dr. Beans from Boston*.

In the spring of 1941, Dinah Scott let "the cock-eyed world know that he will make the season of 1941 with the Silas Green Show. Friends may reach him, 1312 Monk street, Brunswick, Georgia." Scott had come up for recognition during the early years of southern vaudeville. He eventually ascended to the role of Silas Green.

On the road in the fall of 1942, Charles Collier was stricken with typhoid fever and died at a hospital in Knoxville, Tennessee, at the age of 61. Minnie D. Singleton, editor of the "Colored Department" of the mainstream daily *Macon Telegraph*, informed that, "During the hour of the funeral the entire cast of the famed Silas Green Show will cease activities in recognition of their beloved owner, as they station for a performance in Paducah, Ky. The old saying, 'The show must go on,' is the message he left with his widow who expects to continue to give the public the same

GEORGIAN ENJOYS BROADWAY

MRS. HORTENSE COLLIER

A leading exponent of the theatrical profession from Brunswick, Ga., who has been visiting the Erskine Hawkinses in New York for the past several days spent much of her time viewing and reviewing Broadway. She is the wife of Charles Collier, owner of the Silas Green shows.

Chicago Defender, March 30, 1940.

high class entertainment in keeping with the standard set by her husband."[620]

Within a year of her husband's death, Hortense Collier sold Silas Green to Charles Morton and two other Athens, Georgia, businessmen, Rodney Harris and Wilbur P. Jones. Morton was the only one with hands-on experience, but in 1944 Wilbur Jones became Silas Green's sole proprietor. Originally from Union Springs, Alabama, Jones had married an Athens girl and made a name for himself as an insurance agent, recognized in fraternal circles as the "Grand Chief of the Improved Order of Samaritans."[621]

Like Eph Williams and Charles Collier before him, Wilbur Jones was a Race man, and he adopted Silas Green as a way of life. For the next fifteen years, he plowed the minstrel show routes eleven months out of the year, covering some 30,000 miles each season, pitching his tent in 240 different towns across fourteen states, and showing to more than 100,000 people.[622] A 1949 *Defender* report assured that Silas Green was "still the apple of Dixie's eye":

> To the starved audiences below the Mason Dixon line the black face Silas and Lilas, with their familiar routine, the hard-working chorus line and the plump soubrette are perennial attractions. Sandwiched in between are headliners like Johnny Hudgins, dancer Crip Heard, and blues singer Cherry Mills . . .
>
> In a Pullman, six trucks and two buses, they transport fifty people including performers, musicians, porter, cook and canvas boys . . . Mr. and Mrs. Jones and the married couples live in the Pullman while the show plays an area. The car is run on a railroads siding and there the company community life of cooking and eating and washing and ironing goes on. Mrs. Jones tends to the marketing for the entire company, keeps an eye on the costumes, takes tickets at night and helps check tickets and money in the morning.
>
> The route of the show is governed by the business seasons in the South. They come into Miami during the height of the tourist season. They strike agricultural areas at harvest time.
>
> During the war the show did tremendous business, but as soon as the allotment checks stopped, Mrs. Jones said they could tell it in the box office. In Mississippi this year they had a good season, because of the bumper cotton crop. In North Carolina, however, where they were scheduled at strawberry harvest time there were no strawberries.

> Largest audiences are in Atlanta where they abandon the tent for an auditorium that seats 7,000.[623]

Jones's daughter Eleanor was four years old when he took over the show, and she toured with her parents every summer until she was thirteen.[624] In a 2005 interview Eleanor Jones Baker recalled the Pullman car that was her childhood summer home:

> It was really the main gathering place, because, all of the women, all of the chorus girls, would stay on the Pullman car, as well as all of the married couples, and that's where you also ate. The man who took charge of the Pullman car was called Mister Harry. And he was responsible for making the beds down at night, and then putting them up in the morning, and there was a cook, and they served breakfast, and they served dinner. And the band members did not stay on the Pullman car. The band members would always stay in the town, and they were given additional money to stay in the town. And we [she and her family] had a stateroom. And then Freddie Durrah, who was also the accountant and managed the money and so forth, also had a stateroom. And then, back in the back of it—it was a long car—was where they put the luggage and so forth, and we had a couple slot machines back there. And the Pullman car moved about once a week. Say, if you went to Birmingham, it would go to the larger places generally, where it could be parked, and then you would play the smaller towns outside, and then come back at night to the Pullman car.[625]

Jones managed to keep his Pullman car on the track until 1953. He may have been the last tent show owner to perpetuate this once pervasive mode of transportation. Indeed, Jones was one of the last of a breed altogether.

Ernest "Punch" Miller, who played trumpet on dozens of 1920s jazz recordings, may have been among the performers who witnessed the end of Silas Green's Pullman car days. Miller was spotted in Mississippi with the Silas Green band in 1952, and he later recalled having spent two and a half years with the show.[626]

In 1954, Jones hauled Silas Green in a convoy of six trucks, three house trailers, a bus, ten passenger cars and a station wagon. A feature article in *Ebony* that fall said the show was "almost as much a part of Dixie as collard greens and barbecued ribs." The reporter enumerated "such diverse fare as a chorus line, table eaters, torch singers and lively situation comedy featuring black face comedians."[627] S. H. Dudley Jr. was the director-producer; Dinah Scott was Silas. *Ebony* described Silas as "a loveable fall guy." Eleanor Baker recalls a "very gullible" character who was always getting involved in money-making schemes, only to get caught up "in some sort of dilemma which he did not have any control over; and he never, of course, got what he thought he was going to get."

In the 1954 edition of the show, "Silas and his friends poke fun at Negro life in metropolitan cities, particularly New York's Harlem where the action frequently takes place at the Seventh avenue and 125th street crossroads." The cast included two new characters, Sasparilla and Savannah, unworldly female counterparts to Silas and Lilas: "Sent down from heaven to straighten out Harlem," Sasparilla and Savannah get into "several beguiling situations," damage their angelic reputations, and "end up in hell."[628]

The March 12, 1955, edition of the *Chicago Defender* informed that a new season was set to open in April at Alexandria, Louisiana, and that S. H. Dudley Jr. was in Chicago, "awaiting call to duty." Readers were reminded that the show had served as a "molding pot for many of the nation's top stars of today. There have been and still are quite a few top names whose beginning can be traced to tent work with 'Silas Green From New Orleans.' And that pot is still boiling and turning 'em out."[629]

By this time, however, Silas Green's molding pot was cooling off. In Eleanor Baker's estimation, "1954 was sort of a watershed, in terms of the downward trend for the show." In 1956, her father was forced to place Silas Green under the umbrella of a white-owned traveling carnival. S. H. Dudley Jr. appears to have bailed out at this point. Jones tried in vain to sell the show before taking it off the road for good in 1958. He attributed the show's ultimate demise to "increased overhead expenses, the popularity of television, and the heightened racial tensions in the South brought on by the 1954 Supreme Court decision in *Brown v. Board of Education* declaring segregation in public schools unconstitutional."[630]

APPENDIX I

Rosters of Alexander Tolliver's Shows

C. W. Park's Musical Comedy Company
August through November 1914

The following persons were members of C. W. Park's Musical Comedy Company for all or part of August through November 1914: C. W. Park, owner; Charles Collier, manager; Alexander Tolliver, producer and stage manager; William "King" Phillips, musical director and orchestra leader; Helen Bumbray, Evelyn White, Tressie Legge, Octavia Rogers, Mabel Tolliver, Artie Belle McGinty, Isaiah A. and Leola Grant, B. B. Joyner, Isaac "Slim" Jones, "Kid Nappie" Lewis, Ed Whitehurst, Walter Smith, Kag Fisher, Doc Perkins, Johnnie Nickelby, John Howard, Henry Austin, Shorty Harris, Sam "Slow Kid" Wade, Walter Hastings, Hattie Newell, Mazie Daye, Fannie Turner, Phoebe Young, Daisy Young, Arthur L. and Ruth Sprague Prince, Maggie Graham, Bill Jones, Henry and Loretta Wooden, Jones and Jones ("Happy" Jones and Clara Smith), Mr. and Mrs. A. A. Wright, Mack Carter, Tony Barefield, Tolliver Quartet (Alexander Tolliver, A. A. Wright, Mack Carter, and Tony Barefield).

Tolliver's Big Show/ Tolliver's Smart Set
1915

The following persons were members of Tolliver's Big Show/Tolliver's Smart Set for all or part of the season beginning in March 1915 and ending in December 1915: Alexander Tolliver, manager, producer, comedian, singer, and skate dancer; Mabel Tolliver, prima donna soprano; Aaron Tolliver, skate dancer, singer, and comedian; Isaiah A. Grant, baritone singer; Leola Grant, singing and dancing soubrette; Carter Lockhart, comedian; Jodie Edwards and Eddie "Peg" Lightfoot, singers, dancers, and comedians; King Williams and his dogs; Arthur Williams, tenor singer; Susie Hawthorne and Cleo Poteet, singing and dancing soubrettes; Gertrude "Ma" and W. M. "Pa" Rainey, singers and comedians; Ada Lockhart, singer; Wayne "Buzzin'" Burton and Little Frank D. Jackson, dancers, singers, and comedians; Alexander L. Lovejoy, dancer, singer, and comedian; Tressie Legge and Artie Belle McGinty, dancers and singers; Nettie Perry, singing and dancing soubrette; the Walton Duo Musical Act (Earl Walton and unidentified partner); Trixie Smith, singer and comedian; Clara Smith, singer and comedian; Evelyn White, singer; the Lewis Brothers ("King Nappie" Lewis and unidentified partner), dancers; Anita Ramsey and Magnolia Brown, sister team; Al and Luella Wells, trapeze artists; Henry and Loretta Wooden, trick bicyclists; H. H. Puggsley, acrobat; Barringer and Barringer; The Gaines Brothers (Charles and Albert Gaines), acrobats; Mrs. Alice Gaines, singer; Rhoda and John McNeal; Frank Chapman; H. B. "Caggie" Howard, pianist and musical director; Freddie Pratt, trombonist; Willie "Tutan" Richardson, trap drummer. One report states that the company had an eight-piece band, but names of the other musicians were not given.

1916

The following performers were members of Tolliver's Big Show/Tolliver's Smart Set for all or any part of the season beginning in January 1916 and ending in

December 1916: Alexander Tolliver, manager and producer; Mabel Tolliver, Aaron Tolliver, Arthur and Mary Francis Williams, Tressie Legge and Artie Belle McGinty, Gertrude "Ma" and William "Pa" Rainey, the Lewis Brothers ("King Nappie" Lewis and Lewis Boyd), Cleo Poteet, Susie Hawthorne Edwards, Susie Cooksey, Eddie "Peg" Lightfoot and Jodie Edwards, Charles H. Coffey, Ed Love, Lena Leggett, Wesley Michel, Elizabeth Kewley, Anita Ramsey and Magnolia Brown, Alice Ramsey, Isaac "Slim" Jones, Daisy Martin and W. M. Floyd, Leroy Knox, John Berry and Telfair Washington, Roxie Caldwell, Jack and Charles Beacham, Davis and Elmore, Pope and Dallas, Alexander Lovejoy and Thompson, Zudora Johnson, Clara Smith, The Musical Seminoles (father and son), Johnny Hudgins and Helen Bumbray, Little Ella Simmons, Evelyn White, Rhoda and John McNeal, Alice Gaines, Ethel Fleming, Kid Owen, Leola Grant and Mattie Lewis, and C. H. Meredith. Novelty acts: Al and Luella Wells, acrobats and trapeze artists; Joe and Mrs. Jalvan, jugglers and magicians; Charles and Albert Gaines, acrobats and wire walkers; Henry and Loretta Wooden, trick cyclists; Great Adams, trick cyclist; Calbo, wire walker and foot juggler. Band: Fred Kewley, leader and clarinet; Arnold Metoyer, cornet; Willie Hightower, cornet; Alvin "Zoo" Robertson, trombone; David Jones, mellophone; H. B. Howard, piano; J. W. Craddock, bass and tuba; John Porter, bass and tuba; Eddie "Rabbit" Robinson, trap drums.

January through September 1917

Alexander Tolliver, Eddie "Peg" Lightfoot and Jodie Edwards, Susie Hawthorne Edwards and Evelyn White, Tressie Legge and Artie Belle McGinty, Telfair Washington and Zudora Johnson, Gertrude "Ma" Rainey, Bessie Smith, George Bell, Willie and Lottie Frost Hightower, and Eddie "Rabbit" Robinson.

November 1917 through April 1918

Alexander Tolliver, Eddie "Peg" Lightfoot, Etheline and Sam Jordan, Beatrice Johnson, Nina Davis, Minstrel Morris, Margaret Duckett, Mrs. Susie Hughes, the Strayhorn Children, Leon Long, Kennett ("Imp of Satan"), W. Henri Bowman, and Prof. Attrice Hughes, musical director and orchestra leader.

July 1919

Mr. and Mrs. Alexander Tolliver, Joe Smith, William Howard, Mr. and Mrs. W. H. Hightower, Eleanor Burleigh, Bobbie Thomas, Hettie V. Snow, Sarah Tolliver, Naoma Preston, Annie Dudley, Jones and Jones, John L. Porter, Eddie "Peg" Lightfoot, Elizabeth Jones, P. Jones, and Leon "Sonny" Gray, stage manager.

APPENDIX II

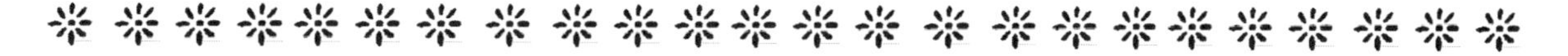

Itinerary of Alexander Tolliver's Big Show/Smart Set

April or May 1915: Charleston, South Carolina (probably one week).
April or May 1915: Winston-Salem, North Carolina (probably one week).
May 1915: Durham, North Carolina (probably one week).
Late May 1915: Asheville, North Carolina (one week).
June 7 through June 13, 1915: Raleigh, North Carolina.
June 14 through June 20, 1915: Greensboro, North Carolina.
June 21 through June 27, 1915: Danville, Virginia.
June 28 through July 18, 1915: Richmond, Virginia.
Late July 1915: Norfolk, Virginia (two weeks).
August 9 through August 21, 1915: Newport News, Virginia.
August 22 through September 4, 1915: Portsmouth, Virginia.
September 5 through September 18, 1915: Norfolk, Virginia.
September 19 through September 25, 1915: Petersburg, Virginia.
September 26 through October 9, 1915: Richmond, Virginia.
October 1915: Roanoke, Virginia.
October 1915: Winston-Salem, North Carolina.
October 25 through October 31, 1915: Sumter, South Carolina.
November 1 through November 7, 1915: Augusta, Georgia.
Probably November 8 through November 14, 1915: Montgomery, Alabama.
Late November to early December 1915: Mobile, Alabama (probably two weeks).
December 1915: New Orleans, Louisiana.
January 1 through February 6, 1916: Temple Theater, New Orleans, Louisiana.
February 26 through about March 26, 1916: New Orleans, Louisiana.
April 3 through April 16, 1916: Birmingham, Alabama.
April 17 through April 23, 1916: Bessemer, Alabama.
April 24 through May 6, 1916: Birmingham, Alabama.
May 8 through May 14, 1916: Atlanta, Georgia.
May 15 through May 21, 1916: Macon, Georgia.
May 22 through May 28, 1916: Savannah, Georgia.
May 29 through June 4, 1916: Charleston, South Carolina.
June 19 through June 25, 1916: Raleigh, North Carolina.
June 26 through July 2, 1916: Petersburg, Virginia.
July 3 through July 9, 1916: Norfolk, Virginia.
July 10 through July 16, 1916: Portsmouth, Virginia.
July 17 through July 23, 1916: Norfolk, Virginia.
July 24 through July 30, 1916: Berkley, Virginia.
July 31 through August 6, 1916: Newport News, Virginia.
August 7 through early September 1916: Richmond, Virginia (five weeks).
Mid-September 1916: Durham, North Carolina.
September 18 through September 24, 1916: Greensboro, North Carolina.
September 25 through October 1, 1916: Winston-Salem, North Carolina.
October 2 through October 8, 1916: Charlotte, North Carolina.
October 16 through October 22, 1916: Augusta, Georgia.
October 23 through October 29, 1916: Charleston, South Carolina.

October 30 through November 5, 1916: Savannah, Georgia.
November 6 through November 12, 1916: Macon, Georgia.
November 13 through November 19, 1916: Atlanta, Georgia.
January 1 through (probably) January 31, 1917: Strand Theater, Jacksonville, Florida.
February and early March 1917: Atlanta, Georgia (three weeks).
March 12 through March 18, 1917: Douglass Theater, Macon, Georgia.
April 9 through April 15, 1917: unidentified theater, Albany, Georgia.
April 16 through April 22, 1917: Dixieland Theater, Charleston, South Carolina.
June 4 through June 9, 1917: Pocahontas, Virginia.
June 11 through June 16, 1917: New Grand Theater, Northfork, West Virginia.
June 18 through June 23, 1917: Keystone, West Virginia.
June 25 through June 27, 1917: Thorp, West Virginia.
June 28 through June 30, 1917: Filbert, West Virginia.
July 2 through July 4, 1917: Gary, West Virginia.
July 5 through July 7, 1917: Anawalt, West Virginia.
July 16 through July 22, 1917: Logan, West Virginia.
July 23, 1917: Montgomery, West Virginia.
July 24, 1917: Thurmond, West Virginia.
July 25 and 26, 1917: Raleigh, West Virginia.
July 27, 1917: Beckley, West Virginia.
July 28, 1917: Layland, West Virginia.
July 30, 1917: Kaymoor, West Virginia.
July 31, 1917: Nutall, West Virginia.
August 1, 1917: Claramount, West Virginia.
August 2, 1917: Ansted, West Virginia.
August 3 and 4, 1917: Fire Creek, West Virginia.
August 6, 1917: Glen Jean, West Virginia.
August 7, 1917: Mt. Hope, West Virginia.
August 8, 1917: Oak Hill, West Virginia.
August 9, 1917: White Oak, West Virginia.
August 10, 1917: Eccles, West Virginia.
August 11, 1917: Tams, West Virginia.
August 13, 1917: Beckley, West Virginia.
August 14, 1917: Raleigh, West Virginia.
August 15 and 16, 1917: Winding, West Virginia.
August 17, 1917: Pemberton, West Virginia.
August 18, 1917: Mullens, West Virginia.
August 20, 1917: Pax, West Virginia.
August 21, 1917: Eccles, West Virginia.
August 22, 1917: Mullens, West Virginia.
August 23, 1917: Bud, West Virginia.
August 24 and 25, 1917: Princeton, West Virginia.
August 27, 1917: McDowell, West Virginia.
August 28, 1917: Northfork, West Virginia.
August 30 through September 1, 1917: Keystone, West Virginia.
September 10 through September 16, 1917: unidentified theater, Philadelphia, Pennsylvania.
September 17 through September 23, 1917: Lincoln Theater, New York City.

APPENDIX III

Circus and Wild West Side Show Annex Band and Minstrel Rosters, 1911–1920

P. G. Lowery's Band and Minstrels (with Hagenbeck and Wallace Circus)
May 1911

P. G. Lowery, cornet soloist, leader; Thomas May, Tom Tolliver, cornets; Fred C. Richardson, James Brown, clarinets; Anatole Victor, Ben W. Lee, altos; E. Venable, A. Valentine, trombones; Paul Halvard, baritone; William May, Tony Barefield, tubas; Junk Edwards, Edward Nevils, drums. Minstrels: Essie Williams, interlocutor; Winona Crigler, Charles Beechum, Junk Edwards, Mr. and Mrs. James Brown.

H. L. Rawles's Band and Minstrels (with Howe's Great London Circus)
May 1911

Al White, first clarinet; H. T. Howard, second clarinet; Ed Tolliver, first alto; A. N. Parker, second alto and violin; Max Shaw, first trombone; Irving Brown, second trombone; E. P. Wood, E♭ bass; J. L. Holmes, snare drum; L. H. Kitchen, bass drum; T. M. Thomas, B♭ cornet; L. H. Gilbert, E♭ cornet and assistant leader; H. L. Rawles, baritone and manager.

R. Roy Pope's Band (with Ringling Brothers Circus)
May 1911

R. Roy Pope, Edward Wisdom, Fred D. Owens, Alex Jackson, Buford Palmer, Jess Baltimore, Walter E. Hinson, P. A. Venable, Preston Duncan, Nathan Stirman, John Mitchell, M. O. Russell.

James Wolfscale's Band and Minstrels (with Forepaugh and Sells Brothers' Circus)
June 1911

James Wolfscale, director, cornet, and violin; Roy Wolfscale, interlocutor and cornet; Troy Wolfscale, trap drummer and alto; Horace Eubanks, clarinet; W. F. Russell, cornet; J. A. Hains, trombone; H. Stratton, bass; W. P. Smith, baritone; H. Brown, bass drum and end man; W. Brown, snare drum and end man; Amos Peoples, alto and end man; Ben Goodall, trombone and end man; Miss C. C. Clements, soubrette; Miss A. Anderson, soubrette.

W. L. Horne's Band and Minstrels (with Young Buffalo's Wild West Show)
July 1911

W. L. Horne, director and B-♭ cornet; H. Hunt, B-flat cornet; A. Grayson, tuba; R. L. Davis, alto; George Ross, second trombone; Jesse Brooks, first trombone; J. Johnson, baritone; T. A. Sulcer, clarinet; Jasper Taylor, traps; Will Moore, bass drum. Minstrels: R. L. Davis, George Ross, William Moore, Jasper Taylor.

Bismark Ferris's Band and Minstrels (with Buffalo Bill Wild West Show)
July 1911

Bismark K. Ferris, clarinet, director; Ben Jackson, solo cornet; William Carr, solo cornet; Edward Howard, first cornet; Reed Connor, alto; James Shaw, baritone; Ulysses Everly, Billy Moore, trombones; John Butler, tuba; Johnny Crabb, small drum; Bud Borders, bass drum; Tony Mays, clarinet. Minstrels: Norris Grigsby and Harrison Blackburn, extreme ends; Bud Borders and Billy Moore, end. Rambler Quartette: Melvin Oglesby, Ed Love, Fred Smart, and Ed Tandy. Reed Connor, interlocutor.

Grant Cooper's Band and Minstrels (with Kit Carson's Buffalo Ranch Wild West Shows)
September 1911

Grant Cooper, trombone, leader; B. C. Campbell, tuba; John Eubanks, Jr., baritone; Lonnie Kyle, alto; A. Turner, cornet, violin; Bert F. DeLeo, cornet; Ernest Williams, snare drum; Peter L. Joiner, bass drum; Minstrels: Mr. and Mrs. P. L. Joiner, Lula Cooper.

R. Roy Pope's Band (with Ringling Brothers Circus)
May 1912

R. Roy Pope, director; Frank Belt, assistant director; P. A. Venable, baritone; Walter Hinson, William Smith, trombones; Alex Jackson, Buford Palmer, altos; Andrew Scott, Preston Duncan, cornets; Nathan Stirman, tuba; M. Lee Perry, snare drum; Jesse Baltimore, bass drum.

W. L. Horne's Band and Minstrels (with Young Buffalo's Wild West Show)
May 1912

W. L. Horne, cornet and violin; T. Boone, cornet; George F. Hill, clarinet; William Moore, alto and comedian; Reginald Horne, comedian; Thomas Edwards, first trombone; W. R. Robinson, second trombone; J. F. Johnson, baritone and violin; A. L. Grayson, tuba; Charles (Shine) Irving, bass drum and comedian; Jasper Taylor, snare drum and comedian; Mrs. W. L. Horne, interlocutor and soubrette; Mrs. Alice Edwards, soubrette.

A. Turner's Band and Minstrels (with Kit Carson's Buffalo Ranch)
June 1912

A. Turner, solo cornet, violin; Frank Burgess, cornet; P. J. "Pick Doo" Langford, alto and comedian; Robert Cain, baritone and interlocutor; B. C. Campbell, bass; Paul Cheatham, snare drum; P. L. Joiner, bass drum and comedian; Mrs. Mae Langford, soubrette; Jack LaVere, ventriloquist.

James A. Harris's Band and Minstrels (with Gollmar Bros. Circus)
July 1912

James A. Harris, first trombone; Tommie Bright, second trombone; William M. Carr, Billy Bright, cornets; Buddy James, baritone; Ulysses Douglass, tuba; Charles F. Brown, alto; Henry Young, bass drum; James J. Jackson, snare drum. Minstrels: James Jackson, W. M. "Billy" Bright, Tommie Bright, Ulysses Douglass; Charles F. Brown, interlocutor.

Bismark Ferris's Satisfied Company (with Two Bills Show)
July 1912

Ed Ritter and Arthur Madison, solo cornets; Ed Howard, first cornet; Reid Connor, alto; Fred Douglass, baritone; George Triggers, first trombone; Arthur Gibbs, second trombone; Tony Mays, Bismark Ferris, clarinets; John Butler, tuba; Johnnie Crabb, small drum; John Wilson, bass drum; Mays, Penn, Madison, and Gibbs, chorus singers.

John Eason's Band and Minstrels (with Yankee Robinson's Circus)
July 1912

John Eason, leader, baritone; Preston Bridgewater, solo cornet; Boise Gray, first cornet; Frank Terry, first trombone; Clarence Stacker, second trombone; Harrison Hall, tuba; James Brooks, alto; A. N. Peterson, clarinet; John Mitchell, snare drum; Sheenie Peterson, bass drum.

P. G. Lowery's Band and Minstrels (with Hagenbeck and Wallace Circus)

August 1912

P. G. Lowery, director; Arthur Wright, solo cornet; Tom May, first cornet; John Tobias, first trombone; Max Shaw, second trombone; Johnnie Haywood, baritone; William May, tuba; Anatole Victor, alto; Elmer Payne, clarinet; Charlie Beechum, snare drum; Willie Lee, bass drum. Minstrels: U. S. Thompson, Charlie Beechum, Irvin Richardson, Alma Richardson, Lizzie Thompson, and Callie Vassar Hill.

James Wolfscale's Band and Minstrels (with Barnum and Bailey Circus)

May 1913

James Wolfscale, Beverly Walker, Roy E. Wolfscale, cornets; Joe E. Herriford, Lewis Ford, clarinets; Troy Wolfscale, Ray Wolfscale, altos; Fred Garland, James McDonald, trombones; Ernest Smith, baritone; Dennis Stratton, bass; Earl Levy, Willie Brown, and J. Ed Hunn, drums; Earl Levy and Willie Brown, eccentric comedians; Ernest Smith and Lewis Ford, singers; J. Ed Hunn, stage manager for the minstrels.

L. K. Baker's Band and Minstrels (with 101 Ranch Wild West Show)

May 1913

L. K. Baker, director, solo cornet; M. Casey, second cornet; A. Parker, first cornet; David Francis, clarinet; Charlie Brown, first alto; S. Ford, second alto; W. F. Washington, first trombone; Willie Nash, second trombone; James Mitchell, baritone; W. H. White, tuba; Ernest Williams, bass drum; James L. Holmes, snare drum.

John Eason's Band and Minstrels (with Frank A. Robbins Circus)

May 1913

John Eason, leader; Charles Creath, cornet; John Adams, alto; William Martin, trombone; King Moody, tuba and comedian; Fred Johnson, snare drum; David C. Smith, bass drum and comedian.

P. G. Lowery's Band and Minstrels (with Hagenbeck and Wallace Show)

June 1913

P. G. Lowery, director; Horace Eubanks, clarinet; Thomas May, A. A. Wright, J. Bryant, cornets; A. Victor, J. L. Edwards, altos; A. G. Fredericks, Earl Granstaff, trombones; A. J. Johnson, baritone; William May, Tony Barefield, bass; Mack Carter, William Hoy, drums. Minstrels: A. A. Wright, stage manager; Carrie Gilbert, Callie Vassar, Mrs. J. L. Edwards, J. L. "Junk" Edwards, U. S. "Slow Kid" Thompson, Tony Barefield, J. Bryant, Mack Carter, Earl Granstaff.

Annex Band and Minstrels (with Howe's Great London Circus)

June 1913

W. S. Jenkins, Lew Gilbert, Dan Terry, cornets; Walter Howard, clarinet; C. V. Johnson, alto; Robert J. Bolden, baritone; Jeff Mackley, tuba; A. B. Niles, trap drum; Johnnie Riddick, bass drum; Lucille Day, Lottie Proyer Riddick, soubrettes; Kid Teddy Johnson, Johnnie Riddick, ends.

James Harris's Band and Minstrels (with Gollmar Bros. Circus)

June 1913

James Harris, trombone, leader; E. M. Hopkins, William Bright, cornet; Perry Gant, clarinet; T. J. Bright, baritone; M. A. Douglass, tuba; Buddie James, alto; Ed Jackson, snare drum; Harry Anderson, bass drum. Minstrels: Harry Henderson, Billie Bright, M. A. Douglass, T. J. Bright; Perry Gant, interlocutor.

P. A. Venable's Band (with Ringling Brothers Circus)
July 1913

P. A. Venable, director, baritone; Preston Duncan, Andrew Scott, I. Patterson, B. Bedenbaugh, cornets; Buford Palmer, Alex Jackson, altos; William Smith, Elbert Hall, trombones; John Mitchell, Richard Jones, drums; G. L. Young, tuba.

William H. Reed's (or Reid's) Band and Minstrels (with Young Buffalo's Wild West Shows)
September 1913

Sam E. Reed, director; William H. Reed, manager and snare drummer; W. B. Cole, solo cornet; Walter Reed, clarinet; Joe Gibbons, baritone; L. E. Wilks, solo tuba; Ben F. Harris, trombone; Wyatt Long, second alto and end man; Martin Enoch, first alto, minstrel; Lawrence Livingston, bass drummer and minstrel.

Prof. Murdock's Band and Minstrels (with Sparks Circus)
End of season 1913

Prof. Murdock, cornet, manager; Thomas Ramsey, cornet; Edward Lankford, alto; Thomas Edward, trombone; Jesse Clark, baritone; William Blake, tuba; Clifford Peeler, drums; Mae Harris, Mrs. Murdock, singers.

James Wolfscale's Concert Band (with Barnum and Bailey Circus)
March 1914

James Wolfscale, leader; Charles Holloway, Ed Farrell, Roy Wolfscale, Albert Franklin, William Carr, Arthur Madison, B. C. McWilliams, cornets; Oscar Lowe, R. J. Scott, W. P. Smith, John Harris, clarinets; Frosty Moore, Troy Wolfscale, Ray Wolfscale, Earl Johnson, Victor Alex, altos; Ernest C. Smith, Dave Lewis, baritone; James McDonald, [?] McShaw, Ed Hall, George Sharp, William Morgan, William Moorehead, Joe Sudler, trombones; Bennie Stratton, John Butler, Bud Campbell, basses; Sonny Grey, timpani; Joe Webb, Ben Wolfscale, Earl Terry, drums and bells.

J. C. Miles's Band and Minstrels (with Jones Bros. and Wilson's Circus)
May 1914

P. M. Williams, J. C. Miles, cornets; Earnest Montague, Samuel Johnson, trombones; Ben Evans, baritone; Charles Brewer, clarinet; Jess Watt, snare drum; James Small, bass drum; Elizabeth "Lizzie" Miles, singer.

James Harris's Band and Minstrels (with Gollmar Bros. Circus)
May 1914

Prof. James A. Harris, director, trombone; Eugene M. Hopkins, Roscoe C. Copeland, cornets; Frank R. Robinson, clarinet; Buddie James, Jim "Captain Jinks" Green, altos; Elmer Scott, baritone; Kilmer Jackson, tuba; Edwin Jackson, trap drummer; Elvis "Slim" Mason, bass drummer; stage manager, Jim Green, minstrel.

"Pop" Adams's Band and Minstrels (with Circle D Wild West Show)
May 1914

C. W. Stripling, cornet soloist; William Bright, solo cornet; Perry Gant, solo clarinet; James A. Willis, baritone; James "King" Moody, tuba; W. H. James, drums; J. E. "Pop" Adams, alto and leader. Minstrels: Harry "Big Boy" Anderson, King Moody, W. H. James.

L. K. Baker's Band and Minstrels (with 101 Ranch Shows)
June 1914

L. K. Baker, leader, solo cornet; M. C. Wilson, solo cornet; A. N. Parker, first cornet; Charles Brown, first alto; Doc Ford, second alto; Frank Washington, trombone; Billy Nash, second trombone; James Mitchell, baritone; Henry White, tuba; William Polk, bass drum; J. Holmes, snare drum; W. D. Cook, clarinet.

Edward Rucker's Band and Minstrels (with Young Buffalo Show)
July 1914

Edward Rucker, director; Babe Lewis, tuba; Dave Stephens, cornet; Congo Cropp, drums; William Sidney, Webster Rucker, trombones; Eddie Porter, baritone; John Briscoe, alto; Ethel Rucker, soubrette.

Eugene Clark's Band (with Robinson's Famous Shows)
August 1914

Prof. Eugene Clark, minstrel, leader; Prof. John B. Forrester, band director and cornetist; John Seawright, first cornet; Benny Williams, second cornet; Hunt Smith, first clarinet; William Brooks, first trombone; Jimmy Washington, second trombone; Alfred Lee, solo alto; Lindsey B. Herndon, baritone; William Tyler, tuba; Joe Dark, "tenor drummer"; William Able, bass drummer.

R. Roy Pope's Annex Band (with Ringling Brothers Circus)
April 1915

Prof. R. Roy Pope, director; Preston Duncan, assistant director; Mrs. E. Ruth Pope, saxophone soloist; I. Patterson, C. Davis, cornets; P. A. Venable, baritone; Ted Morton, tuba; John Mitchell, Harry Mitchell, drums; A. Jackson, B. Palmer, mellophones; W. Smith, W. Hinson, trombones.

A. A. Wright's Band and Minstrels (with Sparks Circus)
April 1915

Prof. A. A. Wright, leader; Toe B. Gray, cornet; Robert Oliver, first clarinet; Isaiah Wilds, James McDonald, trombones; William Bryant, baritone; Mose McQuitty, bass; James Ransom, snare drum; Sam Kennedy, bass drum. Minstrels: James Ransom, Sam Kennedy, extreme ends; A. A. Wright, Rastus Airship, second ends; William Bryant, conversationalist.

John Eason's Band and Minstrels (with Yankee Robinson's Three-Ring Circus)
May 1915

John Eason, leader, baritone, and violin; Charles Creath, cornet; Sam Smith, cornet and violin; Hope Clarkston, trombone and violin; Irvin Brown, trombone; Archie Bell, alto and trap drums; Arnett Nelson, clarinet; Bud Campbell, tuba; Hugh Bowman, snare drum and minstrel; Noah Robinson, bass drum and minstrel; Lena Hulett, vocalist; Mrs. Ozella Smith, vocalist and interlocutor.

James Wolfscale's Band (with Barnum and Bailey Circus)
May 1915

Prof. James Wolfscale, cornet and director; Roy Wolfscale, cornet and assistant director; Albert Franklin, C. Mickens, A. Madison, cornets; Ernest Smith, baritone; Kilmer Jackson, James Dorsey, bass; Fred "Cat" Garland, Steven Robison, William Morehead, trombones; Harvey Holland, trombone and orchestra leader; Ray Wolfscale, Earl Johnson, altos; Leon Gray, Slim Mason, drums; Troy Wolfscale, alto and trap drums.

L. K. Baker's Band and Minstrels (with 101 Ranch)
May 1915

L. K. Baker, cornet and leader; Moses Casey, cornet; Alex N. Parker, cornet, violin, orchestra director; A. F. Washington, cornet, minstrel; Charles Brown, first horn; Samuel Ford, second horn, minstrel; Will Nash, trombone, minstrel; James Mitchell, baritone, minstrel; H. R. Hall, tuba; W. H. White, bass drum, interlocutor; Robert Wilson, small drum and traps.

James A. Harris's Band and Minstrels (with Gollmar Bros. Circus)
May 1915

J. A. Harris, trombone; Steven Dewayne, tuba; Elmer Scott, baritone; Elmer Stuman, alto; E. F. Wanser, first cornet; Claud Williams, William Carr, solo cornets; W. R. Jackson, bass drum; Sam Good, snare drum.

Eugene Clark's Band and Minstrels (with Robinson's Famous Shows)

July 1915

Jerry Martin, director, solo cornet; McKinley Neighbors, solo cornet; Charles Evans, first alto; William Able, second alto; George Artis, first trombone; Thomas Robinson, second trombone; Lindsey B. Herndon, baritone; William Tyler, tuba; Joe Clark, snare drums; Eugene Clark, bass drum, manager. Minstrels: Freddie Clark, buck dancer; Corina Adams, singer; Anna Hicks, interlocutor, singer; Clark Brothers, end men.

L. K. Baker's Annex Band (with 101 Ranch Shows)

November 1915

Prof. L. K. Baker, Mose Casey, A. N. Parker, John Estes, cornets; Charles Brown, S. F. "Doc" Ford, mellophones; P. L. Jenkins, William Nash, trombones; William Israel, tuba; Robert Wilson, snare drum; W. H. White, bass drum.

Wolfscale's Band and Minstrels (with Barnum and Bailey Circus)

Opening the season of 1916

Prof. James Wolfscale, cornet, leader; Thomas Ramsey, Al. Franklin, Joe Sudler, Arthur Madison, cornets; Fred Garland, Harvey Holland, Willie Moorehead, trombones; Ernest C. Smith, baritone; Bennie Stratton, Kilmer Jackson, bass; M. O. Russell, Troy Wolfscale, mellophones; Slim Mason, Sam Good, Earl Johnson, drums and minstrel.

L. K. Baker's Annex Band (with 101 Ranch Shows)

April 1916

L. K. Baker, William Thompson, Moses Casey, cornets; S. F. "Doc" Ford, Master Leslie McCall, mellophones; P. L. Jenkins, William Nash, trombones; James Mitchell, baritone; John Richardson, tuba; W. R. Jackson, snare drum; J. N. Anderson, bass drum.

"Pop" Adams's Annex Band and Minstrels (with Yankee Robinson Shows)

April 1916

Pop Adams, alto and manager; Jay Bryant, cornet and leader; Clarence Williams, cornet; Hope Clarkson, trombone and orchestra leader; Bud Campbell, tuba; Earnest Thyous, trombone and comedian; "Big Boy" Anderson, bass drum and comedian; Frank James, baritone; Jack Turner, snare drum. Minnie Pyle and Sophia Vassar, soubrettes.

Eugene Clark's Band and Minstrels (with La Tena Shows)

May 1916

James Berry, Thomas Robinson, trombones; Grant Smith, tuba; L. Herndon, baritone; Charles W. Evans, alto and saxophone; William Able, alto; McKinley Wayne, A. Calmers, Charles Milton, cornets; Joe Clark, Eugene Clark, drums; Miss Annie Hicks, interlocutor; Edna Barlett, coon shouter; Master Freddie Clark, buck and wing dancer; Joe Clark, comedian.

P. A. Venable Band (with Ringling Brothers Circus)

May 1916

P. A. Venable, baritone, leader; Preston J. Duncan, C. M. Davis, J. C. Fields, C. Washington, cornets; A. P. Jackson, B. L. Palmer, altos; W. F. Smith, T. C. Williams, trombones; H. R. Williams, tuba; John Mitchell, Richard Jones, drums.

A. A. Wright's Band and Minstrels (with Sparks Circus)

May 1916

A. A. Wright, manager; Miss Cleo Poteet, Viola McCoy, soubrettes; William Carr, cornet; Robert Oliver, clarinet; Isaiah Wilds, James McDonald, trombones; William Bryant, baritone; Mose McQuitty, bass; Rastus Airship, comedian and drum; John Wilson, comedian and drum.

R. N. Jackson's Band (with Howe's Great London Shows)

June 1916

R. N. Jackson, leader and cornet; David Phoenix, cornet; Thomas Stevens, clarinet; Jesse McCoy, alto; James Peters, baritone; Frederick A. Douglass, trombone; R. W. Wallace, tuba; B. E. Edwards, snare drum; Roy Gibson, bass drum.

James Harris's Band and Minstrels (with Gollmar Bros. Circus)

June 1916

James A. Harris, Eugene Hopkins, Lewis Fletcher, cornets; Lawrence Denton, clarinet; Eugene Gentry, alto; Elmer Scott, baritone; Otis Wheeler, tuba; James Jackson, snare drum; Edward McNeal, bass drum. Minstrels: James Jackson, stage manager; Elmer Scott, Lewis Fletcher, Otis Wheeler, Eugene Gentry.

J. S. Riggers's Annex Band (with Coop and Lentz Three-Ring Circus)

June 1916

J. S. Riggers, cornet and leader; R. E. Hughes, cornet; J. W. Toomey, saxophone; O. H. Rathman, baritone; H. Carey, tuba; Irving Brown, trombone and violin; Walter Graham, trombone; Frank Nichols, mellophone; George Bell, bass drum; Ned Cumby, trap drums.

P. G. Lowery's Band and Minstrels (with Hagenbeck and Wallace Circus)

September 1916

P. G. Lowery, cornet and director; Thomas May, cornet; W. E. Fields, cornet and baritone; Elmer Payne, clarinet; Maylon Hall, clarinet, 2nd tenor; Dan White, baritone and violin; Edgar Carr, trombone; Irvie Richardson, alto and 1st tenor; William May, tuba; Tony Barefield, tuba and bass solo; William Hoy, trap drums; Jakie Smith, bass drum and comedian; Bennie Jones, comedian; Essie Williams, soprano; Carrie Gilbert Lowery, soprano.

Arthur A. Wright's Band and Minstrels (with John W. Sparks' Big Show)

April 1917

Prof. A. A. Wright, cornet and leader; Robert Oliver, clarinet; Jess Clark, baritone; Edward Carr, trombone; Harrison Hall, tuba; Johnnie Riddick, alto and end man; Rastus Airship, bass drum and buck and wing dancer; John Wilson, snare drum and end man; Cleo Poteet, soubrette; Maggie Dixon, soubrette.

Eugene Clark's Band (with La Tena's Circus)

April 1917

Theodore Boon, cornet and leader; Joe Hobbs, cornet; Roy Quin, alto; Will Henson, trombone; Isaiah Davidson, baritone; Grant Smith, tuba; Joe S (?), drum; Will Able, bass drum; Eugene Dark, manager.

P. G. Lowery's Band and Minstrels (with Hagenbeck and Wallace Circus)

May 1917

P. G. Lowery, conductor, cornet; Tom May, cornet; Charles Creath, cornet and minstrel; Robert Stevenson, cornet and minstrel; D. W. Batsell, clarinet; Mahlon Hall, clarinet and minstrel; Mack Carter, alto and minstrel; William Moore, alto and orchestra leader; James Berry, John Mansfield, trombones; A. C. Cobb, baritone and minstrel; William May, tuba; Charles Beechum, small drum and stage manager (minstrel); James Faulkner, bass drum; Jakie Smith, comedian; Callie Vassar, interlocutor; Carrie Gilbert Lowery, Olga Beecham, minstrels.

R. N. Jackson's Band and Minstrels (with John Robinson Circus)

May 1917

R. N. Jackson, cornet and leader; Richard Jasper, cornet; Fred Douglass, baritone; Jesse McCoy, Charles

Crenshaw, altos; Ermal Coleman, Jerry Martin, trombones; Willis McKinney, drums. Minstrels: Dan Kinsey, Charles English, comedians; E. L. Smith, interlocutor; Essie Williams, soubrette; Morris Taylor, buck and wing dancer. (Note: Band leader Jackson was replaced mid-season by T. E. White, cornet and leader).

T. E. White's Band and Minstrels (with John Robinson Circus)

September 1917

T. E. White, leader and cornet; John W. Webb, cornet; Richard Jasper, Jerry Bush, Raymond Fisher, cornets; Jesse McCoy, alto; Robert Martin, L. B. Herndon, baritones; William Tyler, tuba; Ermal Coleman, trombone; Jerry Martin, trombone; Willie McKinney, snare drum; Dan Kinsey, bass drum. Minstrels: Dan Kinsey, stage manager and comedian; Morris Taylor, dancer and comedian; Essie Williams, singing and straight; E. L. Smith, interlocutor and singing; Albert Allen, comedian.

James Wolfscale's Band (with Barnum and Bailey Show)

June 1917

James Wolfscale, Al Franklin, James Dorsey, W. A. Wilkes, Thomas Ramsey, cornets; Ernest Smith, Abner Good, baritones; Ralph Goodson, Willie Green, trombones; Ray Wolfscale, Frederick Lewis, Earl Johnson, mellophones; Troy Wolfscale, traps; Slim Mason, Leon Gray, Sam Good, drums; Bennie Stratton, Kilmer Jackson, bass.

J. S. Riggers's Band and Minstrels (with Coop and Lentz Circus)

July 1917

J. S. Riggers, cornet, leader; William Carr, cornet and violin; Joe Porter, cornet; A. R. Joshlin, B. Fowler, clarinets; P. D. Langford, alto and comedian; P. Ruthman, baritone; W. Graham, A. Pendleton, trombones; H. Carey, tuba; George Bell, bass drum and comedian; William Garvin, trap drums, Mrs. S. J. Harris, vocalist.

Elmer Payne's Band (with Honest Bill Show)

July 1917

William R. Lacy, Lewis Smith, cornets; Elmer H. Payne, William O. Bell, clarinets; Harrison Baldwin, William Payne, trombones; Robert Hill, Fred Mayes, altos; L. W. Payne, baritone; Calvin White, bass; William Cash, Eirniett (*sic*) Richardson, drums.

Bismark Ferris's Band and Minstrels (with Al G. Barnes Circus)

August 1917

James A. Shackleford, Vernon Elkins, solo cornets; Sam Harris, alto; Roy Gray, baritone; Ashford Hardee, trombone; Jesse Brooks, tuba; Ben Borders, snare drum; Jolly J. Johnson, bass drum; Bismark Ferris, clarinet and conductor. Minstrels: Jolly J. Johnson, Ben Borders, Little Arthur Taylor.

P. A. Venable's Band (with Ringling Brothers Circus)

September 1917

P. A. Venable, baritone and leader; William Smith, Willie Moorehead, trombones; Harry Williams, tuba; M. O. Russell, Alex Jackson, mellophones; Preston Duncan, Clifford Davis, Jimmie Fields, Harry Franklin, cornets; Frank Robinson, snare drum; John Mitchell, bass drum.

L. K. Baker's Band and Minstrels (with Jess Willard–Buffalo Bill Wild West Show)

September 1917

L. K. Baker, bandmaster; Moses Casey, R. N. "Jug" Everly, cornets; W. T. Howard, clarinet; Edward Long, baritone; James Mitchell, bass; P. L. Jenkins, trombone; Pop Adams, alto; James Holmes, traps; Will Nash, trombone and minstrel; Doc Ford, mellophone and minstrel; James Anderson, minstrel.

Robert Clark's Band and Minstrels (with John Robinson Circus)

May 1918

Robert Clark, band and minstrels; W. S. Jenkins, bandleader; W. O. Faulks, Mary Humphrey, Roy Quinn, Evelyn Langston, Will Able, Grant Smith, Mary Smith, T. Gates, E. B. Topp.

James Wolfscale's Band (with Barnum and Bailey)

May 1918

James Wolfscale, Thomas Ramsey, William Malone, R. Patton, Lewis Fletcher, cornet; Ben Goodall, Willie Green, R. Horton, trombone; C. Mills, William Wells, baritone; Ben Stratton, Kilmer Jackson, bass; Sam Reid, N. Tolliver, Earl Smith, mellophone; Johnny Brown, Joseph Walker, clarinet; Troy Wolfscale, trap drum; Clyde Dollar, Bill Jones, drums.

Marcus Veal's Band and Minstrels (with John Robinson's Circus)

June 1918

Marcus Veal, clarinet and bandmaster; Leroy White, first cornet; H. S. Jenkins, second cornet; Buddy James, alto; Archie Blue, alto, minstrel; Frank Tousell, mellophone, minstrel; D. E. James, baritone; W. H. White, bass; Ed Carr, trombone; Honey Boy Evans, snare, traps, and minstrel; G. E. Glasco, bass drum and minstrel.

L. K. Baker's Band (with Hagenbeck and Wallace Circus)

August 1918

L. K. Baker, bandmaster; Mose Casey, cornet; Gene McDonald, cornet; Edgar Long, cornet and minstrel; W. T. Howard, clarinet; Charles A. Scott, alto and minstrel; "Boo Hoo" Carter, alto and minstrel; P. L. Jenkins, trombone; W. H. White, tuba; James A. Faulkner, trap drum.

Prof. Irvin Brown's Band and Minstrels (with Gentry Brothers Circus)

July 1919

Irvin Brown, trombone and bandmaster; W. J. Jackson, cornet; Eddie Alford, cornet; Johnny Bray, baritone; N. M. Turner, alto and trap drum; Phillip R. Perkins, bass drum and minstrel; Fisher Handy, tuba, minstrel; Effie Moore Brady, minstrel, Pearl Alford, minstrel.

R. N. Jackson's Band and Minstrels (with Hagenbeck and Wallace Circus)

July 1919

R. N. Jackson, band director; T. E. White, I. D. Fletcher, cornets; Cecil White, tuba; Lawrence Lee, Samuel Johnson, trombones; Raymond Latimore, clarinet; Marie Jackson, minstrel; Ossir Jackson, minstrel; Lillian Irving, minstrel, Willie Jackson, minstrel; John Jackson, minstrel; Warren Irving, stage manager.

A. A. Wright's Georgia Minstrels (with Sparks Shows)

August 1919

James J. Clarke, director; Kid Gibson, stage manager and comedian; Edward Carr, trombone; Dixie Kidd, drum; Ernest Montague, bandmaster; E. Rodgers, piano; Mamie Burns, violin; Jessie Love, dancer; Ralph Harris, comedian, dancer; Miss Bryant, buck and wing dancer; Mrs. Gibson, singer; Mrs. Montague, singer; Curie Brook, comedian and wooden shoe dancer; Baby Gibson, child performer.

P. G. Lowery's Band (with Ringling Brothers and Barnum and Bailey Circus)

April 1920

P. G. Lowery, cornet, director; Thomas May, cornet, assistant director; R. Q. Dickerson, Richard Jasper, cornets; William Blue, Jr., clarinet; Charles Evans, James Young, altos; Redus Horton, H. M. Lankford, A. H. Bass, trombones; Winston Walker, Alvin "Zoo" Robertson, baritones; William May, bass; Walter Coleman, bass drum; James Holmes, drum.

J. S. Riggers's Band and Minstrels (with Sells-Floto Circus)

May 1920

J. S. Riggers, cornet and director; Tom Howard, R. E. Hughes, cornets; Charles Weaver, Harry Green, clarinets; William Bell, alto and comedian; Preston Hancock, E. L. Duncan, trombones; Otto Washington, baritone; E. J. Mady, bass; Jefferson Thirkles, bass drum and comedian; William Wheeler, trap drummer.

R. N. Jackson's Band and Minstrels (with Hagenbeck and Wallace Circus)

May 1920

A. P. Alexander, tuba; Abner Good, H. L. Rawles, baritones; Frank Blakely, trombone; Jess McCoy, first alto; James Weathers, second alto; James Rucker, third alto; Pal Williams, clarinet; R. N. Jackson, first cornet; James Hollowell, second cornet; Preston Killebrew, small drums; John T. Jackson, bass drum. Minstrels: Mabel Turner, soubrette; Willie Lane; Joseph Jalvan; Leroy Scottie, end; Clarence Turner, John G. Jackson, extreme ends.

Montell Proctor's Band and Minstrels (with Howe's Great London Circus)

June 1920

Montell Proctor, director, cornet; Ike Sanders, trombone; James Gordon, trombone, comedian; Louis Johnson, tuba, comedian; Ed Fisher, tuba; Fred Gordon, alto, comedian; Ed Sherill, alto; Sidney Proctor, Roman Meaux, cornets; Nathaniel Proctor, small drum; James Cowan, large drum, comedian.

F. Bennett Hargrave's Band and Minstrels (with Rhoda Royal Circus and Old Buffalo Wild West Shows)

July 1920

Bert DeLeo, William H. Davis, cornets; Latrille C. Powell, James King, trombones; J. W. Craddock, baritone; J. A. Young, tuba; George Williams and Irene Drum, comedians; Willie Smith, bass drum and comedian; F. Bennett Hargrave, mellophone and manager.

Eugene Clark's Band and Minstrels (with Walter L. Main Show)

July 1920

Louis Gilbert, first cornet, leader; Frank Hobbs, second cornet; Zack Smith, clarinet; Nelson Sharpe, gas pipe [*sic*]; Henry Morgan, baritone; Ed Thomas, drums; Viola Guest, coon shouter; Hazel Alexandria, alto; Gilbert Scott, trombone; Guy Smith, second trombone; Will Able, tuba; Carlton Adams, bass drums, Mamie Evans, soft-shoe dancer; Eugene Clark, minstrel.

R. J. Simmons's Band and Minstrels (with Sparks Circus)

August 1920

R. J. Simmons, leader; Ernest Montague, trombone; Jess Clark, baritone; Tony Barefield, Walter Wardell, tubas; John Wilson, bass drum; Wallace Simmons, snare drum; Edna Thorpe, Sadie Wardell, Viola Lavaughn, Marguerite Montague.

L. K. Baker's Band and Minstrels (with John Robinson Circus)

October 1920

L. K. Baker, leader, cornet; Charles Jones, Buford Palmer, John W. Hopkins, cornets; Frank Sloan, clarinet; L. B. Herndon, first alto; Noble Ragan, second alto; Walter Graham, trombone; Humphrey Nelson, baritone; James Giles, tuba; James Proctor, snare drum; Lucian Merriweather, bass drum.

APPENDIX IV

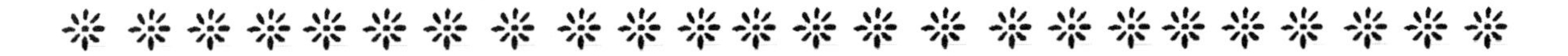

BAND ROSTERS OF ALLEN'S NEW ORLEANS MINSTRELS, THE RABBIT'S FOOT COMPANY, THE FLORIDA BLOSSOMS, AND *SILAS GREEN FROM NEW ORLEANS*, 1900–1940

The rosters listed in this appendix are given verbatim from contemporaneous sources. The ones dated 1900 through 1920 are from the *Indianapolis Freeman*. Those dated 1921 through 1940 are from the *Chicago Defender*. A note on the abundance of typos and spelling variations seems to be in order. Disparate spellings of people's names, place names, etc., run through the entertainment columns of the African American press. At least a few such misrepresentations give the effect of practical jokes: James Reese Europe as "James Reese, of Europe"; Clarence Cameron White as "Clarence Cameron (white)."[1] In his thoroughly researched book on the Creole Band, *Pioneers of Jazz*, Larry Gushee notes that variations of Fred Keppard's name encountered in his newspaper research—Keppert, Keppit—may be phonetic indicators of how it was actually pronounced.[2]

Listings of band rosters were especially vulnerable to spelling anomalies. In the rosters collected here, snare drummer Charles Laurendine suffers through Larndene, Larndie, and Larnee; bandmaster J. H. McCamon endures seven different takes on his last name.[3] To flag every discernible misnomer with a *sic* would hopelessly clog this documentation; to try to iron things out would only introduce new wrinkles. And so, we leave it to the reader to deduce that "Fred Knewly" is Fred *Kewley*, "Will Goss Kennady" is Will *Goff Kennedy*, a "snaw drum" is a *snare* drum, etc. This collection of rosters represents the best available record of the physical makeup of early-twentieth-century tented minstrel bands.

Allen's New Orleans Minstrels

June 2, 1900

"Members of No. 1 band W. G. Bostwick, M. Vassar and Cupper, cornets; F. T. Viccas, clarnette, Pillman and Grady altos, J. W. Jordan and Burton slide trombones, C. Ritcherson baritone, F. Castry tuba. No. 2 band McCanom, W. Hopkins and W. Lee cornets, J. Bryant clarinet, F. Garland and Little Pick altos; Miller and A. Isler slide trombones, S. Johnson euphonium, W. Grant tubas."

January 19, 1901

"Prof. McCamon, bandmaster . . . our two bands, No. 1, J. Lost, drum major; J. Jordan and C. Burton, slide trombones; Castry, tuba; DeMuse, baritone; Guiguesse, saxaphone; L. Glover and Pittman, altos; F. T. Viccas, clarionet; G. B. Brooks and Cooper, cornets; J. Walker, snare drummer; Brown, cymbals; P. Ownes, bass drummer. No. 2, J. Lost drum major; F. Miller and A. Isler, slide trombones; W. Grant, tuba; Sam Johnson, euphonium; C. Garland and W. Davis, altos; W. Lee and Prof. McCammon, cornets; F. T. Cox, snare drummer; J. Bailey, cymbols; C. Barge, bass drummer."

August 3, 1901

"Prof. McCamon's big concert band [is comprised of] F. Miller. A. Isler, J. Jordan, slide trombones; F. Castry, W. Grant, tubas; S. Johnson, D. W. Muse, baritones; G. Pittman, F. Garland, W. Davis, altos;

F. T. Viccas, clarionet; B. Webster, flute and piccolo; Prof. McCamon, G. B. Brooks, W. Cooper, W. Lee, cornets; J. T. Cox, snare drum; J. Fernando, cymbals; C. E. Rue, bass drum."

December 7, 1901

"Prof. McCannon's famous concert band consists of the following members: F. Castry and Wm. Grant, tubas; Sam Johnson, Dee W. Muse, baritones; Arthur Isler, Frank McDade, trombones; Wm. Cooper and McCannon and G. Brooks, cornets; E. C. Pittman and F. Garlin, altos; F. P. Viccars, clarionette; B. Webster, flute; James Cox, snare drummer; Jimmie Wise, cymbals; Chas. Rue, bass drum; Arnte and Roberson, drum majors."

July 4, 1908

"The band consists of J. H. McCamran, leader; Elwood Johnson, solo cornet; G. B. Brooks, E flat cornet; Robert H. Gant, solo alto; Robert Brown, second alto; Robert Miller, third alto; P. L. Jenkins, first trombone; George Willson, second trombone; H. S. Smith, third trombone; Johnnie Jones, baritone; R. O. Henderson, tuba; Charles E. Ruel, bass drum; James T. Cox, snare drum."

November 14, 1908

"J. H. McCamron is bandmaster; Ellwood Johnson, solo cornet; G. B. Brooks, E flat cornet; William Fisher, baritone; Bob Gant, solo alto; Robert Miller, second alto; C. Adam LaRase, third alto; P. L. Jenkins, first trombone; Pearl Mapping, second trombone; Joe Miller, tuba; Charles E. Rul, bass drum; Joe White, snare drum."

December 19, 1908

"J. H. McCamron's big concert band [consists of] Edward Johnson, solo cornet; G. B. Brooks, E flat cornett; Robert H. Gant, solo alto; C. Adam Laruse, third alto; P. L. Jenkins, first trombone; Pearl Moppins, second trombone; William Fisher, euphaum; Joe Miller, tuba; Charles E. Rue, basedrum; Joe White, snare drum."

April 3, 1909

"The instrumentation [of the band] is: J. H. McCammon, leader; G. B. Brooks, E-flat cornet; Ellwood Johnson, first B-flat cornet; William Phillips, clarinet; Robert H. Gant, solo mellophone; Robert Miller, second mellophone; C. A. Larose, third mellophone; P. L. Jenkins, first trombone; Pearl Moppin, second trombone; H. S. Smith, third trombone; William Fisher, euphonium; William (Tuba) Thomas, bass; Ben F. Stevens, snare drum; Charles E. Rue, bass drum."

August 21, 1909

"Our orchestra [is comprised of] Prof. Ellwood Johnson, 1st violin and leader; Robert Gant and Robert Miller, 2nd violins; Wm. Phillips, clarinet; J. C. Singleton, flute; Prof. J. H. McCammon, cornet; P. L. Jenkins, trombone; Wm. (Tuba) Thomas, double bass; B. F. Stevens traps."

January 4, 1913

"Prof. McCamon now has a concert band of seventeen picked men . . . viz: J. H. McCamon, Ellwood Johnson and Edward Alexander, B♭ cornets; G. B. Brooks, E♭ cornet; Wm. Phillips and Fred C. Richardson, B♭ clarinets; Marcus L. Veal, E♭ clarinet; Wm. [S]haw, piccolo; Robert H. Gant, Robert Miller and Prof. J. C. Turner, mellophones; P. L. Jenkins and Amos Gilliard, trombones; William Fisher, euphonium; Mose McQuitty, tuba; A. Laurendine, snare drum; Chas. E. Rue, bass drum."

October 11, 1913

"Roster of the band: J. H. McCamron, director; Boisie Gray, solo cornet; G. B. Brooks, E-flat cornet; Fred Richardson, solo clarinett; Markus Veal, E-flat clarinet; Robert H. Gant, solo mellophone; Robert Miller, second melophone; Louie Watts, third melophone; A. M. Gillard, solo trombone; Joseph V.

Watts, second trombone; William Shaw, piccolo; Mose McGenillie, tuba; Charley Larndene, snare drum; Charles Rue, bass drum."

November 29, 1913

"Our band is composed of Prof. J. H. McCammon, bandmaster and cornet; Boisy Gray, cornet; Paul Brooks, cornet; Robert Gant, melophone; Robert Miller, melophone; Lew Watts, melophone; Mark Veal, clarinet; Henry Fitzglies, clarinet; Amos Gilliard, trombone; Joe Watts, trombone; Mose McQuitty, bass; John Verdun, snare drum; and Charles E. Rue, bass drum."

March 14, 1914

"Have the greatest colored band on the road, bar none. As follows: J. H. McComron, director; Basie Gray, solo cornet; Walter Lee, solo cornet; G. B. Brooks, E flat cornet; William (King) Phillips, solo clarinet; Henry Phillips, second clarinet; Markins Oneal, E flat clarinet; Robert Gant, solo meterphone; Robert Miller, second melerphone; William Fisher E phomm [i.e., euphonium]; Eldridge Collins, first trombone; Pearl Mappins, second trombone; Mase McQuittie, bass; John Walker, snare drum; Chas. E. Rue, base drum."

September 12, 1914

"The band is doing fine. Members: J. H. McCawan, Markus Chaney Veal, Robert H. Gant, Mase McQuity, Daniel Perkins, Charlie E. Rue, John Porter, Lloyd Jackson, Pro. T. A. Homes, Victor Jacobs, Willie Johnson, Boisie Grayes, and they are in line."

October 3, 1914

"Rosters of the band, J. H. McCammon, band master; T. A. Holmes, Boisy Grey, Joe Porter, cornets; Robert H. Gant, melaphone; David Jones, alto; Porter, baritone; Mark Veal, clarinet; Ralph Redmond, trombone; Mose Mc[Quitty], tuba; Charles E. Rue, bass drum; Daniel Perkins, snare drum."

May 29, 1915

"We have an A1 band now. The members are as follows: Arthur Cox, band master and clarinet player; Elmer Moore solo cornet; Napoleon C. Black, alto; Claude Curl, alto; Alfred Williams, baritone; Howard Duffy, trombone; Brent Sparks, tuba; C. A. Gibbs, tuba; Charles Larndie, snare drum; Page Tillman, base drums."

June 5, 1915

"Alonzer Wilson still has the leadership of the orchestra . . . Alonzer Wilson is first violin; J. W. Write, first violin; Albert Williams, second; Arthur Black, second; Arthur Cox, clarinet; Howard Duffie, trombone; J. E. Moore, first cornet; Charles Hervey, second cornet; Brant Sparks, tuba; Charley Larnee, traps."

February 23, 1918

"Band—Prof. Marcus L. Veal, formerly of the Rabbit's Foot Company, clarinetist and director; cornets, Silas C. Elliott and G. W. Mitchell and Leroy White; altos, Buddy James and Hosie Hand; trombones, Arthur C. Gibbs and Edward Carr; tuba, W. H. White; battery, Nathan (Honey Boy) Evans (snare), A. C. Blue, (bass); euphonium, David James, alias Bow Legs."

September 6, 1919

"The band is Prof. Erwin, Shelly McWilliams, Ronald Ingram, cornets; Warner Ford, Jim Green, trombones; Oscar Adams, clarinet; Claude McMurry, trombone; John L. Porter, tuba; Rastus Lenkins, snare; Luke Davis, bass drums."

Rabbit's Foot Company

March 14, 1903

"Following is the roster of the musicians . . . Prof. A. G. Jones, cornetist, leader of band and orchestra; Willie Lewis, cornet, B and O [i.e., band and orchestra]; Lewis Williams, clarinet; Frank Hopkins, first violin and solo alto; E. D. Collins, alto; Will Goff Kennedy, alto; Amos Gaillaird, trombone, B and O; Alfred Hunt, second trombone; Rudolph Reynolds, trombone and second violin; Josiah Gayles, baritone, Wm. Thomas, tuba; Oscar Hicks, traps; C. D. Brooks, bass drum."

August 1, 1903

"The roster of the band is as follows: Trombones, Amos Gillard, Albert H. Hunt; tuba, Rudolph Regnaud; baritone, J. M. Gayles; altos, W. G. Kennedy, E. N. Collins, Frank Hopkins; clarionet, Lewis Williams; cornets, Willie Lewis and A. G. Jones; battery, Fred Goodwin and C. D. Brooks. The orchestra: First violin, Frank Hopkins; second violin, Fred Goodwin; cornets, Willie Lewis and A. G. Jones; clarinet, Lewis Williams; double bass, Rudolph Reynaud; trombone, Amos L. Gillard; traps, Oscar Hicks; flute, Fred Goodwin."

April 29, 1905

"Prof. J. C. Turner, bandmaster and leader of orchestra . . . E. B. Dudley, first violin and alto; W. Lewis, cornet; Fred Goodwin, flute and piccolo; Pearl Moppin, the world's greatest hoop roller, William Johnson and G. S. DesVeny, trombones; Joseph Miller, tuba . . . Oscar Hicks, trap drum; Oasey Goodwin, leader the drum corps."

May 19, 1906

"Our band is small but doing fine . . . Wm. Lewis, captain; cornets, John Gunley, William Lewis; alto, Ed. Collins; clarionet, Philip Williams; baritone, Joseph Gale; trombones, Pearl Moppin, C. T. Cherry; double bass, Benjamin F. Stevens, the only double instrument on the road with any colored show and he is making a big hit with it."

June 1, 1907

"This season we are carrying 20-piece band, consisting of David Bonds, J. Anderson, Fred Goodwin, William Philip, Harvey Perguley, Jenuie Reese, William Fisher, Frank Hopkins and several other members. David Bonds, leader."

June 27, 1908

"Roster of the band is as follows: Prof. D. Anderson, bandmaster; Willie Lewis, solo cornet; E. W. Blake, solo cornet; faithful second cornet Rogers; solo alto G. W. H. Jones; second alto Stewart; third alto Gales; baritone Ben Stephens; tuba Cherry; Frank Perrimont, Ratcliff, trombonest; Joe Means, bass drum and cimbles; Tim More, snaw drum; Williams clairnetist; picalo player Jones; Thompson flute; second clarinet Davis; French horn Jackson; euphunion G. Green; Melowphone, Caswell; obia Jenkins."

April 17, 1909

"Roster of band: R. J. Anderson, bandmaster, cornet; N. E. Perkins, cornet; Sam Stevens, cornet; Harry Lewis, violin and clarinet; Fred Knewly, clarinet; L. Normon, melliphone; Warren Thorn alto; Jesse Reeves, slide trombone; Pelson Dillon, trombone; J. M. Gayles, baritone; Walter Gordon, tuba; William Brown, snare drum and traps; Joe Means, bass drum."

October 15, 1910

"The band members are Prof. M. J. Nettles, Irving Brown, Joseph Gale, W. L. Blake, John W. Brown, Edward Miller, Will Stegall and Grew Baynham."

February 8, 1913

"Our band is under the leadership of Geo. A. Williams and consists of the following players: Geo. A. Williams, A. Townsend and A. Cox, cornets; Ralph Redmond, George Ross, Ed Williams, trombones; Jap Reed, John Allen, altos; William Green, baritone; Wm. Thomas, tuba; Joe White and Charles Burems, drums."

August 30, 1913

"The band is still under the direction of Prof. George Williams. The roster is as follows: W. Lee and

Lonnie Townsend, cornets; Prof. Williams, cornet and saxaphone; Parker Wade and William Green, baritone; Ralph Redmond, trombone and saxaphone; Billy Moore and Fred Pratt, trombone; A. D. King, metaphone; G. Chisolm, clarinet; William Thomas, [tuba]; Joe White and Carter Lockhart, [drums]."

February 14, 1914

"Below is the roster of our Gold Band and orchestra: Ralph S. Redmond, 1st trombone; Freddie Pratt, 2d trombone; B.O.S.S. Hale, 3d trombone; Wm. Thomas, tuba; B. O. Wm. Green, baritone and violin; Frank Reed, 3d alto; W. H. Lee, 2d alto and violin; P. H. Wade, 1st alto; T. W. Barnett, solo clarinetist; B. O. Robert Everly, 1st clarinetist; Norman Mason, 2d cornet; A. D. King, 1st cornet; B. O. Silas C. Elliott, solo cornet; Walter Lee, solo cornet; B. O. Joe White, snare drum; Archie Blue, bass drum; R. J. Anderson, bandmaster."

July 11, 1914

"Below you'll find the roster of the band: Solo cornets, E. W. Blake, Norman Mason; solo clarinet, Robert Young; 2d clarinet and violin, W. M. Lee; solo alto, Frank Jap Reid; 1st alto, Park Wade; 2nd alto, Lew Watts; 1st trombone, Freddie Pratt; 2d trombone, Joseph Watts; 3d trombone, S. S. Hale; baritone and violin, W. M. Green; bass, A. D. King; bass drum, Archie Blue; snare drum, Joseph White; solo trombone and director, Ralph S. Redmond."

April 24, 1915

"Below will be seen the roster of the band: Marcus L. Veal, E flat clarinetist and director; Fred C. Richardson, solo -flat clarinetist; Robert Everly, 1st B flat clarinet; Norman Mason, solo cornet; Bert Deleo, 1st cornet; Lew Watts, 2d cornet; Frank 'Jap' Reed, solo melophone; Park Wade, 1st melophone; Arthur C. Gibbs, 1st trombone; Freddie Pratt, 2d trombone; Joe Watts, 3d trombone; W. M. Green, baritone; Wm. 'tuba' Thomas, bass; Joe White and Archie Blue, drums."

September 18, 1915

"Our band, under the direction of Mark V. Chaney, is a No. 1 band. Members are: Norman Mason, solo cornet; Sam Forester, 1st cornet; Fred Richardson, solo clarinet; Robert Eveiligh, 1st clarinet; Arthur Gibbs, 1st trombone; Laurence Gibbs, 1st trombone; Lawrence Lee, 2nd trombone; Frank J. Reed, 1st alto; Rark Wade, 2nd alto; Herman Green, baritone; Tuba Thomas, tuba; Joe White, snare drum; Chas. C. Price, bass drum."

January 29, 1916

"Our band is exceptionally good. The roster is as follows: Marcus Veale Chaney, leader, E flat cornet; N. K. Mason and Geo. Jefferson, cornets; F. C. Richardson and Master Robert Everleigh, clarinet; Arthur Gibbs and P. L. Jenkins, trombones; Park Wade, mellophone; W. H. White, tuba; Joe White, snare drum, and Chas. E. Rue, bass drum."

April 22, 1916

"Prof. Veals concert band [includes] M. V. Chaney, E-flat clarinet and leader; Messrs Norman Mason and George E. Jefferson, cornets; F. C. Richardson and Robert Everleigh, clarinets; Park Wade, mellophone; P. L. Jenkins and Frank Perryman, trombones; Arthur Gibbs, baritone; W. H. White, tuba; Joseph White, snare drum, and Charles E. Rue, bass drum."

December 2, 1916

"Prof. Veal now has surrounded himself with the following musicians . . . Prof. Veal, clarinet and director; Norman Mason, solo clarinet; Geo. Jeffries, cornet; Robert Everly, clarinet; R. H. Young, clarinet; Arthur Gibbs, trombone; Frank Perryman, trombone; P. Wade, alto; R. L. Lovelace, alto; Dennis West, baritone; W. H. White, tuba; Joe White, snare drum; A. C. Blue, bass drum."

May 22, 1920

"The band is composed of: Frank Green, solo cornet; Claud Forner, first cornet; L. P. Anderson, second cornet; Roman Nelson, second cornet; Joe Armstrong, trombone; Arthur Prince, trombone; Lamar Nelson, bass; George Thayer, baritone; Sam Brown, clarinet; Joe Taylor, piccolo; Walter Hoyt, drum; A. L. Boyn, bass drum."

August 7, 1920

"Line up of the band: Arthur Prince, band master; Frank L. Green, Raymond Nelson and Robert Davis, cornets; Arthur Prince and Armstrong, trombones; George Thair, baritonist; Sam Brown and Wiggins, clarinet; Wallace & Johnson, alto; Lamar Nelson, bass; Hoyt and A. L. Boyd, drummers."

The Florida Blossoms Company

March 2, 1907

"Band roster: Trombones: Geo. B. Roane, Amos Gilliard and Pearl Moppins. Cornets: Dick Anderson and Jas. A. Shackleford. Piccalo and flute: Clarence Jones. Clarinet: F. Purnsley. Baritones: Pete Woods and Frank Hopkins. Tuba: Jos. Miller. Drums: Buddy Glenn, snare; Freddie Goodwin, bass. W. G. Kennedy, alto."

March 16, 1907

"The musical end of the show is in the hands of W. H. Dorsey . . . The personnel is as follows: Geo. B. Rhone, violin and trombone; Clarence (Picolo) Jones, flute and piccolo; Frank Hopkins, violin and baritone; Harvey Purnsley, clarinet; James Shackleford, cornet; R. H. Anderson, cornet; W. G. Kennedy, horn; Amos Gilliard, trombone; Pearl Moppin, trombone; Pete Woods, baritone; Joe Miller, bass; Fred Goodwin, traps; Charles Santana, bass drum."

April 24, 1909

"The following is the personnel of the band: E. B. Dudley, leader and cornet; Walter Childs, cornet; G. E. Crump, cornet; Geo. Motto, clarinet; Wm. Johnson, clarinet; W. G. Kennedy, alto; Eddie Miller, alto; Clarence Stewart, alto; John H. Tobias, trombone; Clifford Prather, trombone; G. A. Christian, baritone; Joe Miller, tuba; Sam West, double B flat monster; Lonnie Fisher, sensational snare drummer; Claude Glover, bass drum."

June 5, 1909

"The [band] roster is as follows: E. B. Dudley, bandmaster and orchestra leader; Walter Child, solo cornet; George Crump, solo cornet; George Motto, clarinet; Clarence Steward and Ed Miller, first and second altos; George Christian, baritone; John H. Tobias, first trombone; Clifford Prater, second trombone; little Joe Miller, tuba; Larney Fisher, snare drum; Cloud Glover, bass drum."

September 11, 1909

"Band: E. B. Dudley and Walter Childs, solo cornet and violin; G. W. Crump first cornet; George W. Motto, first clarinet; George E. Miller, first alto; Tom Fleming, second alto; John Tobias, first trombone; Cliff Prather, second trombone; Georghe Christian, baritone; Little Joe Miller, tuba; Claude Glover, side drum; Nelson Green, bass drum."

November 20, 1909

"The band is composed of the following: E. B. Dudley, band master and cornet; W. H. Childs, solo cornet; Geo. Crump, solo and first cornet; Geo. W. Motto, clarinet; Geo. Christian, baritone; Little Joe Miller and Clarence Steward, altos; John Tobias, first trombone; Clifford Pratter, second trombone; L. L. Fisher, snare drum; Nelson Green, bass drum; Joe White, traps in orchestra."

June 17, 1911

"The band is under the leadership of Mr. Walter H. Childs, assisted by Mr. Briggs Bennett, solo cornet; Geo. Crump, first B-flat cornet; George W. Motto, clarinet; Frank Hopkins, solo alto; Warren Thorn, first alto; George Christian, baritone; Joe Miller, tuba (the little fellow with the big horn); John H. Tobias, first trombone; Clifford Praytor, second trombone; Joe White, snare drum; Clarence Steward, bass drum."

JULY 5, 1913

"The roster is as follows: Walter Childs, solo B♭ cornet; Atler Cox, solo B♭ cornet; George Crump, first B♭ cornet; Richard Reese, clarinet; Warren Thorn, first alto; Alex Rice, second alto; Ward (Dope) Andrews, first trombone and baritone; George Ross, second trombone; Irvin Brown, second trombone; Joe Miller, bass; Harry Jefferson, snare drum; Lonnie Fisher, bass drum."

JULY 31, 1915

"The orchestra: A. Cox, cornetist; Great Rock, violinist; Miss Julia Knox, pianist; J.L. Williams, trombonist; Clifford Peeler, trap drummer, and others."

AUGUST 14, 1915

"Roster of band: Prof. Attler Cox, cornet; Frank Robinson, alto; J. L. Williams, trombone; L. L. Fisher, bass drum and Clifford Peeler, our sensational trap and snare drummer."

DECEMBER 18, 1915

"The band under the direction of Mr. Atlee Cox, cornet; W. R. Twiggs, cornet; Stiffis Thorne, alto; Dan Hull, alto; E. W. Harris, trombone; Albert Driver, trombone; John Ivey, baritone; Little Joe Miller, bass; Cliff Peeler and John Bossenger, drums. The orchestra under the direction of Miss Julia Knox, pianist; Atlee Cox, first cornet; W. R. Twiggs, second cornet; Don Hull, violin; John Ivey, cello; Albert Driver, trombone; Joe Miller, bass; Cliff Peeler, drums."

MARCH 25, 1916

"The band, numbering 13, is as follows: George Ross, Albert Driver, W. Harris, trombones; John Evers, baritone; Little Joe Miller, bass; Robert (Sippi) Miller, alto; Warren Thorne, alto; Walter H. Childs, bandmaster; Alter Cox and W. H. Triggs, cornets; Oscar Lowe, clarinet; Clifford Peeler, D. H. Hull, drums."

MAY 13, 1916

"The band . . . is under the leadership of Walter H. Childs, with the following gentlemen under him: Will Triggs and Arthur Cox, cornets; Oscar Lowe, clarinet; Warren Thorne, alto; Geo. Ross, E. W. Harris, Albert Driver, trombones; John Ivey, baritone; Little Joe Miller, bass; D. H. Hull, bass drum; Cliff Peeler, snare drum."

SEPTEMBER 2, 1916

"Our band under Walter H. Childs, assisted by the following gentlemen: Mr. Geo. Crump, Oscar Lowe, Warren Thorne, D. R. Hull, Clifford Peelee, John Ivey, Joe Miller, Geo. Ross, Albert Driver and Earl Harris, makes the noonday parades a feature."

OCTOBER 14, 1916

"The roster of the band is as follows: Prof. W. H. Childs, W. R. Triggs, Alter Cox, Geo. Crump, cornets; Oscar Lowe, clarinet; Warren Thorne, Walter Smith, altos; Geo. Ross, Albert Driver, Earl Harris, trombones; John Ivey, baritone; Little Joe Miller, bass; D. R. Hull, bass drum and cymbals; Clifford Peeler, snare drum."

APRIL 28, 1917

"The band of fourteen, under the direction of Walter H. Childs, cornet; Cox, cornet; George Crump, cornet; Oscar Lowe, clarinet; Arnett Nelson; clarinet; Warren (Stiffy) Thorne, alto; Louis McCormick, alto; Albert Driver, trombone; Slim Jim Austin, trombone; Clifford Peeler, snare drum; D. R. (Puff) Hull, bass drum; John Grey, baritone; Little Joe Miller, bass."

JULY 21, 1917

"The band is just making a fuss, that's all. They have the jollying Wind Jammers W. R. Triggs, Alter Cox, Arnett Nelson, Oscar Lowe, Warren Thorne, John

Ivey, Little Joe Miller, Slim Jim Austin and Calf Skin beaters Clifford Peeler and D. R. (Puff) Hill."

April 3, 1920

"The band: Prof. J. H. McCamon, Walter Hobbs, James McCory, cornets; D. R. (Puff) Hall, Stuffy Thorne, altos; Arthur Williams, bass drum; Jimmie (Getch) Garrett, snare drum; John Gay, baritone; Little Joe Miller, Tuba; and D. R. Hull, orchestra leader."

July 31, 1920

"The band is playing everything possible. This is the roster: J. H. McCamon, band master and cornet; Gus Aiken, Jimmie McLearey, Walter Hobbs, cornets; Emanuel Cobral, clarinet; D. R. (Puff) Hall, Warren (Stiffy) Thorne, altos; Eugene Aiken, trombone; John Avery, baritone; Little Joe Miller, bass; Arthur Williams, bass drum; Jimmie (Geech) Garrett, snare drum."

September 27, 1924

"Members of the band are: Prof. J. H. Witherspoon, George Gillens and Gregg A. Williams, cornets; John Williams, clarinet; Chick Garnett and George Long, trombones; John Porter, baritone; yours truly [Lamar "Buck" Nelson], tuba; Jack Thompson and Walter Miller, drums."

October 11, 1924

"Roster of band: Prof. James H. Witherspoon, cornet; Gregg Williams, cornet; George Gillen, cornet; John Wilson, clarinet; Arthur (Chick) Garnett, George Long and Warner Ford, trombones; John Porter, baritone; Lamar B. Nelson, tuba; Jack Thompson and Walter Miller, drums."

November 8, 1924

"The roster of band: Prof. J. H. Witherspoon, George Gillen and Gregg A. Williams, cornets; John Wilson, clarinet and saxophone; Arthur (Chick) Garnett, George Long and Warner Ford, trombones; John Porter, baritone; yours truly [Buck Nelson], tuba; Walter Miller and Jock Thompson, drums."

March 28, 1925

"Prof. Elijah Nelson has a band with some real talent. Roster of band is: Prof. E. Nelson, cornet; Sgt. Elmer Moore, cornet; Gregg A. Williams, cornet; Elmer Wheeler, clarinet; Allen Fudge, melaphone; Arthur Gibbs, trombone; Rastus Smith, trombone; Devoe Graden, trombone; John Porter, baritone; Lamar B. Nelson, tuba; Jack Thompson, Walter Miller, drums."

June 13, 1925

"Band has Prof. Elijah Nelson, cornet; Gregg A. Williams, cornet; James G. Buckingham, cornet; Elmer Wheeler, clarinet; Devoe Graden and Rastus Smith, trombones; John L. Porter, baritone; Lamar B. Nelson, tuba; Jockey Thomson and Walter [Miller], drums;. The sax quartet has Elmer Wheeler, Gregg A. Williams, James Buckingham and John L. Porter."

August 1, 1925

"Prof. E. Nelson is doing great work . . . His band at the present time consists of the following: Devore Graden, better known as 'Trombone Red'; Rastus Smith, trombone and cornet; Gregg A. Williams, cornet and alto saxophone; James G. Buckingham, cornet, clarinet and 'C' sax; John L. Porter, baritones and tenor sax; Lamar B. Nelson, tuba; Jack Thompson, drummer; Walter Miller, bass drummer; Elmer Wheeler, clarinet and alto sax."

February 27, 1926

"The roster of the band: Alonzo Williams, George Gillems, Gregg Williams, Elmer Wheeler, Rastus Smith, John Porter, Lamar Nelson, Jock Thompson and Walter Miller."

August 7, 1926

"The line-up still remains the same: Elonzo S. Williams, band leader, cornet and banjo; George

Gillens, cornet; Gregg A. Williams, cornet and saxophone; Sam Williams, clarinet and saxophone; John L. Porter, baritone and tenor saxophone; Devore Graden and Rastus Smith, trombones; Lamar B. Nelson, tuba; little Jock Thompson and and Walter Sapp Miller, drums."

JUNE 9, 1928

"In the band are George Gillians, cornet and band leader; Greg A. Williams, cornet; Eddie Billups, cornet; Elmer Wheeler, clarinet; Buck Nelson, tuba; Jack Thompson, drums; Rastus Smith, trombone; William Mills, trombone; Horsley Dorsey, baritone player."

Silas Green from New Orleans

APRIL 23, 1910

"Our band, under the direction of R. H. Collins [consists of] R. H. Collins, Lunford Davis, R. J. Anderson, cornets; W. G. Kennedy, Napoleon Black, altos; Archie Taylor, Frank Perryman, trombones; Wm. Mayfield, baritone; Sam White, tuba; Tom Price and Page Tillman, battery."

JULY 9, 1910

"The roster of the band is as follows: R. J. Anderson, b-flat cornet; D. L. Davis, b-flat cornet; R. H. Collins, b-flat cornet; F. S. Perdome, e-flat cornet; Wm. H. Mayfield, baritone; Sam White, tuba; Jerry Martin, trombone; Wm. Goff Kennedy, alto; Page Tillman, bass drum; Thos. Price, snare drum."

MAY 25, 1912

"The personnel of the band is as follows: Fred Kewley, clarinet; Wm. Mayfield, cornet; R. H. Collins, cornet; W. G. Kennedy and Lawrence Booker, melophones; John Ivey, baritone; Wm. Fisher, tuba; Happy Charley Lewis, Jerry Martin and Jesse Reeves, trombones; Manzie Williams, snare drum; Babe Steele, bass drum."

FEBRUARY 8, 1913

"Our band, under the leadership of R. H. Collins, numbers thirteen pieces. The roster is as follows: Jessie Reeves, Jerry Martin and Mr. Humboldt, trombonists; William Fisher, bass; John Ivey, baritone; Will Goff Kennedy and L. J. Christohm, alto; William Mayfield, R. H. Collins (leader) and Lawrence Booker, cornet; Mancy Williams, snare drum; Leroy Knox, bass drum, and Fred Kewley, clarinet."

NOVEMBER 22, 1913

"Following is the roster of the band: Fred Kewley, solo clarinet; Chas. Lewis, R. H. Collins and Laurence Booker, cornets; W. G. Kennedy, C. B. Hight and Elliott Wright, altos; Jesse Reeves, Jerry Martin, Bob Bartell and John Brooks, trombones; Frank Hopkins, baritone; Bennie Stratton, tuba; Leroy Knox and Frank Smedley, battery."

DECEMBER 27, 1913

"R. H. Collins is bandmaster and Fred Kewley, clarinet virtuoso, orchestra leader, with the following musicians: Frank Hopkins, first violin; C. B. Hight, second violin; Jesse Reeves, cello; Bennie Stratten, bass, Fred Kewley, clarinet and leader; Lawrence Booker and R. H. Collins, cornets; Jerry Martin, trombone; Walter Hoyt, traps; Charles (Happy) Lewis, our sensational cornet player and character actor, is with us. Jesse Reeves' trombone solos are the feature of our noonday concerts."

FEBRUARY 20, 1915

"The roster of the company [includes] George Smith, bandmaster; Jesse Reeves, leader of orchestra . . . Frank Hopkins, baritone and violin; Isaiah Wilds, trombone and flute; Laurence Booker, cornet and violin; R. J. Mitchell, cornet; Jesse Reeves, trombone; George Smith, cornet; Willie Fisher, tuba; Willie Austin, trombone; Leroy Knox and Ford Wiggins, battery."

April 3, 1915

"Mr. Geo. Smith is leader of the band, which is composed of the following: Jessie Reeves, Sarah Wilds, Slim Austin, trombones; Lawrence Booker, Geo. Smith, R. J. Mitchell, cornetists; Austin Gosser, Will Goss Kennedy, horns; Frank Hopkins, baritone; Wm. Fisher, tuba; Leroy Knox, snare drum; Ford Wiggins, bass drum; Walter Hoyt, trap drums."

March 25, 1916

"The band is under the direction of Enoch W. Blake. Following is the roster: E. W. Blake, leader and cornet; George Smith, cornet; L. Booker, cornet; Austin Dorsey and W. G. Kennedy, altos; William Fisher, tuba; Frank Hopkins, baritone; Jessie Reeves, trombone; Slim Austin, trombone, and usual drums."

December 30, 1916

"Our Musicians, A. D. King and Lawrence Booker, solo cornets; Harold Ferguson, clarinet; Jap Reed and Goff Kennedy, altos; Frank Hopkins, baritone; W. L. Blake, tuba; Jerry Martin, Slim Austin, Harvey McCloudy, Jesse Reeves, trombones; Ford Wiggins and 'Dukie' Hoyt, drums; Frank Smedley, saxophone, and James B. Raymond, drums in orchestra."

July, 7, 1917

"Jeff Smith has taken charge of the band . . . Bob Everleigh and Harold Ferguson comprise our clarinette section; Jessie Reeves and Clarence Penn, trombones; cornets, Jeff Smith and Lawrence Booker; altos, Will Goff Kennedy and Ollie Young (cat on the wire); drums, Ford Wiggins and Walter Hoyt; baritone, Frank Hopkins."

November 17, 1917

"The roster of the band is as follows: Cornets, Jeff Smith, Lawrence Booker; clarinets, Harold Ferguson, Robbie Everleigh; trombones, Jesse Reeves, Clarence Penn; baritone, Frank Hopkins; bass, Brent Sparks; drums, Ford Wiggins and Walter Hoyt."

July 26, 1919

"Mr. Freddie Pratt is still our congenial bandmaster. We have a new acquisition to the show in the person of Samuel Johnson [solo saxophone and cornet]. We still have with us our old standbys in the person of Mr. Lawrence Booker, cornetist; Mr. Milford Butcher, baritone; Mr. John Ridley, alto; Mr. R. T. Horton, alto; Mr. J. W. Horton, trombone; Mr. Walter Hoyt and Mr. Ford Wiggins (Silas Green), drums."

November 1, 1919

"We have with us Freddie Pratt, band leader; Lawrence Booker, Amos Gilliard and Jas. Thomas, cornets; Fred Smith, tuba; Jessie Watts, snare drums; Ford Wiggins, bass drum; Arthur Dorsey and Freddie Pratt, trombones."

May 1, 1920

"The roster of the band is as follows: Lawrence Booker, cornet; Amos Gilliard and Flossie Ingram, trombones; Leon Pettiford, clarinet; Freddie Smith, tuba; James Hudson, saxaphone; Norman Lankford, melophone; Ford Wiggins, snare drum, and Dick Brown, bass drum."

July 10, 1920

"The roster of the [band] is as follows: Lawrence Booker, cornet; James Hudson, saxophone; Leon Pettiford, clarinet; Arthur Dorsey, Amos Gillard, James R. Jackson, trombones; Norman Langford, melaphone; Richard Brown, bass drum; Ford Wiggins, snare drum."

March 10, 1923

"Band: Jas. C. Hudson, saxaphone; Leon Pettiford, clarinet; Stiffy Thorne, alto; Keg Fisher and Frank Hopkins, baritones; Jas. Giles, bass; Walter Graham, Joe Tarres and J. R. Jackson, trombones; Walter Hobbs, cornet; Dukey Hoyt, snare drum; Ford Wiggins, bass drum; Lawrence Booker, cornet and band leader."

April 14, 1923

"Our band is rated one of the best on the road today. The roster is as follows: Clarinet section, Leon Pettiford and Edgar Esley; Frank Hopkins, baritone; Warren (Stiffy) Thorne, alto; Walter Graham and J. R. Jackson, trombones; Jas. Giles, tuba; Dusky Hoyt and Ford Wiggins, drums; Jas. C. Hudson, saxophone; Walter Hobbs and Lawrence Booker, cornets; Lawrence Booker, band leader."

May 31, 1924

"With John Ivey and Prof. Lawrence Booker as director and leader, harmony reigns supreme. James Jackson, William Penney, trombones; Bob Young, Leon Pettyford, clarinets; Frank Hopkins, solo alto; John Ivey, baritone; James Giles, double bass; James Hudson, Johnson Rooks, saxophones; Lawrence Booker, Romey Nelson, Wilbur Scottie, cornets; and the celebrated drummers, Walter H. Hoyle and Ford Wiggins complete the personnel of our band."

October 25, 1924

"The band, etc., has Lawrence Booker, Eddie Billups, Romeo Nelson, Elmer Scott, Mose Penny, Frankie Hopkins, John Ivy, James Giles, John Wilson, Ford Wiggins, James C. Hudson."

January 24, 1925

"The roster of the company's band as follows: cornets, Lawrence Booker, Willie Hobbs, Eddie Billups and Romia Nelson; trombones, Ford Wiggins, Moses Penny, Brooks and J. R. Jackson; baritone, John Ivey, bandmaster; alto, Frankie Hopkins; saxophone, J. C. Hudson; clarinettes, Bob Young and Leon (Buddie) Pettiford; tuba, Jas. Giles; drums, John Wilson; snare drum, Jimmie Garret."

May 23, 1925

"The roster of the band is as follows: Cornets, Romie Nelson, Lawrence Booker, Eddie Billups and Walter Hobbs; clarinets, Bob Young and Leon Pettiford; melophone, Frank Hopkins; saxophone, James Hudson; trombones, 'Chick' Garnett, James R. Jackson and Moses Penny; bass, James Jiles; drums, Ford Wiggins and John Wilson; John Ivy, baritone and leader."

November 11, 1925

"The roster of the band follows: John Ivy, leader and baritone; Lawrence Booker, Romie Nelson, Ed Billups and Walter Hobbs, cornets; Leon Pettiford and E. C. Ealy, clarinets; Frank Hopkins and Archie Blue, mellophones; J. C. Hudson, saxophone; James Jiles, bass; Ford Wiggins, small drum; John Coswell, bass drum."

June 11, 1927

"The roster of the band: Edgar Ealey, first clarinet; Leon Pettaford, second clarinet; James Hudson, saxaphone; Lawrence Booker, Eddie Billops and Sam Johnson, cornets; Dan Hull, Frank Robinson and Walter Hobbs, mellophones; William Penny, Richard Jones and Fount, trombones; William Bryant, baritone; James R. Jackson, bass; Manzie Campbell and Ford Wiggins, drums."

March 28, 1931

"The band and orchestra men, under the leadership of Fount B. Woods, are: George Gillems, Oliver Mason, Holsey Dorsey; Laurence Booker, Moses Penny, Bellaire Jackson, Arthur Gibbs, Sax Roberts, B. Baldwin, Oscar Lowe, Robert Gant, Archer Blue, Mansie Campbell, Ford Wiggins, Mose McQuitty and Johnson Rooks."

March 2, 1935

"Members of the Silas Green orchestra are Oscar Lowe, Fred Durrah, Eddie Billups, Lee Golden, William Bryant, Mose McQuitty, Sergt. A. D. King, Ford Wiggins, Buster Wheeler, Bob Gant and Charley Rue."

August 22, 1936

"The band is headed by Sargent A. D. King and the following: trumpets, Lee Golden, William Harris, Phillmore Hall; trombones, Delbert Payne, William Mills and F. B. Woods; sax and clarinets, Edgar Ealey, Oscar Lowe and Richard Poore; drums, Selma Williams; mellophone, Robert Gant; baritone, William Bryant; tuba, Julius Stroud."

May 22, 1937

"The following compose the band and orchestra: Lee Golden, William Harris, Julius Fields, B. M. Edwards, James Jackson, William Bryant, Richard Poore, Fred Durrah, Edgar Ealey, Oscar Lowe, Robert Gant, Julius Stroud, Charlie Rue, Selma Williams, Ford Wiggins and Lindsey Ramsey."

September 17, 1938

"The following men compose band and orchestra, under the leadership of Edward Washington: Lee Roi Nabors, William Harris, Hillard Witherspoon, George Scott, Julius Fields, Sam Hinton, Robert Block, Richard Poore, Edgar Ealey, Oscar Lowe, William Bryant, Robert Gant, John Blatch, Ford Wiggins, Jack Sims."

March 30, 1940

"Musicians: Eddie Washington, Roy Bowling, William Harris, George Scott, Johnnie Jones, Oliver Mason, A. D. King, Julius Fields, T. H. Jones, B. M. Edwards, John Blotch, William Bryant, Will Brown, Nathan Melvin, Bob Young, Robert Gant, Julius Stroud and Theodore Treville."

NOTES

Notes to Introduction

1. "Miss Bessie L. Gillam," *Indianapolis Freeman*, April 9, 1898.
2. For precedent commentary on coon songs as popular ragtime fare, see William J. Schafer and Johannes Riedel, *The Art of Ragtime: Form and Meaning of an Original Black American Art* (Baton Rouge: Louisiana State University Press, 1973); Edward A. Berlin, *Ragtime: A Musical and Cultural History* (Berkeley: University of California Press), 1980; and Paul Oliver, *Songsters and Saints: Vocal Traditions on Race Records* (Cambridge: Cambridge University Press, 1984).
3. Its etymology as a racial designation remains obscure. The *Dictionary of American Slang* (New York: Thomas Y. Crowell Company, 1967), cites H. L. Mencken's suggestion, in "Designations for Colored Folk," *American Speech*, October 1944, that it "originally came from the name of the animal which Southern Negroes were supposed to enjoy hunting and eating." The *Oxford English Dictionary* notes a precedent colloquial use of "coon" to describe a "sly, knowing fellow" (second edition, 1989, vol. 3, p. 894). For a commentary that attempts to attach this earlier connotation of the word "coon" to the subsequent racial epithet, see John Minton and David Evans, *"The Coon in the Box": A Global Folktale in African-American Context* (FF Communications No. 277) (Helsinki: Suomalainen Tiedeakatemia Academia Scientiarum Fennica, 2001).
4. We examine coon song lyrics in relation to early blues, but we do not attempt a musical analysis. Paul Oliver took a similar approach, and came to some of the same conclusions, in *Songsters & Saints*. Peter Muir is currently completing a musicological study of early blues and proto-blues, including coon songs, to be published by the University of Illinois Press.
5. For an account of the *Freeman*'s early history, see Lynn Abbott and Doug Seroff, *Out of Sight: The Rise of African American Popular Music, 1889–1895* (Jackson: University Press of Mississippi, 2003), pp. xii–xiii.
6. "The Billboard and the Race Press," *Billboard*, December 11, 1920.
7. William Henry Davis, "A Historic Account of Sylvester Russell," *Indianapolis Freeman*, January 1, 1910; "Sylvester Russell Probably To Appear At The Pekin At An Early Date," *Indianapolis Freeman*, March 25, 1911.
8. "Sylvester Russell Dead," *Chicago Defender*, October 11, 1930; Salem Tutt Whitney, "Timely Topics," *Chicago Defender*, October 18, 1930.
9. Sylvester Russell, "The Legitimate Standard of Musical Comedy," *Indianapolis Freeman*, June 1, 1907.
10. Sylvester Russell, "Vaudeville in Boston," *Indianapolis Freeman*, January 8, 1903.
11. Books that have previously dealt with the larger context of black musical comedy in the ragtime era include James Weldon Johnson, *Black Manhattan*, 1930 (New York: Da Capo Press, 1991); Henry T. Sampson, *Blacks in Blackface: A Source Book on Early Black Musical Shows* (Metuchen, NJ: Scarecrow Press, 1980); Henry T. Sampson, *The Ghost Walks: a Chronological History of Blacks in Show Business, 1865–1910* (Metuchen, NJ: Scarecrow Press, 1988); and Thomas L. Riis, *Just Before Jazz: Black Musical Theater in New York, 1890 to 1915* (Washington: Smithsonian Institution Press, 1989).
12. For information on Hogan's early career, see Abbott and Seroff, *Out of Sight*, pp. 433–38. Fine essays on Hogan by Dennis Pash and Chris Ware

appeared in *The Rag-Time Ephemeralist*, vol. 1, no. 1 (1998), pp. 36–52. Ray Buckberry has collected information, as yet unpublished, on Hogan's family and early life in Bowling Green, Kentucky.

13. Information on the early years of circus annex bands and minstrels is given in Abbott and Seroff, *Out of Sight*, pp. 373–80.
14. "A Trip to Coontown," *Indianapolis Freeman*, December 30, 1899.
15. Freddie Pratt, "A Showman's Dream," *Indianapolis Freeman*, February 13, 1915.

Notes to Part I: Coon Songs, Big Shows, and Black Stage Stars of the Ragtime Era

1. Sigmund Spaeth, *A History of Popular Music in America* (New York: Random House, 1948), p. 286.
2. R. W. Thompson, "The Mirror Up To Nature," *Indianapolis Freeman*, December 19, 1896.
3. "Rag Time Music," *New York Age*, quoted in *Indianapolis Freeman*, March 16, 1901.
4. "Tom the Tattler," *Indianapolis Freeman*, May 25, 1901.
5. Sylvester Russell, "S. Coleridge Taylor Answered," *Indianapolis Freeman*, December 31, 1904.
6. S. H. Dudley, "Uncle Dud Writes of Old Stars," *Pittsburgh Courier*, March 3, 1928.
7. Sylvester Russell, "Ernest Hogan Sleeps His Final Sleep," *Indianapolis Freeman*, May 29, 1909.
8. "The Stage," *Indianapolis Freeman*, November 27, 1897.
9. *New York Sun*, reproduced in "Stage," *Indianapolis Freeman*, April 16, 1898.
10. "Stage," *Indianapolis Freeman*, August 6, 1898.
11. "Stage," *Indianapolis Freeman*, October 15, 1898.
12. As late as 1929 the chorus only of "All Coons Look Alike to Me" was included in a collection of *"88" Grand Old Songs* (New York: Shapiro, Bernstein & Co.).
13. Uncle Tom Collins, "Tain't No Lie," Okeh 45132, 1927.
14. "The Southern Singer," *Hippodrome News*, March 25, 1908, quoted in Jim Walsh, "Favorite Pioneer Recording Artists: Clarice Vance, Part I," *Hobbies* (April 1963), p. 35; *Terre Haute Tribune*, April 30, 1913, quoted in Walsh, "Favorite Pioneer Recording Artists: Clarice Vance, Part I," p. 36; Jim Walsh, "Favorite Pioneer Recording Artists: Clarice Vance, Part II," *Hobbies* (May 1963), p. 59.
15. "Miner's Bowery Theatre," *New York Clipper*, January 22, 1898.
16. *Terre Haute Tribune*, April 30, 1913, quoted in Jim Walsh, "Favorite Pioneer Recording Artists: Clarice Vance, Part I," *Hobbies* (April 1963), pp. 35–36.
17. "Clarice Vance the Southern Singer," *New York Dramatic Mirror* ad, February 17, 1900. Reproduced from *Cincinnati Times Star*.
18. "Alhambra," *Variety*, March 10, 1906.
19. For a Clarice Vance discography see Brian Rust, *The Complete Entertainment Discography* (New Rochelle: Arlington House, 1973).
20. *New York Times*, 1938, quoted in Jim Walsh, "Six Comediennes: May Irwin, Fourth of the Six (part 2)," *Hobbies* (July 1963), p. 35.
21. May Irwin, "The Bully," Victor 31642, 1907, reissued on *Music from the New York Stage, 1890–1920, Vol. 1*, Pearl CD GEMM-9050-2 (Great Britain).
22. "Boston's New Productions," *New York Times*, September 3, 1895.
23. "New Acts of the Week," *Variety*, December 7, 1907.
24. "Artie Hall," *New York Dramatic Mirror*, February 3, 1900.
25. *New York Dramatic Mirror*, November 4, 1899.
26. "Stage," *Indianapolis Freeman*, May 11, 1901; June 1, 1901; "Uncle Tom's Cabin," *New York Times*, December 3, 1901. For more on African American pianist and stage manager Luke Pulley, see Abbott and Seroff, *Out of Sight*, p. 56.
27. "Vaudeville Jottings," *New York Dramatic Mirror*, November 16, 1901.
28. "Vaudeville Jottings," *New York Dramatic Mirror*, March 8, 1902.
29. "Tony Pastor's Theatre," *New York Clipper*, February 3, 1900.
30. Sylvester Russell, "Miscellaneous Musings," *Indianapolis Freeman*, February 20, 1904.
31. Sylvester Russell, "A Little of Everything," *Indianapolis Freeman*, March 7, 1903.

32. Arthur R. LaBrew, "Two Nineteenth Century Detroit Musicians: Gillams," *Afro-American Music Review*, vol. 3, no. 1 (June–December 1985), pp. 49–63. For more on Ed Rector see Abbott and Seroff, *Out of Sight*.
33. "The Stage," *Indianapolis Freeman*, January 22, 1898. Both of these titles by white composers have been popularly associated with the origins of ragtime. See Blesh and Janis, *They All Played Ragtime*, pp. 89, 150.
34. "The Stage," *Indianapolis Freeman*, June 22, 1901.
35. "The Stage," *Indianapolis Freeman*, May 19, 1900; "Stage," *Indianapolis Freeman*, November 24, 1900; March 14, 1903; "The Stage," *Indianapolis Freeman*, September 5, 1903. Other titles identified in the *Freeman* as having been sung by Carrie Hall between 1900 and 1905 include "Since You's Got Money," "I Love You 'Cause You've Got Those Winning Ways," "I've Been Livin' Moderate All My Life," "I've Got Troubles of My Own," "Deed I Do," "Ain't Dat Scan'las," "Have You Got Time to Listen to a Hard Luck Tale," "I Don't Want to Be an Actor Man No More," "Ding a Ling Ding," "I'm Sorry Babe," "I'm Getting Awful Lazy," "I Just Can't Help from Loving That Man," "Gone, Gone, Gone," "Money Was Made for Coons to Spend," "You Must Think I'm Santa Claus," "It Ain't the Kind of Grub I've Been Getting Down Home," "Farewell, Mr. Abner Henenway," and "On Your Way."
36. "The Stage," *Indianapolis Freeman*, March 24, 1900; March 31, 1900. "4-11-44" refers to "playing the numbers," or "playing policy." A review of Cole and Johnson's *A Trip to Coontown* in the *Freeman* of April 16, 1898, identifies "Play 4-11-44" as one of the songs in the first part of the show. Several "policy blues" recordings harbor "4-11-44" references, among them Jim Jackson, "Policy Blues," Victor 21268, 1928, reissued on Document DOCD-5114; and Cripple Clarence Lofton, "Policy Blues," Session 10-014, 1943, reissued on RST BDCD-6002. A "4-11-44" song was recorded as late as 1953 by Bobby Mitchell and the Toppers (Imperial 5250).
37. "Stage," *Indianapolis Freeman*, March 23, 1901.
38. "The Stage," *Indianapolis Freeman*, July 4, 1903.
39. "The Stage," *Indianapolis Freeman*, October 8, 1904.
40. "The Stage," *Indianapolis Freeman*, December 1, 1906; January 12, 1907.
41. "The Stage," *Indianapolis Freeman*, June 15, 1907.
42. Howard W. Odum, "Folk-Song and Folk-Poetry as Found in the Secular Songs of the Southern Negroes," *The Journal of American Folklore*, vol. 24, no. 93 (July–September 1911), pp. 255–96; vol. 24, no. 94 (October–December 1911), pp. 351–96. For an earlier assessment of Howard Odum's fieldwork, see David Evans, *Big Road Blues: Tradition and Creativity in the Folk Blues* (Berkeley: University of California Press, 1982).
43. John Queen and Charlie Cartwell, "I Got Mine" (New York: Howley, Haviland & Dresser Pub.), 1901.
44. Andrew B. Sterling and Harry Von Tilzer, "Moving Day" (New York: Harry Von Tilzer Music Publishing Co.), 1906.
45. Odum, "Folk-Song And Folk-Poetry," p. 389.
46. "Notes from Allen, Quine and Oake's New Orleans Minstrels," *Indianapolis Freeman*, October 27, 1900.
47. Chris Smith and Elmer Bowman, "I've Got De Blues" (New York: The Lyceum Publishing Co., 1901). "I've Got De Blues" was popularly employed by African American entertainers. Correspondence in the *Freeman* during 1902 indicates that Daniel Williams was "making a big hit" with it in New York City, while Ida Larkins was featuring it at the Exchange Garden Theater in Jacksonville, Florida, and Will Goff Kennedy was singing it throughout the State of Alabama, en route with the Rabbit Foot Minstrels.
48. Sylvester Russell, "Annual Stage Review," *Indianapolis Freeman*, December 24, 1904.
49. "The Stage," *Indianapolis Freeman*, December 25, 1897.
50. "The Stage," *Indianapolis Freeman*, July 31, 1897.
51. Son House's complete Library of Congress recordings, 1941–1942, including "Am I Right or Wrong," are reissued on Travelin' Man CD 02.
52. Sylvester Russell, "Booker T. Washington On Taylor Music," *Indianapolis Freeman*, July 22, 1905. The specific "class meeting" hymn from which Edmonds extracted "I'm Going to Live Anyhow

Until I Die" may be "River of Jordan"/"I'm Going to Sit at the Welcome Table." Exemplary recorded versions of this jubilee hymn include Fisk University Male Quartette, "River of Jordan," Columbia A1932, 1915, reissued on Document DOCD-5534; Carter Family, "River of Jordan," Victor 21434, 1929, reissued on Rounder CD 1064; and Birmingham Jubilee Singers, "I'm Going to Sit at the Welcome Table," Vocalion 1599, 1930, reissued on Document DOCD-5362. A very interesting later example is Sensational Nightingales, "View That Holy City," Peacock 1774, 1957.

53. Alan Lomax, liner notes to *Roots of the Blues*, New World Records LP NW252, 1977.

54. Pete Hampton, "I'm Going to Live Anyhow Until I Die," Odeon 2433, 1904.

55. Guthrie T. Meade, Jr., with Dick Spottswood and Douglas S. Meade, *Country Music Sources: A Biblio-Discography of Commercially Recorded Traditional Music* (Chapel Hill: University of North Carolina Press, 2002), cites Fisher Hendley, "Nigger Will You Work," Okeh 45012, 1925; Gid Tanner and His Georgia Boys, "Old Time Tunes," Columbia 15059-D, 1925; Georgia Crackers, "The Coon from Tennessee," Okeh 45098, 1927; Charlie Poole and the North Carolina Ramblers, "Coon from Tennessee," Columbia 15215-D, 1928; and Georgia Yellow Hammers, "Tennessee Coon," Victor 21073, 1928.

56. "Pittsburg Press [*sic*]," quoted in "Clermont's Weekly Dots," *Indianapolis Freeman*, November 5, 1904.

57. Meade lists Sam and Kirk McGee, "C-H-I-C-K-E-N Spells Chicken," Vocalion 5150, 1927, reissued on Document DOCD-8036; Kirk McGee and Blythe Poteet, "C-H-I-C-K-E-N Spells Chicken," Gennett 7022; Asa Martin and Arthur Rose, "Ragtime Chicken Joe," ARC 35-10-12, 1933; and Tobacco Tags, "De Way to Spell Chicken," Bluebird 7973, 1939.

58. Mississippi John Hurt, "Chicken," Vanguard VSD-79248, 1967.

59. Sidney L. Perrin and Bob Slater, "Dat's De Way to Spell 'Chicken'" (New York: M. Witmark & Sons), 1902.

60. Sylvester Russell, "Address To Song Publishers," *Indianapolis Freeman*, April 2, 1904.

61. Curtis M. Hinsley, "The World as Marketplace," in Ivan Karp and Steven D. Lavine, eds., *Exhibiting Cultures* (Washington: Smithsonian Press, 1991), p. 363.

62. "The Stage," *Indianapolis Freeman*, June 9, 1900.

63. "I. McCorker," "Minstrels, Comedians and Singers," *Indianapolis Freeman*, May 31, 1902.

64. Paul Oliver, *Songsters and Saints: Vocal Traditions on Race Recordings* (Cambridge: Cambridge University Press, 1984), pp. 55, 56.

65. Banjo Joe, "My Money Never Runs Out," Paramount 12604, 1927, reissued on Document DOCD-5032; Cannon's Jug Stompers, "Money Never Runs Out," Victor 23262, 1930, reissued on Document DOCD-5033.

66. Paul J. Knox, "I Don't Care If I Never Wake Up" (Chicago: Will Rossiter), 1899.

67. Irving Jones, "My Money Never Gives Out" (New York: Feist & Frankenhalter), 1900.

68. Bill Moore, "Ragtime Millionaire," Paramount 12636, 1928, reissued on Document DOCD-5062.

69. Ad for "Home Ain't Nothing Like This" on back cover of sheet music for George R. Wilson, "Eat, Drink and Be Merry" (New York: Leo Feist), 1903.

70. "P. B. R. Hendrix's Chicago Notes," *Indianapolis Freeman*, September 26, 1903.

71. Carey B. Lewis, "At The Chicago Theaters," *Indianapolis Freeman*, October 15, 1910.

72. Tony Langston, "Irving Jones Hits," *Chicago Defender*, October 4, 1924.

73. Tim Owsley, "With the Georgias," *Chicago Defender*, August 22, 1925.

74. For a very late reference to the word "coon" in a blues song, see Howlin' Wolf, "Coon on the Moon," *The Back Door Wolf*, Chess LP CH 50045, 1973. Composer credit is ascribed to Eddie Shaw. David Evans reports that "Coon on the Moon" has been carried into the twenty-first century by Memphis blues-bar vocalist Tony Chatman.

75. "Notes of the Black Patti Troubadours," *Indianapolis Freeman*, June 2, 1900.

76. "The Stage," *Indianapolis Freeman*, April 27, 1907.

77. W. Milton Lewis, "Black Patti Troubadours," *Indianapolis Freeman*, February 24, 1906.

78. The "Smart Set" toured the South regularly in later years, during the Salem Tutt Whitney era, but not under the Hogan and McClain regime. In fact, none of Hogan's shows toured in the South.
79. *Chattanooga Daily Times*, April 2, 1908, quoted in "The Stage," *Indianapolis Freeman*, April 11, 1908.
80. C. B. L., "Black Patti Troubadours," *Indianapolis Freeman*, April 18, 1908.
81. For information on Black Patti's early life and career, see John Graziano, "The Early Life and Career of the 'Black Patti': The Odyssey of an African American Singer in the Late Nineteenth Century," *Journal of the American Musicological Society*, vol. 53, no. 3 (Fall 2000), pp. 543–96; and Abbott and Seroff, *Out of Sight*.
82. Sylvester Russell, "Black Patti In New York," *Indianapolis Freeman*, June 30, 1906.
83. "The Stage," *Indianapolis Freeman*, April 30, 1898.
84. "The Stage," *Indianapolis Freeman*, December 25, 1897.
85. "The Stage," *Indianapolis Freeman*, April 30, 1898.
86. "Stage," *Indianapolis Freeman*, June 14, 1902.
87. Sylvester Russell, "The Black Patti Show," *Indianapolis Freeman*, September 17, 1904.
88. Sylvester Russell, "Black Patti In New York," *Indianapolis Freeman*, June 30, 1906.
89. "The Stage," *Indianapolis Freeman*, November 21, 1903.
90. For an oral history–driven account of Ida Forsyne's career, see Marshall and Jean Stearns, *Jazz Dance: The Story of American Vernacular Dance*, 1968 (New York: Schirmer Books, 1978), pp. 250–57.
91. "Proctor's Pleasure Palace," *New York Clipper*, May 22, 1897.
92. "The Stage," *Indianapolis Freeman*, April 30, 1898.
93. *Louisville Courier-Journal*, August 22, 1897. This item was picked up in the *Indianapolis Freeman* of September 11, 1897.
94. "Eight Thousand A Year," *Indianapolis Freeman*, December 24, 1898.
95. "SIWEL," "Ernest Hogan Dead," *Indianapolis Freeman*, May 29, 1909.
96. *Honolulu Evening Bulletin*, quoted in "The Stage," *Indianapolis Freeman*, April 7, 1900.
97. "Vaudeville and Minstrel," *New York Clipper*, September 11, 1897.
98. "The Lawyer and the Actor," *Indianapolis Freeman*, April 20, 1901; Sylvester Russell, "Smart Set in 'Enchantment,'" *Indianapolis Freeman*, November 11, 1902.
99. Gerald Bordman, *American Musical Theatre—A Chronicle* (New York: Oxford University Press, 2001), p. 182.
100. Ernest Hogan advertisement, *New York Clipper*, May 20, 1899; Irving Jones, "I'm Livin' Easy" (New York, F.A. Mills), 1899.
101. For details of Hogan's Australasian adventures, see Abbott and Seroff, *Out of Sight*, pp. 130–37.
102. "The Stage," *Indianapolis Freeman*, August 11, 1900.
103. "New York Journal," quoted in "Stage," *Indianapolis Freeman*, September 1, 1900. It is possible this story was trumped up for publicity purposes. In the *Freeman* of March 29, 1902, columnist "I. McCorker" wrote: "During the race riot in New York a few summers ago, Hogan got his name in print oftener than any other unbleached American in Gotham . . . His name was 'up in the air' as it were."
104. *Bridgeport Standard*, quoted in "The Stage," *Indianapolis Freeman*, October 31, 1903.
105. *New York World*, quoted in "The Stage," *Indianapolis Freeman*, July 8, 1905.
106. Sylvester Russell, "General Stage Gossip," *Indianapolis Freeman*, August 19, 1905.
107. Sylvester Russell, "How Actors Figured at the Business League," *Indianapolis Freeman*, September 2, 1905.
108. "Sylvester Russell Notes," *Indianapolis Freeman*, November 4, 1905. Tom Fletcher's fascinating but occasionally unreliable history, *100 Years in Show Business* (New York: Burdge & Company Ltd, 1954), includes an inscrutable chapter on the Memphis Students.
109. Carle B. Cooke, "New York Stage Comments," *Indianapolis Freeman*, October 14, 1905.
110. Carle B. Cooke, "Professional News Notes," *Indianapolis Freeman*, October 21, 1905.
111. P. B. Ross Hendrix, "Chicago Notes," *Indianapolis Freeman*, November 25, 1905.
112. Sylvester Russell, "The Vocal Music of Three Great Composers," *Indianapolis Freeman*, November 10, 1906.

113. "The Stage," *Indianapolis Freeman*, November 18, 1905.
114. Sylvester Russell, "Ernest Hogan Goes West," *Indianapolis Freeman*, March 24, 1906.
115. Sylvester Russell, "Ernest Hogan in New York," *Indianapolis Freeman*, February 17, 1906.
116. "'Rufus Rastus' at the Majestic," *Brooklyn Citizen*, undated clipping (courtesy Ray Buckberry).
117. R. W. Thompson, "Tom Logan," *Indianapolis Freeman*, September 29, 1906.
118. "The Stage," *Indianapolis Freeman*, January 28, 1899.
119. "Stage," *Indianapolis Freeman*, September 7, 1901.
120. "Stage," *Indianapolis Freeman*, April 5, 1902.
121. "The Stage," *Indianapolis Freeman*, July 23, 1904.
122. "The Rufus Rastus Company In Indianapolis," *Indianapolis Freeman*, September 29, 1906.
123. Ernest Hogan, "The Negro in Vaudeville," *Variety*, December 15, 1906.
124. "Ernest Hogan Home," *Variety*, May 4, 1907.
125. "The Oyster Man," *Indianapolis Freeman*, November 2, 1907.
126. Lester Walton, "Ernest Hogan Compelled to Quit on Account of General Breakdown," *New York Age*, quoted in *Indianapolis Freeman*, January 25, 1908.
127. "The Stage," *Indianapolis Freeman*, September 10, 1898.
128. W. Milton Lewis, "Pencilings," *Indianapolis Freeman*, March 31, 1906.
129. Helen Green, "Snowflake Makes Her Brown Legs Fly," clipping from unidentified New York City newspaper, n.d., probably early February 1906 (courtesy Ray Buckberry).
130. Sylvester Russell, "Ernest Hogan in New York," *Indianapolis Freeman*, February 17, 1906.
131. "The Oysterman," *Indianapolis Freeman*, November 2, 1907.
132. The reference work *American Musical Theatre—A Chronicle* (Oxford University Press, 2001) mistakenly asserts that Hogan always refused to perform in blackface.
133. "SIWEL," "Rambling," *Indianapolis Freeman*, April 10, 1909.
134. Sylvester Russell, "Ernest Hogan Sleeps His Final Sleep," *Indianapolis Freeman*, May 29, 1909.
135. Columnist Charles D. Marshall noted snidely in the *Freeman* of February 15, 1908: "It is stated that Ernest Hogan was baptized in the Catholic church a few days ago. Being done with airships, he took to the water."
136. Lester A. Walton, "Death of Ernest Hogan," *New York Age*, May 27, 1909.
137. "News of the Players," *Indianapolis Freeman*, October 6, 1917; "A Tribute to Ernest Hogan," *Indianapolis Freeman*, October 6, 1917.
138. Bowling Green historian Ray Buckberry has recently made efforts to get Ernest Hogan a Kentucky State Historical marker.
139. George W. Walker, "The Real 'Coon' on the American Stage," *The Theatre Magazine*, August 1906, reprinted in liner notes to *Bert Williams: The Early Years, 1901–1909* (Archeophone Records CD ARCH-5004), 2004.
140. An overall sense of Williams and Walker's career can be assimilated from three successive biographies of Bert Williams: Mabel Rowland, *Bert Williams: Son of Laughter*, 1923; Ann Charters, *Nobody: The Story of Bert Williams* (London: Macmillan, 1970); and Eric Ledell Smith, *Bert Williams: A Biography of the Pioneer Black Comedian* (Jefferson: McFarland & Company, 1992). The various Williams and Walker productions are especially well described by Smith.
141. "I. McCorker," "Minstrels, Comedians and Singers," *Indianapolis Freeman*, May 31, 1902.
142. "The Stage," *Indianapolis Freeman*, March 13, 1897.
143. "Koster & Bial's," *New York Clipper*, November 26, 1898.
144. Sylvester Russell, "An Hour With The Walkers," *Indianapolis Freeman*, September 23, 1905.
145. "The Stage," *Indianapolis Freeman*, February 17, 1900.
146. "Abyssinia's Star Actress," *Indianapolis Freeman*, October 6, 1906.
147. She was identified as Aida in the *Freeman* of November 30, 1907. The *Freeman* of February 15, 1908, mentioned "Aida Overton Walker—who used to be Ada."
148. "The Phrenologist Coon," Victor 992, Monarch 992; "My Little Zulu Babe," Monarch 1084;

"In My Castle on the River Nile," Victor 991, Monarch 991. Bert Williams's complete recorded output is reissued on Archeophone CDs ARCH 5002–5004.

149. Sylvester Russell, "A Review of the Stage," *Indianapolis Freeman*, December 28, 1901.
150. Deep River Boys, "Castle on the Nile," Pilotone 5153, circa 1946, reissued on Waldorf LP 33-108. Other recorded versions include Camp Hill Male Quartet, "My Castle on the Nile," V-Disc 469, circa 1944, and Wonder State Harmonists (a white string band), "My Castle on the Nile," Vocalion 5346, 1928.
151. J. W. Johnson, Bob Cole and Rosamond Johnson, "My Castle on the Nile" (New York: Jos. W. Stern & Co.), 1901.
152. J. Harry Jackson, "Stage," *Indianapolis Freeman*, October 25, 1902.
153. J. D. Howard, "The Williams & Walker Show," *Indianapolis Freeman*, December 27, 1902.
154. Williams recorded "All Going Out and Nothing Coming In" for Victor in 1901 (reissued on Archeophone CD 5004).
155. "Stage," *Indianapolis Freeman*, February 7, 1903.
156. "Stage," *Indianapolis Freeman*, February 28, 1903.
157. "The Stage," *Indianapolis Freeman*, July 4, 1903.
158. Sylvester Russell, "A Word Endowed Prominent Stage Factors And Renown," *Indianapolis Freeman*, October 1, 1904.
159. Sylvester Russell, "Sylvester Russell Notes," *Indianapolis Freeman*, October 14, 1905.
160. Sylvester Russell, "The Mistakes of Williams and Walker," *Indianapolis Freeman*, April 14, 1906.
161. Williams recorded "Nobody" for Columbia in 1906 and again in 1913.
162. "Dorothy," "Williams and Walker Glee Club," *Indianapolis Freeman*, October, 20, 1906.
163. See Abbott and Seroff, *Out of Sight*, pp. 293, 307, for more information concerning Edith Pond's Midnight Stars.
164. See Dixon, Godrich, & Rye, *Blues and Gospel Records, 1890–1943*, 4th Ed. (Oxford: Oxford University Press, 1997), pp. 244–45. The complete recorded output is reissued on Document DOCD-5356.
165. "The Stage," *Indianapolis Freeman*, August 19, 1905. One of the sixteen members' names is missing from this report.
166. Sylvester Russell, "Gotham Stage Gossip," *Indianapolis Freeman*, September 9, 1905.
167. "The Passing of Negro Dialect," *Indianapolis Freeman*, April 27, 1907.
168. Sylvester Russell, "The Mistakes of Williams and Walker," *Indianapolis Freeman*, April 14, 1906.
169. "Indianapolis Has Seen Bandana Land," *Indianapolis Freeman*, February 13, 1909.
170. Burton M. Beach, "Williams And Walker A Hit In New York," *Indianapolis Freeman*, February 15, 1908.
171. "Booker T. Washington Sees 'Bandana Land,'" *Indianapolis Freeman*, February 15, 1908.
172. "Dr. Washington Likes Bert Williams' Work," *Chicago Broad Ax*, October 1, 1910.
173. J. D. Howard, "Bandana Land And Its People," *Indianapolis Freeman*, February 20, 1909.
174. "Dorothy," "Women In Bandanna Land," *Indianapolis Freeman*, February 13, 1909.
175. "National and Local Theatrical and Stage Notes," *Chicago Broad Ax*, September 30, 1911.
176. Sylvester Russell, "Mr. Cole and the Johnsons," *Indianapolis Freeman*, August 16, 1902.
177. "I. McCorker," "Minstrels, Comedians and Singers," *Indianapolis Freeman*, May 31, 1902.
178. For information on Sam T. Jack's Creole Burlesque Company, 1891–1895, see Abbott and Seroff, *Out of Sight*, pp. 151–70.
179. See Abbott and Seroff, *Out of Sight*, pp. 386–88, for more on Billy Jackson's Minstrels' 1894–1895 engagement at Worth's Museum.
180. "Vaudeville and Minstrel," *New York Clipper*, May 29, 1897.
181. "Vaudeville and Minstrel," *New York Clipper*, June 12, 1897. The story of Cole vs. Voeckel and Nolan is recounted by Juli Jones Jr. in "The Nervous Breakdown of Mr. George Walker, The Famous Comedian," *Indianapolis Freeman*, March 20, 1909.
182. Alec Johnson, "Mysterious Coon," Columbia 14378-D, 1928, reissued on *Mississippi String Bands and Associates, 1928–1931* (Document BDCD-6013).
183. "The Stage," *Indianapolis Freeman*, March 11, 1899.

184. "A Trip to Coontown," *Indianapolis Freeman*, December 30, 1899.
185. "Stage," *Indianapolis Freeman*, October 20, 1900.
186. A January 13, 1906, report in *Variety* placed Billy Johnson at Keeney's Theater in New York: "The ex-member of the Cole and Johnson combination is supported by four colored girls . . . The act opens in a jungle scene . . . Johnson next does a plantation song before a cornfield drop . . . a ballroom scene closes the sketch . . . 'Evolution of the Negro' is the title." Johnson died on September 12, 1916, in an apparent fall from the balcony of the Pioneer Club on State Street in Chicago. In a eulogy in the *Freeman* of September 23, 1916, Sylvester Russell described a large funeral, with James "Slap" White presiding at the organ.
187. Sylvester Russell, "Mr. Cole and the Johnsons," *Indianapolis Freeman*, August 16, 1902.
188. "Stage," *Indianapolis Freeman*, November 8, 1902.
189. A. H. Reed, "Cole And Johnson," *Indianapolis Freeman*, January 3, 1903.
190. "The Co-Stars Who Will Present New Musical Comedy," *Indianapolis Freeman*, July 7, 1906.
191. "Cole and Johnson Show," *Indianapolis Freeman*, March 23, 1907.
192. "'Starring' No Joke," *Indianapolis Freeman*, April 20, 1907.
193. "The Stage," *Indianapolis Freeman*, October 27, 1906.
194. "Cole and Johnson in 'The Red Moon,'" *Indianapolis Freeman*, November 14, 1908.
195. "Cole and Johnson's Red Moon Co.," *Indianapolis Freeman*, December 26, 1908; J. D. Howard, "Cole and Johnson," *Indianapolis Freeman*, November 21, 1908.
196. J. D. Howard, "Cole and Johnson," *Indianapolis Freeman*, November 21, 1908.
197. "The Red Moon Show," *Indianapolis Freeman*, October 24, 1908.
198. J. D. Howard, "Cole and Johnson," *Indianapolis Freeman*, November 21, 1908.
199. Cary [*sic*] B. Lewis, "Cole And Johnson At Avenue Theater, Louisville," *Indianapolis Freeman*, November 28, 1908.
200. Sylvester Russell, "Eighth Annual Review," *Indianapolis Freeman*, January 9, 1909.
201. "Wealth Of The Stage People," *Indianapolis Freeman*, March 27, 1909.
202. *Indianapolis Freeman*, July 17, 1909; "Sylvester Russell's Review," *Indianapolis Freeman*, September 25, 1909; "Tribbles [*sic*] Is Very Much Missed," *Indianapolis Freeman*, December 25, 1909.
203. Sylvester Russell, "Cole And Johnson Make A Hit In The Red Moon," *Indianapolis Freeman*, November 27, 1909.
204. "'The Red Moon,'" *Indianapolis Freeman*, December 18, 1909.
205. Sylvester Russell, "Tenth Annual Review," *Indianapolis Freeman*, December 25, 1909.
206. "Red Moonbeams," *Indianapolis Freeman*, December 25, 1909.
207. Sylvester Russell, "Welcome Death! Slogan of Robert Cole," *Indianapolis Freeman*, August 12, 1911.
208. Aida Overton Walker continued in mainstream vaudeville. The *Freeman* of May 16, 1914, placed her at Hammerstein's in New York, where she and Lackey Grant "offered the prevailing ballroom dancing act" backed by "their own colored orchestra. But their turn differs from their Caucasian contemporaries in that they open with the Maxine [*sic*] and the Hesitation Tango to follow. Then comes the Negro Drag and finally what is called a Jiggeree." The *Freeman* of October 17, 1914 broke the news of her unexpected death: "Mrs. Walker had been ill with a nervous breakdown for about a week."

Notes to Part II: The Spirit of the Smart Set

1. *Sydney Referee*, July 12, 1899. For information on Hogan and McClain's activities during the 1890s, see Abbott and Seroff, *Out of Sight*.
2. *Pacific Commercial Advertiser*, quoted in "Stage," *Indianapolis Freeman*, March 29, 1902.
3. "SIWEL," "Ernest Hogan Dead," *Indianapolis Freeman*, May 29, 1909.

4. *Oxford English Dictionary* (Oxford: Clarendon Press), second edition, 1989, vol. 15, p. 776.
5. "Stage," *Indianapolis Freeman*, November 8, 1902.
6. The recordings of the Dinwiddie Quartet are reissued on Document DOCD-5061 and DOCD-5288. For information on the Dinwiddie Quartet, see Tim Brooks, *Lost Sounds: Blacks and the Birth of the Recording Industry, 1890–1919* (Urbana: University of Illinois Press, 2004), pp. 155–59.
7. "Stage," *Indianapolis Freeman*, November 15, 1902.
8. Sylvester Russell, "'Smart Set' in New York," *Indianapolis Freeman*, November 22, 1902.
9. "Stage," *Indianapolis Freeman*, March 21, 1903.
10. Juli Jones Jr., "The Nervous Breakdown of Mr. George W. Walker, the Famous Comedian," *Indianapolis Freeman*, March 20, 1909.
11. Sylvester Russell, "Ernest Hogan Sleeps His Final Sleep," *Indianapolis Freeman*, May 29, 1909. There may have also been a financial motive for Hogan's decision to leave the Smart Set. A "Notice" in the *New York Times*, February 7, 1903, said, "Ernest Hogan, showman and actor, who resides at 136 West Fifty-Third Street, has filed a petition in bankruptcy, with liabilities to the amount of $6,324 and no assets."
12. Will Milton Lewis, "The 'Smart Set,'" *Indianapolis Freeman*, March 18, 1905.
13. For information on McIntosh's 1890s career, see Abbott and Seroff, *Out of Sight*.
14. *Columbus Press*, quoted in "The Stage," *Indianapolis Freeman*, November 18, 1899.
15. Sylvester Russell, "Smart Set In Hartford," *Indianapolis Freeman*, October 24, 1903.
16. "A Southern Paper Praises," *Indianapolis Freeman*, November 28, 1903.
17. "The Stage," *Indianapolis Freeman*, January 16, 1904.
18. "The Stage," *Indianapolis Freeman*, December 19, 1903.
19. "Crescent Theatre," *New Orleans Daily Picayune*, November 15, 1903.
20. "'The Smart Set' at the Crescent Theatre," *New Orleans Daily Picayune*, November 16, 1903.
21. "Amusements," *New Orleans Daily Picayune*, November 19, 1903.
22. J. Ed Green, "Obsequies of Tom McIntosh," *Indianapolis Freeman*, March 12, 1904.
23. R. W. Thompson, "Dudley In The 'Spotlight,'" *Indianapolis Freeman*, February 9, 1907.
24. "Comedian of Texas Birth," *Indianapolis Freeman*, March 26, 1910. Race recordings of the title Dudley reportedly sang on the street corners of Dallas include "These Bones Goin' Rise Again," The Jubilee Gospel Team, QRS 7013 and Paramount 12835, 1928, reissued on Document DOCD-5591; "Dese Bones Gonna Rise Again," Golden Gate Jubilee Quartet, Bluebird 8123, 1939; "Dese Bones Gwine Rise Again," Bronzemen, Standard Program Library U143 (ET), 1939, reissued on Document DOCD-5501; "Eva and Adam [*sic*]," Selah Jubilee Quartet, Continental 6037, 1946; "Dese Bones Shall Rise Again," 4 Knights, Langworth VGS 40 (ET); and "Them Bones Shall Rise Again," Silver Echo Quartet, Arco 1201, 1949. A parody version, "G. Burns Is Gonna Rise Again" was recorded in Memphis in 1928 by T. C. Johnson and "Blue Coat" Tom Nelson, Okeh 8577 (as by Johnson-Nelson-Porkchop). Hillbilly recordings include John D. Foster, "These Bones Gwine Rise Again," Gennett 6976, 1929; Arthur Cornwall and John Gibson, "My Bones Is Gonna Rise Again," Champion 16379, 1931; David McCarn and Howard Long, "My Bone's Gonna Rise Again," Victor 23577, 1931 (as by Dave & Howard); and several versions by Frank and James McCravy (see Meade pp. 68–69).
25. *New York Clipper*, January 2, 1897.
26. "The Stage," *Indianapolis Freeman*, December 25, 1897.
27. "The Stage," *Indianapolis Freeman*, June 10, 1899.
28. "The Stage," *Indianapolis Freeman*, October 14, 1899; November 18, 1899.
29. "Stage," *Indianapolis Freeman*, April 27, 1901.
30. "Stage," *Indianapolis Freeman*, December 14, 1901.
31. "Stage," *Indianapolis Freeman*, February 8, 1902.
32. "Stage," Indianapolis Freeman, March 22, 1902; April 26, 1902.
33. "Stage," *Indianapolis Freeman*, April 19, 1902; April 26, 1902.
34. "Stage," *Indianapolis Freeman*, June 7, 1902; June 28, 1902.
35. "Stage," *Indianapolis Freeman*, August 9, 1902.

36. "Stage," *Indianapolis Freeman*, September 13, 1902. It was further noted that Dudley was "very much grieved, on reaching Shreveport . . . to learn that his father had been dead for nearly a year."
37. "Stage," *Indianapolis Freeman*, October 18, 1902.
38. "The Stage," *Indianapolis Freeman*, August 8, 1903.
39. "The Stage," *Indianapolis Freeman*, November 28, 1903.
40. "The Stage," *Indianapolis Freeman*, August 22, 1903.
41. Their marriage appears not to have been announced in the *Freeman*, but the edition of November 28, 1903, mentions "Mrs. Alberta Ormes-Dudley."
42. J. Ed Green, "Obsequies Of Tom McIntosh," *Indianapolis Freeman*, March 12, 1904.
43. "The Stage," *Indianapolis Freeman*, April 30, 1904; June 11, 1904.
44. Sylvester Russell, "'Smart Set' In Newburg," *Indianapolis Freeman*, October 15, 1904.
45. Sylvester Russell, "A Review of Mr. Dudley," *Indianapolis Freeman*, July 28, 1906.
46. "The Stage," *Indianapolis Freeman*, March 11, 1911.
47. "S. H. Dudley Head Of The Smart Set Fined One Dollar And Cost For Assaulting Sylvester Russell," *Chicago Broad Ax*, March 11, 1911.
48. Will Milton Lewis, "The 'Smart Set,'" *Indianapolis Freeman*, March 18, 1905.
49. Will Milton Lewis, "The 'Smart Set,'" *Indianapolis Freeman*, March 18, 1905.
50. "The 'Smart Set' Cullings," *Indianapolis Freeman*, November 12, 1904.
51. Will Milton Lewis, "The 'Smart Set,'" *Indianapolis Freeman*, March 18, 1905.
52. "Louisville's Weekly Events," *Indianapolis Freeman*, December 10, 1904.
53. W. Milton Lewis, "The Smart Set Company," *Indianapolis Freeman*, December 23, 1905.
54. "Smart Set Notes," *Indianapolis Freeman*, October 20, 1906.
55. "'The Smart Set' Coming To Park Theatre," *Indianapolis Freeman*, January 26, 1907.
56. "The Stage," *Indianapolis Freeman*, August 11, 1906.
57. "Smart Set Company," *Indianapolis Freeman*, November 17, 1906. James "Tim" Brymn remained an important contributor to Dudley's road-show enterprises for the next several years. In the spring of 1921 Tim Brymn and His Black Devil Orchestra recorded several jazz titles for the Okeh label. A *Billboard* report of April 16, 1921, made mention of the recording sessions while noting that Brymn's band of twenty-four pieces had begun its third season at the Hotel Shelburne, Brighton Beach, New York.
58. "The Smart Set," *Indianapolis Freeman*, October 6, 1906.
59. "Smart Set Notes," *Indianapolis Freeman*, October 20, 1906.
60. "Smart Set Notes," *Indianapolis Freeman*, November 24, 1906.
61. "Smart Set Notes," *Indianapolis Freeman*, November 3, 1906.
62. "Smart Set Company," *Indianapolis Freeman*, November 17, 1906.
63. "The Smart Set Presents 'Black Politician,'" *Indianapolis Freeman*, February 9, 1907.
64. Sylvester Russell, "The Black Politician," *Indianapolis Freeman*, April 6, 1907.
65. Eubie Blake, Joe Jordan, and Charles Thompson, "Old Black Crow," on *Golden Reunion in Ragtime*, Stereo Oddities LP 1900, 1962.
66. R. C. McPherson (Cecil Mack), Chris Smith, Billy B. Johnson, and Elmer Bowman, "All In, Down and Out (Sorry I Ain't Got It, You Could Get It, If I Had It)" (New York: Gotham-Attucks Music Company), 1906. For more on the Gotham-Attucks Music Publishing Company, see Wayne D. Shirley, "The House of Melody: A List of Publications of the Gotham-Attucks Music Company at the Library of Congress," *The Black Perspective in Music*, vol. 15, no. 1 (Spring 1987), pp. 79–112.
67. Bert Williams, "All In Down and Out," Columbia 30039, 1906; Blue Harmony Boys, "All In Down and Out," Paramount 12976, 1929, reissued on Document DOCD-5392.
68. Glen Alyn, *I Say Me for a Parable: The Oral Autobiography of Mance Lipscomb, Texas Bluesman*, 1993 (New York: Da Capo Press, 1994), pp. 42, 191.
69. Alyn, p. 191.
70. Tim E. Owsley, "Crown Garden," *Indianapolis Freeman*, January 13, 1912.

71. Jasper T. Taylor, "Chas. Geyer's Original Dandy Dixie Minstrels," *Indianapolis Freeman*, February 8, 1913.
72. The *Freeman* of September 23, 1916, carried an ad for "'Nobody Knows You When You're Down and Out.' Words and music by Jimmie Cox. Will be published by Williams & Piron, New Orleans, Louisiana."
73. "A Word From Mattie Dorsey," *Indianapolis Freeman*, April 24, 1920.
74. "The Smart Set Opens," *Indianapolis Freeman*, September 21, 1907; "The Smart Set," *Indianapolis Freeman*, November 16, 1907.
75. "The Smart People In Indianapolis," *Indianapolis Freeman*, January 2, 1909.
76. Sylvester Russell, "Opening Of The Smart Set," *Indianapolis Freeman*, October 12, 1907.
77. Juli Jones Jr., "The Smart Set In Chicago," *Indianapolis Freeman*, December 12, 1908.
78. "Smart Set Company," *Indianapolis Freeman*, March 7, 1908.
79. "Stage Notes," *Indianapolis Freeman*, November 22, 1919.
80. "The Stage," *Indianapolis Freeman*, October 10, 1908.
81. Sylvester Russell, "Eighth Annual Review," *Indianapolis Freeman*, January 9, 1909.
82. "The Smart People In Indianapolis," *Indianapolis Freeman*, January 2, 1909.
83. Sylvester Russell, "S. H. Dudley, In 'His Honor, The Barber,'" *Indianapolis Freeman*, January 8, 1910.
84. Bradford, "S. H. Dudley, His Honor, The Barber, And Company," *Indianapolis Freeman*, September 18, 1909.
85. Herbert Everett Amos, "Who Is Who, What And Why, In 'His Honor, The Barber,'" *Indianapolis Freeman*, October 9, 1909.
86. Sylvester Russell, "S. H. Dudley, In 'His Honor, The Barber,'" *Indianapolis Freeman*, January 8, 1910.
87. "Here At Last—'The Smart Set,'" *Indianapolis Freeman*, March 11, 1911; "Dorothy," "Last Week With The Smart Set Company," *Indianapolis Freeman*, April 1, 1911.
88. Sylvester Russell, "The Smart Set In Chicago," *Indianapolis Freeman*, December 10, 1910.
89. "The 'Smart Set' Company," *Indianapolis Freeman*, February 4, 1911.
90. "The Smart Set Company In Indianapolis," *Indianapolis Freeman*, March 18, 1911.
91. "Artie," "Among Player-Folk And Musicians In Washington," *Indianapolis Freeman*, May 4, 1912.
92. R. W. Thompson, "Dudley In The 'Spotlight,'" *Indianapolis Freeman*, February 9, 1907.
93. W. Milton Lewis, "The Smart Set Company," *Indianapolis Freeman*, December 23, 1905.
94. The *Indianapolis Freeman* of December 2, 1911, notified that Whitney "celebrated the anniversary of his thirty-fifth birthday November 15 while in McAlister, Okla."
95. "Notes," *Indianapolis Freeman*, August 6, 1910.
96. "The Stage," *Indianapolis Freeman*, October 9, 1897.
97. "Stage," *Indianapolis Freeman*, October 19, 1901.
98. Salem Tutt Whitney, "Seen and Heard While Passing," *Indianapolis Freeman*, November 7, 1914.
99. "Miscellaneous," *New York Clipper*, June 8, 1901.
100. "Stage," *Indianapolis Freeman*, October 19, 1901.
101. "Stage," *Indianapolis Freeman*, November 29, 1902.
102. "The Stage," *Indianapolis Freeman*, April 2, 1904.
103. "The Stage," *Indianapolis Freeman*, August 12, 1905.
104. "The Stage," *Indianapolis Freeman*, May 13, 1905.
105. S. Tutt Whitney, "S. Tutt Whitney Makes Statement," *Indianapolis Freeman*, January 16, 1909. Original "Puggsley Brothers Tennessee Warblers" member R. C. Puggsley and his talented sons Richmond and Charles H. Puggsley were from Nashville, Tennessee. The 1880 U.S. Census (Davidson County ED 49, P 200), and the 1887 Nashville City Directory both spell the family name Pugsley, while the *Freeman* invariably spells it Puggsley.
106. "The Stage," *Indianapolis Freeman*, August 7, 1909.
107. *Chattanooga Daily Times*, April 2, 1908, quoted in "Black Patti's Dusky Crowd," *Indianapolis Freeman*, April 11, 1908.
108. "Black Patti Troubadours," *Indianapolis Freeman*, August 22, 1908.
109. "Death Of Emma Baynard Whitney," *Indianapolis Freeman*, November 21, 1908.
110. "Lincoln Theater, Knoxville, Tenn," *Indianapolis Freeman*, March 20, 1909.

111. S. Tutt Whitney, "A White Manager With A Colored Show Through The South," *Indianapolis Freeman*, December 28, 1912.
112. "Whitney Stock Company," *Indianapolis Freeman*, June 26, 1909.
113. "The Southern Smart Set Co.," *Indianapolis Freeman*, October 16, 1909.
114. Salem Tutt Whitney, "Seen and Heard While Passing," *Indianapolis Freeman*, November 27, 1920.
115. "The Southern Smart Set Co.," *Indianapolis Freeman*, October 16, 1909.
116. "Southern Smart Set At Denison," *Indianapolis Freeman*, October 23, 1909.
117. "The Southern Smart Set Co.," *Indianapolis Freeman*, October 9, 1909.
118. "Temple Theater," *New Orleans Item*, November 18, 1909; Tim Owsley, "Whitney Musical Comedy Co.," *Indianapolis Freeman*, March 12, 1910; "Temple Theater," *New Orleans Item*, November 18, 1909. Compare the information given in these citations with Zulu Club historian John E. Rousseau's oral history–driven account of the club's origins: "Early in 1909, a group of laborers, who had organized a club named 'The Tramps,' went to the Pythian Temple Theatre to see a musical comedy performed by the Smart Set. The Comedy included . . . a skit about a Zulu tribe . . . As soon as the 'Tramps' saw the skit, they put their heads together in a woodshed on Perdido Street and emerged as 'Zulus.'" See also Lynn Abbott, "Remembering Mr. E. Belfield Spriggins, 'First Man of Jazzology,'" *78 Quarterly*, no. 10 (n.d.), pp. 49–50.
119. "Whitney Musical Comedy Co.," *Indianapolis Freeman*, April 2, 1910.
120. "Whitney Musical Comedy Company Goes To The East," *Indianapolis Freeman*, June 18, 1910; S. Tutt Whitney, "Retrospection," *Indianapolis Freeman*, July 9, 1910.
121. "'Smart Set' Co. (Southern)," *Indianapolis Freeman*, October 15, 1910.
122. "'Smart Set' Co. (Southern)," *Indianapolis Freeman*, October 15, 1910.
123. "Smart Set Company (Southern) Enroute," *Indianapolis Freeman*, December 10, 1910.
124. S. Tutt Whitney, "'The Show's The Thing.' Southern Playhouses," *Indianapolis Freeman*, October 1, 1910.
125. S. Tutt Whitney, "Seen and Heard While Passing," *Indianapolis Freeman*, February 24, 1912.
126. Whitney also wrote a column for the *Chicago Defender*, basically continuing what he had begun in the *Freeman*, from 1918 until just a few days before his death on February 17, 1934.
127. S. Tutt Whitney, "Seen and Heard While Passing," *Indianapolis Freeman*, September 16, 1911.
128. S. Tutt Whitney, "Seen and Heard While Passing," *Indianapolis Freeman*, May 18, 1912.
129. S. Tutt Whitney, "Seen and Heard While Passing," *Indianapolis Freeman*, December 23, 1911.
130. S. Tutt Whitney, "Seen and Heard While Passing," *Indianapolis Freeman*, October 14, 1911.
131. S. Tutt Whitney, "Seen and Heard While Passing," *Indianapolis Freeman*, February 24, 1912.
132. "Southern Smart Set Company," *Indianapolis Freeman*, September 7, 1912; "Smart Set Company Notes," *Indianapolis Freeman*, September 21, 1912.
133. "Smart Set Company Notes," *Indianapolis Freeman*, September 21, 1912.
134. S. Tutt Whitney, "Seen And Heard While Passing," *Indianapolis Freeman*, November 16, 1912. Born in Charleston, South Carolina, in 1876, Leigh Whipper went on to a very long, successful career as a stage and movie actor. An article in the *Memphis World* of August 17, 1943, recalls that he played "'Crooks,' the old field hand" in both the stage and screen versions of *Of Mice and Men*, and that "his most notable characterization was that of Haile Selassie in 'Mission to Moscow.'" He was yet living in 1964, when Marshall Stearns interviewed him in connection with *Jazz Dance*.
135. "The Smart Set," *Nashville Globe*, December 27, 1912.
136. Salem Tutt Whitney, "Seen And Heard While Passing," *Indianapolis Freeman*, September 27, 1913.
137. Salem Tutt Whitney, "Seen And Heard While Passing," *Indianapolis Freeman*, August 22, 1914.
138. "Ar-W-Tee," "The Passing Show In Washington," *Indianapolis Freeman*, September 5, 1914.
139. Salem Tutt Whitney, "Seen And Heard While Passing," *Indianapolis Freeman*, December 12, 1914.

140. Salem Tutt Whitney, "Seen and Heard While Passing," *Indianapolis Freeman*, February 6, 1915.
141. Salem Tutt Whitney, "Seen and Heard While Passing," *Indianapolis Freeman*, May 29, 1915.
142. Sylvester Russell, "Salem Tutt Whitney and the Smart Set Company Triumph at the Grand," *Indianapolis Freeman*, January 1, 1916.
143. Salem Tutt Whitney, "Seen And Heard While Passing," *Indianapolis Freeman*, December 12, 1914.
144. "Alexander Tolliver's Big Show," *Indianapolis Freeman*, November 27, 1915. A list of all performers known to have traveled with Tolliver's Big Show from 1914 through 1918 appears as Appendix I.
145. S. H. Dudley, "A Great Show, Says S. H. Dudley," *Indianapolis Freeman*, July 31, 1915.
146. Salem Tutt Whitney, "Seen and Heard While Passing," *Indianapolis Freeman*, December 4, 1915.
147. When he registered with the Selective Service System in 1917, Tolliver gave his date of birth as July 4, 1887. See World War I Selective Service System Draft Registration Cards, 1917–1918 (Ancestry.com).
148. "Downie's Uncle Tom's Cabin Company," *Indianapolis Freeman*, April 18, 1908.
149. "Cobby," "Philadelphia Stage Letter," *Indianapolis Freeman*, October 2, 1909.
150. Sylvester Russell, "Chicago," *Indianapolis Freeman*, December 31, 1910.
151. "The Auditorium Theater, Philadelphia, Pa.," *Indianapolis Freeman*, November 9, 1912.
152. "The Tolliver Trio," *Indianapolis Freeman*, December 21, 1912.
153. "P. G. Lowery's Dixie Fashion Plate Minstrels," *Indianapolis Freeman*, December 6, 1913.
154. "Lowerc's [*sic*] Dixie Fashion Plate Minstrels," *Indianapolis Freeman*, January 24, 1914.
155. "Gossip Of The Stage," *Indianapolis Freeman*, February 14, 1914.
156. Marshall Stearns interview with Leola "Coot" Grant, Whitesboro, New Jersey, November 5, 1959 (Center for Jazz Studies, Rutgers University).
157. "C. W. Park's Musical Comedy Company," *Indianapolis Freeman*, November 7, 1914.
158. "C. W. Parks-Tolliver Musical Comedy Company," *Indianapolis Freeman*, November 28, 1914. In a "silver shower," nickels and dimes were tossed onto the stage by an appreciative audience.
159. There may be some confusion here, as the Morton Theater was a well-known black vaudeville house, not in Atlanta but in Athens, Georgia.
160. C. Shawl, "Butter Beans & Susie," *Cart*, May 1964, p. 11.
161. Al Wells, "Alexander Tolliver's Big Show," *Indianapolis Freeman*, September 25, 1915.
162. Undated letter from Berta Wood to Marshall Stearns (Center for Jazz Studies, Rutgers University).
163. Al Wells, "Tolliver's Big Show," *Indianapolis Freeman*, July 17, 1915.
164. Marshall and Jean Stearns, *Jazz Dance* (New York: Schirmer, 1968), p. 110.
165. See Lynn Abbott and Doug Seroff, "Bessie Smith: The Early Years," *Blues & Rhythm* no. 70 (June 1992), pp. 8–11.
166. Frankie Jaxon's recordings, originally made for Okeh, Gennett, Vocalion, Decca, and other labels, are reissued on Document CDs DOCD-5073, 5074, 5076, 5258, 5259, and 5260.
167. Al Wells, "Alexander Tolliver's Big Show," *Indianapolis Freeman*, November 13, 1915.
168. Al Wells, "Alexander Tolliver's Big Show," *Indianapolis Freeman*, April 29, 1916.
169. Charles Edward Smith, "Ma Rainey and the Minstrels," *The Record Changer* vol. 14, no. 6 (1955), p. 5.
170. A. Wells, "Tolliver's Musical Comedy Company," *Indianapolis Freeman*, June 12, 1915.
171. Al Wells, "Tolliver's Big Show," *Indianapolis Freeman*, August 28, 1915.
172. Al Wells, "Alexander Tolliver's Big Show," *Indianapolis Freeman*, September 25, 1915.
173. Al Wells, "Alexander Tolliver's Big Show," *Indianapolis Freeman*, September 25, 1915.
174. Al Wells, "Alexander Tolliver's Big Show," *Indianapolis Freeman*, October 30, 1915.
175. Al Wells, "Alexander Tolliver's Big Show," *Indianapolis Freeman*, October 23, 1915. Ma Rainey was not the first to be associated with this slogan. The *Freeman* of January 14, 1911, mentions the male comedy team of "Dude" Kelley and Amon

Davis, "assassinators of the blues, as they style themselves."

176. Al Wells, "Alexander Tolliver's Big Show," *Indianapolis Freeman*, November 6, 1915.
177. Alexander Tolliver, "Answering Mr. Whitney's Success and the Reason Why," *Indianapolis Freeman*, November 27, 1915.
178. "Alexander Tolliver's Big Show," *Indianapolis Freeman*, November 20, 1915.
179. Al Wells, "Alexander Tolliver's Big Show," *Indianapolis Freeman*, December 4, 1915.
180. Al Wells, "Alexander Tolliver's Big Show," *Indianapolis Freeman*, December 4, 1915; "Alexander Tolliver's Big Show," *Indianapolis Freeman*, December 11, 1915. In show business lingo, when "the ghost walked," everyone got paid. Two different explanations of the term are cited in Abbott and Seroff, *Out of Sight*, p. 471, n50.
181. "Alexander Tolliver's Big Show," *Indianapolis Freeman*, November 20, 1915.
182. Al Wells, "Alexander Tolliver's Big Show," *Indianapolis Freeman*, December 18, 1915.
183. Al Wells, "Alexander Tolliver's Big Show," *Indianapolis Freeman*, January 15, 1916.
184. Al Wells, "Alexander Tolliver's Big Show," *Indianapolis Freeman*, January 8, 1916.
185. Al Wells, "Alexander Tolliver's Big Show," *Indianapolis Freeman*, January 29, 1916.
186. Al Wells, "Alex Tolliver's Big Show," *Indianapolis Freeman*, February 5, 1916.
187. Al Wells, "Alexander Tolliver's Big Show," *Indianapolis Freeman*, December 18, 1915; January 15, 1916.
188. Al Wells, "Alex Tolliver's Big Show," *Indianapolis Freeman*, February 26, 1916.
189. As reported in Al Rose and Edmond Souchon, *New Orleans Jazz: A Family Album* (Baton Rouge: Louisiana State University Press, 1967) p. 64.
190. "Cotton Club Orchestra," *Chicago Defender*, April 4, 1925.
191. Lee Collins, *Oh, Didn't He Ramble* (Chicago: University of Illinois Press, 1989), pp. 47, 48.
192. Bill Russell interview with Willie Hightower, June 3, 1958 (Hogan Jazz Archive, Tulane University).
193. Daisy Martin's 1921–1923 recordings were originally issued on Gennett, Okeh, and Banner and have been reissued on Document DOCD-5522 and DOCD-5602.
194. Al Wells, "Alex Tolliver's Big Show," *Indianapolis Freeman*, March 4, 1916.
195. Al Wells, "Alexander Tolliver's Big Show," *Indianapolis Freeman*, March 11, 1916.
196. Al Wells, "Alex Tolliver's Big Show," *Indianapolis Freeman*, March 18, 1916.
197. Al Wells, "Alex Tolliver's Big Show," *Indianapolis Freeman*, March 25, 1916.
198. Al Wells, "Alexander Toliver's Big Show" [*sic*], *Indianapolis Freeman*, April 22, 1916.
199. Al Wells, "Alexander Tolliver's Big Show," *Indianapolis Freeman*, April 8, 1916.
200. Salem Tutt Whitney, "Seen and Heard While Passing," *Indianapolis Freeman*, October 7, 1916.
201. Al Wells, "Alexander Tolliver's Big Show," *Indianapolis Freeman*, April 15, 1916. The Hill Sisters featured young Ethel Purnsley, known at the time as "Mama Stringbeans," and later as Ethel Waters.
202. Al Wells, "Alexander Tolliver's Big Show," *Indianapolis Freeman*, April 22, 1916.
203. *Indianapolis Freeman*, August 19, 1916, quoted in Lynn Abbott, "'Brown Skin, Who You For?' Another Look at Clarence Williams' Early Career," *The Jazz Archivist*, vol. 8, no. 1–2 (December 1993), p. 10.
204. "Notes From New Orleans, La.," *Indianapolis Freeman*, October 28, 1916.
205. Al Wells, "Alexander Tolliver's Big Show," *Indianapolis Freeman*, April 29, 1916; May 6, 1916.
206. Al Wells, "Alexander Tolliver's Big Show," *Indianapolis Freeman*, May 13, 1916.
207. Al Wells, "Alexander Tolliver's Big Show," *Indianapolis Freeman*, May 20, 1916.
208. Al Wells, "Alexander Tolliver's Big Show," *Indianapolis Freeman*, May 27, 1916.
209. L. Walton, "Wooden's Bontons," *Indianapolis Freeman*, July 29, 1916.
210. Al Wells, "Alexander Tolliver's Big Show," *Indianapolis Freeman*, June 17, 1916.
211. Al Wells, "Alexander Tolliver's Big Show," *Indianapolis Freeman*, July 1, 1916.
212. Al Wells, "Alexander Tolliver's Big Show," *Indianapolis Freeman*, July 8, 1916.

213. Al Wells, "Alexander Tolliver's Big Show," *Indianapolis Freeman*, July 22, 1916.
214. Presumably, Prof. Wm Burton was one and the same as William E. "Buddy" Burton, the storied Paramount/Gennett recording artist of the 1920s.
215. Al Wells, "Alexander Tolliver's Big Show," *Indianapolis Freeman*, July 29, 1916.
216. Al Wells, "Alexander Tolliver's Big Show," *Indianapolis Freeman*, August 12, 1916. "Down Home Blues" was a popularly recorded title of the 1920s. Daisy Martin recorded "Everybody's Man Is My Man" in 1921 (Okeh 8008, reissued on Document DOCD-5522).
217. Al Wells, "Alexander Tolliver's Big Show," *Indianapolis Freeman*, August 5, 1916; August 12, 1916. A review in the *Freeman* of October 16, 1915, identified the Two Musical Seminoles as "Paul Sims and little son," with "their tuneful selections on the xylophone, bells, mandolin and guitar. Mr. Sims' typical Indian song and eccentric comedy and the 'pappooses' dancing specialty are features that 'take.'" In the *Freeman* of September 30, 1916, Al Wells reported that the Two Musical Seminoles were leaving Tolliver's Big Show to go "to New York City to make records for Columbia Phonograph Company." It is not known whether any recordings were actually made. The *Chicago Defender* of September 3, 1927, notified that "Paul Seminole" had recently died in Philadelphia: "His son is now playing in a local orchestra in the Quaker City."
218. Al Wells, "Alexander Tolliver's Big Show," *Indianapolis Freeman*, September 9, 1916.
219. Al Wells, "Alexander Tolliver's Big Show," *Indianapolis Freeman*, September 9, 1916.
220. Al Wells, "Alexander Tolliver's Big Show," *Indianapolis Freeman*, September 16, 1916.
221. Al Wells, "Alexander Tolliver's Big Show," *Indianapolis Freeman*, October 7, 1916.
222. Al Wells, "Alexander Tolliver's Big Show," *Indianapolis Freeman*, October 14, 1916.
223. Al Wells, "Alexander Tolliver's Big Show," *Indianapolis Freeman*, October 21, 1916.
224. James White, "Morning Noon and Night" (Chicago: Will Rossiter), 1916.
225. Al Wells, "Alexander Tolliver's Big Show," *Indianapolis Freeman*, November 4, 1916.
226. Al Wells, "Alexander Tolliver's Big Show," *Indianapolis Freeman*, November 4, 1916.
227. Al Wells, "Alexander Tolliver's Big Show," *Indianapolis Freeman*, November 11, 1916.
228. Al Wells, "Alexander Tolliver's Big Show," *Indianapolis Freeman*, November 25, 1916.
229. Al Wells, "Alexander Tolliver's Big Show," *Indianapolis Freeman*, December 9, 1916.
230. "Tolliver's Big Show A Big Hit At The Strand Theater," *Indianapolis Freeman*, January 13, 1917.
231. "Wanted For the Great Tolliver Show!" ad in *Indianapolis Freeman*, February 10, 1917.
232. "Original Tolliver Show Changes Name," *Indianapolis Freeman*, February 17, 1917.
233. "Colored Aristocrats Open In Savannah," *Indianapolis Freeman*, April 7, 1917; "Park's Colored Aristocrats Greatest Show On Road," *Indianapolis Freeman*, April 14, 1917.
234. "C. W. Park's Colored Aristocrats," *Indianapolis Freeman*, May 12, 1917. For more on Mattie Dorsey see Doug Seroff and Lynn Abbott, "Sweet Mattie Dorsey, Been Here, but She's Gone," *78 Quarterly* no. 8 (n.d.), pp. 103–12.
235. "Colored Aristocrats Makes Effort To Quiet Race Riot," *Indianapolis Freeman*, September 1, 1917. For more on Butler "String Beans" May, see Doug Seroff and Lynn Abbott, "The Life and Death of Pioneer Bluesman Butler 'String Beans' May: 'Been Here, Made His Quick Duck, And Got Away," *Tributaries* no. 5 (2002), pp. 9–48.
236. "Theatricals," *Nashville Globe*, September 14, 1917. "J. A. Jackson's Page," in *Billboard*, September 3, 1921, reported that John L. Long, known as "Sweet Papa Long Boy," was general manager of "the C. W. Parks great 'Smart Set' show," of forty people, presently touring North Carolina.
237. "Tolliver's Big Show A Big Hit At Strand Theater," *Indianapolis Freeman*, January 13, 1917.
238. Shortly thereafter, the Kewleys were reported to have taken up residence in Detroit, Michigan, where they appear to have remained through the close of the decade. Little is known of Fred Kewley's subsequent music career.

239. "Wooden's Bon Tons Best Show Seen In Montgomery, Ala.," *Indianapolis Freeman*, May 26, 1917.
240. "Wooden's Bon Ton Company Receives Warm Welcome," *Indianapolis Freeman*, August 11, 1917.
241. "Al Wells' Smart Set Company," *Indianapolis Freeman*, July 31, 1920.
242. "Tolliver's Smart Set The Talk Of Charleston," *Indianapolis Freeman*, May 5, 1917.
243. "Tolliver's Smart Set The Talk Of Charleston," *Indianapolis Freeman*, May 5, 1917.
244. "Cupid Gets Busy On The Tolliver Show," *Indianapolis Freeman*, July 21, 1917.
245. Pete Porter, "Queen Theatre, Chattanooga, Tenn.," *Indianapolis Freeman*, September 22, 1917. The song referred to was probably "I've Got the Blues for Home Sweet Home," words by Wm. Jerome and E. Ray Goetz, music by Geo. W. Meyer (New York: Kalmar, Puck and Abrahams, 1916).
246. "News of the Players," *Indianapolis Freeman*, September 8, 1917.
247. "Musical and Dramatic," *Indianapolis Freeman*, November 3, 1917.
248. "Harris And Mines Write From Hattiesburg, Miss.," *Indianapolis Freeman*, December 15, 1917.
249. Lottie Hightower became the first woman officer of the Musicians Union, Local 208, serving as financial secretary. In 1926, Willie Hightower played cornet with Carroll Dickerson's Sunset Cafe Orchestra alongside Louis Armstrong. The band that recorded for the Black Patti label in 1927 as "Hightower's Nighthawks" was better known around Chicago as "Lottie Hightower and the Eudora Nighthawks." As noted in a Bill Russell interview with the Hightowers (June 3, 1958, Hogan Jazz Archive, Tulane University), "Eudora" referred to a Chicago dancing class, located at Forum Hall, Forty-Third and Calumet.
250. "News Of The Players," *Indianapolis Freeman*, September 15, 1917.
251. A report from A. G. Allen's New Orleans Minstrels in the *Freeman* of September 6, 1919, noted, "The new addition of this great outfit are Eddie (Peg) Lightfoot, the world's premier one-legged dancer, and Leon (Sonny) Gray, formerly stage manager of Tolliver's Smart Set Minstrels." The *Chicago Defender* of July 21, 1923, supplied an appalling addendum to Lightfoot's biography: "Peg was beaten nearly to death by a mob of whites at Erlanger, Ky. He was accused of having insulted a woman and . . . is now confined in the jail hospital in the town mentioned. Peg is reported to have lost an eye in the melee." Lightfoot was still performing with the Rabbit's Foot Minstrels in the mid-1950s.
252. "News of the Players," *Indianapolis Freeman*, December 1, 1917.
253. Salem Tutt Whitney, "Seen and Heard While Passing," *Indianapolis Freeman*, June 12, 1915.
254. Salem Tutt Whitney, "Seen and Heard While Passing," *Indianapolis Freeman*, November 11, 1916.
255. Salem Tutt Whitney, "Seen and Heard While Passing," *Indianapolis Freeman*, March 31, 1917.
256. This may be the same Billie Young who recorded blues titles in 1930, accompanied by Jelly Roll Morton.
257. "Smart Set Show Notes," *Indianapolis Freeman*, April 21, 1917. Juanita Stinette recorded both as a single and in duets with Thomas "Chappie" Chappelle during the early 1920s on the Chappelle and Stinette label, reissued on Document DOCD-5508 and Document DOCD-1015.
258. This unconfirmed report suggests Roberts may have done some recording prior to the one session listed in Rust (Columbia, October 26, 1916, unissued).
259. Salem Tutt Whitney, "Seen and Heard While Passing," *Indianapolis Freeman*, October 20, 1917.
260. David P. Dorsey, "Pittsburgh Theater News," *Indianapolis Freeman*, May 4, 1918. The *Freeman* of March 2, 1918, identified "Irresistible Blues" as a Lucky Roberts composition. The "Irresistible Blues" recorded in 1923 by both Clara Smith (Columbia A3991, reissued on Document DOCD-5364) and Eva Taylor (Okeh 8129, reissued on Document DOCD-5409) was self-published in Nashville, Tennessee, by George E. Jefferson in 1922.
261. Sylvester Russell, "Smarter Set At The Grand," *Indianapolis Freeman*, February 16, 1918.
262. Salem Tutt Whitney, "Seen and Heard While Passing," *Indianapolis Freeman*, July 20, 1918.

263. "Alexander Tolliver Returns Home From The Colors," *Indianapolis Freeman*, October 5, 1918.
264. "Minstrel and Tent Show Talk," *Billboard*, October 4, 1924; October 11, 1924.
265. "Here and There Among the Folks," *Billboard*, November 22, 1924; December 6, 1924.
266. "Buzz's Dope," *Chicago Defender*, January 10, 1925.
267. "J. A. Jackson's Page," *Billboard*, February 7, 1925.
268. "Frolic to Show Northern Brand of Negro Jazz," *New Orleans States*, January 8, 1925, quoted in Lynn Abbott, "'For Ofays Only': An Annotated Calendar of Midnight Frolics at the Lyric Theater," *The Jazz Archivist* vol. 17 (2003), p. 19.
269. Coy Herndon, "Coy Cogitates," *Chicago Defender*, April 3, 1926.
270. Coy Herndon, "Coy Cogitates," *Chicago Defender*, August 18, 1928.
271. "Hits and Bits," *Chicago Defender*, June 7, 1930.
272. Will Milton Lewis, "The 'Smart Set,'" *Indianapolis Freeman*, March 18, 1905.
273. David A. Himmelstein, liner notes to Jaki Byard, *Out Front*, Prestige LP 7397, 1965.

Notes to Part III: Blues for the Sideshow Tent

1. Al Wells, "Negro Novelty Acts," *Indianapolis Freeman*, August 26, 1916.
2. Curtis Hinsley, "The World as Marketplace," in Ivan Karp and Steven D. Lavine, eds., *Exhibiting Cultures* (Washington: Smithsonian Press, 1991), pp. 358–59. Hinsley used this phrase—"a certain ironic distance"—in describing the response of whites to the Dahomean Village exhibit at the 1893 World's Columbian Exposition. See *Out of Sight*, pp. 294–96.
3. F. W. Thompson, "The Mirror Up To Nature," *Indianapolis Freeman*, December 19, 1896.
4. Abbott and Seroff, *Out of Sight*, pp. 373–80.
5. Salem Tutt Whitney, "Seen and Heard While Passing," *Indianapolis Freeman*, January 16, 1915.
6. Clifford Edward Watkins, *Showman: The Life and Music of Perry George Lowery* (Jackson: University Press of Mississippi, 2003), p. 28.
7. "Stage," *Indianapolis Freeman*, February 22, 1902.
8. "The Stage," *Indianapolis Freeman*, May 5, 1900.
9. "The Stage," *Indianapolis Freeman*, June 2, 1900; July 28, 1900; "Stage," *Indianapolis Freeman*, October 6, 1900.
10. "Stage," *Indianapolis Freeman*, September 15, 1900.
11. "The Stage," *Indianapolis Freeman*, July 21, 1900; July 28, 1900.
12. "Stage," *Indianapolis Freeman*, December 1, 1900.
13. "Stage," *Indianapolis Freeman*, September 15, 1900.
14. "The Stage," *Indianapolis Freeman*, May 5, 1900.
15. "Chicago Comment," *Indianapolis Freeman*, February 9, 1918; *Chicago Whip*, July 29, 1922; William Russell interview with Charles Elgar, May 27, 1958 (Hogan Jazz Archive, Tulane University). For more on Elgar see Jean-Christophe Averty, "Music For All Occasions: Chas. A. Elgar," *Storyville* no. 137 (March 1989), pp. 174–88.
16. The Elgar's Creole Orchestra recordings are reissued on Frog CD DGF28, *"Hot Stuff": Black Chicago Big Bands, 1922–29*.
17. "The Stage," *Indianapolis Freeman*, February 18, 1899. At this time Farrell was with Stetson's Uncle Tom's Cabin Company.
18. "The Stage," *Indianapolis Freeman*, July 28, 1900.
19. McQuitty's career was fairly well chronicled in the African American press. The *Chicago Defender* of September 20, 1924, informed that, "Deacon Mose McQuiddy [*sic*], who for ten years has puffed a pizen bass at the Standard and Dunbar theaters up there in Philly," had left to join James "Tim" Brymn's Orchestra with the "Shuffle Along" Company on a tour of eastern theaters. On October 29, 1927, the *Defender* reported that McQuitty had recently closed the season with the annex band of the 101 Ranch Wild West Shows. He spent most of his final years in tented minstrelsy. An indispensable source on McQuitty is Alex Albright, "Mose McQuitty's Unknown Career: A Personal History of Black Music in America," *Black Music Research Bulletin* vol. 11, no. 2 (Fall 1989).
20. "From New York City To Richmond, Virginia With The Ringling Bros.' Circus," *Indianapolis Freeman*, November 13, 1920.

21. "Lowery's Band, Orchestra, Minstrel Show And Other Attractions With The Wallace & Hagenbeck Show," *Indianapolis Freeman*, June 14, 1913.
22. "Afro-American Firemen," *Indianapolis Freeman*, May 9, 1891.
23. "Stage," *Indianapolis Freeman*, September 9, 1900.
24. A brief biography of Solomon P. White in the *Freeman* of October 23, 1897, states that he toured South America with the Spurgeon Great American Show in the winter of 1887. At this time, the assertion that he toured Australia cannot be confirmed.
25. "With The Circuses," *Indianapolis Freeman*, January 28, 1911.
26. For a description of "In Old Kentucky" and its Woodlawn Wangdoodle Pickaninny Band, see Abbott and Seroff, *Out of Sight*, pp. 406–9.
27. "Negro Concert Band With Ringling Bros.' Circus," *Indianapolis Freeman*, January 21, 1911.
28. "Notes From Ringling Bros.' Circus Annex," *Indianapolis Freeman*, July 20, 1912.
29. "Finest Annex On The Road," *Indianapolis Freeman*, May 27, 1911.
30. "Ringling Bros.' Shows in Indianapolis—Roy Pope and His Band," *Indianapolis Freeman*, May 9, 1914.
31. "Ringling Bros. Circus Annex," *Indianapolis Freeman*, May 23, 1914. "Remick's Hits," or "Bits of Remick's Hits," comprised a popular series of contemporary "medley overtures," compiled and arranged by J. Bodwalt Lampe for Tin Pan Alley publisher Jerome H. Remick.
32. "Prof. R. Roy Pope, Band Master, In Indianapolis," *Indianapolis Freeman*, April 10, 1915.
33. "Notes From R. Roy Pope's Band, Ringling Brothers Band, Ringling Bros. Circus," *Indianapolis Freeman*, September 4, 1915.
34. "Ringling Bros. Annex Band," *Indianapolis Freeman*, April 17, 1915.
35. "Stage Gossip," *Indianapolis Freeman*, November 6, 1915.
36. Tim Owsley, "In Dayton," *Chicago Defender*, August 20, 1927.
37. 1870 United States Federal Census (Ancestry.com); "Notes of 101 Ranch Real Wild West," *Indianapolis Freeman*, June 13, 1914.
38. "Interesting Career of Oldest Band and Minstrel Manager," *Indianapolis Freeman*, December 20, 1913, reproduced in *Out of Sight*, p. 378.
39. "Stage," *Indianapolis Freeman*, May 31, 1902; August 23, 1902.
40. "The Stage," *Indianapolis Freeman*, August 29, 1903.
41. "The Cole Bros. Shows," *Indianapolis Freeman*, June 1, 1907.
42. "Jas. Wolfscale's Band and Vaudeville Company," *Indianapolis Freeman*, April 20, 1912.
43. "Barnum & Bailey Notes," *Indianapolis Freeman*, October 12, 1912.
44. Billy (Lewis), "Seeing Barnum & Bailey's Big Show," *Indianapolis Freeman*, June 19, 1915.
45. *Indianapolis Freeman*, July 19, 1913. "Zip" was the inspiration for Bill Griffith's popular syndicated cartoon character "Zippy the Pinhead." For more, see www.zippythepinhead.com.
46. According to an article in *Billboard*, April 9, 1921, Princess Wee Wee's real name was Harriet Thompson and she hailed from Baltimore, Maryland.
47. "Notes From Wolfscale's Band With Barnum & Bailey Circus," *Indianapolis Freeman*, April 15, 1916.
48. "Here and There Among the Folks," *Billboard*, February 28, 1925.
49. "Whitmans Meet Coolidge," *Chicago Defender*, July 3, 1926. The meeting was reportedly arranged by C. Lucien Skinner of the Crispus Attucks Press Association.
50. "Prof. James Wolfscale's Company With Barnum and Bailey's Greatest Show on Earth," *Indianapolis Freeman*, May 31, 1913.
51. "Notes From Wolfscale's Band And Minstrels, With Barnum & Bailey," *Indianapolis Freeman*, July 12, 1913.
52. "Barnum And Bailey Circus To Have Colored Concert Band," *Indianapolis Freeman*, February 21, 1914.
53. "Notes From Wolfscale's Band," *Indianapolis Freeman*, April 4, 1914.
54. "Notes From Wolfscale's Band, With Barnum And Bailey," *Indianapolis Freeman*, August 8, 1914.
55. "Notes From Wolfscale's Band With Barnum & Bailey Circus," *Indianapolis Freeman*, May 16, 1914;

"Notes From Wolfscale's Band With Barnum & Bailey's Circus," *Indianapolis Freeman*, June 13, 1914; "Notes From Wolfscale's Band With Barnum & Bailey Circus," *Indianapolis Freeman*, July 4, 1914; "Notes From Wolfscales Band With the Barnum & Bailey Circus," *Indianapolis Freeman*, August 8, 1914; "Notes From Wolfscales Band With Barnum & Bailey," *Indianapolis Freeman*, October 17, 1914.

56. "The Lyric Theatre, Kansas City, Mo.," *Indianapolis Freeman*, June 5, 1915; "Around The Town," *Chicago Defender*, May 11, 1918.
57. "Prof. Wolfscale Cancels Engagement With Barnum & Bailey," *Indianapolis Freeman*, March 6, 1915.
58. "Notes From Wolfscale's Band With Barnum & Bailey's Circus," *Indianapolis Freeman*, May 1, 1915.
59. "Notes From Wolfscale's Band With Barnum & Bailey Circus," *Indianapolis Freeman*, October 16, 1915.
60. "Notes from Wolfscale's Band With Barnum & Bailey Circus," *Indianapolis Freeman*, May 22, 1915; Billy [*sic*], "Seeing Barnum & Bailey's Big Show," *Indianapolis Freeman*, June 19, 1915; "Notes From Wolfscale's Band With Barnum & Bailey Circus," *Indianapolis Freeman*, July 31, 1915; October 16, 1915.
61. "Notes From Wolfscale's Band With Barnum & Bailey Circus," *Indianapolis Freeman*, October 16, 1915.
62. "Wolfscale's Band With Barnum and Bailey Circus," *Indianapolis Freeman*, July 29, 1916; "Wolfscale's Band With Barnum and Bailey's Circus," *Indianapolis Freeman*, October 21, 1916. Wayne Shirley notes that the band arrangement of "The Hesitating Blues" was scored by William Grant Still.
63. "Billy," "Seeing Barnum and Bailey's Big Show," *Indianapolis Freeman*, June 19, 1915.
64. "Notes From Wolfscale's Band With Barnum And Bailey's Circus," *Indianapolis Freeman*, October 21, 1916.
65. H. Jones, "Cream City News," *Indianapolis Freeman*, December 22, 1917.
66. "Notes From Wolfscale's Band With Barnum & Bailey Circus," *Indianapolis Freeman*, April 15, 1916.
67. "Notes From Wolfscale's Band With Barnum and Bailey Circus," June 17, 1916.
68. "Notes From Wolfscale's Band With Barnum & Bailey Circus," *Indianapolis Freeman*, April 22, 1916; June 3, 1916.
69. Shelton Brooks, "Walkin' the Dog" (Chicago: Will Rossiter, 1916).
70. "'Moonlight On The Levee,' With Princess Wee Wee, Crowds the Grand Theater—Slim Henderson a Good Dancing Comedian—Tabor & Green Draw Classy Houses All the Week," *Indianapolis Freeman*, January 13, 1917.
71. "Notes From Moonlight On The Levee Company, James E. Wolfscale, Manager," *Indianapolis Freeman*, March 31, 1917.
72. "Notes From Wolfscale's Band With Barnum & Bailey," *Indianapolis Freeman*, June 16, 1917.
73. "Notes From Wolfscale's Band With Barnum & Bailey Circus," *Indianapolis Freeman*, July 7, 1917.
74. "Notes From Princess Wee Wee And Her Jass Band In Moonlight On The Levee Co.," *Indianapolis Freeman*, December 1, 1917.
75. J. H. Gray, "Gibson's New Standard Theatre, Philadelphia," *Indianapolis Freeman*, January 12, 1918.
76. "Notes From Wolfscale's Band—Goes Back To B. & B. Circus," *Indianapolis Freeman*, May 18, 1918.
77. "Band Leader Dead," *Chicago Defender*, October 29, 1921.
78. "Notes from the Sparks' Show," *Indianapolis Freeman*, July 11, 1914; Sam Kennedy, "Sparks' World Famous Shows," *Indianapolis Freeman*, August 1, 1914; "Sparks Circus Closes November 2nd," *Indianapolis Freeman*, October 31, 1914.
79. "Gossip of the Stage," *Indianapolis Freeman*, June 13, 1914; Sam Kennedy, "Sparks' World Famous Shows," *Indianapolis Freeman*, August 1, 1914; "Notes of A. A. Wright Minstrels," *Indianapolis Freeman*, August 29, 1914; "Sparks' Show," *Indianapolis Freeman*, September 26, 1914.
80. Horace Harrison, "News from Georgia Minstrels No. 1," *Indianapolis Freeman*, May 29, 1915; "Mose McQuitty Writes from the Spark's Annex Band," *Indianapolis Freeman*, June 5, 1915.
81. "Mase [*sic*] McQuitty Writes from Sparks' Circus," *Indianapolis Freeman*, April 24, 1915.

82. "Notes from Sparks' Show," *Indianapolis Freeman*, December 4, 1915.
83. This is confirmed at least for the years 1916, 1918 and 1919. No documentation is in hand regarding the Sparks Circus Annex for the year 1917.
84. "Spark's Minstrel," *Indianapolis Freeman*, May 27, 1916.
85. "McQuitty Writes from Sparks Shows," *Indianapolis Freeman*, May 27, 1916.
86. "Ringling Circus News," *Indianapolis Freeman*, October 12, 1912.
87. Billy Lewis, "Looking Sells-Floto Over," *Indianapolis Freeman*, September 26, 1914.
88. Coy Herndon, "Coy Cogitates," *Chicago Defender*, April 14, 1923.
89. James A. Harris should not be confused with James H. Harris, also a trombonist and bandleader, who was associated with Frank Mahara's Minstrels and other companies earlier in the twentieth century.
90. O. F. Wansel, "Seeing the Gollmar Brothers'," *Indianapolis Freeman*, October 16, 1915.
91. "Notes of the J. H. Harris' [*sic*] Band and Minstrel Co. with Gollmar Bros. Shows," *Indianapolis Freeman*, June 6, 1914.
92. O. F. Wansel, "Seeing the Gollmar Brothers," *Indianapolis Freeman*, October 16, 1915; J. T. Jackson, "Notes from J. H. [*sic*] Harris' Band and Minstrels, with Gollmar Brothers' Show," *Indianapolis Freeman*, August 26, 1916; "Notes from James A. Harris' Band and Minstrel Show," *Indianapolis Freeman*, October 7, 1916.
93. See Lynn Abbott and Doug Seroff, "They Cert'ly Sound Good to Me": Sheet Music, Southern Vaudeville, and the Commercial Ascendancy of the Blues," *American Music* vol. 14, no. 4 (Winter 1996), pp. 402–54.
94. "Notes From Prof. John Eason Annex Band And Minstrels, With Yankee Robinson's Circus," *Indianapolis Freeman*, July 27, 1912.
95. "Notes From Prof. Eason's Annex Band And Minstrel—With Yankee Robinson's Circus," *Indianapolis Freeman*, August 10, 1912.
96. "News From Prof. John Eason's Band And Minstrel Show," *Indianapolis Freeman*, October 12, 1912.
97. "Mrs. Lena Hulett Writes From Yankee Robinson's Three-Ring Circus," *Indianapolis Freeman*, May 8, 1915. A roster of Prof. Eason's band can be found in Appendix III.
98. Mrs. Lena Hulett, "Notes From Yankee Robinson's Side Show," *Indianapolis Freeman*, September 4, 1915.
99. Lizzie Miles's complete pre–World War II recorded output is reissued on Document CDs DOCD-5458, DOCD-5459, and DOCD-5460.
100. For more of an overview on Lizzie Miles, see Abbott and Seroff, "Lizzie Miles: Her Forgotten Career in Circus Side-Show Minstrelsy 1914–1918," *78 Quarterly* vol. 1, no. 7 (1992), pp. 57–70.
101. "J. C. Miles Writes From Roanoke, Va.—Alabama Minstrels," *Indianapolis Freeman*, February 14, 1914.
102. Transcript of Dave Garroway conversation with Lizzie Miles, *Wide, Wide World*, February 2, 1958 (Lizzie Miles vertical file, New Orleans Jazz Club Collection, Louisiana State Museum).
103. "Gossip Of The Stage," *Indianapolis Freeman*, May 2, 1914.
104. "J. C. Miles' Band And Minstrels," *Indianapolis Freeman*, May 16, 1914.
105. "J. C. Miles' Band And Minstrels With Jones' Bros. & Wilson's 3-Ring Circus," *Indianapolis Freeman*, June 27, 1914.
106. "Landry" is an Americanization of Lizzie and Edna's shared maiden name, "Landreaux."
107. "J. C. Miles' Band And Minstrels With Jones Bros. Three-Ring Circus," *Indianapolis Freeman*, April 24, 1915.
108. "J. C. Miles' Band And Minstrels With Jones Bros. Circus," *Indianapolis Freeman*, May 15, 1915.
109. "J. C. Miles' Band And Minstrels With Jones Bros. Circus," *Indianapolis Freeman*, June 12, 1915.
110. "J. C. Miles' Band And Minstrels With Jones Bros.' Circus," *Indianapolis Freeman*, December 4, 1915.
111. "J. C. Miles And Company With Cole Bros.' Show," *Indianapolis Freeman*, April 8, 1916.
112. Haley Walker, "J. C. Miles & Co. With Cole Bros.' Circus," *Indianapolis Freeman*, April 22, 1916.
113. "J. C. Miles Band And Minstrels With Cole Bros. Shows," *Indianapolis Freeman*, June 3, 1916.
114. "J. C. Miles & Co. In Colorado Mountains," *Indianapolis Freeman*, August 12, 1916.

115. "J. C. Miles' Band And Minstrels With The Great Cole Bros. World-Toured Shows," *Indianapolis Freeman*, July 7, 1917.
116. "J. C. Miles And Co. Enjoys Treat Of Real 'Spread,'" *Indianapolis Freeman*, July 21, 1917.
117. Bill Russell interview with Amos White, August 23, 1958 (Hogan Jazz Archive, Tulane University).
118. "Noted Bandmaster And Musician Passes Away," *Indianapolis Freeman*, November 2, 1918.
119. World War I Selective Service System Draft Registration Cards, 1917–1918 (Ancestry.com).
120. "Prof. Bismark Ferris Is Satisfied," *Indianapolis Freeman*, November 12, 1910.
121. "Prof. B. Ferris Satisfied Musical Enterprise At Madison Square Garden," *Indianapolis Freeman*, May 14, 1910.
122. "Prof. Bismark Ferris Is Satisfied," *Indianapolis Freeman*, November 12, 1910.
123. "Ferris' Georgia Minstrels With The Buffalo Bill Wild West Show," *Indianapolis Freeman*, July 29, 1911.
124. Sylvester Russell, "Chicago Weekly Review," *Indianapolis Freeman*, July 22, 1911.
125. 1920 United States Federal Census (Ancestry.com).
126. Ragtime Billy Tucker, "Coast Dope," *Chicago Defender*, June 24, 1922. The *Defender* of October 3, 1925, said Bismark Ferris's show of eight musicians, including Amy, Lucille, and Theresa Ferris, had left Southern California "for Oregon, Washington and Canada, where they will fill a 'gang' of fair dates." The 1930 U.S. Census reported Theresa and Amy, then ages twenty-one and twenty-four, living in Los Angeles with their father; both gave their occupations as "musician."
127. According to Donald Russell, *The Wild West* (Amon Carter Museum, 1970), "Young Buffalo" was Cal Lavelle. Vernon C. Seavers was proprietor of Young Buffalo's Wild West Show in 1911, and Seavers and Col. Fred T. Cummins were co-owners in 1912.
128. "W. L. Horne's Minstrels With Young Buffalo Bill Shows," *Indianapolis Freeman*, July 1, 1911.
129. "Keene, N. H.," *Indianapolis Freeman*, July 27, 1912.
130. "Horne's Original Georgia Minstrels, With Young Buffalo's Wild West And. Col. Cummins' Far East," *Indianapolis Freeman*, August 24, 1912.
131. Bill Russell interview with Jasper Taylor, June 30, 1959 (Hogan Jazz Archive, Tulane University).
132. "Gossip Of The Stage," *Indianapolis Freeman*, December 6, 1913.
133. "Gossip Of The Stage," *Indianapolis Freeman*, July 11, 1914.
134. Dave Peyton, "The Musical Bunch," *Chicago Defender*, November 14, 1925.
135. Paul Reddin, *Wild West Shows* (Urbana: University of Illinois Press, 1999), pp. 158–62.
136. Doc Ford, "Notes From 101 Ranch Real Wild West," *Indianapolis Freeman*, October 11, 1913.
137. Billy Lewis, "Seeing The 101 Ranch Shows," *Indianapolis Freeman*, September 12, 1914.
138. Reddin, p. 175.
139. "Notes By Harrison Hall, 101 Ranch Wild West Correspondent," *Indianapolis Freeman*, May 22, 1915.
140. "Prof. L. K. Baker's Annex Band With 101 Ranch Shows," *Indianapolis Freeman*, October 16, 1915.
141. "Prof. L. K. Baker's Annex With 101 Ranch Shows," *Indianapolis Freeman*, October 9, 1915.
142. P. L. Jenkins, "Prof. L. K. Baker's Annex Band With 101 Ranch Shows," *Indianapolis Freeman*, June 24, 1916.
143. Reddin, p. 176.
144. Billy Lewis, "Seeing Jess Willard's Buffalo Bill's Shows," *Indianapolis Freeman*, September 8, 1917.
145. "Prof. L. K. Baker's Annex To Leave New York State," *Indianapolis Freeman*, September 1, 1917.
146. P. L. Jenkins, "Prof. L. K. Baker Annexes With The Jess Willard–Buffalo Bill Shows," *Indianapolis Freeman*, August 4, 1917.
147. "Prof. L. K. Baker's Annex In The Catskill Mountains," *Indianapolis Freeman*, August 25, 1917.
148. P. L. Jenkins, "Prof. L. K. Baker's Annex," *Indianapolis Freeman*, November 3, 1917.
149. It seems unlikely that this is the same "Will Nash" who composed "Snakey Blues," "Lonesome Road Blues," "Glad Cat Rag" and other titles published by Pace and Handy Music Company during this period. In his "Notes to the Collection" of songs compiled in the second edition of W. C. Handy, ed., *Blues: An Anthology*, p. 210, Abbe Niles identifies the author of "Snakey Blues" as "a

Hot Springs, Arkansas, Negro, an old-time blues pianist of parts."

150. "Prof. L. K. Baker's Annex Band With 101 Ranch Shows," *Indianapolis Freeman*, May 13, 1916.
151. Doc Ford, "Notes From The 101 Ranch Real Wild West Annex Band And Minstrels," *Indianapolis Freeman*, May 24, 1913; Sam Ford, "101 Ranch Wild West Show," *Indianapolis Freeman*, July 12, 1913.
152. Billy Lewis, "Seeing Jess Willard's Buffalo Bill's Shows," *Indianapolis Freeman*, September 8, 1917.
153. It was mentioned in the February 21, 1925, edition of *Billboard* that Oskazuma would celebrate his sixtieth birthday on March 5, 1925. For more on Oskazuma, see *Out of Sight*, pp. 312–15.
154. Price Askazuma [*sic*], Black Scout, "Fine Performances Of Superior Shows Attract Large Crowds," *Indianapolis Freeman*, August 18, 1917.
155. "Prince Askazuma Visits The Buffalo Bill Show," *Indianapolis Freeman*, July 28, 1917.
156. "J. A. Jackson's Page," *Billboard*, April 21, 1923.
157. "J. A. Jackson's Page," *Billboard*, November 15, 1924.
158. "Minstrel and Tent Show Talk," *Billboard*, January 26, 1924.
159. "Here and There Among the Folks," *Billboard*, December 6, 1924.
160. "William H. Reed's [*sic*] Band," *Indianapolis Freeman*, September 27, 1913.
161. "Seeing Young Buffalo Bill's Show [*sic*]," *Indianapolis Freeman*, July 25, 1914.
162. "Notes From Prof. L. K. Baker's Band And Minstrels With John Robinson's Circus," *Indianapolis Freeman*, October 16, 1920.
163. "Gossip of the Stage," *Indianapolis Freeman*, March 9, 1912.
164. "With Robinson's Famous Shows," *Indianapolis Freeman*, September 5, 1914.
165. "Eugene Clark's Band And Minstrel, With Robinson's Famous Shows," *Indianapolis Freeman*, July 10, 1915.
166. "Notes From John Robinson's Circus," *Indianapolis Freeman*, August 12, 1916.
167. "'All Well With John Robinson Bunch And Doing Well,' Glad To Say," *Indianapolis Freeman*, September 22, 1917.
168. For example, a November 13, 1920, note said James R. Jackson, "prominent trombone and baritone player, for a number of years connected with E. H. Jones' Alabama Minstrels and Cole Bros. Circus, has given up the band with Silas Green's show and joined the Big Six Orchestra of Greenwood, Miss., playing saxophone."
169. E. L. Smith, "The John Robinson's Circus Bunch Bid Adieu To All For The Season Of 1917," *Indianapolis Freeman*, November 10, 1917.
170. "Marcus Veal's Band And Company With John Robinson's Ten Big Shows," *Indianapolis Freeman*, June 1, 1918.
171. "Gossip Of The Stage," *Indianapolis Freeman*, August 16, 1919.
172. "News Of The Players," *Indianapolis Freeman*, July 31, 1920.
173. "Music And Musicians In and Around Columbus, O.," *Indianapolis Freeman*, February 4, 1911.
174. "Notes From Homes [*sic*] Great London Shows," *Indianapolis Freeman*, August 8, 1914.
175. "Notes From Howe's Great London Shows," *Indianapolis Freeman*, August 22, 1914.
176. Tommy Stevens, "Notes From Howe's Great London Shows," *Indianapolis Freeman*, June 10, 1916.
177. "Notes From Howe's Great London Shows," *Indianapolis Freeman*, June 3, 1916.
178. "Notes From Howe's Great London Show," *Indianapolis Freeman*, September 16, 1916.
179. "Notes From Howe's Great London Shows," *Indianapolis Freeman*, June 3, 1916; Tommy Stevens, "Notes From Howe's Great London Shows," *Indianapolis Freeman*, June 17, 1916.
180. Tommy Stevens, "Notes From Howe's Great London Shows," *Indianapolis Freeman*, July 15, 1916.
181. By this time, Burton was in failing health. He died in Detroit, August 21, 1925.
182. "Notes From P. G. Lowery's Big Minstrel Company And Colored Band," *Indianapolis Freeman*, May 17, 1913.
183. "Harrisburg, Pa., Lowery's Minstrels, the Best Under Canvas," *Indianapolis Freeman*, May 31, 1913.
184. "Lowery's Band, Orchestra, Minstrel Show And Other Attractions With The Wallace &

Hagenbeck Show," *Indianapolis Freeman*, June 14, 1913. This is a reference to the fact that Lowery attended the Boston Conservatory of Music.

185. "Stage Gossip," *Indianapolis Freeman*, March 25, 1916.
186. "Notes From P. G. Lowery's Minstrels," *Indianapolis Freeman*, June 28, 1913.
187. Jelly Roll Morton's Jazz Band, "Someday Sweetheart"/ "London Blues," Okeh 8105, 1923.
188. Billy Lewis, "Seeing a Wonderful Show," *Indianapolis Freeman*, August 30, 1913.
189. Billy Lewis, "Seeing The White Top," *Indianapolis Freeman*, May 4, 1912. "Mammy's Shuffling Dance" is misidentified in the report as "Mamma Shufflin's Dance."
190. "What Lowery's Minstrels Are Doing," *Indianapolis Freeman*, July 11, 1914.
191. "What Lowery's Minstrels Are Doing," *Indianapolis Freeman*, July 11, 1914; "Notes From Hagenbeck-Wallace Circus By Staff," *Indianapolis Freeman*, July 18, 1914.
192. "What Lowery's Minstrels Are Doing," *Indianapolis Freeman*, July 11, 1914; "Notes From Hagenbeck-Wallace Circus By Staff," *Indianapolis Freeman*, July 18, 1914. In *Pioneers of Jazz: The Story of the Creole Band* (Oxford: Oxford University Press, 2005), pp. 91, 100, Lawrence Gushee gives evidence that the "'Mandalay' song" noted in the Creole Band's 1914 repertoire was not Olney Speaks and Rudyard Kipling's "On the Road to Mandalay," from 1907, but Fred Fisher and Albert Bryan's "rather raggy" "I'm on My Way to Mandalay," published by Leo Feist in 1913. This may also have been Callie Vassar's 1914 "Mandalay song."
193. "Hagenbeck Wallace Notes," *Indianapolis Freeman*, October 3, 1914.
194. Callie Vassar's Gennett recordings are reissued on Document CD DOCD-5390, *Richard M. Jones and the Blues Singers*.
195. "Hagenbeck-Wallace Notes," *Indianapolis Freeman*, October 17, 1914.
196. "Granstaff and Davis Hit at 81, Atlanta, Ga.," *Indianapolis Freeman*, December 5, 1915.
197. Brooks, *Lost Sounds*, pp. 358, 360.
198. "Lowery's Bunch Entertained—P. G. Lowery Injured—Closing The Season," *Indianapolis Freeman*, October 24, 1914.
199. "Notes From 101 Ranch Annex Band," *Indianapolis Freeman*, November 7, 1914.
200. "P. G. Lowery Returns To The Circus Field," *Indianapolis Freeman*, March 25, 1916.
201. "Notes From R. Roy Pope's Band, Ringling Brothers Band, Ringling Bros. Circus," *Indianapolis Freeman*, September 4, 1915.
202. "Lowery's Minstrels With Hagenbeck and Wallace Shows," *Indianapolis Freeman*, May 20, 1916; "Notes From P. G. Lowery's Band And Company With The H. And W. Circus," *Indianapolis Freeman*, September 2, 1916.
203. "Lowery's Minstrels With Hagenbeck and Wallace Shows," *Indianapolis Freeman*, May 20, 1916.
204. "Lowery's Band And Minstrels Merit Wins," *Indianapolis Freeman*, August 19, 1916.
205. W. E. Fields, "Notes of the H. & W. Circus," *Indianapolis Freeman*, October 7, 1916.
206. W. E. Fields, "Notes of the H. & W. Circus," *Indianapolis Freeman*, October 7, 1916. Levy Payne's Colored Female Band performed in Ernest Hogan's first musical comedy production, *In Old Tennessee*, in 1895. William H. Young and Nathan B. Young, Jr., *Your Kansas City and Mine* (1950), includes a biographical sketch of Levy and Elmer Payne under the caption, "Mr. Minstrel Himself And Son": "Levy Payne was born on a farm in Ohio, November 18, 1858 [and] was brought to Missouri by his father right after the Civil War . . . His first professional appearance was back in 1881 with the Great Pacific Show, a circus. He played in the sideshow band . . . From 1903 to 1917 he organized and taught local bands in Kansas . . . 1918 through 1923 he and his son Elmer were with the famous Harvey Greater Minstrels." In 1942 Levy Payne quit the road and went home to Kansas City, Kansas, where he played with the local municipal band until he retired in 1948. In 1950 Elmer Payne was president of the Kansas City Musicians Union, Local 627.
207. "Wanted! For Hagenbeck-Wallace Circus Season 1917," *Indianapolis Freeman*, February 3, 1917.

208. "Notes from P. G. Lowery's Band," *Indianapolis Freeman*, September 2, 1915.
209. "Prince Mungo, Descendent Of The Bhogirattes," *Indianapolis Freeman*, September 16, 1911.
210. W. E. Fields, "Notes of the H. & W. Circus," *Indianapolis Freeman*, October 7, 1916.
211. "Payne's Band With Honest Bill Show," *Indianapolis Freeman*, July 14, 1917.
212. "Circus Day," *Indianapolis Freeman*, May 5, 1917.
213. Salem Tutt Whitney, "Seen and Heard While Passing," *Indianapolis Freeman*, January 24, 1920.
214. "Chicago Monogram Theatre," *Indianapolis Freeman*, December 18, 1915; Geo. C. Anderson, "Theatrical News From East St. Louis, Ill.," *Indianapolis Freeman*, January 15, 1916; S. H. Gay (*sic*), "Theatrical News From Atlantic City, N. J.," *Indianapolis Freeman*, July 22, 1916; "Drake and Walker All The Go In Kansas," *Indianapolis Freeman*, May 5, 1917; "Circus Day," *Indianapolis Freeman*, May 5, 1917.
215. D. W. Batsell, "Prof. P. G. Lowery's Band And Co., Hagenbeck-Wallace Circus," *Indianapolis Freeman*, July 7, 1917.
216. "Miss Callie Vassar Was Royally Received At Her Home," *Indianapolis Freeman*, June 30, 1917.
217. D. W. Batsell, "Prof. P. G. Lowery's Band And Co., Hagenbeck-Wallace Circus," *Indianapolis Freeman*, July 7, 1917.
218. "Gossip Of The Stage," *Indianapolis Freeman*, January 13, 1912. D. W. Batsell is almost certainly the Dink Willie Batsell who registered with the Selective Service System at Russellville, Kentucky, on September 12, 1918 (Ancestry.com).
219. "The Stage," *Indianapolis Freeman*, December 3, 1910.
220. "The Stage," *Indianapolis Freeman*, March 4, 1911. For historical background on "Mazeppa" see Wolf Mankovitz, *Mazeppa: The Lives Loves and Legends of Adah Isaacs Menken* (New York: Stein and Day, 1982).
221. "Gossip Of The Stage," *Indianapolis Freeman*, August 19, 1911.
222. "Gossip Of The Stage," *Indianapolis Freeman*, February 3, 1912.
223. "Gossip Of The Stage," *Indianapolis Freeman*, May 25, 1912.
224. "Gossip Of The Stage," *Indianapolis Freeman*, August 24, 1912.
225. "Gossip Of The Stage," *Indianapolis Freeman*, September 7, 1912.
226. "Gossip Of The Stage," *Indianapolis Freeman*, April 26, 1913; "The Batsell & Martin's Minstrels," *Indianapolis Freeman*, April 4, 1914.
227. Earlier references to Batsell's "Alabama Blues" have yet to be located.
228. For more on Lowery's tenure in Nitro, see Watkins, *Showman*, pp. 108–9.
229. Sylvester Russell, "Stage Notes," *Indianapolis Freeman*, September 6, 1919.
230. "F. Bennett Hargrave's Band And Minstrels," *Indianapolis Freeman*, April 3, 1920.
231. "News Of The Players," *Indianapolis Freeman*, June 12, 1920.
232. "Notes From Grant Cooper's Band And Minstrels, With Kit Carson's Buffalo Ranch Wild West Shows," *Indianapolis Freeman*, September 23, 1911.
233. Bert F. DeLeo, "Notes From Royal Rhoda Circus," *Indianapolis Freeman*, July 31, 1920.
234. "Bert F. DeLeo Writes From Rhoda Royal Circus," *Indianapolis Freeman*, October 9, 1920.
235. "Al G. Barnes' Greatest Wild Animal Circus," *Indianapolis Freeman*, March 13, 1920.
236. "Walter L. Main's Shows," *Indianapolis Freeman*, July 31, 1920.
237. "Circus Friends Meet," *Indianapolis Freeman*, July 17, 1920.
238. "P. G. Lowery And His Band With Ringling Bros. Circus," *Indianapolis Freeman*, April 17, 1920.
239. "P. G. Lowery's Band Featured Two New Skidmore Song Hits," *Indianapolis Freeman*, May 8, 1920.
240. "News Of The Players," *Indianapolis Freeman*, May 8, 1920.
241. "From New York City To Richmond, Virginia With the Ringling Bros.' Circus," *Indianapolis Freeman*, November 13, 1920.
242. Alvin Zoo Robertson, "Notes From Homer Butler's Band," *Indianapolis Freeman*, July 26, 1919; "P. G. Lowery's Engagement With The Ringling Bros. And Barnum & Bailey's Combined Shows A Decided Success—Reengaged For 1920," *Indianapolis Freeman*, December 13, 1919.

243. "Stage Notes," *Indianapolis Freeman*, October 16, 1920. For more information on Alvin "Zoo" Robertson see William Russell, "Zue Robertson – King of the Trombone," *Jazz Information* vol. 1, no. 26 (March 15, 1940), p. 3; reprinted in *The Needle* vol. 2, no. 1 (1945), p. 17.
244. Callie Vassar, Charles Creath, and Horace Eubanks all hailed from St. Louis or nearby East St. Louis, Illinois.
245. Tony Langston, "The Grand," *Chicago Defender*, August 30, 1924.
246. "Lowery's Band," *Chicago Defender*, June 4, 1921.
247. "Band Concert," *Chicago Defender*, January 7, 1922.
248. *Industrial High School Record*, vol. 2, no. 1 (November 1922): vol. 2, no. 3 (January 1923).
249. Coy Herndon, "Coy Cogitates," *Chicago Defender*, June 16, 1923.
250. "Ragtime" Billy Tucker, "Coast Dope," *Chicago Defender*, September 29, 1923.
251. Dave Peyton, "The Musical Bunch," *Chicago Defender*, July 16, 1927.
252. Watkins, *Showman*, pp. 119–27.
253. Wright is listed as director in the Ringling Bros. and Barnum & Bailey "Route Book" for 1939.
254. Frank J. Gillis and John W. Miner, eds., *Oh, Didn't He Ramble: The Life Story of Lee Collins, As Told to Mary Collins* (Urbana: University of Illinois Press, 1974), p. 49.

Notes to Part IV: "Under Canvas": African American Tented Minstrelsy and the Untold Story of Allen's New Orleans Minstrels, the Rabbit's Foot Company, the Florida Blossoms, and *Silas Green from New Orleans*

1. "The Stage," *Indianapolis Freeman*, December 19, 1903.
2. "Rialto Topics," *Indianapolis Freeman*, May 23, 1903.
3. "The Stage," *Indianapolis Freeman*, May 23, 1908.
4. "Stage," *Indianapolis Freeman*, November 16, 1901.
5. P. L. Jenkins, "Aboard A. G. Allen's Private Car 999," *Indianapolis Freeman*, July 26, 1913.
6. "Allen's Minstrels," *Indianapolis Freeman*, August 21, 1909.
7. J. B. Norton, "A. G. Allen's Minstrels," *Indianapolis Freeman*, November 1, 1913.
8. Mrs. Frankie C. Latham, "The Sunny Dixie Minstrels," *Indianapolis Freeman*, April 18, 1914; "News From The F. C. Huntington Minstrel Co.," *Indianapolis Freeman*, October 31, 1914; "Barfield's Georgia Minstrels," *Indianapolis Freeman*, April 17, 1915; "Notes From J. C. O'Brien's Famous Georgia Minstrels No. 1," *Indianapolis Freeman*, September 4, 1915.
9. "From The Georgia Smart Set Company," *Indianapolis Freeman*, June 8, 1918.
10. "Notes From Mahoney's Mobile Minstrel Co.," *Indianapolis Freeman*, October 13, 1917; "Notes of the Mobile Minstrels," *Indianapolis Freeman*, December 1, 1917.
11. A *Freeman* report of February 21, 1914, states that they were beginning their twenty-fifth season.
12. "J. C. O'Brien's Minstrels," *Indianapolis Freeman*, January 14, 1911.
13. "J. C. O'Brien's Famous Georgia Minstrels," *Indianapolis Freeman*, December 23, 1911.
14. E. Alfred Drew, "Notes from J. C. O'Brien's Famous Georgia Minstrels," *Indianapolis Freeman*, July 13, 1912. The citation may have intended to say that Warford was playing two titles, "The Blues" and "The Dream."
15. "Notes From J. C. O'Brien's Georgia Minstrels No. 1," *Indianapolis Freeman*, October 30, 1915.
16. "Notes From J. C. O'Brien's Famous Georgia Minstrels," *Indianapolis Freeman*, July 11, 1914.
17. "Notes from J. C. O'Brien's Famous Georgia Minstrels No. 1," *Indianapolis Freeman*, October 24, 1914.
18. "Notes from J. C. O'Brien's Minstrels, No. 1," *Indianapolis Freeman*, October 23, 1915.
19. "Notes From J. C. O'Brien's Famous Minstrel No. 2 Show," *Indianapolis Freeman*, August 7, 1915.
20. "Notes From J. C. O'Brien's Famous Georgia Minstrel Co. No. 2 Show Under Management Of Lew Aronson," *Indianapolis Freeman*, October 16, 1915.
21. "Paul Steal [*sic*] Writing For The J. C. O'Brien Georgia Minstrel No. 1," *Indianapolis Freeman*, March 25, 1916.

22. "Notes From The Georgia Minstrels No. 1," *Indianapolis Freeman*, August 26, 1916.
23. "Notice From J. C. O'Brien's Famous Georgia Minstrels Number One," *Indianapolis Freeman*, November 18, 1916.
24. "Georgia Minstrels No. One In Mississippi," *Indianapolis Freeman*, April 21, 1917.
25. For more on the Yancy and Booker Musical Publishing Company, see David Lee Joyner, "Southern Ragtime and Its Transition to Published Blues" (Phd dissertation, Memphis State University, 1986), pp. 110–13.
26. Edith Wilson, "The West Texas Blues," Columbia A3537, 1921, reissued on Document JPCD-1522; Tampa Blue Jazz Band, "The West Texas Blues," Okeh 4595, 1922; Booker's Jazz Band, "West Texas Blues," Domino 3474, 1924.
27. "Geo. Barrett Writes From J. C. O'Brien's Georgian Minstrels No. 1," *Indianapolis Freeman*, February 27, 1915. In an August 21, 1915, correspondence, the fife and drum corps was qualified as "the Ladies Challenge Drum Corps."
28. "Notes From J. C. O'Brien's Famous Georgia Minstrels No. 1," *Indianapolis Freeman*, August 21, 1915.
29. Prince Ali Mona, "Notes From J. C. O'Brien's Famous Georgia Minstrels No. 1," *Indianapolis Freeman*, April 24, 1915.
30. "Notes From The J. C. O'Brien's Famous Georgia Minstrels," *Indianapolis Freeman*, March 14, 1914.
31. "Notes From J. H. Mahoney's Model Mobile Minstrels," *Indianapolis Freeman*, April 15, 1916.
32. "Robinson's Old Kentucky Minstrels," *Indianapolis Freeman*, December 18, 1915.
33. Dennis West, "Notes From Old Kentucky Minstrels," *Indianapolis Freeman*, December 18, 1915.
34. "Notes of Silas Green Co.," *Indianapolis Freeman*, September 30, 1916.
35. "Notes of Silas Green Co.," *Indianapolis Freeman*, November 18, 1916.
36. Max C. Elliott, "Silas Green and Mobile Minstrels," *Indianapolis Freeman*, November 25, 1916.
37. "Notes From the Big One in the Mississippi Delta," *Indianapolis Freeman*, October 6, 1917.
38. Charles Davis Wright, "Minstrels and Barnum & Bailey at Greenwood, Miss.," *Indianapolis Freeman*, October 27, 1917.
39. Wm. Reid-Connor, "Smart Set Minstrels Notes," *Indianapolis Freeman*, October 27, 1917.
40. Geo. E. Glasco, "A. G. Allen's Greater New Orleans Minstrels, Greenwood, Miss., Geo. W. Quine, Mgr.," *Indianapolis Freeman*, October 20, 1917.
41. "Notes From The Silas Green Shows," *Indianapolis Freeman*, October 20, 1917.
42. "A. G. Allen's Big Minstrel Show," *Indianapolis Freeman*, November 20, 1920.
43. Coy Herndon, "Coy Cogitates," *Chicago Defender*, October 10, 1925.
44. Unidentified Nashville paper, quoted in "The Stage," *Indianapolis Freeman*, May 12, 1900.
45. "The Stage," *Indianapolis Freeman*, May 26, 1900.
46. "Stage," *Indianapolis Freeman*, November 10, 1900.
47. "Stage," *Indianapolis Freeman*, January 5, 1901.
48. "Stage," *Indianapolis Freeman*, February 8, 1902.
49. "Stage," *Indianapolis Freeman*, February 21, 1903.
50. "Stage," *Indianapolis Freeman*, February 28, 1903.
51. "Aboard A. G. Allen's Private Car 999," *Indianapolis Freeman*, March 2, 1912.
52. Joe Norton, "Notes Of Allen's Minstrels," *Indianapolis Freeman*, December 13, 1913.
53. "Stage," *Indianapolis Freeman*, March 29, 1902.
54. P. L. Jenkins, "Aboard A. G. Allen's Private Car '999,'" *Indianapolis Freeman*, March 18, 1911.
55. "Stage," *Indianapolis Freeman*, June 15, 1901.
56. "Aboard A. G. Allen's Private Car, 'Ida May,'" *Indianapolis Freeman*, August 27, 1910.
57. J. B. Norton, "A. G. Allen's Minstrel Show," *Indianapolis Freeman*, July 17, 1915.
58. "Allen's Minstrels," *Indianapolis Freeman*, January 23, 1909.
59. "Stage," *Indianapolis Freeman*, March 30, 1901.
60. "Stage," *Indianapolis Freeman*, July 27, 1901.
61. For more on the death of Joe Ravise, see Abbott and Seroff, *Out of Sight*, p. 397.
62. "The Stage," *Indianapolis Freeman*, February 24, 1900.
63. Sylvester Russell, "Musical And Dramatic," *Indianapolis Freeman*, April 22, 1916.
64. "Stage," *Indianapolis Freeman*, June 7, 1902.

65. "The Stage," *Indianapolis Freeman*, November 14, 1903.
66. "Death of Henry McDade," *Indianapolis Freeman*, June 9, 1906. George McDade eventually left the minstrel profession. The 1930 Federal Census lists him as a lawyer, living in Knoxville with his wife and family.
67. "Pearl Moppins on the Cars," *Chicago Defender*, August 8, 1925.
68. John Chilton, *A Jazz Nursery: The Story of the Jenkins' Orphanage Bands of Charleston, South Carolina* (London: Bloomsbury Book Shop, 1980).
69. P. L. Jenkins, "Aboard A. G. Allen's Private Car 999," *Indianapolis Freeman*, January 4, 1913; January 25, 1913.
70. "Allen's Minstrels," *Indianapolis Freeman*, April 17, 1909.
71. "Allen's Minstrels," *Indianapolis Freeman*, June 19, 1909.
72. "Allen's Minstrels," *Indianapolis Freeman*, June 5, 1909; August 14, 1909.
73. "Aboard A. G. Allen's Private Car, 'Ida May,'" *Indianapolis Freeman*, May 7, 1910.
74. "Allen's Minstrels," *Indianapolis Freeman*, February 27, 1909.
75. "Allen's Minstrels," *Indianapolis Freeman*, November 13, 1909.
76. "Aboard A. G. Allen's Private Car, Ida May," *Indianapolis Freeman*, November 5, 1910.
77. "Aboard A. G. Allen's Private Car 999," *Indianapolis Freeman*, August 17, 1912.
78. P. L. Jenkins, "Aboard A. G. Allen's Private Car 999," *Indianapolis Freeman*, June 28, 1913.
79. "Gossip of the Stage," *Indianapolis Freeman*, June 6, 1914.
80. "The Stage," *Indianapolis Freeman*, August 26, 1899.
81. "The Stage," *Indianapolis Freeman*, September 24, 1898; "Cooperidge's World's Fair Band and Orchestra," *Indianapolis Freeman*, November 14, 1903. It is not presently known if, or how, Milton and William Vassar were related to Callie Vassar, also of St. Louis, Missouri.
82. "The Stage," *Indianapolis Freeman*, December 3, 1898; "Stage," *Indianapolis Freeman*, November 30, 1901; Sylvester Russell, "Chicago Weekly Review," *Indianapolis Freeman*, April 22, 1916; Sylvester Russell, "Chicago Weekly Review," *Indianapolis Freeman*, July 29, 1916.
83. "Stage," *Indianapolis Freeman*, June 22, 1901.
84. "Stage," *Indianapolis Freeman*, December 1, 1900.
85. "Stage," *Indianapolis Freeman*, August 30, 1902.
86. "Joe Norton Writes From North Carolina," *Indianapolis Freeman*, June 6, 1914. Chaney was also known simply as Marcus Veal.
87. "The Stage," *Indianapolis Freeman*, June 4, 1904.
88. "Stage," *Indianapolis Freeman*, April 20, 1901.
89. "The Stage," *Indianapolis Freeman*, March 24, 1900.
90. "The Stage," *Indianapolis Freeman*, May 5, 1900.
91. Abbott and Seroff, *Out of Sight*, p. 92.
92. "Stage," *Indianapolis Freeman*, October 27, 1900.
93. "Aboard A. G. Allen's Private Car, 'Ida May,'" *Indianapolis Freeman*, June 11, 1910.
94. Gid Tanner and His Georgia Boys, "Old Time Tunes," Columbia 15059-D, 1925; Jim Jackson, "I'm Gonna Start Me A Graveyard Of My Own," Vocalion 1164, 1928, reissued on Document DOCD-5114; Furry Lewis, "Furry's Blues," Victor V38519, 1928, reissued on Document DOCD-5004. Pinetop Smith's "Pinetop Blues" (Vocalion 1245, 1928, reissued on Document DOCD-5102) includes the phrase, "I'm gonna buy myself a graveyard of my own." A related theme is "heaven of my own." Bessie Smith recorded a "heaven of my own" verse in "Work House Blues," Columbia 14032-D, 1924, reissued on Frog CD DGF42. Michael Taft's *Web-Concordance of Pre-war Blues Lyrics* references Texas Alexander, "Yellow Girl Blues," Okeh 8801, 1928; Henry Thomas, "Worried Blues," Vocalion 1249, 1928; and Son House, "Preaching the Blues," Paramount 13013, 1930.
95. "Stage," *Indianapolis Freeman*, February 2, 1901.
96. "Aboard A. G. Allen's Private Car, 'Ida May,'" *Indianapolis Freeman*, August 27, 1910.
97. "Aboard A. G. Allen's Private Car 999," *Indianapolis Freeman*, March 2, 1912.
98. "Allen's Minstrels," *Indianapolis Freeman*, December 6, 1913.
99. "The Stage," *Indianapolis Freeman*, October 17, 1903; October 24, 1903. In his autobiography, *Born with the Blues* (New York: Oak Publications, 1965), pp. 19, 32–33, Perry Bradford said he "joined

Allen's New Orleans Minstrels in my home town, Atlanta, Georgia, in the fall of 1907 . . . I stayed with the New Orleans Minstrels until we played a town named Vinita in Oklahoma," where he left in a hurry after getting caught with loaded dice in "a 'crap game' going on in the baggage car." As in Jelly Roll Morton's Library of Congress interviews, Bradford's sense of chronology does not conform to contemporaneous documentation. Entertainers seldom claim to have launched their careers *later* than they actually did, but Bradford appears to have done so. Bradford's date of birth is variously given as 1893 and 1895; either way, he would have been less than ten years old when the *Freeman* first placed him on the road in 1902. According to a bio in the *Chicago Defender* of March 4, 1922, "Perry Bradford was born Feb. 14, 1889, in Montgomery, Ala.," and was taken to Atlanta at age 5: "His theatrical work began in 1902, when he joined Allen's New Orleans Minstrels, and he 'arrived' in Chicago in 1906."

100. "Aboard A. G. Allen's Private Car, 'Ida May,'" *Indianapolis Freeman*, April 16, 1910.
101. "The Stage," *Indianapolis Freeman*, December 9, 1905. For more on Sol Tibbs, see Abbott and Seroff, *Out of Sight*, p. 47.
102. Sol Tibbs, "Mama, Mama Make Cinda 'Haive Herself (New Orleans: Grunwald Co.), 1901.
103. Alec Robertson, "Cindy," transcribed by John Work III and reproduced in John W. Work, Lewis Wade Jones, and Samuel C. Adams, Jr. (Robert Gordon and Bruce Nemerov, eds.), *Lost Delta Found: Rediscovering the Fisk University—Library of Congress Coahoma County Study, 1941–1942* (Nashville: Vanderbilt University Press, 2005), p. 134.
104. "The Stage," *Indianapolis Freeman*, November 11, 1905.
105. "Allen's Minstrels," *Indianapolis Freeman*, February 27, 1909.
106. "The Stage," *Indianapolis Freeman*, December 31, 1904; "Stage," *Indianapolis Freeman*, May 27, 1905. A note from the Vendome Theater in Hamilton, Ohio, in the *Freeman* of January 9, 1909, informed that a performer known as "Shoe Strings" was "singing his own composition [*sic*], 'Ragged But Right.'" "Ragged but Right" was recorded numerous times over the course of several decades by such diverse musicians as Rufus and Ben Quillian, Charlie Slocum and Ikey Robinson, Riley Puckett, Moon Mullican, George Jones, and others.
107. "Aboard A. G. Allen's Private Car 'Ida May,'" *Indianapolis Freeman*, March 12, 1910; "Aboard A. G. Allen's Private Car, 'Ida May,'" August 27, 1910.
108. P. L. Jenkins, "Aboard A. G. Allen's Private Car," *Indianapolis Freeman*, August 12, 1911.
109. Jim Jackson, "I Heard the Voice of a Pork Chop," Victor 21387, 1928, reissued on DOCD-5114; Bogus Ben Covington, "I Heard the Voice of a Pork Chop," Paramount 12693, 1928, reissued on DOCD-5166.
110. "World's [sic] Davis Dead," *Indianapolis Freeman*, November 10, 1917.
111. "Stage," *Indianapolis Freeman*, April 12, 1902.
112. "The Stage," *Indianapolis Freeman*, September 30, 1899.
113. Hattie Garland's recordings have been reissued on Document DOCD-5510.
114. "The Stage," *Indianapolis Freeman*, April 21, 1900; "Augustus Stevens, Female Impersonator," *Indianapolis Freeman*, December 28, 1901.
115. P. L. Jenkins, "Allen's Minstrels," *Indianapolis Freeman*, May 22, 1909.
116. "Allen's Minstrels," *Indianapolis Freeman*, February 27, 1909.
117. "The Stage," *Indianapolis Freeman*, May 5, 1900.
118. "Stage," *Indianapolis Freeman*, February 23, 1901.
119. "Stage," *Indianapolis Freeman*, April 13, 1901.
120. "The Stage," *Indianapolis Freeman*, August 22, 1903.
121. "Stage," *Indianapolis Freeman*, June 14, 1902.
122. "Stage," *Indianapolis Freeman*, December 8, 1900.
123. "Stage," *Indianapolis Freeman*, December 22, 1900.
124. "Stage," *Indianapolis Freeman*, February 16, 1901.
125. Bob Hayes, "Here And There," *Chicago Defender*, August 29, 1942. The *Freeman* of December 19, 1903, noted Billy Arnte traveling with Weaver's Ragtime Opera Company: "He sends regards to Wm Hallback, Williams & Stevens and the A. G. Allen's N. O. Minstrel."
126. P. L. Jenkins, "Aboard A. G. Allen's Private Car '999,'" *Indianapolis Freeman*, September 23, 1911.

127. P. L. Jenkins, "Aboard A. G. Allen's Private Car 999," *Indianapolis Freeman*, January 25, 1913.
128. "The Stage," *Indianapolis Freeman*, August 15, 1908.
129. "The Stage," *Indianapolis Freeman*, July 30, 1900.
130. "The Stage," *Indianapolis Freeman*, January 14, 1905.
131. P. L. Jenkins, "Aboard A. G. Allen's Private Car 999," *Indianapolis Freeman*, August 9, 1913.
132. "Gossip of the Stage," *Indianapolis Freeman*, April 11, 1914.
133. "Stage Gossip," *Indianapolis Freeman*, December 12, 1914. See Appendix V for a roster of the band that brought out the blues with Allen's Minstrels.
134. P. L. Jenkins, "Aboard A. G. Allen's Private Car 999," *Indianapolis Freeman*, March 22, 1913.
135. "J. B. Norton Writes From Allen's Minstrels," *Indianapolis Freeman*, September 12, 1914.
136. "J. B. Norton Writes From Allen's Minstrels," *Indianapolis Freeman*, November 28, 1914.
137. J. B. Norton, "Notes From A. G. Allen's Show," *Indianapolis Freeman*, October 3, 1914.
138. "J. B. Norton Writes From Allen's Minstrels," *Indianapolis Freeman*, November 21, 1914.
139. J. H. McCamon, "J. B. [*sic*] McCamon Writes From The Virginia Minstrels," *Indianapolis Freeman*, May 8, 1915.
140. Chas. E. Rue, "Notes Of A. G. Allen's Minstrels," *Indianapolis Freeman*, May 1, 1915.
141. "Mase [*sic*] McQuitty Writes From Sparks Circus," *Indianapolis Freeman*, April 24, 1915.
142. "Stage Gossip," *Indianapolis Freeman*, May 8, 1915.
143. "De Ridder, La.," *Indianapolis Freeman*, April 24, 1915.
144. "A. G. Allen's Minstrels," *Indianapolis Freeman*, April 24, 1915.
145. J. H. McCamon, "J. B. [*sic*] McCamon Writes From The Virginia Minstrels," *Indianapolis Freeman*, May 8, 1915.
146. "A. G. Allen's Band All Right," *Indianapolis Freeman*, May 22, 1915.
147. J. B. Norton, "A. G. Allen's Big Minstrel Show," *Indianapolis Freeman*, June 5, 1915.
148. J. B. Norton, "A. G. Allen's Big Minstrel Show," *Indianapolis Freeman*, June 5, 1915.
149. J. B. Norton, "A. G. Allen's Minstrel Show," *Indianapolis Freeman*, July 17, 1915.
150. J. B. Norton, "A. G. Allen's Big Minstrel Show," *Indianapolis Freeman*, June 19, 1915.
151. J. B. Norton, "A. G. Allen's Minstrel Show," *Indianapolis Freeman*, July 17, 1915.
152. Dennis West, "Notes From Robinson's Old Kentucky Minstrels," *Indianapolis Freeman*, February 19, 1916.
153. Originally made for Columbia and Gennett between 1924 and 1931, Hezekiah Jenkins's complete recorded output is reissued on Document DOCD-5481 and DOCD-5574.
154. "A. G. Allen's World's Greatest Colored Minstrels," *Indianapolis Freeman*, October 13, 1917.
155. "A. G. Allen's Greater New Orleans Minstrels," *Indianapolis Freeman*, December 22, 1917.
156. Dennis West, "Government Closes Shows: F. S. Wolcott's Rabbit Foot Company and A. G. Allen's Minstrels Must Quit the Road," *Indianapolis Freeman*, January 26, 1918.
157. "Brownlee & Allen's Minstrels," *Indianapolis Freeman*, August 30, 1919.
158. "Brownlee & Allen's Minstrels," *Indianapolis Freeman*, August 30, 1919.
159. "Washburn's Famous Minstrels Encounter Heavy Rain In Mississippi," *Indianapolis Freeman*, November 8, 1919.
160. Leon "Sonny" Gray, "Jottings From A. G. Allen's New Orleans Minstrels," *Indianapolis Freeman*, September 6, 1919. Membership of Prof. Erwin's "wonderful jazz band" with A. G. Allen's Minstrels in 1919 can be found in Appendix V.
161. "Wanted For A. G. Allen's Minstrels," ad in *Indianapolis Freeman*, November 6, 1920.
162. "Allen's Minstrels," *Chicago Defender*, April 21, 1923.
163. "Allen's Minstrels," *Chicago Defender*, June 2, 1923.
164. "A. G. Allen Dead," *Chicago Defender*, January 22, 1927.
165. Winstead is named on 1928 and 1929 orders for advertising placards for A. G. Allen's Minstrels from Hatch Show Print in Nashville. For a fascinating account of Emerson Stowe Winstead and his Mighty Minstrels, see Alex Albright, "Noon Parade and Midnight Ramble," *Good Country People: An Irregular Journal of the Cultures of Eastern North Carolina* (Rocky Mount: North Carolina Wesleyan Press, 1995).

166. "Mr. Lewis Chappelle Dead," *Indianapolis Freeman*, February 18, 1905.
167. "Stage," *Indianapolis Freeman*, January 14, 1899.
168. Charles Wolfe, *Devil's Box* (Nashville: The Country Music Foundation Press, 1997).
169. "The Stage," *Indianapolis Freeman*, April 29, 1899.
170. "The Stage," *Indianapolis Freeman*, June 30, 1900.
171. "Pat Chappell Again," *Florida Times Union And Citizen*, October 1, 1899.
172. "Took the Floor," *Tampa Morning Tribune*, September 28, 1899; *Indianapolis Freeman*, May 5, 1906. Located south of Ybor City and east of what eventually became downtown Tampa, Fort Brooke was annexed into the city of Tampa in 1907. Thanks to Curator Rodney H. Kite-Powell II, Tampa Bay History Center, Tampa, Florida.
173. *Tampa Morning Tribune*, March 13, 1900.
174. "The Stage," *Indianapolis Freeman*, April 7, 1900.
175. "The Stage," *Indianapolis Freeman*, May 12, 1900.
176. "Stage," *Indianapolis Freeman*, September 8, 1900.
177. Sylvester Russell, "A Review of the Stage," *Indianapolis Freeman*, February 15, 1902.
178. "Pat Chappelle Grows Caustic," *Indianapolis Freeman*, March 1, 1902.
179. "Stage," *Indianapolis Freeman*, November 9, 1901.
180. "Stage," *Indianapolis Freeman*, December 7, 1901.
181. "Stage," *Indianapolis Freeman*, August 30, 1902.
182. "William Goff Kennedy Dead After Lingering Illness," *Nashville Globe*, March 15, 1918.
183. "Stage," *Indianapolis Freeman*, September 27, 1902.
184. "Stage," *Indianapolis Freeman*, October 4, 1902.
185. "Stage," *Indianapolis Freeman*, March 7, 1903.
186. "The Stage," *Indianapolis Freeman*, August 8, 1903.
187. "The Stage," *Indianapolis Freeman*, July 11, 1903.
188. "The Stage," *Indianapolis Freeman*, August 29, 1903.
189. *Atlanta Constitution*, quoted in "The Stage," *Indianapolis Freeman*, August 29, 1903.
190. "Stage," *Indianapolis Freeman*, April 18, 1903. A note the following week informed that the walking gents' straw beavers were "made especially for Mr. Chappelle by the Knox hat company."
191. "The Stage," *Indianapolis Freeman*, July 16, 1904.
192. "The Stage," *Indianapolis Freeman*, June 20, 1903.
193. "Stage," *Indianapolis Freeman*, August 1, 1903. For more on Detroit-based pianist and composer Fred S. Stone, see Abbott and Seroff, *Out of Sight*, pp. 256–59; and Nan Bostick and Arthur LaBrew, "Harry P. Guy and the 'Ragtime Era' of Detroit Michigan," *Rag-Time Ephemeralist* vol. 1, no. 2 (1999).
194. "The Stage," *Indianapolis Freeman*, June 11, 1904.
195. "The Stage," *Indianapolis Freeman*, June 20, 1903; July 18, 1903.
196. "The Stage," *Indianapolis Freeman*, April 29, 1905.
197. "The Stage," *Indianapolis Freeman*, April 9, 1904.
198. "The Stage," *Indianapolis Freeman*, April 23, 1904; May 28, 1904.
199. "The Stage," *Indianapolis Freeman*, December 10, 1904.
200. "The Stage," *Indianapolis Freeman*, December 10, 1904.
201. "The Stage," *Indianapolis Freeman*, January 6, 1906.
202. "The Stage," *Indianapolis Freeman*, June 24, 1905.
203. "Theater Royal, Memphis, Tenn.," *Indianapolis Freeman*, April 2, 1910.
204. "The Stage," *Indianapolis Freeman*, January 6, 1906.
205. "The Stage," *Indianapolis Freeman*, May 6, 1905.
206. "'For Rent' Minstrels Shows Under Canvas," *Indianapolis Freeman*, April 27, 1907.
207. "From A Rabbit's Foot Company," *Indianapolis Freeman*, January 25, 1908. Chappelle preceded Alexander Tolliver by a decade as the "P. T. Barnum of his Race."
208. "Business Man Of Rare Ability," *Indianapolis Freeman*, October 23, 1909.
209. "The Stage," *Indianapolis Freeman*, August 25, 1906.
210. John W. Work, *American Negro Songs and Spirituals* (New York: Crown Publishers, 1940), pp. 22–23.
211. "Belmont Street Theater, Pensacola, Fla.," *Indianapolis Freeman*, February 19, 1910; "The Stage," *Indianapolis Freeman*, November 20, 1909.
212. "A Rabbit Foot Comedy Company," *Indianapolis Freeman*, June 27, 1908.
213. "A Rabbit's Foot Comedy," *Indianapolis Freeman*, July 18, 1908. The title "These Dogs of Mine" turns up on 1924 recordings by both Ma Rainey (as "Those Dogs of Mine") and Helen Gross.

214. "Rabbit's Foot Minstrel Co.'s Car Burned," *Indianapolis Freeman*, August 22, 1908.
215. "'A Rabbit's Foot' Company," *Indianapolis Freeman*, March 20, 1909.
216. "The Stage," *Indianapolis Freeman*, May 8, 1909.
217. "Rabbit's Foot Company Gives Bad Show," *Indianapolis Freeman*, July 3, 1909.
218. "'A Rabbit's Foot' Company," *Indianapolis Freeman*, July 24, 1909.
219. "'A Rabbit Foot' Comedy Co.," *Indianapolis Freeman*, December 4, 1909. The three titles associated with Will Goff Kennedy are all coon songs, all published in 1909: "Come After Breakfast" is James "Tim" Brymn, James Burris, and Chris Smith, "Come After Breakfast, Bring 'Long Your Lunch, and Leave 'Fore Supper Time" (New York: Jos. W. Stern & Co.); "Transmag" is James Burris and Chris Smith, "Trans-mag-ni-fi-can-bam-dam-u-ality" (New York: Jerome H. Remick & Co.); and "The Christening" is most likely Cecil Mack and Chris Smith, "Abraham Lincoln Jones or The Christening" (New York: Gotham-Attucks). Thanks to Wayne Shirley for identifying "The Christening."
220. "A Rabbit's Foot Company, Jacksonville, Fla.," *Indianapolis Freeman*, August 13, 1910.
221. "Pat Chappelle's Rabbit's Foot Comedy Company, *Indianapolis Freeman*, September 24, 1910.
222. Mississippi Fred McDowell, "I Wish I Was in Heaven Sittin' Down," Arhoolie LP F1027; Rev. Robert Wilkins, "In Heaven, Sitting Down," Sire/London LP SES 97003, 1968. Thanks to David Evans for assistance.
223. Fleta Jan Brown, "I Wish I Was in Heaven Sitting Down" (M. Witmark and Son), 1908.
224. In 1935 an African American male "jive" or "rhythm" vocal quartet, the Mississippi Mud Mashers, possibly from Biloxi (see "Biloxi, Miss.," *Louisiana Weekly*, April 15, 1939), recorded a song titled "Take My Seat and Sit Down" (Bluebird 5899, reissued on Document DOCD-5550). Delta bluesman Son House used the phrase "I'm gonna take my seat and sit down" in his "Preachin' The Blues—Part II" (Paramount 13013, 1930; reissued on Document DOCD-5002). A song titled "Choose My Seat and Set Down" was recorded by Amy Moss at Natchez, Mississippi, for the Library of Congress on October 18, 1940. In 1956, the Five Blind Boys of Mississippi recorded "Save a Seat for Me" (Peacock 1760, 1956), which makes the request: "If you make it in Glory before I do, save a seat for me." Further, Howard Odum transcribed the phrase, "I wish I wus in de kingdom settin' side o' my Lord," which he collected in either Mississippi or Georgia, as part of a study titled "Religious Folk-Songs of the Southern Negroes," published in *The American Journal of Religious Psychology and Education* vol. 3, no. 3 (July 1909).
225. "'A Rabbit's Foot Co.,' Yazoo City, Miss.," *Indianapolis Freeman*, October 22, 1910.
226. "Notes Of 'A Rabbit's Foot Co.,'" *Indianapolis Freeman*, December 24, 1910.
227. Baby F. Seals, "Discussing Billy M'Clain's Letter," *Indianapolis Freeman*, August 12, 1911.
228. "The One Billy M'Clain In Europe," *Indianapolis Freeman*, July 15, 1911.
229. "A Rabbit Foot Company," *Indianapolis Freeman*, August 19, 1911.
230. Information contained on Fred Swift Wolcott's headstone in Wintergreen Cemetery, Port Gibson, Mississippi.
231. "Wolcott's Fun Factory," *Indianapolis Freeman*, May 14, 1910; "F. G. [*sic*] Wolcott's Fun Factory," *Indianapolis Freeman*, May 28, 1910; "F. S. Wolcott's Fun Factory, Greenville, N. C.," *Indianapolis Freeman*, June 4, 1910.
232. "The Rabbits Foot Musical Comedy Company On Wheels Again," *Indianapolis Freeman*, November 16, 1912.
233. "Boxley, Ga.," *Indianapolis Freeman*, November 30, 1912.
234. Marcellus Henderson, "Rabbit Foot Musical Company At Orlando, Fla.," *Indianapolis Freeman*, January 4, 1913. The title of the afterpiece was also given as "Eliza Jane Spliven's Wedding."
235. "Rabbit's Foot Company," *Indianapolis Freeman*, May 3, 1913.
236. David G. Smith, "The Rabbit Foot Co.," *Indianapolis Freeman*, May 17, 1913.
237. J. M. Means, "A Rabbit's Foot Company," *Indianapolis Freeman*, January 11, 1913.

238. "Cracker Jack Comedy Co.," *Indianapolis Freeman*, November 7, 1914.
239. "Notes—Rabbit Foot Company," *Indianapolis Freeman*, April 26, 1913.
240. "Rabbit's Foot Show Notes," *Indianapolis Freeman*, July 12, 1913.
241. "Gossip Of The Stage," *Indianapolis Freeman*, February 8, 1913.
242. "Notes—Rabbit Foot Company," *Indianapolis Freeman*, April 26, 1913.
243. "From F. S. Wolcott's Rabbit Foot Company," *Indianapolis Freeman*, December 13, 1913.
244. Karl Gert zur Heide, "Mortonia and More," *Doctor Jazz Magazine* no. 189 (June 2005), p. 11.
245. "Notes—Rabbit Foot Company," *Indianapolis Freeman*, April 26, 1913.
246. "Stage," *Indianapolis Freeman*, March 7, 1903.
247. P. L. Jenkins, "F. S. Wolcott's Rabbit Foot Company," *Indianapolis Freeman*, January 29, 1916.
248. "Notes From 'A Rabbit Foot' Company," *Indianapolis Freeman*, November 8, 1913.
249. Freddie Pratt, "Notes From F. S. Wolcott's Rabbit Foot Co.," *Indianapolis Freeman*, February 21, 1914; Freddie Pratt, "Notes From A. Rabbitfoot [*sic*] Co.," *Indianapolis Freeman*, April 11, 1914.
250. Freddie Pratt, "A Rabbit Foot Company," *Indianapolis Freeman*, October 17, 1914.
251. Freddie Pratt, "A Rabbit's Foot Company And 'Gold' Band," *Indianapolis Freeman*, July 11, 1914.
252. "Notes From A Rabbit Foot Co.," *Indianapolis Freeman*, June 6, 1914.
253. Freddie Pratt, "Notes From A Rabbit Foot Company," *Indianapolis Freeman*, June 13, 1914.
254. Dennis West, "Notes From F. S. Wolcott's Rabbit Foot Co.," *Indianapolis Freeman*, January 20, 1917.
255. Freddie Pratt, "F. S. Wolcott's Rabbit's Foot Company," *Indianapolis Freeman*, July 4, 1914; Freddie Pratt, "A Rabbit's Foot Company And 'Gold' Band," *Indianapolis Freeman*, July 11, 1914.
256. Freddie Pratt, "A Rabbit Foot Company," *Indianapolis Freeman*, October 17, 1914.
257. Vernor Massey, "A Rabbit Foot Company," *Indianapolis Freeman*, July 10, 1915.
258. "The Rabbit's Foot Company At Greenville, Miss.," *Indianapolis Freeman*, October 16, 1915.
259. Freddie Pratt, "Notes From F. S. Wolcott Rabbit Foot Co.," *Indianapolis Freeman*, February 14, 1914.
260. Freddie Pratt, "Notes From A Rabbit Foot Company," *Indianapolis Freeman*, March 21, 1914.
261. "Notes From A Rabbit Foot Co.," *Indianapolis Freeman*, April 18, 1914.
262. Frederick Pratt, "Notes From The Rabbit Foot County [*sic*]," *Indianapolis Freeman*, May 9, 1914.
263. Freddie Pratt, "Notes From A Rabbit Foot County [*sic*]," *Indianapolis Freeman*, May 16, 1914.
264. Freddie Pratt, "A Rabbit-Foot Company," *Indianapolis Freeman*, May 23, 1914.
265. "Freddie Pratt Writes From 'A Rabbit Foot. Co.' Helena, Ark.," *Indianapolis Freeman*, November 21, 1914.
266. Norman Mason interviewed by Paul Crawford, February 6, 1960 (Hogan Jazz Archive, Tulane University).
267. George Mitchell interviewed by Bill Russell, July 1, 1959 (Hogan Jazz Archive, Tulane University).
268. Jelly Roll Morton's Red Hot Peppers, 1926 and 1927; New Orleans Bootblacks, 1926; New Orleans Wanderers, 1926; Luis Russell's Red Hot Six, 1926; Ada Brown, 1926; Doc Cook Band, in which he replaced Freddie Keppard, 1926; Johnny Dodds's Black Bottom Stompers, 1927; possibly with Jimmie Noone's Apex Club Orchestra, 1928 and 1929; Earl Hines, 1929; Dixie Rhythm Kings, with Omer Simeon, 1929; Frankie "Half Pint" Jaxon, 1933.
269. Joe Watts, "A Rabbit's Foot Show," *Indianapolis Freeman*, May 22, 1915. Watts also noted that, "All mail for Marcus Veal Chaney will reach him at Box 181, Rolling Fork, Miss."
270. Joe Watts, "A Rabbit's Foot Show," *Indianapolis Freeman*, June 12, 1915.
271. Vernor Massey, "A Rabbit Foot Company," *Indianapolis Freeman*, July 10, 1915.
272. Vernor Massey, "Notes From A Rabbit Foot Co.," *Indianapolis Freeman*, June 26, 1915.
273. Vernor Massey, "Notes From A Rabbit Foot Co.," *Indianapolis Freeman*, June 26, 1915.
274. "A 'Rabbit's Foot Comedy' At Greenwood, Miss.," *Indianapolis Freeman*, October 2, 1915.
275. Quine is first noted with the Foots in *Freeman* correspondence of September 9, 1916.

276. P. L. Jenkins, "F. S. Wolcott's Rabbit Foot Co.," *Indianapolis Freeman*, February 12, 1916.
277. P. L. Jenkins, "F. S. Wolcott's Rabbit Foot Co.," *Indianapolis Freeman*, March 4, 1916.
278. Dennis West, "Notes From F. S. Wolcott's Rabbitfoot Co.," *Indianapolis Freeman*, January 13, 1917.
279. P. L. Jenkins, "F. S. Wolcott's Rabbit Foot Co.," *Indianapolis Freeman*, February 12, 1916; March 4, 1916; "Notes From F. S. Wolcott's Rabbit Foot Co.," *Indianapolis Freeman*, September 2, 1916.
280. P. L. Jenkins, "F. S. Wolcott's Rabbit Foot Co.," *Indianapolis Freeman*, March 4, 1916; April 22, 1916.
281. E. Alfred Drew, "Notes From F. S. Wolcott's Rabbit Foot Minstrels," *Indianapolis Freeman*, September 9, 1916; Dennis West, "Notes From F. S. Wolcott's Rabbit Foot Co.," *Indianapolis Freeman*, December 2, 1916.
282. Dennis West, "Notes From F. S. Wolcott's Rabbit Foot Co.," *Indianapolis Freeman*, January 20, 1917.
283. Al Wells, "Walcott's Rabbit Foot Show Does Good Business," *Indianapolis Freeman*, April 21, 1917.
284. Al Wells, "Wolcott's Rabbit Foot Conjures North Carolina," *Indianapolis Freeman*, June 23, 1917.
285. Dennis West, "Walcott's Rabbits Hop About Over Good Ground," *Indianapolis Freeman*, August 4, 1917; Dennis West, "Walcott's Rabbits Are Back In Alabama," *Indianapolis Freeman*, August 18, 1917.
286. "Government Closes Shows," *Indianapolis Freeman*, January 26, 1918. "David James," the mellophonist mentioned here, may be David Jones of New Orleans, who had recently toured in the band with Tolliver's Smart Set.
287. Port Gibson has been under considerable stress since the enforcement of Civil Rights law. Details can be found in Emilye Crosby, *A Little Taste of Freedom* (Chapel Hill: University of North Carolina Press, 2005).
288. "Glen Sade Place Sold," *Port Gibson Reveille*, April 25, 1918. Thanks to Jerry Bangham of Port Gibson, who brought this and other newspaper items to the authors' attention.
289. World War I Selective Service System Draft Registration Cards, 1917–1918 (Ancestry.com).
290. For instance, an ad that Wolcott placed in the *Port Gibson Reveille* of October 28, 1943, announced: "Rabbit Foot Minstrels has closed 1943 season and will not show in Port Gibson Saturday Night. I Am In Market [*sic*] to buy oil leases, mineral and royalties, at all times. Come see me. F. S. Wolcott, Telephone 104."
291. David Evans, "Since Ol' Gabriel's Time: Hezekiah and the Houserockers," *Louisiana Folklife* vol. 7, no. 2 (October 1982), pp. 1–34.
292. Some confirmation can be found in the Claiborne County Oral History Project interviews conducted by David Crosby, in which Annie Wade said, "Wolcott used to have buildings in Glensage [*sic*], where the performers would stay and practice"; and Nathan Jones said, "Wolcott had a plantation, he had a place. He kept them. They had a job. I don't know how much money they made when they got on the road."
293. Evans, "Since Ol' Gabriel's Time."
294. The building was still standing in the summer of 2006.
295. David Crosby interview with Carl Boren (n.d.).
296. "From The Rabbit Foot Co.," *Indianapolis Freeman*, July 26, 1919.
297. "Notes from Rabbit Foot Co.," *Indianapolis Freeman*, April 3, 1920.
298. Odell Rawlinson, "Notes From S. Walcott Rabbit Foot Company," *Indianapolis Freeman*, May 22, 1920; Odell Rawlinson, "Rabbit Foot Co.," *Indianapolis Freeman*, June 5, 1920; "Notes from F. S. Wolcott's Rabbit Foot Co." *Indianapolis Freeman*, July 17, 1920.
299. "Notes From A. Rabbit Foot Co.," *Indianapolis Freeman*, August 7, 1920.
300. Milton D. Quigless, Sr., "Two Weeks on a Minstrel Show," *Good Country People: An Irregular Journal of the Cultures of Eastern North Carolina* (Rocky Mount: North Carolina Wesleyan College Press, 1995), pp. 91–113.
301. "Minstrel and Tent Show Talk," *Billboard*, March 29, 1924.
302. "Minstrel and Tent Show Talk," *Billboard*, November 8, 1924. In an interview conducted by David Crosby, February 5, 2006, F. S. Wolcott's

daughter Hilda Wolcott Hutchings said that her father at one time owned the Planters Hotel, which still stands on Market Street in Port Gibson. She said it was used as a dining hall for Rabbit's Foot Company members gathering in Port Gibson prior to the annual tour. The "Rabbit's Foot Hotel" and the Planters Hotel are probably one and the same. Any connection between the Planters Hotel and the elusive "big house for performers" described by Pee Wee Whitaker remains speculative.

303. Buzzin' Burton, "Rabbit Foot Minstrels," *Chicago Defender*, February 14, 1925.
304. Coy Herndon, "Coy Cogitates," *Chicago Defender*, May 2, 1925.
305. J. Churchill, "Sleep Baby Sleep"/"Mad Man Blues," Paramount 12091, 1923, reissued on Document DOCD-5532.
306. Joseph Jones, "Says Jonesy," *Chicago Defender*, August 16, 1924.
307. For example, neither Louis Jordan nor Rufus Thomas is mentioned in any known newspaper report.
308. George Guesnon interviewed by Bill Russell, June 10, 1960 (Hogan Jazz Archive, Tulane University). Guesnon did not make clear how long he stayed with the Foots, noting only that he had tried to make a go with a Jackson, Mississippi–based band led by Little Brother Montgomery, "but nothing was happening, so I went on the [Rabbit Foot] show, and when I come off the show, well, that's when I went to New York." It would appear that Guesnon joined some time after October 1936, when he and Little Brother Montgomery recorded together for Decca in New Orleans; and left before April 1940, when he recorded in New York at the head of a small band.
309. Bob Hayes, "Here and There," *Chicago Defender*, November 5, 1938.
310. Jessie Charles interviewed by Richard B. Allen, December 15, 1967 (Hogan Jazz Archive, Tulane University); Lars Edegran, "Jessie Charles Talking to Lars Edegran: An Interview in New Orleans," *Footnote* vol. 6, no. 6 (August-September 1975), pp. 19–27, and vol. 7, no. 1 (October-November 1975), pp. 13–18.
311. Bob Hayes, "Here And There," *Chicago Defender*, June 27, 1942.
312. Bob Hayes, "Here and There," *Chicago Defender*, October 16, 1943.
313. "Rabbit Foot Minstrels To Show Here Wednesday," *Port Gibson Reveille*, July 10, 1943.
314. Interviews with Annie Wade, Harry Parker, and Nathan Jones, conducted by David Crosby for Claiborne County Oral History Project. These interviews are part of the Mississippi Oral History Program. The tapes are deposited at the Center for Oral History and Cultural Heritage, at the University of Southern Mississippi. It may be relevant to note that Nathan Jones was a determined civil rights activist. His leadership role in the struggle for equal rights in Claiborne County, Mississippi, is chronicled in Emilye Crosby's 2005 book, *A Little Taste of Freedom*.
315. Libby Hollingsworth, interviewed by David Crosby for the Claiborne County Oral History Project.
316. Russ Daley, "'Rabbit's Foot' Minstrel One Of Last In Dixie," *New Orleans Item*, July 15, 1954 (clipping in vertical file, Hogan Jazz Archive, Tulane University).
317. "Diamond Teeth Mary," "If I Can't Sell It, I'm Gonna Sit on It," Big Boss CD BB91003. "Diamond Teeth Mary" obituary, *Living Blues* no. 153 (September-October 2000).
318. In fact, the Foots had been hopping around for fifty-six years, since Pat Chappelle's tenuous debut at Paterson, New Jersey, in the fall of 1900.
319. Baker E. Morton, "'Rabbit' Foot' Is 44 Years Old And Still Going Strong," *Louisiana Weekly*, July 7, 1956.
320. Worthia "Showboy" Thomas interviewed by Bill Russell, December 11, 1961 (Hogan Jazz Archive, Tulane University). In later years, Thomas was less inclined to give interviews. He died in 1994.
321. Hosea Sapp (April 13, 1912–February 3, 1988) is present on Roy Milton's Solid Senders' sessions for the Hamp-Tone, Juke Box, and Miltone labels. He also recorded under the name Hosea Sapp and His Solid Six for Plymouth Records in 1949, and with the Johnny Otis Orchestra for Savoy Records

in 1950. Thanks to Bo Berglind, Richard Reicheg, and Billy Vera.

322. Guesnon interviewed by Russell.
323. Thanks to Jim Sherraden of Hatch Show Print for providing access to archival records.
324. "The Stage," *Indianapolis Freeman*, December 22, 1906.
325. Macon City Directory listings, compiled by Washington Library archivist Muriel McDowell-Jackson.
326. Yet standing, the Douglass Theater has been fully restored by the City of Macon. Broadway is now Martin Luther King Boulevard.
327. "Florida Blossoms Co.," *Indianapolis Freeman*, June 6, 1908.
328. "The Florida Blossoms," *Indianapolis Freeman*, October 31, 1908; "Florida Blossoms Show," *Indianapolis Freeman*, January 9, 1909.
329. "The Stage," *Indianapolis Freeman*, November 28, 1908.
330. "The Florida Blossoms," *Indianapolis Freeman*, January 30, 1909.
331. "The Florida Blossoms," *Indianapolis Freeman*, November 14, 1908.
332. Courtesy Muriel McDowell-Jackson, Washington Library, Macon, Georgia.
333. "Florida Blossoms Show," *Indianapolis Freeman*, January 9, 1909.
334. "The Florida Blossoms," *Indianapolis Freeman*, April 24, 1909.
335. "Florida Blossoms Company," *Indianapolis Freeman*, September 11, 1909.
336. Clarence Steward, "Florida Blossoms Company," *Indianapolis Freeman*, July 24, 1909.
337. "Florida Blossom Minstrel," *Indianapolis Freeman*, December 18, 1909.
338. "The Florida Blossoms Company," *Indianapolis Freeman*, November 20, 1909.
339. "The Florida Blossoms Co.," *Indianapolis Freeman*, July 17, 1909.
340. "The Florida Blossoms Company," *Indianapolis Freeman*, November 20, 1909; "Florida Blossom Minstrel," *Indianapolis Freeman*, December 18, 1909. This same song can be heard on 1920s race recordings by Sippie Wallace, Barbecue Bob, and Frankie "Half Pint" Jaxon: Sippie Wallace, "I'm So Glad I'm Brownskin," Okeh 8197, 1924, reissued on Document DOCD-5399; Barbecue Bob, "Chocolate to the Bone," Columbia 14331-D, 1928, reissued on Document DOCD-5046; Frankie "Half Pint" Jaxon, "Chocolate to the Bone," Vocalion 1583, 1930, reissued on Document DOCD-5259.
341. "Coy Herndon, 'The Wizard of Hoopville,'" *Indianapolis Freeman*, December 27, 1913.
342. "Florida Blossom Minstrel," *Indianapolis Freeman*, December 18, 1909.
343. "The Florida Blossoms Company," *Indianapolis Freeman*, July 9, 1910.
344. "The Florida Blossoms En Route," *Indianapolis Freeman*, February 18, 1911.
345. Lawrence L. Fisher, "Florida Blossoms, In and About Washington, D. C.," *Indianapolis Freeman*, May 27, 1911.
346. "The Florida Blossoms Co.," *Indianapolis Freeman*, December 23, 1911.
347. "Gossip Of The Stage," *Indianapolis Freeman*, December 28, 1912.
348. "Notes Of The Florida Blossom Company," *Indianapolis Freeman*, July 5, 1913.
349. "Gossip Of The Stage," *Indianapolis Freeman*, January 31, 1914.
350. "Notes From Pete Worthey's Famous Florida Musical Comedy Co.," *Indianapolis Freeman*, April 20, 1918.
351. "The Florida Blossoms Company," *Indianapolis Freeman*, July 5, 1913.
352. "Uncle Joe," Hall Negro Quartette, Planned Program Service (radio transcription) No. 103, 1936, reissued on Document DOCD-5415. "Old Uncle Joe" was also recorded by the white Macon Quartet, in Atlanta, Georgia, 1927 (Columbia 15211-D), and by the white McKinney Brothers in 1934 (Champion 16830). The McKinney Brothers close their version with a barbershop harmonization of a verse from Bland's "In the Evening by the Moonlight."
353. H. Woodard, "The Douglass Theatre, Macon, Ga.," *Indianapolis Freeman*, March 27, 1915.
354. J. L. Williams, "Notes From The Florida Blossom Show," *Indianapolis Freeman*, July 31, 1915.

355. J. L. Williams, "The Florida Blossom Show," *Indianapolis Freeman*, August 14, 1915.
356. "Notes From Florida-Blossom's Company," *Indianapolis Freeman*, January 1, 1916.
357. J. L. Williams, "The Florida Blossom Show," *Indianapolis Freeman*, August 14, 1915.
358. J. L. Williams, "Notes Of The Florida Blossom Show," *Indianapolis Freeman*, July 31, 1915.
359. J. L. Williams, "The Florida Blossom Show," *Indianapolis Freeman*, August 14, 1915.
360. "Brother Low Down" was recorded by Bert Williams in 1921 (Columbia A3508, reissued on Archeophone ARCH-5002). Bertha Idaho recorded four songs for Columbia in 1928, reissued on Document DOCD-5514.
361. "Notes From The Florida Blossoms Co.," *Indianapolis Freeman*, December 18, 1915.
362. Bessie Smith is identified as a "coon shouter" in numerous *Indianapolis Freeman* reports of 1910–1918. Examples include: "Pekin Theatre, Memphis, Tenn.," September 3, 1910; "Gossip of the Stage," August 12, 1911; and "The New Crown Garden," June 29, 1912. For more on Bessie Smith's early career see Lynn Abbott and Doug Seroff, "Bessie Smith: The Early Years," *Blues & Rhythm* no. 70 (June 1992).
363. "Notes From The Florida Blossoms Co.," *Indianapolis Freeman*, July 29, 1916.
364. "Notes From The Florida Blossoms Co.," *Indianapolis Freeman*, October 14, 1916.
365. "Notes From Florida Blossoms Co.," *Indianapolis Freeman*, March 25, 1916.
366. "Notes From The Florida Blossoms Co.," *Indianapolis Freeman*, June 10, 1916.
367. "Notes From Florida Blossoms Co.," *Indianapolis Freeman*, March 25, 1916.
368. "Notes From The Florida Blossoms Co.," *Indianapolis Freeman*, June 10, 1916.
369. "Notes From Florida Blossoms Co.," *Indianapolis Freeman*, September 2, 1916.
370. "Notes From The Florida Blossoms Co.," *Indianapolis Freeman*, December 2, 1916.
371. "The Florida Blossoms," *Indianapolis Freeman*, September 21, 1918.
372. "Manager Pete Worthey Of Florida Blossoms Receives Bad News," *Indianapolis Freeman*, June 23, 1917.
373. "Notes From Florida Blossoms Company," *Indianapolis Freeman*, July 21, 1917.
374. "Notes From Smith's Old Kentucky," *Indianapolis Freeman*, July 10, 1920.
375. "Notes From Pete Worthey's Famous Florida Musical Comedy Co.," *Indianapolis Freeman*, April 20, 1918.
376. "Notes From Pete Worthey's Famous Florida Musical Comedy Co.," *Indianapolis Freeman*, April 20, 1918.
377. Pete Worthy death certificate (Thanks to Muriel McDowell-Jackson, Archivist, Washington Library, Macon, Georgia).
378. *Freeman* correspondence of July 5, 1919, mentions, "Our manager, Mr. Oscar Rogers, is well pleased with his band and show."
379. "Florida Blossoms Show," *Indianapolis Freeman*, August 2, 1919.
380. "Notes From The Florida Blossoms," *Indianapolis Freeman*, August 28, 1920.
381. "Florida Blossom Co. Notes," *Indianapolis Freeman*, April 3, 1920; "Florida Blossoms Co. Notes," *Indianapolis Freeman*, July 31, 1920; "Notes From The Florida Blossoms," *Indianapolis Freeman*, August 28, 1920.
382. "Florida Blossoms Notes," *Indianapolis Freeman*, April 24, 1920.
383. "Notes From The Florida Blossoms," *Indianapolis Freeman*, August 28, 1920.
384. Chilton, *A Jazz Nursery*, p. 52.
385. "Florida Blossoms," *Chicago Defender*, March 28, 1925.
386. "Gus Smith Writes," *Chicago Defender*, September 19, 1925.
387. Buck Nelson, "Fla. Blossoms," *Chicago Defender*, November 1, 1924.
388. "Minstrel and Tent Show Talk," *Billboard*, March 7, 1925.
389. "Florida Blossoms," *Chicago Defender*, June 13, 1925.
390. "Florida Blossoms," *Chicago Defender*, August 1, 1925.
391. "The Florida Blossoms," *Chicago Defender*, September 26, 1925.
392. "Florida Blossoms," *Chicago Defender*, December 12, 1925.
393. "A Note Or Two," *Chicago Defender*, May 28, 1927.
394. "A Note Or Two," *Chicago Defender*, April 6, 1929.

395. "Jolly" Saunders, "Jolly's Letter," *Chicago Defender*, September 10, 1927. Fat Hayden made one recording in 1939 (Decca 7614), reissued on RST Records JPCD-1509.
396. Jolly Saunders, "Jolly Says," *Chicago Defender*, November 5, 1927.
397. Coy Herndon, "Coy Cogitates," *Chicago Defender*, May 19, 1928.
398. Coy Herndon, "Coy Cogitates," *Chicago Defender*, March 24, 1928. J. C. O'Brien apparently started using trucks to haul his show in 1918. He reported in the January 3, 1920, edition of *Billboard* that during the season of 1919, "The show was transported on fourteen trucks and three seven-passenger touring cars." Noting that "many in the show business predicted a failure for my show transported on trucks," O'Brien was "pleased to say that I have run a truck show two years and could not be handed a one-car railroad show again." In the following week's *Billboard*, O'Brien revealed another use for the trucks: "The stage is made by backing two trucks together, letting down the sides and using extension stringers and jacks. The stage is 20 x 20, and is put up in less than ten minutes."
399. "Osby Mitchell's Letter," *Chicago Defender*, June 9, 1928.
400. "Davis Spiels Dope on Fla. Blossoms," *Chicago Defender*, April 18, 1931.
401. Earl Humphrey interviewed by Richard B. Allen, November 30, 1968 (Hogan Jazz Archive, Tulane University). The *Chicago Defender* of January 16, 1937, lists Humphrey with "Barnett Bros. Circus' 10 piece band."
402. "The Stage," *Indianapolis Freeman*, December 9, 1899.
403. Salem Tutt Whitney's brother J. Homer Tutt recalled in an article published in the August 15, 1936, edition of the *Baltimore Afro-American*, and quoted in Henry T. Sampson, *Blacks in Blackface*, pp. 100–101, that the *Silas Green from New Orleans* Company originated in 1905. However, statements made by Eph Williams in the December 31, 1910, *Indianapolis Freeman*—twenty-five years before Tutt's reminiscence—support contemporaneous documentation that indicates 1907. A more egregious error in Tutt's skewed recollection is his assertion that Charles Collier, who took possession of the show in 1922, was white.
404. The 1920 United States Federal Census gives his birthplace as Tennessee (Ancestry.com). His 1892 Registration of Marriage to Rhoda A. Black specifies Nashville (courtesy Circus World Museum, Baraboo, Wisconsin). The *New York Clipper* of August 2, 1890, noted: "Prof. Williams celebrated the thirtieth anniversary of his birth July 19" (Circus World Museum).
405. Coy Herndon, "Famous Georgias," *Chicago Defender*, December 31, 1921. In a letter from Frank H. Thompson to "Circus Dept., B. B. [Barnum and Bailey]," dated January 1, 1954, in the archive of the Circus World Museum, Thompson reminisced about Williams: "When I first heard of him, he tended bar and Barbered in the Plankington [sic] Hotel Milwaukee Wis."
406. Coy Herndon, "Famous Georgias," *Chicago Defender*, December 31, 1921. An interesting sketch of Prof. Williams appears in Dean Jensen, *The Biggest, the Smallest, the Longest, the Shortest: A Chronicle of the American Circus from Its Heartland* (Madison: Wisconsin House, 1975), pp. 103–7. Unfortunately, Jensen does not cite his sources.
407. "Wisconsin," *New York Clipper*, May 19, 1888; July 28, 1888 (Circus World Museum). For more on the Skerbeck Family see Dr. Robert J. Loeffler, M. G. Gorrow, and George L. Chindahl, "The Skerbeck Family History," *The White Tops* (July-August 1955).
408. "Medford's Circus," *Taylor County Star and News*, April 18, 1891 (Circus World Museum).
409. *New York Clipper*, June 8, 1889 (Circus World Museum). Over the next four years, press reports referred to Prof. Williams's circus under various titles. An ad in the *New York Clipper* of August 2, 1890, reproduced in Abbott and Seroff, *Out of Sight*, p. 98, identified it as "Prof. Williams & Co's. Mammoth Railroad Shows, Equine Wonders and World's Fair Carnival." A sketch in the *Taylor County Star and News* of April 25, 1891, called it "Prof. Williams & Co.'s Consolidated American and German Railroad Shows" (Circus World Museum). The *New York Clipper* of April 15, 1893,

cited "Professor Williams' New Consolidated Railroad Show and Grand Northern Circus" (Circus World Museum).

410. *Taylor County Star and News*, April 25, 1891 (Circus World Museum).
411. *Taylor County Star and News*, February 8, 1896; February 22, 1896 (Circus World Museum).
412. *Taylor County Star and News*, April 17, 1897 (Circus World Museum).
413. "The Stage," *Indianapolis Freeman*, July 10, 1897.
414. "Under the Tents," *New York Clipper*, May 18, 1901 (Circus World Museum).
415. "S. H. Dudley's Jolly Ethiopians," *Indianapolis Freeman*, February 2, 1907.
416. Prof. Eph Williams, "Eph. Williams' Famous Troubadours," *Indianapolis Freeman*, December 31, 1910.
417. Coy Herndon, "Coy Cogitates," *Chicago Defender*, June 27, 1925.
418. Prof. Eph Williams, "Eph. Williams' Famous Troubadours," *Indianapolis Freeman*, December 31, 1910.
419. "Black Patti Troubadours," *Indianapolis Freeman*, August 22, 1908.
420. "Black Patti Troubadours," *Indianapolis Freeman*, March 20, 1909.
421. "The Famous Troubadours," *Indianapolis Freeman*, September 12, 1908.
422. "Williams' Famous Troubadours," *Indianapolis Freeman*, May 15, 1909.
423. "Eph Williams' Famous Troubadours," *Indianapolis Freeman*, April 23, 1910.
424. "Prof. Eph Williams' Famous Troubadours Co.," *Indianapolis Freeman*, July 9, 1910.
425. Edward Baskin, "Notes From Prof. Eph Williams' Famous Troubadours," *Indianapolis Freeman*, April 13, 1912; "Notes From Eph Williams' Famous Troubadours," *Indianapolis Freeman*, May 25, 1912.
426. "Prof. Eph Williams' Famous Troubadours," *Indianapolis Freeman*, May 7, 1910.
427. "Prof. Eph Williams' Famous Troubadours Co.," *Indianapolis Freeman*, July 9, 1910.
428. Prof. Eph Williams, "Eph. Williams' Famous Troubadours," *Indianapolis Freeman*, December 31, 1910.
429. "Prof. Eph Williams' Famous Troubadours, Silas Green Company," *Indianapolis Freeman*, August 9, 1913.
430. "Prof. Eph. Williams' Original Silas Green Co. En Route," *Indianapolis Freeman*, March 18, 1911. *Freeman* reports of January 6, 1906, and October 13, 1917, state that R. J. Dickie Anderson was from Yazoo City, Mississippi.
431. "Notes From Prof. Eph. Williams' Famous Troubadours Co. En Route," *Indianapolis Freeman*, May 27, 1911.
432. "Notes From 'Eph Williams' Troubadours,'" *Indianapolis Freeman*, April 15, 1911.
433. "Notes From Eph Williams' Famous Troubadours At Birmingham, Ala.," *Indianapolis Freeman*, November 18, 1911.
434. R. C. Puggsley, "Week Before Christmas," *Indianapolis Freeman*, January 13, 1912.
435. "Gossip Of The Stage," *Indianapolis Freeman*, July 20, 1912.
436. "Gossip Of The Stage," *Indianapolis Freeman*, January 11, 1913.
437. La Vola, "Prof. Eph Williams' Famous Troubadours And Silas Green Co.," *Indianapolis Freeman*, December 20, 1913.
438. "Notes From Prof. Eph. Williams' Troubadours," *Indianapolis Freeman*, March 2, 1912.
439. "Notes From Prof. Eph Williams' Famous Troubadours," *Indianapolis Freeman*, May 4, 1912.
440. "Notes Aboard Eph Williams' Show Car," *Indianapolis Freeman*, February 8, 1913.
441. Edward Baskin, "Notes From Prof. Eph Williams' Famous Troubadours," *Indianapolis Freeman*, April 13, 1912.
442. Edward Baskin, "Notes From Prof. Eph Williams' Troubadours," *Indianapolis Freeman*, April 20, 1912.
443. Marvelous La Vola, "Notes From Eph Williams' Troubadours," *Indianapolis Freeman*, November 1, 1913; "Prof. Eph Williams Sends Christmas Greetings To All, Also His Wife, Family And Entire Co.," *Indianapolis Freeman*, December 25, 1915.
444. "Continuous Tour Of Prof. Eph Williams' Famous Troubadours And The Original Silas Green Co.," *Indianapolis Freeman*, May 17, 1913.

445. "Notes From Eph. Williams' Silas Green Company," *Indianapolis Freeman*, September 6, 1913.
446. "Continuous Tour Of Prof. Eph Williams' Famous Troubadours And The Original Silas Green Co.," *Indianapolis Freeman*, May 17, 1913.
447. "Notes From Prof. Eph Williams' Famous Troubadours And Original Silas Green Company," *Indianapolis Freeman*, September 20, 1913.
448. La Vola, "Prof. Eph. Williams' Famous Troubadours," *Indianapolis Freeman*, November 8, 1913.
449. "Notes From Prof. Eph Williams 'Silas Green' Company," *Indianapolis Freeman*, December 27, 1913.
450. "Continuous Tour Of Prof. Eph Williams' Famous Troubadours And The Original Silas Green Co.," *Indianapolis Freeman*, May 17, 1913.
451. La Vola, "Prof. Eph Williams' Silas Green Company," *Indianapolis Freeman*, October 18, 1913.
452. "Notes From Prof. Eph Williams 'Silas Green' Company," *Indianapolis Freeman*, December 27, 1913.
453. "Gossip of the Stage," *Indianapolis Freeman*, February 7, 1914.
454. "From Eph Williams' Troubadours," *Indianapolis Freeman*, February 14, 1914.
455. "Prof. Eph Williams' Famous Troubadour and Silas Green Co.," Indianapolis Freeman, March 7, 1914.
456. "Prof. Eph Williams," *Indianapolis Freeman*, March 21, 1914.
457. "Notes from the Silas Green Company," *Indianapolis Freeman*, July 4, 1914.
458. "Jenkins And Jenkins Having Success," *Indianapolis Freeman*, January 18, 1913.
459. "Notes From Silas Green Co.," *Indianapolis Freeman*, August 8, 1914.
460. "Bluefield Colored Institute—R. P. Sims, Principal," *Indianapolis Freeman*, May 29, 1915.
461. Geo. W. Smith, "Notes From Prof. Eph Williams Silas Green Co.," *Indianapolis Freeman*, February 27, 1915.
462. Leon the Magician, "Prof. Eph Williams' Silas Green Company," *Indianapolis Freeman*, April 3, 1915.
463. "Chauncey," "Notes From 'Eph Williams' Troubadours,'" *Indianapolis Freeman*, July 10, 1915.
464. "Silas Green In The Allegheny Mountains 2,000 Feet Above Sea Level," *Indianapolis Freeman*, June 17, 1916.
465. "Notes From The Silas Green Company," *Indianapolis Freeman*, December 9, 1916; Abbott and Seroff, "The Life and Death of Pioneer Bluesman Butler 'String Beans' May," *Tributaries: Journal of the Alabama Folklife Association* no. 5 (2002), pp. 35–36.
466. "Excerpts from Prof. Eph Williams' Silas Green Co.," *Indianapolis Freeman*, December 30, 1916.
467. "Excerpts From Prof. Eph. Williams' Silas Green Co.," *Indianapolis Freeman*, December 30, 1916.
468. "Norfolk, Va.," *Indianapolis Freeman*, May 12, 1917.
469. "Means and Means Have Feature Act With Silas Green Company," *Indianapolis Freeman*, June 10, 1916; "News Of The Players," *Indianapolis Freeman*, December 23, 1916.
470. "News Of The Players," *Indianapolis Freeman*, January 13, 1917.
471. "A. L. B.," "Silas Green Show Has Packed Houses In West Virginia," *Indianapolis Freeman*, July 28, 1917.
472. "A. L. B.," "Death Claims One Of The Oldest Employees In Prof. Eph. Williams Silas Green Co.," *Indianapolis Freeman*, October 27, 1917.
473. "A. L. B.," "Death Claims One Of The Oldest Employees In Prof. Eph. Williams Silas Green Co.," *Indianapolis Freeman*, October 27, 1917.
474. "Prof. Eph Williams' Silas Green Company In Mississippi," *Indianapolis Freeman*, December 4, 1915.
475. T. Gunney Lawrence, "Silas Green From New Leans [*sic*] At Eustis, Florida," *Indianapolis Freeman*, March 18, 1916.
476. "Notes of the Silas Green Co.—The Street Parade," *Indianapolis Freeman*, July 15, 1916.
477. Slim Jim Austin, "Doings of Harvey's Greater Minstrels," *Indianapolis Freeman*, October 4, 1919.
478. "News Of The Silas Green Show," *Indianapolis Freeman*, July 29, 1916.
479. "The Grim Reaper, 'Death,' Visits the Silas Green Car," *Indianapolis Freeman*, May 20, 1916.

480. "Notes Of Silas Green Co.," *Indianapolis Freeman*, September 30, 1916.
481. "Notes Of Silas Green Co.," *Indianapolis Freeman*, July 7, 1917; "A. L. B.," "Death Claims One Of The Oldest Employees In Prof. Eph. Williams Silas Green Co.," *Indianapolis Freeman*, October 27, 1917.
482. "Just A Word From Prof. Eph Williams Silas Green Co.," *Indianapolis Freeman*, February 9, 1918.
483. "A. L. B.," "Death Claims One Of The Oldest Employees In Prof. Eph. Williams Silas Green Co.," *Indianapolis Freeman*, October 27, 1917.
484. "A. L. B.," "On The Silas Green Co.," *Indianapolis Freeman*, June 9, 1917.
485. "Gallant Men Among Prof. Eph. Williams' Troopers," *Indianapolis Freeman*, August 25, 1917.
486. "A. L. B.," "Silas Green Co. To Stay Out For The Winter," *Indianapolis Freeman*, October 12, 1918.
487. R. C. Puggsley, "Notes From Eph. Williams' Silas Green Show," *Indianapolis Freeman*, October 26, 1918.
488. "Prof. Eph Williams 'The Hero,'" *Indianapolis Freeman*, May 25, 1918.
489. Sylvester Russell, "Mrs. Eph Williams," *Indianapolis Freeman*, June 22, 1918.
490. "News Of The Silas Green Show," *Indianapolis Freeman*, December 16, 1916.
491. "A. L. B.," "Silas Green Co. To Stay Out For The Winter," *Indianapolis Freeman*, October 12, 1918.
492. "A. L. B.," "Silas Green Co. To Stay Out For The Winter," *Indianapolis Freeman*, October 12, 1918.
493. "Prof. Eph Williams' Big Show Ends Season On Account Of Influenza Epidemic," *Indianapolis Freeman*, October 19, 1918; R. C. Puggsley, "Notes From Eph. Williams' Silas Green Show," *Indianapolis Freeman*, October 26, 1918.
494. R. C. Puggsley, "Notes from Eph Williams Silas Green Show," *Indianapolis Freeman*, October 26, 1918.
495. Adah (*sic*) Lockhart Booker, "Silas Green Company," *Indianapolis Freeman*, July 26, 1919; "Notes From The Pen Of Ada Lockart Booker With Silas Green Co.," *Indianapolis Freeman*, November 1, 1919.
496. Virginia Liston–Sam Gray, "You Can Have It (I Don't Want It)," Okeh 8126, 1924, reissued on Document DOCD-5446. There is no hard evidence to confirm that Flo Russell's "You Can Have It—I Don't Want It" shared anything more than its title with the song Liston and Gray recorded in 1924.
497. "Notes From The Pen Of Ada Lockhart Booker With Silas Green Co.," *Indianapolis Freeman*, November 1, 1919.
498. Adah Lockhart Booker, "Silas Green Company," *Indianapolis Freeman*, July 26, 1919.
499. "Notes From The Pen Of Ada Lockhart Booker With Silas Green Co.," *Indianapolis Freeman*, November 1, 1919.
500. Coy Herndon, "Coy Cogitates," *Chicago Defender*, June 27, 1925.
501. R. C. Puggsley, "Notes From Silas Green Show," *Indianapolis Freeman*, November 13, 1920.
502. It's possible Kentucky Trio member William Coleman was the bass singer of that same name who toured with the famous Excelsior Quartette of the late 1880s and 1890s.
503. Ada Lockhart Booker, "Ideas of the Show World," *Indianapolis Freeman*, June 19, 1920.
504. R. C. Puggsley, "The Passing of Eph Williams," *Chicago Defender*, December 24, 1921. The Hungerford School was said to be located in "Edenville [*sic*], Fla."
505. Coy Herndon, "Famous Georgias," *Chicago Defender*, December 31, 1921.
506. "Collier's Amusement Factory, Macon, Ga.," *Indianapolis Freeman*, November 19, 1910.
507. "Silas Green Co.," *Chicago Defender*, April 14, 1923.
508. Abbott and Seroff, "Bessie Smith: The Early Years," *Blues & Rhythm* no. 70 (June 1992), p. 10.
509. R. C. Puggsley, "Silas Green Show," *Chicago Defender*, September 8, 1923.
510. R. C. Puggsley, "Silas Green Show," *Chicago Defender*, May 31, 1924.
511. Bob Hayes, "Here And There," *Chicago Defender*, August 1, 1936.
512. Coy Herndon, "Coy Cogitates," *Chicago Defender*, June 21, 1924.
513. Coy Herndon, "Coy Cogitates," *Chicago Defender*, July 12, 1924.
514. Coy Herndon, "Coy Cogitates," *Chicago Defender*, July 26, 1924.

515. Coy Herndon, “Coy Cogitates,” *Chicago Defender*, August 16, 1924.
516. Coy Herndon, “Coy Cogitates,” *Chicago Defender*, August 15, 1925.
517. Coy Herndon, “Coy Cogitates,” *Chicago Defender*, September 13, 1924.
518. Coy Herndon, “Coy Cogitates,” *Chicago Defender*, October 25, 1924.
519. Coy Herndon, “Coy Cogitates,” *Chicago Defender*, November 8, 1924.
520. Coy Herndon, “Coy Cogitates,” *Chicago Defender*, September 19, 1925.
521. Harry Hunt, “A Letter,” *Chicago Defender*, December 1, 1928.
522. Coy Herndon, “Coy Cogitates,” *Chicago Defender*, September 6, 1924.
523. Coy Herndon, “Coy Cogitates,” *Chicago Defender*, January 17, 1925.
524. Coy Herndon, “Coy Cogitates,” *Chicago Defender*, February 21, 1925.
525. Coy Herndon, “Coy Cogitates,” *Chicago Defender*, August 15, 1925.
526. Coy Herndon, “Coy Cogitates,” *Chicago Defender*, November 21, 1925.
527. Coy Herndon, “Coy Cogitates,” *Chicago Defender*, June 27, 1925.
528. Coy Herndon, “Coy Cogitates,” *Chicago Defender*, April 25, 1925.
529. Coy Herndon, “Coy Cogitates,” *Chicago Defender*, May 23, 1925.
530. Coy Herndon, “Coy Cogitates,” *Chicago Defender*, September 13, 1924.
531. Coy Herndon, “Coy Cogitates,” *Chicago Defender*, September 12, 1925.
532. Coy Herndon, “Coy Cogitates,” *Chicago Defender*, November 28, 1925.
533. Coy Herndon, “Coy Cogitates,” *Chicago Defender*, December 26, 1925.
534. “Minstrel and Tent Show Talk,” *Billboard*, November 29, 1924.
535. Coy Herndon, “Coy Cogitates,” *Chicago Defender*, November 22, 1924.
536. “The Silas Green Show Makes Hit In Nashville,” *Chicago Defender*, September 5, 1925.
537. Coy Herndon, “Coy Cogitates,” *Chicago Defender*, September 12, 1925. The two titles referred to are Chris Smith, Henry Troy, and Clarence Williams, “Cake Walking Babies from Home” (New York: Clarence Williams Music Publishing Company), 1924; and Cecil Mack and Chris Smith, “Fly Roun’ Young Ladies” (New York: Clarence Williams Music Publishing Company), 1925.
538. Coy Herndon, “Coy Cogitates,” *Chicago Defender*, November 14, 1925. It is possible that Silas Green soubrette Effie Smith Nelson, a principal in the 1925 “telephone exchange” comedy skit, is the same Effie Smith who recorded for such post–World War II labels as Gem, Miltone and Aladdin. One of her biggest hits was a telephone skit titled “Dial That Telephone” (Aladdin 3202, 1953). However, Effie Smith’s obituary in *Living Blues* no. 13 (May-June 1977) states that she was born in 1915.
539. Coy Herndon, “Coy Cogitates,” *Chicago Defender*, May 23, 1925.
540. Coy Herndon, “Coy Cogitates,” *Chicago Defender*, November 21, 1925.
541. “Likes Silas Greene Show,” *Chicago Defender*, September 19, 1925.
542. Coy Herndon, “Coy Cogitates,” *Chicago Defender*, May 29, 1926.
543. “Silas Green Show,” *Chicago Defender*, February 19, 1927.
544. Coy Herndon, “Coy Cogitates,” *Chicago Defender*, April 2, 1927.
545. “Silas Green Show,” *Chicago Defender*, February 19, 1927.
546. “Silas Green Show,” *Chicago Defender*, February 19, 1927. Katie Bryant, misidentified in this citation as “Kittie Bryant,” traveled with Silas Green from 1927 to 1932. When tent show researcher and writer Alex Albright interviewed Katie Bryant Abraham in the 1980s, she shared a stunning collection of some 200 snapshots that she had personally taken during her tenure with the show. Albright has published several of them in various sources, including Alex Albright, “If Not Forgotten Then Misunderstood: The African-American Traveling Minstrel Show,” *Living Blues* no. 108 (March-April 1993), pp. 36–41; Alex Albright, “Classic Blues Under Giant Tents,” *Living Blues* no. 109 (May-June 1993), pp. 46–49;

Alex Albright, "Noon Parade and Midnight Ramble," in *Good Country People* (Rocky Mount: North Carolina Wesleyan Press, 1995), pp. 61–89.

547. "S. H. Gray Radios," *Chicago Defender*, November 12, 1927.
548. Coy Herndon, "Coy Cogitates," *Chicago Defender*, June 11, 1927.
549. "Winstead Has Word to Say About His 12," *Chicago Defender*, June 9, 1934.
550. Coy Herndon, "Coy Cogitates," *Chicago Defender*, April 16, 1927.
551. Coy Herndon, "Coy Cogitates," *Chicago Defender*, October 27, 1928.
552. Coy Herndon, "Coy Cogitates," *Chicago Defender*, May 14, 1927; June 11, 1927.
553. Coy Herndon, "Coy Cogitates," *Chicago Defender*, June 25, 1927.
554. Coy Herndon, "Coy Cogitates," *Chicago Defender*, July 16, 1927.
555. Coy Herndon, "Coy Cogitates," *Chicago Defender*, June 25, 1927.
556. "Critic Sees Silas Green Show," *Chicago Defender*, September 24, 1927.
557. Mildred C. Scott, "Silas Green Show," *Chicago Defender*, September 14, 1929. For more on James H. Wilson, see Abbott and Seroff, *Out of Sight*, pp. 356–57.
558. Coy Herndon, "Coy Cogitates," *Chicago Defender*, November 19, 1927.
559. Coy Herndon, "Coy Cogitates," *Chicago Defender*, December 3, 1927.
560. Coy Herndon, "Coy Cogitates," *Chicago Defender*, November 19, 1927.
561. Lewis and Young, words, Ray Henderson, music, "I'm Sitting on Top of the World" (New York: Leo Feist), 1925.
562. Coy Herndon, "Coy Cogitates," *Chicago Defender*, January 21, 1928.
563. Al Vollmer notifies in "Princess White," *Living Blues* no. 28 (July-August 1976), p. 6, that, "She started in show business as a dancer at age 5, and in 1898 toured Australia and Europe with Salicia Bryan and her Pics." A variant account in Sheldon Harris, *Blues Who's Who* (New York: Da Capo Press), 1979, p. 558, says she "toured with Salica Bryan and Her Pickaninnies working as a toe dancer–singing pick in shows throughout Europe/Australia, 1886–93." Thanks to Al Vollmer for sharing his files on Princess White.
564. Derrick Stewart-Baxter, "Ramblin' Around," *Storyville* no. 56 (December 1974–January 1975), p. 47.
565. "Gray Writes New Songs," *Chicago Defender*, March 10, 1928.
566. Coy Herndon, "Coy Cogitates," *Chicago Defender*, March 3, 1928.
567. Coy Herndon, "Coy Cogitates," *Chicago Defender*, June 16, 1928.
568. Coy Herndon, "Coy Cogitates," *Chicago Defender*, August 18, 1928.
569. Coy Herndon, "Coy Cogitates," *Chicago Defender*, February 11, 1928.
570. "Down in Florida With Tim Owsley," *Chicago Defender*, January 11, 1930.
571. Coy Herndon, "Coy Cogitates," *Chicago Defender*, May 5, 1928.
572. Coy Herndon, "Coy Cogitates," *Chicago Defender*, May 26, 1928.
573. Coy Herndon, "Coy Cogitates," *Chicago Defender*, September 22, 1928.
574. Bob Hayes, "Here & There," *Chicago Defender*, September 11, 1937.
575. Military Records, U.S. Veterans Cemeteries, ca. 1800–2004 (Ancestry.com).
576. "Coy Cogitates," *Chicago Defender*, February 23, 1929. Perhaps this was the Andy Razaf song recorded in 1928 by both Victoria Spivey and Ethel Waters as "My Handy Man."
577. Coy Herndon, "Coy Cogitates," *Chicago Defender*, February 23, 1929.
578. "Silas Green Show Band Broadcasts," *Chicago Defender*, March 30, 1929.
579. Tim Owsley, "Silas Green Show," *Chicago Defender*, April 27, 1929.
580. "Silas Green Company," *Chicago Defender*, March 1, 1930.
581. Tim Owsley, "Silas Green Show Works Year 'Round," *Chicago Defender*, April 12, 1930.
582. Bob Hayes, "Here And There," *Chicago Defender*, December 16, 1939.
583. "Silas Green Show," *Chicago Defender*, December 13, 1930.

584. "Ace Hits of Silas Green Show Listed," *Chicago Defender*, May 23, 1931. Between 1923 and 1925, Ethel Ridley made race recordings for several different companies. They have been reissued on Document DOCD-5353 and RST Records JPCD-1526.
585. "Silas Green Show's New Revue June 25," *Chicago Defender*, June 13, 1931.
586. "Silas Green Shows Close," *Chicago Defender*, February 20, 1932.
587. "Silas Green and Band Play Casino," *Chicago Defender*, April 2, 1932.
588. "Silas Green Shows Ready 4th of April," *Chicago Defender*, March 26, 1932.
589. "Virginia Four Makes 4 Victor Recordings," *Chicago Defender*, January 4, 1930. The Virginia Four's 1929 Victor recordings are reissued on Document DOCD-5543.
590. "Silas Green Shows Ready 4th of April," *Chicago Defender*, March 26, 1932.
591. "Sam H. Gray, Vet. Singer, Passes Away," *Chicago Defender*, June 18, 1932.
592. According to an article in the *Indianapolis Freeman* of August 22, 1914, S. H. Dudley Jr. turned ten years old on August 10, 1914.
593. "'Silas Green' Has a New Show Idea," *Chicago Defender*, May 27, 1933.
594. Tim E. Owsley, "Silas Green Shows Score in the West [i.e., in West Virginia]," *Chicago Defender*, August 26, 1933.
595. Tim E. Owsley, "Three Of The Silas Green Cast Are Wed," *Chicago Defender*, October 7, 1933.
596. "The Silas Green Shows Start Tour," *Chicago Defender*, April 13, 1935. The "Kingfish" referred to here is Louisiana Governor Huey P. Long.
597. "The Silas Green Show Is Red Hot," *Chicago Defender*, June 22, 1935.
598. "Silas Green Notes," *Chicago Defender*, September 21, 1935.
599. "Silas Green And Sissle's Shows Take The Carolinas," *Chicago Defender*, June 8, 1935.
600. Floyd G. Snelson, "'Brownskin Models' Finds The South Warm And Kind To Show," *Chicago Defender*, April 3, 1943.
601. Clyde Bernhardt and the Harlem Blues and Jazz Band, *Sittin' on Top of the World*, Barron LP 401, 1975.
602. Clyde Bernhardt, as told to Sheldon Harris, *I Remember: Eighty Years of Black Entertainment, Big Bands and the Blues* (Philadelphia: University of Pennsylvania Press, 1986), pp. 31, 113–14, 210–19; "Princess White, 95, Jazz Dancer, Singer," *New York Times*, March 23, 1976.
603. "Silas Green Shows Click Down South," *Chicago Defender*, August 3, 1935; "Winsteads Minstrels Score Big," *Chicago Defender*, October 12, 1935.
604. "Silas Green Show Headed For Ga., Fla.," *Chicago Defender*, October 24, 1936.
605. Hortense Collier, "Silas Green Show In Winter Quarters After Great Tour," *Chicago Defender*, February 20, 1937.
606. "Roy Bowling With Silas Green's Shows," *Chicago Defender*, October 9, 1937.
607. "Silas Green Full Of Flesh Artists," *Chicago Defender*, October 16, 1937.
608. "Silas Green Full Of Flesh Artists," *Chicago Defender*, October 16, 1937.
609. For information on Fiddler's early career, see Abbott and Seroff, *Out of Sight*.
610. "Fiddler Is Playing In Omaha, Neb.," *Chicago Defender*, December 17, 1938.
611. "Silas Green Manager Opens Café In South," *Chicago Defender*, September 4, 1937.
612. A Silas Green report in the *Chicago Defender* of July 23, 1938, mentions "Charley Morton, assistant manager." A September 17, 1938, report names "Charlie Morton, manager."
613. Eleanor J. Baker interviewed by Lynn Abbott, May 11, 2005; Thomas L. Riis, "Pink Morton's Theater, Black Vaudeville, and the TOBA," in Josephine Wright and Samuel A. Floyd, Jr., eds., *New Perspectives on Music: Essays in Honor of Eileen Southern* (Warren, Michigan: Harmonie Park Press, 1992).
614. Bob Hayes, "Here And There," *Chicago Defender*, July 23, 1938; "Silas Green Meets With Big Success," *Chicago Defender*, September 17, 1938.
615. Harry Fiddler, "Silas Green In West Virginia," *Chicago Defender*, August 27, 1938.

616. Harry Fiddler, "Silas Green In West Virginia," *Chicago Defender*, August 27, 1938.
617. "Silas Green Ork To Play Greenville," *Chicago Defender*, October 1, 1938.
618. "Silas Green Ends Season in Florida," *Chicago Defender*, March 9, 1940.
619. "Mr. Green & Mr. Bean," *Time*, April 29, 1940.
620. Minnie D. Singleton, "Chas. Collier Famed Showman Final Rites Today at 4 P. M.," *Macon Telegraph*, October 4, 1942 (courtesy Muriel McDowell-Jackson, archivist, Washington Memorial Library, Macon).
621. Ramona Lowe, "'Silas Green From New Orleans' Still The Apple Of Dixie's Eye," *Chicago Defender*, January 29, 1949; Abbott interview with Eleanor Baker.
622. "Silas Green Of New Orleans," *Ebony*, September 1954; "'Silas Green,' Cradle of Show Biz, Still Rolls Along After 70 Years," *Chicago Defender*, March 12, 1955. The 1954 *Ebony* article features several good photographs, including an evocative shot of a segregated audience enjoying the Silas Green Show in Waycross, Georgia. *Ebony*'s editorial board refused our request for permission to reprint this seemingly unique photograph, on the grounds that the material was "too dated."
623. Ramona Lowe, "'Silas Green From New Orleans' Still The Apple Of Dixie's Eye," *Chicago Defender*, January 29, 1949.
624. Eleanor J. Baker wrote the entry on "Silas Green Show" in Charles Reagan Wilson and William Ferris, eds., *Encyclopedia of Southern Culture* (Chapel Hill: University of North Carolina Press, 1989), pp. 223–24. Mrs. Baker has collected materials and oral histories for her book in progress, an insider's perspective on Silas Green.
625. Abbott interview with Eleanor J. Baker.
626. Punch Miller interviewed by Richard B. Allen, September 25, 1959 (Hogan Jazz Archive, Tulane University). Photographer Ralston Crawford snapped two close-ups of Miller with the Silas Green band, reportedly at Clarksdale, Mississippi, circa 1952, which are included in the Ralston Crawford Collection, Hogan Jazz Archive.
627. "Table eaters" were akin to "chair balancers" and "iron jaw" acts. As Eleanor Baker recalls, "They would pick up these tables, with other things piled on them, and they would pick them up with their teeth. And they'd have a dance number around it, and so forth, and they would start with one table, and then they might have two tables, and then they'd put a chair on it, and they were called 'table eaters.'"
628. "Silas Green Of New Orleans," *Ebony*, September 1954, pp. 68–72.
629. "'Silas Green,' Cradle of Show Biz, Still Rolls Along After 70 Years," *Chicago Defender*, March 12, 1955.
630. Baker, "Silas Green Show."

Notes to Appendix IV: Band Rosters of Allen's New Orleans Minstrels, the Rabbit's Foot Company, the Florida Blossoms, and *Silas Green from New Orleans*, 1900–1940

1. "Seen And Heard While Passing," *Indianapolis Freeman*, May 20, 1911; Sylvester Russell, "Chicago Weekly Review," *Indianapolis Freeman*, November 18, 1911.
2. Lawrence Gushee, *Pioneers of Jazz*.
3. It is not known for certain that McCamon is indeed the correct spelling of this venerable minstrel bandmaster's last name. We settled on it because it is, by far, the one most often encountered in the *Freeman*.

GENERAL INDEX

References to illustrations are in *italics.*

SONG INDEX